Rick Steves'
BEST OF
EUROPE
1999

Europe

John Muir Publications
Santa Fe, New Mexico

Other JMP travel guidebooks by Rick Steves
Europe 101: History and Art for the Traveler (with Gene Openshaw)
Rick Steves' Postcards from Europe
Rick Steves' Europe Through the Back Door
Rick Steves' Mona Winks: Self-Guided Tours of Europe's Top Museums
  (with Gene Openshaw)
Rick Steves' Best of Europe
Rick Steves' France, Belgium & the Netherlands (with Steve Smith)
Rick Steves' Germany, Austria & Switzerland
Rick Steves' Great Britain & Ireland
Rick Steves' Russia & the Baltics (with Ian Watson)
Rick Steves' Scandinavia
Rick Steves' Spain & Portugal
Rick Steves' London (with Gene Openshaw)
Rick Steves' Paris (with Gene Openshaw and Steve Smith)
Rick Steves' Phrase Books: German, Italian, French,
  Spanish/Portuguese, and French/Italian/German
Asia Through the Back Door (with Bob Effertz)

John Muir Publications, P.O. Box 613, Santa Fe, NM 87504
Copyright © 1999, 1998, 1997, 1996, 1995 by Rick Steves
Cover copyright © 1999, 1998 by John Muir Publications
All rights reserved.

Printed in the United States of America
First printing January 1999

For the latest on Rick Steves' lectures, guidebooks, tours, and public television series, contact Europe Through the Back Door, Box 2009, Edmonds, WA 98020, tel. 425/771-8303, fax 425/771-0833, Web site: www.ricksteves.com, or e-mail: rick@ricksteves.com.

ISBN: 1-56261-461-4
ISSN: 1096-7702

Europe Through the Back Door Editor Risa Laib
John Muir Publications Editors Krista Lyons-Gould, Jill Metzler
Research Assistance Brian Carr Smith, Steve Smith, Gene Openshaw,
  Tracy Turner, and Risa Laib
Production Marie J. T. Vigil, Rebecca Cook
Design Linda Braun
Cover Design Janine Lehmann
Maps David C. Hoerlein
Printer Banta Company
Cover Photo Il Duomo (cathedral and temple), Siena, Italy;
  Leo de Wys Inc./Jacobs

Distributed to the book trade by
Publishers Group West
Berkeley, California

Europe's Best Destinations

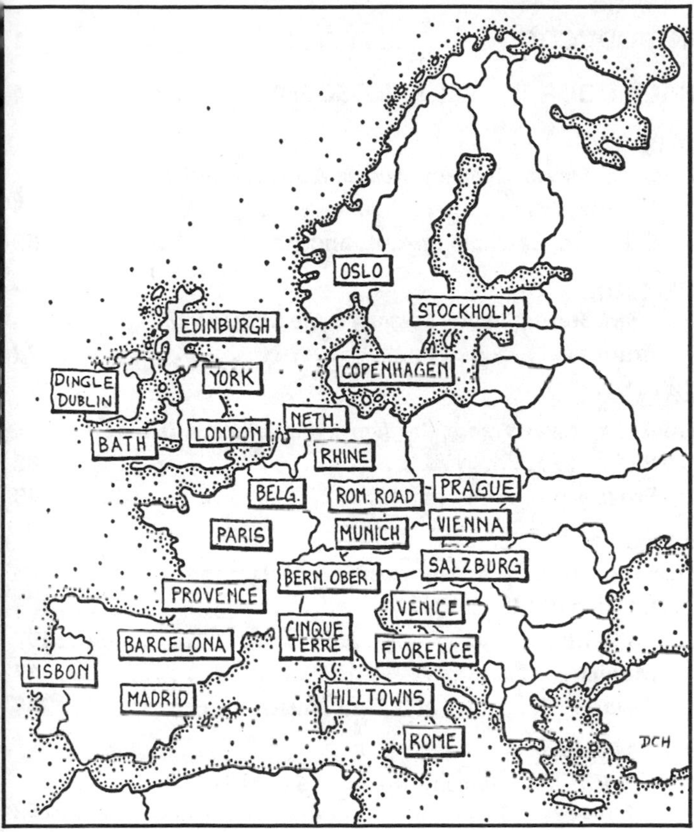

CONTENTS

ITALY
From *Rick Steves' Italy*

THE NETHERLANDS
From *Rick Steves' France, Belgium & the Netherlands*

PORTUGAL
From *Rick Steves' Spain & Portugal*

SCANDINAVIA
From *Rick Steves' Scandinavia*

SPAIN
From *Rick Steves' Spain & Portugal*

SWITZERLAND
From *Rick Steves' Germany, Austria & Switzerland*

INTRODUCTION

This book breaks Europe into its top big-city, small-town, and rural destinations. It then gives you all the information and opinions necessary to wring the maximum value out of your limited time and money in each of them. If you plan two months or less in Europe, this lean and mean book is all you need.

Experiencing Europe's culture, people, and natural wonders economically and hassle-free has been my goal during 25 years of traveling, tour guiding, and travel writing. With this book, I pass on to you the lessons I've learned, updated for 1999.

Rick Steves' Best of Europe is the crème de la crème of places featured in six of my Country Guides. This book is balanced to include a comfortable mix of exciting big cities and cozy small towns: from Paris, London, and Rome to traffic-free Riviera ports, avalanche-zone Alpine villages, and mom-and-pop châteaux. It covers the predictable biggies and mixes in a healthy dose of Back Door intimacy. Along with Leonardo in the Louvre, you'll enjoy Caterina in her Cantina. I've been very selective. For example, rather than listing the countless castles, hill towns, and Riviera resorts, I recommend the best three or four of each.

The best is, of course, only my opinion. But after 25 years of travel writing, lecturing, and tour guiding, I've developed a sixth sense for what tickles the traveler's fancy.

This Information Is Accurate and Up-to-Date

This book is updated every year. Most publishers of guidebooks that cover Europe from top to bottom can afford an update only every two or three years (and even then, it's often by letter). Since this book covers only my favorite places, I am able to personally update it each year. Even with an annual update, things change. But if you're traveling with the current edition of this book, I guarantee you're using the most up-to-date information available. If you're packing an old book, you'll learn the seriousness of your mistake . . . in Europe. Your trip costs at least $10 per waking hour. Your time is valuable. This guidebook saves lots of time.

Planning Your Trip

This book is organized by destinations. Each destination is covered as a mini-vacation on its own, filled with exciting sights and homey, affordable places to stay. In each chapter, you'll find:

Planning Your Time, a suggested schedule with thoughts on how to best use your limited time.

Orientation, including tourist information, city transportation, and an easy-to-read map designed to make the text clear and your arrival smooth.

Sights with ratings: ▲▲▲—Don't miss; ▲▲—Try hard to see; ▲—Worthwhile if you can make it; No rating—Worth knowing about.

Sleeping and Eating, with addresses and phone numbers of my favorite budget hotels and restaurants.

Transportation Connections to nearby destinations by train, bus, or car.

The Appendix is a traveler's tool kit, with telephone tips, a climate chart, and a list of national tourist offices.

Browse through this book, choose your favorite destinations, and link them up. Then have a great trip! You'll travel like a temporary local, getting the absolute most out of every mile, minute, and dollar.

You won't waste time on mediocre sights because, unlike other guidebooks, I cover only the best. Since your major financial pitfalls are lousy, expensive hotels, I've worked hard to assemble the best accommodations values for each stop. And as you travel the route I know and love, I'm happy you'll be meeting some of my favorite Europeans.

Trip Costs

Five components make up your trip cost: airfare, surface transportation, room and board, sightseeing/entertainment, and shopping/miscellany.

Airfare: Don't try to sort through the mess yourself. Get and use a good travel agent. A basic round-trip U.S.A.-to-Europe flight should cost $600–$1,000, depending on where you fly from and when. Always consider saving time and money in Europe by flying "open-jaws" (flying into one city and out of another, such as flying into London and out of Rome).

Surface Transportation: Your best mode depends upon the time you have and the scope of your trip. For many it's a Eurailpass (3 weeks-$718; 1 month-$890; 2 months-$1,260; 15 days in 2 months-$862). Train passes are normally available only outside of Europe. You may save money by simply buying tickets as you go (see Transportation, below).

Drivers can figure $200 per person per week (based on two people splitting the cost of the car, tolls, gas, and insurance). Car rental is cheapest to arrange from the U.S.A. Leasing, for trips over three weeks, is even cheaper.

Room and Board: You can thrive in Europe in 1999 on an overall average of $60 a day per person for room and board. A $60 a day budget allows $10 for lunch, $15 for dinner, and $35 for lodging (based on two people splitting the cost of a $70 double room that includes breakfast). That's doable. Students and tightwads will do it on $40 ($15–20 per bed, $20 for meals and snacks). But budget sleeping and eating require the skills and information covered below (or much more extensively in *Rick Steves' Europe Through the Back Door 1999*).

Sightseeing and Entertainment: In big cities, figure $5 to $10 per major sight, $2 for minor ones, and $25 for splurge experiences (e.g., tours, concerts, gelato binges). An overall average of $15 a day works for most. Don't skimp here. After all, this category directly powers most of the experiences all the other expenses are designed to make possible.

Shopping and Miscellany: Figure $1 per postcard and $2 per coffee, beer, and ice cream cone. Shopping can vary in cost from nearly nothing to a small fortune. Good budget travelers find that this category has little to do with assembling a trip full of life-long and wonderful memories.

Exchange Rates

I've priced things in local currencies throughout this book.

Country	$1 equals roughly...
Austria	12 Austrian schillings (AS)
Belgium	33 Belgian francs (BF)
Czech Republic	32 koruna (kč)
Denmark	7 kroner (kr)
France	5.5 francs (F)
Germany	1.7 Deutsche marks (DM)
Great Britain	.60 pound (£)
Ireland	.70 punt (£)
Italy	1,700 lire (L)
Netherlands	1.7 guilders (f)
Norway	7 kroner (kr)
Portugal	180 escudos ($)
Spain	150 pesetas (ptas)
Sweden	7 kroner (kr)
Switzerland	1.4 Swiss francs (SF)

Prices, Times, and Discounts

The prices in this book, as well as the hours and telephone numbers, are accurate as of late 1998. But Europe is always changing. I know you'll understand that this, like any other guidebook, starts to yellow even before it's printed.

In Europe—and in this book—you'll be using the 24-hour clock. After 12:00 noon, keep going—13:00, 14:00, and so on. For anything over 12, subtract 12 and add p.m. (14:00 is 2 p.m.).

This book lists peak-season hours for sightseeing attractions (July–August). Off-season, roughly October through April, expect

Europe's Best 70 Days

generally shorter hours, more lunchtime breaks, fewer activities, and fewer guided tours in English. If traveling off-season, be careful to confirm opening times.

While discounts for sights and transportation are not listed in this book, seniors (60 and over), students (with International Student Identity Cards), and youths (under 18) can sometimes get discounts—but only by asking.

When to Go

May, June, September, and October are the best travel months. Generally, peak season (July and August) offers the sunniest weather and the most exciting slate of activities—but the worst crowds. During this crowded time, it's best to arrive early in the day or to call your next hotel in advance. (Your fluent receptionist can help you.) As a very general rule of thumb any time of year, the climate north of the Alps is mild (like Seattle) and south of the Alps it's like southern California. For information on weather, check the Climate Chart in the Appendix. If you wilt in the heat, avoid the Mediterranean in the summer. If you want blue skies in the Alps, Britain, and Scandinavia, travel in the height of summer.

Plan your itinerary to beat the heat (spring trip, start in the south and work north) but also to moderate culture shock (start in mild Britain and work south and east) and minimize crowds. Touristy places in the core of Europe (Germany, the Alps, France, Italy, and Greece) suffer most from crowds.

Sightseeing Priorities

Depending on the length of your trip, here are my recommended priorities. Assuming you're traveling by train, I've taken geographical proximity into account.

5 days:	London, Paris
7 days, add:	Amsterdam, Haarlem
10 days, add:	Rhine, Rothenburg, Munich
14 days, add:	Salzburg, Swiss Alps
17 days, add:	Venice, Florence
21 days, add:	Rome, Cinque Terre
24 days, add:	Siena, Bavarian sights
30 days, add:	Arles, Barcelona, Madrid, Toledo
36 days, add:	Vienna, Berlin, Bath/Cotswolds
40 days, add:	Copenhagen, Edinburgh
70 days:	See Europe's Best 70 Days map on p. 4

Red Tape, News, and Banking

Red Tape: You currently need a passport but no visa and no shots to travel in Europe. Crossing borders is easy. Sometimes you won't even realize it's happened. When you do change countries, however, you change money, postage stamps, phone cards, gas prices, ways to flush a toilet, words for "hello," figurehead monarchs, and breakfast breads. Plan ahead for these changes. Coins and stamps are worthless outside their home countries. Just before crossing a border, I use up my coins on gas, candy, souvenirs, or a telephone call home.

News: Americans keep in touch with the *International Herald Tribune* (published almost daily via satellite throughout Europe). Every Tuesday, the European editions of *Time* and *Newsweek* hit the stands with articles of particular interest to European travelers. Sports addicts can get their fix from *USA Today*. News in English will only be sold where there's enough demand: in big cities and tourist centers. If you're concerned about how some event might affect your safety as an American traveling abroad, call the U.S. consulate or embassy in the nearest big city for advice.

Banking: Bring plastic (ATM, credit, or debit cards) along with traveler's checks in dollars.

To get a cash advance from a bank machine, you'll need a four-digit PIN (numbers only, no letters) with your bankcard. Before you go, verify with your bank that your card will work,

Europe's Best Three-Week Trip by Car

Day	Plan	Sleep in
1	Arrive in Amsterdam	Haarlem
2	Amsterdam	Haarlem
3	Haarlem, drive to Rhine	Bacharach
4	Cruise Rhine, Rheinfels Castle	Rothenburg
5	Rothenburg	Munich
6	Munich	Munich
7	Castle Day in Bavaria and Tirol	Reutte
8	Drive to Venice	Venice
9	Venice	Venice
10	Drive to Siena	Siena
11	Florence	Siena
12	Rome	Rome
13	Rome	Rome
14	Cività di Bagnoregio	Vernazza
15	Italian Riviera, Cinque Terre	Vernazza
16	Drive into the Alps, Interlaken	Gimmelwald
17	Alps hike, Jungfrau/Schilthorn	Gimmelwald
18	Bern, Beaune in Burgundy	Beaune
19	Versailles, drop car	Paris
20	Paris	Paris
21	Paris	Paris

While this 21-day itinerary is designed to be done by car, with a few small modifications, it works great by train. The gas and tolls for this trip, if you take all the autobahns, will cost around $600 ($75 for tolls in Italy, $25 in France, $30 for your Swiss autobahn sticker, $10 for your Austria highway sticker, $15 for Austria's Brenner Pass, 3,000 miles at 28 mpg = 107 gallons of gas at $4 a gallon = $430, plus parking—grand total for gas and tolls = $600).

By train, this route would cost about $590 (sample 1999 prices for second-class train tickets: Amsterdam–Frankfurt $90, Frankfurt–Munich $90, Munich–Venice $65, Venice–Rome $50, Rome–Interlaken $90, Interlaken–Paris $110, and Paris–Amsterdam $95). First class is 50 percent more. A 10-days-in-2-months Eurail flexipass ($654), giving you first-class comfort, convenience, and the spontaneity to change your plans, costs only a little more than second-class point-to-point tickets.

Europe's Best Three Weeks

then use it whenever possible. But beware that the distances between these machines can be great, and bring enough traveler's checks as backup.

Visa and MasterCard are more commonly accepted than American Express. Just like at home, credit or debit cards work easily at larger hotels, restaurants, and shops, but smaller businesses prefer payment in local currency.

Regular banks have the best rates for cashing traveler's checks. For a large exchange, it pays to compare rates and fees. Post offices and train stations usually change money if you can't get to a bank.

You should use a money belt. Thieves target tourists. A money belt (call 425/771-8303 for our free newsletter/catalog) provides peace of mind. You can carry lots of cash safely in a money belt.

Don't be petty about changing money. You don't need to waste time every few days returning to a bank or tracking down a cash machine. Change a week's worth of money, get big bills, stuff it in your money belt, and travel!

Travel Smart

Upon arrival in a new town, lay the groundwork for a smooth departure. Reread this book as you travel and visit local tourist information offices. Buy a phone card and use it for reservations, reconfirmations, and double-checking hours. Enjoy the friendliness of the local people. Ask questions. Most locals are eager to point you in their idea of the right direction. Wear your money belt, learn the local currency, and develop a simple formula to quickly estimate rough prices in dollars. Keep a notepad in your pocket for organizing your thoughts, and practice the virtue of simplicity. Those who expect to travel smart, do.

As you read this book, note the days of markets, festivals, and when sights are closed. Anticipate problem days: Mondays are bad in Munich, Dachau, Florence, and Rome; Tuesdays are bad in Paris. Museums and sights, especially large ones, usually stop admitting people 30 to 60 minutes before closing time.

Sundays have the same pros and cons as they do for travelers in the United States. Sightseeing attractions are generally open, shops and banks are closed, and city traffic is light. Rowdy evenings are rare on Sundays. Saturdays in Europe are virtually weekdays with earlier closing hours. Hotels in tourist areas are most crowded on Fridays and Saturdays.

Plan ahead for banking, laundry, post office chores, and picnics. Mix intense and relaxed periods. Every trip (and every traveler) needs at least a few slack days. Pace yourself. Assume you will return.

Tourist Information

The tourist information office is your best first stop in any new city. Try to arrive, or at least telephone, before it closes. In this book, I'll refer to a tourist information office as a TI. Throughout Europe, you'll find TIs are usually well organized and English-speaking.

As national budgets tighten, many TIs have been privatized. This means they become sales agents for big tours and hotels, and their "information" becomes unavoidably colored. While the TI has listings of all the rooms and is eager to book you one, use their room-finding service only as a last resort. Across Europe, room-finding services are charging commissions from hotels, taking fees from travelers, blacklisting establishments that buck their materialistic rules, and are unable to give hard opinions on the relative value of one place over another. The accommodations stakes are too high to go potluck through the TI. By using the listings in this book, you can avoid that kind of "help."

Tourist Offices, U.S.A. Addresses: Each country has a national tourist office in the U.S.A. (see the Appendix for addresses). Before your trip, you can ask for the free general information packet and any specific information you may want (such as city maps and schedules of upcoming festivals).

Recommended Guidebooks

You may want some supplemental information, especially if you'll be traveling beyond my recommended destinations. When you consider the improvements they'll make in your $3,000 vacation, $25 or $35 for extra maps and books is money well spent. Especially for several people traveling by car, the weight and expense are negligible.

The Lonely Planet guides to various European countries are thorough, well researched (though not updated annually), and packed with good maps and hotel recommendations for low- to moderate-budget travelers. The hip, insightful Rough Guide series (by British researchers, not updated annually), and the highly opinionated Let's Go series (annually updated by Harvard students) are great for students and vagabonds. If you're a backpacker with a train pass and interested in the youth and night scene, get Let's Go. The popular, skinny green Michelin guides to most southern countries and French regions are excellent, especially if you're driving. They're known for their city and sightseeing maps, dry but concise and helpful information on all major sights, and good cultural and historical background. English editions are sold locally at tourist shops and gas stations.

Rick Steves' Books and Videos

Rick Steves' Europe Through the Back Door 1999 (John Muir Publications) gives you budget travel tips on minimizing jet lag, packing light, planning your itinerary, traveling by car or train, finding budget beds without reservations, changing money, avoiding rip-offs, outsmarting thieves, hurdling the language barrier, staying healthy, taking great photographs, using your bidet, and much more. The book also includes chapters on my 37 favorite "Back Doors."

Rick Steves Country Guides are a series of eight guidebooks—including this one—covering Europe: Britain & Ireland; France, Belgium & the Netherlands; Italy; Spain & Portugal; Germany, Austria & Switzerland; Scandinavia; and Russia & the Baltics. All but the last two are updated annually and come out each January. If you wish this book covered more of any particular country, my Country Guides are for you.

My new **City Guides** cover Paris and London. With the sleek Eurostar train, London is now just three hours from Paris. Consider combining the two cities (and books) for a great visit.

Europe 101: History and Art for the Traveler (co-written with Gene Openshaw, John Muir Publications, 1996) gives you the story of Europe's people, history, and art. Written for smart people who were sleeping in their history and art classes before they knew they were going to Europe, *101* helps Europe's sights come alive.

Rick Steves' Mona Winks (also co-written with Gene Openshaw, John Muir Publications, 1998) gives you fun, easy-to-follow,

self-guided tours of the major museums and historic highlights
featured in this book, including Amsterdam's Rijksmuseum and
Van Gogh Museum; London's British Museum, British Library,
National Gallery, Tate Gallery, Westminster Abbey, and a
Westminster Walk; Venice's St. Mark's, Doge's Palace, and
Accademia Gallery; Florence's Uffizi Gallery, Bargello,
Michelangelo's *David*, and a Renaissance Walk; Rome's Colos-
seum, Forum, Pantheon, Vatican Museum, and St. Peter's Basil-
ica; Spain's Prado; and Paris's Louvre, the exciting Orsay
Museum, and a tour of Europe's greatest palace, Versailles. If
you're planning on touring these sights, *Mona* will be a valued
friend.

Rick Steves' Phrase Books: After 25 years as an English-
only traveler struggling with other phrase books, I've designed a
series of practical, fun, and budget-oriented phrase books to help
you ask the gelato man for a free little taste and the hotel receptionist for a room with no street noise. If you want to chat with
your cabbie and make hotel reservations over the phone, the
pocket-sized Rick Steves' Phrase Books for French; German;
Italian; Spanish and Portuguese; and French/German/Italian
together will come in very handy (John Muir Publications,
1999).

My television series, *Travels in Europe with Rick Steves*,
includes 52 half-hour shows on Europe. A new series of 13 shows
is planned for 2000. All of the earlier shows are run throughout
the United States on public television stations and on the Travel
Channel. The shows are also available as information-packed
videotapes, along with my two-hour slideshow lectures (call us at
425/771-8303 for our free newsletter/catalog).

Rick Steves' Postcards from Europe (John Muir Publications,
1999), my new autobiographical book, packs 25 years of travel
anecdotes and insights into the ultimate 3,000-mile European
adventure. Through my guidebooks, I share my favorite European discoveries with you. *Postcards* introduces you to my
favorite European friends.

Maps

The maps in this book, drawn by Dave Hoerlein, are concise and
simple. Dave, who is well-traveled in Europe, has designed the
maps to help you locate recommended places and get to the
tourist offices, where you can pick up a more in-depth map (usually free) of the city or region.

European bookstores, especially in tourist areas, have good
selections of maps. For drivers, I'd recommend a 1:200,000 or
1:300,000 scale map for each country. Train travelers can usually
manage fine with the freebies they get with their train pass and at
the local tourist offices.

Railpasses

1999 EURAILPASSES

These passes cover all 17 Eurail countries: Austria, Belgium, Denmark, Finland, France, Germany, Greece, Hungary, Ireland, Italy, Luxembourg, Netherlands, Norway, Portugal, Spain, Sweden, and Switzerland.

	1st cl	1st cl Saver*	2nd cl Youth**
10 days in 2 months flexi	$654	$556	$458
15 days in 2 months flexi	862	732	599
15 consecutive days	554	470	388
21 consecutive days	718	610	499
1 month consec. days	890	756	623
2 months consec. days	1260	1072	882
3 months consec. days	1558	1324	1089

1999 EUROPASSES

All Europasses include France, Germany, Italy, Spain and Switzerland. Up to two of the following extra-cost "zones" may be added: ▼ Austria/Hungary; ▼ Belgium/Netherlands/Luxembourg; ▼ Portugal; ▼ Greece (includes the Brindisi, Italy to Patras, Greece boat).

	1st cl	1st cl Saver*	2nd cl Youth**
5 days in 2 months	$348	$296	$233
6 days in 2 months	$368	$314	$253
8 days in 2 months	$448	$382	$313
10 days in 2 month	$528	$450	$363
15 days in 2 months	$728	$620	$513
With one add-on zone	+$60	+$52	+$45
With two add-on zones	+$100	+$86	+$78

Saverpasses: When 2 or more adults _travel together at all times_, they each save 15% by sharing a Saverpass, compared to buying individual Eurail or Europasses.
**Youthpasses:* Under age 26 only. Kids 4-11 pay half adult fare; under 4: free.

For information on ordering Eurail and Europasses, please call us at 425/771-8303.
For rail 'n drive passes, call Rail Europe at 800/438-7245.

Transportation in Europe

By Car or Train?

Each has pros and cons. Cars are an expensive headache in big cities but give you more control for delving deep into the countryside. Groups of three or more go cheaper by car. If you're packing heavy (with kids), go by car. Trains are best for city-to-city travel and give you the convenience of doing long stretches overnight. By train, I arrive relaxed and well rested—not so by car. A rail 'n' drive pass allows you to mix train and car travel. When thoughtfully used, this pass economically gives you the best of both transportation worlds.

Rail 'n' Drive Passes

1999 FIRST CLASS EURAILDRIVE PASSES
4 first class rail days and 2 car days in a 2 month period.

Car categories	2 adults	1 adult	Extra car day	Extra rail day
Economy	$339	$399	$61	$59
Compact	359	439	80	59
Intermediate	369	459	90	59

Prices are per person. Third and fourth persons sharing car get a 4-day out of 2-month railpass for approx. $280 (kids 4-11: $140). You can add rail days (max. 5) and car days (no limit).

1999 FIRST CLASS EUROPASS DRIVE
3 first class rail days and 2 car days in a 2 month period.

Car categories	2 adults	1 adult	Extra car day	Extra rail day
Economy	$284	$345	$59	$45
Compact	304	379	79	45
Intermediate	314	399	89	45
Small Automatic	334	445	109	45

Prices are per person. You can add rail days (max. 7) and car days (no limit).

For ordering rail 'n drive passes, please call Rail Europe at 800/438-7245.

Traveling by Train

A major mistake Americans make is relating public transportation in Europe to the pathetic public transportation they're used to at home. By rail you'll have the continent by the tail. And every year the trains of Europe are getting speedier and more comfortable. While many simply buy tickets as they go ("point to point"), the various train passes give you the simplicity of ticket-free unlimited travel, and depending on how much travel you do, often offer a tremendous savings over regular point-to-point tickets. The Eurailpass gives you several options (explained in the box on page 11). For a free 40-page Railpass Guide analyzing the railpass and point-to-point ticket deals available both in the U.S.A. and in Europe, call my office at 425/771-8303. This booklet is updated each January. Regardless of where you get your train pass, this information will help you know you're getting the right one for your trip.

Eurailpass and the Europass

The granddaddy of European railpasses, Eurail gives you unlimited rail travel on the national trains of 17 European countries. That's 100,000 miles of track through all of western Europe including Ireland, Greece, and Hungary (but excluding Great Britain and most of eastern Europe). The pass includes many bonuses such as free boat rides on the Rhine, Mosel, Danube, and lakes of Switzerland; several international ferries (Sweden–Finland and Italy–Greece, plus a 50 percent discount on the

Europe by Rail: Time and Cost

This map can help you determine quickly and painlessly whether a railpass is right for your trip. Add up the ticket prices for your route. If your total is about the same or more than the cost of a pass, buy the pass.

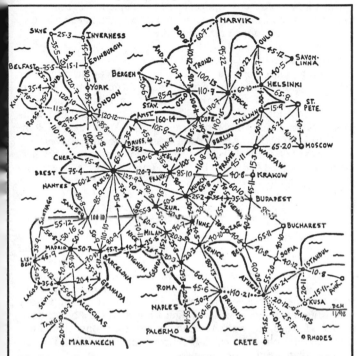

The **first number** between cities = **cost** in $US for a one-way, second-class ticket. The **second number** = number of **hours** the trip takes.

● = Cities served by Eurailpass.

○ = Cities not served by Eurailpass (for example, if you want to go from Munich to Prague, you'll need to pay extra for the portion through the Czech Republic).

Important: These fares and times are based on the Eurail Tariff Guide. Actual prices may vary due to currency fluctuations and local promotions. Local competition can cut the actual price of some boat crossings (from Italy to Greece, for example) by 50 percent or more. For approximate first-class rail prices, multiply the prices shown by 1.5. In some cases, faster trains (like the TGV in France) are available, cutting the hours indicated on the map. Travelers under age 26 can receive up to 1/3 off the second-class fares shown. Eurailpasses are not honored in the United Kingdom, Turkey, or Eastern Europe (except for Hungary).

Ireland–France route); and many buses, including the Romantic Road bus tour through Germany.

The cheaper Europass is more focused than the Eurailpass, covering five countries (France, Germany, Switzerland, Italy, and Spain) with an extra-cost option to add a couple more. Both Eurailpasses and Europasses come in a discounted Saverpass version available to groups of two or more.

Eurail Analysis

Break-even point? For an at-a-glance break-even point, remember that a one-month Eurailpass pays for itself if your route is Amsterdam–Rome–Madrid–Paris on first class or Copenhagen–Rome–Madrid–Copenhagen on second class. A one-month Eurail Youthpass saves you money if you're traveling from Amsterdam to Rome to Madrid and back to Amsterdam. Passes pay for themselves quicker in the north, where the cost per kilometer is higher. Check the map on page 13, Europe by Rail: Time and Cost, to see if your planned travels merit the purchase of a train pass. If it's about even, go with the pass for the convenience of not having to wait in line to buy tickets and for the fun and freedom to travel "free."

Using one Eurailpass versus a series of country passes: While nearly every country has its own mini-version of the Eurailpass, trips covering several countries are usually cheapest with the budget whirlwind traveler's old standby, the Eurailpass, or its budget cousin, the Europass. This is because the more rail days that are included in a pass, the cheaper your per-day cost is. A group of country passes with a few rail days apiece will have a high per-day cost, while a Eurailpass with a longer lifespan offers a better deal overall. However, if you're traveling in a single country, an individual country railpass (such as Francerail or Germanrail) is a better value than a Eurail or Europass.

EurailDrive Pass analysis: The EurailDrive Pass is a great deal compared to the Eurail Flexipass if two are traveling together and would like three days of car rental. When you subtract the cost of a four-day flexi-railpass (based on 80 percent of the cost of a five-day pass), the drive option gives you three driving days at about $14 a day ($7 per person, not including gas or CDW insurance). That's better than the best weekly car rental rate, with the flexibility of a day here and a day there.

Great areas for a day of joyriding include: the Dutch countryside; the Rhine, Mosel, or Bavaria in Germany; the Loire, Burgundy, Alsace, Provence, and the Pyrenees in France; Tuscany, Umbria, the Dolomites in Italy; the hill towns of Andalusia in Spain; Norway's fjord country; or "car hiking" in the Alps. When considering prices, remember that each day of car rental comes with about $30 of extra expenses (CDW insurance, gas, parking) which you'll divide by the number in your party.

Standard European Road Signs

DUH | NO ENTRY FOR CARS | ALL VEHICLES PROHIBITED | NO ENTRY | SPEED LIMIT (IN KM) | YIELD | NO PASSING | DANGER | PARKING

Car Rental

It's cheaper to arrange European car rentals in the United States, so check rates with your travel agent. Rent by the week, with unlimited mileage. If you'll be renting for three weeks or more, ask your agent about leasing, which is a scheme to save on insurance and taxes. I normally rent the smallest, least expensive model. Explore your drop-off options (and costs).

For peace of mind, I spring for the CDW insurance (Collision Damage Waiver, about $10–15 per day), which gives a zero-deductible rather than the standard value-of-the-car "deductible." Ask your travel agent about money-saving alternatives to CDW. A few gold credit cards cover CDW insurance; quiz your credit-card company on the worst case senario. Or consider Travel Guard, which offers CDW insurance for $6 a day (U.S. tel. 800/826-1300).

Driving

For most of Europe, all you need is your valid U.S. driver's license and a car. Ask your rental company whether an international license is required. While gas is expensive, if you keep an eye on the big picture, paying $4 per gallon is more a psychological trauma than a financial one. I use the freeways whenever possible. They are free in the Netherlands and Germany. You'll pay a one-time road fee of about $30 as you enter Switzerland and about $10 for Austria. The Italian autostradas and French autoroutes are punctuated by toll booths (charging about $1 for every 10 minutes). The alternative to these super-freeways often is being marooned in rural traffic. The autobahn/autostrada route usually saves enough time, gas, and nausea to justify its expense. Mix scenic country-road rambling with high-speed autobahning, but don't forget that in Europe, the shortest distance between two points is the autobahn.

Metric: Outside of Britain, get used to metric. A liter is about a quart, four to a gallon. A kilometer is six-tenths of a mile. I figure kilometers to miles by cutting them in half and adding back 10 percent of the original (120 km: 60 + 12 = 72 miles, 300 km: 150 + 30 = 180 miles).

Parking: Parking is a costly headache in big cities. You'll pay about $20 a day to park safely. Ask at your hotel for advice. I keep a pile of coins in my ashtray for parking meters, public phones, Laundromats, and wishing wells.

Telephones and Mail

Smart travelers learn the phone system and use it daily to reserve or reconfirm rooms, find out tourist information, or phone home. Many European phone booths take phone cards rather than coins. Each country sells phone cards good for use in that country's phones. (For example, you can use a Swiss phone card to make local and international calls from Switzerland, but it won't do a thing for you in France.) Buy a phone card from post offices, newsstands, or tobacco shops. Insert the card into the phone, make your call, and the value is automatically deducted from your card. If you use coins instead, have a bunch handy.

Dialing Direct: You'll usually save money by dialing direct. You just need to learn to break the codes.

Here are the general guidelines: When calling long-distance within a country, first dial the area code (which starts with zero), then dial the local number. For example, Munich's area code is 089 and the number of one of my recommended Munich hotels is 264-349. To call it from Frankfurt, dial 089/264-349. When dialing internationally, dial the international access code (of the country you're calling from), the country code (of the country you're calling to), the area code (without the initial zero), and the local number. To call the Munich hotel from the U.S.A., dial 011 (U.S.A.'s international access code), 49 (Germany's country code), 89 (Munich's area code without the zero), then 264-349. To call my office from Munich, I dial 00 (Germany's international access code), 1 (U.S.A.'s country code), 425 (Edmonds' area code), and 771-8303.

There are always exceptions. Some countries do not use area codes, such as Spain, France, Italy, Norway, and Denmark. To make an international call to these countries, dial the international access code of the country you're calling from, the country code of the country you're calling, then the local number in its entirety. (Okay, so there's one exception to the exception; for France, you drop the initial zero of the local number.) To make long-distance calls within any of these countries, simply dial the local number in its entirety (whether you're calling across the street or across the country).

European time is six/nine hours ahead of the east/west coast of the U.S.A. For a listing of international access codes and country codes, see the Appendix.

USA Direct Services: Calling home from Europe is easy with AT&T, MCI, or Sprint calling cards, but since direct dial rates have dropped, calling cards aren't as good a deal as they were a few years ago. It's cheaper to call direct. But if you prefer to use a calling card, here's the scoop: Each card company has a toll-free number in each European country which puts you in touch with an English-speaking operator who takes your card number and the number you want to call, puts you through, and bills your home phone number for the call (about $3 for the first minute, plus a $2.50 service charge, and $1.30 per additional minute). Calling an answering machine is a $5.50 mistake. Avoid this by making a five-second call using a small-value coin or a phone card. For about 25 cents you can get through long enough to make sure an answering machine is off so you can call back using your USA Direct number. For a list of AT&T, MCI, and Sprint calling-card operators, see the Appendix. Definitely avoid using your calling card to make calls between European countries; it's much cheaper to call direct using coins or a phone card.

Mail: To arrange for mail delivery, reserve a few hotels along your route in advance and give their addresses to friends, or use American Express Company's mail services (available to anyone who has at least one Amex traveler's check). Allow 10 days for a letter to arrive. Federal Express makes two-day deliveries—for a price. Phoning is so easy that I've dispensed with mail stops all together.

Sleeping

In the interest of smart use of your time, I favor hotels and restaurants handy to your sightseeing activities. Rather than list hotels scattered throughout a city, I describe my favorite two or three neighborhoods and recommend the best accommodations values in each, from $10 bunks to $150 doubles.

Now that hotels are so expensive and tourist information offices' room-finding services are so greedy, it's more important than ever for budget travelers to have a good listing of rooms and call directly to make reservations. This book gives you a wide range of budget accommodations to choose from: youth hostels, bed-and-breakfasts, guest houses, pensions, small hotels, and splurges. I like places that are clean, small, central, traditional, friendly, and not listed in other guidebooks. Most places I list are a good value, having at least five of these seven virtues.

Rooms with private bathrooms are often bigger and renovated, while the cheaper rooms without bathrooms often will be on the top floor or not yet refurbished. Any room without a bathroom has access to a bathroom in the corridor (free unless otherwise noted). Rooms with tubs often cost more than rooms with showers. All rooms have a sink. Unless I note a difference, the cost of a room includes a continental breakfast. When breakfast is not included, the price is usually posted in your hotel room.

Before accepting, confirm your understanding of the complete price. The only tip my recommended hotels would like is a

Sleep Code

To give maximum information in a minimum of space, I use this code to describe accommodations listed in this book. Prices listed are per room, not per person. When there is a range of prices in one category, the price will fluctuate with the season, size of room, or length of stay.

S = Single room (or price for one person in a double).

D = Double or Twin. Double beds are usually big enough for non-romantic couples.

T = Triple (often a double bed with a single bed moved in).

Q = Quad (an extra child's bed is usually cheaper).

b = Private bathroom with toilet and shower or tub.

t = Private toilet only (the shower is down the hall).

s = Private shower or tub only (the toilet is down the hall).

CC = Accepts credit cards (Visa, MasterCard, American Express). If CC isn't mentioned, assume you'll need to pay cash.

SE = Speaks English. This code is used only when it seems predictable that you'll encounter English-speaking staff.

NSE = Does not speak English. Used only when it's unlikely you'll encounter English-speaking staff.

According to this code, a couple staying at a "Db-6,000 ptas, CC:V, SE" hotel would pay a total of 6,000 pesetas ($40) for a double room with a private bathroom. The hotel accepts Visa or Spanish cash in payment, and the staff speaks English.

friendly, easygoing guest. I appreciate feedback on your hotel experiences.

Hotels

While most hotels listed in this book cluster around $60 to $80 per double, listings range from about $25 (very simple, toilet and shower down the hall) to $150 (maximum plumbing and more) per double. The cost is higher in big cities and heavily touristed cities and lower when off the beaten track. Three or four people can nearly always save lots of money by requesting one big room. Traveling alone can get expensive: a single room is often only 20 percent cheaper than a double. If you'll accept a room with twin beds and you ask for a double, you may needlessly be turned away.

Get in the habit of asking for "a room for two people" if you'll take a twin or a double.

Rooms are generally very safe, but don't leave valuables lying around. More (or different) pillows and blankets are usually in the closet or available on request. Remember, in Europe towels and linen aren't always replaced every day. Drip-dry and conserve.

A very simple continental breakfast is almost always included. (Breakfasts in Europe, like towels and people, get smaller as you go south.) If you like juice and protein for breakfast, supply it yourself. I enjoy a box of juice in my hotel room and often supplement the skimpy breakfast with a piece of fruit and cheese. (A zip-lock baggie is handy for petite eaters to grab an extra breakfast roll and slice of cheese, when provided, for a fast and free light lunch.)

Making Reservations

It's possible to travel at any time of year without reservations, but given the high stakes, erratic accommodations values, and the quality of the gems I've found for this book, I'd highly recommend calling ahead for rooms a day or two in advance as you travel. Even if a hotel clerk says the hotel is full, you can try calling between 9:00 and 10:00 on the day you plan to arrive. That's when the hotel clerk knows who'll be checking out and just which rooms will be available. I've taken great pains to list telephone numbers with long distance instructions (see Telephones above and the Appendix). Use the telephone and the convenient phone cards. Most hotels listed are accustomed to English-only speakers. A hotel receptionist will trust you and hold a room until 16:00 (4:00 p.m.) without a deposit, though some will ask for a credit-card number. Honor (or cancel by phone) your reservations. Long distance is cheap and easy from public phone booths. Don't let these people down—I promised you'd call and cancel if for some reason you won't show up. Don't needlessly confirm rooms through the tourist office; they'll take a commission.

If you know exactly which dates you need and really want a particular place, reserve a room well in advance before you leave home. To reserve from home, call, fax, or write the hotel. Phone and fax costs are reasonable, and simple English is usually fine. To fax, use the form in the Appendix. If you're writing, add the zip code and confirm the need and method for a deposit. A two-night stay in August would be "2 nights, 16/8/99 to 18/8/99"—European dates are written day/month/year, and hotel jargon counts your stay from your day of arrival through your day of departure. You'll often receive a letter or fax back requesting one night's deposit. A credit card and expiration date will usually be accepted as a deposit, though you may need to send a signed traveler's check or a bank draft in the local currency. If your credit card is the deposit, you can pay with your card or cash when you arrive; if you don't show up, you'll be billed for one night. Reconfirm your reservations a day in advance for safety.

Bed-and-Breakfasts

You can stay in private homes throughout Europe and enjoy double the cultural intimacy for about half the cost of hotels. You'll find them mainly in smaller towns and in the countryside (so they are most handy for those with a car). In Germany, look for *Zimmer* signs. For Italian *affitta camere* and French *chambre d'hôte* (CH), ask at local tourist offices. Doubles cost about $50, and you'll often share a bathroom with the family. While your European hosts will rarely speak English (except in Switzerland, the Netherlands, Belgium, and Scandinavia), they will almost always be enthusiastic and a delight to share a home with.

Hostels

For $10 to $20 a night, you can stay at one of Europe's 2,000 youth hostels. While most hostels admit non-members for an extra fee, it's best to join the club and buy a youth hostel card before you go. Except in Bavaria (where you must be under 27 to stay in a hostel), travelers of any age are welcome as long as they don't mind dorm-style accommodations and making lots of traveling friends. Cheap meals are sometimes available, and kitchen facilities are usually provided for do-it-yourselfers. Expect crowds in the summer, snoring, and lots of youth groups giggling and making rude noises while you try to sleep. Family rooms and doubles are often available on request, but it's basically boys' dorms and girls' dorms. Many hostels are locked up from about 10:00 until 17:00, and a 23:00 curfew is often enforced. Hosteling is ideal for those traveling single: prices are by the bed, and you'll have an instant circle of friends. More and more hostels are getting their business acts together, taking credit-card reservations over the phone and leaving sign-in forms on the door for each available room. In the north, many hostels have a new telex reservation system that allows you to reserve and pay for your next hostel from the one before. If you're serious about traveling cheaply, have a card, carry your own sheet, and cook in the members' kitchens.

Camping

For $4 to $10 per person per night, you can camp your way through Europe. "Camping" is an international word, and you'll see signs everywhere. All you need is a tent and a sleeping bag. Good campground guides are published, and camping information is also readily available at local tourist information offices. Europeans love to holiday camp. It's a social rather than a nature experience and a great way for traveling Americans to make local friends. Many campgrounds will have a small grocery and washing machines, and a few even come with discos and mini-golf. Camping is ideal for families traveling by car on a tight budget.

Eating European

Europeans are masters at the art of fine living. That means eating long and eating well. Two-hour lunches, three-hour dinners, and endless hours sitting in outdoor cafés are the norm. Americans eat on their way to an evening event and complain if the check is slow in coming. For Europeans, the meal is an end in itself, and only rude waiters rush you.

Even those of us who liked dorm food will find that the local cafés, cuisine, and wines become a highlight of our European adventure. This is sightseeing for your palate, and even if the rest of you is sleeping in cheap hotels, your taste buds will want an occasional first-class splurge. You can eat well without going broke. But be careful: you're just as likely to blow a small fortune on a mediocre meal as you are to dine wonderfully for $12.

Restaurants

When restaurant hunting, choose a place filled with locals, not the place with the big neon signs boasting "We Speak English and Accept Credit Cards." Look for menus posted outside; if you don't see one, move along. Especially in France and Italy, look for set-price menus (called the tourist menu, *menu del giorno*, *prix-fixe*, or simply *le menu*) that give you several choices among several courses. Combination plates (*le plat* in France, *plato combinado* in Spain) provide house specialties at reasonable prices. Galloping gourmets bring a menu translator. (The *Marling Menu Master*, available in French, Italian, and German editions, is excellent.) These days, tipping is included in the bill in most cafés and restaurants. If it's not, the menu will tell you. Still, it's polite to leave the change (under 5 percent) if the service was good.

When you're in the mood for something halfway between a restaurant and a picnic meal, look for food stands selling take-out sandwiches and drinks, delis with stools or a table, a department store cafeteria, or simple little eateries for fast and easy, sit-down restaurant food. Many restaurants offer a good value, three- to five-course "menu" at lunch only. The same menu often costs much more at dinner.

Picnics

So that I can afford the occasional splurge in a nice restaurant, I like to picnic. Besides the savings, picnicking is a great way to sample local specialties. And, in the process of assembling your meal, you get to plunge into local markets like a European.

Gather supplies early. Many shops close for a lunch break. While it's fun to visit the small specialty shops, local supermarchés give you the same quality with less color, less cost, and more efficiency.

When driving I organize a backseat pantry in a cardboard box with plastic cups, paper towels, a water bottle (the standard, disposable, European half-liter plastic mineral water bottle works fine), a damp cloth in a zip-lock baggie, a Swiss army knife, and a petite tablecloth. To take care of juice once and for all, stow a rack of liter boxes of orange juice in the trunk. (Look for "100%" on the label or you'll get a sickly sweet orange drink.)

Picnics (especially French ones) can be an adventure in high cuisine. Be daring: try the smelly cheeses, midget pickles, ugly pâtés, sissy quiches, and minuscule yogurts. Local shopkeepers are happy to sell small quantities of produce and even slice and stuff a sandwich for you.

A typical picnic for two might be fresh bread (half loaves on request), two tomatoes, three carrots, 100 grams of cheese, (about a quarter-pound, called an *etto* in Italy), 100 grams of meat, two apples, a liter box of orange juice, and yogurt. Total cost for two: about $8.

Stranger in a Strange Land

We travel all the way to Europe to enjoy differences—to become temporary locals. You'll experience frustrations. Certain truths that we find "God-given" or "self-evident," like cold beer, ice in drinks, bottomless cups of coffee, hot showers, body odor smelling bad, and bigger being better, are suddenly not so true. One of the benefits of travel is the eye-opening realization that there are logical, civil, and even better alternatives. A willingness to go local ensures that you'll enjoy a full dose of local hospitality.

If there is a negative aspect to the European image of Americans, we are big, loud, aggressive, impolite, rich, and a bit naive. While Europeans look bemusedly at some of our Yankee excesses—and worriedly at others—they nearly always afford us individual travelers all the warmth we deserve.

Back Door Manners

While updating this book, I heard over and over again that my readers are considerate and fun to have as guests. Thank you for traveling as temporary locals who are sensitive to the culture. It's fun to follow you in my travels.

Send Me a Postcard, Drop Me a Line

If you enjoy a successful trip with the help of this book and would like to share your discoveries, please fill out and send the survey at the end of this book to me at Europe Through the Back Door, Box 2009, Edmonds, WA 98020. I personally read and value all feedback.

For our latest travel information, tap into our Web site: www.ricksteves.com. My e-mail address is rick@ricksteves.com. Anyone is welcome to request a free issue of our *Back Door* quarterly newsletter.

Judging from all the positive feedback and happy postcards I receive from travelers who have used this book, it's safe to assume you're on your way to a great vacation—independent, inexpensive, and with the finesse of an experienced traveler. Thanks, and happy travels!

BACK DOOR TRAVEL PHILOSOPHY
As Taught in *Rick Steves' Europe Through the Back Door*

Travel is intensified living—maximum thrills per minute and one of the last great sources of legal adventure. Travel is freedom. It's recess, and we need it.

Experiencing the real Europe requires catching it by surprise, going casual . . . "Through the Back Door."

Affording travel is a matter of priorities. (Make do with the old car.) You can travel—simply, safely, and comfortably—anywhere in Europe for $60 a day plus transportation costs. In many ways, spending more money only builds a thicker wall between you and what you came to see. Europe is a cultural carnival and, time after time, you'll find that its best acts are free and the best seats are the cheap ones.

A tight budget forces you to travel close to the ground, meeting and communicating with the people, not relying on service with a purchased smile. Never sacrifice sleep, nutrition, safety, or cleanliness in the name of budget. Simply enjoy the local-style alternatives to expensive hotels and restaurants.

Extroverts have more fun. If your trip is low on magic moments, kick yourself and make things happen. If you don't enjoy a place, maybe you don't know enough about it. Seek the truth. Recognize tourist traps. Give a culture the benefit of your open mind. See things as different but not better or worse. Any culture has much to share.

Of course, travel, like the world, is a series of hills and valleys. Be fanatically positive and militantly optimistic. If something's not to your liking, change your liking. Travel is addicting. It can make you a happier American, as well as a citizen of the world. Our Earth is home to nearly 6 billion equally important people. It's humbling to travel and find that people don't envy Americans. They like us, but with all due respect, they wouldn't trade passports.

Globetrotting destroys ethnocentricity. It helps you understand and appreciate different cultures. Travel changes people. It broadens perspectives and teaches new ways to measure quality of life. Many travelers toss aside their hometown blinders. Their prized souvenirs are the strands of different cultures they decide to knit into their own character. The world is a cultural yarn shop. And Back Door Travelers are weaving the ultimate tapestry. Come on, join in!

VIENNA (WIEN)

Vienna is a head without a body. For 600 years the capital of the once-grand Habsburg Empire, she started and lost World War I and, with it, her far-flung holdings. Today you'll find an elegant capital of 1.6 million people (20 percent of Austria's population) ruling a small, relatively insignificant country. Culturally, historically, and from a sightseeing point of view, this city is the sum of its illustrious past. The city of Freud, Brahms, a gaggle of Strausses, Maria Theresa's many children, and a dynasty of Holy Roman Emperors is right up there with Paris, London, and Rome.

Vienna has always been the easternmost city of the West. In Roman times it was Vindobona, on the Danube facing the Germanic barbarians. In medieval times Vienna was Europe's bastion against the Ottoman Turks (a "horde" of 300,000 was repelled in 1683). While the ancient walls held out the Turks, World War II bombs destroyed 22 percent of the city's buildings. In modern times Vienna took a big bite out of the USSR's Warsaw Pact buffer zone. The truly Viennese person is not Austrian but a second-generation Habsburg cocktail, with grandparents from the distant corners of the old empire—Polish, Serbian, Hungarian, Romanian, Czech, or Italian. Vienna is the melting-pot capital of an empire of 60 million—of which only 8 million are Austrian.

In 1900, Vienna's 2.2 million inhabitants made it the world's fifth-largest city (after New York, London, Paris, and Berlin). But the average Viennese mother has 1.3 children, and the population is down to 1.6 million. (Dogs are the preferred "child.")

Some ad agency has convinced Vienna to make Elisabeth, wife of Emperor Franz Josef—with her narcissism and difficulties with royal life—the darling of the local tourist scene. You'll see Sissy all over town. But stay focused on the Habsburgs who mattered.

Of the Habsburgs who ruled Austria from 1273 to 1918, Maria Theresa (ruled 1740–1765) and Franz Josef (ruled 1848–1916) are the most famous. People are quick to remember Maria Theresa as the mother of 16 children (12 survived). This was actually no big deal back then (one of her daughters had 18 kids, and a son fathered 16). Maria Theresa's reign followed the Austrian defeat of the Turks, when Europe recognized Austria as a great power. She was a strong and effective queen. (Her rival, the Prussian emperor, said, "When at last the Habsburgs get a great man, it's a woman.")

Maria Theresa was a great social reformer. During her reign she avoided wars and expanded her empire by skillfully marrying her children into the right families. With daughter Marie Antoinette's marriage into the French Bourbon family (to Louis XVI), for instance, a country that had been an enemy became an ally. (Unfortunately for Marie, she arrived in time for the Revolution, and she lost her head.)

In tune with her age and a great reformer, Maria Theresa's "Robin Hood" policies helped Austria slip through the "age of revolution" without turmoil. She taxed the church and the nobility and provided six years of obligatory education to all children and free health care to all in her realm. She also welcomed the boy genius Mozart into her court.

As far back as the 12th century, Vienna was a mecca for musicians—both secular (troubadours) and sacred. The Habsburg emperors of the 17th and 18th centuries were not only generous supporters of music but fine musicians and composers themselves. (Maria Theresa played a mean double bass.) Composers like Haydn, Mozart, Beethoven, Schubert, Brahms, and Mahler gravitated to this music-friendly environment. They taught each other, jammed together, and spent a lot of time in Habsburg palaces. Beethoven was a famous figure, walking—lost in musical thought—through Vienna's woods.

After the defeat of Napoleon and the Congress of Vienna in 1815 (which shaped 19th-century Europe), Vienna enjoyed its violin-filled belle époque, which shaped our romantic image of the city—fine wine, chocolates, cafés, and waltzes. The waltz was the rage, and "Waltz King" Johann Strauss and his brothers kept Vienna's 300 ballrooms spinning.

This musical tradition that continues in our century leaves some prestigious Viennese institutions for today's tourists to enjoy: the Opera, the Boys' Choir, and the great Baroque halls and churches, all busy with classical and waltz concerts.

Planning Your Time

For a big city, Vienna is pleasant and laid-back. Vienna is worth two days and two nights. Not only is it packed with great sights, but it's also a joy to spend time in. It seems like Vienna was

designed to help people simply meander through a day. To be
grand-tour efficient, you could sleep in and sleep out on the train
(Berlin, Venice, Rome, the Swiss Alps, Paris, and the Rhine are
each handy night trains away). I'd come in from Salzburg via
Hallstatt and spend two days this way:

Day 1:

9:00   Circle the Ring by tram, following the self-guided tour
        (below).

10:00   Tour Opera. (Take care of any TI and ticket needs.)

11:00   Horse lovers tour the Lipizzaner Museum and see the
        horses practicing (at 11:00). Art fans can visit the
        Academy of Fine Arts or the Art Nouveau sights at
        Karlsplatz. People-watchers wander Naschmarkt.

12:00   Lunch at Buffet Trzesniewski or the Rosenberger
        Markt Restaurant.

13:00   Tour Hofburg, visiting Augustinian church, royal
        apartments, treasury, Neue Burg, and Kaisergruft.

16:30   Stroll Kärntner Strasse, tour cathedral, and stroll
        Graben and Kohlmarkt.

19:00   Choose classical music, *Heurige* wine garden, Prater
        amusement park, or an opera performance. Spend
        some time wandering the old center.

Day 2:

9:00   Schönbrunn Palace

13:00   Kunsthistorisches Museum after lunch.

15:00   Your choice of the many sights left to see in Vienna.

Evening See Day 1 evening options.

Orientation (tel. code: 01)

Vienna, or Wien (VEEN) in German, is bordered on three sides
by the Vienna Woods (Wienerwald) and the Danube (Donau). To
the southeast is industrial sprawl. The Alps, which arc across
Europe from Marseilles, end at Vienna's wooded hills. These provide a popular playground for walking and new-wine drinking.
This greenery's momentum carries on into the city. You'll notice
more than half of Vienna is park land, filled with ponds, gardens,
trees, and statue memories of Austria's glory days.

    Think of the city map as a target. The bull's-eye is the cathe-
dral, the first circle is the Ring, and the second is the Gürtel. The
old town snuggles around towering St. Stephan's Cathedral south
of the Donau, bound tightly by the Ringstrasse. The Ring, marking what was the city wall, circles the first district (or *Bezirk*). The
Gürtel, a broader ring road, contains the rest of downtown
(Bezirkes 2–9).

    Addresses start with the *Bezirk*, followed by street and build-
ing number. Any address higher than the ninth *Bezirk* is beyond

the Gürtel, far from the center. The middle two digits of Vienna's postal codes show the district, or *Bezirk*. The address "7, Linden-gasse 4" is in the seventh district, #4 on Linden Street. Its postal code would be 1070. Nearly all your sightseeing will be done in the core first district or along the Ringstrasse. As a tourist, concern yourself only with this small old center, and sprawling Vienna suddenly becomes manageable.

Tourist Information

Beware of "tourist offices" at the train stations, airport, and around town, which are hotel agencies in disguise. Vienna's real tourist office, near the Opera House at Kärntner Strasse 38, is excellent (daily 9:00–19:00, tel. 01/211-140 or 01/513-8892, Web site: http://info.wien.at/). Stop here first with a list of needs and questions. Confirm your sightseeing plans, and pick up the free and essential city map (best of its kind in Europe—use the town center inset, also available at most hotels), the museum brochure (listing hours), the monthly program of concerts, (called "Programm") and the fact-filled *Young Vienna Scene* magazine.

Consider the TI's handy 50-AS *Vienna from A to Z* booklet. Every important building has a numbered flag banner that keys into this guidebook. *A to Z* numbers are keyed into the TI's city map. When lost, find one of the "famous-building flags" and match its number to your map. If you're at a "famous building," check the map to see what other key numbers are nearby, then check the *A to Z* book description to see if you want to go in.

I skip the much promoted 180-AS "Vienna Card," which gives you a three-day transit pass (worth 130 AS) and tiny discounts at museums on the push list (which you probably won't visit).

Arrival in Vienna

By Train at the West Station: Most train travelers arrive at the Westbahnhof. Pick up a free city map at the Reisebüro am Bahnhof. To get to the city center (and most likely, your hotel): catch U-3 subway (buy the 50-AS 24-hour pass from a *Tabak* [tobacco] shop in the station or from a machine—good on all city transit). U-3 signs lead down long escalators to the subway tracks. Catch a train in the direction of U-3-Erdberg. Ride five stops to Stephansplatz, escalate in the exit direction "Stephansplatz," and you hit the cathedral. The TI is a five-minute stroll down the busy Kärntner Strasse pedestrian street.

The Westbahnhof has a grocery store (daily 5:30–23:00), change offices (station ticket windows offer better rates than change offices and are open long hours), storage facilities, and rental bikes (see Getting Around, below).

By Plane: The airport (16 km from town) is connected by 70-AS shuttle buses (3/hr) to either the Westbahnhof (35 min) or the City Air Terminal (20 min) near the river in the old center. Taxis into town cost about 400 AS.

Getting Around Vienna

By Bus, Tram, and Subway: To take simple and economical advantage of Vienna's fine transit system of buses, trams, and sleek, easy subways, buy the 24-hour (50-AS) or 72-hour (130-AS) subway/bus/tram pass at a station machine or at *Tabak* shops near any station. Take a moment to study the eye-friendly city center map on metro station walls to internalize how the metro and tram system can help you. I use it mostly to zip along the Ring (tram #1 or #2) and subway to more outlying sights or hotels. The 15-AS transit map is overkill. All necessary routes are listed on the free tourist city map. Without a pass, either buy individual tickets (17 AS, good for one journey with necessary changes) from metro ticket windows or buy blocks of five tickets for 85 AS (17 AS apiece). Tickets are 20 AS from the driver. Eight-strip, eight-day, 265-AS transit passes, called "8 Tage Umwelt Streifennetzkarte," can be shared (for instance, four people for two days each, a 33 percent savings over the already cheap 24-hour pass).

Stamp a time on your pass as you enter the system or tram (stiff 500-AS fine if caught without a valid ticket). Rookies miss stops because they fail to open the door. Push buttons, pull latches, do whatever it takes. Study your street map before you exit the subway; by choosing the right exit—signposted from the moment you step off the train—you'll save yourself lots of walking.

By Taxi: Vienna's comfortable, honest, and easy-to-flag-down taxis start at 27 AS. You'll pay 90 AS to go from the Opera to the South or West Train Station.

By Bike: Good as the city's transit system is, you may want to rent a bike at any train station (daily 4:00–24:00, 90 AS/day with railpass or train ticket, 150 AS without; rent early in morning before supply runs out). Pedal Power offers rental bikes (350 AS/day for "trekking" bike, 395 AS includes delivery and pickup from your hotel) and 3.5-hour two-language city tours (daily at 10:00, 280 AS includes bike and guide, Austellungsstrasse 3, U-1 to Praterstern and long walk, tel. 01/729-7234).

By Buggy: Rich romantics get around by traditional horse and buggy. You'll see the *Fiakers* clip-clopping tourists on 20-minute (500 AS) or 40-minute (800–1,000 AS) tours.

Helpful Hints

Bank Alert: Banking is expensive in Vienna. Save 3 percent by comparing rates. (Warning: "Rieger Bank" is not a bank; it's an expensive exchange bureau in disguise.) Banks are open weekdays roughly from 8:00 to 15:00 and until 17:30 on Thursday. After hours, you can change money at train stations, the airport, the post office (on Postgasse in city center, open 24 hours daily, also has handy metered phones). Commissions of 100 AS are sadly normal. A happy exception is the American Express Company office, which charges no commissions to change AmExCo checks (Monday–Friday 9:00–17:30, Saturday 9:00–12:00, Kärntner Strasse 21–23, tel. 01/51540). ATMs are abundant.

Post Office: The West and South Train Stations each have full-service post offices (open 4:00–24:00).

English Bookstores: The British Bookshop is at the corner of Weihburggasse and Seilerstätte, and Shakespeare & Co. is at Sterngasse 2, north of the Höher Markt Square (tel. 01/5355-05354).

Telephones: Vienna just changed its 0222 area code to 01. When you encounter 0222 numbers, do the same.

Internet Access: Try Internet Aktiv (8 min walk from West-bahnhof, small sign, Zielergasse 29, tel. 01/526-7389).

City Tours
Walks: The *Walks in Vienna* brochure at the TI describes Vienna's many guided walks. Unfortunately, only a few are in English (130 AS, not including admissions, 90 min, tel. 01/894-5363). Eva Prochaska can book you a private guide who charges 1,230 AS for a half-day (1, Weihburggasse 13–15, tel. 01/513-5294).

Bus Tours: Vienna Line offers hop-on hop-off tours covering the 14 predictable sightseeing stops. Given Vienna's excellent public transportation and this outfit's meager one bus per hour frequency, I'd take this not to hop-on-and-off, but only to get a 2.5-hour narrated (in German and English) orientation drive through town (220 AS, good for two days, for this and more tours, tel: 01/714-1141).

Do-It-Yourself Bus Orientation Tour
▲▲**Ringstrasse Tour**—In the 1860s Emperor Franz Josef had the city's ingrown medieval wall torn down and replaced with a grand boulevard 190 feet wide, arcing nearly three miles around the city's core. The road predates all the buildings that line it. So what you'll see is neo-Gothic, neoclassical, and neo-Renaissance. One of Europe's great streets, it's lined with many of the city's top sights. Trams #1 and #2 circle the whole route and so should you.

This self-service tram tour gives you a fun orientation and a ridiculously quick glimpse of the major sights as you glide by (20-AS, 30-minute circular tour). For an actual look at these sights, consider hiking most of the route. Tram #1 goes clockwise; tram #2, counterclockwise. Most sights are on the outside, so tram #2 is best (sit on right). The tour assumes you're sitting in front of the front car. Ideally, start at the Opera House. With a 24-hour ticket,

Vienna

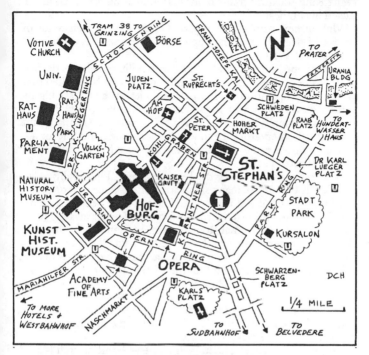

you can jump on and off as you go—trams come every five min-
utes. (Otherwise, buy your 20-AS one-ride ticket as you board.)
Described sights are on the right unless I say "on left." Let's go:
• Just past the Opera (on left): The city's main pedestrian drag,
Kärntner Strasse, leads to the zigzag roof of St. Stephan's Cathe-
dral. This tour makes a 360-degree circle, staying about this far
from that spire.
• At first bend: Look towards the tall fountain. Schwartzenberg
Platz—with its equestrian statue of Prince Charles Schwartzenberg, who battled Napoleon—leads to the Russian monument
(behind the fountain). This monument was built in 1945 as a
forced thanks to the Soviets for liberating Austria from the Nazis.
Formerly a sore point, now it's just ignored.
• Going down Schubertring you reach the huge *Stadtpark* (city
park), which honors 20 great Viennese musicians and composers
with statues. The white and yellow concert hall behind the trees is
the Kursalon, opened in 1867 by the Strauss brothers, who
directed many waltzes here (see Music, below).
• Immediately after next stop: In the park, the gilded statue of

Waltz King Johann Strauss holds his violin as he did when he con-
ducted his orchestra.

• While at next stop at end of park: On the left, a green statue of
Dr. Karl Lueger honors the popular man who was mayor of
Vienna until 1910.

• At next bend: The quaint building with military helmets decorating the windows was the Austrian ministry of war, back when that
was a serious operation. Field Marshal Radetzky, a military big shot
in the 19th century under Franz Josef, still sits on his high horse.

• At next corner: The white-domed building is the Urania, Franz
Josef's 1910 observatory. Lean forward and look behind it for a
peek at the huge red cars of the giant 100-year-old Ferris wheel in
Vienna's Prater Park.

• Now you're rolling along the Danube Canal. This "Baby
Danube" is one of the many small arms of the river that once
made up the Danube at this point. The rest have been gathered
together in a mightier modern-day Danube, farther away. This
was the site of the original Roman town, Vindobona. In three long
blocks, on the left (opposite the BP station), you'll see the ivy-
covered walls and round Romanesque arches of St. Ruprechts, the
oldest church in Vienna (built in the 11th century on a bit of
Roman ruins). By about 1200, Vienna had grown to fill the area
within this ring road.

• Leaving the canal, turning up Schottenring, at first stop: On the
left, the pink and white neo-Renaissance temple of money, the
Börse, is Vienna's stock exchange.

• Next stop, at corner: The huge frilly neo-Gothic church is a
"votive church," built in 1853 as a thanks to God when an assassination attempt on Emperor Franz Josef failed. Ahead on the right
is the Vienna University building, which faces (on the left, behind
the gilded angel) a chunk of the old city wall.

• At next stop: The neo-Gothic city hall, flying the flag of Europe,
towers over Rathaus Platz, a festive site of outdoor movies and
concerts. Immediately across the street (on left) is the Hofburg
Theater, Austria's national theater.

• At next stop: The neo-Greek temple of democracy houses the
Austrian Parliament. The lady with the golden helmet is Athena,
goddess of wisdom. Across the street (on left) is the royal park
called the "Volksgarten."

• At next stop: Ahead on the right is the Natural History Museum,
the first of Vienna's huge twin museums. Next door is the Kunsthistorisches Museum, containing the city's greatest collection of
paintings. A statue of Empress Maria Theresa sits between the
museums, facing the grand gate to the Hofburg, the emperor's
palace (on left). Of the five arches, only the center one was used by
the emperor. The gate, a modern addition, is located where Vienna's medieval city wall once stood.

• Fifty yards after next stop, through a gate in the black iron fence: On the left is the statue of Mozart in the Burggarten, which until 1880 was the private garden of the emperor. A hundred yards farther (on left), Goethe sits in a big, thought-provoking chair playing Trivia with Schiller (on right). Behind the statue of Schiller is the Academy of Fine Arts. Vienna had its share of intellectual and creative geniuses.

• Hey, there's the Opera again. Jump out and see the rest of the city.

Sights—Vienna's Old Center
(Sights are listed in a logical walking order.)

▲▲▲**Opera**—The Staatsoper, facing the Ring, just up from Stephansdom and next to the TI, is a central point for any visitor. While the critical reception of the building 130 years ago led the architect to commit suicide, and though it's been rebuilt since the World War II bombings, it's a dazzling place (60 AS, by guided 35-minute tour only, daily in English, July and August at 11:00, 13:00, 14:00, 15:00, and often at 10:00 and 16:00; other months, afternoons only). Tours are often canceled for rehearsals and shows, so check the posted schedule or call 01/51444 or 01/5144-42959.

The Vienna State Opera, with not the Vienna Philharmonic Orchestra but its farm team in the pit (you can't get into the best orchestra in town without doing time here), is one of the world's top opera houses. There are 300 performances a year—nearly nightly, except in July and August (when the singers rest their voices). Expensive seats are normally sold out. Unless Pavarotti is in town, it's easy to get one of 567 *Stehplatz* (standing-room spots, 20 AS for the very top, better 30-AS spots downstairs). If fewer than 567 people are in line, there's no need to line up early. The *Stehplatz* ticket window in the front lobby opens 80 minutes before each performance (*Stehplatz* information tel. 01/5144-42419). Dress is casual (but do your best) at the standing room bar.

Rick's crude tip: For me, three hours is a lot of opera. But just to see and hear the Opera House in action for half an hour is a treat. You can buy a ticket intending to just drop in for part of the show. Ushers don't mind letting tourists with standing-room tickets in for a short look. Ending time is posted in the lobby—you could drop in for just the finale. If you go for the start or finish, you'll see Vienna dressed up. With all the time you save, consider stopping by . . .

Sacher Café, home of every chocoholic's fantasy, the Sachertorte, faces the rear of the Opera (on Philharmoniker Strasse). A coffee and slice of cake here is 100 AS well invested.

Monument against War and Fascism—Behind the Opera House, on Albertinaplatz, a modern, white split statue is Vienna's monument remembering the victims of the 1938–1945 Nazi rule of Austria. In 1938, Germany annexed Austria, saying Austrians were wanna-be-Germans anyway. Austrians are *not* Germans—never were, never will be. They're quick to tell you that, while Austria was founded in 976, Germany wasn't born until 1870. For seven years (1938–1945), there was no Austria. In 1955, after 10 years of joint occupation by the victorious Allies, Austria regained her independence.

▲**Kärntner Strasse**—This grand mall (traffic-free since 1974) is the people-watching delight of this in-love-with-life city. It points south in the direction of the southern Austrian state of Kärnten (for which it's named). Starting from the Opera, you'll find the TI, city casino (at #41, the former Esterhazy Palace), many fine stores, pastry shops, the American Express Company office (#21–23), and then, finally, the cathedral.

▲▲**St. Stephan's Cathedral**—Stephansdom is the Gothic needle around which Vienna spins. It's survived Vienna's many wars and symbolizes the city's freedom. Locals call it "Steve" (*Steffl*, church open daily 6:00–22:00, tours are in German only, information board near entry has tour schedules and time of impressive 50-minute daily Mass).

Outside, the last bit of the 11th-century Romanesque church can be seen in the west end (above the entry): the portal and the round windows of the towers. The church survived the bombs of World War II but, in the last days of the war, fires from the street-fighting between Russian and Nazi troops leapt to the rooftop; the original timbered Gothic rooftop burnt, and the cathedral's huge bell crashed to the ground. With a financial outpouring of civic pride, the roof of this symbol of Austria was rebuilt in its original splendor by 1952. The ceramic tiles are purely decorative (and each has the name of a local who contributed money to the rebuilding). Photos of the war damage can be seen inside.

The interior is grand in general, but it's hard to get thrilled about any particular bit. An exception is the Gothic sandstone pulpit in the middle of the nave (on left or north). A spiral stairway winds up to the lectern, surrounded and supported by the four Latin Church fathers: St. Ambrose, St. Gerome, St. Gregory, and St. Augustine. The work of Anton Pilgram, this has all the elements of Flamboyant Gothic in miniature. But this was 1515. The Italian Renaissance was going strong in Italy and, while Gothic persisted in the north, the Renaissance spirit had already arrived. Pilgram included a rare self-portrait bust in his work (the guy with sculptor's tools, looking out a window under the stairs). Gothic art was to the glory of God. Artists were anonymous. In the more humanist Renaissance, man was allowed to shine—and artists became famous.

Hundreds of years of history are carved in its walls and buried in its crypt (40 AS, open at odd times, tel. 01/5155-23526). You can ascend both towers, the north (via crowded elevator) and the south (by spiral staircase). The north shows you a big bell (the 21-ton Pummerin, cast from the cannon captured from the Turks in 1683) but a mediocre view (40 AS, daily 9:00–18:00, enter inside). The 450-foot-high south tower, called St. Stephan's Tower, offers a great view—343 tightly wound steps away, up the spiral staircase at the watchman's lookout, 246 feet up (30 AS, daily 9:00–17:30, enter outside and burn about one Sachertorte of calories). From the top, use your *Vienna from A to Z* to locate the famous sights.

The peaceful **Cathedral Museum** (Dom und Diözesen Museum) gives a close-up look at piles of religious paintings, statues, and a treasury (40 AS, Tuesday–Saturday 10:00–16:00, behind the church and past the buggy stand, Stephansplatz 6). Near the church entrance, descend into the Stephansplatz subway stop for a peek into the 13th-century Virgilkapelle.

▲▲**Stephansplatz, Graben, and Kohlmarkt**—The atmosphere of the church square, Stephanplatz, is colorful and lively. At nearby Graben Street (which was once a *Graben* or "ditch"), top-notch street entertainment dances around an exotic plague monument. In medieval times, people did not understand the causes of plagues and figured they were a punishment from God. It was common for survivors to thank God with a monument like this one from the 1600s.

Just beyond the monument is a fine set of Jugendstil public toilets (6 AS). St. Peter's Church faces the toilets. Step into this festival of Baroque (from 1708) and check out the jeweled skeletons—anonymous martyrs donated by the pope.

Kohlmarkt (end of Graben), Vienna's most elegant shopping street (except for "American Catalog Shopping," at #5, second floor), leads left to the palace. Wander down here, checking out the edible window displays at Demel (Kohlmarkt 14). Then drool through the interior (coffee and cake for 100 AS). Shops like this one and the one across the street boast "K. u. K." This means a shop considered good enough for the *König und Kaiser* (king and emperor—same guy).

Kohlmarkt leads to Michaelerplatz. The stables of the Spanish Riding School face this square (left). Notice the Roman excavation in the center. Enter the Hofburg Palace by walking through the gate and into the first square (In der Burg).

Sights—Vienna's Hofburg Palace

▲▲**Hofburg**—The complex, confusing, imposing Imperial Palace, with 640 years of architecture, demands your attention. This first Habsburg residence grew with the family empire from the 13th century until 1913, when the new wing (Neue Burg) was opened. The winter residence of the Habsburg rulers until 1918, it's still the home of the Spanish Riding School, the Vienna Boys' Choir, the Austrian president's office, and several important museums.

While you could lose yourself in its myriad halls and courtyards, I'd focus on three things: the Imperial Apartments, Treasury, and Neue Berg (New Palace).

Orient from **In der Burg Square**. The statue is of Emperor
Franz II (grandson of Maria Theresa and grandfather of Franz
Josef). Behind him is a tower with three kinds of clocks (the yellow
disc shows the stage of the moon tonight). On the right, a door
leads to the Imperial Apartments and Hofburg model. Franz II is
facing the oldest part of the palace. The gate (which used to have a
drawbridge) leads to the 13th-century Swiss Court (named for the
Swiss mercenary guards who used to be stationed here) with the
Schatzkammer (treasury) and the Hofburgkappelle (palace chapel)
—where the Boys' Choir sings the Mass. Continuing out opposite
the way you entered In der Burg, you'll pass through the left-most
tunnel (with a handy sandwich bar—Hofburg Stüberl) to the
Hero's Square and the Neue Burg. Tour the Imperial Apartments
first.

▲▲▲**Imperial Apartments (Kaiserappartements)**—These lavish, Versailles-type "wish-I-were-God" royal rooms are a small,
downtown version of the grander Schönbrunn Palace. If rushed,
and have time for only one, these suffice. The Imperial Apartments share a ticket booth with the Silver and Porcelain Collection (Silberkammer). You can tour either for 80 AS or get a
Kombi-Ticket for 95 AS and see them both (daily 9:00–17:00,
from courtyard through St. Michael's Gate, just off Michaelerplatz, tel. 01/533-7570). While combo tickets are cheap, for most,
the rooms of plates and fancy silverware are not worth the extra 15
AS or time. (Study the great Hofburg model outside near the
ticket line. From there, see enough of the collection through the
window.) Palace visits are a one-way romp through 20 rooms.
You'll find no English information within, but with the following
description, you won't need the 95-AS Hofburg guidebook.

• The first few rooms get you warmed up.

• **The audience chamber:** Three huge paintings would entertain
guests waiting here before an audience with the emperor. Every
citizen had the right to meet privately with the emperor. Paintings in this room show crowds of commoners enthusiastic about
their Habsburg royalty. On the right: The emperor returning to
Vienna celebrating news that Napoleon had begun his retreat in
1809. Left: The return of the emperor from the 1814 Peace of
Paris, the treaty which ended the Napoleonic wars. (The 1815
Congress of Vienna that followed was the greatest assembly of
diplomats in European history. Its goal: to establish peace
through a "balance of power" among nations. While rulers
ignored nationalism in favor of continued dynastic rule, this
worked for about 100 years, when a colossal war wiped out
Europe's royal families.) Center: Less importantly, the emperor

Vienna's Hofburg Palace

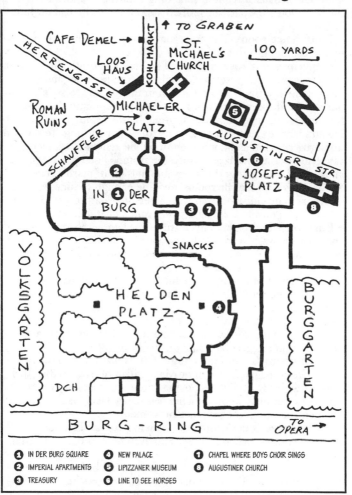

1 IN DER BURG SQUARE **4** NEW PALACE **7** CHAPEL WHERE BOYS CHOIR SINGS
2 IMPERIAL APARTMENTS **5** LIPIZZANER MUSEUM **8** AUGUSTINER CHURCH
3 TREASURY **6** LINE TO SEE HORSES

makes his first public appearance to adoring crowds after recovering from a life-threatening illness (1826). The chandelier is Baroque of Bohemian crystal.

• **Audience room:** Suddenly you were face to face with the emp. The portrait shows Franz Josef (my vote for the greatest Habsburg emperor) in 1915 when he was over 80 years old. Famously energetic, he lived a spartan life dedicated to duty. He'd stand at the high table here to meet with commoners who came to show gratitude or make a request. (Standing kept things moving.) On the table you see a partial list of 56 appointments he had on June 3, 1910.

• **Conference room:** The emperor presided here over the equivalent of cabinet meetings.

• **Emperor Franz Josef's study:** The desk was originally between the windows. Franz Josef could look up from his work and see his lovely empress Elisabeth's reflection in the mirror. "Sissy's" main purpose in life seemed to be to preserve her reputation as a beautiful empress and maintain her fairy-tale hair. In spite of severe dieting and fanatic exercise, age took its toll. After turning 30, she had no portraits painted and was seen in public generally with a delicate fan covering her face. Notice the trompe l'oeil paintings above each door giving the believable illusion of marble relief.

• The walls between the rooms are wide enough to hide servants' corridors. The emperor lived with a personal staff of 14: "3 valets, 4 lackeys, 2 doormen, 2 manservants, and 3 chambermaids."

• **Emperor's bedroom:** This features his famous spartan iron bed and portable washstand (necessary until 1880 when the palace got running water). A small painted porcelain portrait of the newlywed royal couple sits on the dresser. Franz Josef lived here after his estrangement from Sissy. An etching shows the empress—an avid hunter—riding sidesaddle while jumping a hedge. The big ornate stove in the corner was fed from behind. Through the 19th century, this was a standard form of heating.

• **Large drawing room:** See the paintings of the emperor and empress in grand gala ballroom outfits from 1865.

• **The emperor's smoking room:** This is dedicated to the memory of the assassinated Emperor Maximillian of Mexico (bearded portrait, killed in 1867). A smoking room was necessary in the early 19th century, when smoking was newly fashionable but only for men and not in the presence of women.

• **The empress's bedroom and drawing room:** This was Sissy's, refurbished neo-rococo in 1854. She lived here until her death in 1898.

• **Sissy's dressing room:** This was the marital bedroom of the newlywed couple. The open bathroom door shows her huge copper tub. Servants worked two hours a day on Sissy's famous ankle-length hair here. She'd exercise on the wooden structure. While she had a tough time with people, she did fine with animals. Her favorite circus horses, Flick and Flock, prance on the wall.

• **The empress's large drawing room:** The room is painted with Mediterranean escapes, the 19th-century equivalent of travel posters. The statue is of Elisa, Napoleon's oldest sister (by the neoclassical master Canova).

• Around the corner is a room dedicated to the last emperor (Karl, ruled 1916–1918) and empress (Zita, lived 1892–1989). After the abdication of the last Habsburg, Zita lived in exile until her old age, then returned to Austria.

• **Reception room:** This has Gobelin wall hangings, a 1776 gift from Marie Antoinette and Louis XVI in Paris to their Vienese counterparts.

• **The dining room:** It's dinner time, and Franz Josef has called his large family together. The settings are of modest silver. Gold was saved for formal state dinners. Next to each namecard was a menu with the chef responsible for each dish. (Talk about pressure.) While the Hofburg had tableware for 4,000, feeding 3,000 was a typical day. The cellar was stocked with 60,000 bottles of wine—fit for an emperor. The kitchen was huge—50 birds could be roasted on the hand-driven spits at once.

• **Small salon:** The last room is dedicated to Franz Josef's first two heirs: Rudolf (his troubled son, who committed suicide in 1889) and Franz Ferdinand (his liberal nephew, assassinated in Sarajevo, 1914).

▲▲▲**Treasury**—The Weltliche und Geistliche Schatzkammer (secular and Religious Treasure Room) contains by far the best jewels on the Continent. Slip through the vault doors and reflect on the glitter of 21 rooms filled with scepters, swords, crowns, orbs, weighty robes, a 96-inch-tall and 500-year-old unicorn horn (or maybe the tusk of a narwhal), double-headed eagles, gowns, dangles, and gem-studded bangles. Remember that these were owned by the Holy Roman Emperor—a divine monarch.

Study the Throne Cradle (room 5). Napoleon's son was born in 1811 and made king of Rome. The little eagle at the foot is symbolically not yet able to fly, but glory-bound. "Glory" is the star with his dad's big "N" raised high.

The collection's highlight is the 10th-century crown of the Holy Roman Emperor (room 11). The imperial crown swirls with symbolism "proving" that the emperor is both holy and Roman. The jeweled arch over the top is reminiscent of the parade helmet of ancient Roman emperors whose successors the HRE claimed to be. The cross on top says that the HRE rules as Christ's representative on earth. King Solomon's portrait is Old Testament proof that kings can be wise and good. The crown's eight sides represent the celestial city of Jerusalem's eight gates. The jewels on the front panel symbolize the Twelve Apostles. The honorary 13th stone is the HRE.

Two cases in this room have jewels from the reign of Karl der Grosse (Charlemagne), the greatest ruler of medieval Europe. Notice Charlemagne modeling the crown in the tall painting adjacent. Room 12 features a painting of the coronation of Josef II in 1764, wearing the crown and royal garb you've just seen (80 AS, Wednesday–Monday 10:00–18:00, closed Tuesday, follow "Schatzkammer" signs through the black, red, and gold arch leading from the main courtyard into the Schweizerhof, tel. 01/533-7931).

Take advantage of the free and helpful Art-Guide (deposit: passport or 500 AS). Point this infrared computer at display cases to get information.

▲**Neue Burg (New Palace)**—This last grand addition to the palace, from just before World War I, was built for Franz Ferdinand but never used. Its grand facade arches around Heldenplatz, or Hero's Square. Notice statues of the two great Austrian heroes on horseback: Prince Eugene of Savoy (who saved the city from the Turks) and Archduke Charles Schwartzenberg (first to beat Napoleon in a battle, breaking Nappy's image of invincibility and heralding the end of the Napoleonic age). The Neue Burg houses three small but fine museums (same ticket): an armory, historical musical instruments, and classical statuary from ancient Ephesus. The musical instruments are particularly entertaining, and free radio headsets (when they work) play appropriate music in each room. Wait for the German description to finish, and you might hear the instruments you're seeing. Stay tuned in, as graceful period music accompanies your wander through the neighboring halls of medieval weaponry—a killer collection of crossbows, swords, and armor. An added bonus is the chance to wander all alone among those royal Habsburg halls, stairways, and painted ceilings. Gavotte to the music down the royal stairs and out (30 AS for all three collections, Wednesday–Monday 10:00–18:00, closed Tuesday, almost no tourists).

More Sights—Vienna

▲**Lipizzaner Museum**—This is a must for horse lovers. This tidy new museum in the Renaissance Stallburg Palace shows the 400-year history of the famous riding school. Videos show the horses in action (on TVs throughout and in the basement theater—45-minute movie in German, but great horse footage). A highlight for many is the opportunity to view the stable from a museum window and actually see the famous white horses just sitting there looking common (50 AS, daily 9:00–18:00, Reitschulgasse 2 between Josefsplatz and Michaelerplatz, tel. 01/5264-18430). At the end of World War II, knowing that the Soviets were about to take control of Vienna, U.S. General Patton ordered a raid on the stable to save the horses and insure the survival of their fine old bloodlines.

Seeing the Lipizzaner Stallions: While seats for performances of Vienna's prestigious Spanish Riding School are booked long in advance, standing room is usually available the same day (tickets 250–900 AS, standing room 200 AS, one or two shows per week April–June, September, October). Lucky for the masses, training sessions in a chandeliered Baroque hall are open to the public (100 AS at the door, Tuesday–Friday 10:00–12:00 roughly February–June, September–December; occasional rehearsals with music on Saturdays are especially entertaining). The gang lines up early at Josefsplatz gate 2. Save money and avoid the wait by buying admission to the training session together with a ticket to the museum. Or, better yet, simply show up late. Tourists line up for hours to get in at 10:00. Anyone can just waltz in with no wait at all after 11:00. Almost no one stays for the full two hours—except for the horses.

▲**Augustinian Church**—Step into the nearby Augustinerkirche (on Josefsplatz), the church where the Habsburg weddings took place. Don't miss the exquisite Canova tomb (neoclassical, 1805) of Maria Theresa's favorite daughter, Maria Christina, with its incredibly sad white-marble procession. The church has the burial vault for the hearts of the Habsburgs (by appointment only).

▲▲**Kaisergruft, the Remains of the Habsburgs**—Visiting the imperial remains is not as easy as you might imagine. These original organ donors left their bodies—147 in all—in the Kaisergruft (Capuchin Crypt), their hearts in St. George Chapel in the Augustinian Church (church open daily, but to see the goods you'll have to talk to a priest; near the Hofburg, Augustinerstrasse 3), and their entrails in the crypt below St. Stephan's Cathedral. Don't tripe.

Upon entering the Kaisergruft (40 AS, daily 9:30–16:00, behind the Opera on Neuer Markt), buy the 5-AS map with a Habsburg family tree and a chart locating each coffin from the Capuchin brother at the door. The double coffin of Maria Theresa and her husband is worth a close look for its artwork. Don't miss the tomb of Franz Josef and—the latest addition—Empress Zita, buried in 1989.

Rather than chasing down all these body parts, remember that the magnificence of this city is the real remains of the Habsburgs. Pan up. Watch the clouds glide by the ornate gables of Vienna.

▲▲▲**Kunsthistorisches Museum**—This exciting museum across the Ring from the Hofburg Palace showcases the great Habsburg art collection—masterpieces by Dürer, Rubens, Titian, Raphael, and especially Brueghel. There's also a fine display of Egyptian, classical, and applied arts, including a divine golden salt bowl by Cellini. The museum sells a pamphlet on the top 21 paintings (20 AS) and offers English tours (30 AS, 1.5 hours, usually at 11:00 and 15:00 Tuesday–Sunday April–October). The paintings are hung on one floor (95 AS, higher depending on special exhibitions, Tuesday–Sunday 10:00–18:00, Thursday until 21:00, closed Monday, tel. 01/525-240).

Natural History Museum—In the twin building facing the art museum, you'll find moon rocks, dinosaur stuff, and the fist-sized Venus of Willendorf—at 30,000 years old, the world's oldest sex symbol, found in the Danube Valley (50 AS, Wednesday–Monday 9:00–18:00, closed Tuesday, off-season 9:00–15:00).

▲**Academy of Fine Arts**—This small but exciting collection includes works by Bosch, Botticelli, and Rubens; a Venice series by

Guardi; and a self-portrait by 15-year-old Van Dyck (50 AS, Tuesday–Sunday 10:00–16:00, closed Monday, three blocks from the Opera at Schillerplatz 3, tel. 01/5881-6225).

KunstHausWien—This "make yourself at home" modern-art museum is a hit with lovers of modern art. It features the work of local painter/environmentalist Hundertwasser (90 AS, 45 AS on Monday, daily 10:00–19:00; 3, Weissgerberstrasse 13, nearest metro: U-3 Landstrasse, tel. 01/712-0491). Nearby, the one-with-nature Hundertwasserhaus (at Löwengasse and Kegelgasse) is a complex of 50 lived-in apartments. This was built in the 1980s as a breath of architectural fresh air in a city of boring blocky apartment complexes. It's not open to visitors but worth visiting for its fun-loving and colorful patchwork exterior, the Hundertwasser festival of shops across the street, and for the pleasure of annoying its residents.

▲Jugendstil—Vienna gave birth to its own curvaceous brand of Art Nouveau around the turn of the century: Jugendstil. The TI has a brochure laying out Vienna's 20th-century architecture. The best of Vienna's scattered Jugendstil sights: the Belvedere Palace collection; the clock on Höher Markt (which does a musical act at noon); the WC on the Graben; and the Karlsplatz subway stop, where you'll find the gilded-cabbage-domed gallery with the movement's slogan: "To each century its art and to art its liberty." Klimt, Wagner, and friends (who called themselves the Vienna Succession) first exhibited their "liberty style" art here in 1897.

▲Belvedere Palace—The elegant palace of Prince Eugene of Savoy (the still-much-appreciated conqueror of the Turks), and later home of Franz Ferdinand, houses the Austrian Gallery of 19th- and 20th-century art. Skip the lower palace and focus on the garden and the top floor of the upper palace (Oberes Belvedere) for a winning view of the city and a fine collection of Jugendstil art, Klimt, and Kokoschka (60 AS, Tuesday–Sunday 10:00–17:00, closed Monday, entrance at Prinz Eugen Strasse 27, tel. 01/795-570). Your ticket includes the Austrian Baroque and Gothic art in the Lower Palace.

▲▲▲Schönbrunn Palace—Only Schloss Schönbrunn, among Europe's palaces, rivals Versailles. Located 7 kilometers from the center, it was the Habsburgs' summer residence. It is big—1,441 rooms—but don't worry, only 40 rooms are shown to the public. (The families of 260 civil servants actually rent simple apartments in the rest of the palace.)

While the exterior is Baroque, the interior was finished under Maria Theresa in the let-them-eat-cake rococo style. The chandeliers are either of hand-carved wood with gold-leaf gilding or of Bohemian crystal. Thick walls hid the servants as they ran around stoking the ceramic stoves from the back, and so on. Most of the public rooms are decorated in neo-Baroque as they were under Franz Josef (ruled 1848–1916). While World War II bombs rained on the city and the palace grounds, the palace itself took only one direct hit. Thankfully, that bomb, which crashed through three floors, including the sumptuous central ballroom, was a dud.

Choose between the Imperial Tour and the bigger Grand Tour. Both come with free headphones that describe the sights in English as you walk through the rooms on your own. The Imperial Tour covers 22 rooms (90 AS, 30 minutes, the Grand Palace rooms plus apartments of Franz Josef and Elisabeth). I'd recommend the Grand Tour, which covers those 22 rooms plus 18 more (120 AS, 45 minutes, adding the apartments of Maria Theresa). Optional guided tours do all 40 rooms in English (departing roughly every two hours, 25 AS extra). The headphones are so good I'd skip the tour.

Schönbrunn suffers from serious crowd problems. To avoid the long delays, simply make a reservation by telephone (01/8111-3239). You'll get an appointment time and ticket number. Upon arrival, go to the first desk reserved for group leaders, give your number, pick up your ticket and jump in ahead of the masses. If you show up without having called first, wait in line, buy your ticket, read the time listed, and wait until then to enter (which could be tomorrow). Kill waiting time in the gardens or coach museum (palace open daily 8:30–17:45—last entry 17:00, off-season until 17:15—last entry 16:30; take tram #58 from West-bahnhof or U-4 to Schönbrunn, tel. 01/8111-3239). Crowds are worst around 10:00 and on weekends; it's least crowded from 12:00–14:00 and after 16:00.

Coach Museum Wagenburg: The Schönbrunn coach museum is a 19th-century traffic jam of 50 impressive royal car-riages and sleighs. Highlights include silly sedan chairs, the death-black hearse carriage (used for Franz Josef in 1916 and most recently for Empress Zita in 1989), and an extravagantly gilded imperial carriage—pulled by eight Cinderella horses (30 AS, daily 9:00–18:00, off-season 10:00–16:00 and closes on winter Mondays, 200 meters from the palace).

Palace Gardens: A stroll through the emperor's garden with countless commoners (after strolling through all the Habsburgs tucked neatly into their crypts) is a celebration of the natural (and necessary) evolution of civilization from autocracy into real democracy. We're doing good. The sculpted gardens (with a palm house, 45 AS, 9:30–18:00) lead past Europe's oldest zoo (Tier-garten, 100 AS, built by Maria Theresa's husband for the enter-tainment and education of the court in 1752) up to the Gloriette, a purely decorative monument celebrating an obscure Austrian mili-tary victory and offering a fine city view (and an expensive cup of coffee). The park is free and open until dusk.

Honorable Mention—There's much, much more. The city museum brochure lists everything. If you're into butterflies, Esperanto, undertakers, tobacco, clowns, fire fighting, Freud, or the homes of dead composers, you'll find them all in Vienna. Several good museums that try very hard but are submerged in the greatness of Vienna include: **Historical Museum of the City of Vienna** (Tuesday–Sunday 9:00–16:30, Karlsplatz), **Folkloric Museum of Austria** (8, Laudongasse 15, tel. 01/438-905), and **Museum of Military History**, one of Europe's best if you like swords and shields (Heeregeschichtliches Museum; Saturday–Thursday 10:00–16:00, closed Friday; 3, Arsenal, Objekt 18). The **Albertina Museum**, with its great collection of sketches and graphic art, is closed for a few years. **Shopping:** The best-value shopping street, with more than 2,000 shops, is Mariahilfer Strasse. **Vienna Woods:** For a walk in the Vienna Woods, catch the U-4 subway to Heiligenstadt then bus #38A to Kahlenberg, where there are great city views and a café terrace overlooking the city. From there it's a peaceful 45-minute downhill hike to the *Heurigen* of Nussdorf or Grinzing to enjoy some wine.

Top People-Watching and Strolling Sights

▲**City Park**—Vienna's Stadtpark is a waltzing world of gardens, memorials to local musicians, ponds, peacocks, music in bandstands, and local people escaping the city. Notice the Jugendstil entry at the Stadtpark subway station. The Kursalon orchestra plays Strauss waltzes nightly in summer (see Music, below).
▲**Prater**—Vienna's sprawling amusement park tempts any visitor with its huge 220-foot-high, famous, and lazy Ferris wheel (*Riesenrad*), roller coaster, bumper cars, Lilliputian railroad, and endless eateries. This is a fun, goofy place to share the evening with thousands of Viennese (daily 9:00–24:00 in summer, U-Bahn: Praterstern). For a local-style family dinner, eat at Schweizerhaus (good food, great beer) or Wieselburger Bierinsel.
Sunbathing—Like most Europeans, the Austrians worship the sun. Their lavish swimming centers are as much for tanning as for swimming. For the best man-made island beach scene, head for the "Danube Sea," Vienna's 20 miles of beach along Danube Island (subway: Donauinsel).
▲**Naschmarkt**—Vienna's ye olde produce market bustles daily, near the Opera along Wienzeile Street. It's likably seedy and surrounded by sausage stands, Turkish *döner kebab* stalls, cafés, and theaters. Each Saturday it's infested by a huge flea market where, in olden days, locals would come to hire a monkey to pick little critters out of their hair (Monday–Friday 6:00–18:30, Saturday 6:00–17:00). For a picnic park, walk a block down Schleifmuhlgasse.

Summer Music Scene

Vienna is Europe's music capital. It's music *con brio* from October through June, with things reaching a symphonic climax during the Vienna Festival each May and June. Sadly, in July and August, the

Boys' Choir, the Opera, and many more music companies are—
like you—on vacation. But Vienna hums year-round with live classical music. In the summer, you have these basic choices:

Touristy Mozart and Strauss Concerts—If the music comes to
you, it's touristy—designed for flash-in-the-pan Mozart fans. Pow-
dered-wig orchestra performances are given almost nightly in
grand traditional settings (400–600 AS). Pesky wigged and powdered Mozarts peddle tickets in the streets with slick sales pitches
about the magic of the venue and the quality of the musicians.
Second-rate orchestras, clad in historic costumes, perform the
greatest hits of Mozart and Strauss. While there's not a local person in the audience, the tourists generally enjoy the evening.

Strauss in the Kursalon—Two rival companies offer Strauss concerts inside the Kursalon, where the Waltz King himself directed
wildly popular concerts 100 years ago. To accommodate antsy
groups, concert tickets are sold in two sections: 20:00–21:00 and
21:30–22:30 (260 AS for one with a glass of wine, 490 AS for both,
tel. 01/718-9666; for the other company, tel. 01/710-5580). Or pick
up the brochures from racks all over town. Shows are a touristy mix
of ballet, waltzing, 15-piece orchestra in wigs and old outfits, and a
chance to get on the floor and waltz yourself. On balmy summer
evenings, the concert moves into the romantic garden.

Serious Concerts—These events, including the Opera, are listed
in the monthly *Programm* (available at the TI). Tickets run from
300 to 700 AS (plus a stiff 25 percent booking fee when booked in
advance or through a box office like the one next to the TI behind
the Opera). If you call a concert hall directly, they can advise you
on the availability of (cheaper) tickets at the door. Vienna takes
care of its starving artists (and tourists) by offering cheap standing-
room tickets to top-notch music and opera. Locals are amazed at
the stiff prices tourists pay to see otherwise affordable concerts.

Vienna's Summer of Music Festival assures that even from
June through September you'll find lots of top-notch concerts,
choirs, and symphonies (special *Klang Bogen* brochure at TI; tickets at the Wien Ticket pavilion off Kärntner Strasse next to the
Opera House, or go directly to the location of the particular event,
tel. 01/4000-8410 for information).

▲▲Vienna Boys' Choir—The boys sing (heard but not seen, from
a high balcony) at Mass in the Imperial Chapel (Hofburgkapelle) of
the Hofburg (entrance at Schweizerhof) at 9:15 on Sundays, except
from July through mid-September. Seats must be reserved at least
two months in advance (60–280 AS), but standing room inside is free
and open to the first 60 who line up. Rather than line up early, you
can simply swing by and stand in the narthex just outside, from
where you can hear the boys and see the Mass on a TV monitor.
Boys' Choir concerts (on stage in the Konzerthaus) are also given
Fridays at 15:30 in May, June, September, and October (390–430

AS, tel. 01/5880-4141, fax 011-431-587-1268 from the United States or write Reisebüro Mondial, Faulmanngasse 4, 1040 Wien). They're nice kids but, for my taste, not worth all the commotion.

Vienna's Cafés and Wine Gardens

▲**Viennese Coffeehouse**—In Vienna the living room is down the street at the neighborhood coffeehouse. This tradition is just another example of the Viennese expertise in good living. Each of Vienna's many long-established (and sometimes even legendary) coffeehouses has its individual character (and characters). They offer newspapers, pastries, sofas, elegance, a smoky ambience, and a "take all the time you want" charm for the price of a cup of coffee. You may want to order *malange* (with a little milk) rather than *schwarzer* (black).

My favorites are: **Café Hawelka**, with a rumpled, "brooding Trotsky" atmosphere, paintings on the walls by struggling artists who couldn't pay, a saloon-wood flavor, chalkboard menu, smoked velvet couches, an international selection of newspapers, and a phone that rings for regulars (8:00–2:00, Sunday from 16:00, closed Tuesday, Dorotheergasse 6, just off the Graben); crowded **Café Central**, with Jugendstil decor and great *Apfelstrudel* (8:00–20:00, closed Sunday, Herrengasse 14); the Jugendstil **Café Sperl**, dating from 1880 (7:00–23:00, closed Sunday in summer, Gumpendorfer 11, just off Naschmarkt); and the basic, untouristy **Café Ritter** (daily 8:00–20:00, Mariahilfer Strasse 73, at the Neubaugasse subway stop near several of my recommended hotels).

▲**Wine Gardens**—The *Heurige* is a uniquely Viennese institution celebrating the *Heurige*, or new wine. It all started when the Habsburgs let Vienna's vintners sell their own wine tax-free for 300 days a year. Several hundred families opened *Heurigen* (wine-garden restaurants) clustered around the edge of Vienna, and a tradition was born. Today they do their best to maintain their old-village atmosphere, serving the homemade new wine (the last vintage, until November 11) with light meals and strolling musicians. For a *Heurige* evening, rather than go to a particular place, tram to the wine-garden district of your choice and wander around, choosing the place with the best ambience.

Of the many *Heurige* suburbs, **Grinzing** (tram #38 or #38A) is the most famous and lively—but it comes with too many tour buses. **Nussdorf** is less touristy but still characteristic and popular with locals (two fine places are right at the end of tram D). Pfarrplatz has many decent spots. **Beethoven's home** in Heiligenstadt comes with crowds and live music (Pfarrplatz, tram #38A or #37 and a 10-minute walk, tel. 01/371-287). While Beethoven lived here in 1817 (to be near a spa he hoped would cure his worsening deafness), he composed his Sixth Symphony (*Pastoral*). These suburbs are all within a 15-minute stroll of each other.

Gumpoldskirchen is a small medieval village farther outside of Vienna with more *Heurige* ambience than tourists. Ride the commuter train from the Opera to Gumpoldskirchen and you'll find plenty of places to choose from.

At any *Heurige*, fill your plate at a self-serve cold-cut buffet (75–125 AS for dinner). Waitresses will then take your wine order (30 AS per quarter-liter). Many locals claim it takes several years of practice to distinguish between *Heurige* and vinegar. For a near-*Heurige* experience right downtown, drop by Gigerl Stadtheuriger (see Eating, below).

Nightlife

If old music or new wine isn't your thing, Vienna has plenty of alternatives. For an up-to-date rundown on fun after dark, get the TI's free *Young Vienna Scene* booklet. An area known as the "Bermuda Dreieck" (Triangle), north of the cathedral between Rotenturmstrasse and Judengasse, is the hot local nightspot, with lots of classy pubs, or *Beisl* (such as Krah Krah, Salzamt, and Kitch, and Bitter) and popular music spots. On a balmy summer evening, the most lively scene is at Danube Island.

Sleeping in Vienna
(12 AS = about $1, tel. code: 01)

Sleep Code: **S** = Single, **D** = Double/Twin, **T** = Triple, **Q** = Quad, **b** = bathroom, **t** = toilet only, **s** = shower only, **CC** = Credit Card (Visa, MasterCard, Amex). English is spoken at each place.

Call accommodations a few days in advance. Most places will hold a room without a deposit if you promise to arrive before 17:00. My recommendations stretch mainly along the likeable Mariahilfer Strasse from the Westbahnhof (West Station) to the town center. Unless otherwise noted, prices include a continental breakfast. Street addresses start with the district. Postal code is 1XX0, with XX being the district.

Sleeping Outside the Ring, along Mariahilfer Strasse

Lively Mariahilfer Strasse connects the West Station with the center. The U-3 subway line, starting at the Westbahnhof, goes down Mariahilfer Strasse to the cathedral. The very Viennese Mariahilfer Strasse is a comfortable and vibrant area filled with local shops and cafés. Most are within a few steps of the subway station just one or two stops from the West Bahnhof. The first three are relatively luxurious splurges followed by you-get-what-you-pay-for good budget values.

Pension Mariahilf is a four-star place offering a clean aristocratic air in an affordable and cozy pension package. Its 12 rooms are spacious and feel new, but with a Jugendstil flair. With four stars, everything's done right—the latest American magazines and

Vienna: Hotels Outside the Ring

1 FUNFHAUS	**8** NEUSTIFTGASSE
2 BUDAI	**9** BELIEVE IT OR...
3 LINDENHOF	**10** WILD
4 HARGITA	**11** ANDREAS
5 ASTRON SUITE	**12** IBIS WIEN
6 QUISISANA	**13** MARIAHILF
7 HILDE WOLF	

even free Mozart Balls at the reception desk (Sb-800 AS, Db-1,300 AS, Tb-1,700 AS, including an all-you-can eat breakfast, at U-3 Neubaugasse station, Mariahilfer Strasse 49, tel. 01/586-1781, fax 01/5861-78122, warmly run by Frau and Herr Ender).

Hotel Ibis Wien, a modern highrise hotel with American charm, is ideal for anyone tired of quaint old Europe. Its 340 cookie-cutter rooms are bright, comfortable, and modern, with all the conveniences. It has a friendly, spirited staff, lots of smoke-free rooms, some easy-access rooms and air conditioning—rare in this price range (Sb-890 AS, Db-1,090 AS, Tb-1,290 AS, breakfast extra, CC:VMA, elevator, three blocks from the Westbahnhof and metro station at Mariahilfer Gürtel 22–24, A-1060 Wien, tel. 01/59998, fax 01/597-9090, e-mail: mariahilf@hotel-ibis.co.at).

Astron Suite Hotel Wien/Atterseehaus, a new business- and family-friendly place, has 54 apartment-like suites. Each has a separate living room, two TVs, full modern bathroom, large desk and full kitchenette. (Suites for two adults and up to two children-1,880 AS, breakfast extra, CC:VMA, non-smoking rooms, elevator, at the U-3 Sieglergasse subway stop, Mariahilferstrasse 78, A-1070 Wien, tel. 01/5254-6000, fax 01/5254-60015, e-mail: wienatterseehaus@astron-hotels.de). Nearby they have a second, bigger suite hotel with the same prices and rooms (Mariahilferstrasse 32, tel. 01/521-720).

Pension Lindenhof is worn but clean, filled with plants, and run with a unique combination of Bulgarian and Armenian warmth (S-370 AS, Sb-470 AS, D-620 AS, Db-840 AS, cheaper in winter, hall showers-20 AS, most rooms are spacious; 7, Lindengasse 4, 1070 Wien, take U-3 Neubaugasse to Stiftgasse, tel. 01/523-0498, fax 01/523-7362).

Pension Hargita, with 19 generally small, bright, and tidy rooms (mostly twins), is handy—right at the U-3 Zieglergasse stop—and next to a sex shop (S-400 AS, Ss-450 AS, D-600 AS, Ds-700 AS, Db-800 AS, Ts-850 AS, Tb-1,050 AS, Qb-1,100 AS, breakfast-40 AS, cheaper for longer stays off-season, U-Bahn: Zieglergasse, on corner of Mariahilfer Strasse and Andreasgasse at 7, Andreasgasse 1, 1070 Wien, tel. 01/526-1928, fax 01/526-0492).

Budai Ildiko, in a Jugendstil building with a vintage elevator, has high-ceilinged rooms, classy furnishings, and a warm, homey feeling (three rooms, S-350 AS, D-560 AS, T-820 AS, Q-1,050 AS, no breakfast but free coffee, laundry-20 AS; 7, Lindengasse 39/5, 1070 Wien, tel. 01/523-1058, tel. & fax 01/526-2595, run by a charming Hungarian woman, Frau Budai SE).

Privatzimmer Hilde Wolf is another homey place one floor above an ugly entry, with four huge rooms like old libraries. Hilde loves her work, will do your laundry if you stay two nights, and even offers to baby-sit if traveling parents need a break. From the Westbahnhof, take tram #6 or #18 five stops to Eichenstrasse, then tram #62 six stops to Paulanergasse. For a real home in Vienna, unpack here (S-450 AS, D-650 AS, T-955 AS, Q-1,225 AS, with a big, friendly, family-style breakfast, prices through 1999; three blocks off Naschmarkt near U-2 Karlsplatz, 4, Schleifmühlgasse 7, 1040 Vienna, tel. 01/586-5103, reserve by phone and CC; if you can't make it, call to cancel).

Pension Quisisana is tired and ramshackle, but cheap and sleepable for vagabonds (S-330 AS, Ss-380 AS, D-520 AS, Ds-600–640 AS, Db-700–740 AS, third person-260 AS, 6, Windmuhlgasse 6, 1060 Wien, tel. 01/587-7155, fax 01/587-715-633).

Pension Funfhaus is big, clean, stark, and quiet. Although the neighborhood is rundown, this place is a great value (S-390 AS, Sb-470 AS, D-570 AS, Db-650 AS, T-850 AS, Tb-920 AS, two-bedroom apartments for four-1,130 AS, closed mid-November–February; 15, Sperrgasse 12, 1150 Wien, tel. 01/892-3545 or 01/892-0286, fax 01/892-0460, Frau Susi Tersch SE). Half the rooms are in the fine main building and half are in the annex, which has good rooms but is near the train tracks and a bit scary on the street at night. From the station, ride tram #52 or #58 two stops or walk seven blocks away from downtown on Mariahilfer Strasse, to Sperrgasse.

Sleeping Six Blocks North of Mariahilfer Strasse

Jugendherbergen Neustiftgasse is a cheery and well-run youth hostel. They'll hold rooms until 16:00, have a lock-out period from 9:00–16:00, a 1:00 curfew, and 65-AS meals (805 AS per person plus 40 AS for non-members, includes sheets and breakfast, three- to six-bed rooms; 7, Myrthengasse 7, 1070 Wien, tel. 01/523-6316, fax 01/523-5849, e-mail: oejhv-wien-jgh-neustiftg. @oejhv.or.at). They try to accommodate couples and families with private rooms but can make no promises.

Believe It or Not is across the street—a friendly and basic place with two big coed rooms for up to 10 travelers under age 30. It's locked up from 10:30 to 12:30, has kitchen facilities, and no curfew (160 AS per bed, 110 AS November–Easter; 7, Myrthengasse 10, no sign, ring apt. #14, tel. 01/526-4658, run by Gosha).

Pension Wild has 14 decent rooms (though some have a stale smell) and a good, keep-it-simple-and-affordable attitude (S-450 AS, Ss-550 AS, D-590 AS, Ds-690 AS, Db-890 AS, T-860 AS, Ts-960 AS, reserve with CC:VMA but pay cash, elevator, kitchen privileges, near U-2 Rathaus; 8, Langegasse 10, 1080 Vienna, tel. 01/406-5174, fax 01/402-2168).

Pension Andreas is past-its-prime classy and quiet, but a bit smoky (40 rooms, St-690 AS, Ds-850 AS, Db-930 AS, big Db-990 AS, big-family room deals, elevator, CC:VMA, near U-2 Rathaus at 8, Schlösselgasse 11, 1080 Wien, tel. 01/405-3488, fax 01/4053-48850).

Sleeping within the Ring, in the Old City Center

These places offer less room per schilling but are comfortable and right in the town center, with elevators and near the subway. The first four are nearly in the shadow of St. Stephan's Cathedral, on or near the Graben, where the elegance of Old Vienna strums happily over the cobbles. The next two listings are near the Opera (subway: Karlsplatz) just off the famous Kärntner Strasse, near the tourist office and five minutes from the cathedral. If you can afford it, staying here gives you the best classy Vienna experience. The last two are past the cathedral, closer to the Danube Canal.

At **Pension Nossek**, an elevator takes you above any street noise into Frau Bernad's and Frau Gundolf's world, where the children seem to be placed among the lace and flowers by an interior designer. Right on the wonderful Graben, this is the best value of these first three (Ss-700 AS, Sb-850 AS, small Db-1,200

Hotels in Central Vienna

1 PENSION NOSSEK

2 PENSION DR GEISSLER

3 PENSION PERTSCHY

4 PENSION NEUER MARKT

5 PENSION SUZANNE

6 HOTEL ZUR WIENER STAATSOPER

7 SCHWEIZER PENSION SOLDERER

8 ROSENBERGER MARKT RESTAURANT

9 SACHER CAFE

10 MUSIC FESTIVAL TICKET KIOSK

11 GIGERL STADTHEURIGER

12 BREZEL-GWOLB

AS, big Db-1,300 AS, apartment-1,600 AS; 1, Graben 17, tel. 01/5337-0410, fax 01/535-3646).

Pension Pertschy is bigger and more hotelesque than the others. Its big rooms are huge (ask to see a couple), and those on the courtyard are quietest (Sb-800 AS, Db-1,180–1,440 AS depending on size, apartments with kitchenette for the same price—just ask, cheaper off-season, extra person-300 AS, CC:VM; 1, Habsburgergasse 5, tel. 01/53449, fax 01/534-4949).

Pension Neuer Markt has narrow halls caused by a mickey-mouse cramming on of bathrooms to each room, but the rooms are comfy and pleasant and the location is great (Ds-1,150 AS, Dt-950 AS, Db-1,400 AS, prices soft when slow, CC:VMA; 1, Seiler-gasse 9, 1010 Wien, tel. 01/512-2316, fax 01/513-9105, Edith SE).

Pension Suzanne, as Baroque and doily as you'll find in this price range, is wonderfully located a few yards from the Opera. Suzanne is quiet, with pink elegance bouncing on every bed (Sb-850–880 AS, Db-1,050–1,300 AS, third person-500 AS, huge discounts in the winter, reserve with CC but cash preferred; a block from the Opera, U-Bahn to Karlsplatz—Opera exit, 1, Walfis-chgasse 4, 1010 Wien, tel. 01/513-2507, fax 01/513-2500, expertly run by Frau Strafinger).

Hotel zur Wiener Staatsoper is quiet, rich, and hotelesque. Its smallish rooms come with high ceilings, chandeliers, and fancy carpets on parquet floors—a good value for this locale and ideal for people whose hotel taste is a cut above mine (Sb-1,100 AS, Db-1,600 AS, Tb-1,900 AS, family deals, CC:VMA; 1, a block from the Opera at Krugerstrasse 11, 1010 Wien, tel. 01/513-1274, fax 01/5131-27415).

Schweizer Pension Solderer, in the family for three genera-tions, is warmly run by two friendly sisters, Monica and Anita. Enjoy the homey feel, 11 big, comfortable rooms, parquet floors, and lots of tourist info (S-450 AS, Ss-700 AS, Sb-800 AS, D-700 AS, Ds-860 AS, Db-980 AS, elevator, laundry-150 AS, nonsmoking, Heinrichs-gasse 2, 1010 Wien; from West station, take U-3 to Volkstheater, then U-2 to Schottenring; tel. 01/533-8156, fax 01/535-6469).

Pension Dr. Geissler has basic rooms in the center (S-450–580 AS, Sb-650–850 AS, D-600–780 AS, Ds-620–980 AS, Db-800–1,180 AS, prices vary with season, CC:VMA; 1, Postgasse 14, 1010 Wien; U-Bahn: Schwedenplatz; tel. 01/533-2803, fax 01/533-2635).

Eating in Vienna

The Viennese appreciate the fine points of life, and right up there with the waltz is eating. The city has many atmospheric restaurants. As you ponder the Slavic and eastern European specialties on menus, remember that Vienna's diverse empire may be gone, but its flavor lingers.

On nearly every corner, you can find a colorful *Beisl* (Viennese tavern) filled with poetry teachers and their students, couples loving without touching, housewives on their way home from cello lessons, and waiters who thoroughly enjoy serving hearty food and good drink at an affordable price. Ask at your hotel for a good *Beisl*.

All my recommended eateries are within a five-minute walk of the cathedral.

Gigerl Stadtheuriger offers a near-*Heurige* experience (a la Grinzing, see above) without leaving the center. Just point to what looks good. Food is sold by the weight (cheese and cold meats cost about 35 AS/100 grams, salads are about 15 AS/100 grams—price sheet is posted: 10 *dag* = 100 grams). They also have menu entrees, along with spinach strudel, quiche, *Apfelstrudel*, and, of course, casks of new and local wines. Meals run from 100 AS to 150 AS (daily 11:00–24:00, indoor/outdoor seating, behind cathedral, a block off Kärntner Strasse, a few cobbles off Rauhensteingasse on Blumenstock, tel. 01/513-4431).

Brezel-Gwölb, a wonderfully atmospheric wine cellar with outdoor dining on a quiet square, serves delicious light meals, fine *Krautsuppe*, and old-fashioned local dishes. It's ideal for a romantic late-night glass of wine (daily 11:30–1:00, Ledererhof 9, take Drahtgasse off Am Hof, tel. 01/533-8811). Around the corner, **Zum Scherer Sitz u. Stehbeisl** is just as untouristy, with indoor or outdoor seating, a soothing woody atmosphere, intriguing decor, and local specialties (Monday–Saturday 11:00–1:00, Sunday 17:00–24:00, Judenplatz 7, near Am Hof).

These **wine cellars** are fun and touristic but typical, in the old center of town, with reasonable prices and lots of smoke. **Melker Stiftskeller**, the least touristy, is a *Stadtheurige* in a deep and rustic cellar with hearty, inexpensive meals and new wine (Monday–Saturday 17:00–24:00, closed Sunday, halfway between Am Hof and the Schottentor subway stop at Schottengasse 3, tel. 01/533-5530). Closer to the Graben, **Stadtbeisl** offers a good mix of value, local cuisine, and atmosphere (open nightly, Naglergasse 21, tel. 01/533-3507). **Zu den Drei Hacken** is famous for its local specialties (Monday–Friday 9:00–24:00, Saturday 10:00–24:00, closed Sunday, indoor/outdoor seating, CC:VA, Singerstrasse 28). The touristy **Pürstner** restaurant is pleasantly drenched in Old World atmosphere but doesn't encourage lingering (daily 11:00–24:00, indoor/outdoor seating, 150-AS meals, a block away at Riemergasse 10, tel. 01/512-6357). **Augustinerkeller** is fun, reasonably priced, and touristy with live music nightly (daily 10:00–24:00, next to the Opera under the Albertina Museum on Augustinerstrasse).

For a fast, light, and central lunch, **Rosenberger Markt Restaurant**, a popular highway chain, has an elegant super-branch a block toward the cathedral from the Opera. This place, while not cheap, is brilliant: friendly and efficient, with special theme

rooms to dine in, offering a fresh, smoke-free, and healthy cornucopia of food and drink (daily 11:00–23:00, lots of fruits, vegetables, fresh-squeezed juices, just off Kärntner Strasse at
Maysedergasse 2, ride the glass elevator downstairs). You can stack
a small salad or veggie plate into the tower of gobble for 30 AS.

Buffet Trzesniewski is justly famous for its elegant and cheap
finger sandwiches (9 AS) and small beers (9 AS). Three sandwiches
and a *kleines Bier* (*Pfiff*) make a fun, light lunch (Monday–Friday
8:30–19:30, Saturday 9:00–17:00, just off the Graben, nearly across
from the brooding Café Hawelka, on Dorotheergasse).

Naschmarkt, five minutes beyond the Opera, is Vienna's best
Old World market, with plenty of fresh produce, cheap local-style
eateries, cafés, and *döner kebab* and sausage stands (Monday–Friday
6:00–18:30, Saturday until 17:00, closed Sunday).

Wherever you're eating, some vocabulary will help. Try the
grüner Veltliner (dry white wine, any time), *Traubenmost* (a heavenly
grape juice on the verge of wine, autumn only, sometimes just
called *Most*), and *Sturm* (barely fermented *Most*, autumn only). The
local red wine (called *Portuguese*) is pretty good. Since the Austrian
wine is often very sweet, remember the word *Trocken* (dry). You can
order your wine by the *Viertel* (quarter-liter) or *Achtel* (eighth-liter).
Beer comes in a *Krugel* (.5 liter) or *Seidel* (.3 liter).

Transportation Connections—Vienna

Vienna has two main train stations: the Westbahnhof, serving
Munich, Salzburg, Melk, Switzerland, and Budapest; and the Südbahnhof, serving Italy, Budapest, and Prague. The third station,
Franz Josefs, serves Krems and the Danube Valley (but Melk is
served by the Westbahnhof). Subway line U-3 connects the Westbahnhof with the center, tram D takes you from the Südbahnhof
and from the Franz Josefs to downtown, and tram #18 connects
West and South Stations. Train info: tel. 01/1717.

By train to: Melk (hrly, 75 min), **Krems** (10/day, 1 hr),
Salzburg (hrly, 3 hrs), **Innsbruck** (3/day, 5.5 hrs), **Budapest**
(3/day, 3 hrs), **Prague** (4/day, 5.5 hrs), **Munich** (10/day, 4.5 hrs),
Berlin (2/day 14 hrs), **Zurich** (4/day, 9 hrs), **Rome** (3/day, 14
hrs), **Venice** (6/day, 9 hrs), **Frankfurt** (7/day, 7.5 hrs), **Amsterdam** (2/day, 14 hrs).

To eastern Europe: Vienna is the springboard for a quick trip
to Prague and Budapest—three hours by train from Budapest (360
AS, 580 AS round-trip, free with Eurail) and 5.5 hours from Prague
(488 AS one-way, 976 AS round-trip, 652 AS with Eurail). Visas are
not required. Purchase tickets at most travel agencies (such as the
Austrian National Travel Office at Operngasse 3–5, tel. 01/588-
6238, or Intropa, next to the TI on Kärntner Strasse).

SALZBURG, SALZKAMMERGUT, AND WEST AUSTRIA

Enjoy the sights and sounds of Salzburg, Mozart's hometown, then commune with nature in the Salzkammergut, Austria's *Sound of Music* country. Amid hills alive with the S.O.M., you'll find the tiny town of Hallstatt, as pretty as a postcard (and not much bigger).

SALZBURG

With a well-preserved old town, gardens, churches, and lush sur-roundings, set under Europe's biggest intact medieval castle, its river adding an almost seaside ambience, Salzburg is forever smil-ing to the tunes of Mozart and *The Sound of Music*.

This town knows how to be popular. Eight million tourists crawl its cobbles each year. That's a lot of Mozart balls. But all that popularity has led to a glut of businesses hoping to catch the tourist dollar, and an almost desperate greediness. The town's cre-ative energy is invested in ways to soak the tourist rather than share its rich cultural heritage. Salzburg makes for a pleasant visit, but for most, a day is plenty. With a few exceptions, it's hard to get English information, and music costs about 350 AS per event.

Planning Your Time

While Vienna measures much higher on the Richter scale of sight-seeing thrills, Salzburg is simply a joy—a touristy and expensive joy. If you're going into the nearby Salzkammergut lake country anyway, you don't need to take the *Sound of Music* tour. But this tour kills a nest of sightseeing birds with one ticket (city overview, *S.O.M.* sights, a luge ride, and a fine drive through the lakes). If you're not planning a detour through the lakes, allow half a day for this tour. That means a minimum of two nights for Salzburg. Of course, the nights are important for concerts and swilling beer in atmospheric local gardens. The actual town sights are mediocre. It's the town itself—a Baroque treat—that you should enjoy. If you like to get away from it all, bike down the river or hike across the Mönchsberg.

Orientation (tel. code: 0662)

Salzburg, a city of 150,000 (Austria's fourth-largest), is divided into old and new. The old town, sitting between the Salzach River and the 1,600-foot-high hill called Mönchsberg, is a bundle of Baroque holding all the charm and most of the tourists.

Tourist Information: Salzburg's tourist offices are helpful (at the train station; on Mozartplatz in the old center—daily 9:00–20:00, less off-season; on freeway entrances; and at airport, tel. 0662/88987, Web site: www.salzburginfo.or.at). Get a city map (10 AS), a list of sights with current hours, and a schedule of events. The TI sells a "Salzburg Card" (200 AS for a 24-hour bus pass and 24 hours free entrance to all the city sights), which pays for itself after two admissions and one bus ride. Book a concert upon arrival. The TIs also book rooms (30-AS fee, or 60 AS for three people or more).

Arrival in Salzburg: The Salzburg station makes it easy. The TI is at track 2A. Downstairs is the place to leave bags, rent bikes, buy tickets, and get train information (at Reisebüro am Bahnhof). This lower street level faces the bus station (where buses #1, #5, #6, and #51 go to the old center; get off at the first stop after you cross the river). To walk downtown (15 minutes), leave the station ticket hall near the Bankomat through the door marked "Zentrum" and walk absolutely straight down Rainerstrasse, which leads you under the tracks past Mirabellplatz, changes its name to Dreitaltigkeitsgasse, and takes you to the *Staatsbrücke* (bridge), which deposits you in the old town. For a more dramatic approach, leave the same way but follow the tracks to the river, turn left, and walk the riverside path toward the castle.

American Express: The Amex office holds mail for their check or credit card users, and doesn't charge a commission for cashing Amex checks (Monday–Friday 9:00–17:30, Saturday 9:00–12:00, Mozartplatz 5, A-5010 Salzburg, tel. 0662/8080).

Getting Around Salzburg

By Bus: Single-ride tickets are sold on the bus for 20 AS. Daily passes (*Tageskarte*) cost 40 AS (good for one calendar day only). Bus information: tel. 0662/872-145.

By Bike: Salzburg is bike friendly. From 7:00 until midnight, the train station rents good road bikes for 50 AS and mountain bikes for 150 AS; without a railpass or train ticket, you'll pay 50 AS more (no deposit required, pay at counter #3, pick it up at "left luggage"). Georg, who runs Velo-Active, rents bikes on Residenzplatz under the Glockenspiel in the old town. He offers carriers of this book a one-day rental for 150 AS (daily 9:00–19:00, less off-season, passport number for security, extra charge for mountain bikes, tel. 0663/868-827). Two companies now offer bike tours of Salzburg (details at TI).

By Funicular and Elevator: The old town is connected to Mönchsberg (and great views) via funicular and elevator. The funicular whisks you up to the imposing Hohensalzburg fortress (69 AS includes fortress admission). The elevator on the east side of the old town propels you to Café Winkler, the recommended Naturfreundehaus (see Sleeping, below), and lots of wooded paths (27 AS round-trip).

Helpful Hints: A good laundromat is two blocks from recommended Linzergasse hotels (weekdays 7:30–18:00, Saturday 8:00–12:00, self-service or drop-off service, on Wolf-Dietrich Strasse). The post office is just off Rezidenz Platz behind the cathedral.

Sights—Salzburg's Old Town

▲▲**Old Town Walking Tour**—The two-language, one-hour guided walks of the old town are informative and worthwhile if you don't mind listening to a half-hour of German (80 AS, start at TI on Mozartplatz daily at 12:15, not on winter Sundays, tel. 0662/847-568), but you can easily do it on your own. Here's a basic old-town orientation walk (start on Mozartplatz in the old town):

Mozartplatz features a statue of Mozart erected in 1842. Mozart spent most of his first 20 years (1756–1777) in Salzburg. The tourist information office and American Express Company face this square. Salzburg was the greatest Baroque city north of the Alps. Walk to the next square with the huge fountain.

Residenz Platz: Salzburg's energetic Prince-Archbishop Wolf Dietrich (who ruled from 1587–1612) was raised in Rome, counted the Medicis as his buddies, and had grand Renaissance ambitions for Salzburg. After a convenient fire destroyed much of the old town, he set about building "the Rome of the North." This square, with his new cathedral and palace, was the center-piece of his new, Italian-designed Baroque city. A series of inter-connecting squares lead from here through the old town.

For centuries, Salzburg's leaders were both important church leaders and princes of the Holy Roman Empire, hence their title—mixing sacred and secular authority. Wolf Dietrich abused his power and spent his last five years imprisoned in the Salzburg castle.

The fountain is as Italian as can be, with a Triton matching Bernini's famous *Triton Fountain* in Rome. As the north became aware of the exciting things going on in Italy, things Italian were respected. Local architects even Italianized their names in order to raise their rates.

Dietrich's palace, the **Residenz**, is connected to the cathedral

Salzburg

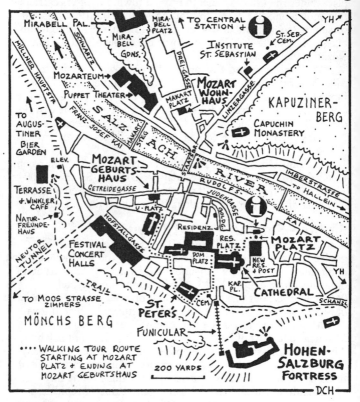

by a skyway. A series of fancy rooms is open to visitors with a headphone guide (60 AS, tel. 0662/8042-2690). The Residenz also has an art gallery.

Opposite the Residenz is the new Residenz, which has long been a government administration building (and post office with a handy bank of pay phones). Atop the new Residenz is the famous **Glockenspiel**, or bell tower. Its carillon of 35 17th-century bells (cast in Antwerp) chimes throughout the day and plays a tune (that changes each month) at 7:00, 11:00, and 18:00. There was a time when Salzburg could afford to take tourists to the top of the tower to actually see the big adjustable barrel turn . . . pulling the right bells in the right rhythm—a fascinating show.

Look back past Mozart's statue to the 4,220-foot-tall Gaisberg (the forested hill with the television tower). A road leads to the top for a commanding view. It's a favorite destination for local bikers.

Opposite the church is a picnic-friendly grocery store with an orange awning (Monday–Friday 8:30–18:00, Saturday 8:00–17:00). Walking under the Prince-Archbishop's skyway, step into Domplatz, the cathedral square.

Salzburg Cathedral, built in the 17th century, claims to be the first Baroque building north of the Alps (free, daily 10:00–18:30). The dates on the iron gates refer to milestones in the church's history: In 774 the previous church (long since destroyed) was founded by St. Virgil, to be replaced in 1628 by the church you see today. In 1959 the reconstruction was completed after a bomb blew through the dome in World War II.

Check out the organ draped over the entrance; it was played only when the archbishop walked in and out of the cathedral. Gape up. The interior is marvelous. Concert and Mass schedules are posted at the entrance; Sunday Mass (10:00) is famous for its music.

Under the skyway, a stairway leads down to the excavation site under the church with a few second-century Christian Roman mosaics and the foundation stones of the previous Romanesque and Gothic churches (20 AS, Wednesday–Sunday 9:00–17:00). The Cathedral (or *Dom*) Museum has a rich collection of church art (entry at portico).

The cathedral square is surrounded by "ecclesiastical palaces." The statue of Mary (1771) is looking away from the church, but if you stand in the rear of the square immediately under the middle arch, you'll see how she's positioned to be crowned by the two angels on the church facade.

From the arch, walk back across the square to the front of the cathedral and turn right (going past the underground public toilets) to the next square, where you'll see locals playing chess on the giant board. Past the chessboard, a small road leads up to the castle (and castle lift). On the right, a gate reading "St. Peter" leads past a traditional old bakery (near the waterfall, hard to beat their rock-like Roggenbrot) and into a cemetery.

St. Peter's Cemetery is a collection of lovingly tended mini-gardens (butted up against the Mönchberg's rock wall). The graves are cared for by relatives; anyone residing in the cemetery for more than 30 years without living kin gets dug up. Early Christian catacombs are carved into the rock wall above the graveyard (12 AS, 10:30–15:30). This was where the von Trapp family hid out in the *S.O.M.* movie. Walk through the cemetery and out the opposite end. Drop into St. Peter's Church, a Romanesque basilica done up beautifully Baroque. Continue (through arch opposite hillside, left at church, second right, past public WC, another square and church) to Universitätsplatz, with its busy open-air produce market. This is Salzburg at its liveliest and most real (mornings, daily except Sunday). Take one of several covered arcades from here to Getreidegasse.

Getreidegasse was old Salzburg's lively and colorful main drag. Famous for its old wrought-iron signs, it still looks much as it did in Mozart's day. *Schmuck* means jewelry. Wolfgang was born on this street. Find his very gold house.

▲**Mozart's Birthplace (Geburtshaus)**—Mozart was born here in 1756. It was in this building that he composed most of his boy-genius works. This most popular Mozart sight in town, filled with scores of scores, portraits, and old keyboard instruments and violins, is almost a pilgrimage. If you're a fan, you'll have to check it out. It's right in the old town on colorful Getreidegasse #9 (70 AS, or 110 AS for combined ticket to Mozart's *Wohnhaus*—see below, daily 9:00–18:00, shorter hours off-season). Note the cobbled entryway. All Salzburg used to be paved this way.

▲**Hohensalzburg Fortress**—Built on a rock 400 feet above the Salzach River, this castle, one of Europe's mightiest, dominates Salzburg's skyline and offers great views of the city and surrounding hills. The castle interior is so-so unless you catch a tour (35 AS admission plus 30 AS for a tour; confirm that it will be in English as well as German). Check out the sound-and-vision show. The museum has the noisiest floorboards in Europe, but even so, the princess had a chastity belt. You can see it next to other gruesome torture devices that need no explanation. You can walk up to the fortress, but the funicular is effortless (34 AS round-trip, every 10 minutes, 69 AS includes fortress admission, castle open daily 8:00–19:00, 9:00–18:00 off-season, tel. 0662/842-430).

▲**The Hills Are Alive Walk**—For a most enjoyable approach to the castle, consider riding the elevator to the Café Winkler and walking 20 minutes through the woods high above the city to Festung Hohensalzburg (stay on the high paved paths, or you'll have a needless climb back up to the castle).

Sights—Across the River

▲▲**Mozart's Wohnhaus (a.k.a. Mozarts Ton- und Filmmuseum)**—Even better than the birthplace is this newly renovated museum, previously Mozart's second home (his family moved here when he was 17). A headphone, free with admission, lets you hear English throughout. Along with the usual scores and old pianos, the highlight is an intriguing film that leaves you wanting to know more about Mozart and his remarkable family (65 AS, or 110 AS for combined ticket to birthplace, guidebook-59 AS, daily 10:00–18:00, just over the river at Marktplatz 8, tel. 0662/8894040).

▲**Mirabell Gardens and Palace (Schloss)**—The bubbly gardens are always open and free. You may recognize the statues featured in the *S.O.M.* To properly enjoy the lavish Mirabell Palace, get a ticket to a *Schlosskonzert*. Baroque music flying around a Baroque hall is a happy bird in the right cage. Tickets are around 400 AS and are rarely sold out (tel. 0662/848-586).

More Sights—Salzburg

▲▲**Riverside Bike Ride**—The Salzach River has smooth, flat, and scenic bike paths along each side. On a sunny day, I can think of no more shout-worthy escape from the city. Hallein is a pleasant destination (with a salt-mine tour, 9:00–17:00, about 15 kilometers away, the north or new-town side of river is most scenic). Even a quickie ride from one end of town to the other gives you the best possible views of Salzburg. In the evening, it's a hand-in-hand, floodlit-spires world.

▲▲*Sound of Music* **Tour**—I took this tour skeptically (as part of my research chores) and liked it. It includes a quick but good general city tour, stops for a luge ride (in season, fair weather, 35 AS extra), hits all the *S.O.M.* spots (including the stately home, gazebo, and wedding church), and shows you a lovely stretch of the Salzkammergut. The Salzburg Panorama Tours Company charges 350 AS for the four-hour, English-only tour (from Mirabellplatz daily at 9:30 and 14:00, tel. 0662/874-029, Web site: www.panoramatours.at; ask for a reservation and a free hotel pickup if you like; travelers with this book who buy their tickets with cash at the Mirabellplatz ticket booth get a 10 percent discount on this and any other tour they do). This is worthwhile for *S.O.M.* fans without a car, or those who won't otherwise be going into the Salzkammergut. Warning: Many think rolling through the Austrian countryside with 30 Americans singing "Doe, a deer" is pretty schmaltzy. And local Austrians don't understand all the commotion.

There are several similar and very competitive tour companies that offer every conceivable tour of and from Salzburg (Mozart sights, Berchtesgaden, salt mines, Salzkammergut lakes and mountains). Some hotels have their brochures and get a healthy commission. Bob's Tours runs minibus tours (two different tours: *S.O.M.* or Berchtesgaden and Bavarian Alps, Kaigasse 19, tel. 0662/849-511).

▲**Hellbrunn Castle**—The attractions here are a garden full of clever trick fountains and the sadistic joy the tour guide gets from soaking tourists. The archbishop's mediocre 17th-century palace is open by tour only (30 AS, 2/hrly, 20 minutes). His Baroque garden, one of the oldest in Europe, is pretty enough and now features the "I am 16, going on 17" gazebo (70 AS for the 35-minute tour and admission, daily 9:00–17:30, until 22:00 in July and August, until 16:30 in April and October, closed November–March, tel. 0662/820-372). The castle is three miles south of Salzburg (bus #55 from station or downtown, 2/hrly, 20 min). It's fun on a sunny day or with kids, but, for many, it's a lot of trouble for a few water tricks.

Music Scene

▲▲**Salzburg Festival**—Each summer from late July to the end of August, Salzburg hosts its famous Salzburger Festspiele, founded in

1920 partly to employ Vienna's musicians in the summer. This fun and festive time is crowded, but there are plenty of beds (except for a few August weekends). Except for the big shows, tickets are normally available the day of the concert (ticket office on Mozartplatz, in TI). You can contact the Austrian National Tourist Office in the United States for specifics on this year's festival schedule and tickets (Box 1142, New York, NY 10108, tel. 212/944-6880, fax 212/730-4568, Web site: www.anto.com), but I've never planned in advance and have enjoyed great concerts with every visit.

▲▲**Musical Events outside of Festival Time**—Salzburg is busy throughout the year with 2,000 classical performances in its palaces and churches annually. Pick up the events calendar at the TI (free, comes out monthly). Whenever you visit, you'll have a number of concerts to choose from. There are nearly nightly concerts at the Mirabell Palace and up in the fortress (both with open seating and 400-AS tickets, concerts at 19:30 or 20:30, doors open 30 minutes early). The *Schlosskonzerte* at the Mirabell Palace offer a fine Baroque setting for your Mozart (tel. 0662/848-586). The fortress concerts, called *Festungskonzerte*, are held in the "prince's chamber" (usually chamber music—a string quartet, tel. 0662/825-858 to reserve, you can pick up tickets at the door). This medieval-feeling room atop the castle has windows overlooking the city. The extra 34-AS round-trip lift gives you a chance to enjoy a stroll through the castle courtyard and enjoy the grand city view.

The afternoon "5:00 Concert" next to St. Peter's is cheaper, since it features young artists (120 AS, daily except Wednesday, 45 minutes, tel. 0662/8445-7619). While the series is named after the brother of Joseph Haydn, it features music from various masters.

The Marionette Theater performs operas with fine marionettes and recorded music (350–480 AS, nearly nightly May–September, tel. 0662/872-406).

Sleeping in Salzburg
(12 AS = about $1, tel. code: 0662, zip code: 5020)
Sleep Code: **S** = Single, **D** = Double/Twin, **T** = Triple, **Q** = Quad, **b** = bathroom, **t** = toilet only, **s** = shower only, **CC** = Credit Card (Visa, MasterCard, Amex).

Finding a room in Salzburg, even during the music festival, is usually easy. Unless otherwise noted, all my listings come with breakfast and at least some English is spoken. The more expensive places charge more during the music festival (late July and August).

Sleeping in (or above) the Old Town
Gasthaus zur Goldenen Ente, run by the family Steinwender, is a great splurge if you'd like to sleep in a 600-year-old building

above a fine restaurant as central as you can be on a pedestrian street in old Salzburg. Somehow the 15 modern and comfortable doubles fit into this building's medieval-style stone arches and narrow stairs (Sb-680 AS and Db-980 AS with this book, higher prices in high season, extra person-450 AS, parking deals, CC:VMA, elevator, Goldgasse 10, tel. 0662/845-622, fax 0662/ 845-6229). The breakfast is buffet-big and their restaurant is a treat (see Eating, below).

Hotel Restaurant Weisses Kreutz is a classy, comfy, family-run place on a cobbled back street near the castle (Sb-700 AS, Db-900-1,200 AS, Tb-1,600, CC:M, reserve ahead, Bierjodlgasse 6, tel. 0662/845-641, fax 0662/845-6419).

Gasthof Hinterbrühl is a smoky, ramshackle old place with a handy location, minimal plumbing, and not a tourist in sight (S-420 AS, D-520 AS, T-600 AS, plus optional 50-AS breakfast, above a bar that can be noisy, workable parking, CC:V, on a village-like square just under the castle at Schanzlgasse 12, tel. 0662/846-798).

Naturfreundehaus, also called "Gasthaus Bürgerwehr," is a local version of a mountaineer's hut. It's a great budget alternative in a forest guarded by singing birds and snuggled in the remains of a 15th-century castle wall overlooking Salzburg, with magnificent town and mountain views (D-280 AS, 120 AS per person in four- to six-bed dorms, breakfast-30 AS, dinner-68–108 AS, curfew-1:00, open May–September, Mönchsberg 19, two minutes from the top of the 27-AS round-trip Mönchsberg elevator, tel. 0662/841-729). High above the old town, it's the stone house to the left of the glass Café Winkler.

Sleeping on Linzergasse and near Kapuzinerberg

All of these listings are a 15-minute walk from the train station in the "new" section of town, across the river from the old town. The first four are on lower Linzergasse, directly across the bridge from Mozartville. Its bustling crowds of shoppers overwhelm the few shy cars that venture onto it. The last two listings are farther from the city center (a 10-minute walk).

Institute St. Sebastian is close to the old town and newly renovated, offering the town's best doubles and dorm beds for the money (Sb-380 AS, Db-660 AS, Tb-900 AS, elevator, Linzergasse 41, enter through arch at #37, tel. 0662/871-386, fax 0662/8713-8685). They usually have rooms available, as well as 210-AS spots in 10-bed dorms (30 AS less if you have sheets, no lock-out time, lockers, free showers). Anyone is welcome to use the self-service kitchen on each floor. Fridge space is free; just ask for a key. This friendly, clean, historic building has lots of spacious public areas and a roof garden. The doubles come with modern baths and head-to-toe twin beds. Some Mozarts are buried in the courtyard.

Hotel Goldene Krone is big, quiet, and creaky-traditional but modern, with comforts rare in this price range (Sb-500–570 AS, D-700–800 AS, Db-850–970 AS, Tb-1,000–1,300 AS, elevator, Linzergasse 48, tel. 0662/872-300).

Hotel zum Jungen Fuchs turns on troglodytes. It's very plain but clean and wonderfully located in a funky, dumpy old building (S-280 AS, D-380 AS, T-480 AS, no breakfast, across from Institute St. Sebastian at Linzergasse 54, tel. 0662/875-496).

Hotel Trumer Stube is a comfy little hotel-pension just off Linzergasse with clean new rooms and a friendly can-do reception (Sb-725 AS, Db-1,250 AS, Tb-1,380 AS, Qb-1,750 AS, higher in August, lower in winter, CC:VMA, elevator, parking-100 AS, Bergstrasse 6, tel. 0662/874-776, fax 0662/874-326, e-mail: hotel.trumer-stube.sbg@eunet.at).

Pension Bergland is a classy oasis of calm, with rustic rooms and musical evenings (Ss-480 AS, Sb-560 AS, two dim D-640 AS, Db-860–920 AS depending on size, Tb-1,060 AS, music room open 17:00–21:30, bike rental, English library, Laundromat nearby, Rupertgasse 15, southeast of the station, tel. 0662/872-318, fax 0662/872-3188, e-mail: pkuhn@sol.at, run by Peter Kuhn).

Gasthaus Ganslhof, three blocks away from the Bergland, is a bit run-down but comfortable and back in the real world with Motel 6 ambience and a parking lot (Sb-480 AS, Db-800 AS, 150 AS more per person in the summer, elevator, TV and phone, CC:VMA, Vogelweiderstrasse 6, tel. 0662/873-853, fax 0662/8738-5323).

Bed-and-Breakfasts

These are generally roomy, modern, comfortable, and come with a good breakfast, easy parking, and plenty of tourist information. Off-season, competition softens prices. They are a bus ride from town, but with a day pass and the frequent service, this shouldn't keep you away. Unsavory *Zimmer* skimmers lurk at the station. If you have a reservation, ignore them. If you need a place . . . they need a customer.

Brigitte Lenglachner fills her big, traditional home with a warm welcome (S-290 AS, D-480 AS, bunk bed D-390 AS, Db-550 AS, T-690 AS, apartment available, two-night minimum, breakfast in room, Scheibenweg 8, tel. & fax 0662/438-044). It's in a chirpy neighborhood a 10-minute walk northwest of the station: from the station, cross the pedestrian Pioneer Bridge, turn right, walk along the river 200 meters, then take a left to Scheibenweg 8. If her place is booked, skip her referrals.

Trude Poppenberger's three pleasant rooms share the same long mountain-view balcony (S-280 AS, D-480 AS, T-720 AS; if you stay two nights she'll do your laundry for 80 AS; Wachtelgasse 9, tel. & fax 0662/430-094). It's a 20-minute walk northwest of the station, near Brigitte's place (or she'll pick you up for free).

Zimmer on Moosstrasse: The street called Moosstrasse, southwest of Mönchsberg, is lined with *Zimmer*. Those farther out are farmhouses. From the station, catch bus #1 and change to bus #60 immediately after crossing the river. From the old town, ride bus #60 (get off after the American High School at Sendleweg). If you're driving from the center, go through the tunnel, straight on Neutorstrasse, and take the fourth left onto Moosstrasse.

Maria Gassner rents 10 sparkling clean, comfortable rooms in her modern house (St-250 AS, Sb-400 AS, D-440 AS, Db-500 AS, big Db-600 AS, 10 percent more for one-night stays, family deals, CC:VM, 60-AS coin-op laundry, Moosstrasse 126-B, tel. 0662/824-990, fax 0662/822-075).

Frau Ballwein offers cozy, charming rooms in an old farmhouse (S-200 AS, Ss-240 AS, D-400 AS, Db-480 AS, farm-fresh breakfasts, Moosstrasse 69A, tel. & fax 0662/824-029).

Haus Reichl also has good rooms (Db-550 AS, Tb-800 AS, Qb-1,000 AS, family deals, Q rooms have balcony and view, between Ballwein and Bankhammer B&Bs at Reiterweg 52, tel. & fax 0662/826-248).

Ziller Family Farm rents three huge rooms with kitchenettes in a kid-friendly, horse-filled environment (Db-600 AS, minimum two nights, Moosstrasse 76, tel. 0662/824-940, Gabi SE).

Helga Bankhammer rents recently renovated, pleasant rooms in a farmhouse with farm animals nearby (D-450 AS, Db-500 AS, Moosstrasse 77, tel. & fax 0662/830-067).

Gästehaus Blobergerhof is rural and comfortable (Sb-350 AS, Db-550 AS, 10 percent more for one-night stays, CC:VM; breakfast buffet, bike rental, laundry service, will pick up at station, Hammerauerstrasse 4, Querstrasse zur Moosstrasse, tel. 0662/830-227, fax 0662/827-061).

Sleeping near the Train Station

Pension Adlerhof, a plain and decent old place, is two blocks in front of the train station but a 15-minute walk from the sightseeing action. It has a quirky staff and well-maintained rooms (S-400–420 AS, Sb-590 AS, D-650 AS, Db-790 AS, Elisabethstrasse 25, tel. 0662/875-236, fax 0662/873-6636).

Gottfried's International Youth Hotel, a.k.a. "the Yo-Ho," is the most fun, handy, and American of Salzburg's many hostels (D-360 AS, Q-160 AS per bed, or six- to eight-bed dorm-140 AS, sheets not required but rentable-20 AS, five blocks from the station toward the center at Paracelsusstrasse 9, tel. 0662/879-649). This easygoing place speaks English first, has cheap meals, lockers, a laundry, tour discounts, and a 1:00 curfew; plays *The Sound of Music* free daily at 13:30; runs a lively bar; and welcomes anyone of any age. Expect a non-stop noisy, smoky, party atmosphere.

Eating in Salzburg

Salzburg boasts many inexpensive, fun, and atmospheric places to eat. I'm a sucker for big cellars with their smoky Old World atmosphere, heavy medieval arches, time-darkened paintings, antlers, hearty meals, and plump patrons. These places are famous with visitors but also enjoyed by the locals.

Gasthaus zum Wilder Mann is the place if the weather's bad and you're in the mood for Hofbräu atmosphere and a hearty, cheap meal at a shared table in one small, well-antlered room (Monday–Saturday 11:00–21:00, closed Sunday, smoky, two minutes from Mozart's place—enter from Getreidegasse 20 or Griesgasse 17, tel. 0662/841-787). For a quick 100-AS lunch, get the *Bauernschmaus*, a mountain of dumplings, kraut, and peasant's meats.

Krimplestätter employs 500 years of experience serving authentic old-Salzburger food in its authentic old-Austrian interior or its cheery garden (10:00–24:00, closed Monday all year and winter Sundays, Müllner Hauptstrasse 31, 10 minutes north of the old town near the river). For fine food with a wild finale, eat here and drink at the nearby Augustiner Bräustübl.

Augustiner Bräustübl, a monk-run brewery, is rustic and crude. On busy nights it's like a Munich beer hall with no music but the volume turned up. When it's cool, you'll enjoy a historic setting with beer-sloshed and smoke-stained halls. On balmy evenings you'll eat under trees in a pleasant outdoor beer garden. Local students mix with tourists eating hearty slabs of schnitzel with their fingers or cold meals from the self-serve picnic counter (daily 15:00–23:30, Augustinergasse 4, head up Müllner Hauptstrasse northwest along the river, and ask for "Müllnerbräu," its local nickname). Don't be fooled by second-rate gardens serving the same beer nearby—this huge, 1,000-seat place is in the Augustiner brewery. Order carefully, prices can sting. Pick up a half-liter (28–32 AS) or full-liter mug (56–64 AS) of the great beer, pay the lady, and give Mr. Keg your empty mug. For dessert, after a visit to the strudel kiosk, enjoy the incomparable floodlit view of old Salzburg from the nearby pedestrian bridge, and then stroll home along the river.

Stiftskeller St. Peter has been in business for more than 1,000 years. It's classier (with strolling musicians), more central, and a good splurge for traditional Austrian cuisine in medieval sauce (daily 11:00–24:00, outdoor and indoor seating, meals 100–200 AS, CC:VMA, next to St. Peter's church at the foot of Mönchsberg, tel. 0662/841-268).

Gasthaus zur Goldenen Ente (see Sleeping, above) serves great food in a classy, subdued hotel dining room. The chef, Robert, specializes in roast duck (*Ente*) and seafood, along with "Salzberger Nockerl," the mountainous sweet soufflé served all over town. It's big enough for four (Monday–Friday 11:00–21:00, closed Saturday and Sunday, Goldgasse 10, tel. 0662/845-622).

Stieglkeller is a huge, atmospheric institution that has several rustic rooms and outdoor garden seating with a great rooftop view of the old town (daily 10:00–22:00, 50 yards uphill from the lift to the castle, Festungsgasse 10, tel. 0662/842-681). They offer the latest *S.O.M.* spin-off—a *Sound of Music* dinner show, featuring songs from the movie and local dances (520 AS includes dinner, 360 AS for show only when booked in advance, daily May–September, tel. 0662/832-029). Since the Stieglkeller has lots of rooms, you can skip the show and still enjoy the restaurant.

Picnics: The University Square, just behind Mozart's house, hosts a bustling morning **produce market** daily except Sunday.

Lunch: Classy Salzburg delis serve good, cheap, sit-down lunches on weekdays. Have them make you a sandwich or something hot, toss in a carrot, a piece of fruit, yogurt, and a box of milk, and sit at a small table with the local lunch crowd.

Café Glockenspiel, on Mozartplatz 2, does a good, if pricey, lunch (80–160 AS). The following cheaper places are all just across the river from the old town: **Frauenberger** is friendly, picnic-ready, and inexpensive, with indoor or outdoor seating (Monday–Friday 8:00–14:00, across from Linzergasse 16). **Spicy Spices** is a vegetarian-Indian lunch take-out (with a few tables) restaurant serving tasty curry and rice boxes, samosas, organic salads and fresh juices (Wolf-Dietrich Strasse 1). **Mensa Aicherpassage** serves some of Salzburg's cheapest meals in the basement (Monday–Friday 11:30–14:30, go under arch, enter metal door to "Mozarteum," and go down one floor).

Transportation Connections—Salzburg

By train to: Innsbruck (every 2 hrs, 2 hrs), **Vienna** (2/hrly, 3.5 hrs), **Hallstatt** (hrly, 50 min to Attnang Puchheim, 20-minute wait, 1.5 hrs to Hallstatt), **Reutte** (every 2 hrs, 4 hrs, transfer in Innsbruck), **Munich** (hrly, 90 min).

SALZKAMMERGUT LAKE DISTRICT AND HALLSTATT

Commune with nature in Austria's Lake District. "The hills are alive," and you're surrounded by the loveliness that has turned on everyone from Emperor Franz Josef to Julie Andrews. This is *The Sound of Music* country. Idyllic and majestic, but not rugged, it's a gentle land of lakes, forested mountains, and storybook villages, rich in hiking opportunities and inexpensive lodging. Settle down in the postcard-pretty, fjord-cuddling town of Hallstatt.

Planning Your Time

While there are plenty of lakes, Hallstatt is really the only one that matters. One night and two hours to browse is all you'll need to fall in love. To relax or take a hike in the surroundings, give it two nights and a day. It's a good stop between Salzburg and Vienna. A visit here (with a bike ride along the Danube and the two big cites—Salzburg and Vienna) balances out your Austrian itinerary.

Orientation (tel. code: 06134)

Lovable Hallstatt is a tiny town bullied onto a ledge between a selfish mountain and a swan-ruled lake, with a waterfall ripping furiously through its middle. It can be toured on foot in about 10 minutes. The town is one of Europe's oldest, going back centuries before Christ. The charm of Hallstatt is the village and its lakeside setting. Go there to relax, nibble, wander, and paddle. (In August, tourist crowds trample much of Hallstatt's charm.) The lake is famous for its good fishing and pure water (8 km by 2 km, 125 meters deep at 508 meters altitude).

Tourist Information: The TI can always find you a room. Its holiday "guest card" gives you free parking (Monday–Friday 9:00–17:00, weekends 10:00–14:00, less off-season, tel. 06134/8208).

Arrival in Hallstatt: Hallstatt's train station is a wide spot on the tracks across the lake. *Stefanie* (a boat) meets you at the station and glides across the lake into town (23 AS, with each train until 18:40—don't arrive after that). The boat ride is gorgeous. Last departing boat-train connection leaves Hallstatt at 18:15.

Helpful Hints: Laundromat is at the camping place near the bathing island (wash, dry, and soap, 100 AS). Post office is below the TI.

Sights—Hallstatt

Prehistory Museum—The humble Prehistory Museum adjacent to the TI is interesting because little Hallstatt was the important salt-mining hub of a culture that spread from France to the Balkans during what archaeologists call the "Hallstatt Period" (800–400 B.C.). Back then, Celtic tribes dug for precious salt, and Hallstatt was, as its name means, the "home of salt." Your 50-AS Prehistory Museum ticket also gets you into the cute Heimatmuseum of folk culture (daily 10:00–18:00 in summer). Historians like the English booklet that covers both museums (25 AS). The Janu sport shop across from the TI recently dug into a prehistoric site, and now its basement is another small museum (free).

▲▲**Hallstatt Church and Cemetery**—Hallstatt has two churches. The Protestant church is at lake level. The more interesting Catholic church, with a giant St. Christopher (protector of us travelers) on its outside wall, overlooks the town from above. From near the boat dock, hike up the covered wooden stairway to the church. The lovely church has 500-year-old altars and frescoes dedicated to the saints of mining and salt. Space is so limited in

Hallstatt that bones have only 12 peaceful buried years in the church cemetery before making way for the freshly dead. The result is a fascinating chapel of bones in the cemetery (*Beinhaus*, 10 AS, daily 10:00–18:00). Each skull is lovingly named, dated, and decorated, with the men getting ivy, and the women, roses. They stopped this practice in the 1960s, about the same time the Catholic Church began permitting cremation.

▲▲**Salt Mine Tour**—If you have yet to do a salt mine, Hallstatt's is as good as any. You'll ride a steep funicular high above the town (97 AS round-trip), take a 10-minute hike, put on old miners' clothes, take an underground train, slide down the banisters, and listen to an English tape-recorded tour while your guide speaks German (135 AS, daily 9:30–16:30, closes early off-season, no children under age 4, tel. 06134/8251). The well-publicized ancient Celtic graveyard excavation sites nearby are really dead. The scenic 50-minute hike back into town is (with strong knees) a joy.

▲**Boating, Hiking, and Spelunking**—Those into relaxation can rent a sleepy electric motorboat to enjoy town views from the water (75 AS/30 minutes, 120 AS/one hour, one or two people, two speeds: slow and stop, rental place next to the ferry dock). Mountain lovers, hikers, and spelunkers keep busy for days using Hallstatt as their home base. Get information from the TI on the various caves with their ice formations, the thunderous rivers, mountain lifts, nearby walks, and harder hikes. The best short and easy walk is the two-hour round-trip up the Echerntal Valley to a waterfall and back. With a car, consider hiking around nearby Altaussee (flat, three-hour hike) or along Grundlsee to Tolpitzsee. Regular buses connect Hallstatt with Gosausee for a pleasant walk around that lake. The TI can recommend a great two-day hike with an overnight in a nearby mountain hut.

Sleeping in Hallstatt
(12 AS = about $1, tel. code: 06134, zip code: 4830)

Hallstatt's TI can almost always find you a room. July and August can be tight, and early August is worst. A bed in a private home costs about 200 AS with breakfast. It's hard to get a one-night advance reservation. But if you drop in and they have a spot, they're happy to have you. Prices include breakfast, lots of stairs, and a silent night. "*Zimmer mit Aussicht?*" means "Room with view?"—worth asking for.

    Gasthof Simony is my stocking-feet-tidy, 500-year-old favorite, right on the square with a lake view, balconies, creaky wood floors, slip-slidey rag rugs, antique furniture, a lakefront garden, and a huge breakfast. Call friendly Susan Scheutz for a reservation. For safety, reconfirm a day or two before you arrive (Sb-500 AS, Db-850 AS, price can vary according to the plumbing, view, season, and length of stay, 250 AS for third person, cheaper for families, Markt

Salzkammergut and Hallstatt

105, tel. 06134/8231, SE). Downstairs, Frau Zopf runs a traditional Austrian restaurant; try her delicious homemade desserts.

Pension Seethaler is a homey old lodge with 45 beds and a breakfast room mossy with antlers, perched above the lake on the parking-lot side of town (215 AS per person in S, D, T, or Q, 280 AS/person in rooms with private bath, 20 AS cheaper if you stay more than one night, no extra for views, Dr. Morton Weg 22, tel. 06134/8421, fax 06134/84214, Frau Seethaler).

Pension Sarstein has 25 beds, mostly in (sometimes dirty) rooms with flower-bedecked lake-view balconies, in a charming building a few minutes' walk along the lake from the center, run by friendly Frau Fisher. You can swim from her lakeside garden (D-420

AS, Ds-520 AS, Db-620 AS with this book; one-night stays cost 20 AS per person extra; Gosaumühlstrasse 83, tel. 06134/8217). Her sister, friendly **Frau Zimmermann**, runs a small *Zimmer* (as her name implies) in a 500-year-old ramshackle house with low beams, time-polished wood, and fine lake views just down the street (D-400 AS, T-600 AS, can be musty, Gosaumühlstrasse 69, tel. 06134/8309). These elderly women speak almost no English, but you'll find yourself caught up in their charm and laughing together like old friends.

Helga Lenz has a big, sprawling, woodsy house on top of the town with great lake and town views and a neat garden perch. It's ideal for those who sleep well in tree houses (D-360 AS, T-540 AS, Q-720 AS, 20 AS more for one-night stays, high above the paddleboat dock at Hallberg 17, tel. 06134/8508, SE).

Gasthof Zauner is a business machine offering modern pine-flavored rooms with all the comforts on the main square, and a restaurant specializing in grilled meat and fish (Db-1,200 AS, CC:VM, Marktplatz 51, tel. 06134/8246, fax 06134/82468).

Gasthaus Mühle Naturfreunde-Herberge has the best cheap beds in town and is clearly the place to eat well on a budget—great pizzas (145 AS per bed with sheets in two- to 20-bed coed dorms, 110 AS if you BYO hostel sheet, 40-AS breakfast, closed in November, restaurant closed on Wednesday, Kirchenweg 36, below the tunnel car park, tel. & fax 06134/8318, run by Ferdinand Törö). "Nature's friends' houses" are found throughout the Alps. Like mountaineers' huts, they're a good, basic, fun bargain.

The nearby village of Obertraun is a peaceful alternative to Hallstatt in August. You'll find plenty of *Zimmer* and a luxurious hostel (182-AS beds with breakfast, tel. 06131/360).

Transportation Connections—Hallstatt
By train to: Salzburg (hrly, 90 min to Attnang Puchheim, short wait, 50 min to Salzburg), **Vienna** (hrly, 90 min to Attnang Puchheim, short wait, 2.5 hrs to Vienna). Daytrippers to Hallstatt can check bags at the Attnang Puchheim station. But connections there and back can be very fast—about five minutes. Have three 10-AS coins ready for the lockers.

Route Tips for Drivers
From Salzburg to Hallstatt (50 miles): Get on the Munich–Wien Autobahn (blue signs), head for Vienna, exit at Thalgau, and follow signs to Hof, Fuschl, and St. Gilgen. The road to Hallstatt leads first past Fuschlsee (mediocre Sommerrodelbahn summer luge ride, 40 AS, open when dry, April–mid-October 10:00–17:00, at Fuschl an See, tel. 06226/8452), to St. Gilgen (pleasant but touristy), to Bad Ischl (the center of the Salzkammergut with a spa, salt-mine tour, casino, the emperor's villa if you need a Habsburg

history fix, and a good tourist office, tel. 06132/23520), and along Hallstattersee to Hallstatt.

Hallstatt is basically traffic-free. Park in the middle of the tunnel at the "P-1" sign and waterfall. If this is full, try the lake-side lot (P-2, a pleasant five-minute lakeside walk from the town center) just after the tunnel. If you're traveling off-season and staying downtown, you can drive in and park by the boat dock (your hotel "guest card" gives you permission).

BRUGES (BRUGGE)

With Renoir canals, pointy gilded architecture, time-tunnel art, and stay-awhile cafés, Bruges is a heavyweight sightseeing destination, as well as a joy. Where else can you ride a bike along a canal, munch mussels, wash them down with the world's best beer, savor heavenly chocolate, and see Flemish Primitives and a Michelangelo, all within 300 yards of a bell tower that rings out "Don't worry, be happy" jingles every 15 minutes? And there's no language barrier.

The town is "Brugge" (broo-gha) in Flemish. It's "Bruges" (broozh) in French and English. Before it was Flemish or French, the name was a Viking word for "wharf" or "embarkment." Right from the start, Bruges was a trading center. By the 14th century Bruges' population was 35,000, in a league with London, and the city was the most important cloth market in northern Europe. By the 16th century the harbor had silted up and the economy had collapsed. In the 19th century a new port, Zeebrugge, brought renewed vitality to the area. Today Bruges prospers mainly because of tourism: it's a uniquely well-preserved Gothic city and a handy gateway to Europe. It's no secret, but even with the crowds it's the kind of city where you don't mind being a tourist.

Planning Your Time

Bruges needs at least two nights and a full, well-organized day. Even non-shoppers enjoy browsing here, and the Belgian love of life makes a hectic itinerary seem a little senseless. With one day, the speedy visitor could do this: 9:30–Climb the belfry, 10:00–Catch the minibus orientation town tour, 11:00–Tour the Burg sights (visit the TI if necessary), 12:15–Walk to the brewery, have lunch, and catch the 13:00 tour, 14:30–Walk through the

Beguinage, 15:00–Tour the Memling Museum (six paintings),
15:45–See the Michelangelo in the church, 16:00–Tour the
Groeninge Museum (closes at 17:00). Rent a bike for an evening
ride through the quiet backstreets (or take a 900BF half-hour
horse-and-buggy tour or catch a canal-boat tour). Lose the
tourists and find a dinner. (If this schedule seems insane, skip the
belfry and the brewery.)

Orientation (tel. code: 050)
The tourists' Bruges (you'll be sharing it) is contained within a
one-kilometer-square canal, or moat. Nearly everything of interest
and importance is within a cobbled and convenient swath between
the train station and Market Square (a 15-minute walk).
      Tourist Information: The main office is on Burg Square
(Monday–Friday 9:30–18:30, Saturday and Sunday 10:00–12:00
and 14:00–18:30; off-season closes at 17:00, tel. 050/448-686, public WC in courtyard). The other TI is at the train station office
(daily 10:30–13:15 and 14:00-18:30, off-season closes at 17:00 and
on Sunday). Both TIs sell a great 25BF all-inclusive Bruges visitors guide with a map and listings of all of the sights and services.
The free *Exit* includes a monthly calendar of the many events the
town puts on to keep its hordes of tourists entertained. It's entirely
in Dutch but almost readable (i.e., *Harmonieconcert*). Skip the TI's
"combo" museum ticket. They also have train schedule information and specifics on the various kinds of tours available. Bikers
will want the *5X On The Bike Around Bruges* map/guide for 20BF,
showing five routes through the countryside.
      Cyber Café: An Internet café is at Katelijnestraat 67, halfway
between the station and Market Square near Walplein (tel.
050/349-352, e-mail: Kdenys@unicall.be). Word processing and
printing are also available: 60BF for 15 minutes.
      Laundromat: You'll find it at Gentportstraat 28 (daily
7:00–22:00, English instructions). All the machines use 20BF
coins; you'll need about 10 total.

Arrival in Bruges
By Train: From the train, you'll see the square belfry tower on
the main square. Upon arrival, stop by the station TI to pick up
the Bruges visitors guide (map in centerfold). Most buses (all those
marked "CENTRUM") go right to Market Square (40BF ticket,
buy from driver, good for an hour). The taxi fare to most hotels is
250BF. It's a 20-minute walk from the station to the center: Cross
the busy street and canal in front of the station, head up Oostmeers, and turn right on Steenstraat to reach Market Square. You
could rent a bike at the station for the duration of your stay
(325BF/day with a 500BF deposit), but other bike rental shops are
closer to the center (see below).

By Car: Park at the train station for just 100BF a day and pretend you arrived by train; show your parking receipt on the bus to get a free ride into town. The pricier underground parking garage at t'Zand costs 350BF/day.

Helpful Hints

Change traveler's checks at Best Change (daily 9:00–21:00, until 19:00 in winter, just off Market Square on Steenstraat). The post office is on Market Square near the belfry (Monday–Friday 9:00–19:00, Saturday 9:00–12:00). Shops are open from 9:00 to 18:00, a little later on Friday. Grocery stores are usually closed on Sunday. Market day is Wednesday morning (Market Square) and Saturday morning (t'Zand). On Saturday and Sunday afternoons there is a flea market along Dijver in front of the Groeninge Museum. October through March is off-season (when some museums close on Tuesday). A botanical garden blooms in the center of Astrid Park.

Sights—Bruges

Bruges' sights are listed here in walking order: from Market Square to the Burg, to the cluster of museums around the Church of Our Lady, to the Beguinage (a 10-minute walk from beginning to end). Like Venice, the ultimate sight is the town itself, and the best way to enjoy that is to get lost on the backstreets away from the lace shops and ice-cream stands.

Market Square (Markt)—Ringed by banks, the post office, lots of restaurant terraces, great old gabled buildings, and the belfry, this is the modern heart of the city. Most city buses go from here to the station. Under the belfry are two great Belgian French-fry stands and a quadrilingual Braille description and model of the tower. In its day, a canal went right up to the central square of this formerly great trading center.

▲▲**Belfry (Belfort)**—This bell tower has towered over Market Square since 1300. In 1486 the octagonal lantern was added, making it 88 meters high—that's 366 steps (daily 9:30–17:00, October–March closed 12:30–13:30, ticket window closes 45 minutes before closing times, WC in courtyard). The view is worth the climb and the 100BF. Survey the town. On the horizon you can see the towns along the coast. Just before you reach the top, peek into the carillon room. The 47 bells can be played mechanically with the giant barrel and movable tabs (as they do on each quarter-hour), or with a manual keyboard (as it does for regular concerts) with fists and feet rather than fingers. Be there on the quarter-hour when things ring. It's *bellissimo* at the top of the hour. Carillon concert times are listed at the base of the belfry (usually Wednesday, Saturday, and Sunday 14:15–15:00). With your back to the belfry, turn right on Breidelstraat to get to Burg Square.

Central Bruges

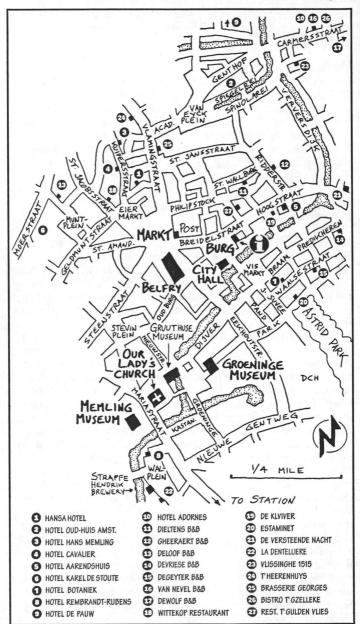

1. HANSA HOTEL
2. HOTEL OUD-HUIS AMST.
3. HOTEL HANS MEMLING
4. HOTEL CAVALIER
5. HOTEL AARENDSHUIS
6. HOTEL KAREL DE STOUTE
7. HOTEL BOTANIEK
8. HOTEL REMBRANDT-RUBENS
9. HOTEL DE PAUW

10. HOTEL ADORNES
11. DIELTENS B&B
12. GHEERAERT B&B
13. DELOOF B&B
14. DEVRIESE B&B
15. DEGEYTER B&B
16. VAN NEVEL B&B
17. DEWOLF B&B
18. WITTEKOP RESTAURANT

19. DE KLVIVER
20. ESTAMINET
21. DE VERSTEENDE NACHT
22. LA DENTELLIERE
23. VLISSINGHE 1515
24. T'HEERENHUYS
25. BRASSERIE GEORGES
26. BISTRO T'GZELLEKE
27. REST. T'GULDEN VLIES

▲▲**Burg Square**—The opulent square called Burg is Bruges' civic center, historically the birthplace of Bruges and the site of the ninth-century castle of the first Count of Flanders. Today it's the scene of outdoor concerts and home of the TI (with a pay WC, 10BF). It's surrounded by six centuries of architecture. Sweeping counterclockwise 360 degrees, you'll go from Romanesque (the round arches and thick walls of the brick basilica in the corner, best seen inside the lower chapel), to the pointed Gothic arches of the Town Hall (with its "Gothic Room"), to the well-proportioned Renaissance windows of the Old Recorder's House (next door, under the gilded statues), and past the TI and the park to the elaborate 17th-century Baroque of the Provost's House.

▲**Basilica of the Holy Blood**—Originally the Chapel of Saint Basil, it is famous for its relic of the blood of Christ, which, according to tradition, was brought to Bruges in 1150 after the Second Crusade. The lower chapel (through door labeled *Basiliek*) is dark and solid—a fine example of Romanesque style (with some beautiful statues). The upper chapel (separate entrance, climb the stairs) is decorated Gothic and is often filled with appropriately contemplative music. An English flier tells about the relic, art, and history. The small but sumptuous Basilica Museum contains the gem-studded hexagonal reliquary that carries the relic on its yearly Ascension Day trip through the streets of Bruges (museum is next to upper chapel, 40BF, daily 9:30–11:50 and 14:00–17:50; shorter hours and closed Wednesday afternoon off-season).

▲**City Hall's Gothic Room**—Built around 1400, this is the oldest room in the Low Countries. Your ticket gives you a room full of old town maps and paintings, and a grand, beautifully restored "Gothic Hall." Its painted and carved wooden ceiling features hanging arches (explained by an English flier). The free ground-level lobby is a picture gallery of Belgium's colonial history, from the Spanish Bourbon king to Napoleon (100BF, includes admission to Renaissance Hall, daily 9:30–16:30, closed 12:30–14:00 during off-season, Burg 12).

Renaissance Hall (Brugse Vrije)—This is just one ornate room with an impressive Renaissance chimney. If you're into heraldry, the symbolism, explained in the free English flier, makes this worth a five-minute stop. If you're not, you'll wonder where the rest of the museum is (100BF, includes admission to City Hall, daily 9:30–12:30 and 13:15–16:40, longer lunch until 14:00 in winter, entry in corner of square).

From Burg to Fish Market to View—From Burg, walk under the Goldfinger family down Blinde Ezelstraat. Just after you cross the bridge, the persistent little fish market (Vismarkt) is on your left. Take an immediate right to Huidevettersplein, a tiny, picturesque, and restaurant-filled square. Continue a few steps to Rozenhoed-kaai street, where you can get a great photo of the belfry reflected in the canal. Can you see its tilt? It leans about four feet. Down the canal (past a flea market on weekends) looms the huge brick spire of the Church of Our Lady (tallest brick spire in the Low Countries). Between you and the church are the next three museums.

▲▲▲**Groeninge Museum**—This diverse and classy collection shows off mostly Flemish art from Memling to Magritte. While it has plenty of worthwhile modern art, the highlights are its vivid and pristine Flemish Primitives. ("Primitive" here means before the Renaissance.) Flemish art is shaped by its love of detail, its merchant patrons' egos, and the power of the Church. Lose yourself in the halls of Groeninge: Gaze across 15th-century canals, into the eyes of reassuring Marys, and through town squares littered with leotards, lace, and lopped-off heads (200BF, daily 9:30–17:00, closed 12:30–14:00 and Tuesday October–March, Dijver 12). The **Brangwyn Museum** (Arentshuis), next door, is only interesting if you are into lace or the early-20th-century art of Brangwyn (80BF, daily 9:30–17:00, closed 12:30–14:00 and Tuesday during off-season, Dijver 16).

▲**Gruuthuse Museum**—A wealthy brewer's home, this is a sprawling smattering of everything from medieval bedpans to a guillotine. There's no information inside, so to understand the crossbows, dark old paintings, and what a beer merchant's doing with box seats peeking down on the altar of the Church of Our Lady next door, you'll have to buy or browse through the 600BF guidebook (130BF, daily 9:30–17:00, shorter hours off-season, Dijver 17).

▲▲**Church of Our Lady**—The church stands as a memorial to the power and wealth of Bruges in its heyday. A delicate *Madonna and Child* by Michelangelo is near the apse (to the right, if you're facing the altar). It's said to be the only Michelangelo statue to leave Italy in his lifetime (cloth money). If you like tombs and church art, pay to wander through the apse (60BF, Michelangelo free, art-filled apse Monday–Friday 10:00–11:30 and 14:30–16:30, closes at 16:00 on Saturday, Sunday 14:30–16:30, on Mariastraat).

▲▲**St. Jans Hospital/Memling Museum**—Beyond the Church of Our Lady is a medieval hospital with six much-loved paintings by the greatest of the Flemish Primitives, Hans Memling. His *Mystical Wedding of St. Catherine* triptych deserves a close look. Catherine and her "mystical groom," the baby Jesus, are flanked by a headless John the Baptist and a pensive John the Evangelist. The chairs are there so you can study it. If you understand the Book of Revelations, you'll understand St. John's wild and intricate vision. The Reliquary of St. Ursula, an ornate little mini-church in the same room, is filled with impressive detail (100BF, daily 9:30–17:00, off-season closed 12:30–14:00 and Wednesday, Mariastraat 38).

▲▲**Straffe Hendrik Brewery Tour**—Belgians are Europe's beer connoisseurs. This fun and handy tour is a great way to pay your respects. The happy gang at this working family brewery gives entertaining and informative 45-minute/four-language tours (usually by friendly Inge, 140BF including a beer, piles of very steep steps, a great rooftop panorama, daily on the hour 11:00–17:00, occasionally skipping 14:00, October–March 11:00 and 15:00 only, one block past church and canal, take right down skinny Stoofstraat to #26 on Walplein square, tel. 050/332-697). Originally Henri Maes, this delicious brew is now known as Straffe Hendrik (strong Henry). They remind their drinkers: "The components of the beer are vitally necessary and contribute to a well-balanced life-pattern. Nerves, muscles, visual sentience, and a healthy skin are stimulated by these in a positive manner. For longevity and life-long equilibrium, drink Straffe Hendrik in moderation!"

Their bistro, where you'll be given your included-with-the-tour beer, serves a quick and hearty lunch plate (the 150BF "bread with paste and vegetables" is the best value, although the 250BF "meat selection and vegetables" is a beer-drinker's picnic for two). You can eat indoors with the smell of hops or outdoors with the smell of hops. This is a great place to wait for your tour or to linger afterward—just watch out for the medieval whoopee cushions on the tables.

▲▲**Beguinage**—For military (and various other) reasons, there were more women than men in the medieval Low Countries. Towns provided Beguinages, dignified places in which these "Beguines" could live a life of piety and service (without having to take the same vows a nun would). You'll find Beguinages all over Belgium and Holland. Bruges' Beguinage almost makes you want to don a habit and fold your hands as you walk under its wispy trees and whisper past its frugal little homes. For a thin slice of Beguinage life, walk through the simple museum (Beguine's House, 60BF with English flier, daily 10:00–12:00 and 13:45–17:00, shorter hours off-season).

Minnewater—Beyond the Beguinage is Minnewater, an idyllic, clip-clop world of flower boxes, canals, swans, and tour boats packed like happy egg cartons. Beyond that is the train station.

Almshouses—Walking from the Beguinage back to the center, you might detour along Nieuwe Gentweg to visit one of about 20 almshouses in the city. At #8, go through the door (free) into the peaceful courtyard. This was a medieval form of housing for the poor. The rich would pay for someone's tiny room here in return for lots of prayers.

Bruges' Experiences

Chocolate—Bruggians are connoisseurs of fine chocolate. You'll be tempted by chocolate-filled display windows all over town.

Godiva is the best big-factory/high-price/high-quality local brand, but for the finest small-family operation, drop by **Maitre Chocolatier Verbeke**. While Mr. Verbeke is busy downstairs making chocolates, Mrs. Verbeke makes sure customers in the shop get the chocolate of their dreams. Ask her to assemble a bag of your favorites. (The smallest amount sold is 100 grams—about seven pieces—for 82BF). Most are pralines, which means they're filled. While the "hedgehogs" are popular, be sure to get a "pharaoh's head." Pray for cool weather, since it's closed when it's very hot. (Open at least in the mornings on Tuesday, Wednesday, Friday, and Saturday; open cooler afternoons as well; a block off Market Square at Geldmuntstraat 25; can ship overseas except during hot summer months, tel. 050/334-198.)

Lace and Windmills by the Moat—A 10-minute walk from the center to the northeast end of town brings you to four windmills strung out along a pleasant grassy setting on the "big moat" canal (between Kruispoort and Dampoort, on the Bruges side of the moat). One of the windmills (St. Janshuismolen) is open for visitors (40BF, 9:30–12:30 and 13:15–17:00, closed October–March, at the end of Carmersstraat).

To actually see lace being made, drop by the nearby Lace Centre, where ladies toss bobbins madly while their eyes go bad (60BF includes afternoon demonstrations and a small lace museum called Kantcentrum, as well as the adjacent Jerusalem church; Monday–Friday 10:00–12:00 and 14:00–18:00, until 17:00 Saturday, closed Sunday, Peperstraat 3). The Folklore Museum, in the same neighborhood, is cute but forgettable (80BF, daily 9:30–17:00, less off-season, Rolweg 40). To find either place, ask for the Jerusalem church.

▲▲Biking—While the sights are close enough for easy walking, the town is a treat to bike through, and you'll be able to get away from the tourist center. Consider a peaceful evening ride through the backstreets and around the outer canal. Rental shops have maps and ideas. The TI sells a handy *5X On The Bike Around Bruges* map/guide for 20BF; it narrates five different bike routes (ranging from 18–30 kilometers) through the idyllic nearby countryside. The best basic trip is 30 minutes along the canal out to Damme and back. The Netherlands/Belgium border is a 40-minute pedal beyond Damme. Two shops rent bikes in the center of town: 70BF/one hour, 150BF/four hours, 250BF/day. Both offer free city maps and child seats. **Popelier Eric's** doesn't require any kind of deposit and sells a good-quality map of the countryside for 80BF (daily 9:00–21:00 in summer, 10:00–19:00 in winter, 50 meters from the Church of Our Lady at Mariastraat 26, tel. 050/343-262). **'T Koffie Boont Je** asks for a deposit of 1,000BF, your passport, or a credit-card imprint. They sell an annoying double-sided photocopy of the TI's biking brochure for

20BF; the map is on one side and the directions—inconveniently—are on the other (Hallestraat 4, closer to the belfry, tel. 050/338-027). The less central **De Ketting** rents bikes for less (150BF/day, Gentpoortstraat 23, tel. 050/344-196).

Bryggia, My Love **Multivision Show**—(This might close in 1999.) Shown in a former neo-Gothic church, this multiscreen film tells of Bruges' Golden Age under the Dukes of Burgundy (mid-1300s–mid-1400s). Dial your audiophone to English and sit near the back to see all of the screens. The 30-minute show, which is informative yet uneven, beats standing in the rain. Parents might find a medieval grope or two objectionable (190BF, daily 10:00–17:00 April–October, shows every hour on the hour, Vlamingstraat 86, tel. 050/347-572). The same company offers a medieval dinner show—skip it.

Dolfinarium—At Boudewijnpark, just outside of town, dolphins make a splash at 11:00, 14:00, and 16:00 (275BF, Debaeckestraat 12, call to confirm show times, tel. 050/383-838). The theme park's roller-skating rink is open in the afternoon (and turns into an ice-skating rink off-season). From Bruges, catch the "Sint Michiels" bus #7 or #17 from Kuipersstraat.

Tours of Bruges

Bruges by Bike—The Backroad Bike Company leads daily bike tours through the nearby countryside (550–650BF, 30 km, three hrs, tel. 050/370-470, fax 050/374-960). Shorter, longer, and evening tours are available.

Bruges by Boat—The most relaxing and scenic (if not informative) way to see this city of canals is by boat, with the captain narrating. Boats leave from all over town (170BF, 10:00–18:00, copycat 35-minute rides).

City Minibus Tours—"City Tour Bruges" gives 50-minute/380BF rolling overviews of the town in a 13-seat, three-skylight minibus, with dial-a-language headsets and earphones. The tour leaves hourly (on the hour, 10:00–19:00 in summer, until 18:00 in spring and fall) from Market Square. The audio is clean, and the narration gives a good history as you tour the town the lazy way.

Bus Tours of Countryside—**Quasimodo Tours** is a hip outfit offering those with extra time two all-day tours through the rarely visited Flemish countryside. The "Flanders Fields" tour on Sunday, Tuesday, and Thursday from 9:00 to 16:30 concentrates on WWI battlefields, trenches, memorials, and poppy-splattered fields. On Monday, Wednesday, and Friday from 9:00 to 16:00, it's "Triple Treat": the port of Damme, a castle, monastery, brewery, and chocolate factory; and sampling the treats—a waffle, chocolate, and beer. Tours are offered in English only (1,400BF, 1,100BF for people under 26, CC:VM, 29-seat nonsmoking bus, lunch included, lots of walking, pick-up at your hotel or the train station, tel. 050/370-470 to book, fax 050/374-960). **Sightseeing Line** offers a bus trip to Damme and a boat ride back (660BF, daily April–June at 14:00 and 16:00, two hours, leaves from Market Square).

Walking Tours—Local guides walk small groups through the core of town daily in July and August (150BF, depart from TI at 15:00, or 1,500BF with private guide by reservation at the TI). The tours, while earnest, are heavy on history and in two languages, so they may be less than peppy. Still, to propel you beyond the pretty gables and canal swans of Bruges, they are good medicine.

Sleeping in Bruges
(33BF = about $1, tel. code 050, zip code: 8000)
Sleep Code: **S** = Single, **D** = Double/Twin, **T** = Triple,
Q = Quad, **b** = bathroom, **t** = toilet only, **s** = shower only,
CC = Credit Card (Visa, MasterCard, Amex). Everyone speaks English.

Most places are located between the train station and the old center, with the most distant (and best) being a few blocks beyond Market Square to the north and east. B&Bs offer the best value (below). All include breakfast, are on quiet streets, and (with two exceptions) keep the same prices throughout the year. Assuming you'll arrive at Market Square by foot or bus, I'll give hotel directions using a 12-hour clock, as if you were standing with your back to the belfry.

Hotels
Hansa Hotel offers 20 rooms in a completely modernized old building. It's bright and tastefully decorated in elegant pastels, and has all the amenities. This is a great splurge, with best prices Sunday through Thursday nights (Sb-3,000–3,900BF, Db-3,500–4,200BF, extra bed-1,250BF, nonsmoking, CC:VMA, elevator, Niklaas Desparsstraat 11, a block north of Market Square, tel. 050/338-444, fax 050/334-205, e-mail: information@hansa.be, run by Johan and Isabelle). Head for Vlamingstraat at 1:00 and take the first left.

Hotel Oud-huis Amsterdam is a classy canalside splurge that seamlessly mixes antiques and chandeliers with modern comforts (Sb-4,750–6,750BF, Db-5,750–7,750BF, five-minute walk from Market Square at Spiegelrei 3, tel. 050/341-810, fax 050/338-891).

Hotel Hans Memling is newly remodeled. There's Mozart in the morning and Beethoven in the afternoon. The giant living/breakfast room is palatial, while the 17 huge upstairs bedrooms are decorated in a classy modern style (Sb-4,200BF, Db-4,900BF, Tb-5,900BF, Qb-6,600BF, CC:VMA, cheaper in winter, buffet breakfast, elevator, Kuipersstraat 18, two blocks north of Market, easy phone reservations if arriving before 18:00, tel. 050/471-212 fax 050/471-210). At 11:00, take Sint Jakobsstraat for one block, then angle right through Eiermarkt Square to Kuipersstraat.

Hotel Cavalier, across the street from Hans Memling, has less character but serves a hearty buffet breakfast in a royal setting (Sb-1,800BF, Db-2,300BF, Tb-2,800BF, Qb-3,200BF, two lofty "backpackers' doubles" on the fourth floor for 1,600BF, CC:VMA, Kuipersstraat 25, tel. 050/330-207, fax 050/347-199, run by friendly Viviane De Clerck).

Hotel Aarendshuis, an old merchant's mansion, is well-worn but comfortable. It's family run with spacious rooms, dingy carpets, chandeliered public places, and a small garden (prices vary with size and luxury: Sb-2,200BF, Db-3,000–4,000BF, Tb-4,000BF, Qb-5,000BF, kids under 10 free, grand boil-your-own-eggs buffet breakfast included, dinner available, carpark-300BF, elevator, CC:VMA, two blocks off Burg Square at Hoogstraat 18, tel. 050/337-889, fax 050/330-816). Immediately to your right at 4:00, take Briedelstraat, which becomes Hoogstraat.

Hotel Karel de Stoute has pleasant rooms in a 15th-century house with carved railings and a huge chandelier (Sb-2,450BF, Db-2,950BF, Tb-3,600BF, Qb-4,500BF, CC:VMA, Moerstraat 23, tel. 050/343-317, fax 050/344-472). Take Sint Jakobsstraat at 11:00, first left on Geldmuntstraat, first right on Geerwijnstraat, then left on Moerstraat.

Hotel Botaniek has three stars, nine fine rooms, and a quiet location a block from Astrid Park. This hotel is basic, small, and comfy. Rooms have TVs and phones, and some have a fridge at no extra cost — ask (Sb 2,400BF, Db 2,800BF, Tb 3,400BF, CC:VMA, Waalsestraat 23, tel. 050/341-424, fax 050/345-939). Immediately to your right at 4:00, take Briedelstraat to Burg, then Blinde Ezelstraat (under Goldfinger family); continue straight (with fish market on your left) for two blocks to Waalsestraat.

Hotel Rembrandt-Rubens has 18 rooms in a creaky 500-year-old building, with tipsy floors, a mysterious floor plan, tacky rooms, elephant tusks, a gallery of creepy old paintings, and probably the holy grail in a drawer somewhere (S-1,000BF, Ss-1,400BF, one D-1,500BF, Ds-2,000BF, Db-2,300BF, Tb-2,900BF, Qb-3,800BF, locked up at 24:00, on a quiet square between the Memlings and the brewery at Walplein 38, tel. 050/336-439). The breakfast room (which must have been the knights' hall) overlooks a canal (while Rembrandt and Rubens overlook you from an ornately carved and tiled 1648 chimney). There's a little warmth behind Mrs. DeBuyser's crankiness. The hotel has been in her family for 50 years. At 8:00, take Steenstraat two blocks to the square, turn left on Mariastraat, then right on Walstraat.

Hotel De Pauw is family-run with straightforward rooms on a quiet street across from a church (two D-1,800BF, Db-2,100–2,350BF, CC:VMA, cable TV and phones, Sint Gilliskerk-hof 8, tel. 050/337-118, fax 050/345-140).

Hotel Adornes is a great value with 20 comfy new rooms in a 17th-century canalside house. They offer free parking and free loaner bikes and the rooms come with all the comforts (Sb-2,600–3,400BF, Db-2,800–3,600BF depending upon size, CC:VMA, near Van Nevel B&B, below, and Carmersstraat at St. Annarei 26, tel. 050/341-336, fax 050/342-085).

Hotel t'Keizershof is a dollhouse of a hotel that lives by its motto, "Spend a night, not a fortune." It's simple and tidy, with eight small, cheery rooms split between two floors, a shower and toi-let on each (S-925BF, D-1,350BF, T-1,980BF, Q-2,380BF free and easy parking, laundry service-300BF, Oostmeers 126, a block in front of train station, tel. 050/338-728, run by Stefaan and Hilde).

Hotel Maison Printaniere, outside of Bruges, has seven doubles (D-from 1,350BF, Db-from 1,850BF, CC:VM, Kapelleweg 7, 8200 Brugge Sint Andries, 20-minute walk from station or take bus #25 "Olympia" to the stop "Vogelzang," tel. 050/385-067, fax 050/380-081).

Bed-and-Breakfasts

These places offer the best value. Each is central, is run by people who enjoy their work, and offers lots of stairs and three or four doubles you'd pay 2,000 to 2,200BF for in a hotel.

Koen and Annemie Dieltiens are a friendly couple who enjoy translating for the guests who eat a hearty breakfast around a big table in their bright, homey, comfortable house. They are a wealth of information on Bruges (S-1,200BF, Sb-1,500BF, D-1,500BF, Db-1,800BF, T-2,000BF, Tb-2,300BF, Qb-2,800BF, nonsmoking, free street parking, Sint-Walburgastraat 14, three blocks east of Market Square, reserve in advance for this popular place, tel. 050/334-294, fax 050/335-230, e-mail: koen.dieltiens @skynet.be). At 1:00, take Philipstockstraat, turn left on Wapen-makersstraat, then take first right. The Dieltiens also rent a cozy studio and apartment for two to six people in a nearby 17th-century house (two pay 10,500BF per week for studio, 12,000BF for apartment, prices higher for shorter stays and more people; cheaper off-season).

Paul and Roos Gheeraert, around the corner from the Diel-tiens, live on the first floor while their guests take the second. With big, bright, comfy rooms, this is a fine value (Sb-1,400BF, larger Sb-1,600BF, Db-1,600BF, larger Db-1,800BF, Tb-2,300BF; rooms have coffee makers, some have fridge; Ridderstraat 9, four blocks east of Market, tel. 050/335-627, fax 050/345-201, e-mail: paul.gheeraert@skynet.be). The Gheeraerts also rent two modern apartments across the street (minimum three nights).

Chris Deloof's rooms are a good bet in the old center. The ones with showers are more elegant, but the upstairs A-frame lofty room is fun (Ss-1,300BF, D-1,800BF, Ds-2,000BF, pleasant breakfast room, Geerwiynstraat 14, tel. 050/340-544, fax 050/343-721, e-mail: chris.deloof@ping.be). The upstairs rooms, which share a kitchenette/microwave, are great for a family or group (Qb-3,500BF). At 11:00, take Sint Jakobsstraat to the first left on Geldmuntstraat, then first right on Geerwiynstraat.

The **Van Nevel family** rents two attractive top-floor rooms with built-in beds in a 16th-century house (S-1,200–1,500BF, D-1,500–1,800BF, Carmersstraat 13, 10-minute walk from Market Square, tel. 050/346-860, fax 050/347-616, e-mail: robert.vannevel@village.uunet.be). Robert enthusiastically shares the culture and history of Bruges with his guests. Take Vlamingstraat at 1:00, turn right on Academiestraat, continue on Spinolarei (runs along right side of canal), and turn right on Carmersstraat.

Yvonne De Vriese rents three tidy but neglected B&B rooms on a corner overlooking two canals (one S-1,000BF, D-1,500BF, Db-1,800BF, 500BF extra for third or fourth person; breakfast served in your room; canal views come with mosquitoes; CC:VMA, free parking, Predikherenstraat 40, four blocks east of Burg Square, take bus #6 or #16 from station and get off at the first stop on Predikheren Rei, tel. 050/334-224). At 4:00, take Breidelstraat to Burg Square, go through archway, pass fish market, and turn left on Braambergstraat, which becomes Predikherenstraat.

Jan Degeyter, a block away, rents two airy, spacious, wood-floored rooms on a quiet street (Db-1,800BF, Tb-2,300BF, Qb-2,800BF, CC:VMA, Waalsestraat 40, tel. 050/331-199, fax 050/347-857).

Arnold Dewolf's B&B is in a stately, quiet neighborhood on a dead-end street. To keep the peace, the rooms lack TVs and radios (S-900BF, D-1,300BF, one big family room-1,400–2,200BF depending on the number of people, free parking, Oostproostse 9, 20-minute walk from center, near the windmills, tel. 050/338-366). Follow directions to Van Nevel's (above), continue on Carmersstraat, turn left on Peterseliestraat, then right on Leestenburg to Oostprootse.

Hostels

Bruges has several good hostels offering beds for around 380BF in two- to eight-bed rooms (singles go for around 550BF). Pick up the hostel info sheet at the station TI. Smallest, loosest, and closest to the center are: the dull **Snuffel Travelers Inn** (Ezelstraat 47, tel. 050/333-133), the **Bauhaus International Party Hotel** (Langestraat 135, tel. 050/341-093), and the funky **Passage** (Dweerstraat 26, tel. 050/340-232; its hotel next door has 1,200BF doubles). Bigger, more modern, and less central are: **International Youth**

Hostel Europa (Baron Ruzettelaan 143, tel. 050/352-679), **IYH Herdersbrug** (Louis Coiseaukaai 46, tel. 050/599-321), and **Merkenveld Scout Center** (Merkenveldweg 15, tel. 050/277-698).

Eating in Bruges

Specialties include mussels cooked a variety of ways (one order can feed two people), fish dishes, grilled meats, and French fries. Touristy places on the square are affordable; candle-cool bistros flicker on backstreets.

Wittekop is very Flemish, specializing in the beer-soaked equivalent of beef bourguignon (18:00–24:00, closed Sunday and Monday, terrace in the back, Sint Jakobsstraat 14). **De Kluiver** offers great "seasnails in spiced bouillon" simmered in a whispering jazz ambience (19:00–1:00, closed Wednesday and Thursday, Hoogstraat 12). For jazz and hearty budget spaghetti (210BF), head for **Estaminet**, on the northern border of peaceful Astrid Park (open from 11:30 on, closed Monday afternoon and all day Thursday, Park 5). Another jazzy place to join locals for dinner is **De Versteende Nacht Jazzcafe** on Langestraat 11 (19:00–2:00, closed Sunday and Monday).

Locals like **La Dentelliere** for its good Flemish food, service, and prices (CC:VMA, Wijngaardstraat 33, tel. 050/331-898); and **Vlissinghe 1515**, a pub at Blekersstraat 2, for its friendly atmosphere (open from 11:30 on, closed Tuesday). Two restaurants popular for their high-quality lunch specials (345BF) are the classy **'t Heerenhuys** (12:00–14:30, closed Thursday and Sunday, Vlamingstraat 53, tel. 050/346-178) and **Brasserie Georges** (12:00–14:30, closed Sunday, Vlamingstraat 58, tel. 050/343-565).

Bistro 't Gezelleke (next door to the Van Nevel B&B and near Bauhaus hostel) offers fine fresh food at bring-'em-in prices (weekdays 12:00–24:00, Saturday from 18:00, closed Sunday, Carmersstraat 15, tel. 050/338-102). **Restaurant 't Gulden Vlies**, just off Burg, is also good (from 19:00 on, closed Monday and Tuesday, Mallebergplaats 17).

Picnics: Geldmuntstraat is a handy street when you're hungry. A block off Market Square on Geldmuntstraat, **Pickles Frituur** serves the best sit-down fries in town. A block farther, past the Verbeke chocolate shop, the **Nopri Supermarket** is great for picnics (push-button produce pricer lets you buy as little as one mushroom, open 9:00–18:00, closed Sunday). The small **Delhaize grocery** is on Market Square opposite the belfry (8:00–12:00 and 13:30–18:00, closed Sunday). **Selfi** has cheap sandwiches to go (Breidelstraat 16, between Burg and Market Square). For midnight munchies, head to the tiny **Nightshop grocery** just off Market Square (daily 14:00–2:00, Philipstockstraat 14).

Frietjes: These local French fries are a treat. Proud and tra-

ditional *frituurs* serve tubs of fries and various local-style shish
kebabs. Belgians dip their *frietjes* in mayonnaise, but ketchup is
there for the Yankees (along with spicier sauces). For a quick,
cheap, and scenic meal, hit a *frituur* and sit on the steps or
benches overlooking Market Square, about 50 yards past the
post office.

Beer: Belgium boasts more than 350 types of beer. Straffe
Hendrik (strong Henry), a potent local brew, is, even to a Bud
Lite kind of guy, obviously great beer. Among the more unusual of
the others to try: Kriek (a cherry-flavored beer), Dentergems (with
coriander and orange peel), and Trappist (a dark, monk-made
beer). Non–beer drinkers enjoy Kriek and Frambozen Bier (the
cherry- and raspberry-flavored beers). Each beer is served in its
own unique glass. Any pub carries the basic beers, but for a selection of more than 300 types, drink at **t'Brugs Beertje**
(16:00–1:00, closed Wednesday, Kemelstraat 5). When you've finished those, step next door, where **Dreupel Huisje "1919"** serves
more than 100 Belgian gins and liqueurs (closed Tuesday).
Another good place to gain an appreciation of the Belgian beer
culture is **de Garre**, off Breidelstraat (between Burg and Markt)
on the tiny Garre alley (daily 12:00–24:00).

Transportation Connections—Bruges

From nearby Brussels, all of Europe is at your fingertips. Train
info: tel. 050/382-382.

By train to: Brussels (2/hrly, 1 hr), **Ghent** (3/hrly, 20 min),
Oostende (3/hrly, 15 min), **Köln** (6/day, 4 hrs), **Paris** (3 direct
highspeed Thalys trains/day, 2.5 hrs, 400BF supplement for
Eurail), **Amsterdam** (hrly, 3.5 hrs).

Trains from England: Bruges is an ideal "welcome to
Europe" stop after London. Take the Eurostar train from London
to Brussels under the English Channel (6/day, 3 hrs), then transfer
to Bruges (hrly, 1 hour). Or, if you'd prefer to cross the Channel
by boat, catch the London–Dover train (2 hrs, from London's
Victoria station), then the catamaran to Oostende (2 hrs; train station at Oostende catamaran terminal), then the Oostende–
Bruges train (15 min). Five boats run daily (900BF one way, same
price for the cheap five-day return ticket; call at least three days in
advance to book with credit card, otherwise just call to reserve a
seat and pay at the dock; CC:VMA, tel. 059/559-955).

PARIS

Paris offers sweeping boulevards, sleepy parks, world-class art galleries, chatty crêpe stands, Napoleon's body, sleek shopping malls, the Eiffel Tower, and people-watching from outdoor cafés. Climb the Notre-Dame and the Eiffel Tower, cruise the Seine and the Champs-Élysées, and master the Louvre and Orsay museums. Save some after-dark energy for one of the world's most romantic cities. Many people fall in love with Paris. Some see the essentials and flee, overwhelmed by the huge city. With the proper approach and a good orientation, you'll fall head over heels for Europe's capital city.

Planning Your Time:
Paris in One, Two, or Three Days

Day 1
Morning: Follow "Historic Core of Paris Walk" (see Sights, below) featuring Île de la Cité, Notre-Dame, Latin Quarter, and Sainte-Chapelle.
Afternoon: Tour Louvre Museum.
Evening: Cruise Seine River or take illuminated Paris by Night bus tour.

Day 2
Morning: Métro to Arc de Triomphe and walk down the Champs-Élysées.
Midday: Tour Orsay Museum.
Afternoon: Catch the RER from Orsay to Versailles. To avoid crowds, see the park first and the palace late.
Evening: Enjoy Trocadero scene and ride up Eiffel Tower.

Day 3
Morning: Follow "Marais Walk" (below).
Afternoon: Tour Rodin Museum and nearby Les Invalides (Napoleon's Tomb and Military Museum).
Evening: Explore Montmartre and Sacre Coeur.

Daily Reminder
Monday: Orsay, Rodin Museum, and Versailles are closed; the Louvre is more crowded because of this. Many small stores don't open until 14:00. Some restaurants close on Mondays. It's discount night at most cinemas.
Tuesday: The Louvre, L'Orangerie, Marmottan, and most other national museums are closed today. Versailles and the Orsay can be jammed.
Wednesday: All museums are open. The weekly *Pariscope* entertainment magazine comes out today.
Thursday: All museums are open.
Friday: All museums are open. Afternoon trains and roads leaving Paris are crowded; TGV reservation fees are much higher.
Saturday: Candlelight visits of Vaux-le-Vicomte (May–October); otherwise avoid weekend crowds at area châteaus. Paris department stores are busy.
Sunday: Organ concerts at St. Sulpice and possibly at other churches. Free evening concert at the American Church (18:00). The fountains run at Versailles. Some museums are two-thirds price all day (Louvre, Orsay, Cluny, Picasso). The Marais is the place to window shop and café hop; many of Paris' stores are closed on Sunday, but as this is the Jewish Quarter, it hops.

Orientation
Paris is split in half by the Seine River, divided into 20 *arrondissements* (proud and independent governmental jurisdictions), and circled by a ring-road freeway (the *périphérique*). You'll find Paris easier to negotiate if you know which side of the river you're on, which *arrondissement* you're in, and which subway (Métro) stop you're closest to. If you're north of the river (above on any city map), you're on the Right Bank (*rive droite*). If you're south of it, you're on the Left Bank (*rive gauche*).

Arrondissements are numbered, starting at Notre-Dame (ground zero) and moving in a clockwise spiral out to the ring road. The last two digits in a Parisian zip code are the *arrondissement* number, and the notation for the Métro stop is "Mo."

In Parisian jargon, Napoleon's tomb is on *la rive gauche* (the Left Bank) in the 7ème (seventh *arrondissement*), zip code 75007, Mo: Invalides. Paris Métro stops are used as a standard aid in giving directions, even for those not using the Métro.

Paris Overview

TRAIN STATIONS / GARES:

① **ST-LAZARE** TO NORMANDY

② **NORD** TO LONDON & BRUSSELS VIA EUROSTAR, TO N. EUROPE

③ **L'EST** TO E. FRANCE, S. GERMANY, SWITZERLAND, AUSTRIA

④ **LYON** TO S.E. FRANCE & ITALY

⑤ **D'AUSTERLITZ** TO S.W. FRANCE, LOIRE & SPAIN

⑥ **MONTPARNASSE** TO NORMANDY, BRITTANY, CHARTRES, TGV TO LOIRE & S.W. FRANCE

ARRONDISSEMENTS (DISTRICTS)

Tourist Information

Avoid the Paris TIs—long lines, short information, and a 5F charge for maps. This book, the *Pariscope* magazine (described below), and one of the freebie maps available at any hotel are all you need. The main TI is at 127 avenue des Champs-Élysées (daily 9:00–20:00), but the TIs at the Louvre, Eiffel Tower, and train stations Gare de Lyon and Gare de Montparnasse are handier (daily 8:00–20:00).

The *Pariscope* weekly magazine (or one of its clones, 3F at any newsstand, explained below) lists museum hours, special art exhibits, concerts, music festivals, plays, movies, and nightclubs.

For a complete list of museum hours and scheduled English museum tours, pick up the free *Musées, Monuments Historiques, et Expositions* booklet from any museum.

While Paris is littered with free maps, they don't show all the streets. You may want the huge Michelin #10 map of Paris. For an extended stay we prefer the pocket-size and street-indexed *Paris Practique* (40F). For supplemental background on the city, sights, and neighborhoods, you may want to buy an additional guidebook. The *Michelin Green Guide*, which is somewhat scholarly, and the more readable *Paris Access Guide* are both well-researched. *Mona Winks*, a guidebook by Rick Steves and Gene Openshaw, is particularly heavy on Paris, with extensive self-guided walking tours of the Louvre, Orsay, Versailles, and the Historic Core of Paris.

There are many English-language bookstores in Paris where you can pick up guidebooks (for nearly double their American price). A few are: Shakespeare and Company (12:00–24:00, lots of used travel books, 37 rue de la Boucherie, across the river from Notre-Dame), W. H. Smith (248 rue de Rivoli), and Brentanos (37 avenue de L'Opéra).

The American Church is a nerve center for the American èmigrè community and distributes the *Free Voice*, a handy and insightful monthly English-language newspaper, with useful reviews of concerts, plays, and current events in Paris; and *France—U.S.A. Contacts*, an advertisement paper full of useful information for those looking for work or long-term housing (facing the river between Eiffel and Orsay at 65 quai d'Orsay, Mo: Invalides).

Arrival in Paris

By Train: Paris has six train stations, all connected by Métro and bus, most with banks and TIs, and none that will check bags (blame terrorism). Hop the Métro to your hotel (see Getting Around Paris, below).

Paris' train stations serve many different destinations. The Gare de l'Est handles the east, the Gare du Nord and Gare St. Lazare serve northern and central Europe, the Gare d'Austerlitz and Gare du Lyon cover southern Europe, and the Gare Montparnasse handles western France and TGV service to France's southwest. (Any train station can give you the schedule information you need, make reservations, and sell tickets for any destination.) Buying tickets is handier from a SNCF neighborhood office (e.g.: Louvre, Orsay, Versailles, airports) or at your neighborhood travel agency, and it's worth their small fee (SNCF signs in their window indicate they sell train tickets).

By Plane: For detailed information on getting from Paris' airports to downtown Paris (and vice versa), see Transportation Connections at the end of this chapter.

Helpful Hints

Theft Alert: Use your money belt, and never carry a wallet in your back pocket or a purse over your shoulder. Thieves thrive in tourist areas, subway stations, and on the Métro.

Museums: Most museums offer reduced prices and shorter hours on Sunday. Many begin closing rooms 45 minutes before the actual closing time. For the fewest crowds, visit very early, at lunch, or very late. The best Impressionist art museums are the Orsay, Marmottan, and L'Orangerie (each described below). Most museums have slightly shorter hours October through March. French holidays can really mess up your sightseeing plans (Jan. 1, May 1, May 8, July 14, Nov. 1, Nov. 11, and Dec. 25). See Daily Reminder, above, for other "closed" days.

Paris Museum Pass: In Paris there are two classes of sightseers: those with a museum pass and those without. Serious sightseers save time (less time in lines) and money by getting this pass. Sold at museums, main Métro stations, and tourist offices, it pays for itself in two admissions and gets you into sights with no lining up (one day-80F, three consecutive days-160F, five consecutive days-240F). Included sights (and admission prices without the pass) you're likely to visit: Louvre (45F), Orsay (39F), Sainte-Chapelle (32F), Arc de Triomphe (35F), Army Museum and Napoleon's Tomb (37F), Carnavalet Museum (35F), Conciergerie (28F), Sewer Tour (32F), Cluny Museum (30F), Notre-Dame towers (30F) and crypt (32F), L'Orangerie (30F), Picasso Museum (30F), Rodin Museum (28F), and the elevator to the top of the Grand Arche de La Defense (40F). Outside Paris, the pass covers the Palace of Versailles (45F), its Grand Trianon (25F), and Château Chantilly (35F). Notable sights not covered: Marmottan Museum, Eiffel Tower, Montparnasse Tower, the ladies of Pigalle, and Disneyland Paris. Tally it up—but remember, an advantage of the pass is that you skip to the front of the line—saving hours of waiting in the summer (though everyone must pass through the slow-moving metal detector lines at a few sights). And with the pass, you'll pop painlessly into sights that you're walking by (even for a few minutes) that might otherwise not be worth the expense (e.g., Notre-Dame crypt, Cluny Museum, Conciergerie, Victor Hugo's House). The free museum and monuments directory that comes with your pass lists the latest hours, phone numbers, and specifics on what kids pay. The cut-off age for free entry varies from 5 to 18. Most major, serious art museums let young people up to age 18 in for free. If buying a pass at a museum with a long line, skip to the front and find the sales window.

Local Guides: Arnaud Servignat (tel. 01 42 57 03 35, fax 01 42 62 68 62, e-mail: arnoud.saigon@wanadoo.fr) and Marianne Siegler (tel. 01 42 52 32 51) are licensed local guides who free-lance for individuals and families ($150/4 hrs, $250/day).

Telephone Cards: Pick up the essential France *télécarte* at any *tabac* (tobacco shop), post office, or tourist office (*une petite carte* is 42F; *une grande* is 98F). Smart travelers check things by telephone. Most public phones use these cards.

Useful Telephone Numbers: American Hospital, 01 46 41 25 25; American pharmacy, 01 47 42 49 40 (Mo: Opéra); Police, 17; United States Embassy, 01 43 12 22 22; Paris and France directory assistance, 12; AT&T operator, 0800 99 00 11; MCI, 0800 99 00 19; Sprint, 0800 99 00 87.

Toilets: Carry small change for pay toilets, or walk into any outdoor café like you own the place and find the toilet in the back. Remember, the toilets in museums are free and generally the best you'll find. Modern super-sanitary street booths provide both relief and a memory.

Getting Around Paris

By Métro: Europe's best subway is divided into two systems—the Métro (puddle-jumping everywhere in Paris) and the RER (which makes giant speedy leaps around town and connects suburban destinations). You'll be using the Métro for most of your trips.

In Paris you're never more than a 10-minute walk from a Métro station. One ticket takes you anywhere in the system with unlimited transfers. Save 40 percent by buying a *carnet* (car-nay) of 10 tickets for 48F at any Métro station (a single ticket is 8F). Métro tickets work on city buses, though one ticket cannot be used as a transfer between subway and bus.

The Mobilis ticket (30F) allows unlimited travel for a single day on all bus and Métro lines. If you're staying longer, the *Carte d'Orange* pass gives you free run of the bus and Métro system for one week (75F and a photo, ask for the *Carte d'Orange Coupon Vert*) or a month (254F, ask for the *Carte d'Orange Coupon Orange*). These pass prices cover only central Paris; you can pay more for passes covering regional destinations (e.g., Versailles). The weekly pass begins Monday and ends Sunday, and the monthly pass begins the first day of the month and ends the last day of that month, so mid-week or mid-month purchases are generally not worthwhile. All passes can be purchased at any Métro station (most have photo booths).

To get to your destination, determine which "Mo." stop is closest to it and which line or lines will get you there. The lines have numbers, but they're best known by their direction or end-of-the-line stop. (For example, the La Defense/Château de Vincennes line runs between La Defense in the west and Vincennes in the east.)

Once in the Métro station, you'll see blue-and-white signs directing you to the train going in your direction (e.g., direction: La Defense). Insert your ticket in the automatic turnstile, pass through, then reclaim and keep your ticket until you exit the

Paris

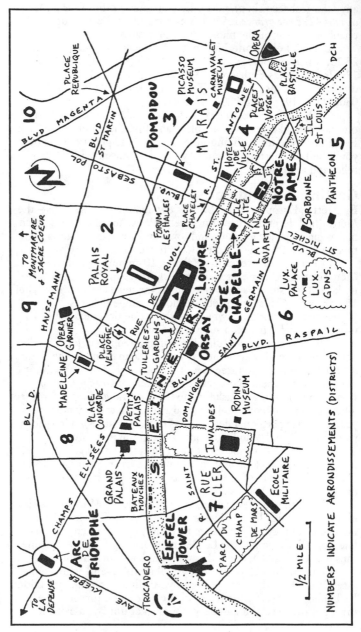

system (fare inspectors accept no excuses from anyone). Transfers are free and can be made wherever lines cross. When you transfer, look for the orange *correspondence* (connections) signs when you exit your first train, then follow the proper direction sign.

Before you *sortie* (exit), check the helpful *plan du quartier* (map of the neighborhood) to get your bearings, locate your destination, and decide which *sortie* you want. At stops with several *sorties*, you can save lots of walking by choosing the best exit.

Thieves thrive in the Métro. Be on guard. For example, a pocket picked as you pass through a turnstile leaves you on the wrong side and the thief strolling away. Any jostle or commotion (especially when boarding or leaving trains) is likely the sign of a thief or team of thieves in action. Paris is most dangerous late at night.

Paris has a huge homeless population and over 12 percent unemployment; expect a warm Métro welcome by panhandlers, musicians, and those selling magazines produced by the homeless community.

By RER: The RER (*Réseau Express Régionale*, ehr-uh-ehr) suburban train system (thick lines on your subway map identified by letters A, B, C, and so on) works like the Métro but is much speedier because it makes only a few stops within the city. One Métro ticket is all you need for RER rides within Paris. You can transfer between the Métro and RER systems with the same ticket. Unlike the Métro, you need to insert your ticket in a turnstile to exit the RER system. To travel outside the city (to Versailles or the airport, for example) you'll need to buy a separate, more expensive ticket at the station window before boarding, and make sure your stop is served by checking the signs over the train platform (not all trains serve all stops).

By City Bus: The trickier bus system is worth figuring out. Métro tickets are good on both bus and Métro, though you can't use the same ticket to transfer between the two systems. One ticket gets you anywhere in central Paris, but if you leave the city center (shown as section 1 on the diagram on board the bus), you must validate a second ticket. While the Métro shuts down at about 00:30, some buses continue much later. Schedules are posted at bus stops. Handy bus-system maps are available in any Métro station (*plan des autobus*) and are provided in your *Paris Pratique* map book if you invest.

Big system maps, posted at each bus and Métro stop, display the routes. Individual route diagrams show the exact route of the lines serving that stop. Major stops are painted on the side of each bus. Enter through the front doors. Punch your Métro ticket in the machine behind the driver, or pay the higher cash fare. Get off the bus using the rear door. Even if you're not certain you've figured it out, do some joyriding (outside of rush hour). Lines #24,

#63, and #69 are Paris' most scenic routes and make a great introduction to the city. Bus #69 is particularly handy, running between the Eiffel Tower, the recommended hotels around rue Cler, the Orsay Gallery, the Louvre, the Marais/Bastille area (more recommended hotels), and Père Lachaise Cemetery. The most handy bus routes are listed for each hotel area recommended (below).

By Taxi: Parisian taxis are almost reasonable. A 10-minute ride costs about 50F (versus about 5F to get anywhere in town on the Métro). You can try waving one down, but it's easier to ask for the nearest taxi stand ("oo ay la tet de stah-see-oh taxi") or ask your hotel to call for you. Higher rates are charged from 22:00 to 6:30, all day Sunday, and to the airport. If you call from your hotel the meter starts as soon as the call is received. Taxis are tough to find on Friday and Saturday night, especially after the Métro closes (around 00:30).

By Foot: Be careful out there! Parisian drivers are notorious for ignoring pedestrians. Never assume you have the right of way, even in a crosswalk. When crossing a street, keep your pace constant and don't stop suddenly. Parisian drivers carefully calculate your speed and will miss you, provided you don't alter your route or pace.

Organized Tours of Paris

Bus Tours: Paris Vision offers handy bus tours of Paris, day and night (advertised in hotel lobbies); their "Illuminated Paris" tour is explained in Entertainment, below. Paris also has a "hop-on, hop-off" bus service called **Open Deck Tours** that connects all the major sights and includes a running commentary; you can get off at a site, explore, and catch a later bus (170F, buy from driver, good for two days, 2 buses per hour). You'll see these bright yellow topless double-decker buses all over town.

Boat Tours: Several companies offer one-hour boat cruises on the Seine. The **Bateaux-Mouches** boats depart every 30 minutes (from 10:00–23:00, best at night) from the pont de l'Alma, the pont Neuf, and Eiffel Tower (40F, 20F for children under age 14, tel. 01 42 25 96 10). Offered from June–September only, the **Bateau-Bus** is a river bus that connects five stops along the river: Eiffel Tower, Orsay, Louvre, Notre-Dame, and place de la Concorde (60F, 30F for youth, departures every 45 minutes from about 10:00–19:00; pick up a brochure at any TI).

Walking Tours: Use the walking tours described in this book and be your own guide. Or, consider Paris Walking Tours, which offers a daily walk for 60F. Choose from architecture, Montmartre, Hemingway's Paris, Medieval Paris, French Revolution, museum tours (admission extra), and more (tel. 01 48 09 21 40, fax 01 42 43 75 51, Web site: http://ourworld.compuserve com/homepages/Pariswalking).

Sights—The "Historic Core of Paris" Walk

(This information is distilled from the Historic Paris Walk chapter in *Rick Steves' Mona Winks*, by Gene Openshaw and Rick Steves.) Allow four hours for this self-guided tour, including sightseeing. Start where the city did—on the Île de la Cité, facing the Notre-Dame; follow the dotted line on the "Core of Paris" map. To get to the Notre-Dame, ride the Métro to Cité, Hôtel de Ville, or St. Michel, and walk to the square facing the . . .

▲▲**Notre-Dame Cathedral**—The 700-year-old cathedral is packed with history and tourists. Study its sculpture (Notre-Dame's forte) and windows, take in a Mass, eavesdrop on guides, and walk all around the outside. (Free, daily 8:00–18:45; treasury-15F, daily 9:30–17:30. Ask about the free English tours, normally Wednesday and Thursday at noon and Saturday at 14:30.) Sunday Masses are at 8:00, 8:45, 10:00, 11:30, 12:30, and 18:30. Climb to the top for a great gargoyle's-eye view of the city; you get 400 steps for only 30F (entrance on outside, north tower open 9:30–17:30, closed at lunch and earlier off-season). There are clean 2.70F toilets in front of the church near Charlemagne's statue.

The **Cathedral facade** is worth a close look. The church is dedicated to "Our Lady" (Notre-Dame). Mary is center stage—cradling Jesus, surrounded by the halo of the rose window. Adam is on the left, and Eve is on the right.

Below Mary and above the arches is a row of 28 statues known as the Kings of Judah. During the French Revolution, these Biblical kings were mistaken for the hated French kings. The citizens stormed the church, crying, "Off with their heads!" All were decapitated but have since been recapitated.

Speaking of decapitation, look at the carving above the doorway on the left. The man with his head in his hands is St. Denis. Back when there was a Roman temple on this spot, Christianity began making converts. The fourth-century bishop of Roman Paris, Denis, was beheaded. But these early Christians were hard to keep down. The man who would become St. Denis got up, tucked his head under his arm, and headed north until he found just the right place to meet his maker: Montmartre, which means "mountain of the martyr." The Parisians were convinced of this miracle, Christianity gained ground, and a church soon replaced the pagan temple.

Medieval art was OK if it embellished the house of God and told Bible stories. For a fine example, move to the base of the central column (at the foot of Mary, about where the head of St. Denis could spit if he was real good). Working around from the left, find God telling a barely created Eve, "Have fun but no apples." Next, the sexiest serpent I've ever seen makes apples *à la mode*. Finally, Adam and Eve, now ashamed of their nakedness, are expelled by an angel. This is a tiny example (featuring a story most of us know) in a church covered with meaning.

Core of Paris

Now move to the right and study the carving above the central portal. It's the end of the world, and Christ sits on the throne of Judgment (just under the arches, holding his hands up). Below him an angel and a demon weigh souls in the balance. The "good" stand to the left, looking up to heaven. The "bad" ones to the right are chained up and led off to . . . Versailles on a Tuesday. The "ugly" ones must be the crazy sculpted demons to the right, at the base of the arch.

Wander through the interior. You'll be routed around the ambulatory, much as medieval pilgrims would have been. Don't miss the rose windows filling each of the transepts. Back outside, walk around the church through the park on the riverside for a close look at the flying buttresses.

The neo-Gothic 90-meter spire is a product of the 1860 reconstruction. Around its base are apostles and evangelists (the green men) as well as Viollet-le-Duc, the architect in charge of the work. Notice how the apostles look outward, blessing the city, while the architect (at top, seen from behind the church) looks up, admiring his spire.

The archaeological **crypt** is a worthwhile 15-minute stop with your museum pass (enter 100 yards in front of church, 32F, 50F with Notre-Dame's tower, daily 10:00–18:00, closes at 16:30 October–April). You'll see Roman ruins, trace the street plan of the medieval village, and see diagrams of how the earliest Paris grew and grew, all thoughtfully explained in English.

If you're hungry near Notre-Dame, the only grocery store on the Île de la Cité is tucked away at 16 rue Chanoinesse, one block north of the church (9:00–13:30 and 16:00–20:30, closed Sunday). Nearby Île St. Louis has inexpensive *crêperies* and grocery stores open daily on its main drag. Plan a picnic for the quiet bench-filled park immediately behind the church (public WC).

Behind the Notre-Dame, squeeze through the tourist buses, cross the street, and enter the iron gate into the park at the tip of the island. Look for the stairs and head down.

▲▲Deportation Memorial (Mémorial de la Déportation)— This memorial to the 200,000 French victims of the Nazi concentration camps draws you into their experience. As you descend the steps, the city around you disappears. Surrounded by walls, you have become a prisoner. Your only freedom is your view of the sky and the tantalizing glimpse of the river below.

Enter the single-file chamber ahead. Inside, the circular plaque in the floor reads, "They descended into the mouth of the earth and they did not return." A hallway stretches in front of you, lined with 200,000 lighted crystals, one for each French citizen that died. Flickering at the far end is the eternal flame of hope. The tomb of the unknown deportee lies at your feet. Above, the inscription reads, "Dedicated to the living memory of the 200,000 French deportees sleeping in the night and the fog, exterminated in the Nazi concentration camps."

Above the exit as you leave is the message you'll find at all Nazi sights: "Forgive but never forget." (Free, daily 8:30–21:45, weekends and holidays from 9:00, sometimes closes 12:00–14:00, shorter hours off-season, east tip of the island near Île St. Louis, behind Notre-Dame, Mo: Cité.)

Île St. Louis—Back on street level, look across the river to the Île St. Louis. If the Île de la Cité is a tug laden with the history of Paris, it's towing this classy little residential dinghy laden only with boutiques, famous sorbet shops, and characteristic restaurants (see Eating in Paris, below). This island wasn't developed until much later (18th century). What was a swampy mess is now harmonious Parisian architecture. The pedestrian bridge, Pont Saint Louis, connects the two islands leading right to rue Saint Louis en l'Île. This spine of the island is lined with interesting shops. A short stroll takes you to the famous Bertillon ice-cream parlour (#31). Loop back to the pedestrian bridge along the parklike quays (walk north to the river and turn left). This walk is about as romantic as Paris gets.

Before walking to the opposite end of the Île de la Cité, loop through the Latin Quarter (as indicated on the map). From the Deportation Memorial cross the bridge onto the Left Bank and enjoy the riverside view of the Notre-Dame and window shop among the green book stalls, browsing through used books, vintage posters, and souvenirs. At the little park and church (over the bridge from the front of Notre-Dame), venture inland a few blocks, basically arcing through the Latin Quarter and returning to the island two bridges down at place St. Michel.

▲**Latin Quarter**—This area, which gets its name from the language used here when it was an exclusive medieval university district, lies between the Luxembourg Gardens and the Seine, centering around the Sorbonne University and boulevards St. Germain and St. Michel. This is the core of the Left Bank—it's crowded with international eateries, far-out bookshops, street singers, and jazz clubs. For colorful wandering and café-sitting, afternoons and evenings are best (Mo: St. Michel).

Along rue Saint-Severin you can still see the shadow of the medieval sewer system. (The street slopes into a central channel of bricks.) In the days before plumbing and toilets, when people still went to the river or neighborhood wells for their water, "flushing" meant throwing it out the window. Certain times of day were flushing times. Maids on the fourth floor would holler "*Garde de l'eau!*" ("Look out for the water!") and heave it into the streets, where it would eventually be washed down into the Seine.

The **Cluny Museum** (also known by its new name: Musée National du Moyen Age), a treasure trove of medieval art, fills the old Roman baths, offering close-up looks at stained glass, Notre-Dame carvings, fine goldsmithing and jewelry, and rooms of tapestries—the best of which is the exquisite *Lady with the Unicorn.* In five panels, a delicate-as-medieval-can-be noble lady introduces a delighted unicorn to the senses of taste, hearing, sight, smell, and touch (30F, Wednesday–Monday 9:15–17:45, closed Tuesday, 6 place Paul-Painlevé near the corner of boulevards St. Michel and St. Germain, tel. 01 53 73 78 00, Mo: Cluny).

Place St. Michel (facing the St. Michel bridge) is the traditional core of the Left Bank's artsy, liberal, hippie, Bohemian district of poets, philosophers, winos, and tourists. In less commercial times, place St. Michel was a gathering point for the city's malcontents and misfits. Here, in 1871, the citizens took the streets from the government troops, set up barricades *Les Miz*–style, and established the Paris Commune. In World War II the locals rose up against their Nazi oppressors (read the plaques by the St. Michael fountain). And in the spring of 1968, a time of social upheaval all over the world, young students—battling riot batons and tear gas—took over the square and demanded change.

From place St. Michel, look across the river and find the spire of Sainte-Chapelle church and its weathervane angel (below). Cross the river on the St. Michel bridge and continue along boulevard du Palais. On your left you'll see the high-security doorway to Sainte-Chapelle. But first, carry on another 30 meters and turn right at a wide pedestrian street, the rue de Lutece.

Cité "Métropolitain" Stop—Of the 141 original turn-of-the-century subway entrances, this is one of 17 survivors now preserved as a national art treasure. The curvy, plant-like ironwork is a textbook example of Art Nouveau, the style that rebelled against the erector-set squareness of the Industrial Age (e.g., Mr. Eiffel's tower).

The flower market right here on place Louis Lepine is a pleasant detour. On Sundays this square chirps with a busy bird market. And across the way is the Prefecture de Police, where Inspector Clouseau of *Pink Panther* fame used to work, and where the local resistance fighters took the first building from the Nazis in August 1944, leading to the Allied liberation of Paris a week later.

Pause here to admire the view. Sainte-Chapelle is a pearl in an ugly architectural oyster, part of a complex of buildings that includes the Palace of Justice (to the right of Sainte-Chapelle, behind the fancy gates). Return to the entrance of Sainte-Chapelle. You'll need to pass through a metal detector to get in. Free toilets are ahead, on the left. The line into the church may be long. (Museum card holders can go directly in; pick up the excellent English info sheet.) Enter the humble ground floor. . . .

▲▲▲Sainte-Chapelle—The triumph of Gothic church architecture is a cathedral of glass like no other. It was speedily built from 1242 to 1248 for St. Louis IX (France's only canonized king) to house the supposed Crown of Thorns. Its architectural harmony is due to the fact that it was completed under the direction of one architect in only six years—unheard of in Gothic times. (Notre-Dame took more than 200 years to build.)

The design clearly shows an Old Regime approach to worship. The basement was for staff and other common folk. Royal Christians worshiped upstairs. The ground-floor paint job, a 19th-century restoration, is a reasonably accurate copy of the original.

Climb the spiral staircase to the *Chapelle Haute*. Fill the place with choral music, crank up the sunshine, face the top of the altar, and really believe that the Crown of Thorns was there, and this becomes one awesome space.

"Let there be light." In the Bible, it's clear: Light is divine. Light shining through stained glass was a symbol of God's grace shining down to earth. Gothic architects used their new technology to turn dark stone buildings into lanterns of light. The glory of Gothic shines brighter here than in any other church.

There are 15 separate panels of stained glass (6,500 square feet—two-thirds of it 13th-century original), with more than 1,100 different scenes, mostly from the Bible. In medieval times, scenes like these helped teach Bible stories to the illiterate.

The altar was raised up high to better display the relic—the Crown of Thorns—around which this chapel was built. The supposed Crown cost King Louis three times as much as this church. Today it is kept in the Notre-Dame Treasury and shown only on Good Friday.

Louis' little private viewing window is in the wall to the right of the altar. Louis, both saintly and shy, liked to go to church without dealing with the rigors of public royal life. Here he could worship still dressed in his jammies.

Lay your camera on the ground and shoot the ceiling. Those pure and simple ribs growing out of the slender columns are the essence of Gothic.

Books in the gift shop explain the stained glass in English. There are concerts (120F) almost every summer evening. (32F, daily 9:30–18:00, off-season 10:00–17:00, call 01 48 01 91 35 for concert information, Mo: Cité.)

Palais du Justice—Back outside, as you walk around the church exterior, look down and notice how much Paris has risen in the 800 years since Sainte-Chapelle was built. You're in a huge complex of buildings that has housed the local government since ancient Roman times. It was the site of the original Gothic palace of the early kings of France. The only surviving medieval parts are the Sainte-Chapelle church and the Conciergerie prison.

Most of the site is now covered by the giant Palais de Justice, home of France's supreme court (built in 1776). "*Liberté, Egalité, Fraternité*" over the doors is a reminder that this was also the headquarters of the revolutionary government.

Now pass through the big iron gate to the noisy boulevard du Palais and turn left (toward the Right Bank). On the corner is the site of the oldest public clock (1334) in the city. While the present clock is said to be Baroque, it somehow still manages to keep accurate time.

Turn left onto Quai de l'Horloge and walk along the river. The round medieval tower just ahead marks the entrance to the Conciergerie. Pop in to visit the courtyard and lobby (free). Step past the serious-looking guard into the courtyard.

Conciergerie—The Conciergerie, a former prison, is a gloomy place. Kings used it to torture and execute failed assassins. The leaders of the Revolution put it to similar good use. The tower next to the entrance, called "the babbler," was named for the painful sounds that leaked from it.

Look at the stark lettering above the doorways. This was a no-nonsense revolutionary time. Everything, even lettering, was subjected to the test of reason. No frills or we chop 'em off.

Step inside; the lobby, with an English-language history display, is free. Marie-Antoinette was imprisoned here. During a busy eight-month period in the Revolution, she was one of 2,600 prisoners kept here on their way to the guillotine. The interior, with its huge vaulted and pillared rooms, echoes with history but is pretty barren (28F, daily 9:30–18:30, 10:00–17:00 in winter, good English descriptions). You can see Marie-Antoinette's cell, housing a collection of her mementos. In another room, a list of those made "a foot shorter at the top" by the "national razor" includes ex-King Louis XVI, Charlotte Corday (who murdered Marat in his bathtub), and the chief revolutionary who got a taste of his own medicine, Maximilien Robespierre.

Back outside, wink at the flak-vested guard, fake right, and turn left. Listen for babbles, and continue your walk along the river. Across the river you can see the rooftop observatory—flags flapping—of the Samaritaine Department store, where this walk will end. At the first corner, veer left past France's supreme court building and into a sleepy triangular square called place Dauphine. Marvel at how such quaintness could be lodged in the midst of such greatness as you walk through the park to the end of the island. At the equestrian statue of Henry IV, turn right onto the bridge and take refuge in one of the nooks on the Eiffel Tower side.

Pont Neuf—This "new bridge" is now Paris' oldest. Built during Henry IV's reign (around 1600), its 12 arches span the widest part of the river. The fine view includes the park on the tip of the island (note Seine tour boats), the Orsay Gallery, and the Louvre. These turrets were originally for vendors and street entertainers. In the days of Henry IV, who originated the promise of "a chicken in every pot," this would have been a lively scene.

Directly over the river, the first building you'll hit on the Right Bank is the venerable old department store, Samaritaine.

▲**Samaritaine Department Store Viewpoint**—Enter the store and go to the rooftop. Ride the glass elevator from near the Pont Neuf entrance to the ninth floor (you'll be greeted by a W.C., check out the sink). Pass the 10th-floor *terrasse* for the 11th-floor *panorama* (tight spiral staircase; watch your head). Quiz yourself. Working counterclockwise, find: the Eiffel Tower, Invalides/Napoleon's Tomb, Montparnasse Tower, Henry IV statue on the tip of the island, Sorbonne University, the dome of the Panthéon, Sainte-Chapelle, Notre-Dame, Hôtel de Ville (city hall), Pompidou Center, Sacré-Coeur, Opéra, and Louvre. The Champs-Élysées leads to the Arc de Triomphe. Shadowing that—even bigger, while two times as distant—is the Grand Arche la Defense. You'll find light, reasonably priced, and incredibly scenic meals on the breezy terrace, and a supermarket in the basement. (Rooftop view is free, daily 9:30–19:00, tel. 01 40 41 20 20. Mo: Pont Neuf.)

Sights—Paris' Museums near the Tuileries Gardens

The newly renovated Tuileries Gardens was once private property of kings and queens. Paris' grandest public park links these museums:

▲▲▲**Louvre**—This is Europe's oldest, biggest, greatest, and maybe most-crowded museum. There is no grander entry than through the pyramid, but metal detectors create a long line at times. To avoid the line, either use the nearby entrance over the Richelieu wing (facing the pyramid with your back to the Tuileries Garden, go to your left, which is north; under the arches you'll find the Richelieu entrance and escalator down), or enter the Louvre directly from the Métro stop "Palais Royale Musée de Louvre." Signs to "Musée du Louvre" put you in a slick underground shopping mall that connects with the Pyramid. (Don't get off at the "Louvre Rivoli" Métro stop, which is farther away.)

Pick up the free *Louvre Handbook in English* at the information desk under the pyramid as you enter. Don't try to cover the museum thoroughly. The 90-minute English-language tours, which leave six times daily except Sunday, boil this overwhelming museum down to size (33F, tour tel. 01 40 20 52 09, Web site: www. louvre.fr). Clever new 30F digital audio tours (after ticket booths, at top of stairs) give you a receiver and a directory of about 130 masterpieces, allowing you to dial a (rather dull) commentary on included works as you stumble upon them. Rick Steves' and Gene Openshaw's museum guidebook, *Rick Steves' Mona Winks* (buy in the United States), includes a self-guided tour of the Louvre.

If you can't get a guide, start in the Denon wing and visit these highlights, in this order: Michelangelo's *Slaves*, Ancient Greek and Roman (Parthenon frieze, *Venus de Milo*, Pompeii mosaics, Etruscan sarcophagi, Roman portrait busts, Nike of Samothrace); Apollo Gallery (jewels); French and Italian paintings in the Grande Galerie (a quarter-mile long and worth the hike); the *Mona Lisa* and her Italian Renaissance roommates; the nearby neoclassical collection (*Coronation of Napoleon*); and the Romantic collection, with works by Delacroix (*Liberty at the Barricades*—see your 100F note) and Géricault (*Raft of the Medusa*).

Cost: 45F, 26F after 15:00 and on Sunday, those under 18 enter free. Tickets good all day. Reentry allowed.

Hours: Wednesday through Monday 9:00 to 18:00, closed Tuesday, all wings open Wednesday until 21:45, Richelieu Wing (only) open until 22:00 on Monday. Galleries start closing 30 minutes early. Closed January 1, Easter, May 1, November 1, and Christmas Day. Crowds are worst on Sunday, Monday, Wednesday, and mornings. Save money and avoid crowds by visiting in the afternoon. (You can enter the pyramid for free until 21:30. Go

Louvre Area

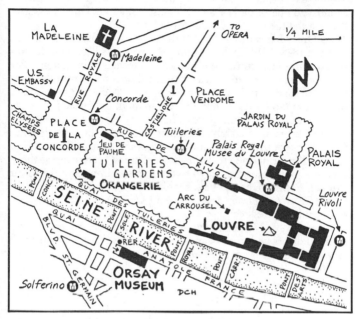

in at night and see it glow.) Tel. 01 40 20 53 17 or 01 40 20 51 51 for recorded information.

The newly-renovated Richelieu wing and the underground shopping mall extension add the finishing touches to Le Grand Louvre Project (that started in 1989 with the pyramid entrance). To explore this most recent extension of the Louvre, enter through the pyramid then walk toward the inverted pyramid and uncover a post office, a handy TI and SNCF office, glittering boutiques and a dizzying assortment of good-value eateries (up the escalator), and the Palais-Royal Métro entrance. Stairs at the far end take you right into the Tuileries Gardens, a perfect antidote to the stuffy, crowded rooms of the Louvre.

▲**L'Orangerie**—This small, quiet, and often-overlooked museum houses Monet's waterlilies, many famous Renoirs, and a scattering of other great Impressionist works. The round rooms of waterlilies are two of the most enjoyable rooms in Paris (30F, Wednesday–Monday 9:45–17:15, closed Tuesday, in Tuileries Gardens near the place de la Concorde, Mo: Concorde, tel. 01 42 97 48 16).

Jeu de Paume—This one-time home to the Impressionist art collection (now located in the Musée d'Orsay) hosts rotating exhibits of top contemporary artists (38F, Tuesday 12:00–21:30,

Wednesday–Friday 12:00–19:00, weekends 10:00–19:00, closed
Monday; on place de la Concorde, just inside the Tuileries Gardens on the rue de Rivoli side; Mo: Concorde).

▲▲▲**Orsay Museum**—Paris' 19th-century art museum (actually,
art from 1848–1914) includes Europe's greatest collection of Impressionist works. The museum is housed in a former train station (Gare
d'Orsay) across the river and 10 minutes downstream from the Louvre. (The RER-C train line zips you right to "Musée d'Orsay"; the
Métro stop "Solferino" is three blocks south of the Orsay.)

Start on the ground floor. The "pretty" conservative establish-
lishment art is on the right. Then cross left into the brutally truth-
ful and, at that time, very shocking art of the realist rebels and
Manet. Then ride the escalators at the far end (detouring at the
top for a grand museum view) to the series of Impressionist rooms
(Monet, Renoir, Dégas, et al). Don't miss the Grand Ballroom
(room 52, *Arts et Decors de la IIIème République*) and Art Nouveau
on the mezzanine level.

Cost: 39F, 27F for the young and old, under 18 free, tickets
good all day. The booth near the entrance gives free floor plans in
English. English-language tours usually run daily except Sunday at
11:30, cost 38F, take 90 minutes, and are also available on audiotape. City museum passes are sold in the basement; if there's a
long line you can skip it by buying one there, but you can't skip
the metal detector line into the museum. Tel. 01 40 49 48 48.

Hours: Tuesday, Wednesday, Friday, Saturday 10:00 to 18:00,
Thursday 10:00 to 21:45, Sunday 9:00 to 18:00, closed Monday.
Museum opens at 9:00 June 20 through September 20. Last entrance
is 45 minutes before closing. Galleries start closing 30 minutes early.
The Orsay is very crowded Tuesdays, when the Louvre is closed.

Sights—Southwest Paris: The Eiffel Tower Neighborhood

▲▲▲**Eiffel Tower**—It's crowded and expensive but worth the
trouble. Go early (arrive by 9:30) or late in the day (after 18:00) to
avoid most crowds; weekends are worst. Pilier Nord (the north pillar) has the biggest elevator and, therefore, the fastest moving line.

It's 1,000 feet tall (six inches taller in hot weather), covers 2.5
acres, and requires 50 tons of paint. The Tower's 7,000 tons of
metal are spread out so well at the base that it's no heavier per
square inch than a linebacker on tiptoes. Visitors to Paris may find
Mona Lisa to be less than expected, but the Eiffel Tower rarely
disappoints, even in an era of skyscrapers.

Built a hundred years after the French Revolution (and in the
midst of an industrial one), the Tower served no function but to
impress. Gustave Eiffel won an architectural contest at the 1889
Centennial world's fair by beating out such rival proposals as a
giant guillotine. To a generation hooked on technology, the

Eiffel Tower to Invalides

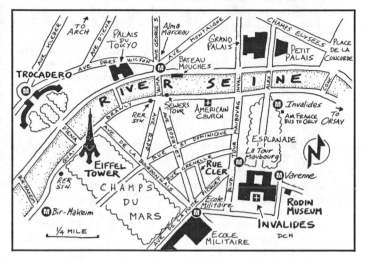

Tower was the marvel of the age, a symbol of progress and of man's ingenuity. To others it was a cloned-sheep monstrosity. The writer Maupassant routinely ate lunch in the tower just so he wouldn't have to look at it.

Delicate and graceful when seen from afar, it's massive—even a bit scary—from close up. You don't appreciate the size until you walk toward it—like a mountain, it seems so close but takes forever to reach. There are three observation platforms, at 200, 400 and 900 feet. The higher you go the more you pay. Each requires a separate elevator (and a line), so plan on at least 90 minutes if you want to go to the top and back. The view from the 400-foot-high second level is plenty. Begin at the first floor, read the informative signs (in English) describing the major monuments, see the entertaining free movie on the history of the tower, and consider a drink overlooking all of Paris at the café or at the reasonable restaurant Altitude 95 (decent 100F meals until 20:00, and Paris' best view bar). Take the elevator to the second floor for even greater views. As you ascend through the metal beams, imagine being a worker, perched high above nothing, riveting this giant erector set together.

On top you can see all of Paris, aided by a panorama guide. On a good day you can see 40 miles. It costs 20F to go to the first level, 40F to the second, and 57F to go all the way for the 1,000-foot view (not included with museum pass). On a budget? You can climb the stairs to the second level for only 12F (summers daily 9:00–24:00, off-season 9:30–23:00, tel. 01 44 11 23 23, Mo: Trocadero, RER: Champs de Mars).

The best places from which to view the tower are Trocadero square (a 10-minute walk north, across the river) and the long, grassy fields of the Champ-du-Mars (to the south). After about 21:00 the gendarmes look the other way as Parisians stretch out or picnic on the grass. However impressive it may be by day, it's an awesome thing to see at twilight, when the tower becomes engorged with light, and virile Paris lies back and lets night be on top.

For another great view, especially at night, enjoy the tower (and the wild in-line skating scene) by approaching via the Trocadero Métro stop. The big J-number panal clicks down the days (j for *jour*) until the new millenium.

▲**Paris Sewer Tour (Egouts)**—This quick and easy visit takes you along a few hundred yards of underground water tunnel lined with interesting displays, well-described in English, explaining the evolution of the world's longest sewer system. (If you lined up Paris' sewers they would reach beyond Istanbul.) Don't miss the slide show, the fine W.C.s just beyond the gift shop, and the occasional tours in English (32F, 11:00–17:00, closed Thursday and Friday, where the Pont de l'Alma hits the Left Bank, tel. 01 47 05 10 29).

▲▲**Les Invalides: Napoleon's Tomb and Army Museum**— The emperor lies majestically dead inside several coffins under a grand dome—a goose-bumping pilgrimage for historians. Napoleon is surrounded by the tombs of other French war heroes and Europe's greatest military museum in the Hôtel des Invalides. Follow signs to the "crypt," where you'll find Roman Empire–style reliefs listing the accomplishments of Napoleon's administration. The restored dome glitters with 26 pounds of gold (37F, daily 10:00–18:00, off-season 17:00, tel. 01 44 42 37 67, Métros: La Tour Maubourg or Varennes).

▲▲**Rodin Museum**—This user-friendly museum is filled with passionate works by the greatest sculptor since Michelangelo. See *The Kiss*, *The Thinker*, *The Gates of Hell*, and many more. Don't miss the room full of work by Rodin's student and mistress, Camille Claudel. (28F, 18F on Sunday; 5F for gardens only, which may be Paris' best deal as many works are well-displayed in the beautiful gardens; 9:30–17:45, closed Monday and at 17:00 off-season, 77 rue de Varennes, tel. 01 44 18 61 10, Mo: Varennes, near Napoleon's Tomb.) There's a good self-serve cafeteria as well as idyllic picnic spots in the family-friendly back garden.

▲▲**Marmottan**—In this private, intimate, less-visited museum you'll find more than 100 paintings by Claude Monet (thanks to his son Michel), including the *Impressions of a Sunrise* painting that gave the movement its start—and name (40F, 10:00–17:30, closed Monday, no museum pass, 2 rue Louis Boilly, Mo: La Muette, follow the museum signs six blocks through a park to the museum,

tel. 01 42 24 07 02). Combine this fine museum with a stroll down
one of Paris' most pleasant shopping streets, the rue de Passy
(from la Muette Mo. stop).

Sights—Southeast Paris: The Latin Quarter

▲**Latin Quarter**—This Left Bank neighborhood just opposite the
Notre-Dame is the Latin Quarter. (For more information and a
walking tour, see "Historic Core of Paris" walk above.) This was a
center of Roman Paris. But its touristic fame relates to the Latin
Quarter's intriguing artsy, bohemian character. This was perhaps
Europe's leading university district in the middle ages—home,
since the 13th century, to the prestigious Sorbonne University.
Back then, Latin was the language of higher education. And, since
students here came from all over Europe, Latin served as their lin-
guistic common denominator. Locals referred to the quarter by its
language: Latin. In modern times this was the center of Paris' café
culture. The neighborhood's main boulevards (St. Michel and St.
Germain) are lined with cafés—once the haunts of great poets and
philosophers, but now the hang-out of tired tourists. While still
youthful and artsy, the area has become a tourist ghetto filled with
cheap North African eateries.

St. Germain des Prés—A church was first built on this site in
A.D. 452. The church you see today was constructed in 1163. The
area around the church hops at night with fire-eaters, mimes, and
scads of artists (Mo: St. Germain-des-Prés).

▲**St. Sulpice Organ Concert**—For pipe-organ enthusiasts, this is a
delight. The Grand-Orgue at St. Sulpice has a rich history, with a
line of 12 world-class organists (including Widor and Dupre) going
back 300 years. Marcel Dupre started the tradition of opening the
loft to visitors after the 10:30 service on Sundays. Daniel Roth continues to welcome guests in three langueages while playing five key-
boards at once. The 10:30 Sunday Mass is followed by a 20-minute
recital at 11:40. If you're lucky, at 12:00 the small unmarked door
will open (left of entry as you face the rear) and allow visitors to
scamper like sixteenth notes up spiral stairs to a world of 6,000 pipes,
where they can watch the master perform the next Mass, friends
warming his bench, and a committee scrambling to pull and push
the 110 stops (Mo: St. Sulpice or Mabillon).

▲**Luxembourg Gardens**—Paris' most beautiful, interesting, and
enjoyable garden/park/recreational area is a great place to watch
Parisians at rest and play. Bring your kids to the playground or
afternoon puppet shows (*guignols*). Challenge the card and chess
players to a game (near the tennis courts) or find a free chair near
the main pond and take a breather. Notice any pigeons? A poor
Ernest Hemingway used to hand-hunt (read: strangle) them here.
The grand neoclassical-domed **Panthéon** is a block away and is
only worth entering if you have a museum pass. The park is open

until dusk (Mo: Odéon). If you enjoy the Luxembourg Gardens and want to see more, visit the more elegant Parc Monceau (Mo: Monceau) and the colorful Jardin des Plantes (Mo: Jussieu).

▲**Montparnasse Tower**—This 59-floor superscraper—it's cheaper and easier to get to the top than it is to that of the Eiffel Tower—offers one of Paris' best views, since the Eiffel Tower is in it and the Montparnasse tower isn't. Buy the photo guide to the city, then go to the rooftop and orient yourself (42F, daily in summer 9:30–23:00, off-season 10:00–22:00, disappointing after dark, entrance on rue l'Arrivé, Mo: Montparnasse). This is efficient when combined with a day trip to Chartres, which begins at the Montparnasse train station.

Sights—Northwest Paris: Champs-Élysées and Arc de Triomphe to La Defense

▲▲**Place de la Concorde and the Champs-Élysées**—This famous boulevard is Paris' backbone and greatest concentration of traffic. All of France seems to converge on the place de la Concorde, the city's largest square. It was here that the guillotine took the lives of thousands—including King Louis XVI. Back then it was called the place de la Revolution.

Catherine de Medici wanted a place to drive her carriage, so she started draining the swamp that would become the Champs-Élysées. Napoleon put on the final touches, and it's been the place to be seen ever since. The Tour de France bicycle race ends here, as do all parades (French or foe) of any significance. While the boulevard has become a bit hamburgerized, a walk here is a must. Take the Métro to the Arc de Triomphe (Mo: Étoile) and saunter down the Champs-Élysées (Métro stops every few blocks: FDR, George V, and Étoile).

▲▲▲**Arc de Triomphe**—Napoleon had the magnificent Arc de Triomphe commissioned to commemorate his victory at the Battle of Austerlitz. There's no triumphal arch bigger (50 meters high, 40 meters wide). And, with 12 converging boulevards, there's no traffic circle more thrilling to experience—either behind the wheel or on foot (take the underpass). An elevator or a spiral staircase leads to a cute museum about the arch and a grand view from the top, even after dark (35F, Tuesday–Saturday 9:00–23:00, Sunday and Monday 9:30–18:00, tel. 01 43 80 31 31, Mo: Étoile).

▲**Grande Arche de La Defense**—The centerpiece of Paris' ambitious skyscraper complex (La Defense) is the Grande Arche. Built to celebrate the 200th anniversary of the 1789 French Revolution, the place is big—38 floors on more than 200 acres. It holds offices for 30,000 people. Notre-Dame Cathedral could fit under its arch. The La Defense complex is an interesting study in 1960s land-use planning. More than 100,000 workers commute here daily, directing lots of business and development away from downtown and allowing central Paris to retain its more elegant feel. This aspect makes sense to most Parisians, regardless of whatever else they feel about the controversial complex. You'll enjoy city views from the Arche elevator (40F includes a film on its construction and art exhibits, daily 9:00–20:00, off-season 9:00–19:00, tel. 01 49 07 27 57, Métro or RER: La Defense, follow signs to Grande Arche).

Sights—North Paris: Montmartre

▲**Sacré-Coeur and Montmartre**—This Byzantine-looking church, while only 130 years old, is impressive. It was built as a "praise the Lord anyway" gesture, after the French were humiliated by the Germans in a brief war in 1871. The church is open daily until 23:00. One block from the church, the place du Tertre was the haunt of Toulouse-Lautrec and the original Bohemians. Today it's mobbed by tourists and unoriginal Bohemians, but still fun. Wander down the rue Lepic to the two remaining windmills (once there were 30). Rue des Saules leads to Paris' only vineyard. Métros: Anvers (one Métro ticket buys your way up the funicular and avoids the stairs) or the closer but less scenic Abbesses. A taxi to the top of the hill saves time and sweat.

Pigalle—Paris' red light district, the infamous "Pig Alley," is at the foot of Butte Montmartre. Ooh la la. More shocking than dangerous. Walk from place Pigalle to place Blanche, teasing desperate barkers and fast-talking temptresses. In bars a 1,000F bottle of cheap champagne comes with a friend. Stick to the bigger streets, hang on to your wallet, and exercise good judgment. Cancan can cost a fortune, as can con artists in topless bars. After dark, countless tour buses line the streets, reminding us that tour guides make big bucks by bringing their groups to touristic nightclubs like the famous Moulin Rouge (Mo: Pigalle and Abbesses).

Sights—Northeast Paris: Marais Neighborhood and More

To better appreciate this area and connect its sights, take our "Marais Walk," described later in this chapter.

▲**Picasso Museum (Hôtel Salé)**—This is the world's largest collection of Pablo Picasso's paintings, sculpture, sketches, and ceramics, and includes his personal collection of Impressionist art. It's well-explained in English and worth ▲▲▲ if you're a fan (30F, Wednesday–Monday 9:30–18:00, closed Tuesday, 5 rue Thorigny, tel. 01 42 71 25 21, Mo: St. Paul or Chemin Vert).

▲**Carnavalet Museum**—The tumultuous history of Paris is well-displayed in this converted Marais mansion. Explanations are in French only, but most displays are somewhat self-explanatory. You'll see paintings of Parisian scenes, French Revolution paraphernalia, old Parisian store signs, a guillotine, a model of 16th-century Île de la Cité (notice the bridge houses), and rooms full of 15th-century

Parisian furniture. The medieval and revolution rooms are the most interesting (35F, included with museum pass, Tuesday–Sunday 10:00–17:00, closed Monday, 23 rue de Sévigné, tel. 01 42 72 21 13, Mo: St. Paul).

Promenade Plantée Park—This three-mile garden walk was once a train track and is now a joy. It runs from the place de la Bastille (Mo: Bastille) along Avenue Daumesnil to Saint-Mandé (Mo: Michel Bizot). Part of the park is elevated and part consists of just walking along the street till you pick up the next segment. From the place de la Bastille, take Avenue Daumesnil (past the opera building) to the intersection with avenue Ledru Rollin, then walk up the stairs and through the gate (hours vary with season, open roughly 8:00–20:00).

▲Père Lachaise Cemetery—Littered with the tombstones of many of the city's most illustrious dead, this is your best one-stop look at the fascinating and romantic world of the "permanent Parisians." The place is confusing, but maps will direct you to the graves of Chopin, Molière, and even the American rock star Jim Morrison (who died in Paris). In section 92, a series of statues memorializing the war makes the French war experience a bit more real (helpful 10F maps at the flower store near entry, across the street from Métro stop, closes at dusk, Mo: Père Lachaise or bus #69).

▲Pompidou Center—(Closed for renovation until 2000.) Europe's greatest collection of far-out modern art, the Musée National d'Art Moderne is housed in this colorfully exoskeletal building. After so many Madonnas and Children, a piano smashed to bits and glued to the wall is refreshing. It's a social center with lots of people, street theater, and activity inside and out—a perpetual street fair. Ride the escalator for a free city view from the café terrace on top and don't miss the free exhibits on the ground floor (35F, 24F for the young and old, Monday and Wednesday–Friday 12:00–22:00, weekends and most holidays 10:00–22:00, closed Tuesday, tel. 01 44 78 12 33, Mo: Rambuteau). Kids of any age enjoy the fun, colorful fountain (called *Homage to Stravinsky*) next to the Pompidou Center.

Sights— Marais Walks

This walk takes you through one of Paris' most characteristic quarters. When in Paris, the natural inclination is to concentrate only on the big sights. But to experience Paris you need to experience a vital neighborhood. This is a good one, containing more pre-Revolutionary buildings than anywhere else in town.

Ride the Métro to Bastille and follow the dotted path outlined on the Marais map in this chapter. This walk is about three miles long. Allow two hours, and add another hour if you visit the Carnavalet Museum.

At **place de la Bastille** there are more revolutionary images in the Métro station murals than on the square. Exit the Métro following signs to rue Saint Antoine (not the signs to rue Saint Antoine du Faubourg). Ascend onto a noisy square dominated by the bronze *Colonne de Juillet* (July Column). Victims of the revolutions of 1830 and 1848 are buried in a vault 55 meters below this gilded statue of liberty. The actual Bastille, a royal fortress-then-prison that once symbolized old regime tyranny and now symbolizes the Parisian emancipation, is long gone. While only a brick outline of the fortress' round turrets survives (under the traffic where rue Saint Antoine hits the square), the story of the Bastille is indelibly etched on the city's psyche.

For centuries the Bastille was used to defend the city (mostly from its own people). On July 14, 1789, the people of Paris stormed the prison, releasing its seven prisoners and hoping to find arms. They demolished the brick fortress and decorated their pikes with the heads of a few bigwigs. By shedding blood, the leaders of the gang made sure it would be tough to turn back the tides of revolution. Ever since, the French have celebrated July 14th as their independence day—Bastille Day.

The flashy, glassy-grey, and controversial **Opéra-Bastille** dominates (some say overwhelms) the square. Designed by the Canadian architect Carlos Ott, this latest Parisian grand project was opened with great fanfare by François Mitterrand on the 200th Bastille Day, July 14, 1989.

Turn your back to the statue and, passing the Banque de France on your right (good rates, long lines, opposite a fine map of the area on your left), head straight down the busy rue Saint Antoine about four blocks into the Marais.

The **Marais** neighborhood, still filled with pre-Revolutionary lanes and buildings, is more characteristic than touristy (unlike the Latin Quarter). It's medieval Paris. This is how much of the city looked until, in the mid-1800s, Napoleon III had Baron Haussmann blast out the narrow streets to construct broad boulevards (wide enough for the guns and marching ranks of the army, too wide for revolutionary barricades).

Leave rue Saint Antoine at #62 and turn right through two elegant courtyards of **Hôtel de Sully** (62 rue Saint Antoine, open until 19:00, good Marais map on corridor wall). Originally a swamp (*marais*), during the reign of Henry IV it became the hometown of the French aristocracy. In the 17th century, big shots built their private mansions (*hôtels*) like this one—close to Henry's place des Vosges. *Hôtels* that survived the revolution now house museums, libraries, and national institutions. The aristocrats may be gone, but the Marais—which until recently was a dumpy Bohemian quarter—is today a thriving, trendy but real community, and a joy to explore.

To get to the **place des Vosges** park, continue through the

Marais Walk

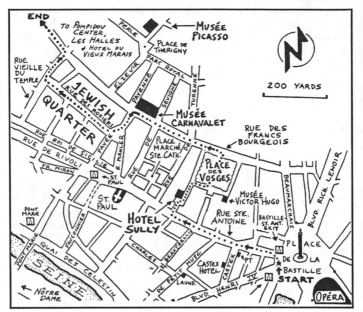

Hôtel de Sully. The small door on the far right corner of the second courtyard pops you out into one of Paris' finest squares (closes at dusk). Walk to the center, where Louis XIII sits on a horse surrounded by locals enjoying their community park. Children frolic in the sandbox, lovers warm benches, and pigeons guard their fountains, while trees shade this retreat from the glare of the big city. Henry IV built this centerpiece of the Marais in 1605. As hoped, this turned the Marais into Paris' most exclusive neighborhood. **Victor Hugo** lived at #6; you can visit his house (18F, corner closest to the Bastille).

To leave the square, walk behind Louis' horse to the arcade. Follow it left past art galleries and antique shops onto the boutique-filled rue des Francs Bourgeois (the store at #17 sells used silver, often from famous restaurants, by weight). Browse two blocks off the place des Vosges to the corner of rue de Sévigné, where you'll see the Musée Carnavalet (on right).

The **Carnavalet Museum**, focusing on the history of Paris, is housed inside a Marais mansion with classy courtyards and statues (35F, Tuesday–Sunday 10:00–17:00, closed Monday, 23 rue de Sévigné; for more information see Sights—Northeast Paris, above).

To continue the Marais walk, go another block along rue des

Francs Bourgeois (peeking through the gate on the right) and turn left at the post office. (The **Picasso Museum**, described more fully in Sights—Northeast Paris, above, is up one block to the right: 30F, Wednesday–Monday 9:30–18:00, closed Tuesday, 5 rue Thorigny.) From rue Pavée, bend right onto rue Rosiers, which runs straight for three blocks through Paris' Jewish Quarter. It's lively every day except Saturday.

The **Jewish Quarter** is lined with colorful shops and kosher eateries. Jo Goldenberg's delicatessen/restaurant (first corner on left, at #7—scene of a terrorist bombing in darker times) is worth poking into. You'll be tempted by kosher pizza and plenty of 20F falafel-to-go (*emporter* = to go) joints. Rue Rosiers dead-ends into rue du Vieille du Temple. Turn right.

Frank Bourgeois is waiting at the corner postcard/print shop. Turn left on rue des Francs Bourgeois. This road leads past the national archives (peek inside the courtyard) and turns into rue Rambuteau.

The pipes and glass of the **Pompidou Center** reintroduce you to our century. Pass that huge building on your left to join the fray in front of the center (also called the Centre Beaubourg). Survey this popular spot from the top of the sloping square. A tubular series of escalators leads up the building (closed for renovation until 2000).

The Pompidou Center follows with gusto the 20th-century architectural axiom "form follows function." To get a more spacious and functional interior, the guts of this exoskeletal building are draped on the outside and color coded: vibrant red for people lifts, cool blue for air-conditioning, eco-green for plumbing, don't-touch-it yellow for electrical stuff, and white for bones. Enjoy the adjacent *Homage to Stravinsky* fountain. Jean Tingley designed this new-wave fountain as a tribute to the composer. . . . Every fountain represents one of his hard-to-hum scores.

With your back to the Pompidou Center's escalators, walk the cobbled pedestrian mall and cross the busy boulevard Sebastopol to the ivy-covered pavilions of Les Halles. After 800 years as Paris' down-and-dirty central produce market, this was replaced by a glitzy but soulless modern shopping center in the late 1970s. The most endearing layer of the mall is its grassy rooftop park. The fine Gothic Saint Eustache church overlooking this contemporary scene has a famous 8,000-pipe organ. The Louvre and Notre-Dame are just a short walk away. The mall is served by Paris' busiest Métro hub (the Chatelet-Les Halles station)

Best Shopping

Forum des Halles is a huge subterranean shopping center. It's fun, mod, and colorful, but lacks a soul (Mo: Halles). The Galleries Lafayette behind the opera house is your best elegant, Old World, one-stop Parisian department store/shopping center. Also, visit the

Printemps store and the historic (as well as handy) Samaritaine
department store in several buildings near Pont Neuf. Ritzy shops
surround the Ritz Hotel at place Vendôme (Mo: Tuileries).

Disappointments de Paris

While Paris can drive you in-Seine with superlatives, here are a
few negatives to help you manage your limited time:

La Madeleine is a big, stark, neoclassical church with a postcard facade and a postbox interior. The famous aristocratic deli
behind the church, Fauchon, is elegant, but so are many others
handier to your hotel.

The old **Opéra Garnier** has a great Chagall-painted ceiling
but is in a pedestrian-mean area. Don't go to American Express
(behind the Opéra) just to change money. You'll get a better rate
at many other banks.

Paris' **Panthéon** (nothing like Rome's) is another stark neoclassical edifice filled with mortal remains of great Frenchmen
who mean little to the average American tourist.

The **Bastille** is Paris' most famous nonsight. The square is
there, but confused tourists look everywhere and can't find the
famous prison of Revolution fame. The building's gone and the
square is good only as a jumping-off point for the "Marais Walk"
(see below) or the Promenade Plantée Park (see Sights—Northeast Paris, above).

The **Latin Quarter** is a frail shadow of its characteristic self.
It's more Tunisian, Greek, and Woolworth's than old-time Paris.
The café life that turned on Hemingway and endeared Boul Miche
and Boulevard St. Germain to so many poets is also trampled by
modern commercialism.

Day Trips: Châteaus near Paris

The region around Paris (the Île de France) is dotted with sumptuous palaces. Paris' booming upper class made this the heartland
of European château building in the 16th and 17th centuries. Most
of these châteaus were lavish hunting lodges—getaways from the
big city. The only thing they defended were noble and royal egos.
Consider these two very different châteaus, both ▲▲▲ sights:
Versailles (for grandeur) and Vaux-le-Vicomte (for intimacy).

Palace of Versailles

Every king's dream, Versailles was the residence of the French
king and the cultural heartbeat of Europe for about 100 years—
until the Revolution of 1789 ended the notion that God deputized
some people to rule for Him on Earth. Louis XIV spent half a
year's income of Europe's richest country turning his dad's hunting lodge into a palace fit for a divine monarch. Louis XV and
Louis XVI spent much of the 18th century gilding Louis XIV's

Versailles

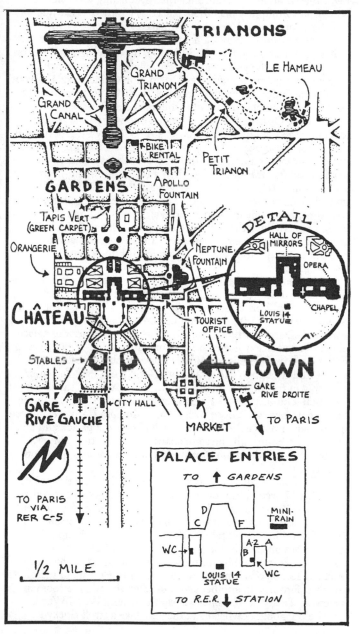

lily. In 1837, about 50 years after the royal family was evicted, King Louis Philippe opened the palace as a museum. Europe's next-best palaces are Versailles wannabes.

Information: There's a helpful TI across the street from Versailles' R.G. station (tel. 01 39 50 36 22), two information desks on the approach to the palace, and a very helpful TI at entrance C. The useful brochure, "Versailles Orientation Guide," explains your sightseeing options. Versailles info: tel. 01 30 84 76 18 or 01 30 84 74 00. W.C. and phones are near the main entrance.

Ticket Options: The self-guided one-way palace romp, including the Hall of Mirrors, costs 45F (35F after 15:30, on Sunday, or for those over 60 or ages 18–25; under 18 free). To supplement this with a guided tour through the other sections, you'll need to pay the 45F base price, then add 25F for a one-hour guided tour, 37F for a 90-minute guided tour, or 30F for a self-guided Walkman-cassette tour. (Tip: If you're waiting for your tour time, have finished a tour, or have a Paris Museum Card, you can go directly into the main palace with no line at the A2 gate and explore the palace on your own.) In the gardens, you can see the Grand and Petit Trianon palaces for 30F total (payable at the site).

Hours: Tuesday through Sunday 9:00 to 18:30, closed Monday; 9:00 to 17:30 October through April; last entry 30 minutes before closing. Versailles is especially crowded Tuesday through Sunday 10:00 to 15:00. To minimize crowds and get a reduced entry ticket, arrive after 15:30. Tour the gardens after the palace closes. The palace is great late. On my last visit, at 18:00, I was the only tourist in the Hall of Mirrors . . . even on a Tuesday.

Time to Allow: Six hours round-trip from Paris (an hour each way in transit, two hours for the palace, two for the grounds).

Self-Guided Tour: For the basic self-guided tour, join the line at entrance A1. Those with a Paris Museum Card are allowed in through entrance A2 without a wait. Enter the palace and take a one-way walk through the state apartments from the "King's Wing," through the magnificent Hall of Mirrors, and out via the "Queen's Wing."

The Hall of Mirrors was the ultimate hall of the day—250 feet long, 17 arched mirrors matching 17 windows with royal garden views, 24 gilded candelabra, eight busts of Roman emperors, and eight classical-style statues (seven of them actually ancient originals). The ceiling is decorated with stories of Louis' triumphs. Imagine this place filled with silk gowns and powdered wigs, lit by thousands of candles. The mirrors—a luxurious rarity at the time—were a reflection of a time when aristocrats felt good about their looks and their fortunes. In another age altogether, this was the room in which the Treaty of Versailles was signed, ending World War I.

Before going downstairs at the end, take a stroll clockwise

around the long room filled with the great battles of France murals.
If you don't have *Rick Steves' Mona Winks*, the guidebook called *The
Châteaux, The Gardens, and Trianon* gives a room-by-room rundown.

Guided Tours: For a guided tour, pay the 45F base-price
admission at the same time you pay for your tour (at entrance D).
The 60- or 90-minute tours, led by an English-speaking art historian, take you through sections of Versailles not included in the
base-price visit. Groups are limited to 30. Of the several tours
offered, the 90-minute version covering Louis XV and Louis
XVI's apartments and the opera is best. Pay and get your tour
appointment at entrance D. Tour times are normally all allotted
for the day by 13:00. Tours leave from entrance F.

Walkman Tour: If you're in a hurry, the self-guided
Walkman-cassette tour of the king's chamber (25F, entrance C, last
entry at 15:00) covers Louis XIV's rooms and is a good option.

Palace Gardens: The gardens offer a world of royal amusements. Outside the palace is the L'Orangerie. Louis, the only one
who could grow oranges in Paris, had an orange grove on wheels
that could be wheeled in and out of his greenhouses according to
the weather. A promenade leads from the palace to the Grand
Canal, an artificial lake that, in Louis' day, was a mini-sea with
nine ships, including a 32-cannon warship. France's royalty used
to float up and down the canal in Venetian gondolas.

While Louis cleverly used palace life at Versailles to "domes-
ticate" his nobility, turning otherwise meddlesome nobles into
groveling socialites, all this pomp and ceremony hampered the
royal family as well. For an escape from the public life at Versailles, they built more intimate palaces as retreats in their garden.
Before the revolution there was plenty of space to retreat—the
grounds were enclosed by a 25-mile-long fence.

The beautifully restored **Grand Trianon Palace** is as sumptuous as the main palace but much smaller. With its pastel pink
colonnade and more human scale, this is a place you'd like to call
home. (See hours and prices below).

The nearby **Petit Trianon**, which has a fine neoclassical
exterior with a skippable interior, was Marie Antoinette's favorite
residence.

You can almost see princesses bobbing gaily in the branches
as you walk through the enchanting forest, past the white marble
temple of love (1778) to the queen's fake-peasant **hamlet** (interior
not tourable). Palace life really got to Marie Antoinette. Sort of a
back-to-basics queen, she retreated further and further from her
blue-blooded reality. Her happiest days were at the hamlet, under
a bonnet, tending her perfumed sheep and her manicured gardens
in a thatch-happy wonderland.

Getting Around the Gardens: It's a 30-minute hike from the
palace, down the canal, past the two mini-palaces to the hamlet. You

can rent bikes (30F/hr). The pokey tourist train, which costs only 10F, runs between the canal and château (30F, 5/hrly, four stops, you can hop on and off as you like; nearly worthless commentary).

Garden Hours and Admissions: Except for fountain-filled Sundays (below), the gardens are free and open from 7:00 to sunset (as late as 21:30). Grand and Petit Trianon are open May through September Tuesday through Sunday from 10:00 to 18:00, and are closed Monday (off-season 10:00–17:00, Grand Trianon-25F, Petit Trianon-15F, 30F for both). The park is picnic-perfect. Food is not allowed into the palace, but those with a picnic can check bags (and picnics) at doors A or C. There's a kiosk selling good sandwiches, and there's a decent restaurant on the canal in the gardens.

Fountain Spectacles: Every Sunday, May through October, music fills the king's backyard and the garden's fountains are in full squirt (from 11:15–11:35, and from 15:30–17:00, 25F garden admission on these days only). Louis had his engineers literally reroute a river to fuel these fountains. They are impressive.

Getting to Versailles: From Paris, take the RER-C train (26F round-trip, 30 min) to "Versailles R.G.," not "Versailles C.H.," which is farther from the palace. Trains, usually named "Vick," leave about five times an hour for the palace. Get off at Versailles Rive Gauche (the end of the line). RER-C trains leave from these RER/Metro stops: "Invalides" (Napoleon's Tomb, Military Museum, Rodin Museum), "Champ de Mars" (Eiffel Tower), "Musée d'Orsay," "St. Michel" (Notre-Dame, Latin Quarter), and "Gare d'Austerlitz." Leaving the station, turn right, then turn left on the major boulevard (10-minute walk). Your Eurailpass is not good on the RER trains (instead get a ticket for the turnstiles; keep this ticket to get out upon arrival). When returning look through the windows past the turnstiles for the departure board. Any train leaving Versailles goes as far as downtown Paris (they're marked "all stations until Austerlitz"). If you're uncertain, confirm with a local by asking, "À Paris?" (To Paris?).

The 100F Paris–Versailles taxi fare is economic for groups of three or four, or for people with more money than time. To cut your park walking by 50 percent, consider having the taxi drop you at the Hamlet (Hameau).

Town of Versailles (zip code: 78000): After the palace closes and the tourists go, the prosperous, wholesome town of Versailles feels a long way from Paris. The central market thrives on Tuesday, Friday, and Saturday until 13:00 (place du Marché; leaving the RER station, turn right and walk 10 minutes). Consider the wisdom of picking up or dropping your rental car in Versailles rather than in Paris. In Versailles, the Hertz and Avis offices are at the Gare des Chantiers (Versailles C.H., served by Paris' Montparnasse station). Versailles makes a fine homebase; see Versailles accommodations under Sleeping, below.

Vaux-le-Vicomte

While Versailles is most travelers' first choice for its sheer historic weight, Vaux-le-Vicomte offers a more lavish interior and a far better sense of 17th-century château life. Sitting in a huge forest with magnificent gardens and no urban sprawl in sight, Vaux-le-Vicomte gave me just a twinge of palace envy.

Vaux-le-Vicomte was the architectural inspiration of Versailles and set the standard for European châteaus to come. The proud owner, Nicolas Fouquet (Louis XIV's finance minister) threw a château-warming party. Louis was so jealous that he arrested his host, took his architect (Le Vau), artist (Le Brun), and landscaper (Le Notre), and proceeded with the construction of the bigger and costlier (but not necessarily more splendid) palace of Versailles. Monsieur Fouquet is thought to be Alexandre Dumas' man in *The Man in the Iron Mask*, which was recently filmed here.

Vaux-le-Vicomte is a headache to get to (see below) but a joy to tour. While the gift shop's 25F souvenir booklet has helpful information, the château's rooms have English explanations. Start with the fine horse carriages exhibit (*equipages*) in the old stables. Wax figures and an evocative soundtrack get you in the proper mood. Next, stroll like a wide-eyed peasant across the drawbridge and up the front steps into the château. You'll notice candles. Over 1,300 flicker for candlelit night visits.

As you wander through Fouquet's dream-home, you'll understand Louis' jealousy. Versailles was a rather simple hunting lodge when this was built. Since Louis confiscated everything, the furniture is not original. It's from other palaces in the area. You'll see cozy bedrooms upstairs, and grand living rooms downstairs, including a billiards room, library, card room, and dining room. The kitchen and wine cellar are in the basement.

Survey the garden from the back steps of the palace. This was the landscaper Le Notre's first claim to fame. This garden set the standards for sculpted French gardens. He integrated ponds, shrubbery, flowers, and trees in a style that would be copied in palaces all over Europe. Take the 30-minute walk (one way) to the Hercules viewpoint, atop the grassy hill way in the distance. Rent golf carts (Club Cars, 80F for 45 minutes) to make the trip easier. Picnics are not allowed.

Hours and Admission: The château is open daily March through October 10:00 to 13:00 and 14:00 to 18:00 (gardens don't close midday), less in winter (tel. 01 64 14 41 90). Steep 56F admission; 30F for gardens only.

The candlelit visits (*visites aux chandelles*) are worth the 75F entry. (20:30–24:00 May–October on Saturdays and holidays except July 14—call to ask about any upcoming holidays; there are many in May. The last train to Paris leaves Melun at about 22:00.)

The fountains run April through October on the second and last Saturday of each month from 15:00 to 18:00. A good indoor/outdoor café-restaurant, offering reasonable prices and good salads, is inside the first courtyard.

Getting to Vaux-le-Vicomte: To reach Vaux-le-Vicomte by car or by a train and taxi combination, head for the city of Melun. RER trains run to Melun from Paris' Gare du Nord and Chatelet stations. Faster Banlieue trains leave from Paris' Gare de Lyon (43F one-way, 35 min). Taxis make the 10-minute drive from Melun's station to Vaux-le-Vicomte (85F weekdays, 100F evenings and Sundays, taxi phone number posted above taxi stand). Ask a staff person at the château to call a cab for your return, or schedule a pick-up time with your driver. In either direction, split the cab fare with other travelers. Melun's TI is a block from the train station, past the ugly concrete building (Tuesday–Saturday 10:00–12:00 and 14:00 to 18:00, closed Sunday and Monday, 2 avenue Gallieni, tel. 01 64 37 11 31).

Sleeping near Vaux-le-Vicomte: The modern but handy IBIS Hotel is between Melun and the chateau (Db-300F, less on weekends, tel. 01 60 68 42 45, fax 01 64 09 62 00).

More Day Trips from Paris

▲▲▲**Chartres**—In 1194 a terrible fire destroyed the church at Chartres with the much-venerated veil of Mary. With almost unbelievably good fortune, the monks found the veil miraculously preserved in the ashes. Money poured in for the building of a bigger and better cathedral—decorated with 2,000 carved figures and some of France's best stained glass. The cathedral feels too large for the city because it was designed to accommodate huge crowds of pilgrims. One of those pilgrims, an impressed Napoleon, declared after a visit in 1811: "Chartres is no place for an atheist." Rodin called it "the Acropolis of France." British Francophile Malcolm Miller or his impressive assistant give great "Appreciation of Gothic" tours Monday through Saturday, usually at noon and 14:45 (verify times in advance, no tours off-season, call TI at 02 37 21 50 00). Each 40F tour is different; many people stay for both tours. Just show up at the church (daily 7:00–19:00).

Explore Chartres' pleasant city center and discover the picnic-friendly park behind the cathedral. The helpful TI, next to the cathedral, has a map with a self-guided tour of Chartres (daily 9:30–18:45). Chartres is a one-hour train trip from the Gare Montparnasse (71F one-way, 10/day, last train on Saturday departs at about 19:00). Upon arrival, confirm your return schedule to avoid an unplanned night in Chartres.

▲**Giverny**—Monet spent 43 of his most creative years (1883–1926) here at the Camp David of Impressionism. Monet's gardens and home are split by a busy road. Buy your ticket, walk through the gardens, and take the underpass into the artist's famous lilypad land. The path leads you over the Japanese Bridge, under weeping willows, and past countless scenes that leave artists aching for an easel. For Monet fans, it's strangely nostalgic. Back on the other side, continue your visit with a wander through his more robust and structured garden and his mildly interesting home. The jammed gift shop at the exit is the actual skylit studio where Monet painted his waterlily masterpieces.

While lines may be long and tour groups may trample the flowers, true fans still find magic in those lilypads. Avoid crowds by arriving after 16:00 (35F, 25F for gardens only, April–October Tuesday–Sunday 10:00–18:00, closed Monday and off-season, tel. 02 32 51 28 21). Take the Rouen-bound train from Paris' Gare St. Lazare station to Vernon (about 140F round-trip, long gaps in service, know schedule before you go). To get from the Vernon train station to Monet's garden (four kilometers away), take the Vernon–Giverny bus (5/day, scheduled to meet most trains), hitch, taxi (60F), or rent a bike at the station (55F, busy road). Get return bus times from the ticket office in Giverny or ask them to call a taxi. Big tour companies do a Giverny day trip from Paris for around $60.

The new **American Impressionist Art Museum** (100 yards from Monet's place) is devoted to American artists who followed Claude to Giverny. Giverny had a great influence on American artists of Monet's day. This bright, modern gallery is well-explained in English, has a good little Mary Cassatt section, and gives Americans a rare chance to see French people appreciating our artists (same price and hours as Monet's home, pleasant café).

▲▲**Disneyland Paris**—Europe's Disneyland is basically a modern remake of California's, with most of the same rides and smiles. The main difference is that Mickey Mouse speaks French (and you can buy wine with your lunch). My kids went ducky. Locals love it. It's worth a day if Paris is handier than Florida or California. If possible, avoid Saturday, Sunday, Wednesday, school holidays, and July and August. The park can get very crowded. When 60,000 have entered, they close the gates (tel. 01 64 74 30 00 for the latest). After dinner, crowds are gone, and you'll walk right onto rides that had a 45-minute wait three hours earlier. Food is fun but expensive. Smuggle in a picnic.

Disney brochures are in every Paris hotel. The RER (40F each way, direct from downtown Paris to Marne-la-Vallee in 30 minutes) drops you right into the park. The last train back into Paris leaves shortly after midnight. (200F for adults, 155F for kids ages 3–11, 25F less in spring and fall. Daily 9:00–23:00 late June–early September and Saturday and Sunday off-season, shoulder-season weekdays 9:00–19:00, off-season 10:00–18:00, tel. 01 60 30 60 30, fax 01 60 30 60 65 for park and hotel reservations.)

To sleep reasonably at the huge Disney complex, try **Hotel Sante Fe** (780F family rooms for two to four people includes breakfast, less off-season; ask for their hotel-and-park package deal). If all this ain't enough, a new Planet Hollywood restaurant opened just outside the park a five-minute walk from the RER stop.

Sleeping in Paris
(5.5F = about $1)

Sleep Code: **S** = Single, **D** = Double/Twin, **T** = Triple, **Q** = Quad, **b** = bathroom, **t** = toilet only, **s** = shower only, **CC** = Credit Card (Visa, MasterCard, Amex), * = French hotel rating system (0–4 stars).

French hotels are rated by stars (indicated in this chapter by an *). One star is simple, two has most of the comforts, and three is, for this book, plush. Old, characteristic, budget Parisian hotels have always been cramped. Retrofitted with elevators, toilets, and private showers (as most are today), they are even more cramped. Even three-star hotel rooms are small, and generally not worth the extra expense in Paris. Some hotels include the hotel tax (*taxe de sejour*, about 5F per person per day), though most will add this to your bill. Almost every hotel accepts Visa and MasterCard. Fewer take American Express. Two-star hotels are required to have an English-speaking staff. Nearly all hotels listed will have someone who speaks English.

Quad rooms usually have two double beds. Recommended hotels have an elevator unless otherwise noted. Because rooms with double beds and showers are cheaper than rooms with twin beds and baths, room prices vary within each hotel. To keep things manageable, I've focused on three safe, handy, and colorful neighborhoods (listing good hotels, restaurants, and helpful hints for each).

You can save about 100F by finding the increasingly rare room without a private shower, though some hotels charge for down-the-hall showers. Breakfasts cost 20F to 50F extra. Café or picnic breakfasts are cheaper. Singles (except for the rare closet-type rooms that fit only one twin bed) are simply doubles used by one person. They rent for only a little less than a double.

Conventions clog Paris in September (worst), October, May, and June. Reserve in advance during these months. July and August are no problem. Most hotels accept telephone reservations, require prepayment with a credit-card number, and prefer a faxed follow-up to be sure everything is in order. Get advice for safe parking from your hotel. Meters are free in August. Garages are plentiful (90–140F per day, with special rates through some hotels). Self-serve Laundromats are common; ask your hotelier for the nearest one (*Où est un laverie automatique?*; ooh ay uh lah-vay-ree auto-mah-teek).

Sleeping in the Rue Cler Neighborhood
(7th arrondissement, Mo: École Militaire, zip code: 75007)

Rue Cler, a village-like pedestrian street, is safe, tidy, and makes me feel like I must have been a poodle in a previous life. How such coziness lodged itself between the high-powered government/business district and the expensive Eiffel Tower and Invalides areas, I'll never know. Living here ranks with the top museums as one of the city's great experiences. (But if you're into nightlife, consider one of the other two neighborhoods I list.)

Rue Cler is the glue that holds this pleasant neighborhood together. From rue Cler you can walk to the Eiffel Tower, Les Invalides, the Seine, and the Orsay and Rodin Museums. The first six hotels listed below are within camembert-smelling distance of rue Cler, the others are within a five-minute stroll. Warning: The first two hotels are popular with my readers.

Hôtel Leveque** has been entirely renovated. But, with a helpful staff and a singing maid, it's still cozy. It's a fine value with the best location on the block, comfortable rooms, cable TV, hair dryers, safes, an ice machine, and tasteful decor throughout (Sb-270F, Db-380–450F, Tb-550F, breakfast-35F but free for readers of this book, CC:VMA, 29 rue Cler, tel. 01 47 05 49 15, fax 01 45 50 49 36, Web site: http://interresa.ca/hotel/leveque/fr, e-mail: hotellev@clubinternet.fr). Laurence at the front desk speaks English.

Hôtel du Champs de Mars**, with charming, pastel rooms, is an even cosier rue Cler option. The hotel has a Provence-style small-town feel from top to bottom. Rooms are comfortable and a very good value. Single rooms can work as tiny doubles (Db-390–420F, Tb-505F, CC:VMA, cable TV, hair dryers, etc., 30 yards off rue Cler at 7 rue du Champs de Mars, tel. 01 45 51 52 30, fax 01 45 51 64 36, Web site: www: adx.fr/hotel-du-champ-de-mars, e-mail: stg@club-internet.fr, owners Françoise and Stephane SE).

Hôtel la Serre*, across the street from the Hotel Leveque, is a shabby hotel with some renovated rooms, well-worn hallways, no elevator, and a charming location. Request to see your room before you pay; refunds are rarely given (D-270F, Db-390–400F, Tb-520F, cable TV, CC:VM, 24 rue Cler, tel. 01 47 05 52 33, fax 01 40 62 95 66, e-mail: laserre@easynet.fr).

Hôtel Relais Bosquet*** is bright, spacious, and a bit upscale with sharp, comfortable rooms (Db-550–900F, most at 750F, CC:VMA, 19 rue du Champs de Mars, tel. 01 47 05 25 45, fax 01 45 55 08 24, e-mail: Webmaster@relais-bosquet.com). The similar **Hotel Beaugency***** offers similar comfort for less (Db-720F, includes a buffet breakfast, 21 rue Duvivier, tel. 01 47 05 01 63, fax 01 45 51 04 96).

Hôtel Le Valadon**, on a quiet street with a plain lobby and

Rue Cler Hotels

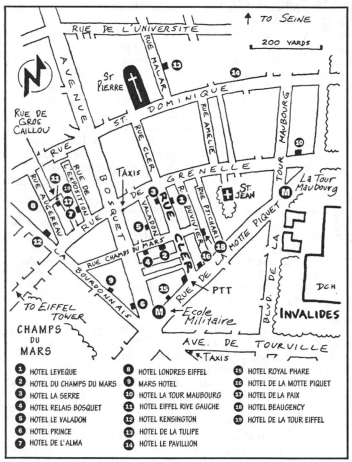

Map legend:

1. HOTEL LEVEQUE
2. HOTEL DU CHAMPS DU MARS
3. HOTEL LA SERRE
4. HOTEL RELAIS BOSQUET
5. HOTEL LE VALADON
6. HOTEL PRINCE
7. HOTEL DE L'ALMA
8. HOTEL LONDRES EIFFEL
9. MARS HOTEL
10. HOTEL LA TOUR MAUBOURG
11. HOTEL EIFFEL RIVE GAUCHE
12. HOTEL KENSINGTON
13. HOTEL DE LA TULIPE
14. HOTEL LE PAVILLION
15. HOTEL ROYAL PHARE
16. HOTEL DE LA MOTTE PIQUET
17. HOTEL DE LA PAIX
18. HOTEL BEAUGENCY
19. HOTEL DE LA TOUR EIFFEL

spacious, comfy rooms, has a shy, modern Parisian cuteness and a friendly staff (Db-410–530F, Tb-560F, CC:VM, 16 rue Valadon, tel. 01 47 53 89 85, fax 01 44 18 90 56).

These listings are a five-minute walk west of rue Cler and are listed in order of proximity.

Hotel Prince**, just across avenue Bosquet from École Militaire Métro, has a "we-try-harder" spirit and good-value rooms, many of which overlook a busy street (Db-430–510F, CC:VM, 66 avenue Bosquet, tel. 01 47 05 40 90, fax 01 47 53 06 62 friendly owner Christof SE).

Hôtel de l'Alma*** is a tight and tidy place with 32 delightful look-alike rooms, all of which come with a TV and minibar (Sb-400F, Db-450F, breakfast included, no triples but a kid's bed can be moved in for free, popular with Mexican and Russian groups, CC:VMA, 32 rue de l'Exposition, tel. 01 47 05 45 70, fax 01 45 51 84 47).

Hôtel Eiffel Rive Gauche** is quiet, unassuming, and is being renovated into a fair value (Ds-260F, Db-420–460F, CC:VM, 6 rue du Gros-Caillou, tel. 01 45 51 24 56, fax 01 45 51 11 77).

Hotel Londres Eiffel*** was just renovated with cheerful attention to detail. Its small, cozy rooms are comfortable (and some have Eiffel views), and its friendly owners seem eager to please (Sb-495F, Db-595F, Tb-725F, extra bed-70F, CC:VMA, 1 rue Augerau, tel. 01 45 51 63 02, fax 01 47 05 28 96).

Mars Hôtel** has a richly decorated lobby, spacious—if well-worn—rooms, and a beam-me-up-Maurice coffin-sized elevator. The front rooms look out on the Eiffel Tower (large Sb-320F, Db-380F, Twin/b-480F, CC:VM, 117 avenue de la Bourdonnais, tel. 01 47 05 42 30, fax 01 47 05 45 91).

Hôtel La Tour Maubourg*** is particularly romantic. It lies alone five minutes east of rue Cler, just off the Esplanade des Invalides, and feels like a slightly faded, elegant manor house with spacious Old World rooms. It overlooks a cheery green lawn within sight of Napoleon's tomb (Sb-550–650F, Db-690–850F, suites for up to four-900–1,400F, prices include breakfast with fresh-squeezed juice, prices reduced mid-July–mid-August, CC:VM, at the La Tour Maubourg Métro stop, 150 rue de Grenelle, tel. 01 47 05 16 16, fax 01 47 05 16 14, e-mail: victor@worldnet.fr).

These places are lesser values but, in this fine area, acceptable last choices: Hôtel de la Tour Eiffel** (Sb-330F, Db-380F, Tb-480F, CC:VMA, 17 rue de l'Exposition, tel. 01 47 05 14 75, fax 01 47 53 99 46, Muriel SE); Hôtel Kensington**, near the Mars Hotel (Sb-315F, Db-400–500F, extra bed-80F, CC:VMA, 79 avenue de La Bourdonnais, tel. 01 47 05 74 00, fax 01 47 05 25 81); Hôtel de la Tulipe** (Db-580F, overpriced and wood-beamed with a leafy courtyard, 33 rue Malar, tel. 01 45 51 67 21, fax 01 47 53 96 37); quiet Hotel le Pavillon with a small court-yard (Db-460F, family suites-575F, 54 rue St. Dominique, tel. 01 45 51 42 87, fax 01 45 51 32 79); Hôtel Royal Phare** (Db-310–410F, facing École Militaire Métro stop, 40 avenue de la Motte Piquet, tel. 01 47 05 57 30, fax 01 45 51 64 41); Hôtel la Motte Piquet** (Db-350–440F, duplex suites-730F, CC:VM, 30 avenue de la Motte Piquet, tel. 01 47 05 09 57, fax 01 47 05 74 36); and simple, quiet Hôtel de la Paix, run agreeably by English-speaking Noël (S-175F, Ds-310F, Db-345F, Tb-475F, no elevator, 19 rue du Gros-Caillou, tel. 01 45 51 86 17).

Rue Cler Orientation

Become a local at a rue Cler café for breakfast or join the afternoon crowd for une bière pression (a draft beer). On rue Cler you
can eat and browse your way through a street full of tart shops,
delis, cheeseries, and colorful outdoor produce stalls (see Eating,
below). For an after-dinner cruise on the Seine, it's just a short
walk to the river and the Bâteaux Mouches.

Your neighborhood TI is at the Eiffel Tower (daily
11:00–18:00 May–September, tel. 01 45 51 22 15). The Métro station (École Militaire) and a post office with phone booths are at
the end of rue Cler, on avenue de la Motte Piquet. Taxi stands are
on avenue de Tourville at avenue la Motte Piquet (near the Métro
stop), and on avenue Bosquet at rue St. Dominique. The Banque
Populaire (across from Hôtel Leveque) changes money and has an
ATM. Rue St. Dominique is the area's boutique street.

The American Church and College is the community center
for Americans living in Paris (65 quai d'Orsay, tel. 01 47 05 07 99).
The interdenominational service at 11:00 on Sunday, the coffee
hour after church, and the free Sunday concerts (18:00) are a great
way to make some friends and get a taste of émigré life in Paris. Stop
by and pick up copies of the Free Voice and France–U.S.A. Contacts
newspapers for information on housing and employment through
the community of 30,000 Americans living in Paris.

Afternoon *boules* (lawn bowling) on the esplanade des
Invalides is a relaxing spectator sport. Look for the dirt area to the
upper right as you face the Invalides.

Helpful bus routes: Line 69 runs along rue St. Dominique
and serves Les Invalides, Orsay, Louvre, Marais, and Père-
Lachaise cemetery. Line 92 runs along avenue Bosquet and
serves the Arc de Triomphe and Champs-Élysées in one direction and the Montparnasse tower in the other. Line 49 runs on
boulevard La Tour Maubourg and serves St. Lazaire and Gard
du Nord stations.

Sleeping in the Marais Neighborhood
**(4th arrondissement, Mo: St. Paul or Bastille,
zip code: 75004)**

Those interested in a more Soho/Greenwich, gentrified, urban-
jungle locale would enjoy making the Marais their Parisian
home. The Marais is a more happening locale than rue Cler. It's
narrow medieval Paris at its finest. Only 15 years ago it was a
forgotten Parisian backwater, but now the Marais is one of Paris'
most popular residential areas. It's a 15-minute walk to Notre-
Dame, Île St. Louis, and the Latin Quarter.

Grand Hôtel Jeanne d'Arc**, a cozy, welcoming place with
thoughtfully appointed rooms on a quiet street, is a fine value and
a haven for connoisseurs of the Marais (small Db-310F, Db-

Marais Neighborhood

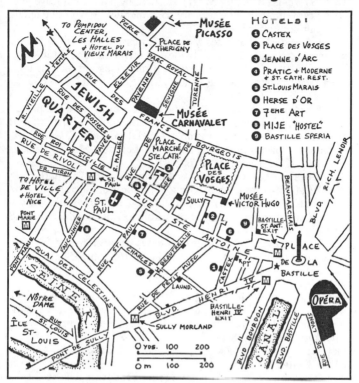

To Pompidou Center, Les Halles + Hotel du Vieux Marais

Musée Picasso

Place de Thérigny

Parc Royal

JEWISH QUARTER

Musée Carnavalet

Place Marché Ste. Cath.

Place des Vosges

Musée Victor Hugo

St. Paul

To Hôtel de Ville + Hotel Nice

Notre Dame

Île St-Louis

Sully Morland

Bastille-Henri IV Exit

Place de la Bastille

Opéra

HÔTELS:
① Castex
② Place des Vosges
③ Jeanne d'Arc
④ Pratic + Moderne + St. Cath. Rest.
⑤ St. Louis Marais
⑥ Herse d'Or
⑦ 7ème Art
⑧ MIJE "Hostel"
⑨ Bastille Speria

400–490F, Tb-530F, Qb-590F, extra bed 75F, CC:VM, 3 rue Jarente, Mo: St. Paul, tel. 01 48 87 62 11, fax 01 48 87 37 31). Sixth-floor rooms have a view.

Hotel Bastille Speria*** feels family-run while offering a serious business-type service. Its spacious lobby and 45 rooms are modern, cheery, and pastel; and it's English-language-friendly, from the *Herald Tribunes* in the lobby to the history of the Bastille in the elevator (Sb-525–550F, Db-570–635F, Tb-770F, extra bed-120F, CC:VMA, 1 rue de la Bastille, Mo: Bastille, tel. 01 42 72 04 01, fax 01 42 72 56 38, e-mail: speria@micronet.fr).

Hôtel Castex** is pleasant, clean, cheery, and run by the friendly Perdigao family (Miguel and Vasco). This place is a great value, with comfortable rooms, many stairs, and a great location on a relatively quiet street (Ss-240F, Sb-260–290F, Ds-320–340F, Db-340–360F, Tb-460F, CC:VM, no elevator, 5 rue Castex, just off place de la Bastille and rue Saint Antoine, Mo: Bastille, tel. 01

42 72 31 52, fax 01 42 72 57 91). Reserve by phone and leave your credit-card number. The security code marked on your key opens the front door after hours.

Hôtel de la Place des Vosges**, quasi-classy with a linoleum/antique feel, is ideally located on a quiet street (Sb-350F, Db-450–510F, CC:VMA, 12 rue de Biraque, just off the elegant place des Vosges and just as snooty, Mo: St. Paul, tel. 01 42 72 60 46, fax 01 42 72 02 64).

Hotel des Chevaliers***, one block northwest of the place des Vosges, offers pleasant and comfortable rooms with all the comforts from hair dryers to cable TV (Db-630–820F, CC:VMA, skip the overpriced breakfast, 30 rue de Turenne, Mo: St. Paul, tel. 01 42 72 73 47, fax 01 42 72 54 10).

Hotel de la Herse D'Or is dumpy, industrial-strength, three-coats-of-paint simple, with a good location, tortured floor plan, and hard-to-beat prices (S-160F, D-200F, Db-280F, showers 10F, no elevator, 20 rue Saint Antoine, Mo: Bastille, tel. 01 48 87 84 09, fax 01 48 87 94 01).

Hotel Sévigné** provides basic two-star comfort at fair prices with the cheapest breakfast in Paris: 16F (Sb-355F, Db-375F, CC:VM, 2 rue Malher, Mo: Bastille, tel. 01 42 72 76 17, fax 01 42 78 68 26).

Hôtel Pratic* has a slightly Arabic feel in its cramped lobby. The tidy rooms are simple but not confined, stairs are many, and it's right on a great people-friendly square. Single rooms are bare, tiny, and depressing (S-180F, D-245F, Ds-290F, Db-340F, no elevator, 9 rue d'Ormesson, Mo: St. Paul, tel. 01 48 87 80 47, fax 01 48 87 40 04).

The bare-bones and dumpy **Hôtel Moderne**, next to the Hôtel Pratic, might be better than a youth hostel if you need privacy. The only thing *moderne* about it is the name—which is illegible on the broken sign (D-170F, Ds-190F, Db-220F, 3 rue Caron, Mo: St. Paul, tel. 01 48 87 97 05).

Grand Hotel du Loiret** is a fair value with easy-going management. While it's popular with American students, it's renovating many of its rooms so that they'll no longer be in the student price range (S-190F, Sb-250–350F, D-220F, Db-300–400F, Tb-400F, Qb-500F, CC:VMA, 8 rue des Garcons Mauvais, Mo: Hotel de Ville, tel. 01 48 87 77 00, fax 01 48 04 96 56).

Hôtel de 7ème Art**, a Hollywood-nostalgia place, is run by young, hip Marais types, with average rooms, a full-service café/bar, and Charlie Chaplin murals (Sb-300F, Db-420–490F, a few large double rooms at 670F, CC:VMA, 20 rue St. Paul, Mo: St. Paul, tel. 01 44 54 85 00, fax 01 42 77 69 10).

Hôtel de Nice** is a cozy "Marie Antoinette-does-tie-dye" place with lots of thoughtful touches on the Marais' busy main drag (Sb-380F, Db-480F, Tb-600F, CC:VM, 42 bis rue de Rivoli,

Mo: Hotel de Ville, tel. 01 42 78 55 29, fax 01 42 78 36 07). Twin rooms, which cost the same as doubles, are roomier but on the street side (effective double-pane windows).

Hotel de la Bretonniere*** is my favorite splurge in the Marais with elegant decor; tastefully decorated rooms with an antique, open-beam coziness; and an efficient, helpful staff (standard Db-640F, Db with character-790F, elegant Db suites-980F, the standard Db has enough character for me, CC:VMA, between rue du Vielle du Temple and rue des Archives at 22 rue Sainte Croix de la Bretonnerie, Mo: Hotel de Ville, tel. 01 48 87 77 63, fax 01 42 77 26 78, www: HoteldelaBretonnerie.com).

Hotel Caron de Beaumarchais***, renovated into an 18th-century Marais manor house, is charming from the Louis XVI fireplace in the lobby to the period furniture in each room (Db-690–770F, CC:VMA, air-conditioning, 12 rue Vielle du Temple, Mo: Hotel de Ville, tel. 01 42 72 34 12, fax 01 42 72 34 63).

Hotel Rivoli Notre Dame***, another nicely remodeled three-star place with all the comforts, is centrally located in the Marais (Db-660–715F, CC:VMA, 19 rue du Bourg Tibourg, Mo: Hotel de Ville, tel. 01 42 78 47 39, fax 01 40 29 07 00, Web site: www.hotelrivolinotredame.com).

Hotel de Vieux Marais**, tucked away on a quiet street near the Pompidou Center, offers renovated rooms with air-conditioning (Sb-500F, Db-660–690F, extra bed-100F, CC:VM, just off rue des Archives at 8 rue du Platre, Mo: Hotel de Ville, tel. 01 42 78 47 22, fax 01 42 78 34 32).

MIJE "Youth Hostels": The Maison Internationale de la Jeunesse des Étudiants (MIJE) runs three classy old residences in the Marais for travelers under age 30. Each offers simple, clean, single-sex, mostly four-bed rooms for 126F per bed, including shower and breakfast. Singles cost 200F. Rooms are locked from 12:00 to 15:00 and at 1:00. MIJE Fourcy (cheap dinners, 6 rue de Fourcy, just south of the rue Rivoli), MIJE Fauconnier (11 rue Fauconnier), and the best, MIJE Maubisson (12 rue des Barres), share one telephone number (tel. 01 42 74 23 45) and the same Métro stop (St. Paul). Reservations are accepted at all three hostels.

Marais Orientation

The nearest TIs are in the Louvre and Gare de Lyon (arrival level, open 8:00–20:00, tel. 01 43 43 33 24). The Banque de France changes money; it offers good rates but sometimes long lines (where rue Saint Antoine hits the place de la Bastille, Monday–Friday 9:00–11:45 and 13:30–15:30). Most banks, shops, and other services are on rue Saint Antoine between Métro stops St. Paul and Bastille. You'll find one taxi stand on the north side of Saint Antoine where it meets rue Castex, and another on the south side of Saint Antoine in front of the St. Paul church.

The new Bastille opera house, Promenade Plantée Park, place des Vosges (Paris' oldest square), and the Jewish Quarter (rue des Rosiers) are all nearby. The Marais' main drag, rue Saint Antoine, starts at the Bastille and leads west toward the hopping Beaubourg/Les Halles area. Paris' biggest and best budget department store is BHV, next to the Hôtel de Ville. Marais post offices are on rue Castex and on the corner of rues Pavée and Francs Bourgeois. (See "Bastille/Marais/Beaubourg Walk," above, for more information on this area.)

Helpful bus routes: Line 69 on rue Saint Antoine takes you to the Louvre, Orsay, Rodin, and Invalide museums, and ends at the Eiffel Tower. Line 86 runs down boulevard Henri IV crossing the Île St. Louis and serving the Latin Quarter along boulevard St. Germain. Line 65 serves the Gares Austerlitz, Est, and Nord from the place de la Bastille.

Sleeping in the Contrescarpe Neighborhood
(5th arrondissement, Mo: place Monge, zip code: 75005)
This lively, colorful neighborhood—just over the hill from the Latin Quarter and behind the Panthéon—is walking distance from Notre-Dame, Île de la Cité, Île St. Louis, Luxembourg Gardens, and the grand boulevards St. Germain and St. Michel. The rue Mouffetard and delightfully Parisian place Contrescarpe are the heart and soul of this area. Rue Mouffetard is a market street by day and touristy restaurant row by night. Fewer tourists sleep here and I find the hotel values consistently better than most other neighborhoods. These hotels are listed in order by proximity to the Seine River.

The low-energy, bare-bones **Hôtel du Commerce** is run by Monsieur Mattuzzi, who must be a pirate gone good (S-130F, D-140F, Ds-150F, Ts-210F, Qs-260F, showers-15F, no elevator, takes no reservations, call at 10:00 and he'll say *"oui"* or *"non,"* 14 rue de La Montagne Ste. Geneviève, Mo: Maubert-Mutualité, tel. 01 43 54 89 69). This 300-year-old place (with vinyl that looks it) is a great rock-bottom deal and as safe as any dive next to a police station can be. In the morning, the landlady will knock and chirp, *"Restez-vous?"* ("Are you staying tonight?")

Hôtel des Grandes Écoles** is as good as a two-star Parisian hotel gets (and better than most three-star hotels). It's idyllic and peaceful, with three buildings protecting a flowering garden courtyard. This romantic place is deservedly popular, so call well in advance (Db-520–670F, Tb-620–770F, Qb-670–870F, 75 rue de Cardinal Lemoine, Mo: Cardinal Lemoine, tel. 01 43 26 79 23, fax 01 43 25 28 15, run by mellow Marie.)

Hôtel Central* is unprententious with a charming location, a steep and slippery castlelike stairway, simple rooms (all with shower, though toilets are down the hall), so-so beds, and plenty of smiles.

Contrescarpe Hotels

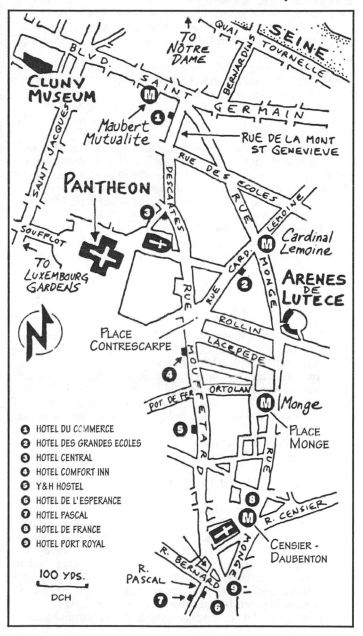

SEINE

QUAI

TO
NÔTRE
DAME

BLVD.

SAINT

BERNARDINS

TOURNELLE

CLUNY
MUSEUM

GERMAIN

Ⓜ

❶

Maubert
Mutualite

SAINT JACQUES

RUE DE LA MONT
ST GENEVIEVE

RUE DES ECOLES

PANTHEON

DESCARTES

RUE

LEMOINE

❸

SOUFFLOT

Ⓜ

RUE CARD.

Cardinal
Lemoine

TO
LUXEMBOURG
GARDENS

ARENES
DE
LUTECE

RUE

RUE

MONGE

❷

N

ROLLIN

PLACE
CONTRESCARPE

LACEPEDE

❹

MOUFFETARD

POT DE FER

ORTOLAN

Ⓜ Monge

❺

PLACE
MONGE

RUE

❶ HOTEL DU COMMERCE
❷ HOTEL DES GRANDES ECOLES
❸ HOTEL CENTRAL
❹ HOTEL COMFORT INN
❺ Y&H HOSTEL
❻ HOTEL DE L'ESPERANCE
❼ HOTEL PASCAL
❽ HOTEL DE FRANCE
❾ HOTEL PORT ROYAL

❽

Ⓜ

R. CENSIER

CENSIER -
DAUBENTON

MONGE

R. BERNARD

❼

R.
PASCAL

100 YDS.

DCH

❾

❻

It's a fine budget value (Ss-165–190F, Ds-240–270F, no elevator, 6 rue Descartes, Mo: Cardinal Lemoine, tel. 01 46 33 57 93).

The hotels listed below lie on or at the bottom of the rue Mouffetard (Mo: Cardinal Lemoine) and often have rooms when others don't.

Hotel Comfort Inn**, with its modern chain-hotel rooms, seems out of place in this nonconformist area, but it's brilliantly located right on the rue Mouffetard, a stone's throw from the place Contrescarpe and the late-night action (Sb-535F, Db-620F, CC:VM, 56 rue Mouffetard, Mo: Cardinal Lemoine, tel. 01 43 36 17 00, fax 01 43 36 25 78).

Y&H Hostel offers a great location, easygoing English-speaking management, and basic but acceptable hostel-like conditions (100F-beds in four-bed rooms, 120F-beds in double rooms, 15F for sheets, rooms closed 11:00–17:00 though reception stays open, reservations must be paid in advance, 80 rue Mouffetard, Mo: Censier-Daubenton, tel. 01 45 35 09 53, fax 01 47 07 22 24).

Hotel de l'Esperance** gives you nearly three stars for the price of two. It's quiet, fluffy, and comfortable, with thoughtfully appointed rooms complete with canopy beds, hair dryers, cable TV, and a flamboyant owner (Sb-380–410F, Db-410–480F, Tb-550F, CC:VM, rue Pascal 15, Mo: Censier-Daubenton, tel. 01 47 07 10 99, fax 01 43 37 56 19).

Hotel Pascal* is a good value with simple, clean rooms, small double beds, and miniscule bathrooms (S-200F, Db-300F, Tb-450F, Qb-600F, funky studio lofts with kitchenettes-450F, 20 rue Pascal, Mo: Censier-Daubenton, tel. 01 47 07 41 92, fax 01 47 07 43 80, e-mail: hotpascal@mail.opsion.fr).

Hotel de France**, on a busy street, has fine, modern rooms and hardworking, helpful owners (Sb-360F, Db-410–430F, CC:VM, 108 rue Monge, Mo: Censier-Danbeutontel. 01 47 07 19 04, fax 01 43 36 62 34). Its best and quietest rooms are *sur le cour* (on the courtyard).

Hotel Port Royal* is a budget traveler's dream with helpful owners and spotless, comfortable rooms at great prices (S-180–225F, D-225F, Db-335–350F, CC:VM, 8 boulevard de Port Royal, Mo: Gobelins, tel. 01 43 31 70 06, fax 01 43 31 33 67).

Contrescarpe Orientation

The nearest TI is at the Louvre Museum. The post office (PTT) is between rue Mouffetard and rue Monge at 10 rue de l'Épée du Bois. Place Monge hosts a colorful outdoor market on Wednesday, Friday, and Sunday until 13:00. The street market at the bottom of rue Mouffetard bustles daily from 8:00 to 12:00 and 15:30 to 19:00 (five blocks south of Contrescarpe), and the lively place Contrescarpe hops in the afternoon and well after dark.

The flowery Jardin des Plantes park is close by and great

for afternoon walks, as are Luxembourg Gardens, which justify the 15-minute walk. The doorway at 49 rue Monge leads to a hidden Roman arena (**Arènes de Lutèce**). Today, *boules* players occupy the stage while couples cuddle on the seats. Walk to the Panthéon, admire it from the outside (it's not worth paying to go in), and go into the wildly beautiful St. Étienne-du-Mont church.

Sleeping near Paris, in Versailles
For a laid-back alternative to Paris within easy reach of the big city by RER-C train (5/hrly, 30 min, use Versailles C.H. station), Versailles can be a good overnight stop. Parking is free and easy.

Hôtel Le Cheval Rouge**, built in 1676 as Louis XIV's stables, now houses tourists comfortably. It's a block behind the place du Marche in a quaint corner of town on a large quiet courtyard (Ds-275F, Db-340–390F, extra bed-90F, CC:VMA, 18 rue Andre Chenier, 78000 Versailles, tel. 01 39 50 03 03, fax 01 39 50 61 27).

Ibis Versailles**, a slick business-class place, offers all the comfort with none of the character (Db-390–490F, CC:VMA, across from RER station, 4 avenue du Gen. de Gaulle, tel. 01 39 53 03 30, fax 01 39 50 06 31).

Hotel du Palais, facing the RER station, has cheap and handy beds; get one off the street. It's a pink and funky place, dumpy enough to lack stars but proud enough to put candy on the beds (D-170F, Ds-220F, Db-250F, 30F per additional person, miles of stairs, 6 place Lyautey, tel. 01 39 50 39 29, fax 01 39 50 80 41).

Hotel d'Angleterre** is a peaceful, well-worn old place near the palace (Db 300 350F, extra bed-60F, CC:VM, first-floor rooms are best, 2 rue de Fontenay, tel. 01 39 51 43 50, fax 01 39 51 45 63).

Eating in Paris
Paris is France's wine and cuisine melting pot. While it lacks a style of its own, it draws from the best of France. Paris could hold a gourmet's Olympics—and import nothing.

Picnic or go to bakeries for quick take-out lunches, or stop at a café for a lunch salad or *plat du jour*, but linger longer over dinner. You can eat well, restaurant-style, for 100F to 140F. Your hotel can also recommend nearby restaurants in the 60F to 100F range. Remember, cafés and simple small restaurants are happy to serve a *plat du jour* (garnished plate of the day, about 60F) or a chef-like salad (35–50F) day or night. Famous places are often overpriced, overcrowded, and overrated. Find a quiet neighborhood and wander, or follow a local recommendation. Restaurants open for dinner around 19:00. Small local favorites get crowded after 21:00.

Cafeterias and Picnics

Many Parisian department stores have huge supermarkets hiding
in the basement and top-floor cafeterias offering not really cheap
but low-risk, low-stress, what-you-see-is-what-you-get meals. For
picnics, you'll find handy little groceries (*épiceries*) and delis (*char-
cuteries*) all over town but rarely near famous sights. Good picnic
fixings include roasted chicken, drinkable yogurt, fresh bakery
goods, melons, and exotic pâtés and cheeses. Great take-out deli-
type foods like gourmet salads and quiches abound. Boulangeries
make good, cheap mini-quiches and sandwiches. While wine is
taboo in public places in the United States, it's *pas de problème* in
France. The budget eating tips in this book's introduction will
save piles of francs in Paris.

Good Picnic Spots: The pedestrian bridge, Pont des Arts,
with unmatched views and plentiful benches; and the park under
the Eiffel Tower are my favorite dinner-picnic places. Bring your
own dinner feast and watch the riverboats or the Eiffel Tower
light up the city for you. The Palais Royal (across the street from
the Louvre) is a good spot for a peaceful and royal picnic. Also try
the little triangular Henry IV Park on the west tip of the Île de la
Cité, people-watching at the Pompidou Center, the elegant place
des Vosges (closes at dusk) in the Marais neighborhood, the gardens at the Rodin Museum, and Luxembourg Gardens.

Restaurants

The Parisian eating scene is kept at a rolling boil. Entire books
(and lives) are dedicated to the subject. If you are traveling outside
of Paris, save your splurges for the countryside, where you'll enjoy
better cooking for less money. I've listed places that conveniently
fit a busy sightseeing schedule and places near recommended
hotels. If you'd like to visit a district specifically to eat, consider
the many romantic restaurants that line the cozy Île St. Louis'
main street and the colorful, touristic-but-fun string of eateries
along rue Mouffetard behind the Panthéon.

Eating in the Rue Cler Neighborhood

Restaurants: The rue Cler neighborhood isn't famous for its
restaurants. That's why I eat here. Several small family-run places
serve great dinner *menus* for 100F and *plats du jour* for 60 to 80F.

Café du Marché, with the best seats, coffee, and prices on rue
Cler, serves hearty salads and great 60F *plats du jour* for lunch or
dinner. Arrive before 19:30 or wait at the bar. A chalkboard listing
the plates of the day—each a meal—will momentarily be hung in
front of you (at the corner of rue Cler and rue Champs du Mars).

Leo le Lion has been run by Mimi for 20 years and must be
the friendliest place in the neighborhood. A warm, charming souvenir of old Paris, it's popular with locals. The 105F *menu* comes

with a first course that could feed two for an entire meal (but no splitting), and a fully garnished main course (closed Sunday, 23 rue Duvivier, tel. 01 45 51 41 77).

Vegetarians will appreciate the Mediterranean cuisine at **7ème Sud**, though the restaurant can be smoky (at the corner of rue de Grenelle and rue Duvivier).

Thoumieux, the neighborhood's classy, traditional Parisian *brasserie*, is deservedly popular (82F and 160F *menus*, complete á la carte, 79 rue St. Dominique, tel. 01 47 05 49 75).

For a special dinner, survey the handful of fine places that line rue de l'Exposition (between rue St. Dominique and rue de Grenelle): **Restaurant La Serre**, at #29, has fun ambience (*plats* 50–70F, daily from 19:00, often a wait after 21:00, good onion soup and duck specialties, tel. 01 45 55 20 96, Marie-Alice and Philippe SE). Across the street at #28, **Le P'tit Troquet** is popular with locals and ideal for a last-night splurge—allow 150F per person for dinner (closed Sunday and Monday, tel. 01 47 05 80 39). The quieter **La Maison de Cosima** at #20 offers a refined, creative French cuisine and excellent 100F and 150F *menus* that include a vegetarian option (closed Sunday, tel. 01 45 51 37 71, run by friendly Helene). The softly-lit tables and red velvet chairs of **Auberge du Champ de Mars** at #18 draw a romantic crowd in search of a good value (100F *menu* only, limited wine menu, closed Sunday, tel. 01 45 51 78 08).

Around the corner, just off rue de Grenelle, the friendly and unpretentious **La Varanque** is a good budget bet with 60F *plats* and an 80F *menu* (27 rue Augereau, tel. 01 47 05 51 22).

Ambassade du Sud-Ouest, a wine and food boutique/ restaurant, specializes in French Southwest cuisine such as *daubes de canard*–duck meatballs (46 avenue de la Bourdonnais, tel. 01 45 55 59 59). **L'Ami de Jean** is a lively place to sample Basque cuisine (closed Sunday, 27 rue Malar, tel. 01 47 05 86 89).

Picnicking: Rue Cler is a movable feast that gives "fast food" a good name. The entire street is clogged with connoisseurs of good eating. Only the health-food store goes unnoticed. A festival of food, the street is lined with people whose lives seem to be devoted to their specialty: Stacking polished produce, rotisserie chicken, crêpes, or cheese squares.

For a magical picnic dinner, assemble it in no fewer than six shops on rue Cler and lounge on the best grass in Paris (the police don't mind after dark) with the dogs, Frisbees, a floodlit Eiffel Tower, and a cool breeze in the Parc du Champs de Mars.

The **crêpe stand** next to the Café du Marche does a wonderful top-end dinner crêpe for 25F. An Asian deli, **Traiteur Asie** (across from Hôtel Leveque; another is across from the Hotel de Champs de Mars), has tasty low-stress, low-price take-out treats. Its two tables offer the cheapest place to sit, eat, and enjoy the rue Cler ambience. For quiche, cheese pie, or a pear/chocolate tart, try **Tarte Julie's** (take-out or stools, 28 rue Cler). The elegant **Flo Prestige** *charcuterie* (at École Militaire Métro stop) is open until 23:00 and offers mouthwatering meals to go. **Real McCoy** is a little shop selling American food and sandwiches (194 rue de Grenelle). There's a small late-night grocery on rue de Grenelle at rue de l'Exposition.

The bakery (*boulangerie*) on the corner of rue Cler and rue de Champs de Mars is the place for a fresh baguette, sandwich, tiny quiche, or *pain au chocolat*, but the almond croissants at the *boulangerie* on rue de Grenelle at rue Cler make my day. The bakery at 112 rue St. Dominique is in a league by itself and worth the detour, with classic decor and tables to enjoy your *café au lait* and croissant.

Cafés and Bars: If you want to linger over coffee or a drink at a sidewalk café, try **Café du Marché** (see above), **Petite Brasserie** (opposite #53 rue Cler), or the traditional **La Terasse** café (at École Militaire Métro). **Café La Roussillon**, peopled and decorated belle epoque, also offers a quintessential café experience. Sip a 7F wine at the bar or enjoy the good bistro fare at a table (hearty 50F *plats du jour* and salads, corner of Grenelle and Cler). **Le Sancerre** wine bar/café is wood beam–warm and ideal for a light lunch or dinner (great omelets), or just for a glass of wine after a long day of sightseeing. You'll be served by the owner, whose cheeks are the same color as his wine (open until 21:30, 22 avenue Rapp, tel. 01 45 51 75 91). The almost no-name **Maison Altmayer** is a hole-in-the-wall place for a drink quietly festooned with reality (9:00–19:30, 6 rue du Gros Caillou, next to Hôtel Eiffel Rive Gauche). Cafés like this originated (and this one still functions) as a place where locals enjoyed a drink while their heating wood, coal, or gas was prepared for delivery.

Nightlife: This sleepy neighborhood is not the place for night-owls, but there are three notable exceptions: **Café du Marché** (above) hops with a Franco-American crowd until about midnight. **O'Brien's Pub** is an upscale and popular Parisian rendition of an Irish pub (77 St. Dominique). **Café Thoumieux** is a new hip, happening place with big-screen sports and a young international crowd (4 rue de la Comete, Mo: Latour Maubourg).

Eating in the Marais Neighborhood

The windows of the Marais are filled with munching sophisticates. The place du Marche Ste. Catherine, a tiny square midway between the St. Paul Métro and place des Vosges, is home to several good places. **Le Marais Ste. Catherine** is a good value (100F *menu*, daily from 19:00, extra seating in their candlelit cellar, 5 rue Caron, tel. 01 42 72 39 94), though many seem willing to pay 30F more for the *menu* at **Le Marche** (2 place Marche Ste. Catherine, tel. 01 4 77 34 88). Just off the square, **l'Auberge de Jarente** offers a well-respected and traditional cuisine (117F *menu*, closed

Sunday and Monday, 7 rue Jarente, tel. 01 42 77 49 35).

Dinners beneath the candlelit arches of the place des Vosges are *très* romantic: **Nectarine** at #16 serves fine salads, quiches, and *plats du jour* day and night; while **Ma Bourgogne** is where locals go for a splurge (at the northwest corner, daily, tel. 01 42 78 44 64).

For a fast, cheap change of pace, eat at (or take-out from) the Chinese/Japanese **Delice House**. Two can split 200 grams of chicken curry (or whatever, 26F) and a heaping helping of rice (20F). There's lots of seating, with pitchers of water at the ground-floor tables and a roomier upstairs (81 rue Saint Antoine, open until 21:00).

Near Hôtel Castex, the restaurant **La Poste** and the *crêperie* across the street (13 rue Castex) offer inexpensive, light meals (both closed on Sunday). I like **La Bastoche**'s cozy ambience and good 100F *menu* (7 rue Saint Antoine, tel. 01 48 04 74 34). Across the street, **Le Paradis de Fruit** serves organic foods to young locals (on the small square at rues Tournelle and Saint Antoine). Several cafés on the Boulevard Henri IV (**Brasserie Le Reveil** at #29, near rue Castex) offer reasonable *plats du jour* and salads.

Wine lovers shouldn't miss the excellent Burgundy wines and exquisite, though limited *menu* selection at the cozy **Au Bourguignon du Marais** (52 rue Francois Miron, call by 19:00 to reserve, tel. 01 48 87 15 40).

For a worthwhile splurge, try the romantic and traditional **L'Excuse** (185F *menu*, closed Sunday, 14 rue Charles V, call ahead, tel. 01 42 77 98 97). Across the street, **L'Énoteca** has lively and reasonable Italian cuisine in a relaxed, open setting (across from Hôtel du 7ème Art at 20 rue St. Paul, closed Sunday, tel. 01 42 78 91 44).

Vegetarians will appreciate the fine cuisine at **Picolo Teatro** (closed Monday, 6 rue des Ecouffes, tel. 01 42 72 17 79), and at **l'As du Falafel**, which serves the best falafel on the rue Rosier at #34.

Picnicking: Hobos and connoisseurs picnic at the peaceful park at place des Vosges (closes at dusk). Connoisseurs prefer the busy gourmet take-out places all along rue Saint Antoine, such as **Flo Prestige** (open until 23:00, on the tiny square where rue Tournelle and rue Saint Antoine meet). Hobos stretch their francs at the supermarket in the basement of the Monoprix department store (close to place des Vosges on rue Saint Antoine). A few small grocery shops are open until 23:00 on the rue Saint Antoine (near intersection with rue Castex). An open-air market, held Sunday morning, is just off the place de la Bastille on boulevard Richard Lenoir.

For a cheap breakfast, try the tiny *boulangerie/pâtisserie* where the hotels buy their croissants (coffee machine, 3F; 10F baby quiches, 5F *pain au chocolat*, one block off place de la Bastille at corner of rue Saint Antoine and rue de Lesdiguieres).

Cafés and Bars: This hip area is overrun with atmospheric cafés and bars (open generally till 2:00), most of which lie north of rue Saint Antoine and rue Rivoli. Here are a few keys areas to consider for café sitting: along the rue du Vielle du Temple; at the rue de la Croix Bretonnière and the rue Tresor; or on the rue Rosiers for ethnically hip cafés like the **Hamman** cyber-café (4 rue des Rosiers, on the pleasant place du Marche Ste. Catherine). The *trés* local wine bar at **Au Temps des Cerises** is amiably run and a welcoming if smoky place (rue du Petit Musc and rue de Cerisaie, around the corner from the Hôtel Castex).

Nightlife: The streets running north of rue Saint Antoine and Rivoli play host to a lively after-hours scene. Wander rue du Vielle du Temple, rue de la Croix Bretonnière, and rue des Archives. **Le Vieux Comptoir** is tiny, lively and not too hip (just off the place des Vosges at 8 rue Biraque). **La Perla** is trendy with Parisian yuppies in search of the perfect margarita (26 rue Francois Miron). **Auld Alliance**, Paris' only Scottish pub, feels a bit like a frat house in Paris with Scottish barmen (80 rue Francois Miron).

Eating in the Contrescarpe Neighborhood

Rue Mouffetard and rue du Pot-de-Fer are lined with inexpensive, lively, and forgettable restaurants. Study the many *menus*, compare crowds, then dive in. **Le Jardin d'Artemis** is one of the better inexpensive values on the rue Mouffetard at #34 (85F *menu*). **Restaurant l'Epoque**, a fine neighborhood restaurant, has excellent-value *menus* at 68F and 118F (one block off place Contrescarpe at 81 rue Cardinal Lemoine, tel. 01 46 34 15 84). **Restaurant Le Vigneron** is well respected and serves traditional French cuisine (20 rue du Pot-de-Fer); and **Savannah Café's** creative Mediterranean cuisine attracts a loyal, artsy crowd (27 rue Descartes, tel. 01 43 29 45 77). **Le Jardin des Pâtes** is popular with vegetarians, serving pastas and salads at fair prices (4 rue Lacepede, near Jardins des Plantes, tel. 01 43 31 50 71). **Café Tournebride** serves delicious salads (104 rue Mouffetard).

Cafés: Brasserie La Chope, a classic Parisian *brasserie* right on the place Contrescarpe, is popular until the wee hours. Indoor and outdoor seating is people-watching good. **Café Le Mouffetard** is in the thick of the street-market hustle and bustle (at the corner of rue Mouffetard and rue de l'Arbalete). At **Café de la Mosque** you'll feel like you've been beamed to Morocco in this purely Arab café. Order a mint tea, pour in the sugar, and enjoy the authentic interior and peaceful outdoor terrace (2 rue Daubenton, behind the mosque).

Eating in the Latin Quarter

La Petite Bouclerie is a cozy place with classy family cooking (70F *menu*, closed Monday, 33 rue de la Harpe, center of touristy

Latin Quarter, tel. 01 43 54 18 03). The popular **Restaurant Polidor** is an old turn-of-the-century-style place, with great *cuisine bourgeois*, a vigorous local crowd, and a historic toilet. Arrive at 19:00 to get a seat in the restaurant (65F *plat du jour*, 100F *menus*, 41 rue Monsieur le Prince, midway between Odéon and Luxembourg Métro stops, tel. 01 43 26 95 34).

Eating on the Île St. Louis

Cruise the island's main street for a variety of good options from cozy *crêperies* to romantic restaurants. Sample Paris' best sorbet and ice cream at any place advertising *les glaces Berthillon*; the original Berthillon shop is at 31 rue St. Louis en l'Île.

All listings below are on rue St. Louis en l'Île. **Café Med** at #53 serves inexpensive salads and crêpes in a delightful setting. My romantic splurge is **Le Tastevin** (150F and 220F *menus*, #46, tel. 01 43 54 17 31). **La Castafiore** at #51–53 serves fine Italian dishes in a cozy setting (160F *menu*). For crazy, touristy, cellar atmosphere and hearty fun food, feast at **La Taverne du Sergeant Recruiter**. The "Sergeant Recruiter" used to get young Parisians drunk and stuffed here, then sign them into the army. It's all-you-can-eat, including wine and service, for 190F (daily from 19:00, #41, tel. 01 43 54 75 42). There's a near-food-fight clone next door at **Nos Ancêtres Les Gaulois** ("Our Ancestors the Gauls," 190F, daily at 19:00, tel. 01 46 33 66 07).

Eating near the Pompidou Center

The **Mélodine** self-service is right at the Rambuteau Métro stop. **Dame Tartine** overlooks the Homage to Stravinsky fountain, serves a young clientele, and offers excellent, cheap, lively meals. The popular **Café de la Cité** fills one long line of tables with locals enjoying their 44F lunches and 65F dinner specials (22 rue Rambuteau, tel. 01 48 04 30 74).

Elegant Dining on the Seine

La Plage Parisienne is a nearly dress-up riverfront place popular with locals, serving elegant, healthy meals at good prices (Port de Javel-Haut, Mo: Javel, tel. 01 40 59 41 00).

Parisian Entertainment

Paris is most beautiful after dark. Save energy from your day's sightseeing and get out at night. Whether it's a concert at Sainte Chapelle, a boat ride on the Seine, a elevator up the Arc de Triomphe, or a late-night café, experience the city of light lit. The *Pariscope* magazine (3F at any newsstand) offers a complete weekly listing of music, cinema, theater, opera, and other special events. The *Free Voice* newspaper, in English, has a monthly review of Paris entertainment (available at any English-language bookstore,

French-American establishments, or the American Church at 65 quai d'Orsay, Mo: Invalides, tel. 01 47 05 07 99).

Music

Jazz Clubs

With a lively mix of American, French, and international musicians, Paris has been an internationally acclaimed jazz capital since World War II. You'll pay from 30–130F to enter a jazz club (one drink may be included; if not, expect to pay 30–60F per drink; beer is cheapest). See *Pariscope* magazine under "Musique" for listings, and the American Church's *Free Voice* paper for a good monthly review (in English). Music starts after 22:00 in most of clubs. Here are good bets:

Caveau de la Huchette, the handiest characteristic old jazz club for visitors, fills an ancient Latin Quarter cellar with live jazz and frenzied dancing every night (60F weekday, 70F weekend admission, 30F drinks, open 21:30–2:30 or later, closed Monday, 5 rue de la Huchette, tel. 01 43 26 65 05).

Au Duc des Lombards is one of the most popular and respected jazz clubs in Paris (42 rue des Lombards, Mo: Chatelet, 20-minute walk from place des Vosges).

At **Le Cave du Franc Pinot**, enjoy a glass of chardonnay at the main floor wine bar, then drop downstairs for a cool jazz scene. (1 quai de Bourbon, centrally located on Île St. Louis, Mo: Pont Marie, tel. 01 46 33 60 64).

The **American Church** regularly plays host to fine jazz musicians for the best price in Paris (65 quai d'Orsay, Mo: Invalides, RER-C: Pont de l'Alma, tel. 01 47 05 07 99).

Come to **Le Sunset** for more traditional jazz—Dixieland, Big Band—and fewer crowds (near Au Duc des Lombards, 60 rue des Lombards, Mo: Chatelet, tel. 01 40 26 46 60).

All Jazz Club, more expensive than the rest, is a hot club in the heart of the St. Germain area, attracting a more mature crowd in search of recognizable names (7 rue St. Benoit, Mo: St. Germain-des-Près, tel. 01 42 61 53 53).

Classical Concerts

For classical music on any night, consult *Pariscope* magazine; the "Musique" section under "Concerts Classique" lists concerts (free and fee). Look for posters at the churches. Churches that regularly host concerts include St. Sulpice, St. Germain-des-Près, Basilique de Madeleine, St. Eustache, and Sainte Chapelle. It's worth the 90–130F entry to hear Mozart surrounded by the stained glass of the tiny Sainte Chapelle. The Galleries Lafayette department store offers concerts. Many are free (*entrée libre*), such as the Sunday Atelier concert sponsored by the American Church (18:00, 65 quai d'Orsay, Mo: Invalides, RER: Pont de l'Alma, tel. 01 47 05 07 99).

Opera

Paris is home to two fine operas. The **Opéra Garnier**, Paris' first opera house, hosts opera and ballet performances. Come here for less expensive tickets and grand Belle Epoque decor (Mo: Opéra, tel. 01 44 73 13 99). The **Opéra de la Bastille** is the massive modern opera house that dominates place de la Bastille. Come here for state-of-the-art special effects and modern interpretations of classic ballets and operas (Mo: Bastille, tel. 01 43 43 96 96). For tickets, call 01 44 73 13 00, or go to the opera ticket offices, open 11:00–18:00.

Bus Tours

Paris Illumination Tours, run by Paris Vision, connects all the great illuminated sights of Paris with a 100-minute bus tour in 12 languages. Double-decker buses have huge windows, but Moulin Rouge customers get the most desirable front seats. You'll stampede on with a United Nations of tourists, get a hand-held audio stick, and listen to a tape-recorded spiel (interesting but occasionally hard to hear). Uninspired as it is, this provides a fine first-night overview of the city at its floodlit scenic best. Left seats are marginally better. Visibility is fine in the rain. You're on the bus entirely except for one five-minute cigarette break at the Eiffel Tower viewpoint (150F-adult, 75F-ages 4 to 11, free-under 3, second adult pays only 100F on 20:30 tours, departures at 20:30 nightly all year, and 22:00 April–October only, departs from Paris Vision office at 214 rue de Rivoli, across street from Mo: Tuileries). These trips are sold through your hotel (brochures in lobby) or direct at the address listed above (tel. 01 42 60 30 01, fax 01 42 86 95 36, Web site: www.parisvision.com).

Seine River Cruises

The **Bateaux-Mouches** offer one-hour cruises on huge glass boats with departures (every 30 minutes from 10:00–23:00) from the pont de l'Alma, the centrally-located pont Neuf, and from right in front of the Eiffel Tower (40F, 20F-under age 14, tel. 01 42 25 96 10).

Walks

Go for a walk to best appreciate the city of light. Break for ice cream, pause at a café, and enjoy the sidewalk entertainers as you join the post-dinner Parisian parade. Consider these:

Trocadero and Eiffel Tower

These monuments glimmer at night. Take the Métro to the Trocadero stop, follow *sortie Tour Eiffel* signs, and join the party on place de la Trocadero for a magnificent view of the glowing Eiffel Tower. It's a festival of gawkers, drummers, street acrobats, and entertainers. Pass the fountains and walk across the river to the base of the tower, worth the effort even if you don't go up. If you spring for the elevator, go to the 1st floor (20F) where the view is best at night and pause for a break at the Altitude 95 restaurant/bar. For more info, see Eiffel Tower under Sights—Southwest Paris

Notre-Dame, Île St. Louis, and the Latin Quarter

From the elegant Île St. Louis to the fire-breathing Latin Quarter, this evening stroll covers 1.5 miles. Start by strolling the main street of the tiny island, Île St. Louis. Have dinner at a classy café (see Eating) or at least an ice-cream cone at Berthillon. Cross the foot bridge to the neighboring island (Île de la Cite) and take an immediate left across the bridge (pont de l'Archeveque) to the Left Bank. Turn right (for great views of Notre-Dame) and drop down to the riverbank. After walking the length of the Notre-Dame along the riverbank, climb back up to street level and venture into Left Bank. Here (opposite the cathedral), the tangle of small, people-filled lanes leads eventually to the big busy boulevard St. Germain (if lost, ask for that street). At boulevard St. Germain, turn right and head toward St. Germain-des-Près church. You'll pass mimes, fire-breathers, musicians, and expensive cafés. From St. Germain-des-Près, the Métro or city bus (bus 86 to Marais, 63 to rue Cler) takes you home.

Transportation Connections—Paris

Paris is Europe's transportation hub. You'll find trains and buses (day and night) to most any French or European destination. Paris has six central rail stations, each serving different regions. For train schedule information, call 08 36 35 35 35 (3F/min).

Gare St. Lazare: Serves Upper Normandy. To **Rouen** (15/day, 75 min), **Honfleur** (6/day, 3 hrs, via Lisieux then bus), **Bayeux** (9/day, 2.5 hrs), **Caen** (12/day, 2 hrs).

Gare Montparnasse: Serves Lower Normandy and Brittany, and offers TGV service to the Loire Valley and southwestern France. To **Chartres** (10/day, 1 hr), **Mont St. Michel** (2/day, 4.5 hrs, via Rennes), **Dinan** (7/day, 3 hrs, via Rennes and Dol), **Bordeaux** (14/day, 3.5 hrs), **Toulouse** (7/day, 5 hrs, possible transfer in Bordeaux), **Albi** (6.5 hrs, via Toulouse), **Carcassonne** (6.5 hrs, via Toulouse), **Tours** (14/day, 1 hr).

Gare d'Austerlitz: Provides non-TGV service to the Loire Valley, southwestern France, Spain, and Portugal. To **Amboise** (8/day, 2.5 hrs), **Sarlat** (5/day, 5.5 hrs), **Cahors** (5/day, 7 hrs), **Barcelona** (3/day, 13 hrs), **Madrid** (5/day, 16 hrs), **Lisbon** (1/day, 24 hrs).

Gare du Nord: Serves northern France and international destinations. To **Brussels** (10/day, 3.5 hrs), **Bruges** (3/day, 2.5 hrs), **Amsterdam** (10/day, 5.5 hrs), **Copenhagen** (3/day, 16 hrs),

Koblenz on the Rhine (3/day, 7 hrs), **London** via the Eurostar Chunnel (12/day, 3 hrs, Full fare: $219-first class/$149-second class; nonexchangeable Leisure Ticket: $179-first class/$109-second class; call 800/EUROSTAR in the U.S. for more info).

Gare de l'Est: Serves eastern France and points east. To **Colmar** (6/day, 5.5 hrs, transfer in Strasbourg or Mulhouse), **Strasbourg** (10/day, 4.5 hrs), **Reims** (8/day, 2 hrs), **Verdun** (5/day, 3 hrs), **Munich** (4/day, 8.5 hrs), **Vienna** (3/day, 13 hrs), **Zurich** (4/day, 6 hrs).

Gare du Lyon: Offers TGV and regular service to southeastern France, Italy, and other international destinations. To **Beaune** (8/day, 2–3 hrs), **Dijon** (13/day, 90 min), **Chamonix** (3/day, 9 hrs, transfer in Lyon and St. Gervais, one direct and very handy night train), **Annecy** (8/day, 4-7 hrs), **Lyon** (12/day, 2.5 hrs), **Avignon** (10/day, 4 hrs), **Arles** (10/day, 5 hrs), **Nice** (8/day, 7 hrs), **Venice** (5/day, 11 hrs), **Rome** (3/day, 15 hrs), **Bern** (5/day, 5 hrs).

Buses: Long-distance bus lines provide a cheaper, if less comfortable and less flexible, means of transportation to major European cities. The principal bus station in Paris is the Gare Routière du Paris-Gallieni (avenue du General de Gaulle, in suburb of Bagnolet, Mo: Gallieni, tel. 01 49 72 51 51). Eurolines buses depart from here.

Charles de Gaulle Airport

Paris' primary airport has three main terminals (T-1, T-2, and T-9). Those flying to or from the United States will probably use T-1. (Air France uses T-2; charters dominate T-9.) Terminals are connected every few minutes by a free *navette* (bus).

At T-1 you'll find an American Express cash machine, an automatic bill changer (at baggage claim 30), and an exchange window (at baggage claim 18). A bank (with barely acceptable rates) and an ATM machine are near gate 16. At the Meeting Point you'll find the TI, which has free Paris maps and information (open until 23:00); and Relais H, where you can buy a *télécarte* (phone card). Car rental offices are on the arrival level from gates 10 to 22; the SNCF (train) office is at gate 22. For flight information, call 01 48 62 22 80.

Transportation between de Gaulle Airport and Paris: There are three efficient public-transportation routes, taxis, and a couple of airport shuttle services linking the airport's T-1 terminal and central Paris. The free *navette* runs between gate 28 and the **RER Roissy Rail** station, where a train zips you into Paris' subway system in 30 minutes (48F, stops at Gare du Nord, Chatelet, St. Michel, and Luxembourg Gardens). The **Roissy Bus** runs every 15 minutes between gate 30 and the old Paris Opéra (stop is on rue Scribe, in front of American Express), costs 45F (use the automatic ticket machine), and takes 40 minutes, but can be jammed. The **Air France Bus** leaves every 15 minutes from gate 34 and serves the Arc de Triomphe and the Porte Maillot in about 40 minutes for 60F, and the Montparnasse Tower in one hour for 75F (from any of these stops, you can reach your hotel by taxi). For most people the RER Roissy Rail works best. A **taxi** ride with luggage costs about 230F; there is a taxi stand, often with long waits, at gate 16. (The RER Roissy Rail, Roissy Bus, and Air France bus described above serve T-2 as efficiently and economically as T-1.) The Disneyland Express bus departs from Gate 32.

For a stress-free trip between either of Paris' airports and downtown, an **airport shuttle minivan** is ideal for single travelers or families of four or more (costs roughly 120F for one person, 90F per person for two or more, 45F for kids under 12). Reserve from home and they'll meet you at the airport. Paris Shuttle Services (tel. 01 49 62 78 78, fax 01 49 62 78 79, e-mail: pas@magic.fr); or even better, Airport Shuttle (tel. 01 45 38 55 72, fax 01 43 21 35 67, Web site: www.parisanglo.com/clients/ashuttle.html, e-mail: ashuttle@clubinternet.fr).

Skipping Paris: A new TGV rail station (located at T-2, take *navette* from T-1, gate 26) links this airport at blistering speeds with Lille to the north and Lyon, Avignon, Nîmes, Marseille, and Montpellier to the south, without passing through Paris. You can transfer easily from these cities to many other French and European destinations.

Sleeping at or near Charles de Gaulle Airport: Those with early flights can sleep in T-1 at Cocoon (60 "cabins," Sb-250F, Db-300F, CC:VM, tel. 01 48 62 06 16, fax 01 48 62 56 97). Take the elevator down to "boutique level" or walk down from the departure level; it's near the Burger King. You get 16 hours of silence buried under the check-in level with TV and toilet. Hôtel IBIS, at the Roissy Rail station, offers more normal accommodations (Db-420F, CC:VMA, free shuttle bus to either terminal takes two minutes, tel. 01 49 19 19 19, fax 01 49 19 19 21).

Drivers who want to stay near the airport can consider the pleasant city of Senlis, a 15-minute drive. Hostellerie de la Porte Bellon is adequate (Sb-215F, Db-365–420F, CC:VM, 51 rue Bellon, tel. 03 44 53 03 05, fax 03 44 53 29 94).

Orly Airport

This airport feels small. Orly has two terminals: Sud and Ouest. International flights arrive at Sud. After exiting baggage claim (near gate H) you'll be greeted by signs directing you to city transportation, car rental, and so on. Turn left to enter the main terminal area and you'll find exchange offices with barely acceptable rates, an ATM machine, the ADP (a quasi–tourist office that offers free city maps and basic sightseeing information), and an SNCF

French rail desk (sells train tickets and even Eurailpasses). Downstairs is a sandwich bar, bank (lousy rates), newsstand (buy *télécarte* phone card), and post office (great rates for cash or American Express traveler's checks). For flight info on any airline serving Orly, call 01 49 75 15 15.

Transportation Between Paris and Orly Airport: There are four efficient public-transportation routes, taxis, and a couple of airport shuttle services linking Orly and central Paris. The **Air France bus** (outside gate F) runs to Paris' Invalides Métro stop (40F, 4/hrly, 30 min), and is best for those staying in or near the rue Cler neighborhood (from the Invalides terminal, take the Métro two stops to École Militaire to reach recommended hotels). The **Jetbus #285** (outside gate F, 24F, 4/hrly) is the quickest way to the Paris subway, and the best way to the recommended hotels in the Marais and Contrescarpe neighborhoods (take Jetbus to Villejuif Métro stop, buy a carnet of 10 Métro tickets, then take the Métro to the Sully Morland stop for the Marais area or the Cardinal Lemoine stop for the Contrescarpe area). If you're staying elsewhere in Paris, consider the **RER**; you can reach two different RER lines from Orly. The shuttle bus from Gate H (35F, 4/hrly) takes you to the RER C-2 line at the Port du Rungis/Aeroport d'Orly station (serving Gare d'Austerlitz, St. Michel, Musée d'Orsay, Invalides, and Eiffel Tower); the Orly bus (30F, 4/hrly) takes you to the Denfert-Rochereau RER-B line (serving Luxembourg Gardens, St. Michel, and Gare du Nord). The Orlyval trains are overpriced (57F) and unnecessary to reach central Paris. Allow 150F for a **taxi** into central Paris.

An **airport shuttle minivan** is ideal for single travelers or families of four or more (costs roughly 120F for one person, 90F per person for two or more, 45F for kids under 12). Reserve from home and they'll meet you at the airport. Try Paris Shuttle Services (tel. 01 49 62 78 78, fax 01 49 62 78 79, e-mail: pas@magic.fr); or even better, Airport Shuttle (tel. 01 45 38 55 72, fax 01 43 21 35 67, Web site: www.paris-anglo.com/clients/ashuttle.html, e-mail: ashuttle@clubinternet.fr).

Sleeping near Orly Airport: The only reasonable airport hotel is the IBIS (Db-400F, CC:VMA, tel. 01 46 87 33 50, fax 01 46 87 29 92). The Hilton offers more comfort for a price (Db-660F, tel 01 45 12 45 12, fax 01 45 12 45 00). Both offer free shuttle service to the terminal. If you have a car you'll find a variety of fast-food hotels within a few minutes drive of Orly. Chartres and Versailles are convenient to Orly by car—beware of rush hour on the freeways. Check Versailles hotels under Sleeping, above.

PROVENCE

This magnificent region is shaped like a wedge of quiche. From its sunburnt crust fanning out along the Mediterranean coast from Nîmes to Nice, it stretches north along the Rhône Valley to Orange. The Romans were here in force and left many ruins—some of the best anywhere. Seven popes; great artists such as van Gogh, Cézanne, and Picasso; and author Peter Mayle all enjoyed their years in Provence. Provence offers a splendid recipe of arid climate (but brutal winds known as the mistral), captivating cities, exciting hill towns, and remarkably varied landscapes.

Wander through the ghost town of ancient Les Baux and under France's greatest Roman ruin, the Pont du Gard. Spend your starry, starry nights where van Gogh did, in Arles. Explore its Roman past, then find the linger-longer squares and café corners that inspired Vincent. Some may prefer Avignon's more elegant feel and softer edge as a home base. Youthful but classy Avignon bustles in the shadow of its brooding popes' palace. It's a short hop from Arles or Avignon into the splendid scenery and villages of the Côtes du Rhône that make Provence so popular today.

Planning Your Time

Make Arles or Avignon your base (Italophiles prefer Arles, while poodles pick Avignon). Avignon (well-connected to Arles by train) is the regional transportation hub for destinations north of Arles: Pont du Gard, Uzès, and Orange. You'll want a full day for sightseeing in Arles (ideally on a Wednesday or Saturday, when the morning market rages), a half day for Avignon, and a day or two for the villages and sights in the countryside.

Provence

Provence Market Days

Provençal market days offer France's most colorful and tantalizing outdoor shopping. Here's a list to help plan your excursions.

Monday: Cadenet (near Vaison la Romaine), Cavaillon

Tuesday: Avignon, Tarascon, Gordes, Vaison la Romaine, Beaumes de Venise

Wednesday: Arles, Avignon, St. Remy, Violes (near Vaison la Romaine)

Thursday: Carianne (near Vaison la Romaine), Nyons, Orange, Avignon, Beaucaire, Vacqueyras, Isle sur la Sorgue

Friday: Remoulins (Pont du Gard), Carpentras, Bonnieux, Visan, Châteauneuf-du-Pape

Saturday: Arles, Avignon, Oppède, Valreas

Sunday: Avignon, Isle sur la Sorgue, Uzès, Coustelet, Beaucaire

Getting Around Provence

The yellow Michelin map to this region is essential for drivers. Public transit is fairly good: frequent trains link Avignon, Arles, and Nîmes; Les Baux is accessible by bus from Arles; and the Pont du Gard and Uzès are accessible by bus from Avignon. The TIs in Arles and Avignon have information on bus excursions to regional sights that are hard to reach *sans* car (95F half-day, 150F all-day).

Cuisine Scene—Provence

The almost extravagant use of garlic, olive oil, herbs, and tomatoes makes Provence's cuisine France's liveliest. To sample it, order anything *à la Provençale*. Among the area's spicy specialties are ratatouille (a thick mixture of vegetables in an herb-flavored tomato sauce), *brandade* (a salt cod, garlic, and cream mousse), aioli (a garlicky mayonnaise often served atop fresh vegetables), *tapenade* (a sauce of puréed olives, anchovies, tuna, and herbs), *soupe au pistou* (vegetable soup with basil, garlic, and cheese), and *soupe à l'ail* (garlic soup). Look also for *riz Camarguaise* (rice from the Camargue) and *taureau* (bull meat). Banon (wrapped in chestnut leaves) and Picodon (nutty taste) are the native cheeses. Provence also produces some of France's great wines at relatively reasonable prices. Look for Gigondas, Sablet, Côte du Rhône, and Côte de Provence. If you like rosé, try the Tavel. This is the place to splurge for a bottle of Châteauneuf-du-Pape.

ARLES

By helping Julius Caesar defeat Marseille, Arles earned the imperial nod and was made an important port city. With the first bridge over the Rhône, Arles was a key stop on the Roman road from Italy to Spain, the Via Domitia. After reigning as a political center of the early Christian church (the seat of an archbishop for centuries) and thriving as a trading city on and off until the 18th century, Arles all but disappeared from the map. Van Gogh settled here a hundred years ago but left only memories. American bombers destroyed much of Arles in World War II, but today Arles thrives again. Today this compact city is alive with great Roman ruins, some fine early-Christian art, an eclectic assortment of museums, made-for-ice-cream pedestrian zones, squares that play hide-and-seek with visitors, and too many cars. Arles is a fine springboard for Provence explorations.

Tourist Information: Arles has two TIs. The one at the train station is relaxed and easy by car (Monday–Saturday 9:00–13:00 and 14:00–18:00, closed Sunday). The main TI on esplanade Charles de Gaulle is a high-powered mega-information site (Monday–Saturday 9:00–19:00, Sunday 9:00–13:00 April 1–September 30; closed 12:00–14:00 and at 18:00 off-season; tel. 04 90 18 41 20). Pick up the free *Arles et Vincent Van Gogh* and the *Guide Touristique 1999*, and ask about bullfights and bus excursions to regional sights.

Supermarket: Place Lamartine has a big handy Monoprix

supermarket/department store (Monday–Saturday 8:30–19:25, closed Sunday).

Banks: Several banks change money on place de la République, across from St. Trophime.

Laundry: A Laundromat is at 12 rue Portagnel (Monday–Saturday 8:00–12:00 and 14:00–19:00). Another, nearby on 6 rue Cavalarie (near place Voltaire, daily 7:00–21:00, later once you're in), has a confusing central command panel: 20F for wash (push machine number on top row), 10F for 25 minutes of dryer (push dryer number on third row five times slowly), 2F for flakes (button #11). Dine at the recommended La Giraudiere restaurant, one block away, while you clean.

Arrival in Arles

By Train and Bus: Both stations sit side by side on the river, a 10-minute walk from the city center. To reach the old town, walk to the river and turn left.

By Car: Follow signs to *centre-ville*, then be on the lookout for signs to the *gare SNCF* (the train station; go there for the TI). You'll come to a huge roundabout (place Lamartine) with a Monoprix department store to the right. There is parking on the left, along the base of the wall. Pay attention to no-parking signs on Wednesday and Saturday until 13:00—they mean it. Theft is a problem; park at your hotel if possible. Take everything out of your car for safety. From place Lamartine, walk into the city through the two stumpy towers.

Getting Around Arles

Arles faces the Mediterranean more than Paris. Its spaghetti streetplan disorients the first-time visitor. Landmarks hide in the medieval tangle of narrow, winding streets. Everything is deceptively close. While Arles sits on the Rhône, it completely ignores the river. The elevated riverside walk does provide a direct route to the excellent ancient history museum and an easy return to the station. Hotels have free city maps, but Arles works best if you simply follow the numerous street-corner signs pointing you toward the sights and hotels of the town center. Racing cars seem to enjoy Arles' medieval lanes, turning sidewalks into tightropes and pedestrians into leaping targets.

By Minibus: The free "Starlette" shuttle minibus, which circles the town's major sights twice an hour, is worthwhile only to get to or from the distant ancient history museum, though I prefer the 20-minute walk along the river (just wave at the driver and hop in; Monday–Saturday 7:30–19:30, never on Sunday).

By Bike and Car: The Peugeot store rents bikes (15 rue du Pont, tel. 04 90 96 03 77) as does the newsstand next to the main TI (tel. 04 90 96 44 20). You can rent cars at Avis (at the train station, tel. 04 90 96 82 42) and Europcar (downtown at 15 boulevard Victor Hugo, tel. 04 90 93 23 24).

By Taxi: Arles' taxis charge a minimum flat 50F fee. Nothing in town is worth a taxi ride (figure 100F to Les Baux).

Sights—Arles

Arles' *Global Billet* covers all the sights (55F, sold at each sight). Otherwise, it's 15F per sight and museum (35F for the ancient history museum). While any sight is worth a few minutes of your time, many aren't worth the individual admission. For the small price of a *Global Billet*, the city is yours. (All sights except the Arlatan folk museum are open June 1–September 15 9:00–19:00; April, May, and September 16–30 9:00–12:30 and 14:00–19:00; otherwise 10:00–12:30 and 14:00–17:30; closed one hour earlier in winter.) See the Musée Arlatan listing, below, for its hours. The excellent and free *Arles et Vincent Van Gogh* brochure (available at the TI) takes you on several interesting walks through Arles using pavement markers as guides; by far the most interesting walk follows the footsteps of Vincent van Gogh.

▲▲**Place du Forum**—This café-crammed square, while always lively, is best at night. Named for the Roman Forum that stood here, only two columns from a second-century temple survive. They are incorporated into the wall of the Hotel Nord Pinus. (After a few drinks at the Café van Gogh, the corner of that hotel actually starts to look phallic.) Van Gogh hung out here under these same plane trees. In fact, his *Starry Starry Night* was painted from this square. The bistros on the square, while no place for a fine dinner, put together a good salad, and when you sprinkle in the ambience, that's 45F well spent. The guy on the pedestal is Frederic Mistral; in 1904 he received the Nobel Prize for literature. He used his prize money to preserve and display the folk identity of Provence at a time when France was rapidly centralizing. (He founded the Arlatan museum—see below.)

▲▲**Wednesday and Saturday Markets**—On these days until around noon, Arles' ring road (boulevard Emile Combes on Wednesday, boulevard Lices on Saturday) erupts into an outdoor market of fish, flowers, produce, and you-name-it. Join in, buy flowers, try the olives, sample some wine, and slap a pickpocket. On the first Wednesday of the month it's a grand flea market.

▲▲▲**Ancient History Museum (Musée de L'Arles Antique)**— The sights of Roman Arles make maximum sense if you start your visit in this superb, air-conditioned museum. Models and original sculpture (with the help of the free English handout) re-create the Roman city of Arles, making workaday life and culture easier to imagine. Notice what a radical improvement the Roman buildings were over the simple mud-brick homes of pre-Roman peoples. Models of Arles' arena even illustrate the movable stadium cover,

Arles

- ❶ HÔTEL RÉGENCE + LAUNDROMAT
- ❷ HÔTEL MUSÉE
- ❸ HÔTEL CALENDAL
- ❹ HÔTEL D'ARLATAN
- ❺ HÔTEL TERMINUS ET VAN GOGH
- ❻ HÔTEL ST. TROPHIME
- ❼ HÔTEL VOLTAIRE
- ❽ HÔTEL LAMARTINE
- ❾ HÔTEL LA GALLIA
- ❿ HÔTEL DE L'AMPHITHEATRE

good for shade and rain. While virtually nothing is left of Arles' chariot racecourse, the model shows how it must have rivaled Rome's Circus Maximus. Jewelry, fine metal and glass artifacts, and fine mosaic floors make it clear that Roman Arles was a city of art and culture. The finale is an impressive row of pagan and early

Christian sarcophagi (second to fifth centuries). In the early days of the Church, Jesus was often portrayed beardless and as the good shepherd—with a lamb over his shoulder.

Built at the site of the chariot racecourse, this museum is a 20-minute walk from Arles along the river. Turn left at the river and follow it to the big modern building just past the new bridge—or ride the free Starlette shuttle bus. (35F, daily 9:00–19:00 April–September, otherwise Wednesday–Monday 10:00–18:00 and closed Tuesday, tel. 04 90 18 88 88.)

▲▲**Roman Arena (Amphithéâtre)**—Nearly 2,000 years ago, gladiators fought wild animals here to the delight of 20,000 screaming fans—cruel. Today matadors fight wild bulls to the delight of local fans—still cruel. While the ancient third row of arches is long gone, three towers survive from medieval times, when the arena was used as a fortress. In the 1800s it corralled 200 humble homes and functioned as a town within the town. Today modern gladiators fight bulls, and if you don't mind the gore, it's an exciting show. Climb the tower. Walk through the inner corridors of this 440-by-350-foot oval and notice the similarity to 20th-century stadium floor plans.

▲▲**Bullfights (Courses Camarguaise)**—Occupy the same seats fans have been sitting in for 1,900 years, and take in one of Arles' most memorable treats—a bullfight *à la Provençale*. Three classes of bullfights take place here. The *course protection* is for aspiring matadors; it's a daring dodge-bull game of scraping hair off the angry bull's nose for prize money offered by local businesses (no blood). The *trophée de l'avenir* is the next class, with amateur matadors. The *trophée des as excellence* is the real thing *à la* Spain: outfits, swords, spikes, and the whole gory shebang (tickets 30–50F; Saturday, Sunday, and holidays April–early October; skip the "rodeo" spectacle; tel. 04 90 96 03 70 or ask at TI). There are nearby village bullfights in small wooden bullrings nearly every weekend (TI has schedule).

Classical Theater (Théâtre Antique)—Precious little survives from this Roman theater, which served as a handy town quarry throughout the Middle Ages. Two lonely Corinthian columns look from the stage out over the audience. The 10,000 mostly modern seats are still used for local concerts and festivals. Take a stroll backstage through broken bits of Rome.

▲▲**St. Trophime Cloisters and Church**—This church, named after a third-century bishop of Arles, sports the finest Romanesque west portal (main doorway) I've seen anywhere.

But first enjoy the place de la République. Sit on the steps opposite the church. The Egyptian obelisk used to be the centerpiece of Arles' Roman Circus. Watch the peasants—pilgrims, locals, buskers—nothing new about this scene. Like a Roman triumphal arch, the church trumpets the promise of Judgment Day. The tympanum is filled with Christian symbolism. Christ sits in majesty surrounded by symbols of the four evangelists (Matthew—the winged man, Mark—the winged lion, Luke—the ox, and John—the eagle). The 12 apostles are lined up below Jesus. Move up closer. This is it. Some are saved and others aren't. Notice the condemned—a chain gang on the right bunny-hopping over the fires of hell. For them the tune trumpeted by the three angels on the very top isn't a happy one. Ride the exquisite detail back to a simpler age. In an illiterate medieval world long before the vivid images of our Technicolor age, this message was a neon billboard over this town's everything square. A chart just inside the church (on the right) helps explain the carvings. On the right side of the nave, a fourth-century early-Christian sarcophagus is used as an altar.

The adjacent cloisters are the best in Provence (15F, enter from the square, 20 meters to the right of the church). Enjoy the sculpted capitals of the rounded Romanesque columns (12th century) and the pointed Gothic columns (14th century). The second floor offers only a view of the cloisters from above.

Musée Réattu—Highlights of this mildly interesting museum are a fun collection of 70 Picasso drawings (some two-sided, and all done in a flurry of creativity) and a room of Henri Rousseau's Camargue watercolors.

▲**Musée Arlatan**—This cluttered folklore museum, given to Arles by Monsieur Mistral, is filled with interesting odds and ends of Provence life. The employees wear the native costumes. It's like a failed turn-of-the-century garage sale: You'll find shoes, hats, wigs, old photos, bread cupboards, and the beetle-dragon monster. If you're into folklore, this museum is for you (daily 9:00–12:00 and 14:00–19:00 April–September, otherwise closes at 17:00).

Fondation Van Gogh—A two-star sight for his fans, this small gallery features works by several well-known contemporary artists who pay homage to Vincent through their thought-provoking interpretations of his art (30F, daily 10:00–19:00 April 1–September 30, otherwise 10:00–12:30 and 14:00–17:00; facing the Roman arena at #24).

Sleeping in Arles
(5.5F = about $1, zip code: 13200)
Sleep Code: **S** = Single, **D** = Double/Twin, **T** = Triple, **Q** = Quad, **b** = bathroom, **t** = toilet only, **s** = shower only, **CC** = Credit Card (Visa, MasterCard, Amex), **SE** = Speaks English, **NSE** = No English, * = French hotel rating system (0–4 stars).

Hôtel Régence** sits right on the river with immaculate and comfortable rooms, good beds, and easy access to the train station and safe parking. Helpful and gentle Sylvie speaks English (one Ds-150–180F, Db-200–280F, Tb-250–335F, Qb-330F; choose river view or quiet, air-conditioned courtyard rooms; CC:VM, 5 rue

Marius Jouveau—from place Lamartine turn right immediately after passing through the towers; tel. 04 90 96 39 85, fax 04 90 96 67 64).

Hotel de l'Amphitheatre** is small, friendly, and *très* cozy with thoughtfully decorated and air-conditioned rooms and a pleasant atrium breakfast room. It's located one block from the arena on a relatively quiet street (Db-290–350F, Tb-420F, 25F garage, CC:VMA, 5 rue Diderot, tel. 04 90 96 10 30, fax 04 90 93 98 69, SE).

Hôtel du Musée** is a quiet, delightful manor house hideaway with air-conditioned rooms and a terrific courtyard terrace. Its friendly owners, M. and Mme. Dubreuil, speak some English (Sb-220F, Db-280–320F, Tb-350–400F, Qb-450F, parking-40F, mostly air-conditioned rooms, CC:VMA, 11 rue de la Grande Prieure, follow signs to Musée Réattu, tel. 04 90 93 88 88, fax 04 90 49 98 15).

Hôtel Calendal** is *très Provençale*, with a tranquil outdoor garden, smartly decorated rooms, and three-star ambience for the price of two (Db-260–460F, Tb-380–470F, Qb-490F, garage-50F, air-conditioned rooms with strong beds and modern bathrooms, CC:VMA, located above the arena at 22 place Pomme, tel. 04 90 96 11 89, fax 04 90 96 05 84, SE).

Hôtel d'Arlatan***, one of France's more affordable classy hotels, comes with a beautiful lobby, courtyard terrace, and air-conditioned, antique-filled rooms. In the lobby of this 15th-century building, a glass floor looks down into Roman ruins (Db-460–800F, Db/suites-1,000–1,400F, garage-70F, elevator, very central, CC:VMA, a block off the place du Forum at 26 rue du Sauvage, tel. 04 90 93 56 66, fax 04 90 49 68 45, e-mail: info@hotel-arlatan.fr, SE).

Hotel Terminus et Van Gogh* has bright, cheery rooms facing a busy square at the gate of the old town a block from the train station. English-speaking Joelle proudly posts photos and pictures showing that her building is in the painting of van Gogh's house, which was bombed in WWII (D-145F with no shower available, Ds-180F, Db-220F, CC:VM, 5 place Lamartine, tel. & fax 04 90 96 12 32).

Hotel St. Trophime** is another fine, very central place with a grand entry, large rooms, and helpful owners (Sb-210F, Db-290–320F, CC:VM, 16 rue de la Calade, near the place de la Republique, tel. 04 90 96 88 38, fax 04 90 96 92 19).

Starving artists can afford these two clean but spartan places: **Hôtel Voltaire*** rents 12 dumpy rooms with great balconies overlooking a caffeine-stained square a block below the arena (D-120–130F, Ds-140F, add 40F per person for three or four, CC:VM, 1 place Voltaire, tel. 04 90 96 13 58). **Hôtel La Gallia** is another sleepable cheapie (Ds-125–145F, above a friendly café, 22 rue de l'Hôtel de Ville, tel. 04 90 96 00 63).

Sleeping near Arles in Fontvielle

Many drivers prefer setting up in the peaceful village of Fontvielle, just 10 minutes from Arles and Les Baux. For weekly rentals at a farmhouse just outside Arles, contact English-speaking Sylvie at the **Domaine de la Foret**. She offers several comfortable two-bedroom apartments with a family-friendly feel (nightly-450F, weekly in summer-2,500F, weekly off-season-2,000F, D-82 route de L'Agueduc, 13990 Fontvielle, tel. 04 90 54 70 25, fax 04 90 54 60 50).

Eating in Arles

On place du Forum the **Le Bistro Arlesien**, **Le Pub** (good 45F *salade niçoise*), and **L'Estaminet** serve basic food with great atmosphere. **L'Olivier** offers exquisite *Provençale* cuisine (150F *menu*, near the Hotel du Musee, 1 bis rue Reattu, reserve ahead, tel. 04 90 49 64 88). For fine, reasonably priced regional cooking, head to the relaxed and friendly **La Giraudiere** (closed Tuesday, 85F *menu*, 55 rue Condorcet on place Voltaire, tel. 04 90 93 27 52). Vegetarians love **La Vitamine**'s salads and pastas (closed weekends, just below place du Forum on 16 rue Dr. Fanton, tel. 04 90 93 77 36). Almost next door, **La Paillotte** specializes in tradional *Provençale* cuisine (90F *menu*, 28 rue Dr. Fanton). **Le Criquet** is cheap, fun, and good, one block from Hôtel Calendal at 12 Porte de Laure.

Transportation Connections—Arles

By bus to: Les Baux (4/day, 30 min; departs Arles' bus station and #16 boulevard Clemenceau in downtown Arles). Service is reduced November through March and on Sunday and holidays (tel. 04 90 49 38 01).

By train to: Paris (two direct TGVs, 4.5 hrs; otherwise, transfer in Avignon, 8/day, 5.5 hrs), **Avignon** (8/day, 20 min, check for afternoon gaps), **Carcassonne** (8/day, 3 hrs, usually with painless transfer in Narbonne), **Beaune** (3/day, 5 hrs, transfer in Lyon), **Nice** (8/day, 3 hrs, likely transfer in Marseille), **Barcelona** (3/day, 7 hrs, at least one transfer), **Italy** (3/day, via Marseille and Nice; from Arles it's 5 hrs to Ventimiglia on the border, 9 hrs to the Cinque Terre, 9 hrs to Milan, 11 hrs to Florence, 13 hrs to Venice or Rome). Train info: tel. 04 90 96 43 94.

AVIGNON

Famous for its nursery rhyme, medieval bridge, and brooding Palace of the Popes, contemporary Avignon bustles and prospers behind its walls. During the 68 years (1309–1377) that Avignon played Franco Vaticano, it grew from an irrelevant speck on the map to the thriving city it still is. Today this city combines a young, hip student population with a white-collar, sophisticated city feel. Street mimes play to crowds enjoying Avignon's slick cafés and chic boutiques. If you're here any time in July, save evening time for Avignon's rollicking theater festival and reserve your hotel early. The streets throng with jugglers, skits, and singing, as visitors from around the world converge on Avignon.

The cours Jean Jaurés (which turns into the rue de la République) leads from the train station to place de l'Horloge and the Palace of the Popes, forming Avignon's spine. Climb to the parc de Rochers des Doms for a fine view, enjoy the people scene on place de l'Horloge, and meander the back streets. Avignon's shopping district fills the pedestrian streets where rue de la République meets the place de l'Horloge. Walk across the Pont Daladier (bridge) for a great view back on Avignon and the Rhône River.

Tourist Information: The main TI is between the train station and the old town at 41 cours Jean Juarés (Monday–Friday 9:00–18:00, Saturday 9:00–12:00 and 14:00–17:00, tel. 04 90 82 65 11, e-mail: information@avignon.fr), while a smaller branch is just inside the city wall at the entrance to Pont St. Bénezet (same hours as main TI). They have regional bus and train schedules and information on Isle sur la Sorgue and the wine villages north of Avignon and the Luberon.

Arrival in Avignon

By Train: In front of the bus or train station, the main drag—the cours Jean Juarés that becomes rue de la République—leads into the old city center (20-minute walk, TI on right in a few blocks).

By Car: Drivers enter Avignon following *centre-ville* signs. Park along the wall close to the Pont St. Bénezet (ruined old bridge) and use that TI. Hotels have advice for smart overnight parking.

Sights—Avignon

▲**Palace of the Popes (Palais des Papes)**—In 1309 a French pope was elected (Pope Clement V). At the urging of the French king, His Holiness decided he'd had enough of unholy Italy. So he loaded up his carts and moved out of the chaos north to Avignon for a steady rule under a friendly, supportive king. The Catholic Church literally bought Avignon, then a two-bit town, and popes resided here until 1403. From 1378 on, there were twin popes, one in Rome and one in Avignon, causing a split in the Catholic Church that wasn't fully resolved until 1417.

The pope's palace is two distinct buildings, one old and one older. Along with lots of big, barren rooms, you'll see brilliant frescoes, enormous tapestries, and remarkable floor tiles. While scheduling your day around the English tour times (several per day) can be a hassle, guided tours can be worthwhile. (49F, includes a guided tour or a self-guided Walkman tour, occasional supplements for special exhibits, daily 9:00–19:00 April–November

1, until 20:00 summer, off-season 9:00–12:45 and 14:00–18:00, ticket office closes one hour earlier, tours in English twice daily March–October, call 04 90 27 50 74 to confirm.)

▲**Musée du Petit Palais**—This palace superbly displays collections of 14th- and 15th-century Italian painting and sculpture. Since the Catholic Church was the patron of the arts in those days, all 350 paintings deal with Christian themes. Visiting this museum before going to the Palace of the Popes gives you a sense of art and life during the Avignon papacy. Notice the improvement in perspective in the later paintings (30F, Wednesday–Monday 9:30–18:00 in summer, otherwise 9:30–12:00 and 14:00–18:00, closed Tuesday).

▲**Parc de Rochers des Doms and Pont St. Bénezet**—Hike above the Palace of the Popes for a panoramic view over Avignon and the Rhône valley. At the far end drop down a few steps for a good view of the Pont St. Bénezet. This is the famous "sur le Pont d'Avignon," whose construction and location were inspired by a shepherd's religious vision. Imagine a 22-arch, 3,000-foot-long bridge extending across two rivers to that lonely Tower of Philippe the Fair (the bridge's former tollgate on the distant side). The island the bridge spanned is now filled with campgrounds. You can pay 15F to walk along a section of the ramparts and do your own jig on the bridge (good view), but it's best appreciated from where you are. The castle on the right, the St. André Fortress, was once another island in the Rhône. Cross Daladier Bridge for the best view of the old bridge and Avignon's skyline.

Sleeping in Avignon
(5.5F = about $1, zip code: 84000)

The cozy and almost elegant **Hôtel Blauvac**** is in the pedestrian zone on 11 rue de La Bancasse (Db-335–410F, Tb/Qb-400–500F, CC:VMA, one block off rue de la République, tel. 04 90 86 34 11, fax 04 90 86 27 41). Right on the loud rue de la République at #17, the bright and cheery **Hotel Danelli**** offers modern and comfortable rooms in shiny surroundings at Parisian prices (Db-425F, Tb-460F, CC:VM, tel. 04 90 86 46 82, fax 04 90 27 09 24). **Hotel Medieval**** is good, central, and reasonable (Db-240–340F, 15 rue Petite Saunerie, tel. 04 90 86 11 06, fax 04 90 82 08 64). The clean, compact, and friendly **Hôtel Mignon*** is simpler, but a good value (Ss-150F, Db-220F, Tb-250F, 12 rue Joseph Vernet, tel. 04 90 82 17 30, fax 04 90 85 78 46). **Hôtel Splendid*** rents firm beds near the station, on the small park near the TI (Ss-140–190F, Ds-170–220F, 17 rue Agricol Perdiguier, tel. 04 90 86 14 46, fax 04 90 85 38 55). Across the street at #17, **Hotel du Parc*** is another good value (Ds-140–170F, Db-180F, tel. 04 90 82 71 55, fax 04 90 85 64 86). For reliable, ultramodern comfort and a great location, try one of two **Hotel Mercures***** (Db-

400–650F). One is just inside the walls near the Pont St. Bénezet
(Quartier de la Balance, tel. 04 90 85 91 23, fax 04 90 85 32 40);
the other is near the Palace of the Popes (Cité des Papes, 1 rue
Jean Vilar, tel. 04 90 86 22 45, fax 04 90 27 39 21).

Transportation Connections—Avignon
By train to: Arles (8/day, 20 min), **Orange** (hrly, 15 min), **Nîmes**
(hrly, 21 min), **Nice** (10/day, 4 hrs; a few direct, but most require
transfer in Marseille), **Carcassonne** (10/day, 3 hrs, possible transfer in Narbonne), **Paris**' Gare de Lyon (10 TGVs/day, 4 hrs),
Barcelona (2/day, 5 hrs, possible transfer in Narbonne; direct
night train is convenient).

    Bus service to Pont du Gard and **Uzès** (3/day, 1 hr) can
leave you stranded for hours. Consider visiting the Pont du Gard,
then continuing on to Uzès or Nîmes (both merit exploration) and
returning to Avignon from there (trains run hourly from Nîmes to
Avignon). Make sure you're waiting for the bus on the right side
of the road at the Pont du Gard (ask at the small inn: "Nîmes?
Uzès? Avignon? *Par ici*?"). The Avignon TI has all schedules. Service is reduced or nonexistent on Sunday and holidays. The bus
station (tel. 04 90 82 07 35) is adjacent to the train station (tel. 08
36 35 35 35).

Sights—Provence
▲▲▲**Les Baux**—This rock-top ghost town is worth visiting for
the lunar landscape alone. In summer, arrive by 9:00 or after 17:00
to avoid the crowds. A 12th-century regional powerhouse with
6,000 fierce residents, Les Baux was razed in 1632 by a paranoid
Louis XIII, afraid of these trouble-making upstarts. What remains
are a reconstructed "live city" of tourist shops and snack stands,
and the "dead city" ruins carved into, out of, and on top of a 600-
foot-high rock. Spend most of your time in the dead city—it's
most dramatic and enjoyable in the morning or early-evening
light. Don't miss the slide show on van Gogh, Gaugin, and
Cézanne in the small chapel near the entry. Spend some time in
the small museum as you enter (good exhibits) and pick up the
English explanations before exploring the dead city. In the tourist-
trampled live city, you'll find artsy shops, several interesting
Renaissance homes, and a fine exhibit of paintings by Yves Brayer
(20F), who spent his final years here. (Entrance to the dead city
costs 35F; fee includes entry to all the town's sights; 9:00–19:00
Easter–October, until 20:00 in summer, otherwise 9:30–17:00;
pick up the excellent brochure, *A Sense of Place*, at the TI, tel. 04
90 54 34 39.) To best experience the bauxite rock quarries and
enjoy a great view of Les Baux, drive or hike one kilometer up D-
27 and sample wines with atmosphere at the **Caves de Sarragnan**
(tel. 04 90 54 33 58).

If tempted to spend the night, try the enchanting **Hotel Reine Jeanne****, 50 yards on your right after the main entry (Db-270–330F, great family suite-520F, ask for the *chambres avec terasse*, *menus* from 110F, CC:VM, 13520 Les Baux, tel. 04 90 54 32 06, fax 04 90 54 32 33). **Le Mas de L'Esparou** is a three-star *chambre d'hôte* with five rooms and a swimming pool one mile from Les Baux (Db-380F, route de St. Rémy de Provence, 13520 Les Baux, tel. 04 90 54 41 32).

Four daily buses serve Les Baux from Arles' train station, and two daily buses (summers only) leave from Avignon. Les Baux is 15 kilometers northeast of Arles, just past Fontvielle.

St. Rémy—This *très Provençale* town is a scenic ride just over the hill from Les Baux. Here you'll find the crumbled ruins of **Glanum**, a once thriving Roman city located at the crossroads of two ancient trade routes between Italy and Spain, and the mental ward where Vincent van Gogh was sent after cutting off his ear. Glanum is just outside St. Rémy, on the road to Les Baux (D-5). Walk to the gate and peek in to get a feel for its scale. The ruins are worth the effort if you have the time and haven't been to Pompeii or Ephesus (33F, daily 9:00–12:00 and 14:00–19:00 April–September, otherwise 9:30–12:00 and 14:00–17:00). Across the street, opposite the entrance, is a Roman arch and tower. The arch marked the entry into Glanum. The tower is a memorial to the grandsons of Emperor Augustus, located there to remind folks of them when entering or leaving Glanum.

Across the street from Glanum is the still-functioning mental hospital that housed van Gogh (Clinique St. Paul). Wander into the small chapel and intimate cloisters. Vincent's favorite walks outside the hospital are clearly signposted. If St. Rémy charms you into a longer visit, sleep just outside town at the tranquil **Canto Cigalo** (Db-280–340F, chemin Canto Cigalo, tel. 04 90 92 14 28, fax 04 90 92 24 48). Wednesday is market day in St. Rémy.

▲▲▲**Pont du Gard**—One of Europe's great treats, this remarkably well-preserved Roman aqueduct was built before the time of Christ. It was the missing link of a 35-mile canal that, by dropping one foot for every 300, supplied 44 million gallons of water to Nîmes daily. While the top is now closed to daredevils, just walking under it is a marvel. Study it up close—there's no mortar, just expertly cut stones. Signs direct you to "panaromas" above the bridge on either side. The best view of the aqueduct is from the cool of the river below, floating flat on your back—bring a swimsuit and sandals for the rocks (always open and free). Consider renting a canoe from Collas to Remoulins (two-hour trip, 175F per two-person canoe; shuttle included to bus stop, car park, or Remoulins; Collas Canoes, tel. 04 66 22 85 54). Buses run from Nîmes, Uzès, or Avignon. Combine Uzès and the Pont du Gard for an ideal day excursion from Avignon. By car, the Pont du Gard is an easy 30-minute drive due west of Avignon (follow signs to Nîmes) and 45 minutes northwest of Arles (via Tarascon). Park on the *rive gauche* side (you'll see signs).

Uzès—An intriguing, less-trampled town near the Pont du Gard, Uzès is best seen slowly on foot, with a long coffee break in its mellow main square, the place aux Herbes (not so mellow during the colorful Sunday morning market). Check out the Tour Fenestrelle and the Duché de Uzès. Uzès is a short hop west (by bus) of the Pont du Gard and is well-served from Nîmes (9/day) and Avignon (3/day).

The Camargue—This is one of the few truly "wild areas" of France, where pink flamingos, wild bulls, and the famous white horses wander freely amid rice fields and lagoons. Skip it. The Camargue's biggest town is Aigue Mortes. That means "dead town," and it should stay that way.

▲▲**Orange**—This most northern town in Provence is notable for its Roman arch and theater. Its 60-foot-tall Roman arch (from 25 B.C.) shows off Julius Caesar's defeat of the Gauls in 49 B.C. Its best-preserved Roman theater in existence still seats 10,000. Of particular interest is its 120-foot-high stage wall, the likes of which you'll see nowhere else (34F, daily 9:00–18:30 April–early October, 9:00–12:00 and 13:30–17:00 in winter; ticket includes entrance to the city museum across the street, which has more Roman art; Orange TI tel. 04 90 34 70 88). Trains run hourly between Avignon and Orange (15 min ride; bus #2 takes you the mile from the Orange station to the old town center).

RHINE AND MOSEL VALLEYS

These valleys are storybook Germany, a fairy-tale world of Rhine legends and robber-baron castles. Cruise the most castle-studded stretch of the romantic Rhine as you listen for the song of the treacherous Lorcley. For hands-on castle thrills, climb through the Rhineland's greatest castle, Rheinfels, above the town of St. Goar. Then, for a sleepy and laid-back alternative, mosey through the neighboring Mosel Valley.

In the north you'll find the powerhouse city of Köln (Cologne) with Germany's greatest Gothic cathedral, best collection of Roman artifacts, a world-class art museum, and a good dose of German urban playfulness. Bustling Köln merits a visit, but spend your nights in a castle-crowned village. On the Rhine, stay in St. Goar or Bacharach. On the Mosel, choose Zell.

Planning Your Time

The Rhineland does not take much time. The blitziest tour is an hour at the Köln cathedral and an hour looking at the castles from your train window. For a better look, however, cruise in, tour a castle or two, sleep in a genuine medieval town, and take the train out. With limited time, cruise less and be sure to get into a castle.

Ideally, spend two nights here, sleep in Bacharach, cruise the best hour of the river (from Bacharach to St. Goar), and tour the Rheinfels Castle. Those with more time can bike the river-side bike path. With two days and a car, visit the Rhine and the Mosel. With two days by train, see the Rhine and Köln. With three days, do all three, and with four days include a sleepy night in the Mosel River Valley.

Rhine and Mosel Valleys

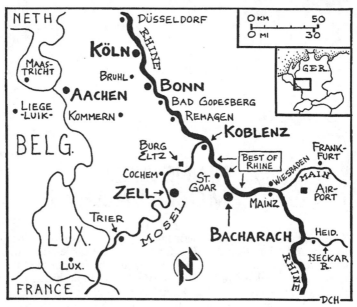

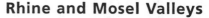

THE RHINE

Ever since Roman times, when this was the Empire's northern boundary, the Rhine has been one of the world's busiest shipping rivers. You'll see a steady flow of barges with 1,000- to 2,000-ton loads. Tourist-packed buses, hot train tracks, and highways line both banks.

Many of the castles were "robber-baron" castles, put there by petty rulers (there were 300 independent little countries in medieval Germany) to levy tolls on passing river traffic. A robber-baron would put his castle on, or even in, the river. Then, often with the help of chains and a tower on the opposite bank, he'd stop each ship and get his toll. There were 10 customs stops between Mainz and Koblenz alone (no wonder merchants were early proponents of the creation of larger nation-states).

Some castles were built to control and protect settlements, and others were the residences of kings. As times changed, so did the lifestyles of the rich and feudal. Many castles were abandoned for more comfortable mansions in the towns.

Most Rhine castles date from the 11th, 12th, and 13th centuries. When the pope successfully asserted his power over the German emperor in 1076, local princes ran wild over the rule of their emperor. The castles saw military action in the 1300s and

1400s, as emperors began reasserting their control over Germany's many silly kingdoms.

The castles were also involved in the Reformation wars, in which Europe's Catholic and "protesting" dynasties fought it out using a fragmented Germany as their battleground. The Thirty Years' War (1618–1648) devastated Germany. The outcome: each ruler got the freedom to decide if his people would be Catholic or Protestant, and one-third of Germany was dead. Production of Gummi Bears ceased entirely.

The French—who feared a strong Germany and felt the Rhine was the logical border between them and Germany—destroyed most of the castles prophylactically (Louis XIV in the 1680s, the revolutionary army in the 1790s, and Napoleon in 1806). They were often rebuilt in neo-Gothic style in the Romantic Age—the late 1800s—and today are enjoyed as restaurants, hotels, hostels, and museums. Check out the Rhine Web site at www.loreleytal.com.

Getting Around the Rhine

While the Rhine flows from Switzerland to Holland, the stretch from Mainz to Koblenz hoards all the touristic charm. Studded with the crenelated cream of Germany's castles, it bustles with boats, trains, and highway traffic. Have fun exploring with a mix of big steamers, tiny ferries, bikes, and trains.

By Boat: While many travelers do the whole trip by boat, the most scenic hour is from St. Goar to Bacharach. Sit on the top deck with your handy Rhine map-guide (or the kilometer-keyed tour in this chapter and enjoy the parade of castles, towns, boats, and vineyards.

There are several boat companies, but most travelers sail on the bigger, more expensive, and romantic Köln–Düsseldorf (K-D) line (free with Eurail, otherwise about 15 DM for the first hour, then progressively cheaper per hour, the recommended Bacharach–St. Goar trip costs 15 DM one-way, 18 DM round-trip, tel. 06741/1634 in St. Goar). Boats run daily in both directions from April through October, with fewer boats off-season. Complete, up-to-date schedules are posted in any station, Rhineland hotel, TI, or current Thomas Cook Timetable. Purchase tickets at the dock five minutes before departure. The boat is never full. (Confirm times at your hotel the night before.)

The smaller Bingen-Rüdesheimer line is 25 percent cheaper than K-D (Eurail not valid, buy tickets on the boat, tel. 06721/14140), with three two-hour round-trip St. Goar–Bacharach trips daily in summer (12 DM one-way, 16 DM round-trip; departing St. Goar at 11:00, 14:10, and 16:10; departing Bacharach at 10:10, 12:30, and 15:00).

Drivers have these options: (1) skip the boat; (2) take a

Best of the Rhine

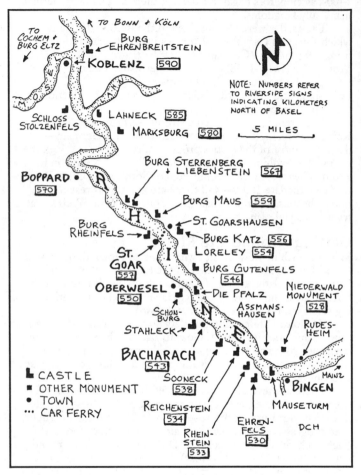

TO BONN + KÖLN

TO COCHEM + BURG ELTZ

BURG EHRENBREITSTEIN

◄ KOBLENZ 590

NOTE: NUMBERS REFER TO RIVERSIDE SIGNS INDICATING KILOMETERS NORTH OF BASEL

5 MILES

SCHLOSS STOLZENFELS

■ LAHNECK 585

■ MARKSBURG 580

BURG STERRENBERG + LIEBENSTEIN 567

BOPPARD ●
570

BURG MAUS 559

BURG RHEINFELS

ST. GOARSHAUSEN

BURG KATZ 556

LORELEY 554

ST. GOAR 557

BURG GUTENFELS 546

OBERWESEL 550

DIE PFALZ

NIEDERWALD MONUMENT 528

SCHÖNBURG

ASSMANS-HAUSEN

STAHLECK ►

RÜDES-HEIM

BACHARACH 543

MAINZ

SOONECK 538

● BINGEN

REICHENSTEIN 534

MAUSETURM

RHEIN-STEIN 533

EHREN-FELS 530

DCH

■ CASTLE
■ OTHER MONUMENT
● TOWN
··· CAR FERRY

round-trip cruise from St. Goar or Bacharach; (3) draw pretzels and let the loser drive, prepare the picnic, and meet the boat; (4) rent a bike, bring it on the boat for free, and bike back; or (5) take the boat one way and return by train.

By Train: Hourly milk-run trains down the Rhine hit every town: St. Goar–Bacharach, 12 min; Bacharach–Mainz, 60 min; Mainz–Frankfurt, 45 min. (Some train schedules list St. Goar but not Bacharach as a stop, but any schedule listing St. Goar also stops at Bacharach. Tiny stations are unmanned—buy tickets on the train.)

1999 Rhine Cruise Schedule

Koblenz	Boppard	St. Goar	Bacharach
—	9:00	10:15	11:35
9:00	10:50	12:05	13:15
11:00	12:50	14:05	15:15
14:00	15:50	17:05	18:15
11:05	11:30	11:50	12:10*
13:00	11:40	10:45	10:00
14:20	13:10	12:15	11:30
—	14:00	13:15	12:30
18:00	16:40	15:45	15:00
20:00	18:50	18:00	17:20

** Hydrofoil, Koblenz-Bacharach, 30 DM with Eurail,
70 DM without.*
*Note: Schedule applies May through September and mostly
April and October; no boats run November through March.*

By Bike: In Bacharach try Pension Lettie (15 DM/day, 10
DM/4 hrs, no deposit for guests, otherwise passport or credit-card
imprint, tel. 06743/2115), Hotel Gelberhof (20 DM/day for 10-
speeds, 25 DM for "trekking" bikes, 5 DM for child's seat, tel.
06743/910-100, ring bell when closed), or Hotel Hillen (15 DM/
day, 10 DM/half-day, cheaper for guests, 20 bikes). In St. Goar you
can rent bikes at the Golf Pavilion along the Rhine (13 DM/day, 10
DM/4 hrs, 50 DM or passport as deposit, April–October 10:00–
21:00, tel. 06741/1360). The best riverside bike path is from Bacharach to Bingen. The path is also good from St. Goar to Bacharach,
but it's closer to the highway. Consider sailing to Bingen and biking
back, visiting Rheinstein Castle (you're on your own to wander the
well-furnished castle) and Reichenstein Castle (admittance with
groups), and maybe even taking a ferry across the river to Kaub
(where a tiny boat shuttles sightseers to the better-from-a-distance
castle on the island). While there are no bridges between Koblenz
and Mainz, several small ferries do their job constantly and cheaply.

Sights—The Romantic Rhine
(These sights are north to south, Koblenz to Bingen.)
▲▲▲**Der Romantische Rhein Blitz Zug Fahrt**—One of
Europe's great train thrills is zipping along the Rhine in this fast
train tour. Here's a quick and easy, from-the-train-window tour

(also works for car, boat, or bike) that skips the syrupy myths and the life story of Dieter von Katzenelnbogen that fill normal Rhine guides. For more information than necessary, buy the handy *Rhine Guide from Mainz to Cologne* (7-DM book with foldout map, at most shops).

Sit on the left (river) side of the train going south from Koblenz. While nearly all the castles listed are viewed from this side, clear a path to the right window for the times I yell, "Crossover!"

You'll notice large black-and-white kilometer markers along the riverbank. I erected these years ago to make this tour easier to follow. They tell the distance from the Rhinefalls where the Rhine leaves Switzerland and becomes navigable. Now the river-barge pilots have accepted these as navigational aids as well. We're tackling just 36 miles of the 820-mile-long Rhine. Your Blitz Rhine Tour starts at Koblenz and heads upstream to Bingen. If you're going the other direction, it still works. Just hold the book upside down.

Km 590: Koblenz—This Rhine Blitz starts with the Romantic Rhine thrills—at Koblenz. Koblenz is not a nice city (it was really hit hard in World War II), but its place as the historic *Deutsche-Ecke* (German corner)—the tip of land where the Mosel joins the Rhine—gives it a certain historic charm. Koblenz, Latin for "confluence," has Roman origins. Walk through the park, noticing the reconstructed memorial to the Kaiser. Across the river, the yellow Ehrenbreitstein Castle now houses a hostel. It's a 30-minute hike from the station to the Koblenz boat dock.

Km 585: Burg Lahneck—Above the modern Autobahn bridge over the Lahn River, this castle (*Burg*) was built in 1240 to defend local silver mines, ruined by the French in 1688 and rebuilt in the 1850s in neo-Gothic style. Burg Lahneck faces the yellow Schloss Stolzenfels (out of view above the train, a 10-minute climb from the tiny car park, open for touring, closed Monday).

Km 580: Marksburg—This castle (black and white with the three modern chimneys behind it, just after town of Spay) is the best-looking of all the Rhine castles and the only surviving medieval castle on the Rhine. Because of its commanding position, it was never attacked. It's now open as a museum with a medieval interior second only to the Mosel's Burg Eltz (9 DM, daily 10:00–17:00, call ahead to see if a rare English tour is scheduled, tel. 02627/206).

Km 570: Boppard—Once a Roman town, Boppard has some impressive remains of fourth-century walls. Notice the Roman tower just after the Boppard train station and the substantial chunk of Roman wall just before. Boppard is worth a stop. Just above the main square are the remains of the Roman wall. Below the square is a fascinating church. Notice the carved Romanesque crazies at the doorway. Inside, to the right of the entrance, you'll

River Trade and Barge Watching

The river is great for barge watching. Since ancient times this has been a highway for trade. Today, the world's biggest port (Rotterdam) waits at the mouth of the river. Barge workers are almost a subculture. Many own their own ships. The captain (and family) live in the stern. Workers live in the bow. The family car often decorates the bow like a shiny hood ornament. In the Rhine town of Kaub, there's even a boarding school for the children of the Rhine merchant marine. The flag of the boat's home country flies in the stern (German, Swiss, Dutch—horizontal red, white, and blue, or French—vertical red, white, and blue). Logically, imports go upstream (Japanese cars, coal, and oil) and exports go downstream (German cars, chemicals, and pharmaceuticals). A clever captain manages to ship goods in each direction.

At this point tugs can push a floating train of up to five barges at once. Upstream it gets steeper and they can push only one at a time. Before modern shipping, horses dragged boats upstream (the faint remains of the tow paths survive at points along the river). From 1873 to 1900 they actually laid a chain from Bonn to Bingen, and boats with cog-wheels and steam engines hoisted themselves slowly upstream. Today, 265 million tons are shipped each year along the 528 navigable miles from Basel on the Swiss border to Rotterdam on the Atlantic.

While riverside navigational aids are ignored by camera-toting tourists, they are of vital interest to captains who don't wish to meet the Loreley. Boats pass on the right unless they clearly signal otherwise with a large blue sign. Since downstream ships can't stop or maneuver as freely, upstream boats are expected to do the tricky do-si-do work. Cameras monitor traffic all along and relay warnings of oncoming ships via large triangular signals posted before narrow and troublesome bends in the river. There may be two or three triangles per sign post, depending upon how many "sectors," or segments, of the river are covered. The lowest triangle indicates the nearest stretch of river. Each triangle tells if there's a ship in that sector. When the bottom side of a triangle is lit, that sector is empty. When the left side is lit, an oncoming ship is in that sector.

see Christian symbols from Roman times. Also notice the painted arches and vaults. Originally most Romanesque churches were painted this way. Down by the river, look for the high water (*Hochwasser*) marks on the arches from various flood years. (You'll find these flood marks throughout the Rhine and Mosel Valleys.)

Km 567: Burg Sterrenberg and Burg Liebenstein—These are the "Hostile Brothers" castles (across from Bad Salzig). Take the wall between the castles (actually designed to improve the defenses of both castles), add two greedy and jealous brothers and a fair maiden, and create your own legend. The castles are restaurants today.

Km 559: Burg Maus—The Maus ("Mouse") got its name because the next castle was owned by the Katzenelnbogen family. ("Katz" means "cat.") In the 1300s it was considered a state-of-the-art fortification . . . until Napoleon had it blown up in 1806 with state-of-the-art explosives. It was rebuilt true to its original plans around 1900.

Km 557: St. Goar and Rheinfels Castle—Cross to the other side of the train. The pleasant town of St. Goar (gwahr) was named for a sixth-century hometown monk. It originated in Celtic times (really old) as a place where sailors would stop, catch their breath, send home a postcard, and give thanks after surviving the seductive and treacherous Loreley crossing. St. Goar is worth a stop to explore its mighty Rheinfels Castle (For information on a guided castle tour and accommodations, see below.)

Km 556: Burg Katz—From the town of St. Goar, you'll see Burg Katz (Katzenelnbogen) across the river. Together, Burg Katz (b. 1371) and Rheinfels Castle had a clear view up and down the river and effectively controlled traffic. There was absolutely no duty-free shopping on the medieval Rhine. Katz got Napoleoned in 1806 and rebuilt around 1900. Today it's a convalescent home.

About km 555: You'll see the statue of the Loreley, the beautiful but deadly nymph (see legend below), at the end of a long spit—built to give barges protection from vicious icebergs that occasionally rage down the river in the winter. The actual Loreley, a cliff, is just ahead.

Km 554: The Loreley—Steep a big slate rock in centuries of legend and it becomes a tourist attraction, the ultimate Rhinestone. The Loreley (two flags on top, name painted near shoreline), rising 450 feet over the narrowest and deepest point of the Rhine, has long been important. It was a holy site in pre-Roman days. The fine echoes here—thought to be ghostly voices—fertilized the legendary soil.

Because of the reefs just upstream (at km 552), many ships never made it to St. Goar. Sailors (after days on the river) blamed their misfortune on a *wunderbares Fräulein* whose long blonde hair almost covered her body. Heinrich Heine's *Song of Loreley* (the *Cliffs Notes* version is on local postcards) tells the story of a count who sent his men to kill or capture this siren after she distracted his horny son, causing him to drown. When the soldiers cornered the nymph in her cave, she called her father (Father Rhine) for help. Huge waves, the likes of which you'll never see today, rose from the river and carried Loreley to safety. And she has never been seen since.

But alas, when the moon shines brightly and the tour buses are parked, a soft, playful Rhine whine can still be heard from the Loreley. As you pass, listen carefully ("Sailors . . . sailors . . . over my bounding mane").

Km 552: Killer reefs, marked by red-and-green buoys, are called the "Seven Maidens."

Km 550: Oberwesel—Cross to the other side of the train. Oberwesel was a Celtic town in 400 B.C., then a Roman military station. It now boasts some of the best Roman wall and tower remains on the Rhine and the commanding Schönburg castle. Notice how many of the train tunnels have entrances designed like medieval turrets—they were actually built in the Romantic 19th century. OK, back to the riverside.

Km 546: Burg Gutenfels and Pfalz Castle: the Classic Rhine View—Burg Gutenfels (see the white painted "Hotel" sign) and the ship-shape Pfalz Castle (built in the river in the 1300s) worked very effectively to tax medieval river traffic. The town of Kaub grew rich as Pfalz raised its chains when boats came and lowered them only when the merchants had paid their duty. Those who didn't pay spent time touring its prison, on a raft at the bottom of its well. In 1504 a pope called for the destruction of Pfalz, but a six-week siege failed. Notice the overhanging "outhouse" (tiny white room with the faded medieval stains between the two wooden ones). Pfalz is tourable but bare and dull (3-DM ferry from Kaub, 4 DM, Tuesday–Sunday 9:00–13:00, 14:00–18:00, closed Monday, tel. 06774/570).

In Kaub a green statue honors the German General Blücher. He was Napoleon's nemesis. In 1813, as Napoleon fought his way back to Paris after his disastrous Russian campaign, he stopped at Mainz—hoping to fend off the Germans and Russians pursuing him—by controlling that strategic bridge. Blücher tricked Napoleon. By building the first major pontoon bridge of its kind, here at the Pfalz Castle, he crossed the Rhine and outflanked the French. Two years later Blücher and Wellington teamed up to defeat Napoleon once and for all at Waterloo.

Km 544: The "Raft Busters"—Immediately before Bacharach, at the top of the island, buoys mark a gang of rocks notorious for busting up rafts. The Black Forest is upstream. It was poor, and wood was its best export. Black Foresters would ride log booms down the Rhine to the Ruhr (where their timber fortified coal mine shafts) or to Holland (where logs were sold to ship builders). If they could navigate the sweeping bend just before Bacharach and then survive these "raft busters," they'd come home reckless and romantic, the German folkloric equivalent of American cowboys after payday.

Km 543: Bacharach and Burg Stahleck—Cross to the other side of the train. Bacharach is a great stop (see details and accommodations below). Some of the Rhine's best wine is from this town, whose name means "altar to Bacchus." Local vintners brag that the medieval Pope Pius II ordered it by the cartload. Perched above the town, the 13th-century Burg Stahleck is now a hostel.

Km 540: Lorch—This pathetic stub of a castle is barely visible from the road. Notice the small car ferry (3/hrly, 10 min), one of several between Mainz and Koblenz, where there are no bridges.

Km 538: Castle Sooneck—Cross back to the other side of the train. Built in the 11th century, this castle was twice destroyed by people sick and tired of robber-barons.

Km 534: Burg Reichenstein, and Km 533: Burg Rheinstein—Stay on the other side of the train to see two of the first castles to be rebuilt in the Romantic era. Both are privately owned, tourable, and connected by a pleasant trail.

Km 530: Ehrenfels Castle—Opposite Bingerbrück and the Bingen station, you'll see the ghostly Ehrenfels Castle (clobbered by the Swedes in 1636 and by the French in 1689). Since it had no view of the river traffic to the north, the owner built the cute little *Mäuseturm* (Mouse Tower) on an island (the yellow tower you'll see near the train station today). Rebuilt in the 1800s in neo-Gothic style, today it's used as a Rhine navigation signal station.

Km 528: Niederwald Monument—Across from the Bingen station on a hilltop is the 120-foot-high Niederwald monument, a memorial built with 32 tons of bronze in 1877 to commemorate "the re-establishment of the German Empire." A lift takes tourists to this statue from the famous and extremely touristy wine town of Rüdesheim.

Our tour is over. From Bingen, you can continue your journey (or return to Koblenz) by train or boat.

BACHARACH

Bacharach, once prosperous from the wine and wood trade, is now just a pleasant half-timbered village working hard to keep its tourists happy.

The lightweight TI is on the main street—look for the "i" sign (Monday–Friday 9:00–12:30, 13:30–17:00, Saturday 10:00–12:00, tel. 06743/1297). They have a blurry photocopied town map with an English history.

The Jost beer stein "factory outlet" carries everything a shopper could want. It has one shop across from the church in the main square and a slightly cheaper shop a block away on Rosenstrasse 16 (Monday–Friday 8:30–18:00, Saturday 8:30–17:00, Sunday 10:00–17:00, ships overseas, 10 percent discount with this book, CC:VMA, tel. 06743/1224).

Get acquainted with Bacharach by taking a walking tour. You

Bacharach

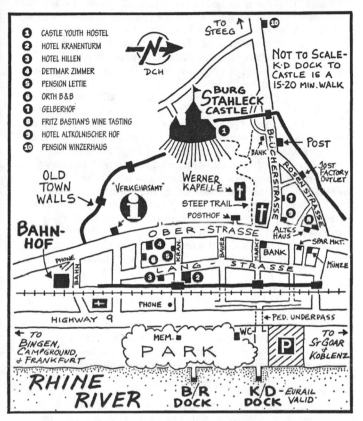

1 CASTLE YOUTH HOSTEL
2 HOTEL KRANENTURM
3 HOTEL HILLEN
4 DETTMAR ZIMMER
5 PENSION LETTIE
6 ORTH B&B
7 GELBERHOF
8 FRITZ BASTIAN'S WINE TASTING
9 HOTEL ALTKOLNISCHER HOF
10 PENSION WINZERHAUS

NOT TO SCALE—
K-D DOCK TO
CASTLE IS A
15-20 MIN. WALK

TO STEEG

BURG STAHLECK CASTLE

POST

JOST FACTORY OUTLET

OLD TOWN WALLS

VERKEHRSAMT

WERNER KAPELLE

STEEP TRAIL
POSTHOF

BLÜCHERSTRASSE

ROSENSTRASSE

BAHN-HOF

OBER - STRASSE

ALTES HAUS

SPAR MKT.

LANG - STRASSE

BAUER

MARKT

BANK

MÜNZE

PHONE

HIGHWAY 9

PHONE

PED. UNDERPASS

TO BINGEN, CAMPGROUND, & FRANKFURT

MEM.

PARK

WC

P

TO St GOAR & KOBLENZ

RHINE RIVER

B/R DOCK

K/D DOCK

—EURAIL VALID

can hire Herr Rolf Jung, retired headmaster of the Bacharach school (50 DM, 1.5 hrs, tel. 06743/1519, speaks excellent English), or take a self-guided walk, below.

Sights—Bacharach

▲▲**Introductory Bacharach Walk**—Start at the Köln-Düsseldorf ferry dock (next to a fine picnic park). View the town from the parking lot—a modern landfill. The Rhine used to lap against Bacharach's town wall (just over the present-day highway). Every few years, the river floods, covering the highway under several feet of water. The castle on the hill is a youth hostel. Two of its original 16 towers are visible from here (up to five if you look real hard). The huge roadside wine keg declares this town was built on the wine trade.

Reefs up the river forced boats to unload upriver and reload here. Consequently, Bacharach became the biggest wine trader on the Rhine. A riverfront crane hoisted huge kegs of prestigious "Bacharach" wine (which in practice was from anywhere in the region). The tour buses next to the dock and the flags of the biggest spenders along the highway remind you today's economy is basically tourism.

At the big town map and public WC, take the underpass, ascend on the right, and walk under the train tracks through the medieval gate (one out of an original six 14th-century gates) and to the two-tone Protestant church, which marks the town center.

From this intersection, Bacharach's main street (Ober-strasse) goes right to the half-timbered red-and-white Altes Haus (from 1368, the oldest house in town) and left to the TI and train station. To the left (or south) of the church, the golden horn hangs over the old Posthof. (The post horn symbolizes the postal service throughout Europe. In olden days, when the post man blew this, traffic stopped, and the mail sped through.) Step into the courtyard. Notice the fascist eagle (from 1936, on the left doorstep as you enter) and the fine view of a chapel and church. This post station dates from 1724, when stagecoaches ran from Köln to Frankfurt.

Two hundred years ago this was the only road along the Rhine. Napoleon widened it to fit his cannon wagons. The steps alongside the church lead to the castle. Return to the church.

Inside the church you'll find grotesque and brightly painted capitals and a mix of round Romanesque and pointed Gothic arches. In the upper left corner some medieval frescoes survive where an older Romanesque arch was cut by a pointed Gothic one.

Continue down Oberstrasse past the Altes Haus to the old mint (*Münze*), marked by a crude coin in its sign. Across from the mint, the wine garden of Fritz Bastian is the liveliest place in town after dark. Above you in the vineyards stands a ghostly black-and-gray tower—your destination.

Wander 30 meters up Rosenstrasse to the well. Notice the sundial and the wall painting of 1632 Bacharach with its walls intact. Climb the tiny-stepped lane behind the well up into the vineyard and to the tower. The slate steps deposit you at a view-point atop the stubby remains of the old town wall just above the tower's base.

A grand medieval town spreads before you. When Frankfurt had 15,000 residents, medieval Bacharach had 6,000. For 300 years (1300–1600) Bacharach was big, rich, and politically powerful.

From this perch you can see the chapel ruins and six of the nine surviving city towers. Visually trace the wall to the castle, home of one of seven electors who voted for the Holy Roman Emperor in 1275. To protect their own power, these elector princes did their best to choose the weakest guy on the ballot. The elector from Bacharach helped select a two-bit prince named Rudolf von Habsburg (from a two-bit castle in Switzerland). The underestimated Rudolf brutally silenced the robber-barons along the Rhine and established the mightiest dynasty in European history. His family line, the Habsburgs, ruled the Austro-Hungarian Empire until 1918.

Plagues, fires, and the Thirty Years' War (1618–1648) finally did Bacharach in. The town has slumbered for several centuries, with a population of about a thousand.

In the mid-19th century, artists and writers such as Victor Hugo were charmed by the Rhineland's romantic mix of past glory, present poverty, and rich legend. They put this part of the Rhine on the old "grand tour" map as the "Romantic Rhine." Victor Hugo pondered the ruined 15th-century chapel, which you can see under the castle. In his 1842 travel book, *Rhein Reise* (*Rhine Travels*), he wrote, "No doors, no roof or windows, a magnificent-skeleton puts its silhouette against the sky. Above it, the ivy-covered castle ruins provide a fitting crown. This is Bacharach, land of fairy tales, covered with legends and sagas."

A path leads along the wall, up the valley, to the next tower, and down onto the street. The road leads under the gate and back into the center. If you're enjoying the Romantic Rhine, thank Victor Hugo and company.

Sleeping on the Rhine
(1.7 DM = about $1)
Sleep Code: **S** = Single, **D** = Double/Twin, **T** = Triple, **Q** = Quad, **b** = bathroom, **t** = toilet only, **s** = shower only, **CC** = Credit Card (Visa, MasterCard, Amex), **SE** = Speaks English, **NSE** = No English. All hotels speak some English. Breakfast is included unless otherwise noted.

The Rhine is an easy place for cheap sleeps. *Zimmer* and *Gasthäuser* with 30-DM beds abound (and *Zimmer* normally discount their prices for longer stays). Several exceptional Rhine-area hostels offer 20-DM beds (for travelers of any age). Each town's helpful TI is eager to set you up, and finding a room should be easy any time of year (except for wine-festy weekends in September and October). Bacharach and St. Goar, the best towns for an overnight stop, are about 10 miles apart, connected by milk-run trains, river boats, and a riverside bike path. Bacharach is less touristy, St. Goar has the famous castle (see St. Goar, below). Parking in Bacharach is simple along the highway next to the tracks (3-hour daytime limit is generally not enforced).

Sleeping in Bacharach
(tel. code: 06743, zip code: 55422)

Hotels
Hotel Kranenturm gives you castle ambience without the climb. It offers the best combination of comfort and hotel privacy with *Zimmer* warmth, central location, and medieval atmosphere. Run by hardworking Kurt Engel, his intense but friendly wife, Fatima, and faithful Schumi (shoo-mee), this hotel is actually part of the medieval fortification. Its former *Kran* (crane) towers are now round rooms—great for medievalists. When the riverbank was higher, cranes on this tower loaded barrels of wine onto Rhine boats. Hotel Kranenturm is five yards from the train tracks, but a combination of medieval sturdiness, triple-paned windows, and included earplugs makes the riverside rooms sleepable (Sb-60–65 DM, Db-90–95 DM, Tb-125–130 DM, Qb-160–165 DM with this book, plus 10 DM for rooms with a TV, cheaper price for stays of two nights, kid-friendly, Rhine views come with train noise, back rooms—some with castle views—are quieter, laundry service, CC:VMA but prefer cash, Langstrasse 30, tel. 06743/1308, fax 06743/1021, e-mail: hotel-kranenturm @t-online.de). Kurt, a great cook, serves fine 15- to 20-DM dinners. Trade travel stories on the terrace with new friends over dinner, letting screaming trains punctuate your conversation. Kurt's big-enough-for-three Kranenturm ice-cream special is a delight (10 DM). For a quick trip to Fiji in a medieval German cellar, check out his tropical bar. Drivers park along the highway at the Kranenturm tower. Eurailers walk down Oberstrasse, then turn right on Kranenstrasse.

Hotel Hillen, a block south of the Hotel Kranenturm, has less charm and more train noise, with friendly owners and lots of rental bikes. To minimize train noise ask for "ruhige Seite," the quiet side, (S-45 DM, Sb-60 DM, D-80 DM, Db-90 DM, Tb-126 DM, 10 percent less for two nights, 10 percent more with CC, Langstrasse 18, tel. 06743/1287, fax 06743/1037).

Hotel Altkölnischer Hof, a grand old building on the main square, rents 20 rooms with modern furnishings and bathrooms, some with balconies. Public rooms are old-time elegant (Sb-90–95 DM, Db-110–130 DM, Db with terrace-140 DM, with balcony-150–160 DM, 10 percent discount for three-night stays, TV and phones in rooms, elevator, attached restaurant, CC:VA, tel. 06743/1339 or 06743/2186, fax 06743/2793).

Hotel Gelberhof has spiffy public spaces but tired rooms (S-55 DM, Sb-75–85 DM, small Db-110 DM, Db-120–140 DM, possible cash or two-night discounts, popular with groups, elevator, bike rental, CC:M, Blücherstrasse 26, tel. 06743/910-100, fax 06743/910-1050, e-mail: gelberhof@fh-bingen.de).

Pensions and Private Rooms

At **Pension Lettie,** effervescent and eager-to-please Lettie offers four cheery, newly remodeled rooms (Sb-55 DM, Db-75 DM, Tb-110 DM with this book and cash, cheaper price is for longer stays, strictly non-smoking, no train noise, a few doors inland from Hotel Kranenturm, Kranenstrasse 6, tel. & fax 06743/2115, e-mail: pension.lettie@t-online.de). Lettie speaks great English (worked for the U.S. army before we withdrew), does laundry (16 DM per load), and rents bikes (15 DM/day, non-guests leave a passport or credit-card imprint).

Entrepreneurial **Annelie und Hans Dettmar** rent six smoke-free rooms in a modern house on the main drag in the center (big Sb-50 DM, Db-60 DM, Tb-75 DM, Qb-100 DM, free use of two old bikes, laundry-17 DM, Oberstrasse 8, tel. & fax 06743/2661, SE). One room is huge, easily fits a family of four, and has a kitchenette (20 DM to use it). Skip their other building up the hill; it's a long, steep walk away. Readers give this couple mixed reviews, but their place is handy for those who need a smoke-free option. Their son Jürgen runs the adjacent bakery and rents five fine rooms on the main square opposite the Altes Haus at **Pension Braustube** (Db-60 DM, Tb-90 DM, Oberstrasse 64, tel. & fax 06743/1715 or call his parents' B&B, SE).

Ursula Orth offers five small, bright rooms in her home around the corner from the Dettmars' in the town center—perhaps the best cheap beds in town (Sb-30 DM, Db-55–60 DM, Tb-75 DM for one night and less for two, non-smoking, Rooms 4 and 5 on ground floor—easy access, Spurgasse 3, tel. 06743/1557, some English spoken).

The home of **Herr und Frau Theilacker** is a German-feeling *Zimmer* with comfortable rooms and no outside sign. It's likely to have a room when others don't (S-30 DM, D-60 DM, in the town center behind the Altes Haus at Oberstrasse 57, tel. 06743/1248, NSE).

Pension Winzerhaus is a 10-room place run by Herr Petrescu. It's 200 yards up the valley from the town gate, so the location is less charming, but it has no train noise and easy parking. Rooms are simple, clean, and modern (Sb-50 DM, Db-85 DM, Tb-90 DM, Qb-95 DM, 10 percent off with this book, free bikes for guests, Blücherstrasse 60, tel. 06743/1294, fax 069/283-927).

Bacharach's hostel, Jugendherberge Stahleck, is a 12th-century castle on the hilltop, 500 steps above Bacharach, with a royal Rhine view. Open to travelers of any age, this is a newly redone gem with eight beds and a private modern shower and WC in each room. A steep 15-minute climb on the trail from the town church, the hostel is warmly run by Evelyn and Bernhard Falke (FALL-kay), who serve hearty, 9-DM buffet, all-you-can-eat dinners. The hostel pub serves cheap local wine until midnight

(24-DM dorm beds with breakfast and sheets, 6 DM extra without a card or in a double, couples can share rooms, groups pay 32 DM per bed with breakfast and dinner, no smoking in rooms, easy parking, beds normally available but call and leave your name, they'll hold a bed until 18:00, tel. 06743/1266, SE).

Eating in Bacharach

Several places offer good, inexpensive, and atmospheric indoor or outdoor dining in Bacharach. **Hotel Kranenturm** (see above) and **Altes Haus** (the oldest building in town, on main square, 20-DM dinners, closed Wednesday) are both excellent. **Kurpfälzische Münze** serves good 20- to 30-DM dinners nightly (in the old mint, across the street from the Altes Haus, claims to be even older). **Weingut zum Gruner Baum** offers delicious dinners and cold lunches (also next to Altes Haus with good ambience indoors and out). And the **Posthof** beer garden has good, cheap pub grub, served outside in the courtyard.

Wine Tasting: Drop in on entertaining Fritz Bastian's **Weingut zum Grüner Baum** wine bar (just past the Altes Haus, evenings only, closed Thursday, tel. 06743/1208). The president of the local vintner's club, Fritz has a calling to give travelers an understanding of the subtle differences among the Rhine wines. Groups of two to 10 people pay 26 DM for a "carousel" of 15 glasses of 14 different white wines, one lonely red, and a basket of bread. Your mission: team up with others with this book to rendezvous here after dinner. Spin the lazy Susan, share a common cup, and discuss the taste. Fritz insists, "After each wine, you must talk to each other."

ST. GOAR

St. Goar is a classic Rhine town—its hulk of a castle overlooking a half-timbered shopping wonderland and leafy riverside park busy with sightseeing ships and contented strollers. From the boat dock, the main drag—a pedestrian mall—cuts through town before winding up to the castle. Rheinfels castle, once the mightiest on the Rhine, is the single best Rhineland ruin to explore.

The St. Goar TI offers free left-luggage service (Monday–Friday 8:00–12:30, 14:00–17:00, Saturday 10:00–12:00 May–October, closed Sunday and earlier in winter, tel. 06741/383). You can rent a bike at the Golf Pavilion near the river (13 DM/day).

St. Goar's waterfront park is hungry for a picnic. The small EDEKA supermarket on the main street is fine for picnic fixings (Monday–Friday 8:00–19:00, Saturday 8:00–16:00, closed Sunday).

The friendly and helpful Montag family in the shop under Hotel Montag has Rhine guidebooks (Koblenz–Mainz), fine steins, and copies of this year's *Rick Steves' Germany, Austria & Switzerland* guidebook. They also run the cuckoo clock shop across the street (marked by the world's biggest free-hanging cuckoo clock)

St. Goar

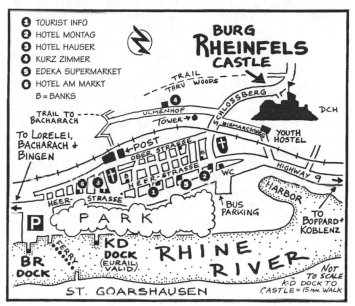

0 TOURIST INFO
2 HOTEL MONTAG
3 HOTEL HAUSER
4 KURZ ZIMMER
5 EDEKA SUPERMARKET
6 HOTEL AM MARKT
   B = BANKS

BURG RHEINFELS CASTLE

TRAIL THRU WOODS

SCHLOSSBERG

DCH

TRAIL TO BACHARACH

ULMENHOF TOWER

BISMARCKWEG

YOUTH HOSTEL

To LORELEI, BACHARACH & BINGEN

POST

OBER STRASSE

HEER-STRASSE

WC

HIGHWAY 9

HEER - STRASSE

BUS PARKING

HARBOR

TO BOPPARD & KOBLENZ

P

P A R K

KD DOCK (EURAIL VALID)

R H I N E RIVER

BR DOCK

FERRY

NOT TO SCALE
K-D DOCK TO CASTLE = 15 MIN. WALK

ST. GOARSHAUSEN

and offer 10 percent off any of their souvenirs for travelers with this book.

For a good two-hour hike from St. Goar, catch the ferry across to St. Goarshausen, hike to the Katz castle, and traverse along the hillside from there to the top of the Loreley. From the Loreley the trail winds down to the river and then takes you back to the St. Goarshausen-to-St. Goar ferry (4/hrly, 3-DM round-trip).

Sights—St. Goar's Rheinfels Castle

▲▲▲**Self-guided Tour**—Sitting like a dead pit bull above St. Goar, this mightiest of Rhine castles rumbles with ghosts from its hard-fought past. Burg Rheinfels (built in 1245) withstood a siege of 28,000 French troops in 1692. But in 1797 the French Revolutionary army destroyed it.

Rheinfels was huge, the biggest on the Rhine, then used as a quarry. Today this hollow but interesting shell offers your single best, hands-on ruined castle experience on the river (5 DM, daily 9:00–18:00, last entry at 17:00; Saturday and Sunday only in winter; gather 10 English-speaking tourists and get a nearly free English tour, tel. 06741/7753). The cruel castle map is worth .30 DM to help follow the guided tour below. The English booklet is not worth 3.50 DM. If planning to explore the underground passages, bring a flashlight, buy a tiny one (5 DM at entry), or do it by candlelight (museum sells candles with matches, 1 DM). To get to the castle from St. Goar's boat dock or train station, take a steep 15-minute hike, a 7-DM taxi ride (11 DM for a minibus, tel. 06741/93100), or goofy tourist train (3 DM, 3/hrly, from square between station and dock, complete with lusty music).

Rather than wander aimlessly, visit the castle by following this tour: From the ticket gate walk straight and uphill. Pass Grosser Keller on left (where we'll end this tour), walk through an internal gate past "zu den gedeckten Wehrgängen" on right (where we'll pass later) to the museum (daily 9:00–12:00, 13:00–17:00) in the only finished room of the castle.

1. Museum and castle model: The seven-foot-tall carved stone ("Keltische Säule von Pfalzfeld") immediately inside the door—a tombstone from a nearby Celtic grave—is from 600 years before Christ. There were people here long before the Romans . . . and this castle. The chair next to the door is an old library chair. Fold it up and it becomes stairs for getting to the highest shelves.

The castle history exhibit in the center of the room is well described in English. At the far end is a model reconstruction of the castle showing how much bigger it was before Louis XIV destroyed it. Study this. Find where you are. This was the living quarters of the original castle, which was only the smallest ring of buildings around the tiny central courtyard (13th century, marked by red well). The ramparts were added in the 14th century. In 1605 the entire fortress was completed. The vast majority of the place was destroyed in 1796. It has had no military value since. While no WWII bombs were wasted on this ruin, it served St. Goar as a quarry for generations. The basement of the museum shows the castle pharmacy and an exhibit on the Rhine icebergs.

(From the museum, walk 30 meters directly out, slightly uphill into the castle courtyard.)

2. Medieval castle courtyard: Five hundred years ago the entire castle circled this courtyard. The place was self-sufficient and ready for a siege with a baker, pharmacy, herb garden, animals, brewery, well (top of yard), and livestock. During peace time, 300 to 600 people lived here—during a siege as many as 4,500. The walls were plastered and painted white. Bits of the original 13th-century plaster survive.

(Continue through courtyard, out "Erste Schildmauer," turn left into the next courtyard below German flag and two old, black, upright posts. Find the pyramid of stone catapult balls.)

3. Castle garden: Catapult balls like these were too expensive not to recycle. If ever used, they'd be retrieved after the battle. Across from the balls is a well: essential for any castle during the age of sieging. The old posts are for the ceremonial baptizing of new members of the local trading league. While this guild goes back centuries, today it's a social club that fills this court with a huge wine party the first weekend of each August.

(If weary, skip to 5; otherwise, climb to the castle's best viewpoint up where the German flag waves.)

4. Highest castle tower lookout: Enjoy a great view of the river, castle, and the forest that was once all part of this castle. Remember, the fortress once covered five times the land it does today. Originally this castle was no bigger than the two you see over the river. Notice how the other castles don't poke above the top of the Rhine canyon. That would make them easy for invading armies to see.

(Return to the catapult balls, walk down the road, through the tunnel, veer left through the arch marked "zu den Gedeckten Wehrgängen," go down two flights of stairs and turn left into the dark covered passageway. We now begin a rectangular walk taking us completely around the perimeter of the castle.)

5. Covered defense galleries: Soldiers—the castle's "minute men"—had a short commute: defensive positions on outside, home in the holes below on the left. Even though these living quarters were padded with straw, life was unpleasant. A peasant was lucky to live beyond age 28.

(Continue straight through the gallery and to the corner of the castle, where you'll see a white painted arrow at eye level.)

6. Corner of castle: Look up. A three-story, half-timbered building originally rose beyond the highest stone fortification. The two stone tongues near the top just around the corner supported the toilet. (Insert joke here.) Turn around. The crossbow slits below the white arrow were once steeper. The bigger hole on the riverside was for hot pitch, etc.

(Follow that white arrow along the outside to the next corner. Midway, you'll pass stairs leading down "zu den Minengängen." Adventurers with flashlights can detour here. You may come out around the next corner. Otherwise, stay with me, walking level to the corner. At the corner, turn left.)

7. Thoop . . . you're dead. Look ahead at the smartly placed crossbow arrow slit. While you're lying there, notice the stone work. The little round holes were for scaffolds used as they built up. They indicate this stonework is original. Notice also the fine stonework on the shoots. More boiling oil . . . now you're toast too. Continue along. At the railing look up the valley and uphill where the fort existed. Below, just outside the wall, is land where attackers would gather. Tunnels filled with explosives ran under the land just outside the walls. With clever thin slate roofs, the force of their detonation went up, killing masses of attackers without damaging the actual castle. In 1626, a handful of underground Protestant Germans blew 300 Catholic Spaniards to—they figured—hell. You can explore these underground passages from the next courtyard.

(Continue along perimeter, jog left, go down five steps and into a huge open field. You may detour here into the passageway marked "13 Hals Graben," or farther to the right and down. The old wooden bridge is actually modern. Continue around the castle through two arches and through the rough entry to "Verliess" on the left.)

8. Prison: This is one of six dungeons. You walked through a door prisoners only dreamed of 400 years ago. They came and went through the little square hole in the ceiling. The holes in the walls supported timbers that politely gave as many as 15 residents something to sit on to keep them out of the filthy slop that gathered on the floor. Twice a day they were given bread and water. Some prisoners actually survived five years in here. The town could torture and execute. The castle had permission only to imprison criminals in these dungeons.

(Continue through next arch, under white arrow, turn left and walk 40 yards to the *Schlachthaus*.)

9. Slaughterhouse: A castle was prepared to survive a six-month siege. With 4,000 people, that's a lot of provisions. The cattle that lived within the walls were slaughtered here. Notice the drainage gutters for water and blood. "Running water" came through from above . . . one bucket at a time.

(Back outside, climb the modern stairs on left. A skinny cool passage leads you into . . .)

10. The big cellar: This "Grosser Keller" was a big pantry. When the castle was smaller, this was the original moat—you can see the rough lower parts of the wall. The original floor was five feet deeper. When the castle expanded, the moat became the cellar. Above the entry, holes mark spots where timbers made a storage loft, perhaps filled with grain. Kegs of wine lined the walls. Part of a soldier's pay was three liters of wine a day. In the back, an arch leads to the wine cellar where finer wine was kept. The castle consumed 200,000 liters of wine a year. The count owned the surrounding farmland. Farmers got to keep 20 percent of their production. Later, in more liberal feudal times, the nobility let them keep 40 percent. Today the German government leaves the workers with 60 percent . . . and provides a few more services.

(Climb out, turn right, and leave. For coffee on a great-view terrace, visit the Rheinfels Castle Hotel, opposite the entrance.)

Sleeping in St. Goar
(tel. code: 06741, zip code: 56329)

Hotel am Markt, well run by Herr and Frau Velich, is a great value. Rustic with all the modern comforts, it features a hint of antler with a pastel flair and bright rooms. It's in the center of town a stone's throw from the boat dock and train station (18 rooms, Ss-65 DM, Sb-80 DM, Db-100 DM, Tb-140 DM, Qb-160 DM, cheaper off-season, open March–November, CC:VMA, Am

Markt 1, tel. 06741/1689, fax 06741/1721, e-mail: hotel_am
_markt_st.goar@t online.de).

Hotel Hauser, facing the boat dock and newly redone, is
warmly run by another Frau Velich (S-42 DM, D-88 DM,
Db-98 DM, Db with Rhine-view balconies-110 DM, show this
book to get these prices, cheaper in off-season, CC:VMA, Heer-
strasse 77, telephone reservations easy, tel. 06741/333, fax
06741/1464, SE).

Hotel Silberne Rose is musty with older decor and some
with Rhine views (Sb-65 DM, Db-90–100 DM, Tb-120–140 DM,
cheaper price for longer stays, CC:VM, across from KD dock,
Heerstrasse 63, tel. 06741/7040, fax 06741/2865).

Hotel Montag is on the castle end of town just across the
street from the world's largest freehanging cuckoo clock. Manfred
Montag, his wife, Maria, and son Mike speak New Yorkish. Even
though Montag gets a lot of bus tours, it's friendly, laid-back, and
comfortable (Sb-70 DM, Db-130 DM, price can drop if things are
slow, CC:VMA, Heerstrasse 128, tel. 06741/1629, fax 06741/2086,
Web site: www.loreleyvalley.com/beerstein-center). Check out
their adjacent crafts shop (heavy on beer steins).

St. Goar's best *Zimmer* deal is the home of **Frau Kurz**, with a
breakfast terrace, fine view, easy parking, and all the comforts of a
hotel (S-34 DM, D-60 DM, Db-70 DM, showers-5 DM, one-
night stays cost extra, confirm prices, honor your reservation or
call to cancel, Ulmenhof 11, tel. & fax 06741/459, some English
spoken). From the train station, it's a steep three-minute hike (exit
left from station, take immediate left at post office, go under tracks
to paved path, take a right partway up stairs, climb a few more
stairs to Ulmenhof).

The Germanly run **St. Goar Hostel**, the big beige building
under the castle, is a good value, with two to 12 beds per room, a
22:00 curfew, and hearty 9.50-DM dinners (20-DM beds with
breakfast, 5-DM sleep sacks, open all day, Bismarckweg 17, tel.
06741/388, SE).

Rheinfels Castle Hotel is the town splurge. Actually part of
the castle, but an entirely new building, this luxury place is good
for those with money and a car (Db-230–255 DM depending on
river views and balconies, CC:VMA, elevator, dress-up restaurant,
Schlossberg 47, tel. 06741/8020, fax 06741/802-802, Web site:
www.talderloreley.de/html/rheinfelsgoar/html, e-mail: rheinfels
.st.goar@t-online.de).

Transportation Connections—Rhine

Milk-run trains stop at all Rhine towns each hour starting around
6:00. Koblenz, Boppard, St. Goar, Bacharach, Bingen, and Mainz
are each about 15 minutes apart. From Koblenz to Mainz takes 75
minutes. To get a faster big train, go to Mainz or Koblenz.

From **Mainz** by train to: **Bacharach/St. Goar** (hrly, 1 hr), **Cochem** (hrly, 2.5 hrs, changing in Koblenz), **Köln** (3/hr, 90 min), **Baden-Baden** (hrly, 2.5 hrs), **Munich** (hrly, 4 hrs), **Frankfurt** (3/hr, 45 min), **Frankfurt Airport** (3/hr, 25 min).

From **Frankfurt** by train to: **Koblenz** (hrly, 90 min), **Rothenburg** (hrly, 3 hrs, transfers in Würzburg and Steinach), **Würzburg** (hrly, 90 min), **Munich** (hrly, 3.5 hrs), **Amsterdam** (8/day, 5 hrs), **Paris** (4/day, 6.5 hrs).

MOSEL VALLEY

The misty Mosel is what many visitors hoped the Rhine would be—peaceful, sleepy, romantic villages slipped between the steep vineyards and the river, fine wine, a sprinkling of castles, and lots of friendly *Zimmer*. Boat, train, and car traffic here is a trickle compared to the roaring Rhine. While the swan-speckled Mosel moseys 300 miles from France's Vosges Mountains to Koblenz, where it dumps into the Rhine, the most scenic piece of the valley lies between the towns of Bernkastel-Kues and Cochem. I'd savor only this section.

Throughout the region on summer weekends and during the fall harvest time, wine festivals with oompah bands, dancing, and colorful costumes are powered by good food and wine.

Getting Around the Mosel Valley

The train zips you to Cochem or Trier in a snap. Regular buses connect the smallest train stations with Mosel villages. The Beilstein-Cochem bus takes 15 minutes (6/day, fewer on weekends, 5.40 DM). Consider a boat ride from Cochem to Zell (KolbLine, 2/day, May–August, except Fridays and Mondays in May and June, 3 hrs, 23 DM one-way, 35 DM round-trip) or Beilstein (5/day, 60 min, 13 DM one-way, 18 DM round-trip, tel. 02673/1515). The K-D (Köln–Düsseldorf) line sails once a day in each direction (May–September, Koblenz to Cochem 10:00–14:30, or Cochem to Koblenz 15:50–20:10, free with Eurail). You can also rent bikes in Cochem from the K-D line kiosk at the dock (summers only) or year-round from Kreutz on Moselstrasse behind the Shell station (7 DM/4 hrs, 14 DM/day, no deposit required, just your passport number). If stranded, many hitchhike.

Sights—Mosel Valley

Cochem—With a majestic castle and picturesque medieval streets, Cochem is the very touristic hub of this part of the river. The Cochem TI has a free town map with history and a walking tour. The pointy Cochem Castle is the work of overly imaginative 19th-century restorers (6 DM, daily mid-March–October 9:00–17:00, 15-minute walk from Cochem, tel. 02671/255). Follow one of the frequent German-language tours (reading English explanation

Mosel Valley

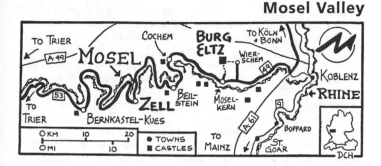

sheets) or call ahead to meet one of the roughly three English tours given daily.

The Cochem TI books rooms (same day only), keeps a thorough 24-hour listing in its window, and offers lots of brochures and concert info (Monday–Friday 10:00–17:00, in summer on Saturday 10:00–15:00 and Sunday 10:00–12:00, off-season closed weekends and at lunch, tel. 02671/3974). The *Moselle Wine Road* flyer is perfect for wine-lovers. Day-trippers can lock or check luggage at the station (2 DM). Many train travelers end up sleeping in Cochem (see Sleeping, below). Stroll along the pleasant paths that line the river. Cochem is right on the train line (to Koblenz, hrly, 60 min; to Trier, hrly, 60 min).

▲▲▲**Burg Eltz**—My favorite castle in all of Europe lurks in a mysterious forest. It's been left intact for 700 years, and is furnished throughout as it was 500 years ago. Thanks to smart diplomacy and clever marriages, Burg Eltz was never destroyed. (It survived one five-year siege.) It's been in the Eltz family for 820 years. The countess arranges for new flowers in each room weekly. The only way to see the castle is with a one-hour tour (included in admission ticket). German tours (with pathetic English fact sheets) go constantly. Organize an English tour. (Corral 20 English-speakers in the inner courtyard—they'll thank you for it. Push the red button on the white porch and politely beg for an English guide. This is well worth a short wait. You can also telephone ahead to see if there's an English-language group scheduled that you could tag along with.)

Reaching Burg Eltz by train, walk one steep hour from Moselkern station (midway between Cochem and Koblen, no lockers at station; trail is slippery when wet, follow white "park and walk" signs) through a pine forest where sparrows carry crossbows, and maidens, disguised as falling leaves, whisper "watch out."

Drivers often get lost on the way to Burg Eltz. Use your map and do this: leave the river at Moselkern (shortest drive) following the white "Burg Eltz Park & Ride" signs through the towns of Münstermaifeld, then Wierschem. The castle parking lot is two kilometers past Wierschem. From the lot, hike 10 minutes downhill or wait for the red castle shuttlebus (2 DM). There are three "Burg Eltz" parking lots; only the Hatzenport lot is close enough for an easy walk (9 DM, daily April–October 9:30–17:30, tel. 02672/950-500).

▲**Beilstein**—Farther upstream is the quaintest of all Mosel towns (see Sleeping, below). Beilstein is Cinderella land. Check out the narrow lanes, ancient wine cellar, resident (and very territorial) swans, and ruined castle. The small 2-DM ferry goes constantly back and forth. Two shops rent bikes for the pleasant riverside roll (toward Zell is best). The TI is in a café (summer Tuesday–Sunday 9:00–19:00, closed Monday, tel. 02673/1417). Four buses a day connect Zell and Beilstein.

▲**Zell**—This is the best Mosel town for an overnight stop (see Sleeping, below). It's peaceful, with a fine riverside promenade, a pedestrian bridge over the water, plenty of *Zimmer*, and a long pedestrian zone filled with colorful shops, restaurants, *Weinstuben* (wine bars), and a fun oompah folk band on weekend evenings on the main square. Walk up to the medieval wall's gatehouse and through the cemetery to the old munitions tower for a village view. The fine little Wein und Heimatmuseum features Mosel history (Wednesday and Saturday 15:00–17:00). Locals know Zell for its Schwarze Katz (Black Cat) wine. (TI open Monday–Friday 8:00–12:30, 13:30–17:00, Saturday 10:00–13:00, off-season closed Saturday, tel. 06542/4031.)

   Franz Josef Weis (who learned his English as a POW in England) gives an entertaining tour of his 40,000-bottle-per-year wine cellar. His witty tour lasts an hour, and you'll want to leave with a bottle or two. (He also rents two luxurious apartments for 95 DM, CC:M) A green flag marks his *Weinkeller* north of town, past the bridge, at Notenau 26 (tel. 06542/5543, fax 06542/5789).

Sleeping on the Mosel
(1.7 DM = about $1)

Sleeping in Cochem
(tel. code: 02671, zip code: 56812)
The little town is strung along the river. Exit right from the station onto Ravenestrasse. A seven-minute walk brings you to the TI (on your left, past the bus lanes). To get to the main square (Markt), continue under the bridge, then angle right and follow Bernstrasse. All rooms come with breakfast.

   Gästezimmer Hüsgen is a good and handy value that welcomes one-night stays (Ss-40–45 DM, D-64 DM, Ds-68 DM, Db-82 DM, family deals, ground-floor rooms, small view terrace,

Ravenestrasse 34, 150 meters from the station, tel. 02671/5817, Andrea SE). Across the street, the **Ravene** offers six rooms varying in size and quality from odd to comfortable (Sb-60 DM, Db-80–100 DM, Tb-133 DM, Ravenestrasse 43, tel. 02671/980-177, fax 02671/91119, some English spoken).

The rustic **Hotel Lohspeicher**, just off the main square, is for those who want a real hotel (and much higher prices, Sb-85–95 DM, Db-170 DM, elevator, CC:VMA, Obergasse 1, on tiny-stepped street off main square, tel. 02671/3976, fax 02671/1772, Ingo SE). **Stolz Zimmer**, up the street, has big rooms that look like they were decorated by an elderly aunt (Ss-30 DM, Sb-35 DM, Ds-60 DM, Db-70 DM, less for stays of three nights or more, Obergasse 20, tel. 02671/1509, friendly Mrs. Stolz NSE).

Haus Andreas has small but modern rooms (S-25 DM, Sb-40 DM, Db-60 DM, Schlosstrasse 9 or 16, tel. 02671/1370 or 02671/5155, fax 02671/1370). From the main square, take Herren-strasse; after a block, angle right uphill on Schlosstrasse.

Sleeping in Zell
(tel. code: 06542, zip code: 56856)
If the Mosel charms you into spending the night, do it in Zell. By car, this is a natural. By train, you'll need to go to Bullay (hourly from Cochem or Trier), where the bus takes you to little Zell (2.60 DM, 2/hrly, 10 min; bus stop is across street from Bullay train station; check yellow MB schedule for times). Its hotels are a disappointment, but its private homes are great. The owners speak almost no English and discount their rates if you stay more than one night. They can't take reservations long in advance for one-night stays; just call a day ahead. My favorites are on the south end of town, a two-minute walk from the town hall square and the bus stop. Breakfast is included.

Gasthaus Gertrud Thiesen is classy, with a TV-living-breakfast room and a river view. The Thiesen house has big, bright rooms and is on the town's first corner overlooking the Mosel from a great terrace (S or D-70 DM, Balduinstrasse 1, tel. 06542/4453, SE). Notice the high-water flood marks on the wall across the street.

Gästezimmer Rosa Mesenich is another friendly little place facing the river a few doors from Thiesen (S-30 DM, Sb-35 DM, D-60 DM, Db-70 DM, Brandenburg 48, tel. 06542/4297).

Friendly **Natalie Huhn**, your German grandmother, has the cheapest beds in town in her simple but comfortable house (S-30 DM, D-60 DM, cheaper for two-night stays, near the pedestrian bridge behind the church at Jakobstrasse 32, tel. 06542/41048).

Weinhaus zum Fröhlichen Weinberg offers cheap, basic rooms (D-70 DM, 60 DM for two or more nights, family *Zimmer*, Mittelstrasse 6, tel. 06542/4308) above a *Weinstube* disco (noisy on

Friday and Saturday nights). **Gästehaus am Römerbad** is also central and a decent value (Db-80 DM, Am Römerbad 5, tel. 06542/41602, Elizabeth Münster).

If you're looking for room service, sauna, pool, and elevator, sleep at **Hotel Grüner Kranz** (Db-160 DM with Mosel views, 140 DM without, elevator, CC:VMA, tel. 06542/98610, fax 06542/986-180). **Weinhaus Mayer**, a classy—if stressed-out—old pension next door, is perfectly central with Mosel-view rooms (13 rooms, Db-120–160 DM, Balduinstrasse 15, tel. 06542/4530, fax 06542/61160).

Sleeping in Beilstein
(tel. code: 02673, zip code: 56814)
Cozier and farther north, Beilstein (BILE-shtine) is very small and quiet (no train; seven buses/day to nearby Cochem, fewer buses on weekends; 15-minute trip). Breakfast is included.

Hotel Haus Lipmann is your chance to live in a medieval mansion with hot showers and TVs. A prizewinner for atmosphere, it's been in the Lipmann family for 200 years. The creaky wooden staircase and the elegant dining hall, with long wooden tables surrounded by antlers, chandeliers, and feudal weapons, will get you in the mood for your castle sightseeing, but the riverside terrace may mace your momentum (five rooms, Db-120–150 DM, tel. 02673/1573, fax 02673/1521).

Gasthaus Winzerschenke an der Klostertreppe is comfortable and a great value, right in the tiny heart of town (Db-75 DM, bigger Db-95 DM, discount for two-night stays, tel. 02673/1354, Frau Sausen).

The half-timbered, riverfront **Altes Zollhaus Gästezimmer** has crammed all the comforts into tight, bright (if a bit musty), and modern rooms (Db-95 DM, deluxe Db-135 DM, 15 DM more on Friday and Saturday, open March–October, tel. 02673/1574 or 02673/1850, fax 02673/1287).

KÖLN
Germany's fourth largest city, big, no-nonsense Köln has a compact and lively center. The Rhine was the northern boundary of the Roman Empire and, 1,700 years ago, Constantine—the first Christian emperor—made "Colonia" the seat of a bishopric. Five hundred years later, under Charlemagne, Köln became the seat of an archbishopric. With 40,000 people living within its walls, it was the largest German city and an important cultural and religious center throughout the Middle Ages. To many, the city is most famous for its toilet water. "Eau de Cologne" was first made here by an Italian chemist in 1709. Even after World War II bombs destroyed 95 percent of it (population down from 800,000 to 40,000), Köln has remained, after a remarkable recovery, a cultural

Köln

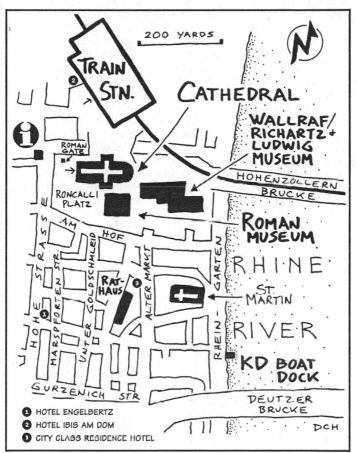

200 YARDS

TRAIN STN.

CATHEDRAL

WALLRAF/ RICHARTZ + LUDWIG MUSEUM

ROMAN GATE

RONCALLI PLATZ

AM HOF

HOHE STRASSE

MARSPFORTEN STR.

UNTER GOLDSCHMIED

RAT-HAUS

ALTER MARKT

RHEIN-GARTEN

HOHENZOLLERN BRUCKE

ROMAN MUSEUM

R H I N E

ST. MARTIN

R I V E R

KD BOAT DOCK

GURZENICH STR

DEUTZER BRUCKE

DCH

❶ HOTEL ENGELBERTZ
❷ HOTEL IBIS AM DOM
❸ CITY CLASS RESIDENCE HOTEL

and commercial center, as well as a fun, colorful, and pleasant-smelling city.

Orientation (tel. code: 0221)

Köln's old town core, bombed out and rebuilt quaint, is traffic free, with a park and bike path along the river. From the cathedral/TI/train station, Hohe Strasse leads into the shopping action. The Roman arch in front of the cathedral reminds us that even in Roman times this was an important trading street and a main road through Köln. In medieval times, when Köln was a major player in the heavyweight Hanseatic Trading

League, two major trading routes crossed here. This "high street" thrived. After complete destruction in World War II, it has emerged—the first pedestrian shopping mall in Germany—once again a thriving trading street. For a quick old town ramble, stroll down Hohe Strasse, go left at the city hall (*Rathaus*) to the river (where K-D Rhine cruises start). Enjoy the quaint old town and waterfront park. The Hohenzollernbrücke (crossing the Rhine at the cathedral) is the busiest railway bridge in the world (30 trains per hour all day long).

Tourist Information: Köln's energetic TI, opposite the church entry, has a list of reasonable private guides and a wealth of brochures (Monday–Saturday 8:00–22:30, Sunday 9:00–22:30, closes at 21:00 in winter, tel. 0221/19433).

Arrival in Köln: Köln couldn't be easier to visit: its three important sights cluster within two blocks of its train station and TI. This super pedestrian zone is a constant carnival of people. There are plenty of 2-DM lockers at the station. If you drive to Köln, follow signs to "Zentrum" and then to the huge Parkhaus Am Dom pay lot under the cathedral.

Sights—Köln's Cathedral

▲▲▲**Cathedral**—The Gothic Dom, or cathedral, Germany's most exciting church, looms immediately up from the train station (daily 7:00–19:00, tel. 0221/9258-4730). The 60-minute English-only tours (7 DM, daily 10:30 and 14:30, not Sunday morning) are reliably excellent. If you are unable to follow a local guide, follow this eight-stop walk:

1. Roman gate and cathedral exterior: The square in front of the cathedral has been a busy civic meeting place since ancient times. A Roman temple stood where the Cathedral stands today. The north gate of the Roman city from A.D. 50 marks the start of Köln's 2,000-year-old main street.

Look for the life-size replica tip of a spire. The real thing is 515 feet above you. The Cathedral facade, while finished according to the original 13th-century plan, is "neo-Gothic" from the 19th century.

(Postcards show the church after the 1945 bombing. The red brick building—to your right as you face the church—is the Diocesan Museum. The Roman museum is beside the church on the right and the art museum is behind that. Step inside the church. Grab a pew in the center of the nave.)

2. Nave: If you feel small, you're supposed to. The 140-feet-tall ceiling reminds us of our place in the vast scheme of things. Lots of stained glass—enough to cover three football fields—fills the church with light, representing God.

The church was begun in 1248. The choir—the lofty area from the center altar to the far end ahead of you—was finished in

Köln Cathedral

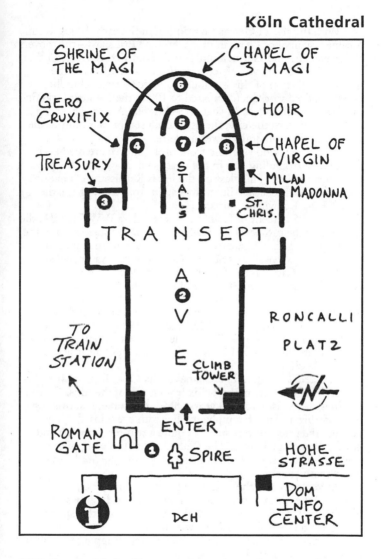

1322. Later, with the discovery of America and routes to the Indies by sea, trade shifted away from inland ports like Köln. Funds dried up and eventually building stopped. For 300 years the finished end of the church was walled off and functioned as a church while the unfinished torso (where you now sit) waited. For centuries the symbol of Köln's skyline was a huge crane that sat atop the unfinished west spire.

With the rise of German patriotism in the early 1800s, Köln became a symbol of German unity. And the Prussians—the movers and shakers behind German unity—mistakenly considered Gothic a German style. They initiated a national tax that funded the speedy completion of this gloriously Gothic German church. Seven hundred workers (compared to 100 in the 14th century) finished the church in just 38 years (1842–1880). And, for a strong first impression to the city, the great train station was built in the shadow of the cathedral's towering spire.

The glass windows in the front of the church are medieval. The glass surrounding you in the nave is not as old, but it's precious nevertheless. The glass on the left is Renaissance. That on the right is 19th-century Bavarian—a gift from Ludwig I, father of "Mad" King Ludwig of touristic fame.

While 95 percent of Köln was destroyed by WWII bombs, the structure of the cathedral survived fairly well. In anticipation of the bombing, the glass and art treasures were taken to shelters and saved. The new "swallow's nest" organ above you was installed to celebrate the Cathedral's 750th birthday in 1998. Relics (mostly skulls) fill cupboards on each side of the nave.

3. Treasury: The treasury is one room filled with mostly medieval reliquaries (bits of chain, bone, cross, cloth, and so on, in gold-crusted glass capsules—3 DM, daily 9:00–17:00). It's fine medieval art but—with no English descriptions—pretty meaningless. The fine little 6-DM book at the door helps (cheapskates read it on the leash).

4. Gero-Crucifix: The Chapel of the Cross features the oldest surviving monumental crucifix from north of the Alps. Carved in 976 with a sensitivity 300 years ahead of its time, it shows Jesus not suffering and not triumphant—but with eyes closed . . . dead. He paid the price for our sins. It's quite a two-fer: great art and powerful theology in one. The Cathedral has three big pilgrim stops: this crucifix, the Shrine of the Magi, and the *Madonna of Milan* (both coming up).

As you step into the oldest part of the church, look for the mosaic of the ninth-century church on the floor. It shows a saint holding the Carolingian Cathedral, which stood on this spot for several centuries before this one was built.

(Continue to the front end of the church, stopping to look at the glass case behind the high altar.)

5. Shrine of the Magi: Relics were a big deal in the Middle Ages. Köln's acquisition of the bones of the Three Kings in the 12th century put it on the pilgrimage map and brought in enough money to justify the construction of this magnificent place. By some stretch of medieval Christian logic, these relics also justified the secular power of the local king. This reliquary, made in about 1200, is the biggest and most splendid I've seen. It's seven feet of gilded silver, jewels, and enamel. Old Testament prophets line the bottom, and 12 New Testament apostles—with a wingless angel in the center—line the top.

Inside sit the bones of the Magi . . . three skulls with golden crowns. So what's the big deal about these three kings of Christmas carol fame? They were the first to recognize Jesus as the savior and the first to come as pilgrims to worship him. They inspired medieval pilgrims and countless pilgrims since. For a thousand years, a theme of this Cathedral is that life is a pilgrimage . . . a search for God.

6. Chapel of the Three Magi: The center chapel, at the far end, is the oldest with the church's oldest window (center, from 1265). It has the typical design: a strip of Old Testament scenes on the left with a theologically and visually parallel strip of New Testament scenes on the right (e.g., on bottom panels: birth of Eve on left, birth of Mary—with her mother Anne on the bed—on right).

Later, glass (which you saw lining the nave) was painted and glazed. This medieval window is actually colored glass, which is assembled like a mosaic. It was very expensive. The size was limited to what pilgrim donations funded. Notice the plain, budget design higher up.

7. Choir: Try to get into the center zone between the high altar and the carved wooden central stalls. This is surrounded by 13th- and 14th-century art: carved oak stalls, frescoed walls, statues painted as they would have been, and original stained glass high above. Study the fanciful oak carvings. The woman cutting the man's hair is a Samson and Delilah warning to the sexist men of the early Church.

8. Chapel of the Virgin: The nearby chapel faces one of the most precious paintings of the important Gothic "School of Köln." *The Patron Saints of Köln* was painted in 1442 by Stefan Lochner. Notice the photographic realism and believable depth. There are literally dozens of identifiable herbs in the grassy foreground. During the 19th century, the city fought to have it in the museum. The Church went to court to keep it. The judge ruled that it can stay in the Cathedral only as long as a Mass is said before it every day. And for over a hundred years, that has happened at 18:00. Lochner was a leader in the School of Köln art style. (For lots more, see the museum described below.)

Overlooking the same chapel, the *Madonna of Milan* (1290) was associated with miracles and a focus of pilgrims for centuries.

As you head for the exit, find the statue of St. Christopher (with Jesus on his shoulder and the pilgrim's staff). Since 1470, pilgrims and travelers have looked up at him and taken solace in the hope that their patron saint is looking out for them. Go in peace.

Church Spire Climb—For 509 steps and 3 DM, you can enjoy a fine city view from the cathedral's south tower. From the Glock-enstube (only 400 steps up) you can see the *Dom's* nine huge bells including Dicke Peter (24-ton "Fat Peter"), claimed to be the largest free-swinging church bell in the world.

Dom Forum—This new visitor center is across from the entry of the church (plenty of info, welcoming lounge with 1-DM coffee, free WC downstairs). They offer an English-language "multi-vision" video on the history of the church daily at 11:30 and 15:30 (20 minutes—starts slow but gets a little better, 3 DM or included with church tour).

Diocesan Museum—This has some of the cathedral's finest art (free, Friday–Wednesday 10:00–17:00, closed Thursday, English description sheet).

More Sights—Köln

▲▲**Römisch-Germanisches Museum**—Germany's best Roman museum offers not a word of English among its elegant and fasci-nating display of Roman artifacts: fine glassware, jewelry, and mosaics (5 DM, Tuesday–Friday 10:00–17:00, Saturday and Sun-day 11:00–17:00, closed Monday, tel. 0221/4590). The permanent collection is downstairs and upstairs. Temporary exhibits (extra ticket) are on the main floor. Budget travelers can view its prize piece, a fine mosaic floor, free from the front window. Once the dining room floor of a rich merchant, this is actually its original position (the museum was built around it). It shows scenes from the life of Dionysus . . . wine and good times, Roman-style. The tall monument over the Dionysus mosaic is the mausoleum of a first-century Roman army officer. Upstairs you'll see a reassem-bled, arched original gate to the Roman city with the Roman ini-tials for the town, "CCAA," still legible, and incredible glassware that Roman Köln was famous for producing.

▲▲**Wallraf-Richartz and Ludwig Museums**—Next door and more enjoyable, you'll find three museums in one slick and modern building for one steep ticket price (10 DM, Tuesday 10:00–20:00, Wednesday–Friday 10:00–18:00, Saturday–Sunday 11:00–18:00, closed Monday, exhibits are fairly well described in English, classy but pricey cafeteria with a reasonable salad bar at entry level, tel. 0221/221-2382). Don't worry about which museum you're in—the floor plan is a mess. Just enjoy the art. (In a few years the Wallraf-Richartz collection will be relocated in its own building a few blocks away near the city hall, and the Ludwig will take over this entire building.)

The **Wallraf-Richartz** (upstairs) features a world-class collec-tion of old masters arranged chronologically, from medieval to northern Baroque and Impressionist. You'll see the best collection anywhere of Gothic School of Köln paintings (1300–1550), offering an intimate peek into those times. Then German, Dutch, Flemish, and French with masters such as Dürer, Rubens, Rembrandt, Hals, Steen, van Gogh, Renoir, Monet, Munch, and Cézanne.

The **Ludwig Museum** offers a stimulating trip through the art of our century (upstairs) and American Pop and post-WWII art (in the basement). Artists featured include German and Russian Expressionists, the Blue Rider school, and Picasso.

The **Agfa History of Photography** exhibit is three rooms with no English. (Don't miss the pigeon with the tiny vintage camera strapped to its chest.)

Assorted Museums—The tourist office has information on lots more museums (from Romanesque churches to the Beatles). The Käthe Kollwitz museum offers the largest collection of this woman's powerful Expressionist art, welling from her experiences living in Berlin during the tumultuous first half of this century (Tuesday–Sunday 10:00–17:00, closed Monday, Neumarkt 18, tel. 0221/227-2363). Chocoholics love the Chocolate Museum, which takes you on a well-described-in-English tour from the plant to the finished product (an easy walk away on the riverfront between Deutzer and Severins bridges, Rheinauhafen 1a, tel. 0221/931-8880). For a thorough visit, consider Köln's two-day museum and transit pass (20 DM, or 36 DM for the entire family). Two-hour German/English city bus tours leave from the TI daily (25 DM, at 10:00, 11:00, and 15:00).

Sleeping in Köln
(tel. code: 0221, zip code: 50667)

Köln is *the* convention town in Germany. Consequently, the town is either jam-packed with hotel prices in the 300-DM range or empty and hungry. In 1999, conventions are scheduled for these dates: Jan. 18–24; Feb. 1–7, 12–14, 22–25; March 7–10, 25–28; April 13–17; all of May; June 2–9; July 23–25; much of August; Sept. 5–19; Oct. 22–29; and much of November. Outside of these dates, the TI can always get you a discounted room in a business-class hotel, and the hotels listed below will honor their fair rates.

Hotel Engelbertz is a fine family-run, 40-room place a five-minute walk from the station and cathedral at the end of the pedestrian mall. Herr Ossendorf promises travelers with my book a Db with breakfast for 100 DM through 1999 (normal price is Db-148–178 DM, CC:VMA, some nonsmoking rooms, elevator, just off Hohe Strasse at Obenmarspforten 1–3, tel. 0221/257 8994, fax 0221/257 8924).

Hotel Ibis am Dom, a huge budget chain with a 66-room modern hotel right at the train station, offers all the comforts in a tidy affordable package without the convention price gouge (Db-99–137 DM without breakfast, CC:VMA, some non-smoking rooms, elevator, Hauptbahnhof, tel. 0221/9128580, fax 0221/138194).

City Class Residence Hotel is a modern, practical place buried nicely in the old town (Db-180–210 DM, CC:VMA, elevator, Alter Markt 55, tel. 0221/9201980, fax 92019899).

Transportation Connections—Köln
By train to: Cochem (every 2 hrs, 1.75 hr), **Bacharach** or **St. Goar** (hrly, 1.5 hrs with one change), **Koblenz** (5/hrly, 1 hr), **Bonn** (4/hrly, 20 min), **Trier** (9/day, 2.5 hrs), **Aachen** (3/hrly, 45 min), **Paris** (2/day, 6 hrs), **Amsterdam** (8/day, 2.5 hrs).

BONN
Bonn was chosen for its sleepy, cultured, and peaceful nature as a good place to plant Germany's first post-Hitler government. Now that Germany is one again, Berlin will resume its position as capital in 1999. Apart from the tremendous cost of switching the seat of government, more than 100,000 jobs are involved, and lots of Bonn families will have some difficult decisions to make.

Today Bonn is sleek, modern, and, by big-city standards, remarkably pleasant and easygoing. Stop here not to see the sparse exhibit at **Beethoven's House** (8 DM, Monday–Saturday 10:00–16:00, Sunday 11:00–16:00, free English brochure, tel. 0228/981-7525) but to come up for a smoggy breath of the real world after the misty, romantic Rhine.

The pedestrian-only old town stretches out from the station and makes you wonder why the United States can't trade in its malls for real, people-friendly cities. The market square and Münster-platz—filled with street musicians—are a joy. People-watching doesn't get much better. The TI faces the station (Monday–Friday 9:00–18:30, Saturday 9:00–17:00, Sunday 10:00–14:00, room-finding service for 5 DM, tel. 0228/773-466).

Hotel Eschweiler is plain but well located, just off the market square on a pedestrian street next to Beethoven's place above a taco joint (S-60 DM, Ss-70 DM, Sb-95 DM, Ds-120 DM, Db-140 DM, show this book for a 10 percent discount, great breakfasts, seven-minute walk from the station, Bonngasse 7, tel. 0228/631-760 or 0228/631-769, fax 0228/694-904).

ROTHENBURG AND THE ROMANTIC ROAD

From Munich or Füssen to Frankfurt, the Romantic Road takes you through Bavaria's medieval heartland, a route strewn with picturesque villages, farmhouses, onion-domed churches, Baroque palaces, and walled cities.

Dive into the Middle Ages via Rothenburg (ROE-ten-burg), Germany's best-preserved walled town. Countless travelers have searched for the elusive "untouristy Rothenburg." There are many contenders (such as Michelstadt, Miltenberg, Bamberg, Bad Windsheim, and Dinkelsbühl), but none holds a candle to the king of medieval German cuteness. Even with crowds, overpriced souvenirs, Japanese-speaking night watchmen, and yes, even with *Schneebälle*, Rothenburg is best. Save time and mileage, and be satisfied with the winner.

Planning Your Time

The best one-day look at the heartland of Germany is the Romantic Road bus tour. Eurail travelers, who get a 75 percent discount, pay only around 30 DM for the ride (daily, Frankfurt to Munich or Füssen, and vice versa). Drivers can follow the route laid out in the tourist brochures (available at any TI). The only stop worth more than a few minutes is Rothenburg. Twenty-four hours is ideal for this town. Two nights and a day is a bit much, unless you're actually relaxing on this trip.

Rothenburg in a day is easy, with four essential experiences: the Medieval Crime and Punishment Museum, the Riemenschneider wood carving in St. Jacob's Church, the city walking tour, and a walk along the wall. With more time there are several mediocre but entertaining museums, walking and biking in the nearby countryside, and lots of cafés and shops. Make a point to spend at least

Rothenburg

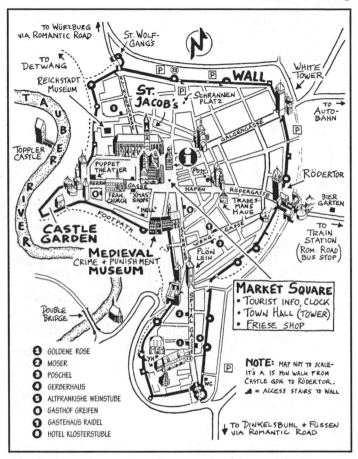

To WÜRZBURG VIA ROMANTIC ROAD

ST. WOLF-GANGS

TO DETWANG

REICHSTADT MUSEUM

TAUBER

TOPPLER CASTLE

RIVER

ST. JACOB'S

PUPPET THEATER

HERRN GASSE

FRAN. CHURCH

XMAS SHOPS

HELL

CASTLE GARDEN

FOOTPATH

MEDIEVAL CRIME + PUNISHMENT MUSEUM

DOUBLE BRIDGE

WALL

WHITE TOWER

SCHRANNEN PLATZ

GALGENGASSE

TO AUTO-BAHN

POST

HAFEN

RÖDERGASSE

RÖDERTOR

TRADES-MANS HAUS

BIER GARTEN

GASSE

WENG

PLÖN LEIN

SPITAL GASSE

YH

WC

TO TRAIN STATION (ROM. ROAD BUS STOP)

MARKET SQUARE
• TOURIST INFO, CLOCK
• TOWN HALL (TOWER)
• FRIESE SHOP

NOTE: MAP NOT TO SCALE - IT'S A 15 MIN WALK FROM CASTLE GDN. TO RÖDERTOR.
▪ = ACCESS STAIRS TO WALL

❶ GOLDENE ROSE
❷ MOSER
❸ POSCHEL
❹ GERBERHAUS
❺ ALTFRANKISHE WEINSTUBE
❻ GASTHOF GREIFEN
❼ GASTEHAUS RAIDEL
❽ HOTEL KLOSTERSTUBLE

↓ TO DINKELSBUHL + FÜSSEN VIA ROMANTIC ROAD

one night. The town is yours after dark, when the groups vacate and the town's floodlit cobbles wring some romance out of any travel partner.

ROTHENBURG

In the Middle Ages, when Frankfurt and Munich were just wide spots on the road, Rothenburg was Germany's second-largest free imperial city, with a whopping population of 6,000. Today it's her best-preserved medieval walled town, enjoying tremendous tourist popularity without losing its charm. Get medievaled in Rothenburg.

Orientation (tel. code: 09861)

To orient yourself in Rothenburg, think of the Rothenburg town map as a human head. Its nose—the castle garden—sticks out to the left, and the neck is the skinny lower part, with the hostel and my favorite hotels in the Adam's apple. The town is a joy on foot. No sight or hotel is more than a 15-minute walk from the train station or each other.

During Rothenburg's heyday, from 1150 to 1400, it was the crossing point of two major trade routes: Tashkent–Paris and Hamburg–Venice. Most of the buildings you'll see were built by 1400. The city was born around its long-gone castle—built in 1142, destroyed in 1356, and now the site of the castle garden. You can see the shadow of the first town wall, which defines the oldest part of Rothenburg, in its contemporary street plan. A few gates from this wall survive. The richest and biggest houses were in this central part. The commoners built higgledy-piggledy (read: picturesquely) farther from the center near the present walls.

Today the great trade is tourism; two-thirds of the townspeople are employed to serve you. Too often Rothenburg brings out the shopper in visitors before they've had a chance to appreciate the historic city. True, this is a great place to do your German shopping, but first see the town. While 2.5 million people visit each year, a mere 500,000 spend the night. Rothenburg is most enjoyable early and late, when the tour groups are gone.

Tourist Information: The TI is on Market Square (Monday–Friday 9:00–12:30, 13:00–18:00, Saturday and Sunday 10:00–15:00 unreliably, shorter hours off-season, tel. 09861/40492, after-hours board lists rooms still available). Pick up a map and the *Sights Worth Seeing and Knowing* brochure (a virtual walking guide to the town). The free "Hotels and Pensions of Rothenburg" map has the greatest detail and names all of the streets. Confirm sightseeing plans and ask about the daily 14:00 walking tour (April–December) and evening entertainment. The best town map is available free at the Friese shop, two doors toward Rothenburg's "nose."

Arrival in Rothenburg: Exit left from the train station, and turn right on the first busy street (Ansbacher Strasse). It'll take you to Rothenburg's Market Square within 10 minutes. Leave luggage in lockers at the station (2 DM). The travel agency in the station is the place to arrange train and *couchette* (sleeper) reservations. Taxis wait at the station and can take you to any hotel for 8 DM.

Tours of Rothenburg

The TI on Market Square offers 90-minute guided **walking tours** in English (6 DM, daily April–October at 14:00 from Market Square). A bit less informative but wonderfully entertaining, the **Night Watchman's Tour** takes tourists on his rounds each evening at 20:00 (6 DM, April–December, in English). This is the best evening activity in town. Or you can hire a private guide. For 85 DM, a local historian—who's usually an intriguing character as well—will bring the ramparts alive. Eight hundred years of history are packed between Rothenburg's cobbles. (Manfred Baumann, tel. 09861/4146, and Anita Weinzierl, tel. 09868/7993, are good guides.) If you prefer riding to walking, **horse-and-buggy rides** last 30 minutes and cost 10 DM per person for a minimum of three people.

Sights—Rothenburg's Town Hall Square

▲▲**Town Hall Tower**—The best view of Rothenburg and the surrounding countryside, and a close-up look at an old tiled roof from the inside are yours for 1 DM and a rigorous (214 steps, 180 feet) but interesting climb (daily 9:30–12:30, 13:00–17:00, off-season weekends from 12:00–15:00 only). Entrance is on Market Square. Women, beware: Some men find the view best from the bottom of the ladder just before the top.

Meistertrunk Show—Be on Market Square at 11:00, 12:00, 13:00, 14:00, 15:00, 20:00, 21:00, or 22:00 for the ritual gathering of the tourists to see the less-than-breathtaking reenactment of the Meistertrunk story. In 1631 the Catholic army took the Protestant town and was about to do its rape, pillage, and plunder thing when, as the story goes, the mayor said, "Hey, if I can drink this entire three-liter tankard of wine in one gulp, will you leave us alone?" The invading commander, sensing he was dealing with an unbalanced people, said, "Sure." Mayor Nusch drank the whole thing, the town was saved, and the mayor slept for three days. Hint: for the best show, don't watch the clock; watch the open-mouthed tourists gasp as the old windows flip open. At the late shows, the square flickers with flash attachments. While you wait for the show, give yourself the spin tour below.

Market Square Spin Tour—Stand at the bottom of Market Square (10 feet below the wooden post) and spin 360 degrees clockwise starting with the city hall tower. Now, do it slower following these notes: 1) The city's tallest tower, at 200 feet, stands atop the old city hall, a white, Gothic, 13th-century building. Notice the tourists enjoying the view from the black top of the tower. 2) When the town had more money and Gothic went out-of-date, a new town hall was built in front of the old one. This is in Renaissance style from 1570. (Access to the old town hall tower is through the middle of the new town hall arcade.) 3) At the top of the square stands the proud Councilors' Tavern (clock tower, from 1466). In its day, the city council drank here. Today it's the tourist office and the focus of all the attention when the little doors on either side of the clock flip open and the wooden figures (from 1910) reenact the Meistertrunk. 4) Across the street, the green building is the oldest pharmacy in town—Löwen Apotheke, from 1374, peek inside. 5) On the bottom end of the square, the grey building is a fine print shop (see Shopping, below, free brandy). 6) Adjoining that is the Baumeister's House with its famous Renaissance facade featuring statues of the seven virtues and the seven vices—the former supporting the latter. 7) The green house below that is the former house of Mayor Toppler, today the fine old Greifen Hotel; next to it is a famous Scottish restaurant. 8) Continue circling to the big 17th-century St. George's fountain. The long metal gutters slid, routing the water into the villagers' buckets. Rothenburg's many fountains had practical functions beyond providing drinking water. The water was used for fighting fires, and the fountains were stocked with fish during times of siege. Two fine buildings behind the fountain show the old-time lofts with warehouse doors and pulleys on top for hoisting. All over town, lofts were filled with grain and corn. A year's supply was required by the city so they could survive any siege. One building is a free art gallery showing off the work of Rothenburg's top artists. The other is another old-time pharmacy. 9) The broad street running under the town hall tower is Herrngasse. The town originated with its castle (1142). Herrngasse leads from the castle (now gone) to Market Square where you stand now.

▲**Historical Town Hall Vaults**—Under the town hall tower is a city history museum that gives a waxy but good look at medieval Rothenburg. With the best English descriptions in town, it offers a look at "the fateful year 1631," a replica of the famous Meistertrunk tankard, and a dungeon complete with three dank cells and some torture lore (3 DM, 9:30–18:00, closed in winter, well described in English).

Sights—Rothenburg

▲▲**Walk the Wall**—Just over a mile around, providing great views and a good orientation, this walk can be done by those under six feet tall and without a camera in less than an hour, and requires no special sense of balance. Photographers go through lots of film, especially before breakfast or at sunset, when the lighting is best and the crowds are fewest. The best fortifications are in the Spitaltor (south end). Walk from there counterclockwise to the "forehead." Climb the Rödertor en route. The names you see along the way are people who donated money to rebuild the wall after World War II.

▲**Rödertor**—The wall tower nearest the train station is the only one you can climb. It's worth the hike up for the view and a fascinating rundown on the bombing of Rothenburg in the last weeks of World War II—the northeast corner of the city was destroyed (2 DM, daily 9:00–17:00, closed off-season, photos, English translation).

▲▲**St. Jacob's Church**—Built in the 14th century, it's been Lutheran since 1544. Take a close look at the Twelve Apostles altar in front (from 1546, left permanently in its open festival day position). Six saints are below Christ. St. James (Jacob in German) is the one with the staff. He's the saint of pilgrims, and this was on the medieval pilgrimage route to Santiago de Compostela in Spain. Study the painted panels. Around the back (upper left) is a great painting of Rothenburg's Market Square in the 15th century—looking like it does today. Before leaving the front of the church, notice the old medallions above the carved choir stalls: the coats of arms of Rothenburg's leading families and portraits of early Reformation preachers.

Next, climb the stairs in the back. Behind the pipe organ stands the artistic highlight of Rothenburg and perhaps the most wonderful woodcarving in all Germany: the glorious 500-year-old, 30-foot-high *Altar of the Holy Blood*. Tilman Riemenschneider, the Michelangelo of German woodcarvers, carved this from 1499 to 1504 to hold a precious rock crystal capsule set in a cross containing a drop of the holy blood (1270). Below, in the scene of the Last Supper, Jesus gives Judas a piece of bread marking him as the traitor while John lays his head on Christ's lap. On the left: Jesus entering Jerusalem. On the right: Jesus praying in the Garden of Gethsemane (2.50 DM, Monday–Saturday 9:00–17:30, Sunday 10:45–17:30, off-season 10:00–12:00 and 14:00–16:00, free helpful English info sheet).

▲▲**Medieval Crime and Punishment Museum**—It's the best of its kind, full of fascinating old legal bits and *Kriminal* pieces, instruments of punishment and torture, even a special cage—complete with a metal gag—for nags. Exhibits are well described in English (5 DM, 80-DM combo includes Imperial City Museum, daily 9:30–17:30, shorter hours in winter, fun cards and posters).

▲**Toy Museum**—Two floors of historic *Kinder*-cuteness is a hit with many (5 DM, 12 DM per family, daily 9:30–18:00, just off Market Square, downhill from the fountain, Hofbronneng 13).

Museum of the Imperial City (Reichsstadt Museum)—This less sensational museum, housed in the former Dominican Convent, gives a more scholarly look at old Rothenburg. Highlights include *The Rothenburg Passion*, a 12-panel series of paintings from 1492 showing scenes leading up to Christ's crucifixion, an exhibit of Jewish culture through the ages in Rothenburg, and a 14th-century convent kitchen (4 DM, daily 9:30–17:30, in winter 13:00–16:00). The convent garden is a peaceful place to work on your tan.

▲▲**Herrngasse and the Castle Garden**—Any town's *Herrngasse*, where the richest patricians and merchants (the *Herren*) lived, is your chance to see its finest old mansions. Wander from Market Square down Herrngasse (past the old Rothenburg official measurement rods on the city hall wall) and drop into the lavish front rooms of a ritzy hotel or two. Pop into the Franciscan Church (free, daily 10:00–12:00, 14:00–16:00, built in 1285—the oldest in town, with a Riemenschneider altarpiece), continue on down past the old-fashioned puppet theater, through the old gate (notice the tiny after-curfew door in the big door and the frightening mask mouth from which hot Nutella was poured onto attackers), through the garden and to the end of what used to be the castle (great picnic spots and Tauber Riviera views at sunset). This is the popular kissing spot for romantic Rothenburg teenagers.

▲**Walk in the Countryside**—Just below the *Burggarten* (castle garden) in the Tauber Valley is the cute, skinny, 600-year-old castle/summer home of Mayor Toppler (2 DM, 13:00–16:00 on Friday, Saturday, and Sunday). On the top floor, notice the photo of bombed-out 1945 Rothenburg. Then walk on past the covered bridge and huge trout to the peaceful village of Detwang. Detwang (from 968, the second-oldest village in Franconia) is actually older than Rothenburg and also has a Riemenschneider altarpiece in its church. For a scenic return, loop back to Rothenburg through the valley along the river, past a café with outdoor tables, great desserts, and a town view to match.

Festivals—Rothenburgers dress up in medieval costumes and beer gardens spill out into the street to celebrate Mayor Nusch's Meistertrunk victory (Whitsun, six weeks after Easter) and 700 years of history in the Imperial City Festival (second weekend in September, with fireworks).

Swimming—Rothenburg has a fine modern recreation center with an indoor/outdoor pool and sauna. It's just a few minutes' walk down the Dinkelsbühl Road (Friday–Wednesday 9:00–20:00, opens at 10:00 on Thursday, tel. 09861/4565).

Sightseeing Lowlights—St. Wolfgang's Church is a fortified Gothic church built into the medieval wall at Klingentor. Its dungeon-like passages and shepherd's dance exhibit are pretty lame (2 DM, daily 10:00–13:00, 14:00–17:00). The cute-looking Bäuerliches Museum (farming museum) next door is even worse. The Rothenburger Handwerkerhaus (tradesman's house, 700 years old) shows the typical living situation of Rothenburg in its heyday (3 DM, daily 9:00–18:00, closed in winter, Alter Stadtgraben 26, near the Markus Tower).

Shopping

Be careful . . . Rothenburg is one of Germany's best shopping towns. Do it here, mail it home, and be done with it. Lovely prints, carvings, wineglasses, Christmas-tree ornaments, and beer steins are popular.

The Käthe Wohlfahrt Christmas trinkets phenomenon is spreading across the half-timbered reaches of Europe. In Rothenburg tourists flock to two Käthe Wohlfahrt Christmas Villages (on either side of Herrngasse, just off Market Square). This Christmas wonderland is filled with enough twinkling lights to require a special electric hookup, instant Christmas spirit mood music (best appreciated on a hot day in July), and American and Japanese tourists hungrily filling little woven shopping baskets with 5-DM to 10-DM goodies to hang on their trees. (OK, I admit it, my Christmas tree sports a few KW ornaments.) Note: Prices have hefty tour-guide kickbacks built into them. The Käthe Wohlfahrt discount store sells damaged and discontinued items. It's unnamed at Kirchgasse 5 across from the entrance of St. Jacob's Church (weekdays 10:00–18:00, less on weekends, tel. 09861/4090).

The Friese shop offers a charming contrast (just off Market Square, west of the TI on the corner across from public WC). Cuckoo with friendliness, it gives shoppers with this book tremendous service: a 10 percent discount, 16 percent tax deducted if you have it mailed, and a free Rothenburg map. Anneliese, who runs the place with her sons, Frankie and Berni, charges only her cost for shipping, changes money at the best rates in town with no extra charge, and lets tired travelers leave their bags in her back room for free. Her pricing is good, but to comparison shop, go here last.

The Ernst Geissendörfer print shop sells fine prints, etchings, and paintings. If you show this book, they'll offer 10 percent off marked prices for all purchases in cash (or credit card purchases of at least 100 DM) and a free shot of German brandy whether you buy anything or not. The shop is on the corner, where Market Square hits Schmiedgasse.

For characteristic wineglasses and oinkology gear, drop by the Weinladen am Plonlein (Plonlein 27).

Shoppers who mail their goodies home can get handy boxes at the post office (Monday–Friday 9:00–12:30, 14:00–17:00, Saturday 9:00–12:00, Milchmarkt 5).

Those who prefer to eat their souvenirs shop the *Bäckereien* (bakeries). Their succulent pastries, pies, and cakes are pleasantly distracting. Skip the good-looking but bad-tasting Rothenburger *Schneebälle*.

Sleeping in Rothenburg
(1.7 DM = about $1, tel. code: 09861, zip code: 91541)
Sleep Code: **S** = Single, **D** = Double/Twin, **T** = Triple, **Q** = Quad, **b** = bathroom, **t** = toilet only, **s** = shower only, **CC** = Credit Card (Visa, MasterCard, Amex), **SE** = Speaks English, **NSE** = No English. Unless otherwise indicated, room prices include breakfast.

Rothenburg is crowded with visitors. But when the sun sets, most retreat to the predictable plumbing of their big-city high-rise hotels. Except for the rare Saturday night, room-finding is easy throughout the year. Unless otherwise noted, enough English is spoken.

Many hotels and guest houses will pick up desperate heavy packers at the station. You may be greeted at the station by the *Zimmer* skimmer trying to waylay those on their way to a reserved room. Resist. If you arrive without a reservation, try talking yourself into one of these more desperate bed-and-breakfast rooms for a youth-hostel price. Be warned: These people are notorious for taking you to distant hotels and then charging you for a ride back if you decline a room. There's a handy Laundromat near the station (Johannitergasse 8, tel. 09861/5177).

Hotels

I like **Hotel Goldene Rose**, where scurrying Karin serves breakfast and stately Henni keeps everything in good order. The hotel has only one shower for two floors of rooms, and the streetside rooms can be noisy, but the rooms are clean and airy and you're surrounded by cobbles, flowers, and red-tiled roofs (one small S-25 DM, S-35 DM, D-65 DM, Ds-83 DM, Db-87 DM in classy annex behind the garden, some triples, and a spacious family apartment: for four-190 DM, for five-225 DM, CC:VMA, closed in January and February, kid-friendly, ground-floor rooms in annex, Spitalgasse 28, tel. 09861/4638, fax 09861/86417, Henni SE). The Favetta family also serves good, reasonably priced meals. Remember to keep your key to get in after they close (at the side gate in the alley). The hotel is a 15-minute walk from the station or a seven-minute (without shopping) walk downhill from Market Square.

Gasthof Greifen, once the home of Mayor Toppler, is a big, traditional, 600-year-old place with large rooms and all the comforts. It's family-run and creaks just the way you want it to (small Sb-64, Sb-80 DM, one big D-74 DM with no shower available, Db-115–135 DM, Tb-180 DM, 10 percent off for three-night stay, CC:VMA, laundry self- or full-service, free and easy parking, half a block downhill from Market Square at Obere Schmiedgasse 5, tel. 09861/2281, fax 09861/86374, Brigitte and Klingler family).

Gasthof Marktplatz, right on Market Square, has eight tidy rooms and a cozy atmosphere (S-38 DM, D-70 DM, Ds-80 DM, Db-88 DM, T-90 DM, Ts-105 DM, Tb-115 DM, Grüner Markt 10, tel. & fax 09861/6722, Herr Rosner SE).

Gästehaus Raidel, a creaky 500-year-old house packed with antiques, offers large rooms with cramped facilities down the hall. Run by grim people who make me want to sing the *Addams Family* theme song, it works in a pinch (S-35 DM, Sb-69 DM, D-69 DM, Db-89 DM, Wenggasse 3, tel. 09861/3115).

Hotel Gerberhaus, a classy new hotel in a 500-year-old building, is warmly run by Inge and Kurt, who mix modern comforts into bright and airy rooms while maintaining the half-timbered elegance. Great buffet breakfasts and pleasant garden in back (Sb-80 DM, Db-100-140 DM depending on size, Tb-165 DM, Qb-185 DM, for five people-210 DM, all with TV and telephones, CC:VM but use cash and you get 5 percent off and a free *Schneeball*, Spitalgasse 25, tel. 09861/ 94900, fax 09861/86555, e-mail: Gerberhaus@

t-online.de). Claudia's café, downstairs, serves good salads and sandwiches.

Hotel Klosterstuble, deep in the old town near the castle garden, is even classier. Jutta greets her guests while husband Rudolf does the cooking (Sb-95 DM, Db-120–160 DM, some luxurious family rooms, 10 DM extra on weekends, discounts for families, buffet breakfast, CC:V, Heringsbronnengasse 5, tel. 09861/6774, fax 09861/6474).

Bohemians enjoy the **Hotel Altfränkische Weinstube am Klosterhof**. Mario and Hanne run this dark and smoky pub in a 600-year-old building. Upstairs they rent six *gemütliche* rooms with upscale Monty Python atmosphere, TVs, modern showers, open-beam ceilings, and *"Himmel"* beds—canopied four-poster "heaven" beds (Sb-79 DM, Db-89 DM, Tb-109–119 DM, most rooms have tubs with hand showers, kid-friendly, CC:VM, walk under St. Jacob's church, take second left off Klingengasse at Klosterhof 7, tel. 09861/6404, fax 09861/6410). Their pub is a candlelit classic, serving hot food until 22:30, closing at 1:00. Drop by on Wednesday evening (19:30–24:00) for the English Conversation Club.

Top Private Rooms

For the best real, with-a-local-family, comfortable, and homey experience, stay with **Herr und Frau Moser** (D-65 DM, T-95 DM, no single rooms, Spitalgasse 12, tel. 09861/5971). This charming retired couple speak little English but try very hard. Speak slowly, in clear, simple English. Reserve by phone and you must reconfirm by phone one day ahead of arrival.

Pension Pöschel is friendly with seven cozy rooms on the second floor of a concrete but pleasant building (S-35 DM, D-60 DM, T-90 DM, small kids free, Wenggasse 22, tel. 09861/3430).

Frau Guldemeister rents two simple ground-floor rooms (Ss-40 DM, Ds with twin beds-60 DM, bigger Db-70 DM, breakfast in room, minimum two-night stay, off Market Square behind the Christmas shop, Pfaffleinsgasschen 10, tel. 09861/8988, some English, takes only telephone reservations no more than a day or two in advance).

Last Resort Accommodations

Pension Kreuzerhof has seven big, modern, ground-floor, motel-style rooms with views of parked cars on a quiet street (Sb-40–50 DM, Db-78–87 DM, Millergasse 6, tel. & fax 09861/3424. **Erich Endress** offers five airy, comfy rooms above his grocery store (S-45 DM, D-80 DM, Db-110 DM, non-smoking, Rodergasse 6, tel. 09861/2331). The **Zum Schmolzer** restaurant at Rosengasse 21 rents 14 well-maintained but drab-colored rooms (Sb-55 DM, Db-90 DM, Stollengasse 29, tel. 09861/3371, fax 09861/7204, SE). **Cafe Uhl** offers 10 fine, slightly frayed rooms over a bakery

(Sb-55–65 DM, Db-95–110 DM, CC:VA, Plonlein 8, tel. 09861/4895, fax 09861/92820). **Gästehaus Flemming** has seven plain, comfortable rooms behind St. Jacob's Church (Db-86, Klingengasse 21, tel. 09861/92380). **Gästehaus Viktoria** is a peaceful and cheery little place with a tiny garden and two rooms (Ds-75 DM, Klingenschütt 4, tel. 09861/87682, Hanne).

In the modern world, a block from the train station, **Pension Willi und Helen Then** is run by a cool guy who played the sax in a jazz band for seven years after the war and is a regular at the English Conversation Club (D-70 DM, Db-80 DM, tel. 09861/5177, fax 09861/86014).

Hostel

The fine **Rossmühle Youth Hostel** has 180 beds in two buildings. The droopy-eyed building (the old town horse-mill, used when the town was under siege and the river-powered mill was inaccessible) houses groups and the hostel office. The adjacent and newly renovated hostel is mostly for families and individuals (22-DM beds, Db-54 DM, 5.50-DM sheets, breakfast included, 9-DM dinners, Muhlacker 1, tel. 09861/ 94160, fax 09861/941-620, e-mail: JHRothen@aol.com, SE). This popular place takes reservations (even more than a year in advance) and will hold rooms until 18:00. Here in Bavaria, hosteling is limited to those under 27, except for families traveling with children under 18.

Sleeping in Nearby Detwang and Bettwar

The town of Detwang, a 15-minute walk below Rothenburg, is loaded with quiet *Zimmer*. The clean, quiet, and comfortable old **Gasthof zum Schwarzen Lamm** in Detwang (D-85 DM, Db-110–130 DM, tel. 09861/6727, fax 09861/86899) serves good food, as does the popular and very local-style Eulenstube next door. **Gästehaus Alte Schreinerei** offers good food and 18 quiet, comfy, reasonable rooms a little farther down the road in Bettwar (Db-76 DM, 8801 Bettwar, tel. 09861/1541, fax 09861/86710).

Eating in Rothenburg

Most places serve meals only from 11:30 to 13:30 and 18:00 to 20:00. At **Goldene Rose** (see Sleeping, above), Reno cooks up traditional German fare at good prices (11:30–14:00, 17:30–21:00, closed Tuesday and Wednesday, in sunny weather the leafy garden terrace is open in the back, Spitalgasse 28).

Galgengasse (Gallows Lane) has two cheap and popular standbys: **Pizzeria Roma** (11:30–24:00, 10-DM pizzas and normal schnitzel fare, Galgengasse 19) and **Gasthof zum Ochsen** (11:30–13:30, 18:00–20:00, closed Thursday, uneven service but decent 10-DM meals, Galgengasse 26). **Landsknechtstuben**, at Galgengasse 21, is pricey but friendly, with some cheaper schnitzel choices.

Gasthaus Siebersturm serves up tasty, reasonable meals in a bright, airy dining room (Spitalgasse). For a break from schnitzel, **Lotus China** serves good Chinese food daily (two blocks behind TI near the church, Eckele 2, tel. 09861/86886). **Gasthaus Greifen** serves typical Rothenburg cuisine at moderate prices (just below Market Square).

There are two **supermarkets** near the wall at Rödertor (the one outside the wall to the left is cheaper, the one inside is nicer).

Evening Fun and Beer Drinking

For beer garden fun on a balmy summer evening (dinner, or later for beer), you have three fine choices: nearby is **Gasthof Rödertor**, just outside the wall at the Rödertor (red gate). In the valley along the river and worth the 20-minute hike is **Unter den Linden** beer garden. A more central and touristy beer garden is behind **Hotel Eisenhut** (nightly until 22:00, access from Burggasse or through the hotel off Herrngasse).

Trinkstube zur Hölle (Hell) is dark and foreboding, serving good ribs from 18:00 and offering thick wine-drinking atmosphere until late (a block past Criminal Museum on Burggasse, with devil hanging out front, tel. 09861/4229). For mellow ambience, try the beautifully restored **Alte Keller's Weinstube** under walls festooned with old pots and jugs (closed Tuesday, Alter Keller 8). Wine lovers enjoy the Glocke Hotel's Stube (Plonlein 1). And perhaps the most elegant place in town is the courtyard of the Baumeister Haus (behind the statue-festooned facade a few doors below Market Square).

Two popular discos are a few doors farther out near the Sparkasse bank (T.G.I. Friday's at Ansbacher 15, in the alley next to the bank, open Wednesday, Friday, and Saturday; the other is Check Point, around the corner from the bank, open Wednesday and Friday–Sunday).

For a rare chance to mix it up with locals who aren't selling anything, bring your favorite slang and tongue-twisters to the **English Conversation Club** at Mario's Altfränkische Weinstube (Wednesday 19:30–24:00, Anneliese from the Friese shop is a regular). This dark and smoky pub is an atmospheric hangout any night but Tuesday, when it's closed (Klosterhof 7, off Klingengasse, behind St. Jacob's church, tel. 09861/6404).

Transportation Connections—Rothenburg

The Romantic Road bus tour takes you in and out of Rothenburg each afternoon (April–October) heading to Munich, Frankfurt, or Füssen (your choice). See the Romantic Road bus schedule later in this chapter.

A tiny train line runs between Rothenburg and Steinach (almost hrly, 15 min, but only until early evening). **Steinach by**

train to: Würzburg (hrly, 30 min), **Munich** (hrly, 2 hrs), **Frankfurt** (hrly, 2 hrs, change in Würzburg). Train connections in Steinach are usually within a few minutes.

ROMANTIC ROAD

The Romantic Road (Romantische Strasse) winds you past the most beautiful towns and scenery of Germany's medieval heartland. Once Germany's medieval trade route, now it's the best way to connect the dots between Füssen, Munich, and Frankfurt.

Wander through quaint hills and rolling villages, and stop wherever the cows look friendly or a town fountain beckons. My favorite sections are from Füssen to Landsberg and Rothenburg to Weikersheim. (If you're driving with limited time, you can connect Rothenburg and Munich by Autobahn, but don't miss these two best sections.) Caution: The similarly promoted "Castle Road" sounds intriguing, but is nowhere near as interesting.

Throughout Bavaria, you'll see colorfully ornamented Maypoles decorating town squares. Many are painted in Bavaria's colors, blue and white. The decorations that line each side of the pole symbolize the crafts or businesses of that town or community. Each May Day they are festively replaced. Traditionally, rival communities try to steal each other's Maypole. Locals will guard their new pole night and day as May Day approaches. Stolen poles are ransomed only with lots of beer for the clever thieves.

Getting Around the Romantic Road

By Bus: The Europa Bus Company runs buses daily between Frankfurt and Munich in each direction (April–October). A second route goes between Dinkelsbühl and Füssen daily. Buses leave from train stations in towns served by a train. The 120-DM, 11-hour ride costs only about 30 DM with a Eurailpass (expect to pay 3 DM extra to stow your bag). Each bus stops in Rothenburg (about 2 hours) and Dinkelsbühl (about an hour) and briefly at a few other attractions, and has a guide who hands out brochures and narrates the journey in English. While Romantic Road bus-tour guides are historically pretty bad, there is no quicker or easier way to travel across Germany and get such a hearty dose of its countryside. Bus reservations are free, easy, and smart—without one you can lose your seat down the road to someone who has one (especially on summer weekends; call 069/79030 one day in advance and leave your name). You can start, stop, and switch over where you like—but you'll be guaranteed a seat only if you reserve each segment.

By Car: Follow the brown "Romantische Strasse" signs.

Sights—Along the Romantic Road
(These sights are south to north.)

Füssen—This town, the southern terminus of the Romantic Road,

Romantic Road

is two miles from the startlingly beautiful Neuschwanstein Castle, worthy of a stop on any sightseeing agenda. (See the Bavaria and Tirol chapter for description and accommodations.)

▲▲**Wieskirche**—Germany's most glorious Baroque-rococo church. Heavenly! It's in a sweet meadow and is newly restored. Northbound Romantic Road buses stop here for 15 minutes. (See the Bavaria and Tirol chapter.)

Rottenbuch—Nondescript village with an impressive church.

▲**Dinkelsbühl**—Rothenburg's little sister is cute enough to merit a short stop. A moat, towers, gates, and a beautifully preserved medieval wall surround this town and its interesting local museum. The Kinderzeche children's festival turns Dinkelsbühl wonderfully on end in mid-July (TI tel. 09851/90240). On Neustädtlein, you'll find 80-DM doubles with bath and TV at friendly Haus Küffner (tel. 09851/1247) and Zur Linde (tel. 09851/3465).

▲▲▲**Rothenburg**—See opening of this chapter for information on Germany's best medieval town.

1999 Romantic Road Bus Schedule (Daily, April–October)

Frankfurt	8:00	—
Würzburg	9:45	—
Arrive Rothenburg	12:45	—
Depart Rothenburg	14:30	—
Arrive Dinkelsbühl	15:25	—
Depart Dinkelsbühl	16:15	16:15
Munich	19:50	—
Füssen	—	20:40
Füssen	8:00	—
Arrive Wieskirche	8:35	—
Depart Wieskirche	8:55	—
Munich	—	9:00
Arrive Dinkelsbühl	12:50	12:45
Depart Dinkelsbühl	—	14:00
Arrive Rothenburg	—	14:40
Depart Rothenburg	—	16:15
Würzburg	—	18:30
Frankfurt	—	20:30

▲**Herrgottskapelle**—This peaceful church, graced with Tilman Riemenschneider's greatest carved altarpiece (daily 9:15–17:30), is one mile from Creglingen and across the street from the Fingerhut thimble museum (daily 9:00–18:00). The southbound Romantic Road bus stops here for 15 minutes, long enough to see one or the other.

Weikersheim—This untouristy town has a palace with fine Baroque gardens (luxurious picnic spot), a folk museum, and a picturesque town square.

WÜRZBURG
A historic city, though freshly rebuilt since World War II, Würzburg is worth a stop to see its impressive Prince Bishop's Residenz, the bubbly Baroque chapel (Hofkirche) next door, and the palace's sculpted gardens.

Orientation (tel. code: 0931)

Tourist Information: Würzburg has a helpful TI just outside the train station (Monday–Friday 10:00–18:00, Saturday 10:00–14:00, closed Sunday) and another TI on Marktplatz (Monday–Saturday 10:00–18:00, tel. 0931/373-98). Their wonderful little *Visitor's Guide* pamphlet covers the tourists' Würzburg well. The produce market near the Marktplatz TI bustles daily except Sunday. Train information tel. 0931/19419.

Sights—Würzburg

▲▲▲**Residenz**—This Franconian Versailles, with grand rooms, 3-D art, and a tennis-court-sized fresco by Tiepolo, is worth a tour. English tours are on weekends at 11:00 and 15:00 (April–October, confirm at TI or call ahead). During the week, the best strategy is to take the TI's walking tour at 11:00, which includes a tour of the Residenz along with a walk through the "old" city (13 DM, Tuesday–Saturday April–October, two hours, all in English, includes admission to Residenz; meet at the TI on Marktplatz). Or buy the 5-DM guide at the Residenz; it's dry and lengthy, but you can use the pictures to figure out what room you're in. No English labels or descriptions are provided. The top sights are the grand staircase with the Tiepolo ceiling, the reconstructed Room of Mirrors (destroyed during World War II), and the grandly Tiepoloed Imperial Hall (5 DM, April–October Tuesday–Sunday 9:00–17:00, November–March 10:00–16:00, closed Monday, last entry 30 minutes before closing, tel. 0931/355-1712).

The elaborate Hofkirche chapel is next door (as you exit the palace, go left) and the entrance to the picnic-worthy garden is just beyond. Easy parking is available. Don't confuse the Residenz (a 15-minute walk from the train station) with the fortress on the hilltop.

Fortress Marienberg—Along with a city history museum, the fortress contains the Mainfränkisches Museum, highlighting the work of Riemenschneider, Germany's top woodcarver and past mayor of Würzburg (3.50 DM, Tuesday–Sunday 10:00–17:00, less off-season, tel. 0931/43016). Riemenschneider fans will find his work throughout Würzburg's many churches (which look closed but are likely open; the sign on the door, *"Bitte Türe schliessen,"* simply means "Please close the doors").

Veitshöchheim—Consider a cruise to Veitshöchheim, five kilometers away, to see the fanciful Baroque gardens and the Summer Residenz (gardens free and open daily 7:00 till dusk; 3 DM for palace, Tuesday–Sunday 9:00–12:00, 13:00–17:00, closed Monday). Catch the boat at the Würzburg dock (13 DM round-trip, leaves hourly, daily 10:00–17:00 April–October) or bus #11 from the Würzburg station (3.20 DM, hourly, 10 min).

Sleeping in Würzburg
(1.7 DM = about $1, tel. code: 0931, zip code: 97070)
All listings include breakfast, and prices are soft off-season.

Hotel-Pension Spehnkuch is the best budget hotel near the station. Overlooking a busy street but quiet behind double-paned windows, it's friendly and comfortable (S-50 DM, D-90 DM, T-130 DM, two minutes' walk from station, exit station and take a right on Rontgenring, at #7, elevator, tel. 0931/54752, fax 0931/54760, SE). **Pension Siegel** is a lesser option (S-46 DM, D-89 DM, from station, go straight on Kaiserstrasse and turn left at Muller store, Reisbrubengasse 7, tel. 0931/52941, fax 0931/52967, NSE).

Three fine hotels cluster within a block on Theaterstrasse. Quieter rooms are in back; front rooms have street noise. **Hotel Barbarossa**, tucked away on the fourth floor, has 17 comfortable rooms (Ss-75 DM, Sb-95 DM, one Ds-110 DM, Db-140 DM, Tb-170 DM, elevator, CC:VMA, Theaterstrasse 2, tel. 0931/321-370, fax 0931/321-3737, e-mail: marchiorello@t-online.de, SE). **Hotel Schönleber** is a cheery vision of pastel yellow (S-70–100 DM, Sb-95–110 DM, D-100 DM, Ds-110 DM, Db-150 DM, hall showers-4 DM, elevator, CC:VMA, Theaterstrasse 5, tel. 0931/12068, fax 0931/16012), and the **Altstadt Hotel** is a slight cut above, with a wonderfully fragrant Italian restaurant below (Ss-85 DM, Sb-95 DM, Ds-110 DM, Db-140 DM, CC:VMA, Theaterstrasse 7, tel. 0931/321-640, fax 0931/321-6464, e-mail: marchiorello@t-online.de, SE).

Sankt Josef Hotel has a more Franconian feel, with a woody restaurant on a quieter street (Sb-92 DM, Db-147–167 DM, CC:VMA, Semmelstrasse 28, coming from station, take left off Theaterstrasse, tel. 0931/308-680, fax 0931/308-6860, e-mail: hotelsanktjosef@at-online.de; NSE). Across the street is the elaborately painted **Hotel zur Stadt Mainz**, dating from 1430. You'll pay 40 to 50 DM more for the privilege of sleeping here (CC:VMA, Semmelstrasse 39, tel. 0931/53155, fax 0931/58510).

FRANKFURT
Frankfurt, the northern terminus of the Romantic Road, is actually pleasant for a big city and offers a good look at today's no-nonsense urban Germany.

Orientation (tel. code: 069)
Tourist Information: For a quick look at the city, pick up a 1-DM map at the TI in the train station (Monday–Friday 8:00–21:00, weekends 9:00–18:00, tel. 069/212-38-849). It's a 20-minute walk from the station down Kaiserstrasse past Goethe's house (great man, mediocre sight, Grosser Hirschgraben 23) to Römerberg, Frankfurt's lively Market Square (or you can take subway U-4 or

U-5 from the station to Römerberg). The TI's brochure, *Frankfurt Welcome*, describes a self-guided walking tour you can take from this square. A string of museums is just across the river along Schaumainkai (Tuesday–Sunday 10:00–17:00, Wednesday until 20:00, closed Monday). The TI also has info on bus tours of the city (44 DM, 10:00 and 14:00 in summer, 14:00 only off-season, 2.5 hrs).

Near the train station, a browse through Frankfurt's red-light district offers a fascinating way to kill time between trains. Wander down Taunusstrasse two blocks in front of the station and you'll find 20 "eros towers," each a five-story-tall brothel filled with prostitutes. Climbing through a few of these may be one of the more memorable experiences of your European trip. It feels safe, the atmosphere is friendly, and browsing is encouraged (40 DM, daily, tel. 069/32422).

Romantic Road Bus: If you're taking the bus out of Frankfurt, you can buy your ticket either in the Deutsches Touring office at the train station (Monday–Friday 7:30–18:00, Saturday 7:30–15:00, Sunday 7:30–14:00, CC:VMA, entrance at Mannheimer Strasse 4, tel. 069/230-735) or pay cash when you board the bus. Eurail and Europass holders, who get a 75 percent discount, pay only about 30 DM (plus 3 DM for one piece of luggage). The bus waits at stall #8 (right of the train station as you leave).

Sleeping in Frankfurt
(1.7 DM = about $1, tel. code: 069, zip code: 60329)
Avoid driving or sleeping in Frankfurt, especially during Frankfurt's numerous trade fairs (about five days a month), which send hotel prices skyrocketing. Pleasant Rhine or Romantic Road towns are just a quick train ride or drive away. But if you must spend the night in Frankfurt, here are some places within a block of the train station (and its handy train to the airport). This isn't the safest neighborhood; be careful after dark. Get a map at the TI, but for a rough idea of directions to hotels, stand with your back to the main entrance of the station: Using a 12-hour clock, Hotel Manhattan is across the street at 10:00, Pension Schneider at 12:00, Hotel Europa and Wiesbaden at 4:00, and the Goldner Stern at 5:00. Breakfast is included in all listings and English is spoken.

Hotel Manhattan, with newly remodeled, sleek, arty rooms, is expensive—best for a splurge on a first or last night in Europe (Sb-135 DM, Db-165 DM, show this book to get a break during non-convention times, elevator, riffraff in front of hotel, CC:VMA, Düsseldorfer Strasse 10, tel. 069/234-748, fax 069/234-532).

Pension Schneider is a strange little oasis of decency and quiet three floors above the epicenter of Frankfurt's red light district, two blocks in front of the train station. The street is safe in spite of the pimps and pushers. Its 10 rooms are big, bright, and comfortable (D-80 DM, Db-100 DM, Tb-110 DM, CC:VMA, elevator, corner of Moselstrasse at Taunusstrasse 43, tel. 069/251071, fax 069/259228).

Hotel Europa, with well-maintained rooms, is a fine value (Sb-80 DM, Db-120 DM, Tb-150 DM, prices soft on weekends, some non-smoking rooms, garage, CC:VMA, Baseler Strasse 17, tel. 069/236-013, fax 069/236-203).

Hotel Wiesbaden has worn rooms and a kind manager (Sb-95 DM, Db-110–135 DM depending on size, Tb-150 DM, a little smoky, elevator, CC:VMA, Baseler Strasse 52, tel. 069/232-347, fax 069/252-845).

Hotel Goldner Stern, a vintage hotel with dim rooms and hallways, is sleepable (S-43–50 DM, D-65–75 DM, hall showers-4 DM, Karlsruherstrasse 8, tel. 069/233-309). It may close before the millennium.

Farther from the station is **Pension Backer** (S-50 DM, D-60 DM, showers-3 DM, near the botanical gardens, Mendelssohn-strasse 92, tel. 069/747992). Take the S-Bahn two stops to Haup-twache, then transfer to U-6 or U-7 for two stops to Westend.

The hostel is open to members of any age (eight-bed rooms, 32 DM per bed with sheets and breakfast, bus #46 from station to Frankenstein Place, Deutschherrnufer 12, tel. 069/619-058).

Transportation Connections—Frankfurt

By train to: Rothenburg (hrly, 3 hrs, changes in Würzburg and Steinach; the tiny Steinach–Rothenburg train often leaves from the "B" section of track, away from the middle of the station, shortly after the Würzburg train arrives; don't miss it; Steinach has no tourism—for good reason), **Würzburg** (hrly, 90 min), **Munich** (hrly, 3.5 hrs), **Baden-Baden** (hrly, 90 min), **Freiburg** (hrly, 2 hrs, change in Mannheim), **Bonn** (hrly, 2 hrs), **Koblenz** (hrly, 90 min), **Köln** (hrly, 2 hrs), **Berlin** (hrly, 5 hrs), **Amsterdam** (8/day, 5 hrs), **Bern** (14/day, 4.5 hrs, changes in Mannheim and Basel), **Brussels** (6/day, 5 hrs), **Copenhagen** (3/day, 10 hrs), **London** (5/day, 9.5 hrs), **Milan** (6/day, 9 hrs), **Paris** (4/day, 6.5 hrs), **Vienna** (7/day, 7.5 hrs).

Frankfurt's Airport

The airport (*Flughafen*) is a 12-minute train ride from downtown (4/hrly, 5.80 DM, ride included in Frankfurt's 8.5-DM, all-day city transit pass or the 13-DM, two-day city pass). The airport is user-friendly, offering showers; baggage check; fair-rate banks with long hours; grocery store; train station; lounge where you can sleep overnight; business lounge (Europe City Club—30 DM to anyone with a plane ticket); easy rental-car pickup; plenty of park-ing; big green meeting-point sign; an information booth; and even McBeer. McWelcome to Germany. Airport English-speaking info:

tel. 069/6901 (will transfer you to any of the airlines for booking
or confirmation). Lufthansa—069/255-255, American Airlines—
069/271-130, Delta—069/664-1212, Northwest—0180/525-4650.

To Rothenburg: Train travelers can validate railpasses or
buy tickets at the airport station and catch a train to Würzburg,
connecting to Rothenburg via Steinach (hrly, 3 hrs). If driving to
Rothenburg, follow Autobahn signs to Würzburg.

Flying Home from Frankfurt: The airport has its own train
station, and many of the trains from the Rhine stop there on their
way into Frankfurt (e.g., hrly 90-min rides direct from Bonn; hrly
2-hr rides from Bacharach with a change in Mainz, earliest train
from Bacharach to Frankfurt leaves just before 6:00). By car, head
toward Frankfurt on the Autobahn and follow the little airplane
signs to the airport (*Flughafen*).

MUNICH (MÜNCHEN)

Munich, Germany's most livable and "yuppie" city, is also one of its most historic, artistic, and entertaining. It's big and growing, with a population of more than 1.4 million. Just a little more than a century ago, it was the capital of an independent Bavaria. Its imperial palaces, jewels, and grand boulevards constantly remind visitors that this was once a political and cultural power-nouse. And its recently-bombed-out feeling reminds us that 75 years ago it provided a springboard for Nazism, and 55 years ago it lost a war.

Orient yourself in Munich's old center with its colorful pedestrian mall. Immerse yourself in Munich's art and history—crown jewels, Baroque theater, Wittelsbach palaces, great paintings, and beautiful parks. Munich evenings are best spent in frothy beer halls, with their oompah bunny-hopping and belching Bavarian atmosphere. Pry big pretzels from no-nonsense, buxom beer maids.

Planning Your Time

Munich is worth two days, including a half-day side trip to Dachau. If necessary, its essence can be captured in a day (walk the center, tour a palace and a museum, and enjoy a beer-filled evening). Those without a car and in a hurry can do the Bavarian castles of Ludwig as a day trip from Munich by tour. Even Salzburg can be a handy day trip from Munich.

Orientation (tel. code: 089)

The tourist's Munich is circled by a ring road (which was the town wall) marked by four old gates: Karlstor (near the train station, known as the *Hauptbahnhof*), Sendlinger Tor, Isartor (near the river), and Odeonsplatz (near the palace). Marienplatz is the city center. A great pedestrian-only street cuts this circle in half, running nearly from Karlstor and the train station through Marienplatz to Isartor. Orient yourself along this east-west axis. Most sights are within a few blocks of this people-filled walk. Ninety percent of the sights and hotels I recommend are within a 20-minute walk of Marienplatz and each other.

Tourist Information

Munich has two helpful TIs: at the train station (Monday–Saturday 9:00–20:00, Sunday 10:00–18:00, Bahnhofplatz 2, tel. 089/233-30-257) and on Marienplatz (Monday–Friday 10:00–20:00, Saturday 10:00–16:00, closed Sunday, tel. 089/233-30-272, Web site: www.muenchen-tourist.de). Have a list of questions ready, confirm sightseeing plans, and pick up brochures. The excellent Munich city map (use the close-up of downtown, with all bus lines) is one of the handiest in Europe. Consider the *Monatsprogramm* (2.50 DM, a German-language list of sights and events calendar), *Hits for Kids* (1 DM), and the free twice-monthly magazine *In München* (lists in German all the movies and entertainment in town, available at TI or any big cinema till supply runs out). The TI can refer you to hotels for a 10 to 15 percent fee, but you'll get a better value with my recommended hotels—contact them directly. If the line at the TI is bad, go to EurAide (below). The only essential item is the TI's great city map (also available at EurAide and many hotels).

EurAide: The industrious, eager-to-help EurAide office in the train station is a wonderful aid for Eurailers and budget travelers (daily in summer 7:45–12:00, 13:00–18:00; in winter it closes at 16:00 on weekdays, 12:00 on Saturday, and all day Sunday; Room 3 at track 11; tel. 089/593-889, fax 089/550-3965, Web site: www.cube.net/kmu/euraide.html, e-mail: euraide@compuserve.com). Alan Wissenberg and his staff know your train travel and accommodations questions and have answers in clear American English. The German rail company pays them to help you design your best train travels. They make reservations and sell train tickets, couchettes, and sleepers. They can find you a room for a 7-DM fee, and they offer the city map and a free newsletter. They sell a "Prague Excursion" train pass, convenient for Prague-bound Eurailers—good for train travel from any Czech border station to Prague and back to any border station within seven days (1st class-90 DM, 2nd class-60 DM, youth 2nd-40 DM; a bit cheaper through their U.S. office: tel. 941/480-1555, fax 941/480-1522). Every Wednesday in June and July, EurAide provides an excellent "Two Castle" tour of Neuschwanstein and Linderhof that includes Wieskirche (frustrating without a car, see below). EurAide is my stop for train and couchette reservations.

Arrival in Munich

By Train: Munich's train station is a sight in itself—one of those places that can turn an accountant into a vagabond. For a quick orientation in the station, use the big wall maps showing the train station, Munich, and Bavaria (through the center doorway as you leave the tracks on the left). For a quick rest stop, the Burger King upstairs has toilets as pleasant and accessible as its hamburgers. A classier and more peaceful hangout is the vast, generally empty, old restaurant opposite track 14. Next door, the post office (which has handy metered phones) is open daily. Sussmann's Internationale Presse (across from track 24) is great for English-language books, papers, and magazines, including *Munich Found* (informative English-speaking residents' monthly, 4 DM). You'll also find two TIs (the city TI and EurAide, see above). The station is connected by U-Bahn, S-Bahn, and buses to the rest of the city (though many hotels listed in this book are within walking distance of the station).

By Plane: There are two good ways to connect downtown Munich and its airport. Either take an easy 40-minute ride on S-8 (from Marienplatz, 14 DM or free with train pass), or hop the Lufthansa airport bus to (or from) the train station (15 DM, 3/hrly, 45 min, buy tickets on bus or from EurAide).

Getting Around Munich

Much of Munich is walkable. To reach sights away from the city center, use the fine tram, bus, and subway systems. Taxis are expensive and generally unnecessary (except perhaps to avoid the time-comsuming trip to Nymphenburg).

By Public Transit: Subways are called U- or S-Bahns. Subway lines are numbered (e.g., S-3 or U-5). Eurailpasses are good on the S-Bahn (actually an underground-while-in-the-city commuter railway). Regular tickets cost 3.50 DM and are good for two hours of changes in one direction. For the shortest rides (one or two stops), get the cheapest 1.80-DM ticket (*Kurzstrecke*). The 8.50-DM all-day pass is a great deal (valid until 6:00 the next morning). The Partner Daily Ticket (for 12.50 DM) is good all day for up to two adults, three kids, and a dog. Tickets are available from easy-to-use ticket machines (which take bills and coins), subway booths, and TIs. The entire system (bus/tram/subway) works on the same tickets. You must punch your own ticket before boarding (stamping a date and time on it). Plainclothes ticket-checkers enforce this "honor system," rewarding freeloaders with stiff 60-DM fines.

Important: All S-Bahn lines connect the Hauptbahnhof (main station) with Marienplatz (main square). At either the station or Marienplatz, follow signs to the S-Bahn (U is not for you) and concern yourself only with the direction (*Richtung*: Hauptbahnhof/Pasing or Ostbahnhof/Marienplatz).

By Bike: Munich—level and compact, with plenty of bike paths—feels good on two wheels. Bikes can be rented quickly and easily at the train station at Radius Bikes (daily 10:00–18:00 May–mid-October, near track 30, tel. 089/596-113). The owner, Englishman Patrick Holder, rents three-speed bikes (5 DM/ hour, 25 DM/day, 30 DM/24 hours, 45 DM/48 hours, mountain bikes 20 percent more; credit-card imprint, 100 DM, or passport for a deposit). Patrick organizes Munich and Dachau tours (see below) and dispenses all the necessary tourist information (city map, bike routes), including a do-it-yourself bike tour booklet (5 DM).

Helpful Hints

Most Munich sights (including Dachau) are closed on Monday. If you're in Munich on Monday, here are some suggestions: visit the Deutsches Museum, BMW museum, or churches; take a walking tour or bus tour; climb high for city views (below); stroll the pedestrian streets; have lunch at the Viktualien Markt (see Eating, below); rent a bike for a spin through Englischer Garten; or day-trip to Salzburg or Ludwig's castles.

Helpful phone numbers: pharmacy (at train station, tel. 089/594-119), train information (tel. 089/19419), U.S. consulate (Königinstrasse 5, tel. 089/28880), American Express Company (tel. 089/290-900), taxi (tel. 089/21610).

There's plenty of online access in Munich. In the station consider the Times Square OnLine Bistro (9 DM/30 min).

Sights—Central Munich

▲▲**Marienplatz and the Pedestrian Zone**—Riding the escalator out of the subway into sunlit Marienplatz (Mary's Square) gives you a fine first look at the glory of Munich: great buildings bombed flat and rebuilt, the ornate facades of the new and old city halls (the Neues Rathaus, built in neo-Gothic style from 1867 to 1910—with the *Glockenspiel*, and the grey, pointy Altes Rathaus), outdoor cafés, and people bustling and lingering like the birds and breeze they share this square with. The not-very-old *Glockenspiel* "jousts" on Marienplatz daily through the tourist season at 11:00, 12:00, and 17:00.

From here the pedestrian mall (Kaufingerstrasse and Neuhau-serstrasse) leads you through a great shopping area, past carnivals of street entertainers and good old-fashioned slicers and dicers, the twin-towering Frauenkirche (built in 1470, rebuilt after World War II), and several fountains, to Karlstor and the train station. One of Europe's first pedestrian zones, this enraged shopkeepers when it was built in 1972. Today it is "Munich's living room." Nine thousand shoppers pass through it each hour . . . and the shopkeepers are very happy. Imagine this street in hometown U.S.A.

In the pedestrian zone around Marienplatz, there are three

Munich Center

HOTELS IN CENTER
❶ BRISTOL   ❸ LINDNER   ★ MARIENPLATZ
❷ MUNCHNER KINDL   ❹ SEIBEL ||||| PEDESTRIAN ZONE

noteworthy churches. **St. Michael's Church**, while one of the first great Renaissance buildings north of the Alps, has a brilliantly Baroque interior. You can borrow the tiny English booklet to read in a pew, see the interesting photos of the bombed-out city center near the entry, and go into the crypt to see King Ludwig II's tomb (2 DM, 40 stark royal tombs and one still-loved-by-romantics "mad" king).

The twin onion domes of the 500-year-old **Frauenkirche** (Church of Our Lady) are the symbol of the city. While much of the church was destroyed in World War II, the towers survived. Gloriously rebuilt since, the church is worth a visit. It was built in Gothic style, but money problems meant the domes weren't added until Renaissance times. These domes were inspired by the typical arches of the Venetian Renaissance. And the church domes we think of as "typically Bavarian" were inspired by these.

St. Peter's Church, the oldest in town, overlooks Marien-platz. Built upon the hill where the first monks founded the city in the 12th century, it has a fine interior with photos of the WWII bomb damage near the entrance. It's a long climb to the top of the spire (no elevator), much of it with two-way traffic on a one-way staircase, but the view is dynamite (2.50 DM, Monday–Saturday 9:00–18:00, Sunday 10:00–18:00). Try to be two flights from the top when the bells ring at the top of the hour (and when your friends ask you about your trip, you'll say, "What?").

▲▲**City Views**—Downtown Munich's three best city viewpoints are from the tops of: 1) St. Peter's Church (described above); 2) Frauenkirche—the highest viewpoint at 350 feet (elevator, 4 DM, Monday–Saturday 10:00–17:00, closed Sunday), and 3) the Neues Rathaus (3 DM, elevator from under the Marienplatz glockenspiel, Monday–Friday 9:00–19:00, weekends 10:00–19:00).

▲**Münchner Stadtmuseum**—The Munich city museum has four floors of exhibits: first floor—on life in Munich through the centuries (including World War II) illustrated in paintings, photos, models; second floor—special exhibits (often more inter-esting than the permanent ones); third floor—historic puppets and carnival gadgets; and fourth floor—a huge collection of musical instruments from around the world (5 DM, 7.50 DM for families, Tuesday–Sunday 10:00–17:00, Wednesday until 20:30, closed Monday, no English descriptions, no crowds, bored and playful guards, three blocks off Marienplatz at St. Jakob's Platz 1, a fine children's playground faces the entry).

▲▲**Alte Pinakothek**—Bavaria's best painting gallery is newly renovated to show off a great collection of European masterpieces (14th–18th centuries, Fra Angelico, Botticelli, da Vinci, Raphael, Dürer, Rubens, Rembrandt, El Greco, and Goya, 7 DM, Tues-day–Sunday 10:00–17:00, closed Monday, U-2 to Königsplatz or tram #27, tel. 089/238-05215).

▲**Neue Pinakothek**—The Alte Pinakothek's hip sister is a twin building across the square showing off paintings from 1800 to 1920: Romantic, Realistic, Impressionism, Jugendstil, Monet, Renoir, van Gogh, Klimt (7 DM, Tuesday–Sunday 10:00–17:00, closed Monday).

▲**Haus der Kunst**—Built by Hitler as a temple of Nazi art, this bold and fascist building now houses modern art, the kind the Führer censored. It's a playful collection—Kandinsky, Picasso, Dalí, and much more from this century (6 DM, Tuesday–Sunday 10:00–17:00, closed Monday, Prinzregentenstrasse 1, at south end of Englischer Garden).

Bayerisches Nationalmuseum—An interesting collection of Riem-enschneider carvings, manger scenes, traditional living rooms, and old Bavarian houses (3 DM, Tuesday–Sunday 9:30–17:00, closed Monday, tram #20 or bus #53 or #55 to Prinzregentenstrasse 3).

▲▲▲**Deutsches Museum**—Germany's answer to our Smith-sonian Institution, the Deutsches Museum traces the evolution of science and technology. With 10 miles of exhibits—from astronomy to zymurgy—even those on roller skates will need to be selective. Blue dots on the floor mark someone's idea of the top 12 stops, but I had a better time just wandering through well-described rooms of historic bikes, cars (Benz's first car . . . a three-wheeler from the 1880s), trains, airplanes (Hitler's flying bomb from 1944), spaceships (step inside a rocket engine), mining, the harnessing of wind and water power, hydraulics, musical instruments, printing, photography, computers, astronomy, clocks . . . it's the Louvre of science and technology.

Most sections are lovingly described in English. The much-vaunted "high voltage" demonstrations (three per day, 15 minutes, all in German) show the noisy creation of a five-foot bolt of light-ning—not that exciting. There's also a state-of-the-art planetarium (German only) and an adjacent IMAX theater (museum entry 10 DM; daily 9:00–17:00; self-serve cafeteria; S-Bahn to Isartor, then walk 300 meters over the river, following signs; tel. 089/217-9369). Save this for a Monday, when virtually all of Munich's museums are closed.

Schwabing—Munich's artsy, bohemian university district, or "Greenwich Village," has been called "not a place but a state of mind." All I experienced was a mental lapse. The bohemians run the boutiques. I think the most colorful thing about Schwabing is the road leading back downtown. U-3 or U-6 will take you to the Münchener-Freiheit Center if you want to wander. Most of the jazz and disco joints are near Occamstrasse. The Haidhausen neighborhood (U-Bahn: Max Weber Platz) is becoming the "new Schwabing."

▲**Englischer Garden**—Munich's "Central Park," the largest on the Continent, was laid out in 1789 by an American. There's a huge beer garden near the Chinese Pagoda. A rewarding respite from the city, it's especially fun on a bike under the summer sun (bike rental at train station). Caution: While a new local law requires sun-worshipers to wear clothes on the tram, this park is sprinkled with nude sunbathers—quite a spectacle to most Americans (they're the ones riding their bikes into the river and trees).

Asam Church—Near the Stadtmuseum, this private church of the Asam brothers is a gooey, drippy masterpiece by Bavaria's top two rococonuts, showing off their popular Baroque-concentrate style. A few blocks away, the small Damenstift Church has a sculptural rendition of the Last Supper so real you feel you're not alone (at intersection of Altheimer Ecke and Damenstiftstrasse, a block south of pedestrian street).

Sights—Residenz

▲**Residenz**—For a long hike through rebuilt corridors of gilded imperial Bavarian grandeur, tour the family palace of the Wittelsbachs, who ruled Bavaria for more than 700 years. With a worthless English guidebook and not a word of English within, it's one of Europe's worst-presented palaces. Think of it as doing laps at the mall, with better art. Follow the "Führungslinie" signs: the first room shows a WWII exhibit. After long, boring halls of porcelain and dishes behind glass, you enter the King's apartments with a little throne-room action. The best Romantic-era dish art is on the top floor (6 DM, Tuesday–Sunday 10:00–16:30, closed Monday, enter on Max-Joseph Platz, three blocks north of Marienplatz).

▲▲**Schatzkammer**—This treasury, next door to the Residenz, shows off a thousand years of Wittelsbach crowns and knickknacks (another 6 DM from the same window, same hours as Residenz, the only English you'll encounter is the "do not touch" signs). Vienna's palace and jewels are better, but this is Bavaria's best, with fine 13- and 14th-century crowns and delicately carved ivory and glass. For a more efficient ramble, consider the eight rooms as one big room and make one long clockwise circle.

▲**Cuvillies Theater**—Attached to the Residenz, this national theater designed by Cuvillies is dazzling enough to send you back to the days of divine monarchs. Visitors see simply the sumptuous interior. There is no real exhibit (3 DM, Monday–Saturday 14:00–17:00, Sunday 10:00–17:00; facing the Residenz entry, go left around the Residenz about a half-block to reach the theater entrance).

Sights—Outer Munich

▲▲**Nymphenburg Palace**—This royal summer palace is impressive only by Bavarian standards. If you do tour it, meditate upon the theme: nymphs. Something about the place feels highly sexed in a Prince Charles kind of way. Two rooms deserve special attention: the riotous rococo Great Hall (at entry, 1756 by Zimmermann) and King Ludwig's Gallery of Beauties. This room (#15, 1825–1848) is stacked with portraits of 36 of Bavaria's loveliest women . . . according to Ludwig. If only these creaking floors could tell a story. Don't miss the photos (in the glass cases) of Ludwig II—the "Mad" King, and his Romantic composer friend Richard Wagner.

The **Amalienburg**—another rococo jewel designed by Cuvillies and decorated by Zimmermann—is 300 meters from the palace. Every rich boy needs a hunting lodge like this. Above the pink and white grand entry notice Diana, goddess of "the chase," flanked by busts of satyrs. Tourists enter around back. Highlights in this tiny getaway include: first room—dog houses under gun cupboards; the fine yellow and silver bedroom—see Vulcan forging arrows for amorous cupids at the foot of the bed; the mini-Hall of

Mirrors—a blue and silver commotion of rococo nymphs and the kitchen with its blue Dutch Bible scene tiles.

The sleigh and coach collection (**Marstallmuseum**, closes from 12:00–13:00) is a huge garage lined with gilded Cinderella coaches. It's especially interesting for "Mad" King Ludwig fans.

The palace park, good for a royal stroll—even better by bike, contains more playful extras such as a bathhouse, pagoda, and artificial ruins (8 DM for everything, less for individual parts, Tuesday–Sunday 9:00–12:30, 13:30–17:00, closed Monday, shorter hours October–March, the 5-DM English guidebook does little to make the palace meaningful; reasonable cafeteria; U-1 direction: Westfriedhof to Rotkreuzplatz, then tram or bus #12 to Romanplatz and a 10-minute walk or tram #17 from downtown or the station direct, tel. 089/179-080).

BMW Museum—The BMW headquarters, located in a striking building across the street from the Olympic Grounds, offers a good museum popular with car buffs (5.50 DM, daily 9:00–17:00, last ticket sold at 16:00, closed much of August, U-3 to the end: Olympia-zentrum, tel. 089/382-23-307). BMW fans may ask about factory tours (unreliable hours).

▲**Olympic Grounds**—Expect construction until 2000. Munich's great 1972 Olympic stadium and sports complex is now a lush park offering a tower (5 DM, commanding but so high it's a boring view from 820 feet, daily 8:00–24:00, last trip 23:30), an excellent swimming pool (5 DM, 7:00–22:30, Monday from 10:00, Thursday closed at 18:00), a good look at its striking "cobweb" style of architecture, and plenty of sun, grass, and picnic potential. Take U-3 to Olympia-zentrum direct from Marienplatz.

▲**Müllersches Volksbad**—This elegant Jugendstil (1901) public swimming pool is just across the river from the Deutsches Museum (5 DM, Rosenheimerstrasse 1, tel. 089/2361-3434).

Tours of Munich: By Foot, Bike, and Bus

Walking Tours—Original Munich Walks, run by the folks who started Berlin Walks, offers two tours: an introduction to the old town and "Infamous Third Reich Sites" (both tours are 15 DM, or 10 DM for those under 26, 2.5 hrs, tel. 0177-227-5901, e-mail: 106513.3461@compuserve.com). The old town tour starts daily at 10:30 early April through October (also at 15:30 May–August, not Sunday) and the Third Reich tour is offered at 10:30 Tuesday, Thursday, and Saturday, June through October (less off-season).

Both tours depart from the EurAide office (track 11) in the train station. There may be more frequent tours in 1999; confirm the schedule, but there's no need to register—just show up. Bring along any city transport ticket (like a *Kurzstrecke*) or buy one from your guide. Renate Suerbaum is a good local guide (140 DM for private two-hour walking tour, tel. 089/283-374).

Bike Tours—Radius Bikes organizes serious guided bike tours covering the best of historic and scenic downtown Munich (April weekends at 12:00, daily May–Sept. 5 at 10:30 and 14:30, daily Sept. 6–Oct. 3 at 12:00, 3 hours, 23 DM regular price, 20 DM with this book in 1999—two per book, tel. 089/596-113). Youth hostelers may prefer the hipper Mike's Bike tours (flyers all over town).

City Bus Tour—Panorama Tours offers one-hour city orientation bus tours (17 DM, daily at 10:00, 11:30, 13:00, 14:30, and 16:00 April–October; 10:00 and 14:30 in winter; live guide speaking German and English; near the train station, Arnulfstrasse 8; tel. 089/5490-7560).

Oktoberfest

When King Ludwig I had a marriage party in 1810, it was such a success that they made it an annual bash. These days the Oktoberfest lasts 16 days, ending with the first full weekend in October. It starts (usually on the third Saturday in September) with an opening parade of more than 6,000 participants and fills eight huge beer tents with about 6,000 people each. A million gallons of beer later, they roast the last ox.

It's crowded, but if you arrive in the morning (except Friday or Saturday) and haven't called ahead for a room, the TI can normally find you a place. The fairground, known as the "Wies'n" (a few blocks south of the train station), erupts in a frenzy of rides, dancing, and strangers strolling arm-in-arm down rows of picnic tables while the beer god stirs tons of beer, pretzels, and wurst in a bubbling caldron of fun. The three-loops roller coaster must be the wildest on earth (best before the beer-drinking).

During the fair, the city functions even better than normal, and it's a good time to sightsee, even if beer-hall rowdiness isn't your cup of tea.

Sights—Near Munich

Castle Tours—Two of King Ludwig's castles, Neuschwanstein and Linderhof, are an easy day trip by tour. Without a tour, only Neuschwanstein is easy (two hours by train to Füssen, 10-minute bus ride to Neuschwanstein). Panorama Tours offers all-day bus tours of the two castles with 30 minutes in Oberammergau (78 DM, plus 19 DM for two castle admissions, live guide, two languages, departing 8:30 from north side of Hauptbahnhof at Arnulfstrasse 8, tel. 089/5490-7560). On Wednesdays in June and July, EurAide operates an all-day train/bus Neuschwanstein– Linderhof–Wies Church day tour (70 DM, 55 DM with a train pass, admissions not included, departs at 7:30 and beats most groups to avoid the long line, tel. 089/593-889). EurAide also sells tickets for Panorama's castle tours (above) at a discount to railpass or ISIC holders. For info on Ludwig's castles, see the Bavaria and Tirol chapter.

Munich Area

Berchtesgaden—This resort, near Hitler's overrated Eagle's Nest getaway, is easier as a day trip from Salzburg (just 20 km away). See Salzburg chapter.

▲**Andechs Monastery**—Where can you find a fine Baroque church in a rural Bavarian setting at a monastery that serves hearty food and perhaps the best beer in Germany, in a carnival atmosphere full of partying locals? It's the Andechs Monastery, crouching quietly with a big smile between two lakes just south of Munich. Come ready to eat tender chunks of pork, huge, soft pretzels, spiraled white radishes, savory sauerkraut, and Andecher monk-made beer that would almost make celibacy tolerable. Everything is served in medieval portions; two people can split a meal. Great picnic center offering first-class views and second-class prices (beer garden open daily 9:45–20:45, dinner until 18:30, church until 19:00, tel. 08152/3760). To reach Andechs from Munich without a car, take the S-5 train to Herrsching and catch a "Rauner" shuttle bus (hourly) or walk two miles from there. Don't miss a stroll up to the church, where you can sit peacefully and ponder the striking contrasts a trip through Germany offers. . . .

▲▲**Dachau**—Dachau was the first Nazi concentration camp (1933). Today it's the most accessible camp to travelers and a very effective voice from our recent but grisly past, warning and pleading "Never Again," the memorial's theme. This is a valuable

Dachau

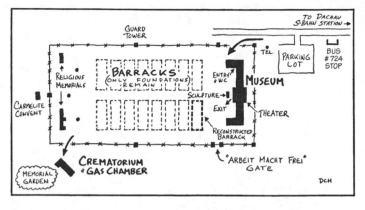

experience and, when approached thoughtfully, well worth the trouble. In fact, it may change your life. See it. Feel it. Read and think about it. After this most powerful sightseeing experience, many people gain more respect for history and the dangers of not keeping tabs on their government.

Upon arrival, pick up the mini-guide and note when the next documentary film in English will be shown (25 minutes, normally shown at 11:30 and 15:30 and often at 14:00). Both the museum and the movie are exceptional. Notice the Expressionist fascist-inspired art near the theater, where you'll also find English books, slides, and a WC. Outside, see the reconstructed barracks and the memorial shrines at the far end (Tuesday–Sunday 9:00–17:00, closed Monday). For maximum understanding, consider the English guided walk (daily in summer at 12:30, 2 hrs, donation, call 08131/1741 to confirm). It's a 45-minute trip from downtown Munich: take S-2 (direction: Petershausen) to Dachau, then from the station, catch bus #724 or #726, Dachau-Ost, to Gedenkstätte (the camp). The two-zone 7-DM ticket covers the entire trip (one-way); with a train pass, just pay for the bus (1.80 DM one-way). Drivers follow Dachauerstrasse from downtown Munich to Dachau-Ost. Then follow the KZ-Gedenkstätte signs. The town of Dachau (TI tel. 08131/84566) is more pleasant than its unfortunate image.

Radius Touristik at the Munich train station offers tours of the Dachau camp (19 DM plus cost of public transportation, May–September Tuesday–Sunday at 14:00, 3.5 hrs, tel. 089/596-113).

Sleeping in Munich
(1.7 DM = about $1, tel. code: 089)
Sleep Code: **S** = Single, **D** = Double/Twin, **T** = Triple, **Q** = Quad, **b** = bathroom, **t** = toilet only, **s** = shower only, **CC** = Credit Card

(Visa, MasterCard, Amex). English is nearly always spoken, unless otherwise noted. Prices include breakfast and increase with conventions and festivals.

There are no cheap beds in Munich. Youth hostels strictly enforce their 26-year-old age limit, and side-tripping in is a bad value. But there are plenty of decent, moderately priced rooms. I've listed places in three areas: within a few blocks of the Hauptbahnhof (central train station), in the old center, and near the Deutsches Museum. Munich is packed during Oktoberfest (late September–early October) and room prices can triple. While (except for Oktoberfest weekends) rooms can be found through the TI, revelers are wise to reserve in advance.

Sleeping near the Train Station

Budget hotels (90-DM doubles, no elevator, shower down the hall) cluster in the area immediately south of the station. It's seedy after dark (erotic cinemas, barnacles with lingerie tongues, men with moustaches in the shadows) but dangerous only to those in search of trouble. Still, I've listed places in more polite neighborhoods, generally a five- or 10-minute walk from the station and handy to the center. Places are listed roughly in order of proximity to the station. The nearest Laundromat is at Paul-Heyse Strasse 21, near the intersection with Landswehrstrasse (daily 7:00–23:00, 8-DM wash and dry, English instructions).

Hotel Haberstock, less than a block from the station, is homey, a little worn, old-fashioned, relatively quiet and a classic old European hotel (S-58–75 DM, Ss-82 DM, Sb-102 DM, D-110 DM, Ds-130 DM, Db-170 DM, good breakfast, CC:VMA, TV-5 DM extra, Schillerstrasse 4, 80336 Munich, tel. 089/557-855, fax 089/550-3634, friendly Alfred at the desk). Ask about weekend and winter discounts.

Hotel Europäischer Hof München is a big business hotel with fine rooms and elegant public spaces (S-91 DM, Sb-121 DM, D-111 DM, Db-141 DM, discount with this book, Bayerstrasse 31, 80335 Munich, tel. 089/551-510, fax 089/5515-1222, e-mail: heh_munich@compuserve.com).

Hotel Schweitz Odeon is comfortable for its price, with a fine buffet breakfast and non-smoking rooms (Sb-95 DM, Db-140 DM, Tb-170 DM, 15-DM garage, elevator, CC:VMA, Goethestrasse 26, from the station walk two blocks down Goethestrasse, tel. 089/539-585, fax 089/550-4383).

Jugendhotel Marienherberge is a pleasant, friendly convent offering the best cheap beds in town to young women only (25-year age limit can flex upward a couple of years, S-40 DM, 35 DM per bed in D and T, 30 DM per bed in four- to seven-bed rooms, non-smoking, open 8:00–24:00, a block from the station at Goethestrasse #9, tel. 089/555-805).

Hotels Near Train Station

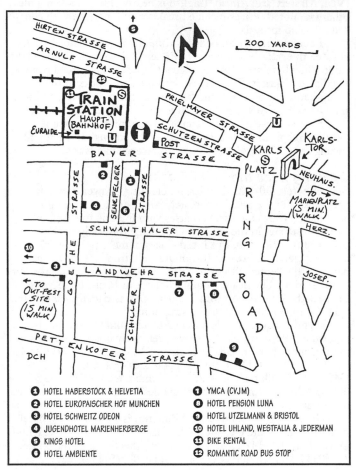

❶ HOTEL HABERSTOCK & HELVETIA	❼ YMCA (CVJM)
❷ HOTEL EUROPAISCHER HOF MUNCHEN	❽ HOTEL PENSION LUNA
❸ HOTEL SCHWEITZ ODEON	❾ HOTEL UTZELMANN & BRISTOL
❹ JUGENDHOTEL MARIENHERBERGE	❿ HOTEL UHLAND, WESTFALIA & JEDERMAN
❺ KINGS HOTEL	⓫ BIKE RENTAL
❻ HOTEL AMBIENTE	⓬ ROMANTIC ROAD BUS STOP

Hotel Helvetia is a backpacker's favorite (S-53–63 DM, D-78–95 DM, Ds-99–115 DM, T-99–120 DM, laundry service, next to Haberstock at Schillerstrasse 6, 80336 Munich, tel. 089/590-685, fax 089/5906-8570).

Kings Hotel, a fancy old business-class hotel, is an elegant splurge and a very good value on weekends. You'll get carved wooden ceilings, canopy beds, chandeliers, a sauna, and the *Herald Tribune* in your room (Db-265 DM, Friday-Saturday-Sunday "King's Weekend" special: Db-165 DM with this book except during fairs, CC:VMA, some non-smoking rooms, ask about their

"Royal Weekend" special: 200 DM for their 400-DM suite, 150 meters north of station at Dachauer Strasse 13, 80335 Munich, tel. 089/551-870, fax 089/5518-7300, Web site: www.king-group .com, e-mail: kingshotel@aol.com).

Hotel Ambiente has dark halls but clean, bright, newly refurbished rooms with all the comforts and a friendly professional staff (Sb-138–182 DM, Db-150–230 DM depending on season, CC:VMA, a block from station at Schillerstrasse 12, 80336 Munich, tel. 089/545-170, fax 089/5451-7200).

YMCA (CVJM), open to people of all ages and sexes, has clean, modern rooms (D-86 DM, T-120 DM, a bed in a shared triple-40 DM, those over 26 pay a 16 percent penalty, free showers, elevator, Landwehrstrasse 13, 80336 Munich, tel. 089/552-1410, fax 089/550-4282, Web site: www.cvjm.org/muenchen/hotel/, e-mail: muenchen@cvjm.org). The cafeteria offers 13-DM dinners (Tuesday–Friday 18:30–22:00).

Hotel Pension Luna is a dumpy building with cheery rooms (S-59 DM, Sb-69 DM, D/twin-90 DM, D-99 DM, Ds-115 DM, T-130 DM, Ts-140 DM, lots of stairs, CC:VA, Landwehrstrasse 5, tel. 089/597-833, fax 089/550-3761).

Hotel Pension Utzelmann has huge rooms, especially the curiously cheap room #6. Each lacy room is richly furnished. It's in a pleasant neighborhood, a 10-minute walk from the station a block off Sendlinger Tor (S-50–65 DM, Ss-85–95 DM, Sb-125 DM, D-90 DM, Ds-110 DM, Db-145 DM, T-125 DM, Ts-150 DM, Tb-175 DM, hall showers-5 DM, Pettenkoferstrasse 6, enter through black iron gate, tel. 089/594-889, fax 089/596-228, Frau Earnst).

Hotel Bristol, nearly next door to Hotel Utzelmann, has renovated, comfortable rooms and is a fine value (Sb-89 DM, Db-129 DM, Tb-160 DM, to get these prices—which are 20–30 DM below the hotel's normal rates—ask for Johannes and mention this book if you call, or show this book if you walk in, non-smoking, hearty buffet breakfast on terrace, bike rental-20 DM/day, parking available, CC:VMA, Pettenkoferstrasse 2, 80336 Munich, one metro stop on U-1 or U-2 from station, tel. 089/595-151, fax 089/591-451, Web site: www.bristol-muc.com, e-mail: hotel@bristol-muc.com). Johannes also has an apartment (45 DM per person, up to four people).

Hotel Uhland, a veritable mansion, is a worthwhile splurge (Sb-110 DM, Db-140 DM, Tb-180 DM, huge breakfast, elevator, Internet access, free parking, Uhlandstrasse 1, 80336 Munich, near the Theresienwiese Oktoberfest grounds, 10-minute walk from the station, tel. 089/543-350, fax 089/5433-5250, e-mail: Hotel_Uhland@compuserve.com, SE). Free use of computer, e-mail, and photocopier.

Pension Westfalia overlooks the Oktoberfest grounds from the top floor of a quiet and elegant old building. Well run by Peter and Mary Deiritz, this is a great value if you prefer sanity and personal touches to centrality (S-65 DM, Sb-90 DM, D-90 DM, Db-110–130 DM, cheaper off-season, extra bed 25 DM, hallway showers-3 DM, buffet breakfast, elevator, CC:VA, Mozartstrasse 23, 80336 Munich, easy parking, U-3 or U-6 to Goetheplatz, tel. 089/530-377, fax 089/543-9120). Around the corner, **Pension Schubert** rents four tidy and simple but elegant rooms (S-50 DM, D-85 DM, Db-95 DM, Schubertstrasse 1, tel. 089/535-087.

Hotel Jederman is a basic well-worn, comfortable old business hotel (S-65–85 DM, Sb-95–160 DM, D-95–145 DM, Db-140–240 DM depending on season, kids' cot-15 DM, CC:VMA, free Internet access, elevator, rental bikes, midway between station and Oktoberfest grounds, tram #18 and #19 at door, Bayerstrasse 95, 80335 Munich, tel. 089/533-617, fax 089/536-506, Web site: www.hotel-jederman.cube.net, e-mail: hotel-jederman@cube.net, Jenke family).

Sleeping in the Old Center

Pension Lindner is clean, quiet, and modern, with pastel-bouquet rooms (S-60 DM, D-95 DM, Ds-120 DM, Db-135 DM, elevator, Dultstrasse 1, just off Sendlinger Strasse, 80331 Munich, tel. 089/263-413, fax 089/268-760, run by cheery Marion Sinzinger). One floor below, the quirky **Pension Stadt Munich** isn't as homey, but is okay if the Lindner is full (four Ds-120 DM, a tad smoky, Dulstrasse 1, tel. 089/263-417, fax 089/267-548, some English spoken).

Pension Seibel has cozy rooms and a friendly, family atmosphere a block off the Viktualienmarkt in a fun neighborhood (S-70 DM, Sb-89 DM, D-99 DM, Db-129 DM, Tb-150 DM, these prices are promised though 1999 only with this book, family apartment for up to five people-45 DM each, soft prices, entirely smoke-free, big breakfast, no elevator, CC:VMA, Reichenbachstrasse 8, 80469 Munich, tel. 089/264-043, fax 089/ 267-803, Moe and Kirstin).

Hotel Münchner Kindl is a jolly place with decent rooms above a friendly local bar (15 rooms, S-80 DM, Sb-110 DM, D-120 DM, Ds-140 DM, Db-160 DM, Tb-195 DM, Qs-200 DM, prices with this book, night noises travel up the central courtyard, no elevator, easy telephone reservations, CC:VM, two blocks off main pedestrian drag from "Thomas" sign at Damenstiftstrasse 16, 80331 Munich, tel. 089/264-349, fax 089/264-526, run by Gunter and English-speaking Renate Dittert, cheery Heinz serves breakfast).

Sleeping near Isartor, the Deutsches Museum, and Beyond

Hotel Isartor is a modern, comfortable, concrete-feeling place beautfully located two minutes' walk from the Isartor S-Bahn stop (26 rooms, Db-160 DM, 10 percent discount with cash in July, August, and slow times, CC:VMA, elevator, refrigerators in rooms, Baaderstrasse 2, 80469 Munich, tel. 089/216-3340, fax 089/298-494, family Pangratz).

Pension Beck is well worn and farther away but a good budget bet (S-from 60 DM, D-82–90 DM, Db-120 DM, rooms for three to five people-42 DM each, free showers; family, youth, and two-night deals; 44 rooms on five floors with no elevator, yellow hall and lots of backpackers, east of Isartor near river and Marienplatz, Thierschstrasse 36, take streetcar #17 direct from station or any S-Bahn to Isartor and 400-meter walk, tel. 089/220-708, fax 089/220-925).

American **Audrey Bauchinger** rents quiet, tidy rooms and spacious apartments east of the Deutsches Museum in a quiet residential area a 20-minute walk from Marienplatz (Ss-45 DM, D-75 DM, one D with private bath across hall-125 DM, Ds-80–105 DM, spacious Db/Tb with kitchenette-160 DM/200 DM, no breakfast included, CC:VMA accepted at 5 percent charge, corner of Schweigerstrasse, at Zeppelinstrasse 37, 81669 Munich, tel. 089/488-444, fax 089/489-1787, e-mail: 106437.3277@ compuserve.com). From the station, take any S-Bahn to Marienplatz, then bus #52 (the only bus there) to Schweigerstrasse.

Familie Jordan Zimmer—The Jordans, now with an empty nest, rent apartments in their home. It's ideal for those driving between Munich and Salzburg (Db-80 DM, 20 min from downtown on the S-5 to Vaterstetten and a two-min walk; from the A-99 Autobahn, take the Vaterstetten exit on the Salzburg side of town, Luitpoldring 8, 85591 Baterstetten, tel. 08106/358-032, SE).

Hostels and Cheap Beds

Munich's youth hostels charge 25 DM in dorms, and 38 DM in doubles (including breakfast and sheets) and strictly limit admission to YH members who are under 27. **Burg Schwaneck Hostel** is a renovated castle (30 minutes from the center, S-7 to Pullach, then follow signs, walking 10 minutes to Burgweg 4, tel. 089/793-0643).

Munich's **International Youth Camp Kapuzinerhölzl** (a.k.a. "The Tent") offers 400 places on the wooden floor of a huge circus tent with a mattress, blankets, good showers, and free tea in the morning for 13 DM to anyone under 25 (flexible). It's a fun experience—kind of a cross between a slumber party and Woodstock (if anyone under 25 knows what that was). Cool ping-pong-and-frisbee atmosphere throughout the day, no curfew at night (open July and August only, confirm first at TI that it's open, then catch tram #17 from Hauptbahnhof to Botanischer Garten, direction: Amalienburgstrasse, and follow crowd down Franz-Schrankstrasse).

Eating in Munich

Munich cuisine is best seasoned with beer. For beer halls, you have two basic choices: the Hofbräuhaus with music and tourists or mellower beer gardens with Germans.

The world's most famous and touristy beer hall is the **Hofbräuhaus** (daily 9:30–24:00, music during lunch and dinner, Platzl 6, five-minute walk from Marienplatz, tel. 089/221-676). Even if you don't eat here, check it out; it's fun to see 200 Japanese people drinking beer in a German beer hall . . . across from a Planet Hollywood. Germans go for the entertainment—to sing "Country Roads," see how Texas girls party, and watch salarymen from Tokyo chug beer. The music-every-night atmosphere is thick; the fat, shiny-leather–bands even get church mice to stand up and conduct three-quarter time with breadsticks. Meals are inexpensive (for a light 10-DM meal, I like the local favorite, *Schweinswurst mit Kraut*); white radishes are salted and cut in delicate spirals; and surly beermaids pull mustard packets from their cleavages. Huge liter beers (called *eine Mass* in German or "*ein* pitcher" in English) cost 10 DM. You can order your beer *helles* (light—but not "lite," what you'll get if you say "*ein* beer"), *dunkeles* (dark), or *Radler* (half lemonade, half light beer). Notice the vomitoriums in the WC. (They have a gimmicky folk evening upstairs in the *Festsaal* nightly at 19:00 for 8 DM, food and drinks are sold from the same menu, tel. 089/290-13-610.)

Weisses Bräuhaus is more local and features good food and the region's fizzy wheat beer (daily 8:00–24:00, Tal 10, between Marienplatz and Isartor, two blocks from Hofbräuhaus). Hitler met with fellow fascists here in 1920 when his Nazi party had yet to ferment.

Augustiner Beer Garden is a sprawling haven for trendy local beer-lovers on a balmy evening (10:00–23:00, across from the train tracks, three loooong blocks from the station, away from the center, on Arnulfstrasse 52). For a true under-the-leaves beer garden packed with locals, this is best.

The tiny **Jodlerwirt** is a woodsy, smart-alecky, yodeling kind of pub. The food is great and the ambience is as Bavarian as you'll find. Avoid the basic ground-floor bar and climb the stairs into the action (accordian act from 19:00, closed Sunday, Altenhofstrasse 4, between the Hofbräuhaus and Marienplatz, tel. 089/221-249). Good food, lots of belly laughs . . . completely incomprehensible to the average tourist.

For a classier evening stewed in antlers and fiercely Bavarian, eat under a tree or inside at the **Nürnberger Bratwurst Glöckl am Dom** (daily 9:30–24:00, 25-DM dinners, Frauenplatz 9, at the rear of the twin-domed cathedral, tel. 089/295-264).

Locals enjoy the **Altes Hackerhaus** for traditional Bayerischer fare with a dressier feel (daily until 24:00, 25–30 DM meals, Sendlingerstrasse 14, tel. 089/260-5026).

For outdoor atmosphere and a cheap meal, spend an evening at the Englischer Garden's **Chinesischer Turm** (Chinese Pagoda) **Biergarten**. You're welcome to BYO food and grab a table or buy

from the picnic stall (*Brotzeit*) right there. Don't bother to phone
ahead: they have 6,000 seats. For a more intimate place with more
local families and fewer tourists, venture deeper into the garden
(past the Isarring road) to the **Hirschau Biergarten.**

For similar BYOF atmosphere right behind Marienplatz, eat at
Viktualien Markt's beer garden. Lunch or dinner here taps you
into about the best budget eating in town. Countless stalls surround
the beer garden and sell wurst, sandwiches, produce, and so on.
This BYOF tradition goes back to the days when monks were
allowed to sell beer but not food. To picnic, choose a table without
a tablecloth. This is a good place to grab the most typical meal in
town: *Weisswurst* (white sausage) with *süss* (sweet) mustard, a salty
pretzel, and *Weissbier*. **Suppenküche** is fine for a small, cozy, sit-
down lunch (soup kitchen, 6–9-DM soup meals, in Viktualien
Markt near intersection of Frauenkirche and Reichenbachstrasse,
everyone knows where it is). For your strudel and coffee, consider
the **Marktcafe** (closed Sunday, 7-DM fresh strudel, on a tiny street
a block below the market, Heiliggeiststrasse 2, tel. 089/227-816).

For a fun and easy (though not cheap) cafeteria meal near
Karlstor on the pedestrian mall, try the **Mövenpick Marche.**
Climb downstairs into the marketplace fantasy and pick up a card.
As you load your tray your card is stamped, choose your table
from several typical Munich themes, and pay after you eat (smoke-
free zones, reasonable small-plate veggie and salad buffets, dis-
tracting men's room, on Neuhauser pedestrian street, across from
St. Michael's church, daily 12:00–22:00).

The crown in its emblem indicates that the royal family
assembled its picnics in the historic and expensive **Alois Dallmayr**
delicatessen (Monday–Friday 9:30–19:30, Saturday 9:00–16:00,
closed Sunday, Dienerstrasse 14, behind the Rathaus). An elegant
café serves light meals behind the bakery on the ground floor.
Explore this dieter's purgatory and put together a royal picnic
to munch in the nearby Hofgarten. To save money, browse at
Dallmayr's but buy in the basement supermarkets of the Kaufhof
stores across Marienplatz or at Karlsplatz.

Transportation Connections—Munich
Munich is a super transportation hub (one reason it was the target
of so many WWII bombs).

By train to: Füssen (10/day, 2 hrs, the 8:53 departure is
good for a Neuschwanstein castle day trip), **Berlin** (6/day, 8 hrs),
Würzburg (hrly, 3 hrs), **Frankfurt** (14/day, 3.5 hrs), **Salzburg**
(12/day, 2 hrs), **Vienna** (4/day, 5 hrs), **Venice** (2/day, 9 hrs), **Paris**
(3/day, 9 hrs), **Prague** (3/day, 7–10 hrs), and just about every
other point in western Europe. Munich is three hours from
Reutte, Austria (every 2 hours, 3 hrs, transfer in Garmisch).

BAVARIA
AND TIROL

Two hours south of Munich, between Germany's Bavaria and Austria's Tirol, is a timeless land of fairy-tale castles, painted buildings shared by cows and farmers, and locals who still yodel when they're happy.

In Germany's Bavaria, tour "Mad" King Ludwig's ornate Neuschwanstein Castle, Europe's most spectacular. Stop by the Wieskirche, a textbook example of Bavarian rococo bursting with curly curlicues, and browse through Oberammergau, Germany's wood-carving capital and home of the famous Passion Play.

In Austria's Tirol, hike to the Ehrenberg ruined castle, scream down a nearby ski slope on an oversized skateboard, then catch your breath for an evening of yodeling and slap-dancing.

In this chapter I'll cover Bavaria first, then Tirol. Austria's Tirol is easier and cheaper than touristy Bavaria. My favorite home base for exploring Bavaria's castles is actually in Austria, in the town of Reutte. Füssen, in Germany, is a handier home base for train travelers.

Planning Your Time

While locals come here for a week or two, the typical speedy American traveler will find two days' worth of sightseeing. With a car and some time you could enjoy the more remote corners, but the basic visit ranges anywhere from a long day trip from Munich to a three-night, two-day visit. If the weather's good and you're not going to Switzerland, be sure to ride a lift to an Alpine peak.

A good schedule for a one-day circular drive from Reutte is: 7:30–breakfast, 8:15–depart, 8:45–arrive at Neuschwanstein, park and hike to the castle for a tour, 12:00–drive to the Wieskirche (20-minute stop) and on to Oberammergau for a stroll and lunch,

Highlights of Bavaria and Tirol

14:00–drive to Linderhof, 14:30–tour Linderhof, 16:30–drive along Plansee back into Austria, 17:30–back at hotel, 19:00–dinner at hotel and perhaps a folk evening. In peak season you might arrive later at Linderhof to avoid the crowds. The next morning you could stroll Reutte, hike to the Ehrenberg ruins, and ride the luge on your way to Innsbruck, Munich, Venice, Switzerland, or wherever.

Getting Around Bavaria and Tirol

By Car: This region is ideal by car. All the sights are within an easy 60-mile loop from Reutte or Füssen.

By Train and Bus: It's frustrating by train. Local bus service in the region is spotty for sightseeing. Without wheels, Reutte, the luge ride, and Wieskirche are probably not worth the trouble. Füssen (with a two-hour train ride to and from Munich every hour, transfer in Buchloe) is three miles from Neuschwanstein

Castle with easy bus and bike connections. Oberammergau (hourly two-hour trains from Munich with one change) has decent bus connections to nearby Linderhof Castle. Oberammergau to Füssen is a pain.

By Tour: If you're interested only in Bavarian castles, consider an all-day organized bus tour of the Bavarian biggies as a side trip from Munich (see Munich chapter).

By Bike: This is great biking country. Many train stations (including Reutte) and hotels rent bikes for about 15 DM a day.

By Thumb: Hitchhiking, always risky, is a slow-but-possible way to connect the public transportation gaps.

FÜSSEN AND NEUSCHWANSTEIN CASTLE, GERMANY

Füssen has been a strategic stop since ancient times. Its main street sits on the Via Claudia Augusta, which crossed the Alps (over Brenner Pass) in Roman times. The town was the southern terminus of the medieval trade route known among 20th-century tourists as the "Romantic Road." Dramatically situated under a renovated castle on the lively Lech River, Füssen just celebrated its 700th birthday.

Unfortunately, in the summer it's entirely overrun by tourists. Traffic can be exasperating, but by bike or on foot it's not bad. Off-season, the town is a jester's delight.

Apart from Füssen's cobbled and arcaded town center, there's little real sightseeing. The striking-from-a-distance castle houses a boring picture gallery. The mediocre city museum in the monastery below the castle exhibits lifestyles of 200 years ago and the story of the monastery, and offers displays on the development of the violin, for which Füssen was famous (5 DM, Tuesday–Sunday 11:00–16:00, closed Monday, explanations in German only). Halfway between Füssen and the border (as you drive, or a woodsy walk from the town) is the Lechfall, a thunderous waterfall with a handy potty stop.

Orientation (tel. code: 08362)

Füssen's train station is a few blocks from the TI, the town center (a cobbled shopping mall), and all my hotel listings.

Tourist Information: The TI has a room-finding service (look for Kurverwaltung, Monday–Friday 9:30–18:00, weekends 9:00–12:30, shorter hours off-season and closed Sunday, tel. 08362/93850, fax 08362/938-520, www.fuessen.de). After hours, try the little self-service info pavilion, near the front of the TI, which dispenses Füssen maps for 1 DM.

Arrival in Füssen: Exit left as you leave the train station and walk a few straight blocks to the center of town and the TI.

Bike Rental: Rad Zacherl, next to the train station, rents road bikes for 14 DM/day (passport number for deposit, Monday–Friday 9:00–12:00 and 14:00–18:00, Saturday 9:00–12:00, mountain bikes-20 DM, Rupprechtstrasse 8.5, tel. 08362/3292).

Sights—Bavaria, near Füssen

(These are listed in driving order from Füssen.)

▲▲▲**Neuschwanstein Castle**—The fairy-tale castle Neuschwanstein looks medieval, but it's only about as old as the Eiffel Tower and feels like something you'd see at a home show for 19th-century royalty. It was built (1869–1886) to suit the whims of Bavaria's King Ludwig II and is a textbook example of the Romanticism that was popular in 19th-century Europe.

Getting to the castle: It's a steep 20- to 30-minute hike to Neuschwanstein from the parking lot. If you arrive by bus, the quickest (and steepest) way to the castle starts in parking lot D. A more gradual ascent starts at the parking lot near the lake (Parkplatz am Alpsee, best for drivers, all lots cost 6 DM). To minimize hiking, you can take advantage of the shuttle buses (3.50 DM up, 5 DM round-trip; drops you off at Mary's Bridge, a steep 10 minutes above the castle) or horse carriages (8 DM up, 4 DM down; slower than walking, stops five minutes short of the castle) that go constantly (watch your step).

Touring the castle: To beat the crowds, see Neuschwanstein, Germany's most popular castle, either by 9:00 or late in the afternoon. The castle is open every morning at 8:30; by 11:00, it's packed. Rushed 35-minute English-language tours are less rushed early. Tours leave regularly, telling the sad story of Bavaria's "mad" king, who drowned under suspicious circumstances at age 41 after nearly bankrupting Bavaria to build his castles. You'll go up and down more than 300 steps through lavish Wagnerian dream rooms, a royal state-of-the-19th-century-art kitchen, the king's gilded-lily bedroom, and his extravagant throne room. You'll see 15 rooms with their original furnishings and fanciful wall paintings. The rest of the castle is unfinished; the king lived here fewer than 200 days before he died (11 DM, daily 8:30–17:30 April–September, 9:30–16:30 October and March, 10:00–16:00 winter, no photography inside). Guided tours are mandatory. To cut down on lines, the plan for 1999 is to give out appointment times for tours; therefore go to the castle's ticket office immediately and pick up a time before hiking up to Mary's Bridge.

After the tour, climb up to Mary's Bridge to marvel at Ludwig's castle, just as Ludwig did. This bridge was quite an engineering accomplishment 100 years ago. From the bridge, the frisky can hike even higher to the "Beware—Danger of Death" signs and an even more glorious castle view. For the most interesting descent (15 minutes longer and extremely slippery when wet), follow signs to the Pöllat Gorge.

Neuschwanstein

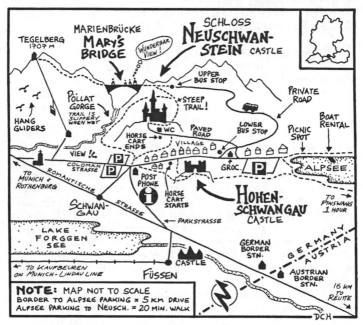

▲▲Hohenschwangau Castle—Standing quietly below Neuschwanstein, the big yellow Hohenschwangau Castle was Ludwig's boyhood home. It's more lived-in and historic, and actually gives a better glimpse of Ludwig's life. There are only three ways to get an English tour: gather 21 people together; wait in line until 20 English speakers join you; or politely ask your German guide to say a few words in English after her German spiels. (Same hours and price as Neuschwanstein but closed in winter.)

The "village" at the foot of the castles lives off the hungry, shopping tourists who come in droves to Europe's "Disney" castle. The little family-run mini-market (open daily) has the makings for a skimpy picnic and a microwave fast-food machine. Picnic in the lakeside park or in one of the old-fashioned rowboats (rented by the hour in summer). The bus stop, post/telephone office, and helpful TI cluster around the main intersection (TI open daily 9:00–18:00, till 17:00 off-season, tel. 08362/819-840).

To give your castle experience a romantic twist, hike or bike over from Austria (trailhead is at the recommended hotel Gutshof zum Schluxen in Pinswang). When the dirt road forks at the top of the hill, go right (downhill), cross the Austrian-German border (marked by a sign and deserted hut), and follow the paved road to the castles. It's an hour's hike one way (can return by bus) or a great circular bike trip. Signposts and books often refer to these castles in the German: *Königsschlösser*.

Buses run between the Füssen train station and Hohenschwangau (2/hrly, 10 minutes, 4.80 DM round-trip), and between Füssen and Reutte (5/day, 30 min, never on Sunday; schedules at TI).

▲**Tegelberg Gondola**—Just north of Neuschwanstein, hang gliders circle like vultures. They jumped from the top of the Tegelberg Gondola. For 27 DM, you can ride high to the 5,500-foot summit and back down (daily from 9:00, last lift at 17:00, closes earlier in winter, tel. 08362/98360). On a clear day, you get great views of the Alps and Bavaria and the vicarious thrill of watching hang gliders and parasailors leap into airborne ecstasy. Tegelberg is a popular take-off point. Weather permitting, scores of German thrill-seekers line up and leap from their launch ramp at the top of the lift. With one leaving every two or three minutes, it's great spectating. Thrill-seekers with exceptional social skills may talk themselves into a tandem ride with a parasailor. From there, it's a steep 2.5-hour hike down to Ludwig's castle.

Tegelberg Luge—Next to the lift is a luge (like a bobsled on wheels; for details see Sights—Tirol, Near Reutte, below). The track, made of stainless steel, is often open when rainy weather shuts the other luges. It's not as fast or scenic as Bichlbach and Biberwier (below), but it's close and cheap (4 DM per run, 10 percent less when using six-trip cards, can be crowded on sunny summer weekends, tel. 08362/98360). A funky cable system pulls lugers to the top without a ski lift.

▲▲**Wies Church (Wieskirche)**—Germany's greatest rococo-style church, Wieskirche ("the church in the meadow") is newly restored and looking as brilliant as the day it floated down from heaven. Overripe with decoration but bright and bursting with beauty, this church is a divine droplet, a curly curlicue, the final flowering of the Baroque movement. The ceiling depicts the Last Judgment.

This is a pilgrimage church. In the early 1700s a carving of Christ too graphic to be accepted by that generation's church was the focus of worship in a peasant's private chapel. Miraculously, it wept. And pilgrims came from all around.

Bavaria's top rococo architects, the Zimmermann brothers, were then commissioned to build the Wieskirche, which features the amazing carving above its altar and still attracts countless pilgrims. Take a commune-with-nature-and-smell-the-farm detour back through the meadow to the car park.

Wieskirche (donation requested, daily 8:00–20:00, less off-season) is 30 minutes north of Neuschwanstein. The northbound Romantic Road bus tour stops here for 15 minutes. Füssen–

Wieskirche buses run several times a day. By car, head north from Füssen, turn right at Steingaden, and follow the signs.

If you can't visit Wieskirche, visit one of the other churches that came out of the same heavenly spray can: Oberammergau's church, Munich's Asam Church, the Würzburg Residenz Chapel, or the splendid Ettal Monastery (free and near Oberammergau).

If you're driving from Wieskirche to Oberammergau, you'll cross the Echelsbacher Bridge, arching 250 feet over the Pöllat Gorge. Drivers should let their passengers walk across and meet them at the other side. Any kayakers? Notice the painting of the traditional village woodcarver (who used to walk from town to town with his art on his back) on the first big house on the Oberammergau side, a shop called Almdorf Ammertal. It has a huge selection of overpriced carvings and commission-hungry tour guides.

▲**Oberammergau**—The Shirley Temple of Bavarian villages and exploited to the hilt by the tourist trade, Oberammergau wears way too much makeup. It's worth a wander only if you're passing through anyway. Browse through the woodcarvers' shops—small art galleries filled with very expensive whittled works—or see folk art at the local Heimatmuseum (TI tel. 08822/2310, closed Saturday afternoon and Sunday off-season).

Visit the church, a poor cousin of the one at Wies. This church looks richer than it is. Put your hand on the "marble" columns. If they warm up, they're painted fakes. Wander through the graveyard. Ponder the deaths that two wars dealt Germany. Behind the church are the photos of three Schneller brothers, all killed within two years in World War II.

Still making good on a deal the townspeople made with God if they were spared devastation by the Black Plague 350 years ago, once each decade Oberammergau performs the Passion Play. The next show is in the year 2000, when 5,000 people a day for 100 summer days will attend Oberammergau's all-day dramatic story of Christ's crucifixion. For the rest of this millennium, you'll have to settle for browsing through the theater's exhibition hall (4 DM, daily 9:30–12:00, 13:30–16:00, closed Monday off-season, tel. 08822/32278), seeing Nicodemus tool around town in his VW, or reading the Book. Oberammergau is connected to Füssen by one direct bus per day (2 hrs).

Gasthaus zum Stern is friendly, serves good food (closed Tuesday in low season), and for this tourist town is a fine value (Sb-45 DM, Db-90 DM, closed November and December, Dorfstrasse 33, 82487 Oberammergau, tel. 08822/867, fax 08822/7027). Oberammergau's modern youth hostel is on the river a short walk from the center (20-DM beds, open all year, tel. 08822/4114).

Driving into town from the north, cross the bridge, take the second left, follow "Polizei" signs, and park by the huge gray Passionsspielhaus. Leaving town, head out past the church and turn toward Ettal on Road 23. You're 20 miles from Reutte via the scenic Plansee.

▲▲**Linderhof Castle**—This was Mad Ludwig's "home," his most intimate castle. It's small and comfortably exquisite, good enough for a minor god. Set in the woods, 15 minutes by car or bus (three per day) from Oberammergau, surrounded by fountains and sculpted, Italian-style gardens, it's the only palace I've toured that actually had me feeling envious. Don't miss the grotto (9 DM, daily 9:00–17:30 April–September, 10:00–16:00 with lunch break off-season, fountains often erupt on the hour, English tours constantly, tel. 08822/3512). Plan for lots of crowds, lots of walking, and a two-hour stop.

▲▲**Zugspitze**—The tallest point in Germany is a border crossing. Lifts from Austria and Germany go to the 10,000-foot summit of the Zugspitze. Straddle two great nations while enjoying an incredible view. There are restaurants, shops, and telescopes at the summit. The 75-minute trip from Garmisch on the German side costs 75 DM round-trip, with family discounts available (buy a combo cogwheel train and cable car ride, tel. 08821/7970). On the Austrian side, from the less crowded Talstation Obermoos, above the village of Erwald, the tram zips you to the top in 10 minutes (420 AS or 61 DM round-trip, daily 8:40–16:40 late May–October, tel. in Austria 05673/2309). The German ascent is easier for those without a car, but buses do connect the Erwald train station and the Austrian lift about hourly. Hikers enjoy the easy 10-km walk around the lovely Elbsee lake (German side, five minutes downhill from cable "Seilbahn").

Sleeping In Füssen, Germany
(1.7 DM = about $1, tel. code: 08362, zip code: 87629)
Sleep Code: **S** = Single, **D** = Double/Twin, **T** = Triple, **Q** = Quad, **b** = bathroom, **t** = toilet only, **s** = shower only, **CC** = Credit Card (Visa, MasterCard, Amex).

Unless otherwise noted, breakfast is included, hall showers are free, and English is spoken. Prices listed are for one-night stays. Some places give a discount for longer stays. Always ask. Competition is fierce, and off-season prices are soft.

Füssen, two miles from Ludwig's castles, is a cobbled riverside oompah treat, but very touristy (notice das sushi bar). It has just about as many rooms as tourists, though, and the TI has a free room-finding service. All places I've listed (except the hostel) are within a few blocks of the train station and the town center. They are used to travelers getting in after the Romantic Road bus arrives (20:40) and will hold rooms for a telephone promise.

Hotel Kurcafé is deluxe, with spacious rooms and all the modern conveniences. Prices vary wildly with the season (July and August are sky-high). But the hotel's bakery can enjoyably ruin your budget any time of year (Sb-95–139 DM, depending on season, Db-125–189 DM, third or fourth person pays 30 DM extra, CC:VMA, on the tiny traffic circle a block in front of the train station at Bahnhofstrasse 4, tel. 08362/6369, fax 08362/39424, e-mail: hotel.kurcafe@t-online.de). The attached restaurant has good, reasonable daily specials.

Hotel Gasthaus zum Hechten offers all the modern comforts in a friendly, traditional shell right under the Füssen Castle in the old-town pedestrian zone (S-60 DM, Sb-75 DM, D-100 DM, Db-110–130 DM, Tb-150 DM, Qb-180 DM, these prices and free parking promised with this book in 1999, cheaper off-season and for multi-night stays, fun mini-bowling alley in basement; from TI, walk down pedestrian street, take second right to Ritterstrasse 6; tel. 08362/91600, fax 08362/916099; Frau Margaret has taken fine care of travelers for 40 years). The attached restaurant Zum Hechten serves hearty Bavarian specialties and specializes in pike (*Hecht*), caught right out of the Lech River.

Gasthof Krone, a rare bit of pre-glitz Füssen also in the pedestrian zone, has dumpy halls and stairs but bright, cheery, comfy rooms (S-53 DM, D-96 DM, extra bed-48 DM, prices drop 6 DM for two-night stays, CC:VMA, from TI, head down pedestrian street, take first left to Schrannenplatz 17, tel. 08362/7824, fax 08362/37505).

Hotel Bräustüberl has clean, bright, newly renovated rooms in a musty old beer hall–type place (Sb-65 DM, Db-110 DM, depending on season, Rupprechtstrasse 5, a block from the station, tel. 08362/7843, fax 08362/38781).

American-run **Suzanne's B&B** does everything exactly right, from eggs laid right in the backyard to local cheese, a great children's yard, affordable laundry, and feel-good balconies (D-80 DM; large Ds with balcony and fridge—120 DM for two, 135 DM for three, 160 DM for four; non-smoking, 10 DM/day bike rental, backtrack two blocks from station, Venetianerwinkel 3, tel. 08362/38485, fax 08362/921-396, e-mail: svorbrugg@t-online.de).

The funky, old, ornately furnished **Pension Garni Elisabeth** exudes an Addams-family friendliness (S-45 DM, D-80–90 DM, Db-120–170 DM, T-120 DM, Tb-150–180 DM, showers-6 DM, Augustenstrasse 10, two blocks from the station toward town, take second left, tel. 08362/6275). Floors creak, dust balls wander, and the piano is never played.

Haus Peters, across the street, is comfy, smoke-free, and friendly but often closed (Db-86 DM, Tb-120 DM, Augustenstrasse 5, tel. 08362/7171).

Füssen Youth Hostel, a fine, German-run youth hostel, welcomes travelers under 27 (two- to six-bed rooms, 22 DM for bed and breakfast, 9 DM for dinner, 5.50 DM for sheets, laundry facilities-7 DM/load, non-smoking, Mariahilferstrasse 5, tel.

08362/7754, fax 08362/2770). From the station, backtrack 10
minutes along the tracks.

Sleeping in Hohenschwangau, near Neuschwanstein Castle (tel. code: 08362, zip code: 87645)

Inexpensive farmhouse *Zimmer* (B&Bs) abound in the countryside
around Neuschwanstein. Look for signs that say "*Zimmer Frei*"
("room free," or vacancy). The going rate is about 80 DM per
double including breakfast. **Pension Weiher** has lots of balconies
and flood-lit Neuschwanstein views (S-35–38 DM, D-77 DM,
Db-95 DM, Hofwiesenweg 11, tel. & fax 08362/81161). **Pension
Schwansee** has clean, basic rooms (Db-100–110 DM, CC:VM,
bike rental, 2.5 km from the castle on the road to Füssen at Park-
strasse 9, 87645 Alterschrofen, tel. 08362/8353, family Strössner).

For more of a hotel, try **Alpenhotel Meier**. In a rural setting
within walking distance of the castle, its rooms have new furnishings and porches (Sb-88 DM, Db-150 DM, Tb-201 DM, two-
night discounts, easy parking, Schwangauerstrasse 37, tel. 08362/
81152, fax 08362/987-028).

Eating in Füssen

Infooday is a clever, modern self-service eatery that sells its hot
meals and salad bar by weight and offers English newspapers (Monday–Friday 10:30–18:30, Saturday till 14:30, closed Sunday, 8
DM/filling salad, 12-DM meals; under the Füssen Castle in Hotel
zum Hechten, Ritterstrasse 6). A couple of blocks away, **Pizza Blitz**
offers good take-out or eat-at-counter pizzas and hearty salads for
about 8 DM apiece (Monday–Saturday 11:00–23:00, Sunday
12:00–23:00, Luitpoldstrasse 14). For more traditional fare, **Hotel
Bräustüberl** (see above) has famous home-brewed beer and a popular kitchen (Tuesday–Sunday 10:00–24:00, closed Monday). For
picnicking, try the Plus supermarket on the tiny traffic circle a
block from the train station (Monday–Friday 8:30–19:00, Saturday
8:00–14:00, closed Sunday, basement level of shopping complex).

Transportation Connections—Füssen

To: Neuschwanstein (2 buses/hrly, 10 min, 4.8 DM round-trip;
taxis cost 15 DM), Reutte (5 buses/day, 30 min, no service on Sunday; taxis cost 35 DM), Munich (hrly, 2 hrs, transfer in Buchloe).

Romantic Road Buses: The northbound Romantic Road
bus departs Füssen at 8:00, and the southbound bus arrives at
Füssen at 20:40 (bus stops at train station).

REUTTE, AUSTRIA
(12 AS = about $1)

Reutte (ROY-teh, rolled "r"), population 5,500, is a relaxed town,
far from the international tourist crowd but popular with Germans

and Austrians for its climate. Doctors recommend its "grade 1" air.
Reutte isn't in any other American guidebook. Its charms are subtle.
It never was rich or important. Its castle is ruined, its buildings have
painted-on "carvings," its churches are full, its men yodel for each
other on birthdays, and lately its energy is spent soaking its Austrian
and German guests in *Gemütlichkeit*. Most guests stay for a week, so
the town's attractions are more time-consuming than thrilling. If the
weather's good, hike to the mysterious Ehrenberg ruins or ride the
luge. For a slap-dancing bang, enjoy a Tirolean folk evening.

Orientation (tel. code: 05672)

Tourist Information: Reutte's helpful TI is a block in front of
the train station (Monday–Friday 8:00–12:00, 13:00–17:00, Saturday 8:30–12:00, tel. 05672/62336 or, from Germany, 0043-
5672/62336). Go over your sightseeing plans, ask about a folk
evening, pick up a city map, and ask about discounts with the
hotel guest cards.

Arrival in Reutte: Head straight out of the station one long
block to the TI. At the TI, turn left to reach the center of town.

Bike Rental: The train station rents bikes for 150 AS, mountain bikes for 200 AS (50 percent discount if you have a railpass).

Laundry: Don't ask the TI about a Laundromat. Unless you
can infiltrate the local campground, Hotel Maximilian, or Gutshof
zum Schluxen (see Sleeping, below), the town has none.

Sights—Reutte

▲▲**Ehrenberg Ruins**—The brooding ruins of Ehrenberg Castle
are a mile outside of Reutte on the road to Lermoos and Innsbruck. This 13th-century rock pile, a great contrast to King Ludwig's "modern" castles, is a super opportunity to let your
imagination off its leash. Hike up from the parking lot at the base
of the hill; it's a 25-minute walk to the castle for a great view from
your own private ruins. (Facing the hill from the parking lot, the
steeper trail is to the right, the easy gravelly road is to the left.)
Imagine how proud Count Meinrad II of Tirol (who built the castle in 1290) would be to know that his castle repelled 16,000
Swedish soldiers in the defense of Catholicism in 1632.

The easiest way down is via the small road leading from the
gully. The car park, with a café/guest house (Gasthof Klaus closed
Wednesday, offers a German-language flyer about the castle and
has a wall painting of the intact castle), is just off the Lermoos/
Reutte road. Reutte is a pleasant one-hour walk away.

Folk Museum—Reutte's Heimatmuseum, offering a quick look at
the local folk culture and the story of the castle, is more cute than
impressive (20 AS, Tuesday–Sunday 10:00–12:00, 14:00–17:00,
closed Monday and off-season, in the Green House on Untermarkt, around the corner from Hotel Goldener Hirsch).

Reutte

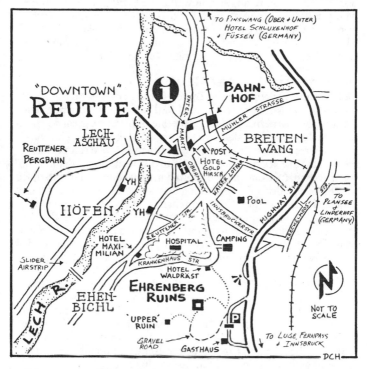

▲▲**Tirolean Folk Evening**—Ask the TI or your hotel if there's a Tirolean folk evening scheduled. About once a week in the summer, Reutte or a nearby town puts on an evening of yodeling, slap-dancing, and Tirolean frolic—usually worth the 80 AS and short drive. Off-season, you'll have to do your own yodeling. There are also weekly folk concerts in the park (ask at TI).

Swimming—Plunge into Reutte's Olympic-sized swimming pool to cool off after your castle hikes (60 AS, daily 10:00–21:00, off-season 14:00–21:00, closed Monday).

Reuttener Bergbahn—This mountain lift swoops you high above the tree line to a starting point for several hikes and to an Alpine flower park with special paths leading you past countless local varieties.

Flying and Gliding—For a major thrill on a sunny day, drop by the tiny airport in Hofen across the river, and fly. A small single-prop plane can buzz the Zugspitze and Ludwig's castles and give you a bird's-eye peek at Reutte's Ehrenberg ruins (two people for 30 minutes 1,350 AS, one hour 2,700 AS, tel. 05672/63207). Or, for something more angelic, how about *Segelfliegen*? For 500 AS, you get 30 minutes in a glider for two (you and the pilot). Just watching the tow-rope launch the graceful glider like a giant, slow-motion rubber-band gun is thrilling (11:00–19:00 late May–October, in good weather only, tel. 05672/71550).

Sights—Tirol, Near Reutte

▲▲**Sommerrodelbahn, the Luge**—Near Lermoos, on the Innsbruck-Lermoos-Reutte road, you'll find two rare and exciting luge courses, or *Sommerrodelbahn*. To try one of Europe's great $5 thrills: take the lift up, grab a sled-like go-cart, and luge down. The concrete course banks on the corners, and even a novice can go very, very fast. Most are cautious on their first run and speed demons on their second. (A woman once showed me her journal illustrated with her husband's dried five-inch-long luge scab. He disobeyed the only essential rule of luging: Keep both hands on your stick.) No one emerges from the course without a windblown hairdo and a smile-creased face. Both places have the same price and hours (70 AS per run, five- and 10-trip discount cards, open weekends from late May and daily mid-June through September or October, weather permitting, 9:00–17:00, closed in wet weather, so call first).

The small and steep luge: Bichlbach, the first course (100-meter drop over 800-meter course), is six kilometers beyond Reutte's castle ruins. Look for a chairlift on the right, and exit on the tiny road at the yellow "Riesenrutschbahn" sign (call first, tel. 05674/5350, or contact the local TI at 05674/5354). If you're without wheels, catch the train from Reutte to Bichlbach (6/day, 20 min) and walk one kilometer to the luge.

The longest luge: The Biberwier Sommerrodelbahn, which is 15 minutes closer to Innsbruck, just past Lermoos in Biberwier (the first exit after a long tunnel), is a better luge and, at 1,300 meters, the longest in Austria. The only drawbacks are its shorter season and that it's open only on weekends until July (9:00–16:30, tel. 05673/2111, local TI tel. 05673/2922). One or two blocks downhill from this luge, behind the Sport und Trachtenstüberl shop, is a wooden church dome with a striking Zugspitze backdrop. If you have sunshine and a camera, don't miss it. Without a car, the bus from Reutte to Biberwier is your best bet (8/day, fewer on Sunday, 30 min, bus stop and posted schedule near Reutte's Hotel Goldener Hirsch on Untermarket). The nearest train station is Lermoos, four kilometers from the luge.

▲**Fallerschein**—Easy for drivers and a special treat for those who may have been Kit Carson in a previous life, this extremely remote log-cabin village is a 4,000-foot-high, flower-speckled world of serene slopes and cowbells. Thunderstorms roll down the valley like it's God's bowling alley, but the pint-sized church on the high ground, blissfully simple in a land of Baroque, seems to promise that this huddle of houses will survive and the river and breeze will just keep flowing. The couples sitting on benches are mostly Austrian vacationers who've rented cabins here. Many of them, appreciating the remoteness of Fallerschein, are having affairs.

For a rugged chunk of local Alpine peace, spend a night in the local Matratzenlager Almwirtschaft Fallerschein, run by Kerle Erwin (120 AS per person with breakfast; open, if weather permits, mid-May–October; 27 cheap beds in a very simple loft dorm, meager plumbing, good, inexpensive meals, 6671 Weissenbach Pfarrweg 18, Reutte, tel. 05678/5142, rarely answered, and then not in English). It's crowded only on weekends. Fallerschein is at the end of a miserable, two-kilometer, fit-for-jeep-or-rental-car-only paved road that looks more closed than it is, near Namlos on the Berwang Road southwest of Reutte.

Sleeping in Reutte, Austria
(12 AS = about $1, tel. code: 05672, zip code: 6600)
For fewer crowds, easygoing locals with a contagious love of life, and a good dose of Austrian ambience, those with a car should home-base in nearby Reutte. (To call Reutte from Germany, dial 0043-5672, then the local number.) You'll drive across the border but probably won't even have to stop. All include breakfast.

Hotels
Reutte is popular with Austrians and Germans who come here year after year for a one- or two-week vacation. The hotels are big and elegant, full of comfy, carved furnishings and creative ways to spend so much time in one spot. They take great pride in their restaurants, and the owners send their children away to hotel management schools.

Hotel Goldener Hirsch, a grand old hotel renovated with a mod Tirolean Jugendstil flair, has sliding automatic doors, minibars, TV with cable in the room, and one lonely set of antlers. The hotel is located right downtown (two blocks from station). For those without a car, this is the most convenient hotel (Sb-550 AS, Db-880 AS, two-night discounts, elevator, grumpy, unpredictable management, decent attached restaurant, CC:VMA, 6600 Reutte-Tirol, tel. 05672/62508 and ask for Monika or Helmut, fax 05672/625-087, e-mail: gold.hirsch@netway.at).

Hotel Maximilian, up the river a mile in the village of Ehenbichl, is a fine splurge that includes the use of bicycles, ping-pong, a children's playroom, and the friendly service of the Koch family. Daughter Gabi speaks fine English. There always seems to be a special event here, and the Kochs host many Tirolean folk evenings (Sb-450 AS, Db-900–960 AS, cheaper for families, laundry service, great restaurant, far from the train station in the next village but can often pick up, A-6600 Ehenbichl-Reutte, tel. 05672/62585, fax

05672/625-8554, e-mail: maxhotel@netway.at). You can use their laundry service even if you're not staying at the hotel.

Pension Hohenrainer is a big, friendly, family-run place offering castle-view balconies (Sb-260–300 AS, Db-560–600 AS). The same family runs the simpler **Gasthof Schlosswirt** across the flowery field (S-180–200 AS, D-360 AS, D with view-400 AS, traditional Tirolean-style restaurant). Both are up the road behind Hotel Maximilian (turn right and continue 100 meters to Unterreid 3, A-6600 Ehenbichl, tel. 05672/62544, fax 05672/62052, e-mail: hohenrainer@aon.at).

Gutshof zum Schluxen, run by friendly and helpful Hermann, gets the "remote-old-hotel-in-an-idyllic-setting" award. This working farm offers good food, modern rustic elegance draped in goose down and pastels, and a chance to pet the rabbit. Its picturesque meadow setting will turn you into a dandelion-picker (Sb-460–540 AS, Db-920–1,080 AS, extra person-220 AS, through 1999 only with this book, discounts for multi-night stays, excellent breakfast, self-service laundry, loaner bikes free for guests, free parking, free e-mail service, no credit cards, A-6600 Pinswang-Reutte, between Reutte and Füssen in the village of Unterpinswang, tel. 05677/8903, fax 05677/890-323, e-mail: schluxen@eunet.at). Schluxen is in the village of Pinswang, between Reutte and Füssen.

Gasthof-Pension Waldrast, separating a forest and a meadow, is warmly run by the Huter family. Its big rooms feel like living rooms, many with fine castle views (Db-about 700 AS, on Ehrenbergstrasse, a half-mile out of town toward Innsbruck, past the campground, just under the castle, 6600 Reutte-Ehenbichl, tel. & fax 05672/62443). The Waldrast is a good coffee stop for non-guests hiking into town from the Ehrenberg ruins.

Zimmer

The tourist office has a list of more than 50 private homes that rent out generally elegant rooms with facilities down the hall, pleasant communal living rooms, and breakfast. Most charge 200 AS per person per night, don't like to rent to people staying fewer than three nights, and speak little if any English. Reservations are nearly impossible for one- or two-night stays. But short stops are welcome if you just drop in and fill in available gaps. The TI can always find you a room when you arrive (free service).

The tiny village of Breitenwang, older and quieter than Reutte, has all the best *Zimmer* (a 20-minute walk from the Reutte train station: at the post office roundabout, follow Planseestrasse past the onion dome to the pointy straight dome; unmarked Kaiser Lothar Strasse is the first right past this church). These three places are comfortable, quiet, and kid-friendly, have few stairs, speak some English, and are within two blocks of the Breitenwang church steeple: **Inge Hosp** (S-200 AS, D-380 AS, an old-fashioned place, includes antlers over the breakfast table, Kaiser Lothar Strasse 36, tel. 05672/62401); her cousins **Walter and Emilie Hosp** across the street (D-400 AS for one night, D-380 AS for two or more, third or fourth person pays 160 AS, Kaiser Lothar Strasse 29, tel. 05672/65377); and **Helene Haissl** (S-190 AS, D-380 AS, 360 AS for a two-night stay, fine rooms, Planseestrasse 63, tel. 05672/ 67913). *Zimmer* charge 15 AS to 20 AS extra for heat in winter—worth it.

Hostels

Reutte has an excellent hostel. If you've never hosteled and are curious (and have a car), try this one. They accept non-members of any age.

The homey, newly renovated **Jugendgästehaus Graben** has two to six beds per room and includes breakfast and sheets (160 AS per bed, Db-400 AS, self-service laundry; from downtown Reutte, cross the bridge and follow the road left along the river, about two miles from Reutte's station—one bus per hour until 18:00; Graben 1, A-6600 Reutte-Höfen, tel. 05672/62644, fax 05672/626-444, e-mail: jgh-hoefen@tirol.com). Frau Reyman keeps the place traditional, clean, and friendly and serves a great 80-AS dinner. No curfew, smoke-free rooms, bus connection to Neuschwanstein. This is a super value.

Eating in Reutte

Each of the hotels takes great pleasure in earning the loyalty of its return guests by serving fine Austrian food at reasonable prices. Rather than go to a cheap restaurant, I'd order low on a hotel menu. For cheap food, the **Metzgerei Storf Imbiss** (Monday–Friday 8:30–15:00), above the deli across from the Heimatmuseum on Untermarkt Street, is good. **Carina** in Breitenwang is a fine Italian restaurant with decent prices (near *Zimmer*, Bachweg 17).

Transportation Connections—Reutte

To: Füssen (6 buses/day, 30 min, no service on Sunday; taxis cost 35 DM), **Garmisch** (2 trains/hr, 60 min), **Munich** (hrly trains, 3 hrs, transfer in Garmisch).

PRAGUE

It's amazing what 10 years of freedom can do. Prague has always been historic. Now it's fun, too. No place in Europe has become so popular so quickly. And for good reason: The capital of the Czech Republic—the only major city of central Europe to escape the bombs of this century's wars—is Europe's best-preserved Baroque city. It's slinky with sumptuous Art Nouveau facades, offers tons of cheap Mozart and Vivaldi, and brews the best beer in Europe. But more than the architecture and traditional culture, it's an explosion of pent-up entrepreneurial energy jumping for joy after 50 years of Communist rule. And its low prices will make your visit enjoyable and nearly stressless.

Planning Your Time

Two days makes the long train ride in and out worthwhile and gives you time to get beyond the sightseeing and enjoy Prague's fun-loving ambience. Many wish they'd scheduled three days for Prague. From Munich, Berlin, and Vienna, it's a six-hour train ride (during the day) or an overnight ride.

With two days I'd spend a morning seeing the castle and a morning in the Jewish Quarter—the only two chunks of sightseeing that demand any brainpower. Spend your afternoons loitering around the Old Town, Charles Bridge, and the Little Quarter and your nights split between beer halls and live music. Keep in mind that state museums close on Monday, and Jewish sites close on Saturday.

History

Medieval Prague: Prague's castle put it on the map in the ninth century. In the 10th century, the region was incorporated into the German "Holy Roman" Empire. The 14th century was

Prague

Prague's Golden Age, when it was one of Europe's largest and most highly cultured cities. During this period Prague built St. Vitus Cathedral and Charles Bridge and established the first university in central Europe.

Bucking the Pope and Germany: Jan Hus was a local

preacher who got in trouble with the Vatican a hundred years before Martin Luther. Like Luther, he preached in the people's language rather than Latin. To add insult to injury, he complained about church corruption. Tried for heresy and burned in 1415, Hus roused nationalist (Bohemian) as well as religious feelings and became a symbol of Czech martyrdom. His followers are Hussites.

Religious Wars: The reformist times of Jan Hus (around 1400, rebelling against both German and Roman control) led to a period of religious wars and ultimately subjugation under Austrian rule. Prague stagnated under the Habsburgs of Austria with the brief exception of Rudolf II's reign.

Under the late 16th-century rule of the Habsburg king Rudolf II, Prague emerged again as a cultural and intellectual center. Johannes Kepler, Tycho Brahe, and others worked here. Much of Prague's great art can be attributed to this Habsburg king who lived not in Vienna but in Prague.

The Thirty Years' War (1618–1648) began in Prague when locals tossed two Catholic/Habsburg officials (Czechs sympathetic to the Germans) out the window of the Prague Castle. Often called "the first world war" because it engulfed so many nations, the 30 years were particularly tough on Prague. During this period, its population dropped from 60,000 to 25,000. The result of this war was 300 years of Habsburg rule: German and Catholic culture, not Czech. Prague was a backwater of Vienna.

Czech Nationalist Revival: The 19th century was a time of nationalism for people throughout Europe, including the Czechs, as the age of divine kings and ruling families was coming to a fitful end. The arts (such as the paintings of Mucha and the building of the massive National Museum atop Wenceslas Square) stirred the national spirit. With the end of World War I the Habsburgs were history, and in 1918 the independent country of Czechoslovakia was proclaimed with Prague as its capital.

Troubled 20th Century: Independence had lasted barely 20 years when the Nazis swept in (1939). Prague escaped the bombs of World War II but went almost directly from the Nazi frying pan into the Communist fire. Almost. A local uprising freed the city from the Nazis on May 8, 1945. The Russians "liberated" them again on May 9.

The Communist chapter of Czech subjugation (1948–1989) was grim. The student and artist-led "Prague Spring" revolt in 1968 was crushed. The charismatic leader Alexander Dubcek was exiled into a job in the back woods, and the years after 1968 were particularly tough. But eventually the Soviet empire crumbled. Czechoslovakia regained its freedom in the 1989 "Velvet Revolution" (so called because there were no casualties). Until 1989, May 9 was the Czech day of liberation. Now Czechs celebrate their liberation on May 8.

In 1993 the Czech and Slovak republics agreed on the "Velvet Divorce" and became two separate countries.

Today, while not without its problems, the Czech Republic is enjoying a growing economy and a strong democracy. Prague has emerged as one of the most popular tourist destinations in Europe. You're about to find out why.

Orientation

Locals call their town "Praha" (pron: pra-ha). It's big, with 1.2 million people, but for the quick visit, think of it as small and focus on the core of the city. I will refer to the tourist landmarks in English (with the Czech name in parentheses). Study the map and learn these key places:

Main Train Station:	*Hlavní Nádraží* (hlav-nee nah-dra-shzee)
Old Town:	*Staré Město* (sta-rey mnyess-toh)
Old Town Square:	*Staroměstské Náměstí* (starro-min-yes-ststi-keh nah-mnyess-tee)
New Town:	*Nové Město* (no-vay mnyess-toh)
Little Quarter:	*Malá Strana* (mah-lah strah-nah)
Jewish Quarter:	*Josefov* (yoo-zef-fohf)
Castle Area:	*Hradčany* (hrad-chah-nee)
Charles Bridge:	*Karluv most* (kar-loov most)
Wenceslas Square:	*Václavske Náměstí* (vah-slawf-skeh nah-mnyess-tee)
The River:	*Vltava* (vul-tah-vah)

The Vltava River divides the west side (castle and Little Quarter) from the east side (train station, Old Town, New Town, and nearly all of the recommended hotels). Prague addresses come with a general zone. Praha 1 is in the old center on either side of the river. Praha 2 is in the new city south of Wenceslas Square. Praha 3 and higher indicates a location farther from the center.

Tourist Information

TIs are at three key locations: at the main train station, on the Old Town Square, and in the West Tower of Charles Bridge (daily 9:00–19:00, until 18:00 on weekends and in winter, tel. 02/2448-2202). They offer maps, information on guided walks and bus tours, and bookings for concerts, hotel rooms, and rooms in private homes. Get the brochure listing all of Prague's museums and hours.

Helpful Hints

Formalities: Travel in Prague is like travel in Western Europe, only it's not covered by the Eurailpass and it seems 15 years behind the times. Americans and Canadians need no visa. Just flash your passport at the border. (U.S. embassy in Prague, tel. 02/5732-0663.)

Rip-offs: Prague's new freedom comes with new scams. There's no particular risk of violent crime, just green, rich tourists getting taken by con artists. Simply be on guard: on trains (thieves on overnight trains and corrupt conductors intimidating Western tourists for a bribe); changing money (tellers anywhere with bad arithmetic and inexplicable pauses while counting back your change); and dealing with taxis (see Getting Around Prague, below). In restaurants, understand the price clearly before ordering.

Telephoning: Czech phones work like any in Europe. For international calls, buy a phone card at a kiosk or your hotel (150 kč). It costs about $1 a minute to call the United States directly (dial 001-area code-number) from a public phone booth that accepts the local phone card. To call Prague from abroad, dial the international code (00 in Europe or 011 in the U.S.), the Czech Republic code (420), then Prague's city code (2), followed by the local number.

Money: 32 Koruna (kč) = about U.S. $1. There is no black market. Assume anyone trying to sell money on the streets is peddling obsolete currency. Buy and sell easily at the station (4 percent fees), banks, or hotels. ATMs are everywhere. Czech money is tough to change in the West. Before leaving the Czech Republic, change your remaining Koruna into your next country's currency (at Prague train station change bureaus).

Local Help: Magic Praha is a tiny travel service run by hard-working English-speaking Lida Steflova. She is a local jack of all trades, helpful with any needs you may have (tel. 02/302-5170, e-mail: mp.ludmila@post.cz).

Best Views: Enjoy "the golden city of a hundred spires" during the early evening when the light is warm and colors rich. Good viewpoints include the castle square, the top of the east tower of Charles Bridge, the Old Town Square clock tower, and the steps of the National Museum overlooking Wenceslas Square.

Language: Czech, a Slavic language, has little resemblance to Western European languages. These days, English is "modern" and you'll find the language barrier minimal. If you speak German, it's helpful. An acute accent means you linger on that vowel. The little carrot above the c, s, or z makes it ch, sh, or zh.

Learn these key Czech words:

Hello/Goodbye (familiar)	*Ahoj* (ah-hoi)
Good day, Hello (formal)	*Dobrý den* (DOH-bree den)
Yes/No	*Ano* (AH-no)/*Ne* (neh)
Please	*Prosím* (proh-zeem)
Thank you	*Děkuji* (dyack-quee)
You're welcome	*Prosím* (proh-zeem)
Where is...?	*Kde je ...?* (gday yeh)
Do you speak English?	*Mluvíte anglicky?*
	(MLOO-vit-eh ANG-litz-key)
krown (the money)	*koruna* (koh-roo-nah)

Arrival in Prague

Prague unnerves many travelers—it's relatively rundown, it's behind the former Iron Curtain, and you've heard stories of rip-offs and sky-high hotel prices. But in reality, Prague is charming, safe, and welcomes you with open cash registers and smiles.

By Train: Prague has several train stations. Most travelers coming from and going to the West use the main station (Hlavní Nádraží) or the secondary station (Holešovice Nádraží; if you arrive here, take metro into town: get off at Hlavní Nádraží for main station, or transfer at Muzeum to green line, stops Můstek and Staroměstská are in Old Town). Trains to other points within the country use Masarykovo or Smíchov stations.

Prague's main train station feels like a big metro station. You'll be met at the tracks by room hustlers (snaring tourists for cheap rooms in the center—illegally). A huge highway (Wilson Boulevard) obliterates the front of the formerly elegant station (go upstairs to see its original Art Nouveau interior). The large low-ceilinged main hall is downstairs: filled with travelers, kiosks, loitering teenagers, and older riff-raff.

Upon arrival by train, change money. Rates vary—compare by asking at two windows what you'll get for $100. Count carefully. At the same window, buy a city map (30 kč, with trams and metro lines marked and tiny sketches of the sights for ease in navigating). You'll be constantly referring to this map. Confirm your departure plans at the train information window. Possibly arrange for a room or tour at TI or the AVE travel agency. The left luggage counter is reportedly safer than the lockers.

To reach the Old Town from the train station, you can catch trams #5, #9, or #26 (to find the stop, walk into the park and head two minutes to the right) or take the metro (downstairs in the station, look for the red "M", two directions: Muzeum or Florenc; take metro to Muzeum, then transfer to green line—stops Můstek and Staroměstská straddle the Old Town). The courageous and savvy get a cabbie to treat them fairly and get to their hotel fast and sweat-free for no more than 130 kč (see below).

By Plane: A couple of minibus services get you from the airport to downtown (or vice versa). The Cedaz minibus costs 100 kč and runs hourly (5:00–22:00) between the airport and Náměstî Rebulicky.

Getting Around Prague

You can walk nearly everywhere. But the metro is slick, the trams fun, and the taxis quick and easy once you're initiated.

Public Transport: The trams and metro work on the same tickets (buy from machines in metro, kiosks, or hotels). For convenience, buy all the tickets you think you'll need for your stay:

Prague Metro

15-minute ticket—8 kč, 60-minute ticket—12 kč, 24-hour ticket—70 kč, three-day pass—180 kč. The metro closes at midnight.

City maps show the tram/bus/metro lines. The metro system is handy and simple (just three lines) but doesn't get to many hotels and sights. Trams come by every couple of minutes. Get used to hopping on and off. Validate your ticket on the bus by sticking it in the machine (which stamps a time on it).

Taxis: The most infamous taxis in Europe are being tamed. While bandito cabbies still have meters that spin like pinwheels, the city has made great strides in civilizing these thugs. While most guidebooks advise avoiding taxis, this is defeatist. I find Prague is a great taxi town and use them routinely. Get the local rate and they're cheap. Use only registered taxis: these are marked by a roof lamp with the word "TAXI" in black on both sides, and the front doors sport a black-and-white checkered ribbon, the company name, license number, and rates (three rows: drop charge—25 kč, per kilometer charge—17 kč, and wait time per minute—4 kč). The key is the tiny "*sazba*" box on the magic meter showing the rate. This should read "1." If a cabbie tries to rip you off, simply pay 100 kč. Let him follow you into the hotel if he

insists you owe him more. (He won't.) The receptionist will defend
you. Rip-offs are most likely around tourist sites and the train station. To remind him to turn on the meter, say "*Zapnete taximetr*"
(zappa-nyet-ay tax-ah-met-er).

City Tours

Prague Walks offers walking tours of the Old Town, the castle,
and Jewish Quarter. Most last two hours and cost 200 kč. Get the
current schedule from any TI (e-mail: pwalks@comp.cz).

Cheap big bus orientation tours provide an efficient once-
over-lightly look at Prague and a convenient way to see the castle.
Premiant City Tours offers 15 different tours including: quick
city (350 kč, 2 hrs, 5/day), grand city (550 kč, 3.5 hrs, 2/day), Jewish Quarter (590 kč, 2 hrs), Prague by night, Bohemian glass,
Terezin Concentration Camp memorial, Karlštejn Castle, český
Krumlov (1600 kč, 8 hrs), and a river cruise. The tours feature live
guides (in German and English) and depart from near the bottom
of Wenceslas Square at Na Príkope 40. Get tickets at an AVE
travel agency, hotel, on the bus, or at Na Príkope 23 (tel. 02/0601-
212625 or 02/2423-0072, Web site: www.sos.cz/premiant).

Tram #22 makes a fine joyride through town. Consider this
as a scenic lead-up to touring the castle. Catch it at metro: Náměstí
Míru, roll through a bit of new town, the Old Town, across the
river and hop out just above the castle.

Self-Guided Walking Tour

The King's Walk (Královská cesta), the ancient way of coronation
processions, is touristy but great. Pedestrian-friendly and full of
playful diversions, it connects the essential Prague sites. The king
would be crowned in St. Vitus Cathedral in the Prague Castle,
walk through the Little Quarter stopping at the Church of St.
Nicholas, cross Charles Bridge, and finish at the Old Town
Square. If he hurried, he'd be done in 20 minutes. Like the main
drag in Venice between St. Mark's and the Rialto bridge, this
walk mesmerizes tourists. Use it as a spine, but venture off it—
especially to eat.

This walk laces together all the following recommended
sights except the Jewish Quarter. From the castle, stairs lead
down into the Little Quarter. They dump you into the Little
Quarter Square and the Church of St. Nicholas. Farther downhill, a medieval gate announces Charles Bridge. Over the river
another gate welcomes you to the Old Town and a well-trod,
shop-lined street under glorious Baroque and Art Nouveau
facades leads to the Old Town Square. For the sake of complete-
ness, extend the King's Walk from there past the Havelska Market and up Wenceslas Square, where a commanding view awaits
from the National Museum steps.

Sights—Prague's Castle Area

▲▲**Prague Castle**—For a thousand years, Czech rulers have ruled from the Prague Castle. It's huge (by some measures, the biggest castle on earth) with a wall more than a kilometer long. And it's confusing with plenty of sights not worth seeing and a newly rebuilt feeling. Rather than worry about rumors that you should spend all day here with long lists of museums within to see, keep things simple. Four stops matter and are explained here: St. Vitus Cathedral, the old Royal Palace, Basilica of St. George, and the Golden Lane. (100 kč for entrance to all sights within, daily 9:00–17:00; the 125 kč audio guide is good but renting it makes it impossible to exit the castle area from the bottom.) To reach the castle by metro, get off at the Malostranská metro stop, climb through the Little Quarter and up the castle steps (Zamecke Schody). Or ride tram #22, which stops above the castle.

Castle Square (Hradčanske Náměstí)—The big square facing the castle offers fine string quartet street music, an awesome city view, and stairs down to the Little Quarter. The National Gallery's collection of European paintings is in the neighboring Sternberg Palace (contains works by Dürer, Rubens, Rembrandt, El Greco, and more—skipable if you're going to Vienna or Munich).

Survey the castle from this square, the tip of a 500-meter-long series of courtyards, churches, and palaces. The offices facing this first courtyard belong to the Czech president, Vaclav Havel (left side). The guard changes on the hour. Walk under the fighting giants, under an arch, and straight into the info center in a small church—buy tickets here.

St. Vitus Cathedral—This cathedral symbolizes the Czech spirit. It was finished in 1929 on about the 1,000th anniversary of the assassination of St. Wenceslas, patron saint of the Czechs. This most important church in Prague houses the crown jewels (thoroughly locked up and out of sight) and the tomb of "Good King" Wenceslas as well as other Czech royalty. Wenceslas's tomb sits in the fancy chapel (on the right). Murals here show scenes of his life. More kings are buried in the royal mausoleum in front of the high altar and in the crypt underneath. The cathedral, a mix of Gothic and neo-Gothic, is 124 meters long and offers a fine view from the top of its spire (daily 9:00–17:00, 287 steps). Notice the fine windows. The rose window above the entry shows the creation. The Art Nouveau window from 1931 is by Czech artist Alfons Mucha (look for Saints Cyril and Methodius, third chapel on left). If you like that, visit the Mucha museum in the Old Town (see below).

Old Royal Palace—This was the seat of the Bohemian princes in the 12th century. While extensively rebuilt, the large hall is late Gothic. It's big enough for jousts—even the spiral staircases were designed to let a mounted soldier gallop up. Look up at the impressive vaulted ceiling, look down on the chapel from the end, and go out on the balcony for a fine Prague view. Is that Paris in the distance? No, it's an observation tower built for an exhibition in 1891 (60 meters tall, a quarter of the height of its big brother in Paris—built in 1889). There's nothing to see downstairs in the palace. Across from palace exit is St. George Basilica.

St. George Basilica and Convent—The first Bohemian convent was established here near the palace in 973. Today the convent houses the Czech Gallery (best Czech paintings from Gothic, Renaissance, and Baroque periods). The basilica is the best-preserved Romanesque church in Prague. St. Ludmila was buried here in 973. Continue walking downhill through the castle grounds. Veer to the left and into a cute lane.

Golden Lane—This street of old buildings, which originally housed goldsmiths, is now filled with gift shops, boutiques, galleries, and cafes. The Czech writer Franz Kafka lived at #22. There's a handy deli/bistro for picnic items at the top and a public WC at the bottom. Beyond that, at the end of the castle, are fortifications beefed up in anticipation of the Turkish attack—the cause for most medieval arms build-ups in Europe—and steps leading down and out into the Little Quarter.

Sights—From the Little Quarter to Charles Bridge

▲▲**Little Quarter (Malá Strana)**—This is the most characteristic fun-to-wander old section of town. It's one of four medieval towns (along with Hradčany, Staré Město, and Nové Město) which eventually grew to become Prague. It centers on the Little Quarter Square (Malostranské Náměstí) with its plague monument and the commanding church.

Church of St. Nicholas—Dominating the Little Quarter, this is the best example of High Baroque in town (daily 9:00–16:00, built 1703–1760, 230-foot-high dome). Normally, every night there are concerts at two venues on this square: in the Church of St. Nicholas and in Lichtenstein Palace across from the church. Charles Bridge is a short walk down Mostecka from the square.

▲▲▲**Charles Bridge (Karluv most)**—This much loved bridge, commissioned by the Holy Roman Emperor Charles IV in 1357, offers one of the most pleasant 500-meter strolls in Europe. Be on the bridge when the sun is low for the warmest people-watching and photography. At one time, the black crucifix (1657) standing near the east end stood alone. The multitude of other saints, near and dear to old Praguers, were added later. Today most are replicas with the originals in museums out of the pollution.

There's a TI at the west end tower (climbable). The tower at the east end is considered one of the finest Gothic gates in existence. Climb it for a fine view but nothing else (30 kč, daily

10:00–18:30). After crossing the bridge, follow the shop-lined street to the Old Town Square.

Sights—Prague's Old Town Square

▲▲▲**Old Town Square**—The focal point for most visits, this has been a market square since the 11th century. It became the nucleus of a town (Staré Město) in the 13th century when its city hall was built. Today the old-time market stalls have been replaced by cafés, touristic horse buggies, and souvenir hawkers.

The Hus Memorial—erected in 1915, 500 years after his burning—marks the center of the square and symbolizes the long struggle for Czech freedom. The Czech reformer Jan Hus stands tall between two groups of people: victorious Hussite patriots and Protestants defeated by the Habsburgs. A mother with her children behind Hus represents the ultimate rebirth of the Czech nation. The steps are a popular local hangout—young Czechs gawking at gawking tourists.

A spin tour from the center gives you a look at architectural styles: Romanesque, Gothic, Renaissance, Baroque, and Art Nouveau.

Spin clockwise from the green domes of the wildly Baroque Church of St. Nicholas. There has been a church on this site since the 12th century. This one, dating from the early 18th century, is now a Hussite church (evening concerts). The Jewish Quarter (Josefov) is a few blocks behind it. Spin to the right past the Hus Memorial and the fine golden and mosaic Art Nouveau facade of the Prague City Insurance Company. Notice the fanciful Gothic Tyn Church with its Disney-esque spires flanking a solid gold effigy of the Virgin Mary. For 200 years after Hus's death, this was the leading Hussite church in Prague (enter through arcade facing the square; a diagram at door locates spots of touristic interest such as the tomb of astronomer Tycho Brahe). Lining the south side of the square is an interesting row of pastel houses. Their Gothic, Renaissance, and Baroque facades are ornamented with interesting statues that symbolize the original use of each building. The pointed 230-foot-tall spire marks the 14th-century Old Town Hall (famous for its astronomical clock—see below). In front of the city hall, 27 white inlaid crosses mark the spot 27 Protestant nobles were beheaded in 1621 after rebelling against Catholic Habsburgs.

▲▲**Old Town Hall Astronomical Clock**—Join the gang, ignoring the ridiculous human sales racks, for the striking of the hour (daily 8:00–20:00) on the 15th-century town hall clock. As you wait for the show, see if you can figure out how the clock works.

With revolving disks and sweeping hands, this clock keeps several versions of time. Two outer rings show the hour: Bohemian time (Gothic numbers, with hours counted from sunset) and our time (24 Roman numerals, XII at the top being noon, XII at the bottom being midnight). Everything revolves around the earth (the fixed middle background, with Prague at the center). Arcing lines and moving spheres combine with the big hand (a sweeping golden sun) and the little hand (the moon showing various stages) to indicate the times of sunset and sunrise. Look for the orbits of the sun and moon as they rise through day (the blue zone) and night (the black zone). If this seems complex today, it must have been a marvel in 1490.

Four statues flank the clock representing 15th-century Prague's four biggest worries: invasion (the Turk), death (skeleton), greed (a moneylender, which used to have "Jewish" features until after World War II, when anti-Semitism became politically incorrect), and vanity (enjoying the mirror).

At the top of the hour, (1) death tips his hourglass and pulls the chord ringing the bell, (2) the windows open and the Twelve Apostles parade by acknowledging the gang of onlookers, (3) the rooster crows, and (4) the hour is rung. The hour is often off because of daylight saving time (which made no sense at all in the 15th century).

Inside the city hall you'll find the main TI, local guides desk, and the opportunity to pay three admissions: for the city hall (by tour only), Gothic chapel (nothing to see except a close-up of the Twelve Apostles and the clock mechanism well-described in English), and the tower (climb for another fine city view).

Sights—Around Wenceslas Square

▲**Havelská Market**—Central Prague's best open-air flower and produce market scene is a block toward the Old Town Square from the bottom of Wenceslas Square. Laid out in the 13th century by King Wenceslas for the German trading community, it keeps hungry locals and vagabonds fed cheaply today.

▲▲**Wenceslas Square (Václavske Náměstí)**—More a broad boulevard than a square, it's named for the statue of King Wenceslas that stands on a horse at the top. The square is a stage for modern Czech history: The Czechoslovak state was proclaimed here in 1918. In 1968 the Soviets put down huge popular demonstrations here. And in 1969 Jan Palach set himself on fire here to protest against the puppet Soviet government. The next day 200,000 local protesters gathered here. Starting at the top (metro: Muzeum), stroll down the square:

The National Museum stands grandly at the top. The only thing exciting about it is the view (60 kč, daily 10:00–18:00, halls of Czech fossils and animals).

St. Wenceslas, commemorated by the statue, is the "good king" of Christmas carol fame. He was never really a king, but the wise and benevolent 10th-century Duke of Bohemia. After being assassinated in 935, he became a symbol of Czech nationalism.

The metro stop (Muzeum) is the crosspoint of two metro lines. From here you could roll a ball straight down the boulevard and through the heart of Prague to Charles Bridge. It is famous locally as the downtown meeting place. They say, "I'll see you under the horse's ass."

Thirty meters below the big horse is a small round garden with a low-key memorial "to the victims of Communism." Pictured here is Jan Palach. The massive demonstrations here in the days following his death led to the overthrow of the Czech Communist government. From the balcony of the Grand Hotel Europa (farther down), Vaclav Havel stood with Alexander Dubcek, hero of the 1968 revolt, and declared the free Republic of Czechoslovakia in December 1989.

Continue people-watching your way downhill. American Express is on the corner (on left, daily 9:00–19:00, money exchange service). The Grand Hotel Europa (halfway down Wenceslas Square) is hard to miss. Notice its Art Nouveau exterior and step inside for the smoky, elegant Old World ambience of its Art Nouveau restaurant (see Sleeping, below).

The bottom of Wenceslas Square meets another fine pedestrian mall. Na Príkope (meaning "the moat") leads from Wenceslas Square right to the Municipal House and the Powder Tower (the Powder Tower sounds interesting but is a dud). City tour buses leave from along this street.

Sights—Prague's Jewish Quarter

▲▲▲Jewish Quarter (Josefov)—The Jewish people were dispersed by the Romans 2,000 years ago. "Time was their sanctuary which no army could destroy" as their culture survived in enclaves throughout the Western world. Jews first came to Prague in the 10th century. The main intersection of Josefov (Maiselova and Siroka Streets) was the meeting point of two medieval trade routes. Jewish traders settled here in the 13th century and built a synagogue.

When the pope declared Jews and Christians should not live together, Jews had to wear yellow badges, and their quarter was walled in, becoming a ghetto. In the 16th and 17th centuries, Prague had the biggest ghetto in Europe with 11,000 inhabitants—nearly half the population of Prague.

The "outcasts" of Christianity relied on profits from moneylending (forbidden to Christians) and community solidarity to survive. While their money protected them, it was also a curse. Throughout Europe, when times got tough and Christian debts to the Jewish community mounted, entire Jewish communities were burned, evicted, or killed.

Within its six gates, Prague's Jewish Quarter was a gaggle of 100 wooden buildings. Someone wrote: "Jews nested rather than dwelled." In the 1780s Emperor Joseph II eased much of the discrimination against Jews. In 1848 the walls were torn down and the neighborhood, named Josefov in honor of the emperor who was less anti-Semitic than the norm, was incorporated as a district of Prague.

In 1897 ramshackle Josefov was razed and replaced with a new modern town—the original 31 streets and 220 buildings became 10 streets and 83 buildings. This is what you'll see today: an attractive neighborhood of fine, mostly Art Nouveau buildings, with a few surviving historic Jewish buildings. In the 1930s some 50,000 Jews lived in Josefov. Today only a couple of thousand remain.

Strangely, the museums of the Jewish Quarter are, in part, the work of Hitler. He preserved Josefov to be his museum of the "exterminated race." Six sites scattered over a three-block area make the tourists' Jewish Quarter. Five, called "the Museum," are treated as one admission. Go early or late, as crowds can be fierce. Your ticket comes with a map locating the sights and five admission appointments. times you'll be let in if it's very crowded. (Without crowds, ignore the times.)

Start at the Maisel Synagogue unless you want to rent the AudioGuide (125 kč, at the Pinkas Synagogue). Westerners pay more than locals: 450 kč (250 kč for the "Museum" and 200 kč for the Old-New Synagogue). The sites are open from Sunday to Thursday 9:00 to 17:30, Friday 9:00 to 14:00 (sometimes later), and closed on Saturday (the Jewish sabbath). The AudioGuide provides a good historic background and an easy-to-follow orientation for each site. There are also occasional live guided walks (often at 10:00, 40 kč). Most stops are wonderfully described in English. These museums are well presented and profoundly moving; for me, this is the most interesting Jewish site in Europe.

Maisel Synagogue—This shows a thousand years of Jewish history in Bohemia and Moravia. Ironically, the collection was assembled from synagogues throughout the region by Nazis planning to archive the "extinct Jewish culture" here in Josefov with a huge museum. Exhibits include topics such as the origin of the Star of David, Jewish mysticism, and the creation of the Prague Ghetto.

Pinkas Synagogue—A site of Jewish worship for 400 years, today this is a moving memorial to the victims of the Nazis. Of the 120,000 Jews living around here in 1939, only 15,000 lived to see liberation in 1945. The walls are covered with the handwritten names of 77,297 local Jews who were sent from here to the gas chambers of Auschwitz. Family names are in gold, followed by the individuals' first names in black, with birthdays and the last date known to be alive (usually the date of transport). Notice how families generally perished together. Climb six steps into the women's gallery. The names near the ceiling in poor condition are from 1953. When the Communists moved in, they closed the synagogue and erased everything. With freedom, in 1989, the Pinkas Synagogue was reopened, and all the names rewritten.

Upstairs is the Terezin Children's Art Exhibit. Terezin, near Prague, was a fortified town of 7,000 Czechs. The Nazis moved these people out and moved in 60,000 Jews, creating their model "Jewish town," a concentration camp dolled up for propaganda purposes. The town's medieval walls, which used to prevent people from getting in, were used by Nazis to prevent people from getting out. Jewish culture seemed to thrive in Terezin as "citizens" put on plays and concerts, published a magazine, and raised their families in ways impressive to Red Cross inspectors. Virtually all of the Jews ended up at Auschwitz. The art of the children of Terezin survives as a poignant testimony to the horror of the Holocaust. While the Communists kept the art away from the public, today it's well displayed and described in English.

Terezin is a powerful day trip from Prague for those interested in touring the concentration camp memorial/museum; you can either take a tour bus (see City Tours, above) or public bus (6/day, 60 min, leaves from Prague's Florenc bus station).

Old Jewish Cemetery—From 1439 until 1787, this was the only burial ground allowed for the Jews of Prague. With limited space and over 100,000 graves, tombs were piled atop each other. With as many as 12 layers, the cemetery became a small plateau. The Jewish word for cemetery means "House of Life"; like Christians, Jews believe that death is the gateway into the next world. Today visitors wander among more than 12,000 evocative stones.

Ceremonial Hall—Leaving the cemetery you'll find a neo-Romanesque mortuary house built in 1911 for the purification of the dead. It's filled with an interesting exhibition on Jewish burial traditions with historic paintings of the cemetery.

Klaus Synagogue—This 17th-century synagogue (also at the exit of the cemetery) is the final wing of this museum, devoted to Jewish religious practices.

Old-New Synagogue—For over 700 years, this has been the most important synagogue and central building in Josefov. Standing like a bomb-hardened bunker, it feels like it's survived plenty of hard times. Stairs take you down to the street level of the 13th century and into the Gothic interior. Built in 1270, it's the oldest synagogue in Europe. Originally called "the New Synagogue," it was renamed "Old-New" as other synagogues were built. The Shrine of the Arc in front is the focus of worship. It holds the sacred scrolls of the Torah, the holiest place in the synagogue. The old rabbi's chair to the right is left empty out of respect. Twelve is a popular number (e.g., windows) because it symbolizes the 12 tribes of Israel. The windows on the left are an 18th-century addition allowing women to view the men-only services.

Art Nouveau

▲▲**Mucha Museum**—I find the art of Alfons Mucha (pron. moo-kah, 1860–1939) insistently likeable. Read about this popular Czech artist's posters which were patriotic banners in disguise, see the crucifixion scene he painted as an eight-year-old, and check out the photographs of his models. Prague isn't much on museums, but if you're into Art Nouveau, this one is great. Run by Mucha's grandson, it's two blocks off Wenceslas Square and wonderfully described and displayed on one comfortable floor (150 kč, daily 10:00–18:00, Panska 7, tel. 02/628-4162, Web site: www.mucha.cz). While the exhibit is well described in English, the 50 kč English brochure on the art is a good supplement. The video is also worthwhile (30 minutes, hourly in English, ask upon entry).

More Art Nouveau—Prague is the best Art Nouveau town in Europe. Check out St. Vitus Cathedral (the Mucha stained-glass window), the main train station (dome on top floor), and the Hotel Europa overlooking Wenceslas Square (inside and out). The Municipal House (Obecní Dům, built 1906–1912, near Powder Tower) features Prague's largest concert hall and a great Art Nouveau café with handy cyber access. On the building's striking facade, look for the *Homage to Prague* mosaic, which stoked cultural pride and nationalist sentiment.

Entertainment

Prague booms with live (and inexpensive) theater, opera, classical, jazz, and pop entertainment. Everything's listed in *Test the Best*, Prague's monthly cultural events program (free at TI). The Prague Spring International Music Festival runs the last three weeks in May.

There must be six or eight classical "tourist" concerts a day in the famous Old Town halls and churches. The music is of the crowd-pleasing sort: Vivaldi, Best of Mozart, Most Famous Arias, and works by local boy Anton Dvorak. Leafleteers are everywhere announcing the evening's events. Concerts typically cost 400 kč, start anywhere from 17:00 to 21:00, last 60 minutes, and are usually quartets (e.g., flute, French horn, cello, violin). Common venues are in the Little Quarter Square (Malostranské Náměstí, at the Church of St. Nicholas and the Prague Academy of Music in the Lichtenstein Palace), at the east end of Charles Bridge (St. Francis Church), and on the Old Town Square (another St. Nicholas Church).

Sleeping in Prague

(32 kč = about $1, tel. code: 02)
Sleep Code: **S** = Single, **D** = Double/Twin, **T** = Triple, **Q** = Quad, **b** = bathroom, **t** = toilet only, **s** = shower only, **CC** = Credit Card (Visa, MasterCard, Amex).

Finding a bed in Prague worries Western tourists. It shouldn't.

You have several options. Capitalism is working as Adam Smith promised: with a huge demand, the supply is increasing, and the price is going up. Peak time is May, June, September, October, Christmas, and Easter. July and August are not too bad. Virtually every place listed speaks English. Reserve by telephone first, follow by a fax to confirm. Generally you simply promise to come and need no deposit.

Room-Booking Services: The city is awash with fancy rooms on the push list and private small-time operators with rooms to rent in their apartments. Numerous booking services connect these places with travelers for a small fee.

At the main train station, **AVE** is a helpful and well-organized booking service (daily 6:00–23:00, tel. 02/2422-3226, fax 02/2423-0783, Web site: www.ave.anet.cz, e-mail: avetours@anet.cz). With the railroad tracks at your back, look for the small window on your right. Their main office is by the taxis on the left (at Wilsonova 8; another AVE office is at Holešovice station). Their push-list board displays three-star hotels with $100 rooms available for half-price. They have a slew of private rooms and small pensions available ($50 pension doubles in the old center, $35 doubles a metro ride away). You can reserve by e-mail, using your credit card as a deposit.

Accotour accommodations booking service, 100 meters toward the National Museum from the main train station, has a line on lots of private rooms all over the Old Town. They charge 120 kč per person per booking. Page through their scrapbook, and take your choice of doubles for as little as $20. They claim they always have rooms available and I believe them. For privacy, comfort, and centrality, I'd recommend one of these rooms over a hostel (Thursday–Tuesday 9:00–17:00, closed Wednesday, Wahingtonova 23, tel. 02/2421-5406).

Three-Star Hotels and Agencies

Prague's three-star–rated hotels come with cookie-cutter standards. They're cheap, perfectly professional, and hotelesque, with English-speaking receptionists, comfortable modern furnishings, modern full bathrooms, included buffet breakfasts, and rarely an elevator. These hotels are often beholden to agencies who have a lock on rooms (generally until six weeks in advance). Agencies get a 30-percent discount and can sell the rooms at whatever they like between that and the "rack rate." Because of these agencies, Prague has a reputation of being perpetually booked up. As they rarely use up their allotment, it almost never is. You need to make reservations either very long in advance—when the few rooms not reserved for agencies are still available, or not long in advance—after the agencies have released their rooms.

These recommended three-star hotels all cost about the same

Prague

Map Legend:

1. PICK UP BUS TOUR (AT #40)
2. MUCHA MUSEUM
3. ACCO TOUR ROOM SERVICE
4. HOTEL JULIAN
5. HOTEL CENTRAL
6. BETLLEM CLUB
7. HOTEL U STARE PANI
8. HOTEL U KLENOTNIKA
9. HOTEL LUNIK
10. HOTEL UNION
11. HOTEL EUROPA
12. PENSION UNITAS
13. EXPRESS PENSION
14. PENSION U MEDVIDKU

and have rooms any normal person would find pleasant. While I've listed them in order of value for the dollar, characteristics such as location and price need to be considered. Hotel Julian and Hotel Union are away from the center; the rest cluster in the Old Town, mainly near metro: Můstek, unless otherwise noted.

Hotel Julian is an oasis of professional, predictable decency in a quiet neighborhood a five-minute taxi or tram ride from the action. Its 29 spacious, well-furnished rooms and big, homey public spaces hide behind a noble neoclassical facade. The staff is friendly and helpful (Sb-2,680 kč, Db-3,080 kč, suite Db-3,680 kč, extra bed-800 kč, CC:VMA, 5-percent discount off best quoted rate with this book, parking lot, elevator, Internet services, non-smoking rooms, Elisky Peskove 11, Prague 5, tel. 02/5731-1150, reception tel. 02/5731-1144, fax 02/5731-1149, e-mail: casjul@vol.cz).

Hotel Central is likeable like an old horse. I stayed there in the Communist days, and it hasn't changed a lot since. Even Charlie is still at the reception desk. The 62 rooms are proletarian plain, but the place is well run and the location, three blocks east of the old square, is excellent (Sb-2,400 kč, Db-3,100 kč, Tb-3,600 kč, CC:VMA, elevator, Rybna 8, Praha 1, metro: Náměstí Republiky, tel. 02/2481-2041, fax 02/232-8404, e-mail: what?).

Bethlem Club is a shiny jewel of comfort on a charming medieval square in the heart of the Old Town across from the Bethlem Chapel where Jan Hus preached his trouble-making sermons. Its 22 modern comfy rooms face a quiet inner courtyard, and breakfast is served in a Gothic cellar (Sb-2,600 kč, Db-3,400 kč, extra bed-400 kč, elevator, Betlémské Náměstí 9, Praha 1, tel. 02/2421-6872, fax 02/2421-8054).

Hotel U Stare Pani is well located in the Old Town above a jazz club that quits around midnight. The bright rooms are pastel cheery and wicker cozy (Db-3,830 kč, apartment Tb-5,760 kč, apartment Qb-6,660 kč, CC:VMA, no elevator, Michalska 9, Praha 1, two blocks from metro: Můstek, tel. 02/267-267, fax 02/267-9841).

Hotel U Klenotnika, with 10 modern and comfortable rooms in a plain building, is the most central of my recommendations—three blocks off the old square (Sb-2,500 kč, Db-3,600 kč, Tb-4,300 kč, CC:VMA, no elevator, Rytirska 3, Praha 1, tel. 02/2421-1699, fax 02/261-782).

Hotel Lunik is a stately no-nonsense place out of the medieval faux-rustic world and in a normal, pleasant business district two stops by metro from the station or a 10-minute walk from Wenceslas Square. It's friendly, spacious, and rents 35 pleasant rooms (Db-2,500 kč, Tb-2,900 kč, CC:VMA, elevator, Londynska 50, Praha 2, tel. 02/2425-3974, fax 02/2425-3986).

Hotel Union is a grand 1906 Art Nouveau building filling its street corner. Like Hotel Lunik, it's away from the touristic center but in a more laid-back neighborhood a direct 10-minute ride to the station on tram #24 or to Charles Bridge on tram #18 (Db-3,350 kč, Nusle Ostrcilovo Náměstí 1, Praha 2, tel. 02/6121-4812, fax 02/6121-4820).

Hotel Europa is in a class by itself. This landmark place, in all the guidebooks for its wonderful 1903 Art Nouveau facade, is the centerpiece of Wenceslas Square. But someone pulled the plug on the hotel about 50 years ago, and it's a mess, not even meriting its two stars. It offers haunting beauty in all the public spaces with 90 dreary, ramshackle rooms and a weary staff (S-1,300 kč, Sb-2,450 kč, D-2,160 kč, Db-3,400 kč, T-2,800 kč, Tb-4,400 kč, CC:VMA, elevator, Václavské Náměstí 25, Praha 1, tel. 02/2422-8117, fax 02/2422-4544).

Pensions

With the rush of tourists into Prague, small six- to 15-room pensions are popping up everywhere. Most have small, basic, clean rooms with no plumbing at all; sinks, showers, and toilets are down the hall. Breakfast is included in the price. These places take bookings no more than a month in advance. All are within 100 meters of each other in the Old Town, close to the Můstek metro station.

Pension Unitas is best—in every guidebook, right in the center, with lots of modern rooms rented from a convent. It's next to the city police station—site of the old Communist secret police headquarters, which still gives locals the creeps. Unitas shares the building with the classy three-star Cloister Inn (Db-3,400 kč—a great value but nearly always booked by agencies, same address and phone as Unitas). The Pension Unitas' 34 rooms are small and tidy with spartan furnishings and no sinks (S-1,020 kč, D-1,200 kč, T-1,650 kč, Q-2,000 kč, T and Q are cramped with bunks in D-sized rooms, book long in advance, Bartolomejska 9, 11000 Praha 1, tel. 02/232-7700, fax 02/232-7709, Web site: www.cloister-inn.cz, e-mail: unitas@cloister-inn.cz). The place was actually a prison recently—Vaclav Havel spent a night here . . . free.

Express Pension is a creative little place renting 16 simple rooms and serving a lousy continental breakfast in the room (D-1,500 kč, two on ground floor and two on fourth floor, Db-2,300 kč, no elevator, Skorepka 5, Praha 1, tel. 02/2421-1801, fax 02/261-672).

Penzion U Medvidku rents seven big plain rooms with no sinks and an indifferent management (D-1,600 kč, Db-2,860 kč, T-2,400 kč, CC:VMA, Na Perstyne 7, Praha 1, tel. 02/2421-1916, fax 02/2422-0930). They run a popular restaurant that has live music until 23:00 nightly.

Eating in Prague

The beauty of Prague is wandering aimlessly through the winding old quarters marveling at the architecture, people-watching, and sniffing out restaurants. You can eat well and cheaply. What you'd pay for a basic meal in Vienna or Munich will get you an elegant meal in Prague. Your basic decision is: traditional dark Czech beerhall-type ambience, elegant Jugendstil turn-of-the-century atmosphere, or a modern place. For traditional, wander the Old Town (Stare Mesto).

I hesitate to recommend a particular place, but since you asked, here are a few places (between the bottom of Wenceslas Square and Charles Bridge) that I enjoyed:

Plzenska Restaurace U Dvou Kocek has cheap, local, no-nonsense, hearty Czech food, great beer, and a local crowd (150 kč for three courses and beer, serving original Pilsner Urquell with traditional music daily until 23:00, under an arcade, facing the tiny square between Perlova and Skorepka Streets, tel. 02/267-729).

Restaurant U Staré Pani is a good place for Czech or

international food (two blocks from metro: Můstek at Michalska
9 in hotel by same name). **Restaurant U Plebana** is a quiet little
place with good service, Czech cuisine, and a more modern yet
elegant setting (daily until 24:00, Betlemske Square 10, tel.
02/2422-9023). **Restaurant Mucha** is smoky with decent but
pricey Czech food in a formal Art Nouveau dining room (300 kč
meals, daily until 24:00, Melantrichova 5, tel. 02/263-586). For a
basic, very local cafeteria, slide your tray down the line with
locals in the Můstek metro station at **37 Patro Fast Food**
(extremely cheap, downstairs under the square). Prices go way
down when you get away from the tourist areas. At least once,
eat in a restaurant with no English menu.

Czech Beer
For many, *pivo* (beer) is the top Czech tourist attraction. After all,
the Czechs invented lager in nearby Pilsen. This is the famous Pilsner Urquell, a great lager available on tap everywhere. Budvar,
another local beer, is the local Budweiser, but it's not related to the
American brew. Czechs are among the world's biggest beer
drinkers—adults drink about 80 gallons a year. The big degree on
bottles and menus marks the beer's heaviness, not its alcohol content
(12 degrees is darker, 10 degrees lighter). The smaller figure shows
alcohol content. Order beer from the tap (*sudove pivo*) in either small
(.3 liter, *male pivo*) or large (.5 liter, *pivo*). In many restaurants a beer
hits your table like a glass of water in the United States. *Pivo* for
lunch has me sightseeing the rest of the day on Czech knees.

Transportation Connections—Prague
Getting to Prague: Those with railpasses need to purchase tickets to cover the portion of their journey from the border of the
Czech Republic to Prague (buy at station before you board train
for Prague). Or supplement your pass with a "Prague Excursion"
pass, giving you passage from any Czech border station into
Prague and back to any border station within seven days. Ask
about this pass (and get reservations) at the EurAide offices in
Munich or Berlin (90 DM first class, 60 DM second class, 40 DM
for youths under 26). EurAide's U.S. office sells these passes a bit
cheaper (tel. 941/480-1555, fax 941/480-1522), or try DER (tel.
847/692-6300) or your travel agent. Direct trains leave Munich for
Prague daily around 7:00, 14:00, and 23:00, arriving five or six
hours later. Tickets cost about 100 DM from Munich or 30 DM
from the border (if you have a railpass covering Germany).

    Prague by train to: Berlin (5/day, 5 hrs), **Munich** (3/day, 5
hrs), **Frankfurt** (3/day, 6 hrs), **Vienna** (3/day, 5 hrs), **Budapest**
(6/day, 9 hrs). Train information: tel. 02/2422-4200. Czech Rail
Agency, tel. 02/800-805.

LONDON

London is more than 600 square miles of urban jungle. With 9 million struggling people—many of whom speak English—it's a world in itself and a barrage on all the senses. On my first visit I felt very, very small. London is much more than its museums and famous landmarks. It's a living, breathing, thriving organism.

London has changed dramatically in recent years, and many visitors are surprised to find how "un-English" it is. Whites are now a minority in major parts of the city that once symbolized white imperialism. Arabs have nearly bought out the area north of Hyde Park. Chinese take-outs outnumber fish-and-chips shops. Many hotels are run by people with foreign accents (who hire English chambermaids), while outlying suburbs are home to huge communities of Indians and Pakistanis. London is learning— sometimes fitfully—to live as a microcosm of its formerly vast empire. With the English Channel Tunnel complete, many see more foreign threats to the Britishness of Britain.

With just a few days here, you'll get no more than a quick splash in this teeming human tidal pool. But, with a quick orientation, you'll get a good taste of its top sights, history, and cultural entertainment, as well as its ever-changing human face.

Have fun in London. Blow through the city on the open deck of a double-decker orientation tour bus, and take a pinch-me-I'm-in-Britain walk through downtown. Ogle the crown jewels at the Tower of London, hear the chimes of Big Ben, and see the Houses of Parliament in action. Hobnob with the tombstones in Westminster Abbey, duck WWII bombs in Churchill's underground Cabinet War Rooms, and brave the earth-shaking Imperial War Museum. Overfeed the pigeons at Trafalgar Square. Visit with Leonardo, Botticelli, and Rembrandt in the National Gallery.

Whisper across the dome of St. Paul's Cathedral and rummage through our civilization's attic at the British Museum. Cruise down the Thames River. You'll enjoy some of Europe's best people-watching at Covent Garden and snap to at Buckingham Palace's Changing of the Guard. Just sit in Victoria Station, at a major tube station, at Piccadilly Circus, or in Trafalgar Square, and observe. Spend one evening at a theater and the others catching your breath.

Planning Your Time

The sights of London alone could easily fill a trip to Britain. It's a great one-week getaway. On a three-week tour of Britain I'd give it three busy days. If you're flying in, consider starting your trip in Bath and make London your British finale. Especially if you hope to enjoy a play or concert, a night or two of jet lag is bad news.

Here's a suggested schedule:

Day 1: 9:00—Tower of London (Beefeater tour, crown jewels), 12:00—Munch a sandwich on the Thames while cruising from Tower to Westminster Bridge, 13:00—Follow the self-guided Westminster–Trafalgar walk (see below) with a quick visit to the Cabinet War Rooms, 15:30—Trafalgar Square and National Gallery, 17:30—Visit National Tourist Information Centre near Piccadilly, planning ahead for your trip, 18:30—Dinner in Soho. Take in a play or 19:30 concert at St. Martin-in-the-Fields.

Day 2: 9:00—If traveling around Britain, spend 30 minutes in a phone booth getting all essential elements of your trip nailed down. If you know where you'll be and when, call those B&Bs now. 9:30—Take the Round London bus tour (consider hopping off for the 11:30 Changing of the Guard at Buckingham Palace), 12:30—Covent Gardens for lunch and people-watching, 14:00—Tour British Museum. Have a pub dinner before a play, concert, or evening walking tour.

Days 3 and 4: Choose among these remaining London highlights: Tour Westminster Abbey, the British Library, Museum of the Moving Image, Imperial War Museum, Tate Gallery, St. Paul's Cathedral, or Museum of London; cruise to Greenwich or Kew; do some serious shopping at one of London's elegant department stores or open-air markets; or consider another historic walking tour.

After considering nearly all of London's tourist sights, I have pruned them down to just the most important (or fun) for a first visit of up to seven days. You won't be able to see all of these, so don't try. You'll keep coming back to London. After 25 visits myself, I still enjoy a healthy list of excuses to return.

Orientation

(downtown tel. code: 0171, suburban: 0181)

To grasp London comfortably, see it as the old town without the

modern, congested sprawl. Most of the visitor's London lies between
the Tower of London and Hyde Park—about a three-mile walk.

Tourist Information

London Tourist Information Centres are located at Heathrow
Airport's Terminal 3 (daily 6:00–23:00, most convenient and least
crowded); in the airport's Terminal 1, 2, and 3 tube stations; at
Victoria Station (crowded and commercial, daily 8:00–18:00,
shorter hours in winter); and at Waterloo International Terminal
Arrivals Hall (daily 8:30–22:30). Like the LTICs, the handier
British Tourist Info Centre (described below) covers London.

Bring your itinerary and a checklist of questions. Pick up these
publications: *London Planner* (a great, free BTA monthly listing all
the sights with latest hours and events), walking-tour schedule fliers,
and a theater guide. Consider buying a Britain map (£1.30) and a
London map (£1.30). The fine London map rivals the £4 maps sold
at newsstands (free from BTA in the United States: tel. 800/462-
2748 or 212/986-2200, 551 Fifth Avenue, seventh floor, New York,
NY 10176, Web site: www.visitbritain.com). The TIs sell BT phone
cards, passes for the tube (subway), long-distance bus tickets and
passes, Great British Heritage Passes, and tickets to plays (steep
booking fee). They also book rooms (avoid their £5 booking fee by
calling direct). Smelling a new source of profit, London TIs are
pushing a 50p-per-minute telephone information service. Avoid it.

The **British Tourist Information Centre** makes gathering
information easy (Monday–Friday 9:00–18:30, Saturday–Sunday
10:00–16:00, just off Piccadilly Circus at 1-3 Lower Regent Street,
tel. 0181/846-9000). Take advantage of its well-equipped London/
England desk, Wales desk (tel. 0171/409-0969), and Ireland desk
(tel. 0171/839-8416 or 0171/493-3201). Gather whatever books,
maps, and information you'll need for your entire trip at the center's extensive bookshop. Consider the *Michelin Green Guide* to
London or Britain (£9). Train travelers can pick up *Let's Go:
Britain and Ireland* (£15, 50 percent higher than the U.S. price)
and hostelers may want the *Youth Hostel Association 1999 Guide*
(£5). Drivers will need a *Britain Road Atlas* (£10). Stock up. You
are your own guide. Be a good one.

The Scottish Tourist Centre (19 Cockspur Street, tel. 0171/
930-8661) and the slick new French National Tourist office
(Monday–Saturday 9:00–17:30, closed Sunday, 179 Piccadilly
Street, tel. 0990-848-848) are nearby.

Helpful Hints

Theft Alert: Be on guard in London more than anywhere else in
Britain for pickpockets and thieves, particularly on public transportation and in places crowded with tourists. Tourists, considered
naive and rich, are targeted.

Changing Money: Standard transaction fees at banks are £2 to £4. American Express offices offer a good rate and change any brand of traveler's checks for no fee. There are several offices (Heathrow Terminal 4 tube station and at 6 Haymarket near Piccadilly, Monday–Friday 9:00–17:30, Saturday 9:00–17:00, Sunday 10:00–16:00, tel. 0171/930-4411). Avoid changing money at exchange bureaus. Their latest scam: They advertise very good rates with a same-as-the-banks fee of 2 percent. But the fine print explains that the fee of 2 percent is for *buying* pounds. The fee for *selling* pounds is 9.5 percent. Ouch!

Telephones: In London dial 999 for emergency help and 192 for directory assistance (free from public phone booths, otherwise 35p). The area code for any downtown London phone number is 0171; for suburban London, 0181. All numbers listed in this chapter with an area code of 0171 can be dialed directly (without the area code) within London. When dialing the suburbs (0181) from downtown (0171), you need to include the area code but it's a toll-free local call. Beware of area codes starting with 08. These are toll numbers with recorded information—usually slow moving and very expensive. Buy a handy BT phone card (£2, £3, £5, £10, or £20) at any newsstand, TI, or post office. It's a big city. If you call sights before heading out, you'll travel smoother and plan for special events or tours. While a few years ago the USA Direct services (AT&T, MCI, and Sprint) were a good value, now you can call the United States much cheaper by simply dialing direct from any phone booth (less than a dollar a minute). And new PIN phone cards (sold at exchange bureaus and in various kiosks) let you call the United States for about 12 pence a minute (that's more than five minutes for a dollar). The card (purchase for a minimum of £5) gives you an access number and a secret personal identification number. It works great from any push-button phone.

What's Up: For the best listing of what's happening (plays, movies, restaurants, concerts, exhibitions, protests, walking tours, shopping, and children's activities) and a look at the trendy London scene, pick up a current copy of *Time Out* (£1.80) at any newsstand. The TI's free monthly *London Planner* lists sights, plays, and events at least as well. For a fun Web site on London's entertainment, theater, restaurants, and news, go to www.thisislondon.com.

Children: *Time Out* has a fine listing of activities great for children and families.

Sunday Morning Activities: Plan your day carefully. Some sights don't open until 14:00 on Sunday. Some Sunday morning activities: a church service at St. Paul's or Westminster Abbey, Original London Sightseeing Bus Tour, a Thames cruise, a walking tour, or open-air markets at Petticoat Lane and Campden Market. "Speaker's Corner" in Hyde Park gets going at noon.

Free Sights: The British Museum, British Library, National Gallery, National Portrait Gallery, and Tate Gallery are always free. The Imperial War Museum, Museum of London, Natural History Museum, and Victoria and Albert Museums are free from 16:30 to closing (17:30 or 18:00), saving you £5 or so.

Travel Bookstores: Stanfords Travel Bookstore is good and stocks current editions of my guidebooks near Victoria Station (52 Grosvenor Gardens), at Covent Gardens (12 Long Acre, tel. 0171/240-3611), and at 156 Regent Street. Dillons Bookstore on the corner of Trafalgar Square is also handy with a fine travel selection.

Arrival in London

By Train: London has eight train stations, all connected by the tube and all with exchange offices and luggage storage. Enter the tube from any station and head to the stop nearest your hotel.

By Bus: The bus station is behind Victoria Station, which has a TI and tube entrance.

By Plane: For detailed information on getting from London's airports to downtown London, see Transportation Connections near the end of the chapter.

Getting Around London

London's taxis, buses, and subway system make a private car unnecessary. In a city this size you must get comfortable with public transportation. Don't be timid.

By Taxi: London is the best taxi town in Europe. Big, black, carefully regulated cabs are everywhere. I never met a crabby cabbie in London. They love to talk and know every nook and cranny in town. I ride one a day just to get my London questions answered. Rides start at £1.40 and cost about £1.50 per tube stop. Connecting downtown sights is quick and easy for about £4 (e.g., St. Paul's to the Tower). For a short ride, three people in a cab travel at tube prices. Groups of four or five should taxi everywhere. If a cab's top light is on, just wave it down. (Drivers flash lights when they see you.) Wave in either direction. They have a tiny turning radius. If waving doesn't work, ask for a taxi stand. Stick with metered cabs. While telephoning a cab gets one in minutes, it's generally not necessary and adds to the cost. London is such a great wave-'em-down taxi town that most cabs don't even have a radio phone.

By Bus: London's extensive bus system is easy to follow if you have a map listing the routes. Get a free map from a TI or tube station. Signs at stops list routes clearly. Conductors are terse but helpful. Ask to be reminded when it's your stop. Just hop on, tell the driver where you're going, pay what he says, grab a ticket, take a seat, and relax. (The best views are upstairs.) Rides start at 90p. If the driver is not taking money, hop in, grab a seat, and the

London

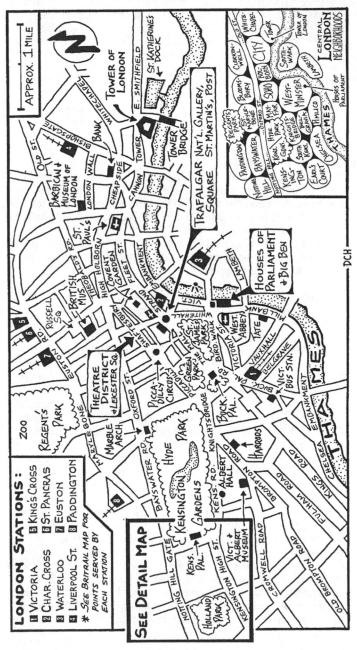

APPROX. 1 MILE

LONDON STATIONS:
1 VICTORIA 5 KING'S CROSS
2 CHAR. CROSS 6 ST. PANCRAS
3 WATERLOO 7 EUSTON
4 LIVERPOOL ST. 8 PADDINGTON

* SEE BRITRAIL MAP FOR POINTS SERVED BY EACH STATION

SEE DETAIL MAP

TRAFALGAR NAT'L. GALLERY, ST. MARTIN'S, POST

Tower of London

St. Katherines Dock

E. SMITHFIELD

TOWER BRIDGE

HOUSES OF PARLIAMENT + BIG BEN

Theatre District + Leicester Sq.

CENTRAL LONDON NEIGHBORHOODS

DCH

conductor will eventually sell you a ticket. If you have a transit pass, get in the habit of hopping buses for quick little straight shots (even just to get to a metro stop). During bump-and-grind rush hours (8:00–10:00 and 16:00–19:00) you'll go faster by tube.

By Tube: London's subway is one of this planet's great peo-ple-movers and the fastest (and cheapest) long-distance transport in town. Any ride in the Central Zone (on or within the Circle Line, including virtually all my recommended sights and hotels) costs £1.30. Avoid ticket-window lines in metro stations by buying tickets from coin-op machines; practice on the punchboard to see how the system works (hit "adult single" and your destination). Again, nearly every ride will be £1.30. (Note: These tickets are valid only on the day of purchase.)

Every city map includes a tube map with color-coded lines and names (free at any station window). Each line has a name (such as Circle, Northern, or Bakerloo) and two directions (indi-cated by end stop). In stations you'll have a choice of two plat-forms per line. Navigate by signs leading to the platforms (usually labeled north, south, east, or west) that clearly list the stops served by each line, or ask a local or an orange-vested staff person for help. Some tracks are shared by several lines, and electronic sign-boards announce which train is next and the minutes remaining until various arrivals. Each train has its final destination or line name above its windshield. Read the system notices clearly posted at the platform; they explain the tube's latest flood, construction, or bomb scare. Bring something to do to pass the waits produc-tively. And always . . . mind the gap.

You can't leave the system without feeding your ticket to the turnstile. Save time by choosing the best street exit (look at the maps on the walls). Remember, "subway" means pedestrian underpass in "English." For tube and bus information, call 0171/222-1234.

London Tube and Bus Passes: These passes, valid on both the tube and buses, are worth considering. The "Travel Card," covering Zones 1 and 2, gives you unlimited travel for a day—starting after 9:30 and anytime on weekends—for £3.50. The all-zone version of this card costs £4.30 (includes Heathrow Airport). The "LT Card," a one-day, two-zone pass with no time restric-tion, costs £4.50. Families save with the one-day "Family Travel Card." The "Weekend Travel Card," for £5.20, costs 25 percent less than two one-day cards. The "7 Day Travel Card" costs £17, covers Zone 1, and requires a passport-type photo (cut one out of any snapshot and bring it from home). All passes are available for more zones, and are purchased as easily as a normal ticket at any station. If you figure you'll take three rides in a day, get a day pass.

If you want to travel a little each day or if you're part of a group, consider buying a *carnet* for £10: you get 10 separate tickets for tube travel in Zone 1 (£1.00 each rather than £1.30).

London Underground

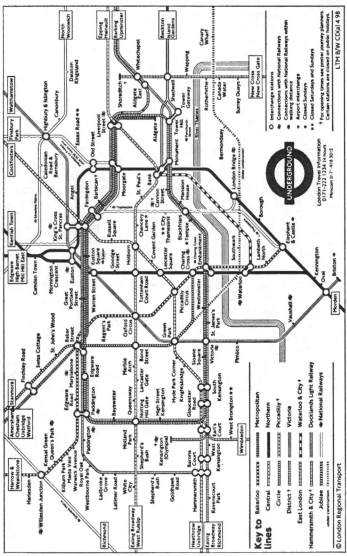

Copyright London Transport Executive

Tours of London

▲▲**Hello London Walk**—To reach the start of this self-guided walk catch a bus to Westminster Bridge (#12 from Notting Hill Gate or #211 from Victoria Station). Sit on the top deck and relax until the first stop east of the bridge. Allow an hour for the following 1.5-mile walk from Westminster Bridge to Piccadilly Circus (includes walking and gawking, not eating or sightseeing).

From Westminster Bridge, walk downstream along the Jubilee Promenade (along the eastern riverbank) for a capital view. Then, for that "Wow, I'm really in London!" feeling, cross the bridge for a close-up view of the Houses of Parliament and Big Ben (floodlit at night). If you ride the tube instead of the bus, the Westminster stop is right at Big Ben. Walk halfway across the bridge for the great view. (Then look for Westminster Pier, offering Thames River cruises, north of the bridge on the Big Ben side.)

To thrill your loved ones (or bug the envious), call home from a pay phone near Big Ben at about three minutes before the hour. You'll find a phone on Great George Street, across from Parliament Square. As Big Ben chimes, stick the receiver outside the booth and prove you're in London: ding dong ding dong . . . dong ding ding dong.

Cross Parliament Street to say hello to Churchill in the park. (He's electrified to avoid the pigeon problem that stains so many other great statues.) To his right is Westminster Abbey with its two stubby, elegant towers.

Walk north up Parliament Street (which turns into Whitehall) toward Trafalgar Square. As you stroll along this center-of-government boulevard, you'll see the thought-provoking cenotaph in the middle of the street, reminding passersby of Britain's many war dead.

Stop at the barricaded and guarded little Downing Street to see the British "White House" at #10, home of the prime minister. Break the bobby's boredom—ask him a question.

Nearing Trafalgar Square, look for the "Queen's Life Guard" (horse guards) behind the gated fence, and the 17th-century Banqueting Hall across the street (details below).

Just before Trafalgar Square, drop into the Clarence Pub for a reasonable meal or pint of whatever you fancy. (Cheaper cafeterias and eateries are on the same block.)

The column topped by Lord Nelson marks Trafalgar Square. The stately domed building on the far side of the square is the National Gallery (free) with its classy café (upstairs in the Sainsbury wing). To the right of the National Gallery is St. Martin-in-the-Fields Church and its Café in the Crypt (see Eating, below).

To get to Piccadilly from Trafalgar Square, take Cockspur Street to Haymarket (passing American Express at 6 Haymarket) then take a short left on Coventry Street.

On colorful Piccadilly, the classy Criterion Brasserie is an affordable splurge for lunch. The National Tourist Information Centre and theaters are nearby, and the Rock Circus and frenetic Pepsi Trocadero Center are within a block (details below). Leicester Square (with its half-price ticket booth for plays) thrives just a few blocks away. For seediness, walk through Soho (north of Shaftesbury Avenue) up to Oxford Street. From Piccadilly or Oxford Circus, you can taxi, bus, or tube home.

▲▲▲**Original London Sightseeing Tour**—This two-hour, once-over-lightly, double-decker bus tour drives by all the most famous sights, providing a stressless way to get your bearings and at least see the biggies. You "hop on and hop off" at any of the 26 stops and catch a later bus (runs about every 10 minutes in summer, every 20 minutes in winter). The basic route comes with a fun, English-only, live guide. (Live guided buses have only a Union Jack on the front of the bus. If the front has many flags, it's a tape-recorded multilingual tour—avoid it). It's an inexpensive form of transport as well as an informative tour. There are daily departures from 9:00 (9:30 in winter) until early evening from Victoria Street (one block north of Victoria Station), Marble Arch, Piccadilly Circus, Trafalgar Square, and so on (£12, £2 off with this book—limit two discounts per book, they'll rip off the corner of this page, reservations unnecessary; buy ticket from the driver, ticket good for 24 hours, tel. 0181/877-1722). Bring a sweater and extra film. Note: If you start at Victoria at 9:30, you can hop off near the end of the two-hour loop at the Buckingham Palace stop (Bressenden Place), a five-minute walk from the palace and the Changing of the Guard at 11:30. The many copycat tours offer about the same service and value.

▲▲**Walking Tours**—Several times every day top-notch local guides lead small groups through specific slices of London's past. Schedule fliers litter the desks of TIs, hotels, and pubs. (The beefy, plain black-and-white *Original London Walks* newsletter lists their extensive daily schedule.) *Time Out* lists many but not all scheduled walks. Simply show up at the announced location, pay £5, and enjoy two chatty hours of Dickens, the Plague, Shakespeare, Legal London, the Beatles, Jack the Ripper, or whatever is on the agenda. "Historic" pub crawls, with a fraction of the information, are a lesser value. "London Walks" is the dominant company (for recorded schedule, tel. 0171/624-3978, Web site: http://london.walks.com). They do private tours for £70.

Chris Salaman, a semiretired guide, loves to tailor walks for special and peculiar interests in London. He offers daylong private walking tours for just £30 per person including lunch, a tube travel card, and museum admissions (tel. 0181/871-9048).

▲▲**Cruise the Thames**—Boat tours with an entertaining commentary sail regularly between Westminster Pier (base of Westminster Bridge under Big Ben) and the Tower of London (£4.40, round-trip £5.60, 3/hrly, 10:20–21:00 in peak season, until 18:00 in winter, 30 min, tel. 0171/930-9033). Similar boats leave Westminster Pier for Greenwich (£5.80, round-trip £7, 2/hrly from 10:00–17:00, 50 min, tel. 0171/930-4097) and Kew Gardens (£6, round-trip £10, 7/day, 90 min, tel. 0171/930-2062). For pleasure and efficiency, consider combining a one-way cruise with a tube ride back.

Sights—Central London

Note: Summer hours are listed. Many sights have slightly shorter hours off-season. Students and seniors should ask for "concessions" (discounts). Since many places run sporadic tours, make a habit of telephoning first.

▲▲**Westminster Abbey**—England's historic coronation church is a crowded collection of famous tombs (including the tomb of the unknown soldier). Like a stony refugee camp waiting outside St. Peter's gates, this is an English hall of fame. Its tombstone history is thick with Richards, Annes, Henrys, Marys, Elizabeths, poets, and so on. The most Gothic-looking decor (like the fine choir in the center) is 19th-century neo-Gothic. Behind the high altar you'll see the historic coronation throne (£5, Monday 9:30–16:45, Tuesday–Friday 9:00–16:45, Saturday 9:00–14:45, also open for half-price on Wednesday 18:00–19:45—the only time photography is allowed, last admission one hour before closing, tube: Westminster, tel. 0171/222-5152). Praying is free—use separate marked entrance.

Well-produced and informative Walkman tours of the abbey cost £2 (offered until 15:00 weekdays, until 13:00 Saturdays). Vergers (the church equivalent of a bat boy) give more entertaining guided tours for £3 (up to 6/day, 90 min, tel. 0171/222-7110 to get times and make a reservation—generally not necessary). Tour themes are the historic church, the personalities buried here, and the great coronations. If you have 90 minutes to spare, either the Walkman or guided tour is worthwhile. Mornings are most crowded. 15:00 is less crowded. Come then and stay for the 17:00 evensong.

Evensong is on Monday, Tuesday, Thursday, and Friday at 17:00, Saturday and Sunday at 15:00. An organ recital is held Sunday at 17:45 (confirm times, tel. 0171/222-5152).

▲▲**Houses of Parliament**—While too tempting to terrorists to be opened wide to tourists, if Parliament is in session you can view debates in either the bickering House of Commons or the gentile House of Lords (Monday, Tuesday, and Thursday 14:30–22:00 with long waits until 18:00, Wednesday 9:30–22:00, Friday 9:30–15:00, use St. Stephen's entrance, tube: Westminster, tel. 0171/219-4272 for current situation).

While it's not worth a long wait and the actual action is generally extremely dull, it is a thrill to be inside and see the British

Central London

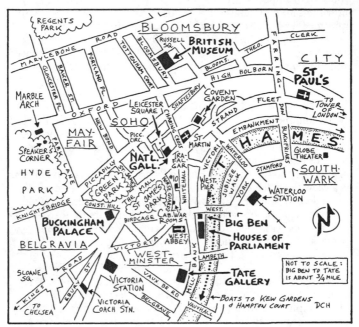

government inaction. The House of Lords has more pageantry, shorter lines, and less-interesting debates (tel. 0171/219-3107 for schedule). If confronted with a too long House of Commons line, see the House of Lords first. Once you've seen the Lords you can often go directly to the Commons. If there's only one line, it's for the House of Commons. Go to the gate and tell the guard you want the Lords. You may slip right in. While other guidebooks tout the U.S. Embassy "entry cards" which get you directly in, they only give out four per day and trying to land one is most likely futile.

After passing security, slip to the left and study the big dark Westminster Hall, which survived the 1834 fire. The hall is 11th century, and its famous self-supporting hammer-beam roof was added in 1397. The Houses of Parliament are located in what was once the Palace of Westminster, long the palace of England's medieval kings before it was largely destroyed by fire in 1834. The palace was rebuilt in Victorian Gothic style after the fire (a move away from neoclassicism back to England's Christian and medieval heritage, true to the Romantic period). Completed in 1860, only a few of its 1,000 rooms are open to the public. For more information about Parliament (or to get a look without actually going in), visit the **Jewel Tower** (across the street, 100 meters from the entry, weekdays 10:00–18:00 in summer) for a video presentation.

The clock tower (315 feet high) is named for its 14-ton bell, Ben. The light above the clock is lit when the House of Commons is sitting. For a hip HOP view, walk halfway over Westminster Bridge.

▲▲**Cabinet War Rooms**—This is a fascinating walk through the underground headquarters of the British government's fight against the Nazis in the darkest days of the Battle for Britain. The nerve center of the British war effort was used from 1939 through 1945. Churchill's room, the map room, and so on, are left just as they were in 1945. For all the blood, sweat, toil, and tears details, pick up the headsets at the entry and follow the included and excellent 45-minute Walkman tour (£4.60, daily 9:30–18:00, last admission 17:15, on King Charles Street just off Whitehall, follow the signs, tube: Westminster, tel. 0171/930-6961).

Horse Guards—The Horse Guards have an 11:00 inspection Monday through Saturday (at 10:00 on Sunday) and a colorful dismounting ceremony daily at 16:00. The rest of the day is terrible for camcorders (on Whitehall, between Trafalgar Square and #10 Downing Street, tube: Westminster). When the weather's bad, all pageantry is canceled.

▲**Banqueting House**—England's first Renaissance building (designed by Inigo Jones around 1620) and one of the few London landmarks spared by the 1666 fire, the House is the only surviving part of the original Palace of Whitehall. Don't miss its Rubens ceiling which, at Charles I's request, drove home the doctrine of the legitimacy of the divine right of kings. In 1649, divine right ignored, Charles I was beheaded on the balcony of this building by a Cromwellian parliament. Admission includes a restful 15-minute audiovisual history which shows the palace in banqueting action, a 30-minute tape-recorded tour that is interesting only to history buffs, and a look at a fancy banqueting hall (£3.50, Monday–Saturday 10:00–17:00, last entry at 16:00, subject to closure for government functions, aristocratic WC, immediately across Whitehall from the Horse Guards, tube: Westminster, tel. 0171/930-4179).

▲▲**Trafalgar Square**—London's central square is a thrilling place to just hang out. Lord Nelson stands atop his 185-foot-tall fluted granite column, gazing out to Trafalgar where he lost his life but defeated the French fleet. Part of this 1842 memorial is made from the melted-down cannons of his victims at Trafalgar. He's surrounded by giant lions, hordes of people, and even more pigeons. Packets of bird-pleasing seed are on sale. The square is the climax of most marches and demonstrations (tube: Charing Cross).

▲▲**National Gallery**—Wonderfully renovated, displaying Britain's top collection of European paintings from 1250 to 1900 (works by Leonardo, Botticelli, Velázquez, Rembrandt, Turner, van Gogh,

National Gallery Highlights

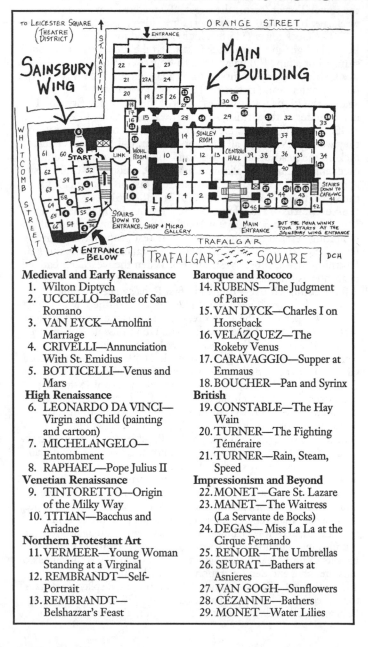

Medieval and Early Renaissance
1. Wilton Diptych
2. UCCELLO—Battle of San Romano
3. VAN EYCK—Arnolfini Marriage
4. CRIVELLI—Annunciation With St. Emidius
5. BOTTICELLI—Venus and Mars

High Renaissance
6. LEONARDO DA VINCI—Virgin and Child (painting and cartoon)
7. MICHELANGELO—Entombment
8. RAPHAEL—Pope Julius II

Venetian Renaissance
9. TINTORETTO—Origin of the Milky Way
10. TITIAN—Bacchus and Ariadne

Northern Protestant Art
11. VERMEER—Young Woman Standing at a Virginal
12. REMBRANDT—Self-Portrait
13. REMBRANDT—Belshazzar's Feast

Baroque and Rococo
14. RUBENS—The Judgment of Paris
15. VAN DYCK—Charles I on Horseback
16. VELÁZQUEZ—The Rokeby Venus
17. CARAVAGGIO—Supper at Emmaus
18. BOUCHER—Pan and Syrinx

British
19. CONSTABLE—The Hay Wain
20. TURNER—The Fighting Téméraire
21. TURNER—Rain, Steam, Speed

Impressionism and Beyond
22. MONET—Gare St. Lazare
23. MANET—The Waitress (La Servante de Bocks)
24. DEGAS— Miss La La at the Cirque Fernando
25. RENOIR—The Umbrellas
26. SEURAT—Bathers at Asnieres
27. VAN GOGH—Sunflowers
28. CÉZANNE—Bathers
29. MONET—Water Lilies

and the Impressionists), this is one of Europe's classiest galleries. While the collection is huge, following the 33-stop route suggested on this map will give you my best quick tour. Don't miss the "Micro Gallery," a computer room even your dad could have fun in (closes 30 minutes earlier than museum). You can study any artist, style, or topic in the museum and even print out a tailor-made tour map. (Free, Monday–Saturday 10:00–18:00, Wednesday until 20:00, Sunday 12:00–18:00, free one-hour tours weekdays at 11:30 and 14:30 and Saturdays at 14:00 and 15:30, on Trafalgar Square, tube: Charing Cross or Leicester Square, tel. 0171/839-3321.) The CD Walkman tours, covering each room and each painting in the gallery at the push of a button, are the best I've used in Europe (£3 donation requested). With these, art lovers could spend four of the best hours of their lives wandering these halls.

National Portrait Gallery—Put off by halls of 19th-century characters who meant nothing to me, I used to call this "as interesting as someone else's yearbook." But a select walk through this five-centuries-long Who's Who of British history is quick, free, and puts a face on the story of England. An added bonus is the chance to admire some great art by painters such as Holbein, Van Dyck, Hogarth, Reynolds, and Gainsborough. The collection is well-described, not huge, and runs in historical sequence from the 16th century on the top floor to today's royal family on the bottom.

Highlights, in order, include: Henry VIII and wives (top floor landing); several fascinating portraits of the "Virgin Queen" Elizabeth I, Sir Francis Drake, Sir Walter Raleigh, and the only real-life portrait of Shakespeare (room 1); Charles I with his head on and Oliver Cromwell (room 2); self-portraits and other portraits by Gainsborough and Reynolds (room 9); the Romantics (Blake, Byron, Wordsworth, and company, room 13); Queen Victoria and her era (rooms 17–21); and the present royal family including the late Princess Diana (first floor landing, rooms 16 and 28). For more information follow the fine CD Walkman tours (donation requested, mostly history rather than art, actual interviews of 20th-century subjects) or the 50p quick overview guidebooklet. (Free, Monday–Saturday 10:00–18:00, Sunday 12:00–18:00, entry just off Trafalgar Square, around the corner from National Gallery and opposite Church of St. Martin-in-the-Fields, tel. 0171/306-0055.)

▲**St. Martin-in-the-Fields**—This church, built in the 1720s with a Gothic spire placed upon a Greek-type temple, is an oasis of peace on wild and noisy Trafalgar Square. St. Martin was a man who cared for the poor. "In the fields" was where the first church stood on this spot (in the 13th century), between Westminster and the city. Stepping inside you still feel a compassion for the needs of the people in this community. The church is famous for its great concerts. Consider a free lunchtime concert (most weekdays at 13:05) or an evening concert (Thursday–Saturday 19:30, £6–15,

tel. 0171/930-0089). Downstairs you'll find a ticket office for concerts, a good shop, a brass-rubbing center, and a fine, budget,
support-the-church cafeteria.

▲▲**Piccadilly Circus**—London's touristy "Town Square" is surrounded by fascinating streets and swimming with youth on the
rampage. The Rock Circus offers a commercial but serious history
of rock music with Madame Tussaud wax stars. It's an entertaining
hour under radio earphones for rock-'n'-roll romantics (£8, daily
10:00–20:00, plenty of photo ops, many enter with a beer-buzz
and sing happily off-key under their headphones—nearly as entertaining as the exhibit itself, tube: Piccadilly Circus). For overstim-
ulation, drop by the extremely trashy Pepsi Trocadero Center's
"theme park of the future" for its Segaworld virtual reality games,
nine-screen cinema, and thundering new IMAX theater (admission
to Trocadero is free; individual attractions cost £2–8; find a discount ticket before paying full price for IMAX; between Coventry
and Shaftesbury, just off Piccadilly). Chinatown, to the east, has
swollen since Hong Kong lost its independence. Nearby Shaftesbury Avenue and Leicester Square teem with fun-seekers, theaters,
Chinese restaurants, and street singers.

Soho—North of Piccadilly, seedy Soho is becoming trendy and is
well worth a gawk. This is London's red-light district where
"friendly models" wait in tiny rooms up dreary stairways and
scantily-clad con artists sell strip shows. While venturing up a
stairway to check out a model is interesting, anyone who goes into
any one of the shows will be ripped off. Every time. Even a £3
show comes with a £100 cover or minimum (as it's printed on the
drink menu) and a "security man." The door has no handle until
you pay. By the way, telephone sex is hard to avoid these days in
London. Phone booths are littered with racy fliers of busty ladies
for sale. Some travelers gather six or eight phone booths' worth of
fliers and take them home for kinky wallpaper.

▲**Covent Garden**—This boutique-ish shopping district is a people-watcher's delight with cigarette-eaters, Punch 'n' Judy acts,
food that's good for you (but not your wallet), trendy crafts, sweet
whiffs of pot, two-tone hair (neither natural), and faces that could
set off a metal detector. For the best lunch deals, walk a block or
two away from the eye of this touristic tornado. Check out the
places along Neal Street and Endell Street—each a block north of
the tube station, and try the "Food is Fun" Dinner Crawl; see
"Eating" below (tube: Covent Gardens).

▲▲▲**British Museum**—This is the greatest chronicle of our
civilization anywhere. Visiting this immense museum is like hiking through Encyclopedia Britannica National Park. After an
overview ramble, cover just two or three sections of your choice
more thoroughly. The Egyptian, Mesopotamian (Assyrian), and
Greek (Parthenon) sections are highlights.

The huge winged lions (which guarded Assyrian palaces 800 years before Christ) guard the museum's three great ancient galleries. For a brief tour, connect these ancient dots:

Start with the Egyptian. Wander from the Rosetta Stone past the many statues. At the end of the hall, climb the stairs to mummyland.

Back at the winged lions, wander through the dark, violent, and mysterious Assyrian rooms. The Nimrud Gallery is lined with royal propaganda reliefs and wounded lions.

The most modern of the ancient art fills the Greek section. Find room #1 behind the winged lions and start your walk through Greek art history with the simple and primitive Cycladian fertility figures. Later, painted vases show a culture really into partying. The finale is the Elgin Marbles. The much-wrangled-over bits of the Athenian Parthenon (from 450 B.C.) are even more impressive than they look. To best appreciate these ancient carvings, read through the orientation material in the tiny intro rooms between rooms 7 and 8. (Free but £2 donation requested, Monday–Saturday 10:00–17:00, Sunday 14:30–18:00, least crowded weekday mornings, guided 90-minute £6 tours offered daily—3/day on Sunday, 2/day in winter—call museum for times, tube: Tottenham Court Road, tel. 0171/636-1555.)

The British Museum is undergoing a major transformation for the millennium and for its 250th birthday in 2003. With more than 6 million visitors a year, Britain's most popular museum is due for an upgrade. The Great Court, unused until now, will become a two-acre glass-domed hub of a new cultural complex. From here you'll enter a reorganized (better-flowing) British museum, a restored and once-again-public Round Reading Room (Marx's hangout), new Ethnographic Galleries (collections on life in Africa, Asia, and the Americas will fill what used to be the British Library quarters), and a bustling people zone of shops and restaurants. For the latest, see www.british-museum.ac.uk.

▲▲**British Library**—Wander through the manuscripts that have enlightened and brightened our lives for centuries in the new and impressive British Library. While containing 180 miles of bookshelves filling London's deepest basement, one beautiful room filled with state-of-the-art glass display cases shows you the treasures: ancient maps, early gospels on papyrus, illuminated manuscripts from the early Middle Ages, the Gütenberg Bible, the Magna Carta, pages from Leonardo's notebooks, and original writing by the titans of English literature, from Chaucer and Shakespeare to Dickens and Wordsworth. There's also a wall dedicated to music with manuscripts from Beethoven to the Beatles. To virtually flip through the pages of a few precious books, drop by the "Turning the Pages" room. (Free, Monday–Saturday 9:30–18:00, Sunday 11:00–17:00, tube to King's Cross/St. Pancras;

leaving station, turn right and walk a block to 96 Euston Road, tel. 0171/412-7332, Web site: www.bl.uk.)

▲**Buckingham Palace**—In order to pay for the restoration of fire-damaged Windsor Castle, the royal family is opening its lavish home to the public until 2000 (£10 to see the state apartments and throne room, open August and September only, daily 9:30–16:30, limited to 8,000 visitors a day—come early to get an appointed visit time, tube: Victoria, tel. 0171/930-4832 to reserve a ticket with your credit card).

▲**Changing of the Guard at Buckingham Palace**—Overrated but almost required (daily April–July at 11:30, generally every even-numbered day August–March, no band when wet). Join the mob at the back side of the palace (the front faces a huge and extremely private park). The pageantry and parading are colorful and even stirring, but the actual changing of the guard is a non-event. It is interesting, however, to see nearly every tourist in London gathered in one place at the same time. Hop into a big black taxi and say, "To Buck House, please." For all the color with none of the crowds, see the Inspection of the Guard ceremony at 11:00 in front of the Wellington Barracks, east of the palace on Birdcage Walk. Afterward, stroll through nearby St. James's Park. For guards' schedule, call 0171/930-4832. (Tube: Victoria, St. James' Park, or Green Park.)

▲▲**Tate Gallery**—One of Europe's great arthouses, the Tate specializes in British painting (14th-century through contemporary), pre-Raphaelites, Impressionism, and modern art (Matisse, van Gogh, Monet, Picasso). Learn about the mystical watercolorist Blake and the romantic, nature-worship art of Turner (free, daily 10:00–18:00, fine £2 CD Walkman tours, free tours weekdays: 11:30—Turner, 14:30—British, and 15:30—Modern, confirm schedule by phone, tel. 0171/887-8000, tube: Pimlico). In 2000 the Tate's modern collection will be moving to the new Tate Modern Art Gallery (on the South Bank) and the current museum will become the Tate Gallery of British Art.

Sights—West London
▲**Hyde Park and Speaker's Corner**—London's "Central Park" has more than 600 acres of lush greenery, a huge man-made lake, the royal Kensington Palace (not worth touring), and the ornate neo-Gothic Albert Memorial across from the Royal Albert Hall. Early afternoons on Sunday, Speaker's Corner offers soapbox oratory at its best (tube: Marble Arch). "The grass roots of democracy" is actually a holdover from when the gallows stood here and the criminal was allowed to say just about anything he wanted to before he swung. I dare you to raise your voice and gather a crowd—it's easy to do.

▲▲**Victoria and Albert Museum**—The world's top collection of decorative arts is a gangly (150 rooms over 12 acres) but surprisingly interesting assortment of artistic stuff from the West as well as Asia and Islam. The V&A grew out of the Great Exhibition of 1851—that ultimate festival celebrating the Industrial Revolution and the greatness of Britain—and was originally for manufactured art. But after much support from Queen Victoria and Prince Albert, it was renamed after the royal couple and its present building was opened in 1909. The idealistic Victorian notion that anyone can be continually improved by education and example remains the driving force behind this museum.

While just wandering works well here, consider catching one of the regular one-hour orientation tours, buying the fine *Hundred Highlights* guidebook, or walking through these ground-floor highlights: Medieval Treasury (room 43, well-described treasury of Middle Age European art), the finest collection of Indian decorative art outside India (room 41), the Dress Gallery (room 40, 400 years of English fashion corsetted into 40 display cases), the Raphael Gallery (room 48a, seven huge watercolor "cartoons" painted as designs for tapestries to hang in the Sistine Chapel; among the greatest art treasures in Britain and the best works of the High Renaissance), reliefs by the Renaissance sculptor Donatello (room 16), a close-up look at medieval stained glass (room 28, much more upstairs), the fascinating Cast Courts (46a and 46b, two giant rooms filled with plaster copies of the greatest art of our civilization—such as *Trajan's Column* and Michelangelo's *David*—made for the benefit of 19th-century art students who couldn't afford to travel), and a hall lined with "great" fakes and forgeries (room 46). Upstairs you can walk through the British Galleries for centuries of aristocratic living rooms. (£5, Monday 12:00–18:00, Tuesday–Sunday 10:00–18:00, and usually Wednesday evenings until 21:30 in summer, free after 16:30, pleasant garden café, tube: South Kensington, a long tunnel leads directly from the tube station to the museum, tel. 0171/938-8500.)

Natural History Museum—Across the street from the Victoria and Albert Museum, this mammoth museum is housed in a giant and wonderful Victorian neo-Romanesque building. Built in the 1870s specifically to house the huge collection (50 million specimens), it presents itself in two halves: the Life Galleries (creepy-crawlies, human biology, origin of the species, "our place in evolution," and awesome dinosaurs) and the Earth Galleries (meteors, volcanoes, earthquakes, and so on). Exhibits are wonderfully explained with lots of creative interactive displays (£6, families £16, free after 16:30 and after 17:00 on weekends, daily 10:00–18:00, Sunday 11:00–18:00, a long tunnel leads directly from the South Kensington tube station to the museum, tel. 0171/938-9123, Web site: www.nhm.ac.uk).

Sights—East London, "The City"

▲▲**The City of London**—When Londoners say "The City," they mean the one-square-mile business, banking, and journalism center that 2,000 years ago was Roman Londinium. The outline of the Roman city walls can still be seen in the arc of roads from Blackfriars Bridge to Tower Bridge. Within the City are 24 churches designed by Christopher Wren. It's a fascinating district to wander but, since nobody actually lives there, it's a ghost town on Saturday and Sunday. An hour in the City's Central Criminal Courts, known as "Old Bailey," is always interesting (Monday–Friday 10:30–13:00, 14:00–16:30, quiet in August, no cameras, no bags, no cloakroom, no kids under 14, at Old Bailey and Newgate Streets, tube: St. Paul's, tel. 0171/248-3277).

▲▲**St. Paul's Cathedral**—Wren's most famous church is the great St. Paul's, its elaborate interior capped by a 365-foot dome. St. Paul's was Britain's World War II symbol of resistance, as Nazi bombs failed to blow it up. (There's a memorial chapel to the heroic firefighters who kept watch over it with hoses cocked.) The crypt (free with admission) is a world of historic bones and memorials, including Admiral Nelson's tomb and interesting cathedral models. This was the wedding church of Prince Charles and the late Princess Diana. Climb the dome for a great city view and some fun in the whispering gallery. Whisper sweet nothings into the wall and your partner (and anyone else) on the far side can hear you. (£4 entry, free on Sunday but restricted viewing due to services, £3.50 extra to climb dome, allow an hour to climb up and down the dome, open daily 9:30–16:30, last entry 16:00, £3.50 for guided 90-minute cathedral and crypt tours offered at 11:00, 11:30, 13:30, and 14:00, or £3 for a Walkman tour anytime, Sunday services at 8:00, 8:45, 11:00, and 15:15, evensongs weekdays at 17:00, tube: St. Paul's, tel. 0171/236-4128.)

▲**Museum of London**—Stroll through London history—from pre-Roman times to the Blitz up through today (£4.30, free after 16:30, Monday–Saturday 10:00–18:00, Sunday 12:00–18:00, tube: Barbican or St. Paul's, tel. 0171/600-3699). This regular stop for the local schoolkids gives the best overview of London history in town.

▲▲**Tower of London**—William I, still getting used to his new title of "the Conqueror," built the stone "White Tower" (1077–1097) to keep the Londoners in line. The tower served as an effective lookout for invaders coming up the Thames. His successors enlarged it to its present 18-acre size. Because of the security it provided, it has served over the centuries as the Royal Mint, the Royal Jewel House, and a prison. You'll find more bloody history per square inch in this original tower of power than anywhere in Britain. Don't miss the entertaining 50-minute Beefeater tour (free, leaving regularly from inside the gate, last one usually at

The City

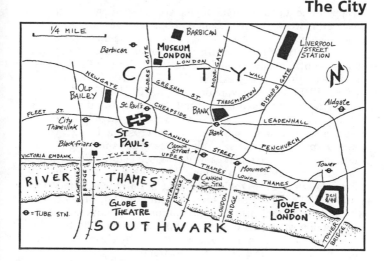

15:30) of this historic fortress, palace, prison, and host to more than 3 million visitors a year. A rare and lovely Norman chapel (St. John's Chapel, 1080) is in the White Tower. At the execution site, Anne Boleyn, Thomas More, Lady Jane Grey, and many others lost their heads. The crown jewels, which date from the Restoration (Cromwell sold or melted down the earlier jewels), are the best on earth; the long midday summer lines are made almost enjoyable by museum videos along the way. Prisoners ranging from unlucky royal rugrats to Sir Walter Raleigh to Rudolph Hess once called the Bloody Tower home. The furnished Medieval Palace is near the entrance to the medieval wall—worth a walk. To avoid the crowds arrive at 9:00 and go straight for the jewels, doing the tour and tower later—or do the jewels after 16:30. The crowd hits after the 9:30 cheap tube passes start. (£9, Monday–Saturday 9:00–18:00, Sunday 10:00–18:00, the long but fast-moving line is worst on Sunday, last entry at 17:00, tube: Tower Hill, tel. 0171/709-0765.) Visitors are welcome on the grounds to worship in the Royal Chapel on Sunday (free, 11:00 service with fine choral music).

Every night at 21:30, with pageantry-filled ceremony, the Tower of London is locked up (as it has been every night for the last 700 years). To attend this free event you need to request an invitation at least five weeks before your visit. Write to: Ceremony of Keys, H.M. Tower of London, London EC3N 4AB. Include your name, number of people (up to seven), requested date, alternative dates, and an international reply coupon (buy at a U.S. post office). Although five week's notice is requested, you might try for an appointment near the end of your trip by sending a stamped envelope addressed to your London hotel once you arrive. **Sights Next to the Tower**—The best remaining bit of London's Roman Wall is just north of the tower (at the Tower Hill tube station). Freshly painted and restored, **Tower Bridge** has an 1894-to-1994 history exhibit (£5.70, daily 10:00–18:30, last entry at 17:15, good view, poor value, tel. 0171/403-3761). **St. Katherine Yacht Harbor**, chic and newly renovated, just east of the Tower Bridge, has mod shops and the classic old Dickens Inn, fun for a drink or pub lunch. If you cross the bridge, you'll find the trendy new Butler's Wharf area with happening restaurants and the Coffee and Tea Museum (see below). From here it's a pleasant riverside walk along the South Bank up to the Globe Theater. **The Docklands** is the latest rage in London's growth. Since the weather blows in from the west, London's bad air ended up in the east. Before pollution was conquered, gritty east London was home only to the poor and a huge harbor (the largest 19th-century port in the world). Newly cleaned up and enjoying fine air, the east end is now trendy.

Sights—South London

The South Bank is rapidly becoming gentrified and a thriving arts and cultural center. From Westminster Bridge to the Tower of London bridge, a slick Jubilee Promenade is a trendy jogging, yuppie pub-crawling walk.

▲▲**Globe Theater**—The original Globe Theater has been rebuilt—half-timbered and thatched—exactly as it was in Shakespeare's time. It's open as a museum and hosts authentic old-time performances of Shakespeare's plays. The theater and exhibit are open to tour when there are no plays (£5, daily 9:00–12:15, 14:00–16:00, includes guided 30-minute tour offered on the half hour; if a play is scheduled, the museum is open only 9:00–12:30; on the south bank directly across the Thames over Southwark Bridge from St. Paul's, tube: Mansion House, tel. 0171/902-1500, for details on seeing a play, see Entertainment, below).

▲▲**Imperial War Museum**—This impressive museum covers the wars of this century, from heavy weaponry to love notes and Varga Girls, from Monty's Africa campaign tank to Schwartzkopf's Desert Storm uniform. You can trace the development of the machine gun, watch footage of the first tank battles, hold your breath through the gruesome WWI trench experience, and buy WWII-era toys in the fun museum shop. Rather than glorify war, the museum does its best to shine a light on the powerful human side of one of mankind's most persistent traits (£5, daily 10:00–18:00, free after 16:30, 90 minutes is enough time for most visitors, tube: Lambeth North, tel. 0171/416-5000).

▲▲**Museum of the Moving Image**—This high-tech, interactive, hands-on museum traces the story of moving images from a caveman's flickering fire to modern TV. There's great footage of the earliest movies and TV shows. Turn-of-the-century-clad staff speak as if silent films are the latest marvel. Don't miss Agit-Train (1919 propaganda film train that brought indoctrination to the far reaches of the early USSR) or the breathtaking 50-years-in-10-minutes montage of magic MGM moments (big screen above the Odeon marquee). Brit movie buffs will enjoy the montage of British cinematic highlights in the large theater. And children will enjoy making their own animated cartoon (£6.25, daily 10:00–18:00, last ticket sold at 17:00, from Embankment tube stop walk across the Thames pedestrian bridge and turn left; it's under the Waterloo bridge, tel. 0171/928-3535).

Bramah Tea and Coffee Museum—Aficionados of tea or coffee will find this small museum fascinating. It tells the story of each drink almost passionately. The owner, Mr. Bramah, comes from a big tea family and wants the world to know how the advent of commercial television with breaks not long enough to brew a proper pot of tea required a faster hot drink. In came the horrible English instant coffee. Tea countered with finely chopped leaves in tea bags, and it's gone downhill ever since. (£3.50, daily 10:00–18:00, in the Butlers Wharf complex just across the bridge from the Tower, tel. 0171/378 0222).

Honorable and Dishonorable Mention

Honorable—**Madame Tussaud's Waxworks** is expensive but dang good (£10, children £6.60, under age five free, combined ticket for Tussaud's and planetarium is £12 for adults, £8 for kids, daily from 9:30, last admission at 17:30, buy ticket at TI—no more than 24 hours in advance—to save a little money and get in with no wait, Marylebone Road, tube: Baker Street, tel. 0171/935-6861). At **Geffrye Decorative Arts Museum** you can walk through British front rooms from 1600 to 1930 (free, Tuesday–Saturday 10:00–17:00, Sunday 14:00–17:00, closed Monday, tube: Liverpool Street, then bus 149 or 242 north, tel. 0171/739-9893). Architects and fans of eclectic knickknacks love the quirky **Sir John Soane's Museum** (free, Tuesday–Saturday 10:00–17:00, 13 Lincoln's Inn Fields, tube: Holborn, tel. 0171/405-2107).

Dishonorable—The venerable BBC broadcasts from Broadcasting House: Of all its productions, its new "BBC Experience" tour for visitors is the worst. Avoid it. On the South Bank, the **London Dungeon**, a much-visited but amateurish attraction, is just a highly advertised, overpriced haunted house—certainly not worth the £10 admission, much less your valuable London time. Wait for Halloween and see one in your hometown to support a better cause. The **Design Museum** (next to the Bramah Tea and Coffee

Museum) and **"Winston Churchill's Britain at War Experience"** (next to the London Dungeon) are disappointments.

More Sights—Outer London

▲**Kew Gardens**—For a fine riverside park and a palatial greenhouse jungle, take the tube or the boat to every botanist's favorite escape, Kew Gardens. While to most visitors the Royal Botanic Gardens of Kew is simply a delightful opportunity to wander among 33,000 different types of plants, it is a hardworking organization committed to understanding and preserving the botanical diversity of our planet. The Kew tube station drops you in a herbal little business community a two-block walk to Victoria Gate (the main garden entry). Watch the five-minute orientation video and pick up a map brochure with a monthly listing of best blooms.

Garden lovers could easily spend all day exploring Kew's 300 acres. For a quick visit, spend a fragrant hour wandering through three buildings: the Palm House—a humid Victorian world of iron, glass, and tropical plants, built in 1844; a Waterlily House that Monet would swim for; and the Temperate House—a modern greenhouse with many different climate zones growing countless cacti, bug-munching carnivorous plants, and more (£4.50, Monday–Saturday 9:30–18:00, Sunday 9:30–19:00, until 16:30 in off-season, galleries and conservatories close 30 minutes earlier, entry discounted to £3 late in day, tube: Kew Gardens, tel. 0181/940-1171). For tea, consider the Maids of Honor (280 Kew Road, near garden entrance, tel. 0181/940-2752).

Hampton Court Palace—Fifteen miles up the Thames from downtown (£16 taxi ride from Kew Gardens) is the 500-year-old palace of Henry VIII. Actually, it was the palace of his minister, Cardinal Wolsey. When Wolsey, a clever man, realized Henry VIII was experiencing a little palace envy, he gave it to his king. The Tudor palace was also home to Elizabeth I and Charles I. Parts were updated by Christopher Wren for William and Mary. The stately palace overlooks the Thames with some impressive Tudor rooms including a Great Hall with its magnificent hammerbeam ceiling. The industrial-strength Tudor kitchen was capable of keeping 600 schmoozing courtesans thoroughly—if not well—fed. The sculpted garden features a rare Tudor tennis court and a popular maze. The palace, fully restored since its 1986 fire, tries very hard to please, but it falls flat to me. The costumed guides seem to be low on energy. The Walkman tours are slow and boring. From the information center in the main courtyard, visitors book times for guided tours or grab Walkmans for taped tours (all free). The Tudor Kitchens, Henry VIII's Apartments, and the King's Apartments are most interesting. The Georgian Rooms are pretty dull. The maze in the nearby garden is a curiosity some find fun. The train (2/hrly, 30 minutes) from London's Waterloo station drops you just across the river from the palace (£10, daily 10:15–18:00, until 16:30 November–March, tel. 0181/781-9500).

Thames Barrier—East of Greenwich, the world's largest movable flood barrier welcomes visitors with an informative and entertaining exhibition (£3.40, Monday–Friday 10:00–17:00, weekends 10:30–17:30; catch 70-minute boat from Westminster Pier, or take 30-minute boat from Greenwich Pier, or train from London's Charing Cross station to Charlton then walk 15 minutes, tel. 0181/305-4188).

Sights—Greenwich

The Tudor kings preferred Greenwich to their other palaces. Henry VIII was born here. Later kings commissioned Inigo Jones and Chris Wren to beautify the place. In spite of its architectural and royal treats, this is England's maritime capital, and visitors go for things salty. And now, as the millennium approaches, the home of the Zero Meridian will be more visited than ever.

Getting to Greenwich is a joy by boat or a snap by tube. You have good choices: Cruise down the Thames from central London's piers at Westminster, Charing Cross, or Tower of London; tube to Island Gardens in Zone 2, free with tube pass, then walk under pedestrian Thames tunnel; or catch the train from Charing Cross station.

Cruise from Westminster to Greenwich. Upon arrival, visit the two great ships and check out the Millennium Experience Visitors Centre. Then walk the shoreline promenade with a possible lunch or drink in the venerable Trafalgar Tavern before heading up to the National Maritime Museum and Old Royal Observatory. Finally, browse the town before catching the tube or train back to London (Greenwich TI tel. 0181/858-6376).

▲▲*Cutty Sark*—The Scottish-built *Cutty Sark* was the last of the great China tea clippers. Handsomely restored, she was the queen of the seas when first launched in 1869. With 32,000 square feet of sail, she could blow with the wind 300 miles in a day. Below deck you'll see the best collection of merchant ships' figureheads in Britain and exhibits giving a vivid peek into the lives of Victorian sailors back when Britain ruled the waves. Stand at the big wheel and look up at the still rigged main mast towering 150 feet above. During summer afternoons costumed storytellers tell tales of the high seas (£3.50, Monday–Saturday 10:00–18:00, Sunday 12:00–18:00; October–April Monday–Saturday 10:00-17:00, Sunday 12:00–17:00, tel. 0181/858-3445, Web site: www.cuttysark.org.uk).

▲*Gipsy Moth IV*—Tiny next to the *Cutty Sark*, the 53-foot *Gipsy Moth IV* is the boat Sir Francis Chichester used for the first solo circumnavigation of the world in 1966 and 1967. Climb through to see the clever and fascinating ways the boat was custom-designed for its historic voyage. Upon Chichester's return, Queen Elizabeth II knighted him in Greenwich using the same sword Elizabeth I had used to knight Francis Drake in 1582 (50p, open Easter–October Monday–Saturday 10:00–18:00, Sunday 12:00–18:00).

Millennium Experience Visitors Centre—The Millennium Experience will take place under a vast dome a mile downriver from Greenwich town. This dome—covering over 20 acres, is the biggest ever built. Throughout 2000, millions will gather here to celebrate British ideas and technology at the birth of the third millennium. Throughout 1999, the Millennium Experience Visitors Centre (next to the *Cutty Sark* in Greenwich) will give visitors a sneak preview of the grand festivities planned. There's plenty of futuristic hoopla as everyone wonders what exactly the Millennium Dome will be filled with (Visitors Centre free, weekdays 11:00–19:00, weekends 10:00–18:00, Web site: www.mx2000.co.uk).

Stroll the Thames to Trafalgar Tavern—From the *Cutty Sark* and *Gipsy Moth*, pass the pier and wander along the Thames on Five Foot Walk (the width of the path) for grand views in front of the Royal Naval College. Founded by William III as a naval hospital and designed by Wren, the college was split in two because Queen Mary didn't want the view from Queen's House blocked. The riverside view's good, too, with the twin-domed towers of the college (one giving the time; the other, the direction of the wind) framing Queen's House and the Old Royal Observatory crowning the hill beyond.

   Continuing downstream, just past the college, you'll see the Trafalgar Tavern. Dickens knew the pub well, and even used it as the setting for the wedding breakfast in *Our Mutual Friend*. Built in 1837 in the Regency style to attract Londoners downriver, the tavern is still popular with Londoners for its fine lunches. And the upstairs Nelson Room is still used for weddings. Its formal moldings and elegant windows with balconies over the Thames are a step back in time (bar meals 10:00–20:00 except Sunday, restaurant meals 12:00–15:00).

   In 1999 the Royal Naval College's buildings will no longer be a military training installation. Whether they'll be open to the public is still uncertain. From the Trafalgar Tavern, walk the two long blocks up Park Walk and turn right onto Ha Ha Walk, which borders the park.

▲Queen's House—This was the first Palladian-style villa in Britain. Designed in 1616 by Inigo Jones for James I's wife, Anne of Denmark, it's the architectural centerpiece of Greenwich. Exploring its Great Hall and Royal Apartments offers a sumptuous look at royal life in the 17th century—or lots of stairs if you're suffering from manor house fatigue (combo ticket to Queen's House,

Maritime Museum, and Observatory costs £5.50, daily 10:00–17:00, off-season 10:30–15:30, tours every 15 minutes).

▲▲▲**National Maritime Museum**—At the largest and most important maritime museum in the world, visitors can taste both the romance and harshness of life at sea. Experience 20th-century naval warfare on a WWII frigate or get to know Britain's greatest naval hero, Nelson, whose display covers both his public career and scandalous private life (don't miss the uniform coat in which he was fatally shot). The museum's ambitious Neptune Court development opens in June 1999; it will greatly increase the number of galleries and better profile the sweep of Empire and the role of the sea in British history (combo ticket to Queen's House, Maritime Museum, and Observatory costs £5.50, daily 10:00–17:00, tel. 0181/312-6565, Web site: www.nmm.ac.uk).

▲▲**Old Royal Observatory**—On December 31, 1999, the eyes of the world will be focused on Greenwich and its observatory. All time is measured from longitude zero degrees, the prime meridian line—the point from which the new millennium will actually begin. However, the observatory's early work had nothing to do with coordinating the world's clocks to GMT, Greenwich mean time. The observatory was founded in 1675 by Charles II to find a way to determine longitude at sea. Today the Greenwich time signal is linked with the BBC (which broadcasts the "pips" worldwide at the top of the hour). Straddle the prime meridian and set your wristwatch to the new digital clock showing GMT to a 10th of a second (and whizzing down the seconds to New Year 2000). See how your foot measures up to *the* foot where the public standards of length are cast in bronze. View historic astronomical instruments and watch the Time Ball, visible from the Thames, drop daily at 13:00.

Finally, enjoy the view: the symmetrical royal buildings, the Thames, the square-mile "City" of London with its skyscrapers and the dome of St. Paul's, the Docklands with its busy cranes, and the Millennium Dome itself (combo ticket to Queen's House, Maritime Museum, and Observatory costs £5.50, daily 10:00–17:00).

Greenwich town—Wander beyond the touristy Greenwich Church Street and Greenwich High Road to where flower stands spill into the side streets, and antique shops sell brass nautical knickknacks. King William Walk, College Approach, Nelson Road, and Turnpin Lane are all worth a look. Covered markets and outdoor stalls are popular year-round as are the covered flea markets. Don't miss the Arts & Crafts Market, an entertaining mini-Covent Garden between College Approach and Nelson Road (daily but busiest on weekends). Greenwich will throb with day-trippers on weekends as the millennium approaches. Visit on a weekday if you can. (TI, 46 Greenwich Church Street, tel. 0181/858-6376).

Shopping in London

▲**Harrods and Harvey Nichols (Big, Fancy English Department Stores)**—Harrods is London's most famous and touristed
department store. Artfully mixing big and classy and filled with
wonderful displays, Harrods has everything from elephants to
toothbrushes. The food halls (with cafeterias) are sights to savor
(10:00–18:00, until 19:00 on Wednesday, Thursday, and Friday,
closed Sunday, Brompton Road, tube: Knightsbridge, tel. 0171/
730-1234). Many readers report that Harrods is now over-priced
(its £1 toilets are the most expensive in Europe), snooty, and teeming with American and Japanese tourists. The nearby Harvey
Nichols store was Princess Diana's favorite and the department
store du jour (tube: Knightsbridge).

For royal window-shopping, cruise nearby King's Road in
Chelsea. Most stores close around 18:00, but many stay open until
20:00 on Wednesday or Thursday, depending on the neighborhood.
▲**Oxford Circus/Regent Street/Piccadilly Circus Shopping
Walk**—From the Oxford Circus tube station, Regent Street leads
past a fun array of diverse places to shop (all on the left-hand side
of street). You'll find: Laura Ashley, Liberty (a big stately local
favorite, 10:00–18:30, closed Sunday, 214 Regent Street), Hamleys
(the biggest toy store in Britain, 10:00–20:00, Sunday 12:00–
18:00), Warner Bros. Studio Store, Beatles Shop (a block behind
Warner Bros., 8 Kingly Street, tel. 0171/434-0464), Waterford
Wedgwood, British Air Travel Shops (9:30–18:00, Saturday
10:00–16:00, accessories, guidebooks, shots, travel agents, British
Air agents, travelers' clinic, WC, and theater ticket agency), a Disney store, Garrard the Crown Jewelers (notice the three royal seals
indicating that this shop is a favorite of the Queen, her mum, and
Prince Charles), the Scotch House (knits, sweaters, wool stuff),
and Piccadilly Circus.

From Piccadilly turn right and wander down Piccadilly Street.
You'll pass Christopher Wren's St. James Church (tiny flea market
and healthy café) and Fortnum & Mason, an extremely classy
department store. Consider a traditional tea in its fourth-floor St.
James Restaurant (£13.50, daily 15:00–17:15, closed Sunday, tel.
0171/734-8040). Relaxing under this plush and elegant tearoom's
chandeliers, you'll get the standard three-tiered silver tea tray: finger sandwiches on the bottom, fresh scones with jam and clotted
cream on the first floor, and decadent pastries and "tartlets" on the
top floor with unlimited tea.

Just past Fortnum & Mason is the French Travel Center, across
the street is the delightful Burlinton Arcade, and a block farther
down is the original "Ritz" Hotel (where the tea is much fancier).
▲**Street Markets**—Antique buffs, people-watchers, and folks who
break for garage sales love London's street markets. The tourist
office has a complete, up-to-date list. The best are Portobello

Road (Saturday 8:30–17:00, antique and flea market, near recommended B&Bs, tube: Notting Hill Gate) and Camden Market (Saturday and Sunday 10:00–17:00; a huge, trendy arts and crafts festival; tube: Camden Town). There's some good early morning market activity somewhere any day of the week. Warning: Street markets attract two kinds of people—tourists and pickpockets. **Famous Auctions**—London's famous auctioneers welcome the curious public. For schedules (most weekdays, closed midsummer), telephone Sotheby's (tel. 0171/493-8080, tube: Oxford Circus) or Christie's (tel. 0171/839-9060, tube: Green Park).

Entertainment and Theater in London

London bubbles with top-notch entertainment seven nights a week. Everything's listed in the monthly *Time Out* magazine, available at newsstands. You can choose from classical, jazz, rock, and far-out music, Gilbert and Sullivan, dance, comedy, Bahai meetings, poetry readings, spectator sports, film, and theater.

London's theater rivals Broadway's in quality and beats it in price. Choose from the Royal Shakespeare Company, top musicals, comedy, thrillers, sex farces, and more. Performances are nightly except Sunday, usually with one matinee a week. Matinees (Wednesday, Thursday, or Saturday) are cheaper and rarely sell out. Tickets range from about £8 to £35.

Most theaters, marked on tourist maps, are in the Piccadilly–Trafalgar area. Box offices, hotels, and TIs carry the handy *Theater Guide* brochure that lists what's playing.

To book a seat, simply call the theater box office directly, ask about seats and dates available, and buy one with your credit card. You can call from the United States as easily as from England (photocopy your hometown library's London newspaper theater section or visit the Web site: www.officiallondontheatre.co.uk). Pick up your ticket 15 minutes before the show.

Ticket agencies are scalpers with an address. Booking through a ticket agency (at most tourist offices or scattered throughout London) is quick and easy, but prices are inflated by a standard 25-percent booking fee. When buying from an agency, see the ticket, read it carefully (your price should be no more than 30 percent over the printed face value; the 17-percent VAT and all other taxes are included in the face value; if your view is restricted it will say on ticket), and understand where you're sitting according to the theater floorplan. Agencies are worthwhile only if a show you've got to see is sold out at the box office. They scarf up hot tickets, planning to make a killing after the show is sold out. U.S. booking agencies get their tickets from another agency, adding even more to your expense by involving yet another middleman. Many tickets sold on the streets are forgeries. With cheap international phone calls and credit cards, there's no reason not to book direct.

Theater lingo: stalls (ground floor), dress circle (first balony), upper circle (second balcony), balcony (sky-high third balcony).

Cheap theater tricks: Most theaters offer cheap returned tickets, standing room, matinee, and senior or student stand-by deals. These "concessions" are indicated with a "conc" or "s" in the listings. Picking up a late return can get you a great seat at a cheap-seat price. Standing room can be very cheap. If a show is "sold out," there's usually a way to get a seat. Call and ask how. The famous (but overrated) "half-price booth" in Leicester Square sells cheap tickets to shows on the push list the day of the show only (Monday–Saturday 14:30–18:30). I buy the second-cheapest tickets directly from the theater box office. Many theaters are so small that there's hardly a bad seat. After the lights go down, "scooting up" is less than a capital offense. Shakespeare did it.

Royal Shakespeare Company—If you'll ever enjoy Shakespeare, it'll be here. The RSC splits its season between the Royal Shakespeare Theatre in Stratford (tel. 01789/295-623) and the Barbican Centre in London (daily 9:00–20:00, credit-card booking, they mail out schedules, tel. 0171/638-8891 or, for recorded information, tel. 0171/628-9760). Tickets range in price from £7 (preview) to £40. The best way to book is direct, by telephone and credit card. You can pick up your ticket at the door. Stand-by tickets for £6 are sold to students and seniors at 9:00 the day of the show. For a complete schedule write to the Royal Shakespeare Theatre, Stratford-upon-Avon, CV37 6BB Warwickshire.

Shakespeare at the New Globe Theater—To see Shakespeare in an exact replica of the theater for which he wrote his plays, attend a play at the Globe. This thatch-roofed, open-air, round theater does the plays as Shakespeare intended (with no amplification). Curtain times from May through September are usually at 14:00 and 19:30, Sunday at 16:00 only, with no plays on Monday. You'll pay £5 to stand and £10 to £20 to sit (on a backless bench). The £5 "groundling" tickets, while the only ones open to rain, are most fun. You're a crude peasant. You can walk around, munch a picnic dinner, lean your elbows on the stage, and even interact with the actors. I've never enjoyed Shakespeare as much as here, performed as it was meant to be in the "wooden O." The theater is on the South Bank directly across the Thames over Southwark Bridge from St. Paul's (tube: Mansion House, tel. 0171/902-1500 to book a ticket with your credit card). Plays are long. Many groundlings leave before the end. If you like, hang out an hour before the finish and beg or buy a ticket off someone leaving early (groundlings are allowed to come and go). The Globe is far from public transport but the courtesy phone in the lobby gets a mini-cab in minutes. Confirm the cost, but they seem to be much cheaper than the official black cabs (£5–6 to Victoria Station).

London Area

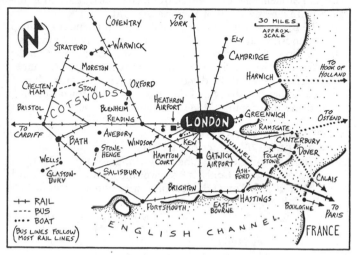

Music—For cheap or free and easy concerts in fine settings, check the listings for lunch concerts given in historic churches around town (listed at TI; especially Wren's St. Bride's Church, tel. 0171/353-1301; and St. Martin-in-the-Fields, most weekdays at 13:05, tel. 0171/930-1862). St. Martin-in-the-Fields also hosts fine evening concerts occasionally by candlelight (see above). For a fun classical event (June–September only), attend a "Prom Concert." This is an annual music festival with almost nightly concerts in the Royal Albert Hall at give-a-peasant-some-culture prices (£3 standing-room spots sold at the door, tel. 0171/589-8212).

Day Trips from London

You could fill a book with the many easy and exciting day trips from London (Earl Steinbicker did: *Daytrips in Britain by Rail, Bus or Car from London and Edinburgh*). Several tour companies take London-based travelers out and back every day. Original London Walks offers a variety of day trips using the train for about £10 plus transportation costs (see their walking-tour brochure). Some big bus tours can be used by those without a car as a "free" way to get to Bath or Stow-on-the-Wold (saving you, for instance, the £28.50 London–Bath train ticket). Evan Evans' tours leave from behind Victoria Station daily at 9:00 (with your bag stowed under the bus), include a full day of sightseeing with £5 to £10 worth of admissions, and leave you in Bath before returning to London (£30 for Stonehenge and Bath; £46 for Salisbury Cathedral, Stonehenge, and Bath; tel. 0181/332-2222). Travelline does a tour of

Bath and Stonehenge for £24 (tel. 0181/668-7261, office in Fountain Square directly south of Victoria Station).

The British rail system uses London as a hub and normally
offers round-trip fares (after 9:30) that cost virtually the same as
one-way fares. "Day return" tickets are best (and cheapest) for day
trips. You can save a little money if you purchase Super Advance
tickets before 14:00 on the day before your trip. But given the
high cost of big-city living and the charm of small-town England,
rather than side-tripping I'd see London and get out.

Sleeping in London
(£1 = about $1.70, tel. code: 0171)
Sleep Code: **S** = Single, **D** = Double/Twin, **T** = Triple, **Q** = Quad,
b = bathroom, **t** = toilet only, **s** = shower only, **CC** = Credit Card
(**V**isa, **M**asterCard, **A**mex). Unless otherwise noted, prices include
a big English breakfast and all taxes.

London is expensive. For £50 ($80) you'll get a sleepable dou-
ble with breakfast in a safe, clean, tiny, dreary place where the
landlords are absent and service is minimal. (Hang up your towel
to dry and reuse.) For £60 you'll get a basic, clean, reasonably
cheery double in a usually cramped, cracked-plaster building, with
a hearty English (as opposed to continental) breakfast. My London
splurges, at £100 to £170, are spacious, thoughtfully appointed
places you'd be happy to entertain or make love in. TVs are nearly
standard in rooms.

Reserve your London room with a phone call or e-mail as soon
as you can commit to a date. Many places will hold a room with no
deposit if you promise to arrive by midday. Others want your credit-
card number as security. Most have expensive cancellation policies.
If you must send a deposit, ask if you can send a signed $100 travel-
er's check. (Leave the "pay to" line blank and include a note explaining that you'll be happy to pay cash upon arrival, so they can avoid
bank charges, if they'll just hold your check until you arrive.)

Sleeping in Victoria Station Neighborhood, Belgravia
The streets behind Victoria Station teem with budget B&Bs. It's a
safe, surprisingly tidy and decent area without a hint of the trashy
touristy glitz of the streets in front of the station. This neighborhood is proud to be part of Belgravia. Even with Margaret Thatcher
living around the corner (you'll see the policeman standing outside
73 Chester Square), this is a classy and peaceful place to call
home in London. Decent eateries abound (see Eating, below). The
cheaper listings are relatively dumpy. Don't expect £80 cheeriness in
a £50 room. Those traveling on a shoestring off-season save a few
pounds by arriving late without a reservation and checking around.
Competition is fierce and prices are often soft, especially for multi-

London, Victoria Station Neighborhood

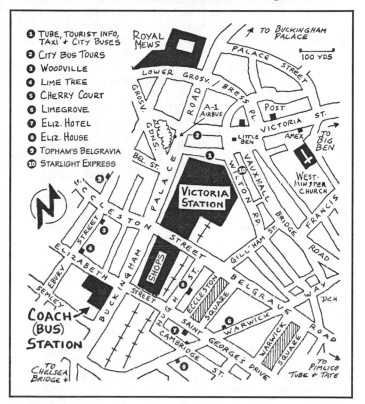

❶ TUBE, TOURIST INFO, TAXI + CITY BUSES
❷ CITY BUS TOURS
❸ WOODVILLE
❹ LIME TREE
❺ CHERRY COURT
❻ LIMEGROVE
❼ ELIZ. HOTEL
❽ ELIZ. HOUSE
❾ TOPHAM'S BELGRAVIA
❿ STARLIGHT EXPRESS

night stays. Particularly for Warwick Way hotels (and in the summer when you'll want the window open at night), request a quiet back room. All are within a five-minute walk of the Victoria tube, bus, and train stations. There's a £8-per-day garage and a nearby launderette (self-serve or full-serve, 3 Westmoreland Terrace, tel. 0171/821-8692).

In **Woodville House** the quarters are dollhouse tight, showers are down the hall, and several rooms are next to the noisy street (doubles are on the quiet backside, twins and singles on the street). But this well-run, well-worn place is a good value with lots of travel tips, and endless tea, coffee, and friendly chat (especially about the local rich and famous) from Rachel Joplin (S-£39, D-£58, bunky family deals—£75–100—for three, four, or five in a room; CC:VM, easy credit-card reservations, 107 Ebury Street, SW1W 9QU, tel. 0171/730-1048, fax 0171/730-2574).

Lime Tree Hotel is enthusiastically run by David and Marilyn Davies. The thoughtfully decorated public areas and rooms are spacious for this area and guests can relax in the peaceful garden off the fun-loving breakfast room (Sb-£70, Db-£90–100, Tb-£120, family room-£140, David will deal in slow times and is good at helping travelers in a bind, CC:VMA, 135 Ebury Street, SW1W 9RA, tel. 0171/730-8191, fax 0171/730-7865). Each room comes with a TV, phone, hair dryer, safe, and teapot.

Cherry Court Hotel, run by the friendly Patel family, offers cramped rooms, tiny bathrooms, and a worthless shrink-wrapped breakfast at youth hostel prices. It's on a quiet street very close to the station (S-£28, Sb-£35, Db-£45, Tb-£65, CC:VMA, no twins—only double beds, pleasant garden, 23 Hugh Street, SW1V 1QJ, tel. 0171/828-2840, fax 0171/828-0393, e-mail: cherryc @globalnet.co.uk).

Cedar Guest House, across the street, is a minimal place with eight rooms at youth-hostel prices. It's run by a Polish organization to help Poles afford London, but all are welcome (D-£38, T-£54, 30 Hugh Street, SW1V 1RP, tel. 0171/828-2625).

Limegrove Hotel, run by harried Joyce, is a little smoky but its nine rooms are a fine value and come with a full English breakfast (S-£26, small D-£36, D-£38, Db-£45, T-£45, Tb-£60, cheaper off-season or for stays of six days or more, 101 Warwick Way, SW1V 4HT, tel. 0171/828-0458). Back rooms are quieter.

Elizabeth House (not related to the Elizabeth Hotel, below) feels institutional and a bit bland—as you might expect from a former YMCA—but the rooms are clean and bright and the price is right (S-£30, D-£50, Db-£60, T-£75, Q-£85, CC:VMA, 118 Warwick Way, SW1 4JB, tel. 0171/630 0741, fax 0171/630 0740).

Tophams Belgravia Hotel packs the formality and service of a top-class hotel into a tight and tangled building beautifully situated on a quiet corner two blocks from Victoria Station. Carefully attired rooms come with all the comforts and carefully attired maids serve breakfast with none of the chat common at funkier places (S-£85, Sb-£110, Db-£120–140, Tb-£155, CC:VMA, 28 Ebury Street, SW1W 0LU, tel. 0171/730 8147, fax 0171/823 5966, Web site: www.tophams.com, e-mail: tophams_belgravia .compuserve.com).

Lesser values near Victoria Station for travelers wanting more comforts: **Quality Hotel Eccleston** is big and modern (Db-£87–100, 82 Eccleston Square, SW1V 1PS, tel. 0171/834-8042, fax 0171/630-8942, e-mail: admin@gb614.u-net.com). Smaller, warmer, and farther from Victoria Station is **Windermere Hotel** (S-£59, Sb-£70, D-£70, Db-£85–100, CC:VMA, 142 Warwick Way, London SW1V 4JE, tel. 0171/834 5163, fax 0171/630 8831, e-mail: 100773.1171@compuserve.com).

Elizabeth Hotel, once a budget bargain, is currently undergoing renovation into a four-star hotel. Its prices will be sky-high, though it will still have a great location and traditional feel, a large elegant lobby with an elevator, airy and pleasant rooms, and free access to the private park the hotel overlooks (call for prices and re-opening info, 37 Eccleston Square, SW1V 1PB, tel. 0171/828-6812, fax 0171/828-6814).

Big, Cheap, Modern Hotels

The Travel Inn chain runs three hotels in London, each of which offers 200-plus cookie-cutter rooms with all the necessary comforts. With long soulless halls and cheesy restaurants and bars, you won't want to savor the ambience, but you can't beat the price for a no-nonsense hotel room (Db-£55 for two adults and up to two children, breakfast extra, book long in advance, no-show rooms are released at 16:00, elevator, some smoke-free and easy-access rooms, CC:VMA, tel. 01582/414-341, fax 01582/400-024 for all). Choose from **London Euston** near the British Library and Euston Station (141 Euston Road, NW1 2AU London) and the much more central **London County Hall**, just across Westminster Bridge from Big Ben, built into the old County Hall building (Belvedere Road, SE1 7PB London). A third Travel Inn, **London Putney Bridge**, is farther away at London's Putney Bridge (tube: Putney Bridge).

"South Kensington," She Said, Loosening His Cummerbund

If you'd like to live on a quiet street so classy it doesn't allow hotel signs, surrounded by trendy shops and colorful restaurants, call "South Ken" your London home. Shoppers like being a short walk from Harrods and the designer shops of King's Road and Chelsea. Budget ethnic eateries line Old Brompton Road (each hotel has restaurant scrapbooks or wall charts). But this ultimate fairy-tale London home-away-from-home comes with a price. When I splurge, I splurge here. Sumner Place is 200 yards from the South Kensington tube station (on Circle Line, two stops from Victoria Station, direct Heathrow connection; at top of the stairs of South Ken tube stop, exit left, cross doubled street, go right two blocks down Old Brompton Road, and turn left onto Sumner Place).

Aster House Hotel has classy rooms, each with a TV, telephone, and fridge. Enjoy breakfast in the whisper-elegant Orangerie, a Victorian greenhouse and lounge in the tidy back garden (Sb-£60–80, third floor Db-£110, Db-£120, deluxe four-poster Db with bath and shower-£135, CC:VM, entirely non-smoking, 3 Sumner Place, SW7 3EE, tel. 0171/581-5888, fax 0171/584-4925, e-mail: asterhouse@btinternet.com, run by manager Simon Tan).

Five Sumner Place Hotel is informal but professional,

"highly commended," and recently voted "the best small hotel in London." You'll talk softly but not feel like you should have dressed up as you wander under the chandeliers out to the Victorian-style conservatory—a greenhouse dressed in blue—for breakfast. Each room in this 150-year-old building is tastefully decorated with traditional period furnishings (Sb-£88, Db-£130–141, third bed is £24 extra, elevator, CC:VMA, easy CC reservations, nonsmoking, 5 Sumner Place, South Kensington, SW7 3EE, tel. 0171/584-7586, fax 0171/823-9962, e-mail: no.5@dial.pipex.com).

Nearby are lesser values for classier travelers: **16 Sumner Place** has over-the-top formality and class (Db-£155–185, CC:VMA, no breakfast room, 16 Sumner Place, London SW7 3EG, tel. 0171/589 5232, fax 0171/584 8615, U.S. tel. 800/592 5387). **Kensington Juries Hotel** is big and stately (Sb/Db/Tb-£99–145 depending upon "availability," breakfast extra, piano lounge, elevator, Queen's Gate, South Kensington, SW7 5LR, tel. 0171/589-6300, fax 0171/581-1492). **The Claverley**, just a couple of blocks from Harrods, is on a quiet street similar to Sumner Place. The rooms are warmly furnished with elegant drapery and all the comforts (S-£70, Sb-£75–115, Db-£110–140, sofa-bed Tb-£160–215, CC:VMA, some balconies, 13-14 Beaufort Gardens, SW3 1PS, tube: Knightsbridge, tel. 0171/589-8541, fax 0171/584-3410, from the United States tel. 800/747-0398).

Sleeping in Notting Hill Gate Neighborhood

Residential Notting Hill Gate has quick and easy bus or tube access to downtown, it's on the A2 Airbus line from Heathrow (second and third stops from airport, after Kensington Hilton), and, for London, is very "homely." Notting Hill Gate has a self-serve launderette, an artsy theater, a late-hours supermarket, and lots of fun budget eateries (see Eating, below). All recommended accommodations are near the Holland Park or Notting Hill Gate tube stations. (Notting Hill Gate is in the central zone and on the Circle Line, handier and 40p cheaper from anywhere in the center than the Holland Park station.)

Westland Hotel is comfortable, convenient, and hotelesque with a fine lounge and a friendly family-run feel. The spacious 1970s-style rooms come with a phone, video-player, hair dryer, and coffee-maker (Sb-£80, Db-£95, cavernous deluxe Db-£110, sprawling Tb-£120, gargantuan Qb-£135, elevator, free garage, CC:VMA, reserve with a credit card, midway between Notting Hill Gate and Queensway tube stations, 154 Bayswater Road, W2 4HP, tel. 0171/229-9191, fax 0171/727-1054). A block away, their **Westland Annex** offers plainer, quieter, cheaper rooms (Sb-£66, Db-£82, family deals also, same front desk and breakfast room as hotel).

Vicarage Private Hotel, understandably popular, is family-

London, Notting Hill Gate Neighborhood

1 WESTLAND HOTEL
2 VICARAGE PRIVATE HOTEL & ABBEY HOUSE HOTEL
3 RAVNA GORA HOTEL
4 NORWEGIAN YWCA
5 MAGGIE JONES RESTAURANT
6 CHURCHILL ARMS PUB
7 LADBROKE ARMS PUB
8 GEALE'S FISH & CHIPS
9 MODHUBON INDIAN REST.

run and elegantly British in a quiet, classy neighborhood. It has 19 rooms furnished with taste and quality, lots of stairs, a TV lounge, and facilities on each floor. Mandy, Richard, and Tere maintain a homey and caring atmosphere. Reserve long in advance with a one-night deposit. There's no better room for the price (S-£40, D-£63, T-£80, Q-£88, a six-minute walk from the Notting Hill Gate and High Street Kensington tube stations, near Kensington Palace at 10 Vicarage Gate, Kensington, W8 4AG, tel. 0171/229-4030, fax 0171/792-5989, Web site: www .londonvicaragehotel.com). **Abbey House Hotel**, next door, is similar but has no lounge and is a bit less cozy (S-£40, D-£65, T-£78, Q-£90, Quint-£100, 11 Vicarage Gate, Kensington, W8 4AG, tel. 0171/727-2594).

Hotel Ravna Gora was formerly the mansion of 18th-century architect Henry Holland. Now it's a large Slavic-run B&B—eccentric and well-worn, but handy for the price. Wry Manda and jocular Rijko offer a royal pre-Tito TV room and a good English breakfast. It has plain, tired rooms, musty shower stalls, a creaky spiral staircase, easy parking, and a Balkan ambience. With the right approach a stay here is a fun memory. With the wrong approach it's a big mistake (S-£30, D-£50, Db-£60, T-£60, Tb-£80, Q-£80, Qb-£88, CC:VM, 50 yards from Holland Park tube station, facing but set back from a busy road, 29 Holland Park Avenue, W11 3RW, tel. 0171/727-7725, fax 0171/221-4282).

Norwegian YWCA (Norsk K.F.U.K.) is for women under 30 only (and men with Norwegian passports). It's an incredible value. Located on a quiet, stately street, it offers smoke-free rooms, a study, TV room, piano lounge, and an open-face Norwegian ambience. All rooms (except singles) have private showers. They have mostly quads, so those willing to share with strangers are most likely to get a place (July–August: Ss-£27, bed in shared double-£25, shared triple-£21 apiece, shared quad-£18 apiece, with breakfast; September–June: same prices but with dinner included; CC:VM, 52 Holland Park, W11 3R5, tel. & fax 0171/727-9897). With each visit I wonder which is easier—getting a sex change or a Norwegian passport?

Sleeping in Other Neighborhoods

Near King's Cross: Methodist International House is a youthful Christian residence filled mostly with Asian and African students. It's great if you want a truly worldwide dorm experience at a price that will bolster your faith. The smoke-free rooms are studious, with a desk and reading lamp. The atmosphere is friendly, safe, clean, and controlled, with a silent study room, reading lounge, TV lounge, game room, and laundry facilities (S-£26, D-£46, a bed in a shared T-£21, includes breakfast and a cafeteria dinner, 81-103 Euston Street, W1 2EZ, reserve long in advance, tel. 0171/380-0001, fax 0171/387-5300. Rooms are most likely available during school breaks, including summer. The included evening "tea" (supper) is great for meeting other residents.

Bloomsbury, near the British Museum: Cambria House, a fine value, is run by the Salvation Army (a plus when it comes to cheap big-city hotels). This smoke-free old building with a narrow maze of halls is all newly painted and super clean, if institutional. The rooms are large and perfectly good. You'll find ample showers and toilets on each floor, a TV lounge, and a warm welcome (S-£27, D-£43, Db-£53, T-£64, CC:VM, north of Russell Square, handy to British Museum at 37 Hunter Street, WC1N 1BJ, tel. 0171/837-1654, fax 0171/837-1229).

Downtown near Baker Street: For a homey alternative in the center, consider renting comfortable well-appointed rooms in this B&B (Db-£80, Tb-£120, strictly smoke-free, at 22 York Street between Baker Street and Oxford Street, tel. 0171/224-3990, fax 0171/224-1990, Liz and Michael).

Near St. Paul's: The **City of London Youth Hostel** is clean, modern, friendly, and well-run. You'll pay about £23 for a bed in two- to five-bed rooms, £25 in a single (CC:VM, cheap meals, 36 Carter Lane, EC4V 5AD, tube: St. Paul's, tel. 0171/236-4965, fax 0171/236-7681).

Near Sloane Square: Hotel Oakley is like a run-down B&B in a fine neighborhood (S-£32, D-£42, Db-£56, CC:VMA, 73 Oakley Street, just off King's Road, 10-minute walk from Sloane Square tube, tel. 0171/352-5599).

South of town: Mary Ward's Guest House is sleepable but very simple. On a quiet street in a well-worn neighborhood south of Victoria near Clapham Common, this beats the hostel. Friendly Mary Ward (Edith Bunker's English aunt) has been renting her five super-cheap rooms to budget travelers for 25 years (S-£12.50, D-£25 with English breakfast, 98 Hambalt Road, Clapham Common, SW4 9EJ London, tel. 0181/673-1077). It's 15 minutes by tube to Clapham Common, then a short bus ride or a 12-minute walk—exit left down Clapham South Road, left on Elms, right on Abbeville Road, left on Hambalt. Rooms in Mary's son's house are an equally good value.

Near Gatwick Airport: The peaceful **Crutchfield Farm B&B** offers three comfortable rooms in a 600-year-old renovated farmhouse. Gillian Blok includes a ride to the airport (Sb-£45, Db-£65, Tb-£75, Qb-£85, two miles from Gatwick Airport—£5 by taxi, 30 minutes by train from London, at Hookwood, Surrey, RH6 0HT, tel. 01293/863-110, fax 01293/863-233). **Barn Cottage**, a converted 17th-century barn in a large garden, has quiet rooms 10 minutes from Gatwick (S-£28, D-£45, Leigh/Reigate/Surrey RH2 8RF, tel. 01306/611-347, warmly run by Pat and Mike Comer). **Lynwood Guest House** (10 minutes by train to Gatwick, 30 minutes by train from London) offers a cozy alternative to big-city lodging in Redhill, a normal workaday English town. It's just a five-minute walk from the train station, but the gracious owner Shanta may pick you up if she's got the car. Ask for a quiet room off the street (Ss-£28, Ds-£42, Db-£45, Tb-£58, Qb-£65, cheaper off-season, 50 London Road, Redhill, Surrey RH1 1LN, tel. 01737/766-894, fax 0171/778-253).

Sleeping and Eating in Hampstead, the Small-Town Alternative

If you must "do" London but wish it were a small town, make Hampstead your home-base-on-the-hill. Just 15 to 30 minutes north of the center by tube (to Hampstead on the sometimes tardy Northern Line) and you're in the former resort of wealthy Londoners—drawn by spas in the 1700s and the brilliant views of London from the popular Hampstead Heath, an 800-acre park.

Hampstead today glows with Georgian village elegance—narrow cobblestone lanes, gas lamps (now electrified), blue plaques noting where Keats, Freud, and other famous locals lived. Even McDonald's has a mock-Tudor facade.

The tube station marks the center of the town. From there, busy High Street cuts downhill though the center. Following it downhill takes you into a cheery business district with side streets flickering with gaslit charm. The hotel is a three-minute walk uphill. The B&B is a brisk 10-minute walk downhill. The Freemason's Arms pub (best for dinner) is a couple of blocks beyond the B&B. And all other pubs and restaurants are within five minutes of the tube station. Everything's near the park.

Make a point to explore the back lanes where you can pop into churches and peek into windows—drapes are left open so their elegant interiors can be envied.

Hampstead Village Guesthouse is run in a laissez-faire style by Anne Marie van der Meer, who rents nine rooms and raised her family in this Victorian house. The homey rooms, most named after her children, lack locks, but come with a phone, miniature fridge, TV, and even a hot-water bottle (S-£32, D-£55, Db-£65, breakfast-£6, CC:VMA only for reservation deposit, payment in cash, nonsmoking, extremely quiet, book well in advance, walk 10 minutes from tube: downhill on High Street, left on Pilgrims Lane to 2 Kemplay Road, Hampstead, London NW3 1SY, tel. 0171/435 8679, fax 0171/794-0254, e-mail: hvguesthouse@ dial.pipex.com).

La Gaffe Hotel is a sweet Italian-run hotel and restaurant right on Heath Street. Rooms are small and well-worn but floral, comfy, and quiet (Sb-£55, Db-£80–115, includes breakfast, TV, phones, nonsmoking, walk uphill from the tube station three minutes to 107 Heath Street, Hampstead, London, NW3 6SS, 0171/435 8965, fax 1071/794-7592, e-mail: la-gaffe@msn.com).

Eating in Hampstead: Freemason's Arms is the place for classy pub grub. If the lighting doesn't make your partner look delicious, the Czech lager will. Set on the edge of the heath with a spacious interior and sprawling beer garden for summer outdoor seating, the Freemason's Arms serves great English food every day (£7 meals, skittles downstairs three nights a week—private but peeking permitted; down High Street, left on Downshire Hill Road to #32, tel. 0171/433-6811).

Down High Street from the tube stop you'll find Hampstead swinging at **The House on Rosslyn Hill** (international cuisine, modern brasserie, young, trendy, popular with locals; meals start at £10, 34 Rosslyn Hill, tel. 0171/435-8037).

French Hampstead cooks a block below the tube station. For a quick bite, **Maison Blanc** not only has the best croissants in town, but also makes great savories like Roquefort and walnut *fougasse* (focaccia pockets) or *tarte Provençal* (tomato, zucchini, and Gruyère mini-quiche); all this plus lovely strong French coffee for £2 to £3, on Hampstead High Street. **Cafe des Arts** serves French food in a rustic candlelit English setting (nightly until 23:00, 82

Hampstead High Street). Next door there's even a little crêpe cart in search of Paris.

There's a handy grocery store next to the tube station. But for real village atmosphere, shop at the **Hampstead Foodhall** on Fitzjohn Avenue. There's no place better for a dinner picnic with a view than Hampstead Heath (a 10-minute hike away).

For a laid-back crowd and a good fireplace to enjoy with your beer, visit the **Holly Bush** pub (no meals but toasted sandwiches, hidden on a quiet lane uphill from tube). For a livelier spit-and-sawdust pub, toss your darts with the locals at **The Flask** (on Flask walk, two blocks below the tube station).

Eating in London

If you want to dine (as opposed to eat), check out the extensive listings in *Time Out* (or the train schedule for Paris). The thought of a £25 meal in Britain generally ruins my appetite, so my London dining is limited mostly to unremarkable but inexpensive alternatives. I've listed places by neighborhood—handy to your sightseeing or hotel.

Your £5 budget choices are pub grub, a café, fish and chips, pizza, ethnic, or picnic. Pub grub is the most atmospheric budget option. Many of London's 7,000 pubs serve fresh, tasty buffets under ancient timbers, with hearty lunches and dinners priced around £5. Ethnic restaurants from all over the world more than make up for England's lackluster cuisine. Eating Indian is "going local" in London. It's also going cheap (cheaper if you order takeout). Chinese and Italian places are not quite the same value. Most large museums (and many churches) have reasonable and handy cafeterias. Of course, picnicking is the fastest and cheapest way to go. Good grocery stores and sandwich shops, fine park benches, and polite pigeons abound in Britain's most expensive city.

Eating near Trafalgar Square

For a tasty meal on a monk's budget in an ancient crypt sitting on somebody's tomb, descend into the **St. Martin-in-the-Fields Café in the Crypt** (Monday–Saturday 10:00–20:00, Sunday 12:00–20:30, £5–7 cafeteria plates, cheaper sandwich bar, profits go to the church; underneath St. Martin-in-the-Fields on Trafalgar Square, tel. 0171/839-4342). Down Whitehall (toward Big Ben), a block from Trafalgar Square, you'll find the touristy but atmospheric **Clarence Pub** (decent grub) and several cheaper cafeterias and pizza joints. For a classy lunch, treat your palate to the pricier **Brasserie** (open daily, on first floor of Sainsbury Wing of the National Gallery). **Simpson's in the Strand** serves a stuffy, aristocratic old-time carvery dinner (where the chef slices your favorite red meat from a fancy trolley at your table) in their

elegant smoky old dining room (£20, daily 12:00–15:00 and
17:30–23:00, tel. 0171/836-9112).

Chandos Bar's Opera Room is amazingly apart from the
tacky crush of tourism around Trafalgar Square. Look for the pub
opposite the National Portrait Gallery (corner of William Street
and St. Martin's Lane) and climb the stairs to the Opera Room.
They serve pub lunches and dinners, and £5 cheese, salad, and
cold plate deals all day long (tel. 0171/836-1401). This is my
favorite rendezvous point around Trafalgar. It's a smoky but wonderfully London scene.

Gordon's Wine Bar is the place to go for a local crowd
and atmosphere. A simple steep staircase leads into a cellar filled
with candlelight, dusty old wine bottles, faded British memorabilia, and local nine-to-fivers (hot meals only for lunch, fine
cheese and salad buffet all day until 21:00—one plate of each
feeds two for £7). While Gordon's is usually crowded, you can
normally corral two chairs and grab the corner of a table
(11:00–23:00, Saturday 17:00–23:00, closed Sunday, two blocks
from Trafalgar Square, bottom of Villiars Street at #47, between
the Embankment and Charing Cross tube stations, tel.
0171/930-1408).

Eating near Piccadilly

Hungry and broke in the theater district? Head for Panton Street
(just off Haymarket, two blocks southeast of Piccadilly Circus) for
a line of decent eateries. **Stockpot**, is a mushy-peas kind of place,
famous and rightly popular for its edible, cheap meals (Monday–
Saturday 8:00–23:00, Sunday 8:00–22:00, 40 Panton Street). The
West End Kitchen (across the street at #5, same hours and menu,
fine seating downstairs) is a direct competitor and just as good.
The original **Stockpot**, a few blocks away, has better atmosphere
(daily noon–23:00, a block north of Shaftesbury near Cambridge
Circus at 18 Old Compton Street).

The palatial **Criterion Brasserie**, serving a two-course menu
for £15 under gilded tiles and chandeliers (12:00–14:30 and
18:00–18:30 only) is right on Piccadilly Circus but a world away
from the punk junk (tel. 0171/930-0488). The **Wren Café** at St.
James Church is exclusively vegetarian, wonderfully green, and in
a pleasant garden next to one of Wren's best churches—peek
inside (Monday–Saturday 9:00–17:00, Sunday 10:00–16:00, two
minutes southwest of Piccadilly Circus at 192 Piccadilly Street, tel.
0171/437-9419).

Near Covent Gardens, the area around Neal Yard is busy
with fun eateries. One of the best is **Food for Thought** (serving
until 20:15, closed Sunday, very good £4 vegetarian meals, smoke-
free, two blocks north of Covent Garden tube stop, 31 Neal
Street, tel. 0171/836-0239).

The Food-Is-Fun Dinner Crawl:
From Covent Garden to Soho

London has a trendy, Generation X scene that most beefeater-seekers miss entirely. For a multicultural moveable feast and a chance to sample some of London's most popular eateries, consider sampling these. To avoid lines, to get in on early specials, and to find waiters happy to let you split a meal, start around 18:00. Prices, while reasonable by London standards, add up. Servings are large enough to share. All are open nightly.

Suggested nibbler's dinner crawl for two: Arrive before 18:00 at Belgo and split the early-bird dinner special: a kilo of mussels, fries with a dark Belgian beer; at Soho Spice Indian, split the "Tandoori selections"; at Yo! Sushi, have beer or sake and a few dishes; slurp your last course at Wagamama; for dessert, people-watch at Leicester Square, where the serf's always up.

Belgo Centraal is a space station world overrun with Trappist monks serving hearty Belgian specialties. The classy restaurant section requires reservations, but just grabbing a bench in the boisterous beer hall is much more fun. Belgians eat as well as the French and as heartily as the Germans. Specialties include mussels, great fries, and a stunning array of dark, blond, and fruity Belgian beers. Belgo actually makes things Belgian trendy—a formidable feat (£12 meals, Monday–Friday 17:00–18:30, "beat the clock" meal specials cost only the time . . . £5–6.30 and you get mussels, fries, and beer; no meal-splitting after 18:30, £5 lunch special daily, one block north of Covent Garden tube station at intersection of Neal and Shelton Streets, 50 Earlham St, tel. 0171/813-2233).

Soho Spice Indian is where modern Britain meets Indian tradition—fine Indian cusine in a trendy jewel-tone ambience (£14 "Tandoori selections" meal is the best "variety" dish and big enough for two, nonsmoking section, five blocks due north of Piccadilly Circus at 124 Wardour Street, tel. 0171/434-0808).

Wagamama Noodle Bar is a mod, watch-it-boiled, pan-Asian slurpathon. As you enter, check out the kitchen and listen to the roar of the basement where a youthful crowd shares benches and waiters take orders with walkie-talkies. Everything's organic—stand against the wall to feel the energy of all this "positive eating" (daily 12:00–23:00, crowded after 20:00, just past the porno and prostitition core of Soho but entirely smoke-free, 10A Lexington Street, tel. 0171/292-0990).

Yo! Sushi is a futuristic Japanese food extravaganza experience. With thumping rock, Japanese cable TV, a 60-meter-long conveyor-belt sushi bar (the world's longest), automated sushi machines, and a robotic drink trolley, just sipping a sake on a barstool here is a trip. For £1 you get unlimited tea (request), water (from spigot at bar, with or without gas), or miso soup. Grab dishes as they rattle by and a drink off the robot (daily 12:00–24:00, two blocks south of Oxford Street, where Lexington Street becomes Poland Street, 52 Poland St., tel. 0171/287-0443).

Soho Soho French Bistro-Rotisserie is a chance to go French in a Matisse-esque setting. The ground floor is a trendy wine bar. Upstairs is an oasis of peace serving £17, three-course French "pre-theater specials"—order from 18:00 to 19:30 (near Cambridge Circus, two blocks east of Charing Cross Road at 11 Frith Street, tel. 0171/494-3491).

Andrew Edmunds Restaurant is a tiny, candlelit place where you'll want to hide your camera and guidebook and act as local as possible. The continental and traditional cooking is worth the splurge (three courses for £20, 46 Lexington Street, Soho, reservations are smart, tel. 0171/437-5708).

Eating near Recommended Victoria Station Neighborhood Accommodations

Here are some places a couple of blocks southeast of Victoria Station where I've enjoyed eating: **Jenny Lo's Tea House** is a simple, for-the-joy-of-good-food kind of place serving up £5 Cantonese meals to locals in the know (Monday–Saturday 12:00–15:00 and 18:00–22:00, 14 Eccleston Street, tel. 0171/259-0399). For pub grub with good local atmosphere, consider the **Plumbers Arms** (filling £5 hot meals and cheaper sandwiches, closed Saturday and Sunday nights, indoor/outdoor seating, 14 Lower Belgrave Street, tel. 0171/730-4067; ask about the murdered nanny—and the distraught wife who ran into the plumber's arms).

Next door, the small but classy **La Campagnola** is Belgravia's favorite budget Italian restaurant (£10 meals, closed Sunday, reservations wise on Thursday and Friday, 10 Lower Belgrave Street, tel. 0171/730-2057). Across the street, the **Maestro Bar** is the closest thing to an English tapas bar I've seen, with salads, sandwiches, and 10 bar stools (very cheap).

The **Ebury Wine Bar** offers a French, smoky ambience and pricey but delicious meals (£15, daily 12:00–15:00 and 18:00–22:30, 139 Ebury Street at intersection with Elizabeth Street, near the coach station, tel. 0171/730-5447). Several cheap places are around the corner on Elizabeth Street (#23 for take-out or eat-in fish and chips).

The **Duke of Wellington** pub is good, if smoky, for dinner (£5 meals, 12:00–15:00 and 18:00–21:30, closed Sunday evening, 63 Eaton Terrace). **Peter's Restaurant** is the cabbie's hangout—cheap food, smoke, and chatter (at intersection of Ebury and Pimlico). Nearby, the **Flamenco** has decent, if pricey, Spanish tapas (54 Pimlico).

For picnics, the nearest supermarket is **J. Sainsbury**, a five-minute walk from Victoria Station (Monday–Saturday 7:30–20:00, Sunday 10:00–16:00, on Victoria Street, just after the intersection with Palace Street). The late-hours **Whistle Stop** grocery at the station has decent sandwiches and a fine salad bar. The **Marche** is an easy cafeteria north of Victoria Station at Bressenden Place.

Eating near Recommended Notting Hill Gate B&Bs

Best classy English meal in London: The rustic and very English **Maggie Jones** serves my favorite £20 London dinner. You'll get solid English cuisine with huge plates of vegetables by candlelight (daily 18:30–23:00, CC:VMA, 6 Old Court Place, just east of Kensington Church Street, near the High Street Kensington tube stop, reservations recommended, tel. 0171/937-6462). If you eat well once in London, eat here (and do it quick, before it burns down).

Good pub grub: The **Churchill Arms** pub is a local hangout with good beer and old-English ambience in front and hearty £5 Thai plates in an enclosed patio in the back (Monday–Saturday 11:00–23:00, 119 Kensington Church Street, tel. 0171/727-4242). The **Windsor Castle Pub** is a great, smoky, and happy scene specializing in traditional sausages and oysters (114 Campden Hill, tel. 0171/243-9551). The smoky **Ladbroke Arms Pub** serves country-style meals that are one step above pub grub in quality and price (daily 12:00–14:30 and 19:00–22:00, great indoor/outdoor ambience, 54 Ladbroke Road, behind Holland Park tube station, tel. 0171/727-6648).

Top fish and chips: The almost-too-popular **Geale's** has long been considered one of London's best fish-and-chips joints (£8 meals, Tuesday–Saturday 12:00–15:00 and 18:00–23:00, 2 Farmer Street, just off Notting Hill Gate behind the Gate Cinema, tel. 0171/727-7969). Get there early for a place to sit (they take no reservations) and the best selection of fish.

Miscellaneous NHG eateries: Costas has eat-in or take-out fish and chips (£5 meals, Tuesday–Saturday 12:00–14:30 and 17:30-10:30, near the Coronet Theatre at 18 Hillgate Street). Next door, the **Hillgate Pub** has good food and famous hot salt-beef sandwiches (daily 11:00–23:00, indoor/outdoor seating, tel. 0171/727-8543). The **Modhubon** Indian restaurant is not too spicy, "vedy vedy nice," and has cheap lunch specials (Sunday–Friday 12:00–15:00 and 18:00–24:00, Saturday 12:00–24:00, 29 Pembridge Road, tel. 0171/727-3399). Next door is a cheap Chinese take-out (daily 17:30–24:00, 19 Pembridge Road) and the tiny **Prost Restaurant and Schnapps Bar** which busily keeps yuppie vegetarians as well as carnivores happy (£10 meals, Monday–Friday 17:30–23:00, weekends 10:30–23:00, 35 Pembridge Road, tel. 0171/727-9620). **Cafe Diana** is a healthy little sandwich shop where you eat surrounded by photos of Princess Diana (5 Wellington Terrace, on Bayswater Road, opposite Kensington Palace Garden Gates).

For a picnic dinner, shop at the **Europe Superstore** (Monday–Saturday 8:30–23:00, Sunday 12:00–18:00, 50 yards west of Notting Hill tube station on Notting Hill Gate).

Just a short tube ride away, you'll find Old Brompton Road and Thurloe Street (each starting at the South Kensington tube station), lined with popular little eateries. Case out the several places along Thurloe Street. At the end you'll find **Daquise**, a smoke-free, authentic-feeling Polish place, ideal if you're in the mood for kielbasa and kraut. It's fast, cheap, faded, family-run, and a part of the neighborhood (daily until 23:30, 20 Thurloe Street, tel. 0171/589-6117).

Transportation Connections—London

Flying into London's Heathrow Airport
Heathrow Airport is user-friendly. Read signs, ask questions. Most flights from the U.S. land at Terminal 3, but British Air's transatlantic flights land at Terminal 4 (same services as 3, but no TI).

In Terminal 3 you'll find: exchange bureaus (24 hours daily, OK rates, £3 fees), an airport terminal information desk (pick up a map and ask questions, but for the official TI, see below), car rental agencies (if you're renting a car, stop to confirm your plans), a £3-a-day baggage-check desk, and a TI. The American Express desk, with better rates than the banks, is in the "underground" at Terminal 4. For Heathrow's flight and transfers information call 0181/759-4321.

Heathrow's TI gives you all the help that London's Victoria Station does, with none of the crowds (daily 8:30–18:00, a five-minute walk from Terminal 3, TI next to tube station, follow signs to the "underground"). If you're riding the airbus into London, have your partner stay with the bags at the terminal. At the TI, get a free simple map and brochures, and buy a subway pass if you're riding the tube into London.

Buses from Heathrow: The National Express Central Bus Station offers direct bus connections to **Cambridge** (hrly, 3.5 hrs, £16), **Cheltenham** (6/day, 2 hrs, £19), **York** (3/day, 6 hrs, £32), **Gatwick** (2/hrly, 1 hr), and **Bath** (9/day, starting at 8:35, 10:35, and so on, 2.5 hrs, £19, direct, tel. 0990-808-080). Or try the slick 2.5-hour Heathrow–Bath bus/train connection via Reading. Buy the £26 ticket at the desk in the terminal (credit cards accepted), then catch the twice-hourly shuttle bus to Reading (RED-ding) to hop on the express train to Bath.

Transportation to London from Heathrow Airport
By Tube (subway): For £3.20 ("free" with £4.30 all-zone, all-day-after-9:30 tube pass) the tube takes you 14 miles to Victoria Station in 45 minutes (6/hrly, one change).

Heathrow and the Four Terminals

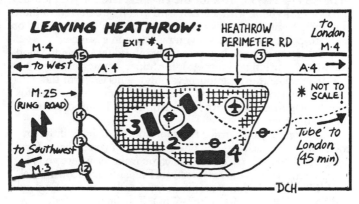

By Airbus: All my recommended hotel neighborhoods are on one of the two airbus lines (serving each terminal, £6, 2/hrly, 5:00–20:00, buy ticket on bus, tel. 0181/400-6655). If you take A1, South Kensington is the third stop, and Victoria Station is the last stop. On A2, the second and third stops cover Notting Hill Gate. The tube works fine, but with baggage I prefer the airbus—no connections underground and a lovely view from the top of the double-decker bus. Ask the driver to remind you when to get off. If you're going to the airport, exact pick-up times are clearly posted at each bus stop.

By Taxi: Taxis from the airport cost about £35. For four this is a deal. Hotels can often line up a cab back to the airport for £28.

By Heathrow Express Train: This new train service zips air travelers between Heathrow and the Paddington Station in town (£5, 4/hrly from 5:10–22:40, 30 min, tel. 0845/600-1515). Unfortunately, Paddington is far from the recommended B&Bs.

Flying into London's Gatwick Airport

More and more flights, especially charters, land at Gatwick Airport, halfway between London and the southern coast. Trains—clearly the best way into London from here—shuttle conveniently between Gatwick and London's Victoria Station (4/hrly, 30 min, £9). Those catching a train for York or Edinburgh can ride a Thameslink train from Gatwick directly to Thameslink King's Cross (100 yards from the King's Cross Station and trains to the north). Gatwick information tel. 01293/535-353.

Trains and Buses

For train schedules and fares for any journey in Britain, call 0345/484-950 from anywhere in Britain (or from the States: dial

011/44/345-484-950). Ask for the cheapest fare for your journey; if you want to book with a credit card you'll be referred to the appropriate rail company's phone number. You'll save money on point-to-point train tickets if you purchase in advance.

To get Apex fares, buy seven days ahead (available for moderate-length or longer journeys); for Super Apex fares, buy 14 days in advance (for long journeys only). This is worth the expense and trouble only if you're willing to pin down dates for your longer trips. For more information, see Transportation in the Introduction.

London, Britain's major transportation hub, has a different train station for each region. The train station you arrive at (or leave from) depends on where you came from (or where you're going). King's Cross covers northeast England and Scotland (tel. 0171/278-2477). Paddington covers west and southwest England and South Wales (tel. 0171/262-6767). For the others, call 0171/928-5100.

National Express's excellent bus service is considerably cheaper than trains. (For a busy signal, call 0990-808-080; or visit the bus station a block south of Victoria Station.)

To Bath: Trains leave London's Paddington Station every hour (at a quarter after) for the £28.50, 75-minute ride to Bath. Consider taking a guided bus tour from London to Stonehenge and Bath, and simply leaving the tour in Bath. Both Evan Evans (tel. 0181/332-2222) and Travelline (tel. 0181/668-7261) offer Stonehenge/Bath day trips from London.

To points north: Trains run hourly from London's King's Cross Station and stop in York (2 hrs), Durham (3 hrs), and Edinburgh (5 hrs). For Cambridge connections, see below.

To Dublin, Ireland: The boat/rail journey takes 10 hours, all day or all night (£40–60). Consider a British Midland flight (Heathrow–Dublin, 10/day, 70 min, about £105 one-way, as little as £70 return for a stay over Saturday, tel. 0345/554-554 or, in the United States, 800/788-0555).

Flights
British Midland, the local discount airline, offers many flights cheaper than train connections. For £120 you can fly round-trip to Dublin, Paris, Amsterdam, or Frankfurt. For the latest, call 0345/554-554 or, in the United States, 800/788-0555.

Crossing the English Channel
By Eurostar Train: The fastest and most convenient way to get from Big Ben to the Eiffel Tower is now by rail. Eurostar is the speedy passenger train that zips you (and up to 800 others in 18 sleek, TGV-type cars) from downtown London to downtown Paris (12/day, 3 hrs) or Brussels (6/day, 3 hrs).

The train goes 100 mph in England and 160 mph on the Continent. The actual tunnel crossing is a 20-minute black, silent, 100 mph nonevent. Your ears won't even pop. You can change at Lille to catch a TGV directly to Paris' De Gaulle Airport or Disneyland Paris. Yes!

Channel fares (essentially the same to Paris or Brussels) are reasonable but complicated. For the latest fares, call 800/EUROSTAR in the United States (or go to www.eurostar.com). The "Leisure" ticket is cheap ($109-second class, $179-first class, 50 percent refundable up to two days before departure). Fully refundable "Full-fare" first class costs $219 including a meal (a dinner departure nets you more grub than breakfast); second class ("standard") costs $149.

Discounts are available for travelers holding railpasses that include France, Belgium, or Britain (about $50 off "Full-fare"); youths under 26 ($70 off second class "Full-fare"); and children under 12 (half the fare of your ticket). Cheaper seats can sell out. You can book your ticket from the United States.

When you're ready to commit to a date and time, book a reservation through your travel agent. Prices do not include FedEx delivery. Note: Britain's time zone is one hour earlier than the Continent's (times listed on ticket are local times).

If you buy your Eurostar ticket in London, here are some sample fares for standard (second-class) travel from London to Paris or Brussels: Those with a railpass pay £45 one-way, any day. Without a railpass, a same-day round-trip on a Saturday or Sunday costs £79. A Leisure ticket, if you stay at least three nights or over a Saturday night, is £119 round-trip. Excursion fares (purchased seven days in advance for travel on Tuedsay, Wednesday, or Thursday, with a round-trip over a Saturday) are cheaper: round-trip for £109, and one-way for £79.

Sample first-class and business-class fares from London to Paris or Brussels: A regular first-class round-trip costs £319, one-way £179. A regular business-class round-trip is £220, one-way £120. A first-class Leisure ticket, if you stay at least three nights or over a Saturday night, costs £199 round-trip.

In Europe get your Eurostar ticket at any major train station or at any travel agency that handles train tickets (expect a booking fee). In Britain you can order your tickets over the phone with a credit card by calling 0345/303-030; pick up your tickets at London's Waterloo station an hour before the Eurostar departure.

By Train, Bus, and Boat: The old-fashioned way of crossing the Channel is very competitive and cheaper than Eurostar; it's also twice as romantic, twice as complicated, and twice as time-consuming. You'll get better prices arranging your trip in London than you would in the United States. Taking the bus is cheapest, and round-trips are a bargain. By bus to Paris or Amsterdam from Victoria Coach Station: £33 one-way, £49 round-trip, 10 hours, day or overnight, on Eurolines (tel. 0990-143-219) or CitySprint (tel. 0990-240-241). By train and ship: £42 one-way overnight, £59 by day, seven hours.

By Plane: Typical fares are £90 regular, £40 student stand by. Call in London for the latest fares.

BATH

Any tour of Britain that skips Bath stinks. Two hundred years ago this city of 80,000 was the trend-setting Hollywood of Britain. If ever a city enjoyed looking in the mirror, Bath's the one. It has more "government-listed" or protected historic buildings per capita than any other town in England. The entire city, built of the creamy warm-tone limestone called "Bath stone," beams in its cover-girl complexion. An architectural chorus line, it's a triumph of the Georgian style. Proud locals remind visitors that the town is routinely banned from the "Britain in Bloom" contest to give other towns a chance to win. Bath's narcissism is justified. Even with its mobs of tourists, it's a joy to visit.

Long before the Romans arrived in the first century, Bath was known for its hot springs. What became the Roman spa town of Aquae Sulis has always been fueled by the healing allure of its 116-degree mineral hot springs. The town's importance carried through Saxon times when it had a huge church on the site of the present-day Abbey and was considered the religious capital of Britain. Its influence peaked in 973 when England's first king, Edgar, was crowned in the Abbey. Bath prospered as a wool town.

Bath then declined until the mid-1600s, when it was just a huddle of huts around the Abbey and a hot springs with 3,000 residents oblivious to the Roman ruins 18 feet below their dirt floors. Then, in 1687, Queen Mary, fighting infertility, bathed here. Within 10 months she gave birth to a son . . . and a new age of popularity for Bath.

The town boomed as a spa resort. Ninety percent of the buildings you'll see today are from the 18th century. Local architect John Wood was inspired by the Italian architect Palladio to build a "new Rome." The town bloomed in the neoclassical style and streets were lined not with scrawny sidewalks but with wide "parades," upon which the women in their stylishly wide dresses could spread their fashionable tails.

Beau Nash (1673–1762) was Bath's "master of ceremonies." He organized both the daily regimen of the aristocratic visitors and the city—lighting and improving security on the streets, banning swords, and opening the Pump Room. Under his fashionable baton, Bath became a city of balls, gaming, concerts, and the place to see and be seen in England. This most civilized place became even more so with the great neoclassical building spree that followed.

Planning Your Time

Bath needs two nights even on a quick trip. There's plenty to do and it's a joy to do it. On a three-week British trip, spend three nights in Bath with one day for the city and one for a side trip to Wells, Glastonbury, and Avebury. Bath could easily fill another day. Ideally, use Bath as your jet-lag recovery pillow and do London at the end of your trip.

Consider starting a three-week British vacation this way:
Day 1: Land at Heathrow. Catch the National Express bus to Bath (9/day, 2.5-hr trip). While you don't need or want a car in Bath, and most rental companies have an office there, those who pick up their cars at the airport can visit Stonehenge on their way to Bath on this day.
Day 2: 9:00—Tour the Roman Baths, 10:30—Catch the free city walking tour, 12:30—Picnic on the open deck of a Guide Friday bus tour, 14:30—Free time in the shopping center of old Bath, 16:00—Tour the Costume Museum.

Orientation (tel. code: 01225)

Bath's town square, three blocks in front of the bus and train station, is a bouquet of tourist landmarks including the Abbey, Roman and medieval baths, and royal Pump Room.

Tourist Information: The TI is in the Abbey churchyard (walk two blocks up Manvers Street from the bus or train station and turn left, Monday–Saturday 9:30–18:00, Sunday 10:00–16:00, shorter hours off-season, tel. 01225/477-101). Pick up the 25p Bath map/mini-guide and the free, packed-with-info *This Month in Bath*, and browse through scads of flyers. There's an American Express outlet in the TI (decent rates, no commission on any checks, open seven days a week).

Arrival in Bath: The Bath train station is a pleasure (small-town charm, an international tickets desk, and a Guide Friday office masquerading as a tourist information service). The bus station is immediately in front of the train station. My recommended B&Bs are all within a 10- or 15-minute walk or a £3.50 taxi ride. For Brock

House and the B&Bs on Marlborough Lane, consider using the Guide Friday city bus tour (described below) as transportation (5/hrly, from Lane 1 of the bus station). Start the tour, jump out, check into your B&B, and hop back on to finish the circle.

Driving within Bath is a nightmare of one-way streets. Nearly everyone gets lost. Ask for advice and minimize driving in town. Streets with no lines allow free unlimited parking.

Car Rental: Avis (behind the station and over the river at Unit 4B Riverside Business Park, Lower Bristol Road, tel. 01225/446-680), Budget (Brassmill Lane, tel. 01225/482-211), and Hertz (at the train station, tel. 01225/442-911) are all trying harder (consider hotel delivery, usually £8). Most offices are a 10-minute walk from most recommended accommodations. Most offices close Saturday afternoon and all day Sunday, complicating weekend pick-ups. Ideally, pick up your car only on the way out and into the countryside. Take the train or bus from London to Bath and rent a car as you leave Bath rather than in London.

Tours of Bath

▲▲**City Bus Tours**—The Guide Friday green-and-cream open-top tour bus makes a 70-minute figure-eight circuit of Bath's main sights with an exhaustingly informative running commentary. For one £7.50 ticket (buy from driver), tourists can stop and go at will for a whole day. The buses cover the city center and the surrounding hills (14 signposted pick-up points, 5/hrly in summer, hrly in winter, about 9:25–18:00, tel. 01225/464-446). This is great in sunny weather and a feast for photographers. You can munch a sandwich, work on a tan, and sightsee at the same time. Several competing hop-on, hop-off tour bus companies offer basically the same tour but in 45 minutes and without the swing through the countryside for a couple pounds less. Generally, the Guide Friday guides are better.

▲▲▲**Walking Tours**—These two-hour tours, offered free by trained local volunteers who want to share their love of Bath with its many visitors, are a chatty, historical gossip-filled joy, essential for your understanding of this town's amazing Georgian social scene. How else will you learn that the old "chair ho" call for your sedan chair evolved into today's "cheerio" greeting? Tours leave from in front of the Pump Room daily at 10:30 (often at 14:00 and 19:00, May–October). For Ghost Walks and Bizarre Bath Comedy Walks, see Evening Entertainment, below. For a private walking tour from a local gentleman who's an excellent guide, contact Patrick Driscoll (2 hours for £40, tel. 01225/462-010).

Sights—Bath

▲▲▲**Roman and Medieval Baths**—Back in ancient Roman times, high society enjoyed the mineral springs at Bath. From

Bath

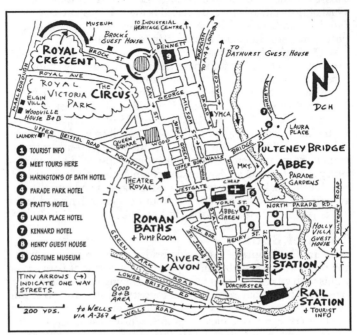

ROYAL CRESCENT

MUSEUM
TO INDUSTRIAL HERITAGE CENTRE
Brock's Guest House
BROCK ST.
BENNETT
TO BATHURST GUEST HOUSE
ROYAL AVE
ROYAL VICTORIA PARK
THE **CIRCUS**
GAY ST.
GEORGE
MILSOM
WALCOT
TO A-46 & LONDON
LANSDOWN
MARLBOROUGH
ELGIN VILLA
WOODVILLE HOUSE B&B
UPPER BRISTOL ROAD

DCH
HENRIETTA
YMCA
LAURA PLACE
LAUNDRY
QUEEN SQUARE
WOOD ST.
QUIET ST.
GREEN ST.
BRIDGE
PULTENEY BRIDGE
MONMOUTH
UPPER BOR. WALLS
MKT.
ABBEY
Parade Gardens

❶ TOURIST INFO
❷ MEET TOURS HERE
❸ HARINGTON'S OF BATH HOTEL
❹ PARADE PARK HOTEL
❺ PRATT'S HOTEL
❻ LAURA PLACE HOTEL
❼ KENNARD HOTEL
❽ HENRY GUEST HOUSE
❾ COSTUME MUSEUM

THEATRE ROYAL
WESTGATE
CHEAP
YORK ST.
ABBEY GREEN
NORTH PARADE RD.
HOLLY VILLA GUEST HOUSE
ROMAN BATHS & Pump Room
ST. JAMES PARADE
LR. BOR. WALLS
HENRY ST.
NEWMARK
MANVERS ST.
PULTENEY ROAD

GREEN PARK
RIVER AVON
SOUTHGATE
BUS STATION

TINY ARROWS (→) INDICATE ONE WAY STREETS.
LOWER BRISTOL RD.
GOOD B&B AREA
DORCHESTER
200 YDS.
to WELLS VIA A-367
WELLS ROAD
RAIL STATION
& TOURIST INFO

Londinium, Romans traveled so often to Aquae Sulis, as the city was called, to "take a bath" that finally it became known simply as Bath. Today a fine Roman museum surrounds the ancient bath. The museum, with its well-documented displays, is a one-way system leading you past Roman artifacts, mosaics, a temple pediment, and the actual mouth of the spring piled high with Roman pennies. Enjoy some quality time looking into the eyes of Minerva, goddess of the hot springs. The included self-guided tour audio-wand makes the visit easy and plenty informative. In-depth 40-minute tours leave from the end of the museum at the edge of the actual bath for those with a big appetite for Roman history (included, on the hour, a poolside clock is set for the next departure time). You can revisit the museum after the tour. (£6.30, £8.40 combo ticket includes Costume Museum at a good savings, a family combo costs £22, daily 9:00–18:00, in August also 20:00–22:00, slightly shorter hours off-season, tel. 01225/477-000.)

▲**Pump Room**—After a centuries-long cold spell, Bath was reheated when the previously barren Queen Mary bathed here and in due course bore a male heir to the throne (1687). Once Bath was back on the aristocratic map, high society soon turned the place into one big pleasure palace. The Pump Room, an elegant Georgian hall just above the Roman baths, offers the visitor's best chance to raise a pinky in this Chippendale elegance. Drop by to sip coffee or tea to the rhythm of a string trio (tea/coffee and pastry for £4, live music all year 10:30–13:00, summers until 17:00, good place for a traditional high tea—after 14:30). Above the newspaper table and sedan chairs a statue of Beau Nash himself sniffles down at you. Now's your chance to have a famous (but forgettable) "Bath bun" and split (and spit) a 45p drink of the awfully curative water. The Pump Room's toilets are open to the discreet public.

A quarter of a million gallons of mineral water still bubble through the spa daily. In 2001 a new spa facility will be opened for the public to once again bathe in Bath.

▲▲**Abbey**—Bath town wasn't much in the Middle Ages. But an important church has stood on this spot since Anglo-Saxon times. In 973, Edgar, the first king of England, was crowned here. Dominating the town center, the present church—the last great medieval church of England—is 500 years old and a fine example of Late Perpendicular Gothic, with breezy fan vaulting and enough stained glass to earn it the nickname "Lantern of the West" (Monday–Saturday 9:00–18:00, from 13:00 on Sunday, concert and evensong schedule posted on the door, worth the £1.50 donation, handy flier narrates a 19-stop tour). The Abbey's Heritage Vaults is a small but interesting exhibit telling the story of Christianity in Bath since Roman times (£2, Monday–Saturday 10:00–16:00, closed Sunday). Take a moment to really appreciate the Abbey's architecture from the Abbey Green square.

▲**Pulteney Bridge and Boats**—Bath is inclined to compare its shop-lined bridge to Florence's Ponte Vecchio. That's pushing it. But to best enjoy a sunny Bath kind of day, pay £1 to go into the Parade Gardens below the bridge (free after 20:00). Across the bridge at Pulteney Weir, tour boats run cruises from under the bridge (£3.80, 50 minutes to Bathampton and back, one boat stops there if you'd like to walk back, the other company has a sundeck ideal for picnics).

▲▲**Royal Crescent and the Circus**—If Bath is an architectural cancan, these are the kickers. These first elegant Georgian "condos" by John Wood (the Elder and the Younger) are well-explained in the city walking tours. "Georgian" is British for "neoclassical," or dating from the 1770s. Stroll the Crescent after dark. Pretend you're rich. Pretend you're poor. Notice the "ha ha fence," a drop in the front yard offering a barrier, invisible from the windows, to sheep and peasants.

▲▲**Georgian House at #1 Royal Crescent**—This museum (on the corner of Brock Street and the Royal Crescent) offers your best look into a period house. It's worth the £3.50 admission to get behind one of those classy exteriors. The volunteers in each room are determined to fill you in on all the fascinating details of Georgian life . . . like how high-class women shaved their eyebrows and pasted on carefully trimmed strips of furry mouse skin in their place (Tuesday–Sunday 10:30–17:00, closed Monday, "no stiletto heels, please," tel. 01225/428-126).

▲▲▲**Costume Museum**—One of Europe's great museums, displaying 400 years of fashion—from Anne Boleyn to Twiggy—one frilly decade at a time, is housed in Bath's elegant Assembly Rooms. Follow the included and excellent CD wand self-guided tour. Learn why Yankee Doodle "stuck a feather in his cap and called it macaroni," and much more (£3.80, cheaper on combo ticket with Roman Baths, daily 10:00–17:00, tel. 01225/477-789).

▲▲**Industrial Heritage Centre**—This is the grand title for Mr. Bowler's Business, a turn-of-the-century engineer's shop, brass foundry, and fizzy-drink factory with a Dickensian office. It's just a pile of meaningless old gadgets until a volunteer guide lovingly resurrects Mr. Bowler's creative genius. Fascinating hour-long tours go regularly; just join the one in session upon arrival. (£3.50, plus a few pence for a glass of genuine Victorian lemonade, daily 10:00–17:00, weekends only in winter, two blocks up Russell Street from the Assembly Rooms, call to be sure a volunteer is available to give a tour, tel. 01225/318-348.) There's a Bath stone exhibit downstairs and a café/shop upstairs.

The Building of Bath Museum—This offers a fascinating look behind the scenes at how the Georgian city was actually built. This is just one large room of exhibits but those interested in construction find it worth the £3 (Tuesday–Sunday 10:30–17:00, closed Monday, near the Circus on a street called "the Paragon," tel. 01225/333-895).

Royal Photographic Society—A hit with shutterbugs, this exhibits the earliest cameras, photos, and their development, along with temporary contemporary exhibits (£3, daily 9:30–17:30, on Milsom Street, tel. 01225/462-841).

▲**American Museum**—I know, you need this in Bath like you need a Big Mac. But this museum offers a fascinating look at colonial and early-American lifestyles. Each of 18 completely furnished rooms (from the 1600s to the 1800s) is hosted by an eager guide waiting to fill you in on the candles, maps, bedpans, and various religious sects that make domestic Yankee history surprisingly interesting. One room is a quilter's nirvana (£5, Tuesday–Sunday 14:00–17:00, closed Monday and November–March, at Claverton Manor, tel. 01225/460-503). The museum is outside of town and a headache to reach if you don't have a car (15-minute walk from the Guide Friday stop or a 10-minute walk from bus #18).

Walking, Biking, and Swimming—The TI has a brochure

describing options. Consider the idyllic walk up the canal path to Bathampton (from downtown, walk over Pulteney Bridge, through Sydney Gardens, turn left on canal, and in 30 minutes you'll hit Bathampton with its much-loved Old George Pub). The Bath skyline walk is a six-mile wander around the hills surrounding Bath (75p leaflet available at TI). Consider taking the river cruise up to Bathampton and walking back (see Pulteney Bridge and Boats, above). From Bathampton it's another two hours along the canal to the fine old town of Bradford-on-Avon, from which a train can zip you back to Bath. You could rent a bike from behind the Bath train station (£9/half day, £14/all day, tel. 01225/442-442) and bike this route. The scenic 12-mile bridle/biking/walking path along the old Bath–Bristol train tracks is also popular. The Bath Sports and Leisure Centre has a swimming pool and more (£2.40, just across the North Parade Bridge, 8:00–22:00, call for free swim times, tel. 01225/462-563).

Shopping—There's great browsing between the Abbey and the Assembly Rooms. Shops close at 17:30, later on Thursday. Interested in antiques? Explore the antique center on Bartlett Street just below the Assembly Rooms. You'll find the most stalls open on Wednesday. For the best deal, pick up the local paper (usually out on Friday) and shop with the dealers at estate sales and auctions listed in the "What's On" section.

Evening Entertainment

This Month in Bath (available at the TI and many B&Bs) lists events and evening entertainment.

Plays—The Theatre Royal, newly restored and one of England's loveliest, offers a busy schedule of London West End–type plays, including many "pre-London" dress rehearsal runs (£10–20, cheap standby tickets, tel. 01225/448-844). You can often get late cancellation seats for sold-out performances (drop by around 18:00).

Bizarre Bath Walks—For a walking comedy act—street theater at its best "with absolutely no history or culture"—follow JJ or Noel Britten on their creative and entertaining Bizarre Bath walk. Their 90-minute "tour," which plays off local passersby as well as tour members, is a kick (£3.50, 20:00 nightly April–September; heavy on magic, careful to insult all kinds of minorities and sensitivities, just racy enough but still good family fun; from the Huntsman pub near the Abbey, confirm time and starting place at TI or call 01225/335-124). Ghost Walks are another way to pass the after-dark hours (£3, 20:00, 2 hrs, unreliably Monday–Friday, tel. 01225/463-618). And for the scholarly types, there are almost nightly historical walks (19:00, 2 hrs, ask at TI).

Drinks—For a good spit-and-sawdust pub, drink real ale at the Star Pub (top of Paragon Street, Bass sold by the jug if you don't want to mess with pints). Or, for maximum entertainment, look

up two particularly musical local residents, Van Morrison and
Peter Gabriel.

Sleeping in Bath
(£1 = about $1.70, tel. code: 01225)
Sleep Code: **S** = Single, **D** = Double/Twin, **T** = Triple, **Q** = Quad,
b = bathroom, **t** = toilet only, **s** = shower only, **CC** = Credit Card
(Visa, MasterCard, Amex).

Bath is one of England's busiest tourist towns. To get a good
B&B, make a telephone reservation in advance. Competition is
stiff, and it's worth asking any of these places for a non-weekend,
three-nights-in-a-row, or off-season deal. Friday and Saturday
nights are tightest—especially if you're staying only one night,
since B&Bs favor those staying longer. If staying only Saturday
night, you're very bad news. There's a laundrette around the corner from Brock's Guest House on the cute pedestrian lane called
Margaret's Buildings, and another, scruffier place on Upper Bristol Road (tel. 01225/429378).

Sleeping near the Royal Crescent
Brock's Guest House will put bubbles in your Bath experience.
Marion Dodd and her husband, Geoffrey, have redone their
Georgian townhouse (built by John Wood in 1765) in a way that
would make the famous architect proud. This charming house is
perfectly located between the prestigious Royal Crescent and the
elegant Circus (Db-£58–68, Tb-£78–82, Qb-£90–95, reserve
with a credit-card number far in advance, strictly nonsmoking,
32 Brock Street, BA1 2LN, tel. 01225/338-374, fax 01225/334-
245, e-mail: marion@brocks.force9.net). If you can't find a sedan
chair, Brock's is a 15-minute uphill walk, £3.50 taxi, or short bus
ride (to Assembly Rooms and short walk) from the station.
Guide Friday buses stop on Brock Street. If you're in a transportation jam, Marion can occasionally arrange a reasonable private car hire.

Woodville House is run by Anne and Tom Toalster. This
grandmotherly little house has three charming rooms, one shared
shower, and a TV lounge. Breakfast is a help-yourself buffet
around a big, family-style table (D-£36, minimum two nights, anyone who smokes at all is not welcome, below the Royal Crescent
at 4 Marlborough Lane, BA1 2NQ, tel. and fax 01225/319-335,
e-mail: AnneToalster@compuserve.com).

Other recommended B&Bs on Marlborough Lane:
Elgin Villa is also a fine value (Ds-£36, Db-£40, minimum two
nights, kids £10 extra, four rooms, parking, nonsmoking, 6 Marlborough Lane, BA1 2NQ Bath, tel. & fax 01225/424-557). They
serve a big continental breakfast in your bedroom. **Athelney
Guest House** (D-£38, three rooms, nonsmoking, parking, 5

Marlborough Lane, tel. & fax 01225/312-031, Sue and Colin Davies) also serves a continental breakfast. **Parkside Guest House** is more upscale, renting five classy Edwardian rooms (Db-£60, nonsmoking, 11 Marlborough Lane, tel. & fax 01225/429-444, Erica and Inge Lynall). The **Marlborough House** is a Victorian place renting five rooms (tel. 01225/318-175, fax 01225/466-127, run by Americans Laura and Charles). **Armstrong House B&B** is closer to town on a busier road, but it's behind double-paned windows and is cozy and well run (five rooms, Db-£50, continental breakfast in room, nonsmoking, 41 Crescent Gardens, Upper Bristol Road, tel. 01225/442-211, fax 01225/460-665, Tony Conradi).

Sleeping behind the Train Station

These pleasant hotels are in a residential neighborhood.

Holly Villa Guest House, with a cheery garden and a cozy TV lounge and an eight-minute walk from the station and center, is enthusiastically and thoughtfully run by Jill McGarrigle (Ds-£40, Db-£48, Tb-£63, prices with this book, seven rooms, strictly nonsmoking, easy parking, 14 Pulteney Gardens, BA2 4HG, tel. 01225/310-331, fax 01225/339-334). From the city center, walk over North Parade Bridge, take the first right, then take the second left. It's a block from a Guide Friday bus stop.

Muriel Guy's B&B is another fine value. It mixes Georgian elegance with homey warmth a 10-minute walk out of town with fine city views (Db-£45, nonsmoking, over the bridge on North Parade Road, left on Pulteney Road, right up Bathwick Hill, on left at 14 Raby Place, tel. 01225/465-120, fax 01225/465-283).

Sleeping in the Town Center

Henry Guest House is a clean and vertical little eight-room, family-run place two blocks in front of the train station on a quiet side street (S-£19, D-£38, T-£57, TVs in rooms, lots of narrow stairs, one shower and one bath for all, 6 Henry Street, BA1 1JT, tel. 01225/424-052). This kind of decency at this price, centrally located, is found nowhere else in Bath.

Harington's of Bath Hotel, with 13 newly renovated rooms on a quiet street in the town center, is run by Susan Pow (Db-£86, family-room deal, slow-time discounts, nonsmoking, lots of stairs, CC:VMA, extremely central at 10 Queen Street, tel. 01225/461-728, fax 01225/444-804).

Parade Park Hotel, with clean rooms and helpful owners, is centrally located (Sb-£45, Db-£55–65, special four-poster Db-£75, Tb-£90, Qb-£105, nonsmoking rooms available, 10 North Parade, BA2 4AL, tel. 01225/463-384, fax 01225/442-322, Nita and David Derrick).

Pratt's Hotel is as proper and old English as you'll find in

Bath. Its creaks and frays are aristocratic. Its public places make you want to sip a brandy, and its 46 rooms are bright, spacious, and come with all the comforts (Sb-£65, Db-£95, prices promised with this book in 1999, dogs £2.95 but children free, CC:VMA, elevator, two blocks immediately in front of the station on South Parade, BA2 4AB, tel. 01225/460-441, fax 01225/448-807, e-mail: martin@prattshotel.demon.co.uk).

Sleeping near Pulteney Bridge

Kennard Hotel is a comfortable hotel with 14 charming Georgian rooms. Richard Ambler runs this place warmly, with careful attention to detail (S-£45, Db-£85–95 depending upon size, non-smoking, CC:VMA, just over Pulteney Bridge at 11 Henrietta Street, BA2 6LL, tel. 01225/310-472, fax 01225/460-054, e-mail: kennard@dircon.co.uk).

Laura Place Hotel is another elegant Georgian place (eight rooms, two on the ground floor, Db-£60–90 from small and high up to huge and palatial, 10-percent discount with cash and this book, family suite, nonsmoking, easy parking, CC:VMA, 3 Laura Place, Great Pulteney Street, just over Pulteney Bridge, tel. 01225/463-815, fax 01225/310-222, Patricia Bull).

Henrietta Hotel is a very plain place in the same elegant neighborhood with nearly no character (10 rooms, Db-£45–65, cash discount when quiet, CC:VM, 32 Henrietta Street, tel. 01225/447-779, fax 01225/444-150).

Cheap Dorm Beds

The **YMCA**, institutional but friendly, and wonderfully central on a leafy square down a tiny alley off Broad Street, has industrial-strength rooms and scuff-proof halls (S-£14, D-£26, T-£39, Q-£52, beds in big dorms-£11, includes breakfast, surcharge for one night, families offered a day nursery for kids under five, cheap dinners, CC:VM, tel. 01225/460-471, fax 01225/462-065, e-mail: info@ymcabath.u-net.com).

Bath Backpackers Hostel (likely to close in 1999) bills itself as a totally fun-packed, mad place to stay. It's an Aussie-run hostel three blocks up from the station renting bunk beds in six- to 10-bed coed rooms (£12 per bed with continental breakfast, non-smoking, no lockers, Internet café, 13 Pierrepont Street, tel. 01225/446-787, fax 01225/446-305).

The **Youth Hostel** is in a grand old building outside of town (£10 per bed without breakfast in two- to 14-bed rooms, bus #18 from the station, tel. 01225/465-674).

Eating in Bath

While not a great pub grub town, Bath is bursting with quaint eateries. There's something for every appetite and budget—just stroll around the center of town. A picnic dinner of take-out fish and chips in the Royal Crescent Park is ideal for aristocratic hoboes.

Eating between the Abbey and the Station

Four fine and popular places share North Parade Passage, a block behind the Abbey: **Tilley's Bistro** serves healthy French, English, and vegetarian meals at great prices with fine atmosphere (three-course meals for £15, smoke-free, nightly 18:30–23:00, North Parade Passage, tel. 01225/484-200). **Sally Lunn's House** is a cutesy, quasi-historic place for expensive doily meals, tea, pink pillows, and lots of lace (£12 meals, nightly, 4 North Parade Passage, tel. 01225/461-634). It's fine for tea and buns, and customers get a free peek at the basement museum (otherwise 30p). Next door, **Demuth's Vegetarian Restaurant** serves good three-course £10 meals (nightly, tel. 01225/446-059). **Crystal Palace Pub**, with hearty meals under rustic timbers or in the sunny courtyard, is a handy standby (meals under £5, daily 12:00–14:30 and 18:00–20:30, closed Sunday; children welcome on the patio, not indoors; 11 Abbey Green, tel. 01225/423-944).

Evans Self-Service Fish Restaurant is the best eat-in or take-out fish-and-chips deal in town (Monday–Wednesday 11:30–18:30, Thursday–Saturday 11:30–20:30, closed Sunday, student discounts, 7 Abbcygate, tel. 01225/463-981). For very cheap meals try **Spike's Fish and Chips** (open very late) and the neighboring café just behind the bus station.

Eating between the Abbey and the Circus

George Street is lined with cheery cateries (Thai, Italian, wine bars, and so on). **Guildhall Market**, across from Pulteney Bridge, is fun for browsing and picnic shopping, with a very cheap cafeteria if you'd like to sip tea surrounded by stacks of used books, bananas on the push list, and honest-to-goodness old-time locals.

Eastern Eye has tasty Indian food under the sumptuous domes of a Georgian auction hall (£15 meals, daily 12:00–14:30 and 18:00–23:00, 8a Quiet Street, tel. 01225/422-323).

The **Green Tree Pub** on Green Street is a rare pub with good grub and a nonsmoking room (lunch only, no children).

Pasta Galore is a bit scruffy but serves decent Italian food (daily 18:00–22:30, good homemade pasta, call to reserve a table—avoid the basement, 31 Barton Street, tel. 01225/463-861). Next door is a cheap and fast Mexican joint.

Devon Savouries serves greasy, delicious take-out pasties, sausage rolls, and vegetable pies (on the main walkway between New Bond Street and Upper Borough Walls). The **Waitrose supermarket**, at the Podium shopping center, is great for groceries (open until 19:00 or 20:00, across from the post office on High Street).

For a classy, intimate setting and "new English" cuisine worth the splurge, dine at **No. 5 Bistro** (main courses with vegetables £12–15, Monday and Tuesday are "bring your own bottle of wine" nights—no corkage charge, Monday–Saturday 18:30–22:00, closed Sunday, just over Pulteney Bridge at 5 Argyle Street, smart to reserve, tel. 01225/444-499).

The **Bathtub Restaurant**, on Grove Street just around the corner from No. 5, is cheaper (£8 meals) and funkier, serving international vegetarian cuisine (nightly 18:00–23:00, tel. 01225/460-593).

Eating near the Circus and Brock's Guest House

Circus Restaurant is intimate and a good value with Mozartian ambience and candlelight prices: £15 for a three-course dinner special including great vegetables and a selection of fine desserts (daily, 34 Brock Street, tel. 01225/318-918, Felix Rosenow).

Woods Restaurant serves modern English cuisine to well-dressed locals in a sprawling candlelit brasserie (£7 lunches, £16 three-course dinners, closed Sunday, 9-13 Alfred Street near Assembly Rooms, tel. 01225/314-812).

On the opposite end of the decency spectrum, the **Chequers Inn** (two blocks up the hill, 50 Rivers Street) is a smoky dive of a pub with cheap, finger-sticking, disgusting grub and darts.

Transportation Connections—Bath

To: London's Paddington station by train (hrly, 75 min, £28.50 one-way or round-trip) or cheaper by National Express bus (hrly, 3 hrs, £19 round-trip £18 one-way, ask about £8 day returns). To get from London to Bath, consider using an all-day Stonehenge and Bath organized bus tour from London. For about the same cost as the train ticket, you can see Stonehenge, tour Bath, and leave the tour before it returns to London (they'll let you stow your bag underneath). Evan Evans (£29.50, tel. 0181/332-2222) and Travelline (£24, tel. 0181/668-7261) offer Stonehenge/Bath day trips from London. Train info tel. 0345/484-950.

London's airports: By National Express bus to **Heathrow Airport** (9/day, at 10:35, 12:35, 13:35, 14:35, 16:35, and so on, 2.5 hrs, £10, tel. 0990-808-080), and **Gatwick** (8/day, 4.5 hrs, change at Heathrow). Trains are faster but more expensive (hrly, 2.5 hrs, £22.50, see London Connections section for details). Coming from Heathrow you can also take the tube from the airport to London's Paddington station, then catch the Exeter train to Bath.

The Cotswolds: By train to **Moreton-in-Marsh** (2.5 hrs, transfers in Didcot Parkway and Oxford). By National Express bus (tel. 0990/808-080) to **Cheltenham** (4/day, 2 hrs), **Stratford** (2/day, 3 hrs), and **Oxford** (3/day, 2 hrs).

Birmingham, points north: By train to **Birmingham** (hrly, 2.5 hrs, transfer in Bristol). From Birmingham, a major transportation hub, trains depart for **Blackpool**, **York**, **Durham**, and **Scotland**. Use a train/bus combination to reach **Ironbridge Gorge**, **North Wales**, and the **Lake District**.

YORK

Historical York is loaded with world-class sights. Marvel at the York Minster, England's finest Gothic church. Ramble through the Shambles, York's wonderfully preserved medieval quarter. Enjoy a walking tour led by an old Yorker. Hop a train at Europe's greatest Railway Museum, travel to the 1800s in the York Castle Museum, and head back a thousand years to Viking York at the Jorvik exhibit.

York has a rich history. In A.D. 71 it was Eboracum, a Roman provincial capital. Constantine was proclaimed emperor here in A.D. 306. In the fifth century, as Rome was toppling, a Roman emperor sent a letter telling England it was on its own, and York became Eoforwic, the capital of the Anglo-Saxon kingdom of Northumbria. A church was built here in 627, and the town was an early Christian center of learning. The Vikings later took the town and from about 860 to 950 it was a Danish trading center called Jorvik. The invading and conquering Normans destroyed then rebuilt the city, giving it a castle and the walls you see today. Medieval York, with 9,000 inhabitants, grew rich on the wool trade and became England's second city. Henry VIII spared the city's fine minster and used York as his Anglican church's northern capital. The Archbishop of York is second only to the Archbishop of Canterbury in the Anglican Church. In the Industrial Age, York was the railway hub of North England. When it was built, York's train station was the world's largest. Today, except for its huge chocolate factory (Kit-Kats are made here), York's leading industry is tourism.

Planning Your Time
York rivals Edinburgh as the best sightseeing city in Britain after London. On even a 10-day trip through Britain, it deserves two nights and a day. For the best 36 hours, follow this plan: Catch the

19:00 city walking tour on the evening of your arrival. The next morning be at Jorvik at 9:00 when it opens (to avoid the midday crowds). The nearby Castle Museum is worth the rest of the morning (10:00–noon, I could spend even more time here). Three options for your early afternoon: shoppers browse the Shambles, train buffs tour the National Railway Museum, and scholars do the Yorkshire Museum. Tour the Minster at 16:00 before catching the 17:00 evensong service. Finish your day with an early evening stroll along the wall and perhaps through the abbey gardens. This schedule assumes you're there in the summer (evening orientation walk) and that there's an evensong on. Confirm your plans with the TI.

Orientation (tel. code: 01904)

The sightseer's York is small. Virtually everything is within a few minutes' walk: the sights, train station, TI, and B&Bs. The longest walk a visitor might take (from a B&B across the old town to the Castle Museum) is 15 minutes.

Bootham Bar, a gate in the medieval town wall, is the hub of your York visit. At Bootham Bar (and on Exhibition Square facing it) you'll find the TI, the starting points for most walking tours and bus tours, handy access to the medieval town wall, Gillygate (lined with good eateries), and Bootham Street, which leads to the recommended B&Bs. (In York, a "bar" is a gate and a "gate" is a street. Go ahead, blame the Vikings.)

Tourist Information: The TI at Bootham Bar sells a 75p "York Map and Guide." Ask for the free monthly *What's On* guide and the monthly "gig guide" for live music (July–August Monday–Saturday 9:00–19:00, Sunday 9:00–18:00; September–June Monday–Saturday 9:00–17:00, Sunday 10.00–17:00, tel. 01904/621-756). The train station TI is smaller but provides all the same information and services (9:00–20:00, less on Sunday).

Arrival in York: Upon arrival, grab a bench at the station and enjoy the enchanting voice of the woman announcer singing the train arrivals. The station is a five-minute walk from town; turn left down Station Road and follow the crowd toward the Gothic towers of the Minster. After the bridge, a block before the Minster, signs to the TI send you left. Recommended B&Bs are a five-minute walk from there. Buses #1, 2, and 3 go from the station to near the TI (St. Leonard's Place). With luggage, consider a quick taxi ride (£3).

Tours of York

▲▲▲**Walking Tours**—Charming local volunteer guides give energetic, entertaining, and free two-hour walks through York (daily, 10:15 all year and 14:15 April–October, plus 19:00 June–August, from Exhibition Square across from the TI). There are many other commercial York walking tours. YorkWalk Tours have reliable guides and many themes (£3, TI has schedule). The various ghost

York

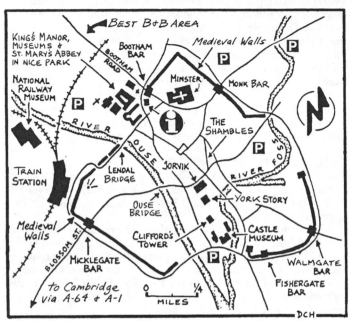

BEST B&B AREA

KINGS MANOR, MUSEUMS & ST. MARYS ABBEY IN NICE PARK

NATIONAL RAILWAY MUSEUM

Medieval Walls

BOOTHAM BAR

BOOTHAM ROAD

MINSTER

MONK BAR

THE SHAMBLES

RIVER OUSE

TRAIN STATION

LENDAL BRIDGE

JORVIK

RIVER FOSS

OUSE BRIDGE

CLIFFORD'S TOWER

YORK STORY

CASTLE MUSEUM

Medieval Walls

BLOSSOM ST.

MICKLEGATE BAR

WALMGATE BAR

FISHERGATE BAR

to Cambridge via A-64 & A-1

0   ¼
MILES

DCH

tours, offered after nightfall, are more fun than informative. York's voluntary guide association can be reached only from 9:30 to 11:30 at 01904/640-780).

▲**Guide Friday Hop-on and Hop-off Bus Tours**—York's Guide Friday offers tour guides on speed who can talk enthusiastically to three sleeping tourists in a gale on a topless double-decker bus for an hour without stopping. Buses make the hour-long circuit, covering secondary York sights that the city walking tours skip—the worka-day perimeter of town. Tickets cost £7.50 on the bus, £6.50 from the TI (hop on and off all day, departures every 10 or 15 minutes from 9:20 until around 18:00, tel. 01904/640-896). While you can hop on and off where you like, the York route is of no value from a trans-portation-to-the-sights point of view. I'd catch it at the Bootham Bar TI and ride it for an orientation all the way around (one hour) or get off at the Railway Museum, skipping the last five minutes. Guide Friday's competitors give you a little less for a little less.

Sights—York
▲**City Walls**—The historic walls of York provide a fine two-mile walk. Walk from Bootham Bar (gate) to Monk Bar for outstanding cathedral views. Open until dusk (barring attacks) and free.

▲▲▲**York Minster**—The pride of York, this largest Gothic church north of the Alps (540 feet long, 200 feet tall) is a brilliant example of how the High Middle Ages were far from dark. The word "minster" means a place from where people go out to minister or spread the word of God.

Your first impression might be the spaciousness and brightness of the nave (built 1280–1350). The nave—from the middle period of Gothic, called "Decorated Gothic"—is one of the widest Gothic naves in Europe. Notice the Great West Window (1338) above the entry. The heart in the tracery is called "the heart of Yorkshire." The mysterious dragon's head (sticking out over the nave) was probably used as a crane to lift a font cover.

The north and south transepts are the oldest part of today's church (1220–1270). The oldest complete window in the minster, with the modern-looking grisaille pattern, is the Five Sisters' Window in the north transept (1260).

The fanciful choir and the east end (high altar) is from the last stage of Gothic, Perpendicular (1360–1470). The Great East Window (1405), the largest medieval glass window in existence, shows the beginning and the end of the world with scenes from Genesis and the Book of Revelation. A chart (on the right, with a tiny, more helpful chart within) highlights the core Old Testament scenes in this hard-to-read masterpiece. Enjoy the art close up on the chart, then step back and find the real thing.

The "foundations" (£2) give you a chance to climb down—archaeologically and physically—through the centuries to see the roots of the much smaller but still huge Norman church (Romanesque, 1100) that stood on this spot, and below that, the Roman excavations. Constantine was proclaimed Roman emperor here in A.D. 306. Peek also at the modern concrete save-the-church foundations and the church treasury.

There are three more extra visits to consider. The chapter house, an elaborately decorated 13th-century Gothic dome, features playful details carved in the stonework (pointed out in the flier that comes with the 70p admission). You can step into the crypt—an actual bit of the Romanesque church excavated in modern times—which features 12th-century Romanesque art (70p), or scale the tower (£2, long climb, great view).

The cathedral is open daily from 7:30 to 20:30 (tel. 01904/624-426). The chapter house, tower, and "foundations" have shorter hours, usually 9:30 to 18:30, less off-season. Follow the "Welcome to the York Minster" flyer and ask about a free guided tour (they go frequently; you can join one in progress). The helpful blue-armbanded Minster guides are happy to answer your questions. While a donation of £2 to visit the church is reasonably requested, by visiting all the small extra spots inside I give that (and more) in the form of those admissions. Just pay for and enjoy all the little extras.

Evensong is a chance to experience the cathedral in musical and spiritual action. Evensong services are held weekdays at 17:00, and 16:00 on Saturday–Sunday (but usually spoken on Monday and when the choir is off).

▲**The Shambles**—This is the most colorful old York street in the half-timbered, traffic-free core of town. Ye olde downtown York, while very touristy, is a window-shopping, busker-filled, people-watcher's delight. Don't miss the more frumpy Newgate Market or the old-time candy store just opposite the bottom end of the Shambles.

▲▲▲**York Castle Museum**—Truly one of Europe's top museums, this is a Victorian homeshow, the closest thing to a time-tunnel experience England has to offer. It includes the 18th-century Kirkgate: a fine collection of old shops well-stocked exactly as they were 150 years ago, along with costumes, armor, an eye-opening Anglo-Saxon helmet (from A.D. 750), and the entertaining "every home should have one" exhibit showing the evolution of vacuum cleaners, toilets, TVs, bicycles, stoves, and so on, from their crude beginnings to now. Follow the arrows to cover everything: a working watermill, prison cells, man traps, WWII fashions, and old toys (£5, Monday–Saturday 9:30–18:00, Sunday 10:00–18:00, less off-season, 1960s cafeteria, shop, car park; the £2.50 guidebook, while not necessary, makes a nice souvenir, tel. 01904/653-611). Clifford's Tower (across from the Castle Museum, not worth the £1.70) is all that's left of York's castle (13th century, site of a 1190 massacre of local Jews—read about this at base of hill). While a stupid stunt, the current record for racing up and down the stairs is 22 seconds.

▲**Jorvik**—Sail the "Pirates of the Caribbean" north and back 800 years and you get Jorvik—more a ride than a museum. Innovative 10 years ago, the commercial success of Jorvik inspired copycat ride/museums all over England. You'll ride a little Disney-type train car for 13 minutes through the re-created Viking street of Coppergate. It's the year 948 and you're in the village of Jorvik. Next your little train takes you through the actual excavation sight that inspired this. Finally you'll browse through a small gallery of Viking shoes, combs, locks, and other intimate glimpses of that redheaded culture (£5, daily from 9:00, last entry at 17:30, November–March last entry at 15:30, tel. 01904/643-211). Avoid hour-long midday waits by going very early or very late. Even past the turnstile there's a 25-minute wait. Some love this "ride"; others call it a gimmicky rip-off. If you're looking for a serious museum, see the Viking exhibit at the Yorkshire Museum. It's better. If you're thinking Disneyland with a splash of history, Jorvik's great. I like Jorvik, but it's not worth a long line.

▲▲**National Railway Museum**—This thunderous museum shows 150 fascinating years of British railroad history. Fanning out from a grand roundhouse is an array of historic cars and engines, including Queen Victoria's lavish royal car and the very first "stagecoaches on rails." There's much more, including exhibits on dining cars, post cars, sleeping cars, train posters, and videos. This biggest and best railroad museum anywhere is interesting even to people who think "Pullman" is Japanese for "tug-o-war" (£5, daily 10:00–18:00, tel. 01904/621-261).

▲**Yorkshire Museum**—Located in a lush and lazy park next to the stately ruins of St. Mary's Abbey, Yorkshire Museum is the city's forgotten serious "archaeology of York" museum. While the hordes line up at Jorvik, the best Viking artifacts are here—with no crowds and in a better historical context. You have to walk through this museum, but the stroll takes you through Roman, Saxon, Viking, Norman, and Gothic York. Its prize piece is the delicately etched 15th-century pendant called the "Middleham Jewel." The video about the creation of the abbey is worth a look (£3.60, daily 10:00–17:00, tel. 01904/629-745).

The Theatre Royal—Fine plays, usually British comedies, entertain the locals (20:00 almost nightly, tickets easy to get from £6–13, St. Leonard's Place next to the TI and a five-minute walk from recommended B&Bs, info tel. 01904/610-041, tickets tel. 01904/623-568).

Honorable Mention—York has a number of other sights and activities (described in TI material) which, while interesting, pale in comparison to the biggies. **Fairfax House** is perfectly Georgian inside (£3.75, Monday–Saturday 11:00–17:30, Sunday 13:30–17:30, closed non-summer Fridays). The **York Story** offers a 45-minute video on the history of York—it's good, straight history (£2, associated with, across the street from, and pushed by the Castle Museum, 10:00–17:00, Sunday 13:00–17:00). The **Hall of the Merchant Adventurers** claims to be the finest medieval guild hall in Europe (from 1361). It's basically a vast half-timbered building with marvelous exposed beams and 15 minutes' worth of interesting displays about life and commerce back in the days when York was England's second city (£2, daily 9:00–17:00, less in winter, below the Shambles off Piccadilly). The **Richard III "Museum"** at Monk Bar is interesting only for Richard III enthusiasts (£1). **The ARC** (Archaeological Resource Center) is a big former church full of genuine archaeological artifacts that visitors—mostly school groups—can study as pretend archaeologists (£3.60, Monday–Friday 10:00–17:00, last admission 15:30; great for kids, welcomes adults; plenty of microscopes, hands-on fun, and helpful volunteers; just off the Shambles on St. Saviourgate, tel. 01904/643-211). The **York Dungeon** is gimmicky but, if you insist on papier-mâché gore, is better than the London Dungeon. The **Antiques Centre** is a fun browse (41 Stonegate near the Minster). Visitors are welcome to buy a pint of beer and watch the action at the **bowling green** near recommended B&Bs (Sycamore Place).

Sleeping in York
(£1 = about $1.70, tel. code: 01904)
Sleep Code: **S** = Single, **D** = Double/Twin, **T** = Triple, **Q** = Quad, **b** = bathroom, **t** = toilet only, **s** = shower only, **CC** = Credit Card (**Visa, MasterCard, Amex**).

I've listed peak-season book-direct prices. Don't use the TI. Outside of July and August some prices go soft.

Sleeping in B&Bs near Bootham Gate
These recommendations are in the handiest B&B neighborhood, a quiet residential neighborhood just outside the old-town wall's Bootham gate, along the road called Bootham. All are within a five-minute walk of the Minster and TI and a 10-minute walk or £3 taxi ride from the station. If driving, head for the cathedral and follow the medieval wall to the gate called Bootham Bar. Bootham "street" leads away from Bootham Bar. These B&Bs are all small, smoke-free, family-run, and come with plenty of steep stairs but no traffic noise. For a good selection, call well in advance. They will generally hold a room with a phone call, and work hard to help their guests sightsee and eat smartly. Most have permits for street parking. And most take no credit cards. Regency Dry Cleaning does small loads for £7 (8:30–18:00, Saturday 9:00–17:00, closed Sunday, 75 Bootham, tel. 01904/613-311). The launderette beyond Gillygate (10-minute walk from B&Bs) is cheaper.

Airden House, the most central of my Bootham-area listings, has eight spacious rooms, a grandfather clock–cozy TV lounge, and brightness and warmth throughout. Susan and Keith Burrows keep their place simple, comfortable, and friendly. They are a great source of local travel tips (D-£40, Db-£48, 1 St. Mary's, York Y03 7DD, tel. 01904/638-915).

The Sycamore, run by Margaret and David Tyce, is a fine value with homey rooms strewn with silk flowers and personal touches. It's at the end of a dead-end opposite a fun-to-watch bowling green (D-£32, Db-£40, family deals, 19 Sycamore Place off Bootham Terrace, YO3 7DW, tel. & fax 01904/624-712).

The Hazelwood is my most hotelesque listing. Ian and Carolyn McNabb run this aggressively spacious old 14-room place in an entrepreneurial way, paying careful attention to details and serving a classy breakfast (Db-£50–53, Db with four-poster-£5 extra, two ground-floor rooms; a fridge, ice, and great travel library in the plush basement lounge; CC:VM, 24 Portland Street, Gillygate, YO3 7EH, tel. 01904/626-548, fax 01904/628-032, e-mail: hzwdyok@aol.com).

Abbeyfields Guest House, with cozy, bright rooms and a quiet lounge, is run and decorated with a masculine sensibility (S-£20, Sb-£28, Db-£48, 19 Bootham Terrace, YO3 7DD, tel. & fax 01904/636-471, Richard and Gwen).

York, Our Neighborhood

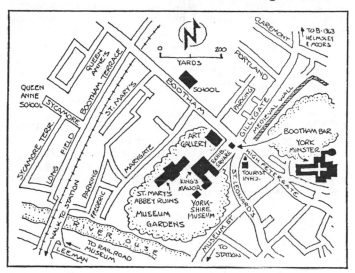

Claremont Guest House is a friendly house offering two delightful rooms and many thoughtful touches. Gill and Martyn Cornell offer laundry service (D-£32, Db-£42, 18 Claremont Terrace off Gillygate, YO3 7EJ, tel. 01904/625-158, e-mail: claremont .york@dial.pipex.com).

White Doves is a cheery little Victorian place with a comfy lounge and four fine rooms (Db-£42–45, family deals, 20 Claremont Terrace off Gillygate, YO3 7EJ, tel. 01904/625-957, Pauline and David Pearce).

23 St. Mary's is a rococo riot. Mrs. Hudson has done everything super-correctly, and offers nine comfortable rooms, a classy lounge, and all the doily touches (Sb-£30–34, Db-£58–64 depending on season and size, 23 St. Mary's, YO3 7DD, tel. 01904/622-738).

Queen Anne's Guest House has six compact, clean, and cheery rooms (D-£30, Db-£34 through 1999 with this book, family deals, 24 Queen Anne's Road, tel. 01904/629-389, Judy and David West).

Crook Lodge B&B is a bit more elegant than the rest with tight and charming rooms (Db-£46–50, 26 St. Mary's, tel. 01904/ 655-614, Susan and John Arnott).

Alcuin Lodge is also good (Db-46, one small top floor D-£35, no kids, CC:VM, 15 Sycamore Place, tel. 01904/632-222, e-mail: Alcuinlodg@aol.com, Susan Taylor).

York's Youth Hotel is well run, with lots of extras like a kitchen, launderette, games, and bar (S-£14, D-£26, £11 in four- to six-bed dorms, sheets and breakfast extra, £1 less for multinight stays, CC:VM, 10-minute walk from station at 11 Bishophill Senior Road, York YO1 1EF, tel. 01904/625-904 or 01904/612-494, e-mail: youth-hotel@ymn.co.uk).

Sleeping in Hotels in the Center of York

Dean Court Hotel, facing the Minster, is a big stately place run by Best Western with classy lounges and spacious rooms (small Db-£99, Db-£115, fancy Db-£125, super-fancy Db-£145, CC:VMA, some nonsmoking rooms, elevator, Doncombe Place, YO1 2EF, tel. 01904/625-082, fax 01904/620-305).

Galtres Lodge Hotel, a block from the Minster, offers cramped hallways but comfy rooms above a restaurant in the old town center (Dt-£50, Db-£65, CC:VM, no kids under 14, nonsmoking, 54 Low Petergate, tel. 01904/622-478, fax 01904/627-804).

Eating in York

Lunch in the Shambles

For cuteness, consider the tiny **St. Crux Parish Hall**, a medieval church now used by a medley of charities selling tea and snacks (at bottom end of the Shambles). For a smoky place with the floor still sticky from last night's spilled beer, the **Golden Fleece** pub is busy at lunch, serving famous Yorkshire pudding and hearty meals. Twee eateries line the street called Pavement. Ye **Olde Starre Inn**, the oldest pub in town, has yet to learn the art of cooking.

Traditional Tea

York is famous for its elegant teahouses. Drop into one around 16:00 for tea and cakes. Ladies love **Betty's Teahouse** (£4, daily 9:00–21:00, mostly nonsmoking, St. Helen's Square, fine people-watching from a window seat, usually a line, wait for a main-floor table), but several others can satisfy your king- or queen-for-a-day desires.

Eating near the Minster

Café Concerto has a loyal following for good reason. Their £15 three-course meal is the best I've had in York (nightly until 22:00, traditional English or Continental cuisine, on Petergate, under Bootham Bar, smart to reserve at 01904/610-478). The **Viceroy of India**—just outside Monkgate and therefore outside the tourist zone—serves great Indian food at good prices to mostly locals (nightly, £8 plates, friendly staff, just past the big old "Bile Beans keep you healthy, bright-eyed, and slim" sign at 26 Monkgate, tel. 01904/622-370). If you've yet to eat Indian on your trip, do it here. **St. Williams Restaurant**, just behind the great east window of the Minster in a wonderful half-timbered 15th-century building, serves quick and tasty lunches and elegant candlelit dinners (two courses-£10, three courses-£15, traditional and Mediterranean, tel. 01904/634-830).

Eating near Bootham Bar and Your B&B

Walk along Gillygate and choose from an enjoyable array of eateries: For authentic Italian, consider **Mama Mia's** (£6–9, daily 11:30–14:00, 17:30–23:00, fun, *domani* service, indoor/outdoor patio, 20 Gillygate, tel. 01904/622-020). **Gillygate Fisheries** is a wonderfully traditional little fish-and-chips joint where tattooed people eat-in and housebound mothers take-out (Mel serves £3 meals, eat your mushy peas; closed Sunday, smoke-free seating, 59 Gillygate). For the closest you'll get to Mexico in Britain, consider **Fiesta Mehicana** (17:30–19:00, sit-down or take-out, 14 Clifford Street, tel. 01904/610-243). There's a pub serving grub on every block. The **Horse and Wagon** on Gillygate has local color and £5 meals. Eat where you see lots of food or go to the **Coach House** (nightly 18:30–21:30, 20 Marygate, tel. 01904/652-780). The people who run your B&B know the latest on what's good.

Transportation Connections—York

By train to: Durham (2/hrly, 40 min), **Edinburgh** (2/hrly, 2 hrs, £43), **London** (2/hrly, 2 hrs, £50), **Bath** (via Bristol, hrly, 5 hrs), **Cambridge** (nearly hrly, 2 hrs with a change in Petersborough), **Birmingham** (8/day, 3 hrs). Train info: tel. 0345-484-950.

 By bus to: Keswick (1/day, 4 hrs, tel. 0990-808-080).

EDINBURGH

Edinburgh, the colorful city of Robert Louis Stevenson, Walter Scott, and Robert Burns, is Scotland's showpiece and one of Europe's most entertaining cities. Historical, monumental, fun, and well-organized, it's a tourist's delight.

Promenade down the Royal Mile through the Old Town. Historic buildings pack the Royal Mile between the castle (on the top) and Holyrood Palace (on the bottom). Medieval skyscrapers stand shoulder-to-shoulder, hiding peaceful courtyards connected to High Street by narrow lanes or even tunnels. This colorful jumble—in its day the most crowded city in the world—is the tourist's Edinburgh.

Edinburgh (ED'n-burah) was once two towns divided by a lake. To alleviate crowding, the lake was drained and a magnificent Georgian city, today's New Town, was laid out to the north. Georgian Edinburgh, like the city of Bath, shines with broad boulevards, straight streets, square squares, circular circuses, and elegant mansions decked out in colonnades, pediments, and sphinxes in the proud, Neoclassical style of 200 years ago.

While the Georgian city celebrated the union of Scotland and England (with streets and squares named after English kings and emblems), "devolution" is the latest craze. In a 1998 election the Scots voted for more autonomy and to bring their parliament home. Though Edinburgh has been the historic capital of Scotland for centuries, parliament has not met in Scotland since 1707. In 2000—while London will still call the strategic shots—Edinburgh will resume its position as home to the Scottish Parliament. And a strikingly modern new parliament building, opening in 2002, will be one more jewel in Edinburgh's crown.

Planning Your Time

While the major sights can be seen in a day, on a three-week tour of Britain I'd give Edinburgh two days.

Day 1: Orient yourself with a Guide Friday bus tour. Do the whole loop, getting off only to tour the Georgian House. After lunch, catch a 14:00 walking tour of the Royal Mile. Finish the afternoon at the National Gallery or browsing through the New Town. Evening: Scottish show, folk pub, or literary pub crawl or haunted walk.

Day 2: Spend the morning touring the castle. The rest of the day is easily spent exploring (downhill) the Royal Mile—museum-going or shopping. If you tour the Holyrood Palace, do it at the end of the day and the bottom of the mile. Family or fun options: Hike up Arthur's Seat or go swimming at the Commonwealth Pool.

Orientation (tel. code: 0131)

The center of Edinburgh holds the Princes Street Gardens park and Waverley Bridge, where you'll find the TI; Waverley Shopping and Eating Center; train station; bus info office, the starting point for most city bus tours; festival office; the National Gallery; and a covered dance-and-music pavilion. Weather blows in and out—bring your sweater.

Tourist Information: The crowded TI has become a profit-seeking business with advice colored by kickbacks. It's central as can be atop the Waverley Market on Princes Street (Monday–Saturday 9:00–19:00, Sunday 10:00–19:00, shorter hours and closed Sunday in off-season, tel. 0131/557-1700, airport TI tel. 0131/333-2167). Ideally, skip it and telephone if you have questions. They have the monthly entertainment *Gig Guide* (free) and brochures on the various Scottish folk shows and walking tours. Their misnamed *Essential Guide to Edinburgh* (which costs £1 and shuffles a little information between lots of ads) has a cruddy little map. *The List*, the best monthly entertainment listing, is sold for £1.50 at newsstands. Book your room direct without the TI's help.

For real information without the sales push, visit the **Old Town Information Centre** at Tron Church (Easter–September, South Bridge at the Royal Mile, great free Royal Mile maps). The **Backpackers' Centre** is a good source of budget travel information (just off High Street at 5 Blackfriars Street).

Sunday Activities: Many sights close on Sunday, but there's still a lot to do: Royal Mile walking tour, city bus tour, Edinburgh Castle, St. Giles Cathedral, Holyrood Palace, Royal Botanic Gardens, and Arthur's Seat hike. The Georgian House and National Gallery open Sunday afternoon.

Arrival in Edinburgh: Arriving by train at Waverley Station puts you in the city center, a few steps from the TI and the city

Edinburgh

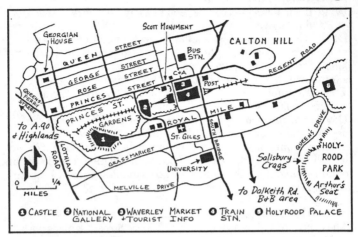

bus to my recommended B&Bs. Both National Express and Scottish Citylink buses use the bus station a block from the train station in the Georgian town on St. Andrew Square.

Edinburgh's slingshot-of-an-airport is 10 miles northwest of the center and well-connected by shuttle buses (LRT "Airline" bus, 4/hrly, 30 min, from Waverley Bridge, £3.20 or £4 with all-day city bus pass, flight info tel. 0131/333-1000, British Midlands tel. 0345/554-554, British Air tel. 0345/222-111). Taxi to airport: £14.

Getting Around Edinburgh

Nearly all Edinburgh sights are within walking distance. City buses are handy and inexpensive (average fare-65p, LRT info office, Old Town end of Waverley Bridge, tel. 0131/555-6363). Tell the driver where you're going, drop exact change into the box or lose the excess, grab your ticket as you board, push the stop button as you near your stop (so your stop isn't skipped), and exit from the middle door. All-day "Freedom Ticket" passes are sold on buses (£2.20—four rides make it worthwhile). Taxis are reasonable (easy to flag down, £1.20 drop charge, 80p extra after 18:00, average ride between downtown and B&B district—£4).

Bus Tours of Edinburgh

▲**Hop-on and Hop-off City Bus Tours**—Two companies, Guide Friday and LRT's "Edinburgh Classic Tour," offer buses that circle the town center—Waverley Bridge, around the castle, Royal Mile, Calton Hill, Georgian New Town, and Princes Street—in about an hour, with pick-ups about every 15 minutes and an informative narration. You can hop on and off all day on one ticket (not for 24 hours). Overlapping can be interesting, since each guide has her own story to tell. On sunny days they go topless (the buses), but can suffer from traffic noise and congestion. First and last buses leave Waverley Bridge at 9:00 and 19:00 in summer. (Guide Friday, £7, tel. 0131/556-2244; Classic Tour, £5.50, tel. 0131/555-6363.)

▲**City Bus Tours**—"City, Sea, and Hills" is the best 90-minute tour of greater Edinburgh (£3.50, Friday and Sunday at 10:30, information at LRT office, on Waverley Bridge, tel. 0131/555-6363). Several all-day bus tours go as far as Loch Ness.

Sights—Edinburgh

▲▲▲**Edinburgh Castle**—The fortified birthplace of the city 1,300 years ago, this imposing symbol of Edinburgh sits proudly on a rock high above the city. While the castle has been both a fort and a royal residence since the 11th century, most of the buildings today are from its more recent use as a military garrison (£6, daily 9:30–18:00, until 17:00 in winter, cafeteria, tel. 0131/225-9846; consider avoiding the long uphill walk from the nearest bus stop by taking a cab to the castle gate).

Entry Gate: Start with the wonderfully droll 30-minute guided introduction tour (free with admission, departs twice an hour from entry, see clock for the next departure). The CD-ROM audio guide is excellent, with four hours of quick digital dial descriptions (free with admission, pick up at entry gate before meeting the live guide). Don't miss the fine WC at the entry (three-time "British Loo of the Year" winner, award plaques near men's entry—ask janitor why they lost last year).

In the castle there are four essential stops: Crown Jewels, Great Hall, National War Memorial, and St. Margaret's Chapel with city view. All are at the highest and most secure point—on or near the castle square—and where your guided tour ends.

The Royal Palace (facing castle square under the flag pole) has two unimpressive rooms (through door reading "1566"). Remember, Scottish royalty only lived here when safety or protocol required. They preferred the Holyrood Palace at the bottom of the Royal Mile. The line of tourists leads from the square directly to the jewels. Skip this line and enter the building around to the left where you'll get to the jewels via a wonderful *Honors of Scotland* exhibition about the crown jewels.

Scotland's Crown Jewels are older than England's. While Cromwell destroyed England's, the Scots hid theirs successfully. Long-time symbols of Scottish nationalism, they were made in Edinburgh—of Scottish gold, diamonds, and gems—in 1540 for a 1543 coronation. They were last used to crown Charles II in 1651. Apparently there was some anxiety about the Act of Union, which dissolved Scotland's parliament into England's to create the United Kingdom in 1707—the Scots locked up and hid their jewels. In 1818 Walter Scott and a royal commission rediscovered the jewels intact.

The **Stone of Scone** sits plain and strong next to the jewels. This is the coronation stone of Scotland's ancient kings (ninth century). Swiped by the English, it sat under the coronation chair at Westminster Abbey from 1296 until 1996. With major fanfare, Scotland's treasured Stone of Scone returned to Edinburgh on November 15, 1996. Talk to the guard for more details.

The Great Hall was the castle's ceremonial meeting place in the 16th and 17th centuries. In modern times it was a barracks and a hospital. While most of what you see is Victorian, two medieval elements survive: the fine hammer-beam roof and the iron-barred peephole (above fireplace on right). This allowed the king to spy on his partying subjects.

The imposing **Scottish National War Memorial** commemorates 148,000 Scottish soldiers lost in WWI, 57,000 lost in WWII, and 750 lost in British battles since. Each bay is dedicated to a particular Scottish regiment. The main shrine, featuring a green Italian marble memorial containing the original WWI rolls of honor, actually sits upon an exposed chunk of the castle rock. Above you, the archangel Michael is busy slaying the dragon. The bronze frieze accurately shows the attire of various wings of Scotland's military. The stained glass starts with Cain and Abel on the left and finishes with a celebration of peace on the right.

St. Margaret's Chapel, the oldest building in Edinburgh, is dedicated to Queen Margaret, who died here in 1093 and was sainted in 1250. Built in the Romanesque style of the Norman invaders in 1130, it is wonderfully simple, with classic Norman zigzags decorating the round arch that separates the tiny nave from the sacristy. Used as a powder magazine for 400 years, very little survives. You'll see an 11th-century Gospel book of St. Margaret's and small windows featuring St. Margaret, St. Columba (who brought Christianity to Scotland via Iona), and William Wallace (the brave defender of Scotland). The place is popular for weddings and, since it seats only 20, particularly popular with brides' fathers.

Belly up to the banister (across the terrace outside the chapel) to enjoy the great view. Below you are the guns that fire the one o'clock salute and a sweet little line of doggie tombstones—the soldier's pet cemetery. Beyond stretches the Georgian New Town (read the informative plaque).

The castle could keep you entertained all day (for instance, below, in the vaults, you can see a fine military museum and Mons Meg—a huge 15th-century siege cannon that fired 500-pound stones nearly two miles). But you've seen the essentials.

When leaving the castle, turn around and look back at the gate. There stand King Robert the Bruce (on the left, 1274–1329) and Sir William Wallace (Braveheart—on the right, 1270–1305). Wallace (newly famous, thanks to Mel Gibson) fought long and hard against English domination before being executed in London—his body cut to pieces and paraded through the far corners of jolly olde England. Bruce beat the English at Bannockburn in 1314. Bruce and Wallace still defend the spirit of Scotland.

Sights—Along the Royal Mile
(In walking order from top to bottom.)

▲▲▲Royal Mile—This is one of Europe's most interesting historic walks. Start at the top and amble down to the palace. I've listed the top sights of the Royal Mile—working downhill.

The Royal Mile, which consists of a series of four different streets—Castlehill, Lawnmarket, High Street, and Canongate—is actually 100 yards longer than a mile. And every inch is packed with shops, cafés, and lanes leading to tiny squares. By poking down the many side-alleys, you'll find a few rough edges of a town well on its way to becoming a touristic mall. See it now. In a few years tourists will be slaloming through the postcard racks on bagpipe skateboards.

Royal Mile Terminology: A "closc" is a tiny alley between two buildings (originally with a door that closed it at night). A close usually leads to a "court" or courtyard. A "land" is a tenement block of apartments. A "pend" is an arched gateway. A "wynd" is a narrow winding lane. And "gate" is from an old Scandinavian word for street.

Royal Mile Walking Tours: Mercat Tours offers two-hour guided walks of the mile—more entertaining than historic (£5, daily at 11:00 and 14:00, from Mercat Cross on the Royal Mile, tel. 0131/661-4541). The guides, who enjoy making a short story long, ignore the big sights, taking you behind the scenes with piles of barely historic gossip, bully-pulpit Scottish pride, and fun but forgettable trivia. For a private guide, consider Robin Sinton (tel. 0131/661-7722) or the Voluntary Guides Association (0131/664-7180).

Castle Esplanade—At the top of the Royal Mile, the big parking lot leading up to the castle was once a military parade ground. It's often cluttered with bleachers under construction for the military tattoo—a spectacular massing of the bands that fills the square nightly for most of August (see Edinburgh Festival, below). At the bottom, on the left, the tiny witch's fountain memorializes 300 women who were accused of witchcraft and burned here. Scotland burned more witches per capita than any other country—17,000 between 1479 and 1722. But in a humanitarian gesture, rather than burning them alive as was the custom in the rest of Europe,

Royal Mile

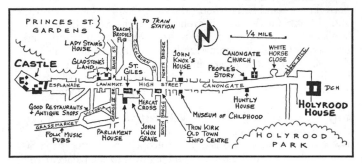

Scottish "witches" were strangled to death before they were burned. The plaque shows two witches: one good and one bad. (For 90 minutes of this kind of Royal Mile trivia, take the guided tour described above.)

Scotch Whiskey Heritage Centre—This touristy ambush is designed only to distill £5 out of your pocket. You get a video history, a little whiskey-keg train-car ride, and a free sample before finding yourself in the shop. People do seem to enjoy it, but that might have something to do with the sample (tel. 0131/220-0441). The **Camera Obscura,** across the street, is just as rewarding.

▲▲**Gladstone's Land**—Take a good look at this typical 16th- to 17th-century merchant's house, complete with a lived-in furnished interior and guides in each room who love to talk (£3, Monday–Saturday 10:00–17:00, Sunday 14:00–17:00). For a good Royal Mile photo, lean out the upper-floor window or climb the entry stairway with the golden eagle.

▲**Writers' Museum at Lady Stair's House**—This interesting house, built in 1622, is filled with manuscripts and knickknacks of Scotland's three greatest literary figures: Robert Burns, Sir Walter Scott, and Robert Louis Stevenson. It's worth a few minutes for anyone and is fascinating for fans (free, Monday–Saturday 10:00–17:00, closed Sunday). Wander around the courtyard here. Edinburgh was a wonder in the 17th and 18th centuries. Tourists came here to see its skyscrapers, which towered 10 stories and higher. No city in Europe was so densely populated as "Auld Reekie."

Deacon Brodie's Tavern—This is a decent place for a light meal (see Eating, below). Read the story of its notorious namesake on the wall facing Bank Street.

▲**St. Giles Cathedral**—Wander through Scotland's most important church. Stepping inside, find John Knox's statue. Look into his eyes from 10 inches away. Knox, the great reformer and founder of austere Scottish Presbyterianism, first preached here in 1559. His insistence that every person should be able to read the word of God gave Scotland an education system 300 years ahead of the rest of Europe. For this reason it was Scottish minds who led the way in math, science, medicine, engineering, and so on. Voltaire called Scotland "the intellectual capital of Europe."

The neo-Gothic Chapel of the Knights of the Thistle (from 1911, in far corner) was built in two years entirely with Scottish material and labor. Find the angel tooting the bagpipes (above the door on right). The Scottish crown steeple from 1495 is a proud part of Edinburgh's skyline (daily 9:00–19:00, until 17:00 off-season, fine café downstairs).

John Knox is buried out back—austerely, under the parking lot, at spot 44. The statue among the cars shows King Charles II riding to a toga party back in 1685.

Parliament House—Stop in to see the grand hall with its fine 1639 hammer-beam ceiling and stained glass. This housed the Scottish Parliament until the Act of Union in 1707 (explained in history exhibition adjacent). Today it's busy with wigged and robed lawyers hard at work in the old library (peek through the door) or pacing the hall deep in discussion. Greater eminence . . . longer wig. The friendly doorman is helpful (free, public welcome Monday–Friday 9:00–16:30, best action mid-mornings Tuesday–Friday, open-to-the-public trials 10:00–16:00—doorman has day's docket, entry behind St. Giles Cathedral near parking spot 21).

Mercat Cross—This stands on the downhill side of the church. Royal proclamations were read from here in the 14th century. Today it's the meeting point of various walking tours. Pop into the police information center, a few doors downhill, for a little local law-and-order history (free, daily 10:00–22:00).

▲**Tron Kirk**—This fine old building houses an interesting (free) Old Town history display and the genuinely helpful Old Town tourist information center (open Easter—September). No crowds. No conflict of interests. Just caring help by an outfit working to better organize and show off Edinburgh's historic Old Town.

▲**Museum of Childhood**—This five-story playground of historical toys and games—called the noisiest museum in the world because of its delighted tiny visitors—is rich in nostalgia and history (free, Monday–Friday 10:00–17:00, closed Sunday). Just downhill is a fragrant fudge shop offering free samples.

▲**John Knox House**—Fascinating for Reformation buffs, this fine 16th-century house offers a well-explained look at the life of the great reformer (£2, Monday–Saturday 10:00–16:30, closed on Sunday). While Knox never actually lived here, it was called "his house" to save it from the wrecking ball in 1850.

▲**People's Story**—This interesting exhibition traces the lot of the working class through the 18th, 19th, and 20th centuries (free,

Monday–Saturday 10:00–17:00, closed Sunday). Curiously, while
this museum is dedicated to the proletariat, immediately around
the back is the tomb of Adam Smith—the author of *Wealth of
Nations* and the father of modern capitalism (1723–1790).

▲**Huntly House**—Another old house full of old stuff, Huntly
is worth a look for its early Edinburgh history and handy
ground-floor WC. Don't miss the original copy of the National
Covenant (written in 1638 on an animal skin) or the sketches of
pre-Georgian Edinburgh with its lake still wet (free, Monday–
Saturday 10:00–17:00, closed Sunday). Just a toot farther downhill is Bagpipes Galore.

White Horse Close—Step into this 17th-century courtyard (bottom of Canongate, on the left, a block before Holyrood Palace). It
was from here that the Edinburgh stagecoach left for London.
Eight days later, the horse-drawn carriage pulled into its destination: Scotland Yard.

▲**Holyrood Palace**—The palace marks the end of the Royal Mile.
The queen spends a week in Scotland each summer and this is her
official residence and office. The abbey—part of a 12th-century
Augustinian monastery—stood here first. It was named for a piece
of the cross brought here as a relic by queen-then-saint Margaret.
Scotland's royalty preferred living here to the blustery castle on the
rock and, gradually, the palace grew. The building is rich in history
and decor. But without information or a guided tour ("there's none
of either," snickered the guy who sells the boring £3.70 museum
guidebooks), you're just another peasant in the dark. Docents in
each room are happy to give you the answer if you know the question. After wandering through the elegantly furnished rooms and a
few dark older rooms filled with glass cases of historic bits and
Scottish pieces that must be fascinating, you're free to wander
through the ruined abbey and the queen's gardens (£5.30, daily
9:30–18:00, shorter hours off-season, closed when the queen's
home—usually 10 days in early July, tel. 0131/556-7371).

More Bonnie Wee Sights

▲**Georgian New Town**—Cross Waverley Bridge and walk
through Georgian Edinburgh. The grand George Street, connecting St. Andrew and Charlotte Squares, was the centerpiece of the
elegantly planned New Town. The entire city plan—laid out in
the late 18th century when George was king—celebrates the
notion of the United Kingdom. Look at the map. You'll see
George Street. Queen Street, Hanover Street (the royal family
surname), and even Thistle and Rose Streets are emblems of the
two happily paired nations.

▲▲**Georgian House**—This refurbished Georgian house, set on
Edinburgh's finest Georgian square, is a trip back to 1796. A
volunteer guide in each room is trained in the force-feeding of

stories and trivia. Start your visit with two interesting videos (architecture/Georgian lifestyles) totaling 30 minutes (£4.30, Monday–Saturday 10:00–17:00, Sunday 14:00–17:00, 7 Charlotte Square, tel. 0131/225-2160).

Princes Street Gardens—This grassy park, a former lake-bed, separates Edinburgh's New and Old Towns and offers a wonderful escape from the city. There are plenty of free concerts and country dances in the summer, and the oldest floral clock in the world. Join the local office workers for a picnic-lunch break.

▲**National Gallery**—This elegant neoclassical building has a small but impressive collection of European masterpieces from Raphael to van Gogh and offers the best look you'll get at Scottish paintings (free, Monday–Saturday 10:00–17:00, Sunday 14:00–17:00, tel. 0131/624-6200).

▲**Walter Scott Monument**—Built in 1840, this elaborate, neo-Gothic monument honors the great author, one of Edinburgh's many illustrious sons. The 200-foot monument shelters a marble statue of Scott. He is surrounded by busts of 16 great Scottish poets and 64 characters from his books. Climb 287 steps for a fine view of the city (£1, Monday–Saturday 9:00–18:00, until 17:00 off-season, closed Sunday).

Royal Botanic Garden—Britain's second-oldest botanical garden, established in 1670 for medicinal herbs, is now one of Europe's best (free, daily 9:30–20:00 in season, £2 "rainforest to desert" tours daily at 11:00 and 14:00, one mile north of the center at Inverleith Row, tel. 0131/552-7171).

▲▲**Arthur's Seat Hike**—A 45-minute hike up the 822-foot volcanic mountain (surrounded by a fine park overlooking Edinburgh), starting from the Holyrood Palace, Commonwealth Pool, or your B&B, gives you a rewarding view. It's the easiest "king of the mountain" feeling I've ever had. You can drive up most of the way from behind (follow the one-way street from the palace, park by the little lake) or run up like they did in *Chariots of Fire*. Ask a local for the best way up.

Brush Skiing—If you'd rather be skiing, the Hillend Ski Centre is an open-all-year hill on the edge of town with a chairlift, T-bar, and rentable skis, boots, and poles (£6/hr with gear, daily 9:30–21:00, less on weekends, probably canceled if it snows, tel. 0131/445-4433).

▲**Royal Commonwealth Games Swimming Pool**—The biggest pool I've ever seen is open to the public, with Café Aqua (overlooking the pool), weight room, sauna (£6 extra), and plenty of water rides, including Europe's biggest waterslide flume (£2.50, Monday–Friday 9:00–21:00, Saturday and Sunday 10:00–16:00, tel. 0131/667-7211).

Edinburgh Crystal—Blowing, molding, cutting, polishing, and engraving, the Edinburgh Crystal Company glassworks tour smashes anything you'll see in Venice (£3, 35-minute tours offered Monday–Friday 9:15–15:30, Saturday and Sunday 11:00–14:30, children under age eight and large dogs are not allowed in for safety reasons). There is a shop full of "bargain" second-quality pieces, a video show, and a cafeteria. A free red minibus shuttle service from Waverley Bridge departs hourly (10:00–15:00) in summer; or you can drive 10 miles south of town on A701 to Penicuik. You can schedule a more expensive super-tour where you actually blow and cut glass (tel. 01968/675-128).

Shopping—The best shopping is along Princes Street (don't miss elegant old Jenner's Department Store), Victoria Street (antiques galore), and the Royal Mile (touristy but competitively priced, shops usually open 9:00–17:30, later on Thursday).

Edinburgh Festival

One of Europe's great cultural events, Edinburgh's annual festival turns the city into a carnival of culture. There are enough music, dance, art, drama, and multicultural events to make even the most jaded traveler drool with excitement. Every day is jammed with formal and spontaneous fun. The official and fringe festivals rage simultaneously for about three weeks each summer, with the Military Tattoo starting a week earlier. Many city sights run on extended hours and those that normally close on Sunday stay open. It's a glorious time to be in Edinburgh.

The official festival (August 15–September 4 in 1999) is more formal and serious, with entertainment by festival invitation only. Major events sell out well in advance (show office at 21 Market Street, £4–45, CC:VMA, booking from April on, tel. 0131/473-2000).

The less-formal **Fringe Festival** features "on the edge" comedy/theater (August 8–30, 1999, ticket/info office just below St. Giles Cathedral on the Royal Mile, tel. 0131/226-5257, bookings tel. 0131/226-5138). Its many events have, it seems, more performers than viewers. Tickets are usually available at the door (or strewn on the streets).

The **Military Tattoo** is a massing of the bands, drums, and bagpipes with groups from all over what was the British Empire. Displaying military finesse with a stirring lone-piper finale, this grand spectacle fills the castle esplanade nightly except Sunday, normally from a week before the festival starts until a week before it finishes: August 6–28 in 1999 (£8–16, CC:VMA, booking starts in January, tel. 0131/225-1188, Friday and Saturday shows sell out, Monday–Thursday shows rarely do). If nothing else, it is a really big show. The BBC airs the Tattoo in a grand TV spectacle throughout Britain once each season (worth watching from anywhere in Britain).

If you do manage to hit Edinburgh during the festival, extend your stay by a day or two and book a room far in advance. While

Fringe tickets and most Tattoo tickets are available the day of the show, you may want to book an official event or two in advance. Do it directly by telephone, leaving your credit-card number. Pick up your ticket at the office the day of the show or at the door just before curtain time. Several publications—including the festival's official schedule, the *Festival Times*, *The List*, *Fringe Program*, and the *Daily Diary*—list and evaluate festival events.

Entertainment in Edinburgh

▲▲**Evening Walking Tours**—These walks, more than a pile of ghost stories, are an entertaining and cheap night out (offered nightly, usually 19:00 and 21:00, easy socializing for solo travelers). The theatrical and creatively staged Witchery Tours are the most established of the ghost tours (£7, 90 min, leave from the Royal Mile, reservations required, book your spot by calling 0131/225-6745). The fascinating-for-those-who-care Literary Pub Tour leaves from the Beehive Pub on Grassmarket (£6, two hours with two actors and three pub stops, nightly in July and August at 18:00 and 20:30, Thursday–Sunday at 19:30 otherwise, Friday only in winter, tel. 0131/226-6665).

▲**Scottish Folk Evenings**—These £35 to £40 dinner shows, generally for tour groups, are held in huge halls of expensive hotels. (Prices are bloated to include 20 percent commissions.) Your "traditional" meal is followed by a full slate of swirling kilts, blaring bagpipes, and Scottish folk-dancing with an "old-time music hall"–type emcee. You can often see the show without dinner for about half-price. The TI has fliers on all the latest venues. Carlton Highland Hotel offers a Scottish folk evening without dinner (£12, at High Street and North Bridge, tel. 0131/556-7277).

▲▲**Folk Music in Pubs**—Edinburgh is a good place for folk music. There's always a pub or two with a folk evening on. The free monthly *Gig Guide* lists most of the live music action. Just off the Royal Mile on South Bridge, the **Tron Tavern and Ceilidh House** is home of the Tron Folk Club. They have nightly ad-lib traditional music from about 22:00 (but doesn't really get going until later, smoky) and a £3–6 candlelit folk concert on Saturday nights (smoke-free, tel. 0131/226-0931). **Whistle Binkies** offers live folk music several nights a week (also near High Street South Bridge at Niddry Street, tel. 0131/557-5114).

Grassmarket Street (below the castle) is sloppy with live music—mostly folk. This noisy nightlife center is fun to just wander through late at night. By the noise and crowds you'll know where to go and where not to. The **Fiddlers Arms** (fiddling on Monday and Thursday, tel. 0131/229-2665), **Biddy Mulligan**, and **White Hart Inn**, among others, all feature regular live folk music. **Finnigan's Wake** specializes in Irish folk music (a block off Grassmarket at 9 Victoria Street, tel. 0131/226-3816).

Theater—Even outside of festival time, Edinburgh is a fine place for lively and affordable theater. Pick up *The List* for a complete rundown of what's on.

Sleeping in Edinburgh
(£1 = about $1.70, tel. code: 0131)
Sleep Code: **S** = Single, **D** = Double/Twin, **T** = Triple, **Q** = Quad, **b** = bathroom, **t** = toilet only, **s** = shower only, **CC** = Credit Card (Visa, MasterCard, Amex).

The annual festival fills Edinburgh each August. Conventions, school holidays, and other surprises can make room-finding tough at almost any time. Call in advance or pay 30 percent extra for a relative dump. For the best prices, book direct (rather than through the greedy TI) and, again, call in advance! "Standard" rooms, with toilets and showers a tissue-toss away, save you £10 a night.

My recommendations are south of town near the Royal Commonwealth Pool, just off Dalkeith Road. This comfortably safe neighborhood is a 20-minute walk or short bus ride from the Royal Mile. All listings are on quiet streets, a two-minute walk from a bus stop, and well-served by city buses. Near the B&Bs you'll find plenty of eateries (see Eating, below), easy free parking, and a handy Laundromat (Monday–Saturday 9:00–17:00, £4 for a self-serve load, £5 if they do it, June–September they'll deliver your clean clothes at the B&B for £1 extra, 208 Dalkeith Road, tel. 0131/667-0825).

To reach the hotel neighborhood from the train station, TI, or Scott Monument, cross Princes Street and wait under the C&A sign (65p, buses #14, #21, #33, #82, #86, or C3; red bus: exact change or pay more; green bus: makes change; ride 10 minutes to first stop 100 yards after the pool, push the button, exit middle door). These buses also stop at the corner of North Bridge and High Street on the Royal Mile. Taxi fare from the station or Royal Mile to the B&Bs is about £4. Room prices are for peak-season 1999 (but not festival time, when they can go higher) and assume you are booking directly and not through a tourist office. Off-season prices go soft. All recommended B&Bs have no traffic noise and are strictly nonsmoking in the bedrooms and breakfast room.

Millfield Guest House, run by Liz and Ed Broomfield, is thoughtfully furnished with antique class, a rare sit-and-chat ambience, and a comfy TV lounge. Since the showers are down the hall, you'll get spacious rooms and great prices (S-£21, D-£35–36, T-£48–52, CC:VM, CC reservation allows for late arrival, 12 Marchhall Road, EH16 5HR, tel. 0131/667-4428). Decipher the breakfast prayer by Robert Burns. Then try the "Taste of Scotland" breakfast option. See how many stone (14 pounds) you weigh in the elegant throne room. This place is worth calling well in advance.

Turret Guest House is teddy-on-the-beddy cozy with a great

Edinburgh, Our Neighborhood

TO EDINBURGH CITY CENTRE (10 MIN BY BUS)

SALISBURY CRAGS →

H O L Y R O O D   P A R K

ARTHUR'S SEAT 823'

BUS # 21

QUEEN'S DRIVE

CLIFFS

LION'S HAUNCH

ST. LEONARD'S ST

HOLYROOD PARK RD

E. PRESTON

BUS # 3, 7, 8, 31, 37 & 81

ROYAL COMMONWEALTH POOL

¼ MILE

S. CLERK

NEWINGTON

SALISBURY RD

MARCHALL PLACE

P R E S T O N F I E L D

MARCHALL ROAD

G O L F   C O U R S E

PRIESTFIELD

MINTO

BLACKET AVE.

BUS # 21, 33, 82, 86

EAST MAYFIELD

QUEEN'S CRESCENT

KILMAURS RD

KIRKHILL

PRIESTFIELD ROAD

DRIVE

PRIESTFIELD AVE

CEMETERY

DCH

DALKEITH ROAD BECOMES A 68 SOUTH TO BORDERS & ENGLAND

❶ MILLFIELD GUEST HOUSE
❷ RAVENSNEUK & BELFORD G.H.
❸ DUNEDIN & KENVIE G. H.
❹ DORSTAN HOTEL
❺ RECOMMENDED EATERIES
❻ LAUNDRETTE, GROCERIES & EATERIES
❼ TURRET GUEST HOUSE
❽ SALISBURY HOTEL
❾ ARD-NA-SAID B&B

ST MAYFIELD

bay-windowed family room and a vast breakfast menu that includes haggis and vegetarian options (S-£18–24, D-£36–40, Db-£42–54, £2-per-person discount with this book, cheaper off-season, 8 Kilmaurs Terrace, tel. 0131/667-6704, Mrs. Jackie Cameron).

Kenvie Guest House, well and warmly run by Dorothy Vidler, comes with lots of personal touches (one small twin-£36, D-£39, Db-£47, family deals, 3 percent more with CC, 16 Kilmaurs Road, EH16 5DA, tel. & fax 0131/668-1964).

The comfortable and very Victorian **Ravensneuk Guest House** is also good (D-£42, Db-£52, 5 percent discount with cash and this book, family deals, CC:VMA, great lounge, 11 Blacket Avenue, EH9 1RR, tel. & fax 0131/667-5347, Chris and Toni Henry).

Highland Park House is simple, bright, and friendly (S-£20, D-£38 with this book, family deals, 16 Kilmaurs Terrace, tel. 0131/667-9204, Margaret and Brian Love).

Ard-Na-Said B&B is an elegant 1875 Victorian house with a comfy lounge and fine rooms (Db-£44–48, family deals, 5 Priestfield Road, EH16 5HH, tel. 0131/667-8754, fax 0131/271-0960, enthusiastically run by Jim and Olive Lyons).

Salisbury Hotel fills a classy old Georgian building with 12 rooms, a large cushy lounge, and even a dumbwaiter in the breakfast room. It's more like a hotel than its neighbors but run with B&B warmth by Brenda Wright (D-£46, Db-£50; D-£48 and Db-£54 in July and August; 5 percent off with cash and this book, CC:VM, 45 Salisbury Road, EH16 5AA, tel. & fax 0131/667-1264, e-mail: brenda.wright@btinternet.com).

Dunedin Guest House is bright, Scottish, and a good value (seven rooms, S-£22–27, Db-£44–54, family deals, strong showers, NASA lighting, TVs with satellite channels in rooms, e-mail access, Scotland and Edinburgh videos in lounge, 8 Priestfield Road, EH16 5HH, tel. 0131/668-1949, fax 0131/668-2181, Annette and Max Preston).

Dorstan Private Hotel is small and personable, but professional and hotelesque with all the comforts. Several of its 14 prim rooms are on the ground floor (Ds-£58, Db-£66, family rooms, CC:VMA, 7 Priestfield Road, EH16 5HJ, tel. 0131/667-6721, fax 0131/668-4644, e-mail: reservations@dorstan-hotel.demon.co.uk, Mairae Campbell).

Priestville B&B is a big old place with charming rough edges (D-£38, Db-£44, family deals, 10 Priestfield Road, tel. 0131/667-2435).

Belford House is a tidy and simple place offering good rooms and a warm welcome (D-£40, Db-£50, family deals, CC:VM, 13 Blacket Avenue, tel. 0131/667-2422, Isa and Tom Borthwick).

Big, Modern, Cheap Hotels in the Center

Ibis Hotel, mid–Royal Mile behind Tron Church, is perfectly located with 97 soulless but clean and comfy rooms and American charm (Db-£55 all year, breakfast is extra, CC:VMA, some nonsmoking rooms, elevator, 6 Hunter Square, EH1 1QW, tel. 0131/240-7000, fax 0131/240-7007). Considering its location and the costs of other hotels in town, this is a great deal.

Travel Inn, the biggest hotel in Edinburgh, has even less character but a great price and a mediocre location about a mile from the Mile. Each of its 280 rooms are modern and comfortable, with a sofa that folds out for two kids if necessary (Db-£40 for two adults and up to two kids under 15, breakfast is extra, CC:VMA, elevators, nonsmoking rooms, weekends booked long in advance, near Haymarket station just west of the castle at 1 Morrison Link, EH3 8DN, tel. 0131/228-9819, fax 0131/228-9836, Web site: www.travelinn.co.uk).

Hostels

Although Edinburgh's hostels are well run, open to all, and provide £10 bunk beds (an £8-12 savings over B&Bs), they don't include breakfast and are scruffy.

Castle Rock Hostel is hip and easygoing, offering cheap

beds, plenty of friends, and a great central location just below the castle and above the pubs with all the folk music (15 Johnston Terrace, tel. 0131/225-9666). They run another backpackers' place at 105 High Street.

For more regulations and less color, try the IYH hostels: **Bruntsfield Hostel** (on a park, six to 10 beds per room, 7 Bruntsfield Crescent, buses #11, #15, and #16 to and from Princes Street, tel. 0131/447-2994) and **Edinburgh Hostel** (four to 22 beds per room, 18 Eglinton Crescent, tel. 0131/337-1120).

Eating in Edinburgh

Eating Along the Royal Mile
Historic pubs and doily cafés with reasonable, unremarkable meals abound. But, since chefs seem to come and go with the seasons, I have no splurge meals to recommend. These are simply handy, affordable places for a good bite to eat (listed in downhill order). **Deacon Brodie's Pub** serves soup, sandwiches, and snacks on the ground floor and good £7 meals upstairs (daily 12:00–22:00, tel. 0131/225-6531). Or munch prayerfully in the **Lower Aisle** restaurant under St. Giles Cathedral (Monday–Friday 10:00–16:30). **Bann's Vegetarian Café** serves carnivore-pleasing veggie cuisine that goes way beyond tofu and granola (daily 10:00–23:00, just off South Bridge behind the Tron Church at 5 Hunter Square, tel. 0131/226-1112). For a break from the touristic grind, consider the **Elephant House** where locals browse newspapers, listen to classic rock, and sip coffee or munch a light meal (daily, three blocks south of Royal Mile at 21 George IV Bridge, tel. 0131/220-5355). **Food Plantation** has good, inexpensive fresh sandwiches to eat-in or take-out (274 Canongate). **Brambles Tea Room** serves light lunches and Starbucks coffee (next to Huntley House at 158 Canongate). **Clarinda's Tea Room**, near the bottom of the Royal Mile, is a charming and tasty place for a break after touring the Mile or palace (daily 9:00–16:45).

Grassmarket Street, below the castle, is lined with sloppy eateries and noisy pubs. This is the place for live folk music. If you want dinner to melt into your beer, eat here.

Lunch in the New Town
Waverley Center Food Court, below the TI and above the station, is a food circus of sticky fast-food joints (including **The Scot's Pantry** for quick traditional edibles) littered with paper plates and shoppers. Local office workers pile into **Lanterna** for good Italian food (family-run, fresh and friendly for lunch or dinner, 83 Hanover Street, two blocks off Princes Street, tel. 0131/226-3090). For a generation, New Town vegetarians have munched salads at **Henderson's Salad Table and Wine Bar**

(Monday–Saturday 8:00–22:45, closed Sunday, nonsmoking section, strictly vegetarian, between Queen and George Streets at 94 Hanover Street, tel. 0131/225-2131). Rose Street has tubs of pubs.

Eating in Dalkeith Road Area, near Your B&B

The following places are within a five-minute walk of the recommended B&Bs. Most are among a cluster of simple eateries within a block of the corner of Newington and Preston Streets. For a fun local atmosphere that makes up for the food and smoke, the **Wine Glass Pub** serves filling "basket meals" (£4, Sunday–Thursday 18:00–20:30). **Chinatown**, next to the Wine Glass, is a delightful little Chinese restaurant (moderate prices, 17:30–23:30, closed Monday, reservations are wise, tel. 0131/662-0555). **Brattisanis** is your basic *chippie* (lousy milkshakes, great haggis, 87 Newington Road). **Chatterbox** is fine for a light meal with tea (8:30–20:00, down East Preston from the pool). **Jade Palace** has tasty Chinese food (takeout only, closed Tuesday, 212 Dalkeith Road). The huge Commonwealth Pool's **Café Aqua** is a noisy cafeteria for hungry swimmers and budget travelers (pass the entry without paying, sit with a poolside view). **Minto Hotel's bar/restaurant** serves a good high tea—hot bar dinner with tea and scones—for £8 (daily 17:00–21:00, corner of Mayfield Terrace and Minto Street, tel. 0131/668-1234).

Transportation Connections—Edinburgh

By train to: Inverness (7/day, 4 hrs), **Oban** (3/day, change in Glasgow, 4.5 hrs), **York** (hrly, 2.5 hrs), **London** (hrly, 5 hrs), **Durham** (hrly, 2 hrs), **Lake District** (south past Carlisle to Penrith, catch bus to Keswick; 6/day, 40 min), **Birmingham** (6/day, 4.5 hrs), **Crewe** (6/day, 3.5 hrs). Train info tel. 0345/484-950.

By bus to: Oban (3/day, 4 hrs, £12), **Fort William** (3/day, 4 hrs, £12), **Inverness** (4/day, 4 hrs, £12). For bus info, call National Express (tel. 0990-808-080) or Scottish Citylink (tel. 0990-505-050).

DUBLIN

With reminders of its stirring history and rich culture on every corner, Ireland's capital and largest city is a sightseer's delight. Dublin's fair city will have you humming "Alive, alive-O."

Founded as a Viking trading settlement in the ninth century, Dublin grew to be a center of wealth and commerce second only to London in the United Kingdom. Dublin, the seat of English rule in Ireland for 700 years, was the heart of a "civilized" Anglo-Irish area (eastern Ireland) known as "the Pale." Anything "beyond the Pale" was considered uncultured and almost barbaric . . . purely Irish.

The Golden Age of English Dublin was the 18th century. Britain was on a roll and Dublin was Britain's second city. Largely rebuilt during this Georgian era, Dublin became an elegant and cultured capital. Everything was OK until nationalism and human rights got in the way. The ideas of the French Revolution inspired Irish intellectuals to buck British rule and, after the revolt of 1798, life in Dublin was never quite the same. But the 18th century left a lasting imprint on the city. Georgian (that's British for neoclassical) squares and boulevards gave the city a grand elegance. The National Museum, National Gallery, and many government buildings are in the Georgian section of town. Few buildings (notably St. Patrick's Cathedral and Christchurch Cathedral) predate this Georgian period.

In the 19th century, with the closing of the Irish Parliament, the famine, and the beginnings of the struggle for independence, Dublin was treated and felt more like a colony than a partner. The tension culminated in the Rising of 1916 and the battle that followed. While many of Dublin's grand streets were left in ruins, the city emerged as the capital of the only former colony in Europe.

While bullet-pocked buildings and dramatic statues keep

memories of Ireland's recent struggle for independence alive, the city is looking to a bright future. Visitors enjoy a big-town cultural scene wrapped in a small-town smile.

Planning Your Time

On a two-week trip through Ireland, Dublin deserves three nights and two days. Consider this sightseeing plan:

Day 1: 9:30—Dublin Experience, 10:30—Trinity College walk, 11:00—Book of Kells and Old Library, 12:00—Browse Grafton Street, lunch there or picnic on St. Stephen's Green, 13:30—National Museum, 15:00—Historical town walk, 17:00—Return to hotel, rest, dinner, 19:30—Evening walk (literary or musical), 22:00—Irish music in Temple Bar area.

Day 2: 10:00—Kilmainham Jail, 12:00—Guinness Brewery tour, 13:30—Lunch (with a faint buzz), 15:00—Tour Dublin Castle, Evening—Catch a play or concert.

Orientation (tel. code: 01)

Greater Dublin sprawls with about 1 million people—nearly a third of the country's population. But the center of touristic interest is a tight triangle between O'Connell Bridge, St. Stephen's Green, and Christchurch Cathedral. Within this triangle you'll find Trinity College (Book of Kells), Grafton Street (top pedestrian shopping zone), Temple Bar (trendy nightlife center), Dublin Castle, and the hub of most city tours and buses.

The River Liffey cuts the town in two. Focus on the southern half (where nearly all your sightseeing will take place). Dublin's main drag, O'Connell Street (near the Abbey Theater and outdoor produce market), stretches from the very central O'Connell Bridge north of the river. Over the river this main city axis continues—mostly as Grafton Street—to St. Stephen's Green. Only the Kilmainham Jail and the Guinness Brewery (both west of the center) are outside your home triangle.

Tourist Information

The TI fills an old church on Suffolk Street (a block off Grafton Street). While packed with tourists, promotional brochures, an American Express office, a café, and traditional knickknacks, it's short on hard info. Less crowded but equally helpful TI branches are on Baggot Street and at the airport (daily 8:00–22:00). To talk to the TI on the phone, you'll pay 60p per minute (1-850-230-230)—welcome to Dublin. The TI gives a free newspaper with a lousy map, lots of advertisements, and the fliers that fill racks all over town. The best extensive publication they offer is *Dublin's Top Visitor Attractions* (which you can buy for £2.50 at the TI bookshop without any wait). This has a map and the latest on all the town's sights (many more than I list here). For a schedule of happenings in town, buy the excellent *In Dublin* at any newsstand (fortnightly, £1.95).

Helpful Hints

Cyber Cafés: On the north side of town, try Global Internet Café (£5/hr, 8 Lower O'Connell St., tel. 01/878-0295). On the south side, try Planet Cybercafé (£4.50/hr, 23 South Great George's Street, tel. 01/679-0583).

Bikes: Bikes can be rented at Dublin Bike Hire (27 North Great Georges Street, tel. 01/878-8473).

Arrival in Dublin

By Train: Trains arrive at Heuston Station (serving the west and southwest) on the west end of town. Dublin's second train station, Connolly Station (serving the north, northwest, and Rosslare), is closer to the center—a 10-minute walk from O'Connell Bridge. Each station has a luggage-check facility.

Bus 90 connects both train stations and the bus station and the city center (60p flat fee, 6/hrly, runs along river).

By Bus: Bus Eireann, Ireland's national bus company, uses the Busaras Central Bus Station next to Connolly Station (catch bus #90 to the city center).

By Ferry: Irish Ferries dock at the mouth of the River Liffey (near the town center) while the Stena Line docks at Dun Laoghaire (easy DART train connections into Dublin, at least 3/hrly, 15 min).

By Plane: From the airport, milk-run buses #41 and #41C go to O'Connell Bridge (£1.10, 3/hrly). The faster Airlink direct bus connects the airport with the Heuston train station and Busaras bus station near Connolly Station (£2.50, 4/hrly, 30 min). Taxis from the airport into Dublin cost about £10.

Getting Around Dublin

You'll do most of Dublin on foot. Big green buses are cheap and cover the city. Most lines start at the four Quays nearest O'Connell Bridge. Tell the driver where you're going and he'll ask for 60p (one to five stops) or 80p (five to 10 stops). The bus office at 59 Upper O'Connell Street has free "route network" maps and sells bus passes (one-day pass-£3.30 adults, £5.50 per family, four-day adult Explorer pass-£10.00, bus information tel. 01/873-4222). DART trains connect Dublin with Dun Laoghaire (ferry terminal and recommended B&Bs, at least 3/hrly, 15 min, £1.10). Taxis seem honest, and they are good sources of information (£4 for most downtown rides).

Tours of Dublin

While the physical treasures of Dublin are mediocre by European standards, the city has a fine story to tell and people with a natural knack for telling it. It's a good town for walking tours—and the competition is fierce for your business. You'll find pamphlets touting creative walks all over town. There are medieval walks, literary walks, Georgian Dublin walks, and more. The two evening walks are great ways to meet other travelers.

Historical Walking Tour—This is your best introductory walk. A group of hardworking history graduates—many who claim to have done more than just kiss the Blarney Stone—fill Dublin's basic historic strip (Trinity College, Old Parliament House, Dublin Castle, and Christchurch Cathedral) with the story of their city from its Viking origin to the present. You stand in front of buildings that aren't much to see but are lots to talk about and listen to your guide's story. Guides talk at length about "the Troubles" and the roots of Ireland's struggle with Britain (£5, two hours, depart from gate of Trinity College, daily 11:00, 12:00, 15:00; Saturday and Sunday only 12:00 in winter; tel. 01/878-0227).

Jameson Literary Pub Crawl—Two actors take 30 or so tourists on a walk stopping at four pubs. Half the time is spent enjoying their entertaining banter which introduces the novice to the high *craic* (conversation) of Joyce, O'Casey, and Yeats. The 2.5-hour tour is punctuated with 20-minute pub breaks (free time). It can be great fun socially, but the content suffers. Meet any night at 19:30 (plus Sunday at noon) in the Duke Pub off Grafton on Duke Street (£6, runs three nights a week in winter, tel. 01/670-5602).

Traditional Irish-Music Pub Crawl—This is like the literary pub crawl but features music. You meet at 19:30 at Gogarty's Pub (in the Temple Bar area) and spend 20 minutes in the upstairs rooms of four pubs listening to two musicians talk about, play, and sing traditional Irish music. While having only two musicians makes the music a bit thin and Irish music aficionados will tell you you're better off just finding a good session, the evening—while touristy—is not gimmicky. The musicians demonstrate four instruments and really enjoy introducing rookies to their art (£6 plus beer, nightly May–October, weekends only in winter, allow 2.5 hours, tel. 01/478-0191).

Hop On/Hop Off Bus Tours—Several companies offer the basic center-of-Dublin orientation. Dublin City Tour (£7, tel. 01/873-4222) and Guide Friday (£7, tel. 01/676-5377) do identical 90-minute circuits of the town allowing you to hop on and hop off at your choice of 10 stops (two buses/hour—mostly topless—with running commentaries; they go to Guinness Brewery but not to Kilmainham Jail). Just hop on and pay the driver. Your ticket's good for the entire day. Buses, which leave about every 10 minutes from about 9:30 to 18:00, are especially enjoyable for photographers on sunny days. One ticket gets you on either company's buses.

Sights—Dublin's Trinity College

▲**Trinity College**—Started in 1592 by Queen Elizabeth I to establish a Protestant way of thinking about God, Trinity has long been Ireland's most prestigious college. Originally the student body was limited to rich, Protestant males. Women were admitted in 1903 and Catholics, while allowed entrance by the school much earlier, were given permission to study at Trinity in the 1970s. Today half of Trinity's 11,000 students are women and 70 percent are culturally Catholic (although only about 20 percent of Irish youth are churchgoing).

▲**Trinity College Tour**—Inside the gate of Trinity, students organize and lead 30-minute tours of their campus. You'll get a rundown on the mostly Georgian architecture, a peek at student life, both in the early days and today, and mostly enjoy a chance to hang out with a witty Irish college kid as he talks about his school (daily 10:00–15:30, the £4.50 tour fee includes the £3.50 fee to see the Book of Kells where the tour leaves you).

▲▲▲**Book of Kells/Trinity Old Library**—The 65-meter-long main chamber of the Old Library (from 1732) is home to an original copy of the 1916 Proclamation of the Irish Republic, the oldest Irish harp (from the 15th century), and, stacked to its towering ceiling, 200,000 of the library's oldest books. The artistic prize of the library—and all Ireland—is the magnificent Book of Kells, stored in the treasury. A first-class exhibit puts the 680-page illuminated manuscript in its historical and cultural context and prepares you for the original book and other precious manuscripts in the collection.

Written on vellum (baby sheepskin) in the ninth century—probably by Irish monks in Iona (Scotland)—and taken to the Irish monastery at Kells in 806 after a series of Viking raids, this enthusiastically decorated copy of the four gospels is arguably the finest piece of art from what is generally called the Dark Ages. It shows how monastic life in this far fringe of Europe was far from dark. The book has been bound into four separate volumes. At any given time, two of the gospels are on display. You'll see four richly decorated 1,200-year-old pages—two text and two decorated cover pages—under glass (£3.50, at Trinity College Library, Monday–Saturday 9:30–17:00, Sunday 9:30–16:30, shorter hours off-season, tel. 01/608-1171). The library also displays the Book of Armagh (A.D. 807) and the Book of Durrow (A.D. 680), neither of which can be checked out.

▲▲**The Dublin Experience**—Shown in a modern building next to the Trinity Old Library, this 40-minute video giving a historic introduction to Dublin is one more tourist movie with the sound turned up. It's good—offering a fine sweeping introduction to the story of Ireland—but pricey and riding on the coattails of the Book of Kells (£3, save a little with a combo Kells/video ticket,

Dublin

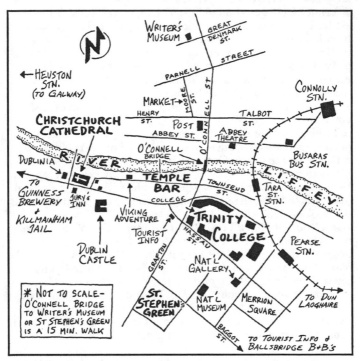

daily 10:00–17:00 on the hour, in the modern arts building next to Trinity College Library).

More Sights—Dublin

▲▲**Dublin Castle**—Built on the spot of the first Viking fortress, this castle was the seat of British rule in Ireland for 700 years (until 1922). Located where the Poddle and Liffey Rivers came together making a black pool ("*dubh linn*" in Irish), Dublin Castle was the official residence of the Viceroy, who implemented the will of the British royalty. Today it's used for fancy state and charity functions. The 45-minute tours offer a room-by-room walk through the lavish state apartments of this most English of Irish palaces (£2.50, about 4/hrly, Monday–Friday 10:00–17:00, weekends 14:00–17:00, tel. 01/677-7129). The tour finishes with a look at the foundations of the Norman tower and the best remaining chunk of the 13th-century town wall.

▲**Dublin's Viking Adventure**—This really is an adventure. You start in a box of seats that transforms into a Viking ship. Your chieftain joins you and suddenly you're in a storm, waves splash, smoke rolls, and you land in a kind of Viking summer camp where you spend 30 minutes being shuttled from one friendly original Dubliner to the next (a trader, a sassy maiden, a monk building a church, and so on). A short film about the Vikings follows with a look at artifacts recently uncovered in the adjacent excavation sight. It feels hokey, but the cast is certainly hardworking and you leave feeling if not having visited a Viking town, at least having visited the set for a B-grade Viking movie. It's on Essex Street a block off the riverside Essex Quay in Temple Bar—exactly where the Vikings established their first Dublin settlement in 841 (£4.75, Tuesday–Saturday 10:00–16:30, closed Sunday and Monday, tel. 01/679-6040).

Dublinia—This tries and fails to be a "bridge to Dublin's medieval past." The amateurish look at the medieval town starts with a goofy 12-minute Walkman tour followed by a few rooms of medieval exhibits, and finishes with a hard-to-follow movie dramatizing medieval political wrangling. Possibly entertaining for a school field trip, it just isn't worth the £4 or time (daily 10:00–17:00, less in winter, tel. 01/679-4611). The ticket does get you a tower-top city view and into Christchurch Cathedral (£1 otherwise).

Christchurch Cathedral—The oldest building in Dublin, the cathedral marks the spot where the Vikings established their town on the river. The first church here was built of wood in 1038 by King Sitric. The present structure dates from a mix of periods: Norman, Gothic, and mostly Victorian neo-Gothic (1870s restoration work). Because of its British past, neither of Dublin's two top churches are Catholic. Christchurch Cathedral and the nearby St. Patrick's Cathedral are both from the Church of Ireland. In Catholic Ireland they feel hollow and are more famous than visit-worthy.

▲▲▲National Museum—Showing off the treasures of Ireland from the Stone Age to the 20th century, this museum is wonderfully digestible under one dome. Ireland's Bronze Age gold fills the center. The prehistoric Ireland exhibit rings the gold, and in a corner you'll find the treasury with the most famous pieces (brooches, chalices, and other examples of Celtic metalwork) and an 18-minute video giving an overview of Irish art through the 13th century. Jumping way ahead, a special corridor features *The Road to Independence* with guns, letters, and death masks recalling the fitful birth of the "Terrible Beauty" (1900–1921 with a focus on the Easter Rising of 1916). The best Viking artifacts in town are upstairs (museum is free, Tuesday–Saturday 10:00–17:00, Sunday 14:00–17:00, closed Monday, between Trinity College and St. Stephen's Green on Kildare Street, tel. 01/677-7444). Greatest-hits tours are given several times a day (£1, 45 minutes, call for schedule).

National Gallery—Along with a hall featuring the work of top Irish painters, this has Ireland's best collection of paintings by the

European masters. It's impressive—unless you've been to London or Paris (free, Monday–Saturday 10:00–17:30, Thursday until 20:30, Sunday 14:00–17:00, tel. 01/661-5133).

Streets, Squares, and Parks—Dublin

▲**Grafton Street**—Once filled with noisy traffic, today Grafton Street is Dublin's liveliest pedestrian shopping mall. You'll find colorful pubs, fancy shops, singing buskers, and lots of browsers. The Powerscourt Townhouse Shopping Centre (nearby on William Street South) is a hit with shoppers. Grafton Street connects Trinity College with St. Stephen's Green.

▲**St. Stephen's Green**—This city park, originally a medieval commons, was enclosed in 1664 and gradually surrounded with fine Georgian buildings. Today it provides 22 acres of grassy refuge for Dubliners.

Merrion Square—This square offers an insider's look at Georgian Dublin. Tour the carefully restored house at **Number 29 Lower Fitzwilliam Street** for a walk through a Dublin home in 1790 (£2.50, Tuesday–Saturday 10:00–17:00, Sunday 14:00–17:00, closed Monday). Notice the fine doors around the square—a Dublin trademark—and the elegant Georgian knobs and knockers.

▲**O'Connell Street and surroundings**—Dublin's grandest street leads from O'Connell Bridge through the heart of north Dublin. Since the 1740s it's been a 45-meter-wide promenade. Ever since the first O'Connell Bridge connected it to the Trinity side of town in 1794, it's been Dublin's main drag. The street, while lined with fast-food and souvenir shops, echoes with history. Much of the fighting during the 1916 Easter Rising and the Civil War a few years later took place here. The imposing **General Post Office** is where Patrick Pearse read the Proclamation of Irish Independence. The GPO building itself—a kind of Irish Alamo—was the rebel headquarters and scene of a five-day bloody siege during the Rising. While there's little to see, its facade remains pockmarked with bullet holes.

The statues lining the street celebrate great figures in Ireland's fight for independence. One monument that didn't—a tall column crowned by a statue of the British hero of Trafalgar, Admiral Nelson—was blown up in 1966 as locals celebrated the 50th anniversary of the Rising.

Make a point to get away from tourists' Dublin. A good way to do that is to stroll the smaller streets north of the Liffey. Just a block west of O'Connell Street, the **Moore Street Market** is a colorful commotion of produce and hawkers. For workaday Dublin, the long pedestrian mall of Mary Street, Henry Street, and Talbot Street is a people-watcher's delight.

Explore. The prestigious **Abbey Theatre**, now a modern, ugly building, is still the much-loved home of the Irish National Theater (a block off the river on Abbey Street). **St. Mary's Pro-Cathedral** is the leading Catholic church in town, but curiously not a cathedral since Christchurch was made one in the 12th century (the pope chose to ignore the fact that it hasn't been Catholic for centuries). The Georgian **Parnell Square** has a Garden of Remembrance honoring the victims of the 1916 Rising.

The **Dublin Writers' Museum** is a must for anyone interested in Irish literature; it features the lives and works of Dublin's greats (£3, daily 10:00–18:00, 18 Parnell Square North, tel. 01/872-2077). With hometown wits such as Swift, Yeats, Joyce, and Shaw, literary fans will have a checklist of residences and memorials to see.

▲▲**Temple Bar**—For many visitors the heart of Dublin is its hot and much-promoted nightlife center, the Temple Bar district. While promoted as Dublin's "Left Bank," it's actually on the right bank (as central as can be and just south of the river). It's a pedestrians-only hive of creative energy day and night. The central Meeting House Square (just off Essex Street) hosts free street theater and is surrounded by interesting cultural centers. For a listing of events, visit the Temple Bar Information Centre (Eustace Street, tel. 01/671-5717). Trendy shops, cafés, theaters, galleries, pubs with live music, and restaurants (Italian, American, and even Irish) vie for your attention. Rather than follow particular recommendations, simply wander the main drag and venture down a few side lanes to see what looks good. Touristy **Gallagher's Boxty House** is a good bet for traditional Irish food (call to get your name on the waiting list at peak times, 01/677-2762). You'd eat their boxty (a stuffed dinner pancake) or Irish stew in anticipation of a famine. The **Bad Ass Café** remains as popular as can be (students-in-a-warehouse ambience, vegetarian and Italian). Pub grub abounds. (To get some folk music away from the tourist crowds, walk five minutes up the river to **Merchants Quay** where, on Lower Bridge Street, you'll find the Merchants Pub and the Brazen Head.) The pedestrian-only Ha' Penny Bridge, named for the half-pence toll originally levied from those who walked it, leads over the Liffey to Temple Bar. ("Bar" means a walkway along the river.)

Sights—Outer Dublin

The Jail and the Guinness Brewery are the only sights outside of the old center. Combine these in one visit.

▲▲▲**Kilmainham Gaol (Jail)**—Opened in 1796 as the Dublin County Jail and a debtors' prison and considered a model in its day, it was used frequently as a political prison by the British. Many of those who fought for Irish independence were held or executed here, including leaders of the rebellions of 1798, 1803, 1848, 1867, and 1916 (most notably Robert Emmett and Charles Stewart Parnell).

The last prisoner to be held here was Eamon de Valera (later president of Ireland). He was released on July 16, 1924, the day Kilmainham was finally shut down. The buildings, virtually in ruins, were restored in the 1960s. Today it's a shrine to the Nathan Hales of Ireland.

Your visit starts with an excellent exhibit on Ireland's fight for independence, followed by a 30-minute video. Then a guide shows you around for another 30 minutes. Touring the cells and places of execution while hearing tales of terrible colonialism and heroic patriotism—alongside Irish schoolkids who know these names well—is moving. Finally the museum explains Victorian prison life and the battle for independence. Don't miss the dimly lit hall off the second floor displaying the stirring last letters patriots sent to loved ones hours before facing the firing squad (£3, daily 9:30–18:00, tours on the hour except last tour at 16:45; off-season Sunday–Friday 10:00–17:00, closed Saturday; £4 taxi, bus #51 or #79 from Aston Quay, tel. 01/453-5984).

▲Guinness Brewery—A visit to the Guinness Hop Store is almost a pilgrimage for many. The home of Ireland's national beer welcomes visitors (for £4) with a museum, video, and drink. Arthur Guinness began brewing the famous stout here in 1759. By 1868 it was the biggest brewery in the world. Today the sprawling brewery fills several city blocks. Around the world Guinness brews more than 10 million glasses a day. You can learn as much or as little about the brewing process as you like. Highlights are the cooperage (with old film clips showing the master wood-kegmakers plying their now extinct trade) and a display of the brewery's clever ads. The video is a well-done ad for the brew that makes you feel almost patriotic as you run down to the sample bar to turn in your coupons for a pint of the real thing (£4, Monday–Saturday 9:30–17:00, Sunday 10:30–16:30, enter on Crane Street off Thomas Street, bus #78A from Aston Quay near O'Connell Bridge, or bus #123 from Dame Street and O'Connell Street, tel. 01/453-6700 ext. 5155). Hop on, hop off bus tours stop here. (Why is there no museum of Irish alcoholism, which is a serious but rarely discussed problem in this land where the social world seems to float in a sea of beer?)

Entertainment and Theater in Dublin

Ireland produced some of the finest writers in both English and Gaelic, and Dublin houses some of Europe's finest theaters. While Handel's *Messiah* was first performed in Dublin (1742), these days Dublin is famous for its rock bands (U2, Thin Lizzie, and Sinead O'Conner all got started here).

You have much to choose from: Abbey Theatre is Ireland's national theater. Gate Theatre does foreign plays as well as Irish classics. Point Theatre, once a railway terminus, is now the country's top live music venue. At the National Concert Hall, the

National Symphony Orchestra performs most Friday evenings.
Street theater takes the stage in Temple Bar on summer evenings.
Folk music rings in the pubs, and street entertainers are everywhere. For the latest, pick up the free *Dublin Event Guide* or a
copy of the twice-monthly *In Dublin* (£2, any newsstand).

Irish Music in nearby Dun Laoghaire
For an evening of pure Irish music, song, and dance, check out the
Comhaltas Ceoltoiri Eireann, an association working to preserve
this traditional slice of Irish culture. It got started when Elvis and
company threatened to steal the musical heart of the new generation. Judging by the pop status of traditional Irish music these days,
Comhaltas accomplished its mission. Their "Fonntrai" evening is a
costumed stage show mixing traditional music, song, and dance (£5,
Monday–Thursday at 21:00 mid-June–August). These are followed
by an informal music session at 22:30. Fridays all year long they
have a Cailidh where everyone dances (£5, 21:30–00:30). Saturday
nights feature an informal session by the fireside. Performances are
held in the Cuturlann na Eireann, near the Seapoint DART stop or
a 20-minute walk from Dun Laoghaire, at 32 Belgrave Square,
Monkstown (tel. 01/280-0295). Their bar is free, and often filled
with music.

Sleeping in Dublin
(£1 = about $1.50, tel. code: 01)
Sleep Code: **S** = Single, **D** = Double/Twin, **T** = Triple, **Q** = Quad,
b = bathroom, **t** = toilet only, **s** = shower only, **CC** = Credit Card
(Visa, MasterCard, Amex).
    Dublin is popular and rooms can be tight. Big and practical
places (both cheap and moderate) are most central at Christchurch
on the edge of Temple Bar. For classy, older Dublin accommodations you'll pay more and stay a bit farther out in the direction of
Ballsbridge (embassy row). For a small-town escape with the best
budget values, side-trip by the convenient DART train (at least
3/hrly, 15 min) from nearby Dun Laoghaire (see below).

Sleeping in Christchurch
These places each face Christchurch Cathedral, a great locale a
five-minute walk from the best evening scene at Temple Bar and
eight minutes from the sightseeing center (Trinity College). Buses
#50, #54, #65, and #77 stop here. For an easy meal near your
hotel, try the popular Leo Burdocks Fish & Chips (2 Werburgh
Street, off Christchurch).
    Jurys Christchurch Inn, like its sister in Galway, is well-
located offering business-class comfort in all its identical rooms.
This no-nonsense, modern, American-style hotel has a winning
keep-it-simple-and-affordable formula. If old is getting old (and

you don't mind big bus-tour groups), you won't find a better value in town. All 180 rooms cost the same: £60 for one, two, or three adults, or two adults and two kids, breakfast not included. Each room has a modern bathroom, direct-dial telephone, and TV. One floor is strictly nonsmoking. Request a room far from the noisy elevator (CC:VMA, Christchurch Place, Dublin 8, tel. 01/454-0000, fax 01/454-0012, United States tel. 800/843-3311). A 234-room **Jurys Custom House Inn** (£60, tel. 01/607-5000) is on Custom House Quay in Dublin.

Kinlay House, across the square from Jurys Christchurch Inn, is its backpackers' equivalent—definitely the place to go for cheap beds with a good location, privacy, and an all-ages-welcome atmosphere. This huge, red-brick, 19th-century Victorian building has 120 metal, prison-style beds in spartan, smoke-free rooms: singles, doubles, and four- to six-bed dorms (generally coed). It fills up most days. Call well in advance, especially for summer weekends (S-£20, D-£30, Db-£34, dorm beds-£13, includes continental breakfast, self-catering kitchen, launderette, left luggage, and so on, Christchurch, 2-12 Lord Edward Street, Dublin 2, tel. 01/679-6644, fax 01/679-7437, e-mail: kindub @usit.ie). If Kinlay is full, a similar place is the well-located **Avalon House** (D-£30, Db-£32, dorm beds-£7.50–10.50, south of Temple Bar at 55 Aungier Street, tel. 01/475-0001, fax 01/475-0303, Web site: www.avalon-house.ie, e-mail: info @avalon-house.ie).

Harding Hotel is a hardwood, 20th-century, Viking-style place with 53 hotelesque rooms. The hotel is as comfortable as Jurys but on a more intimate scale and without the tour-group scene (Sb-£45, Db/Tb-£60, breakfast extra, CC:VM, Copper Alley across the street from Christchurch, tel. 01/679-6500, fax 01/679-6504, Web site: www.iol.ie/usitaccm/, e-mail: harding@usit.ie).

Sleeping East of St. Stephen's Green
The Fitzwilliam rents 13 hotelish rooms in a classy guesthouse (Sb-£45, Db-£80, CC:VMA, 41 Upper Fitzwilliam Street, Dublin 2, tel. 01/662-5155, fax 01/676-7488).

Mespil Hotel is a huge, modern, business-class hotel renting 153 identical three-star rooms, each with all the comforts and at a very good price. Half the rooms overlook a canal greenbelt (Sb, Db, or Tb-£78, continental breakfast-£6, Irish breakfast-£9, elevator, one nonsmoking floor, CC:VMA, Mespil Road, Dublin 4, tel. 01/667-1222, fax 01/667-1244, e-mail: mespil@leehotels.ie).

Albany House is Georgian throughout and completely smoke-free. Each of the 33 rooms is tastefully designed with old elegance and modern comfort. Request the huge "superior" rooms which are the same price (Sb-£70, Db-£100, £80 in slow times, back rooms are generally bigger and quieter, the included breakfast is a healthy first-class continental buffet, CC:VMA, one block south of St. Stephen's Green at 84 Harcourt Street, Dublin 2, tel. 01/475-1092, fax 01/475-1093, e-mail: albany@indigo.ie).

Kilronan House, a classy Georgian-style B&B on a whispy tree-lined street, comes with lots of marble, gilding, chandeliers, and a professional staff (Sb-£50, Db-£80, CC:VM, two blocks south of St. Stephen's Green at 70 Adelaide Road, Dublin 2, tel. 01/755-266, fax 01/782-841).

The next three listings are on Northumberland Road. While Trinity College is only a 15-minute walk away, buses #7, #7A, and #8 (to O'Connell Street) lumber down Northumberland Road to the city center every 10 minutes.

Northumberland Lodge is a quiet, elegant mansion. Bridget and Tony Brady run a tight, comfortable, and friendly ship (Sb-from £55, Db-from £90, CC:VM, 68 Northumberland Road, Ballsbridge, Dublin 4, tel. 01/660-5270, fax 01/668-8679). **Glenveagh Town House** has 13 classy rooms—Victorian upstairs, modern downstairs (Sb-£42, Db-£72, less in slow times, CC:VMA, 31 Northumberland Road, tel. 01/668-4612, fax 01/668-4559). **Bush House**, next door, is small and homey with a pleasant lounge and garden and four rooms mostly on the ground floor (Sb-£46, Db-£66–70, maybe less off-season, CC:VMA, 33 Northumberland Road, tel. & fax 01/668-3927, Diane Armstrong).

Sleeping near the Station
The **Townhouse of Dublin** is a fine basic and comfortable hotel with new furnishings but small rooms located midway between the train station and O'Connell Bridge (Sb-£35–47, D-£50–60, Db-£60–80 depending on season and day of the week, weekends are most expensive, CC:VMA, 47 Lower Gardiner Street, Dublin 1, tel. 01/878-8808, fax 01/878-8787, e-mail: grotter@indigo.ie).

Sleeping in nearby Dun Laoghaire
(tel. code: 01, mail: County Dublin)
The first three listings are a three-minute walk to the Sandycove DART station and a seven-minute walk to the Dun Laoghaire DART station/ferry landing. The rest are closest to the Dun Laoghaire DART station. Except for the first place, all are a bit tattered around the edges. While buses go into Dublin, the DART is much faster (6/hrly in peak times, at least 3/hrly otherwise, 15 min, Eurail valid, £1.10; for a longer stay consider the four-day Explorer ticket covering DART and Dublin buses). The **Dun Laoghaire TI** is in the ferry terminal (daily 10:00–21:00, 9:00–17:00 off-season). The Society of the Preservation of Irish Folk Music has a lively branch in Dun Laoghaire (see above).

Mrs. Kane's B&B is a modern house with three big, cheery rooms and a welcoming guests' lounge. While a few blocks farther

Dun Laoghaire

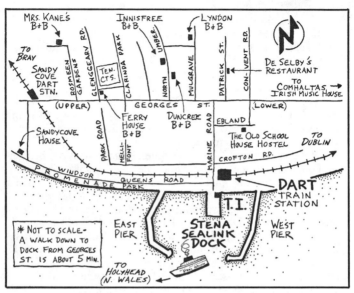

out than the others, it's worth the walk for its great, bright, friendly feeling (Db-£45, completely smoke-free, past Rosmeen Gardens to 2 Granite Hall, tel. & fax 01/280-9105).

Sandycove House, a comfortable old place overlooking a park and the harbor, is run in a no-nonsense kind of way. Its 12 rooms are generally large and fluffy (Sb-£30, Db-£45–47, Db overlooking the sea-£50, CC:VM, a £3 taxi or seven-minute walk from the ferry landing and two blocks from the Sandycove DART station, Marine Road, Sandycove, tel. & fax 01/284-1600).

Lynden B&B, with a classy 150-year-old interior hiding behind a somber front, offers four big rooms run by the charming and energetic Maria Gavin (one S-£17, D-£34, Db-£38, past Mulgrave Street to 2 Mulgrave Terrace, tel. & fax 280-6404). Next door, the similar **Belmont B&B** rents three rooms (D-£34, Db-£39, tel. 01/280-1422).

Innisfree B&B has a fine lounge and six big, bright, and comfy rooms (D-£32, Db-£37, CC:VM, from George Street follow the "Yellow Fever Vaccination Centre" sign to 31 Northumberland Avenue, tel. 01/280-5598, Brendan and Mary Smith). **Duncree B&B** is similar with four mostly large rooms on a quiet street (S-£19.50, D-£35, Db-£39, 16 Northumberland Avenue, tel. 01/280-6118, Mrs. O'Sullivan).

Ferry House B&B is a stately old place facing a quiet square with a tennis court with seven huge rooms and a cozy lounge (D-£42, Db-£46, CC:VM, 15 Clarinda Park North, tel. 01/280-8301, fax 01/284-6530).

The Old School House Hostel is a shoestring traveler's dream-come-true. It's just two blocks from the DART station and ferry landing with incredibly cheap beds in two- to eight-bed rooms and a hardworking and creative staff. Remember, it's a hostel: old carpets, bare walls, and a general scruffiness. Having said that, it's clean with good beds and plenty of privacy and feels secure and safe (£9 bunks in six-bed dorms, £10 in a quad, £24 doubles, less off-season, showers down the hall or in your room for 50p extra, breakfast not included, nonsmoking rooms, self-catering kitchen, restaurant, £3 laundry service, 24-hour staff; CC:VMA; from ferry, go up Marine Road, take first right onto Eblana Avenue; tel. 01/280-8777, fax 01/284-2266, e-mail: info@hostel.ie).

Eating in Dun Laoghaire
George Street, the town's main drag and three blocks inland, has plenty of eateries and pubs, many with live music. Probably the best bet for a good mid-range meal is **De Selby's Restaurant**, serving traditional Irish food, stew, and seafood (£12 meals, nightly 17:00–23:00, a block off George Street at 17 Patrick Street, tel. 01/284-1761). **Scott's** is an Art Nouveau Irish pub with good Irish and Cajun food (nightly until midnight, Georges St. Upr. 17B). The **Purty Kitchen Pub/Restaurant** has good seafood.

Transportation Connections—Dublin
By bus to: Belfast (7/day, 3 hrs), **Ennis** (7/day, 4.5 hrs), **Galway** (10/day, 3.5 hrs), **Limerick** (10/day, 3 hrs), **Tralee** (5/day, 6 hrs). Bus info: tel. 01/836-6111.

By train to: Rosslare (3/day, 3 hrs), **Tralee** (6/day, 4 hrs), **Galway** (4/day, 3 hrs, talking timetable tel. 01/805-4222), **Ennis** (4/day, 4 hrs), **Portrush** (5/day, 5 hrs, £20 one-way, £28 round-trip; stops in Belfast on the way south), **Belfast** (8/day, 2.25 hrs, talking timetable tel. 01/855-4477). The new Dublin–Belfast train connects the two Irish capitals in just over two hours at 90 mph on one continuous welded rail (£17 one-way, £26 round-trip; round-trip the same day only £17, except Friday and Sunday; from the border to Belfast one-way £9, £12 round-trip). Train info: tel. 01/836-6222.

The **Dublin Airport** is well connected to the city center, 12 miles away (see Arrival in Dublin). British Air flies to London's Gatwick Airport (4/day, from £69 return, toll-free tel. 800/626-747 in Ireland, 800/247-9297 in the United States), as do Aer Lingus (tel. 01/705-6705) and British Midland (tel. 01/283-8833 in Ireland, 800/788-0555 in the United States). Dublin Airport info:

tel. 01/814-4222. Ryanair is a new Irish cut-rate airline with unbelievable fares to European destinations (tel. 01/609-7800).

Transportation Connections— Ireland and Britain

Dublin and London: The boat/rail journey takes eight hours (4/day, £40–75). Dublin train info: tel. 01/836-6222.

Dublin and Holyhead: Irish Ferries sails between Dublin and Holyhead in North Wales (2/day, 3 hrs, £25 one-way walk-on fare, Dublin tel. 01/661-0511, Holyhead tel. 0990-329-129).

Dun Laoghaire and Holyhead: Stena Line sails between Dun Laoghaire (near Dublin) and Holyhead in North Wales (5/day, under 2 hrs with new HSS *Catamaran*, £36 one-way walk-on fare, £18 round-trip in a day if you have no baggage, reserve by phone early—they book up long in advance on summer weekends, Dublin tel. 01/204-7777, recorded information tel. 01/204-7799).

Ferry Connections—Ireland and France

Irish Ferries connect Ireland (Rosslare) with France (Cherbourg, and Roscoff) every other day (except January–March). While Cherbourg has the quickest connection to Paris, your overall time between Ireland and Paris is about the same regardless of which port is used on the day you sail. One-way fares vary from £35 to £70 (round-trips are much cheaper). Except for a £4 port tax, Eurailers go half-price and also get beds or cabins for half-price (depending on availability). In both directions departures are generally between 16:00 and 23:00 and arrivals are around midday of the following day. While passengers can nearly always get on, reservations are wise in summer. If you anticipate a crowded departure you can reserve a seat for £5. Beds in a quad start at £10. Doubles (or singles) start at £23. The easiest way to get a bed (except during summer) is from the information desk upon boarding. The cafeteria serves bad food at reasonable prices. Upon arrival in France, buses and taxis connect you to your Paris-bound train (Irish Ferries: Dublin tel. 01/661-0511, recorded info tel. 01/661-0715, Paris tel. 01 44 94 20 40, Web site: www .irishferries.ie, e-mail: info@irishferries.ie, European Ferry Guide Web site: www.youra.com/ferry/intlferries.html).

DINGLE PENINSULA

Dingle Peninsula, the westernmost tip of Ireland, offers just the right mix of far and away beauty, ancient archaeological wonders, and desolate walks or bike rides all within convenient reach of its main town. Dingle Town is just big enough to have all the necessary tourist services and a steady nocturnal beat of Irish folk music.

While the big tour buses clog the neighboring Ring of Kerry before heading east to slobber all over the Blarney Stone, Dingle—while crowded in the summer—still feels like the fish and the farm matter. Fifty fishing boats sail from Dingle, and a faint whiff of peat still fills its nighttime streets.

For 15 years my Irish dreams have been set here on this sparse but lush peninsula where locals are fond of saying "The next parish is Boston." There's a closeness to the land on Dingle. When I asked a local if he was born here, he thought for a second and said, "No, it was about six miles down the road." When I told him where I was from, a faraway smile filled his eyes, he looked out to sea and sighed, "Ah, the shores of Americay."

Dingle feels so traditionally Irish because it's a Gaeltacht, a region where the government subsidizes the survival of the Irish language and culture. While English is always there, the signs, menus, and songs come in Gaelic. Even the local preschool brags "ALL Gaelic."

Of the peninsula's 10,000 residents, 1,300 live in Dingle Town. Its few streets, lined with ramshackle but gaily painted shops and pubs, run up from a rain-stung harbor always busy with fishing boats and yachts. During the day kids—already working on ruddy beer-glow cheeks—roll kegs up the streets and into the pubs in preparation for another night of music and *craic* (fun conversation).

Dingle History

The wet sod of Dingle is soaked with medieval history. In the darkest depths of the Dark Ages, peace-loving, bookwormish monks fled the chaos of the Continent and its barbarian raids. They sailed to the drizzly fringe of the known world—places like Dingle. These monks kept literacy alive in Europe. Charlemagne, who ruled much of Europe in the year 800, imported Irish monks to be his scribes.

It was from this peninsula that the semi-mythical explorer monk, St. Brandon, is said to have set sail in the sixth century in search of a legendary western paradise. Some think he beat Columbus to North America by nearly a thousand years.

Dingle (An Daingean in Gaelic) was a busy seaport in the late Middle Ages. Along with Tralee, it was the only walled town in Kerry and a gateway to northern Spain—a three-day sail due south. Many 14th- and 15th-century pilgrimages left from Dingle for Santiago di Compostela in Spain.

When its position as a medieval trading center ended, Dingle faded in importance. In the last century it was a linen-weaving center. Until 1970 fishing dominated. The only visitors were scholars and students of old Irish ways. In 1970 the movie *Ryan's Daughter* introduced the world to Dingle. The trickle of Dingle fans has grown to a flood in the 1990s as word of its musical, historical, gastronomical, and scenic charms—not to mention its friendly dolphin—has spread.

Planning Your Time

For the shortest visit, give Dingle two nights and a day. It takes about six hours to get there from Dublin, Galway, or the boat dock in Rosslare. I like two nights because you feel more like a local on your second evening in the pubs. You'll need the better part of a day to explore the 30-mile loop around the peninsula by bike, car, or tour bus (see Circular Tour, below). To do any serious walking or relaxing you'll need two or three days. It's not uncommon to find Americans slowing way, way down in Dingle.

Orientation (tel. code: 066)

Dingle is extremely comfortable on foot. The town hangs on a medieval grid of streets between the harborfront (where the Tralee bus stops) and Main Street (three blocks inland). Nothing in town is more than a five-minute walk away. Dingle is so small that street numbers are used only when more than one place is run by a family of the same name. Most locals know most locals, and people on the street are fine sources of information. Remember, tourism is what puts soda bread on the table here and the locals offer a warm and sincere welcome.

Tourist Information: The Bord Failte (TI) is on Strand

Southwest Ireland

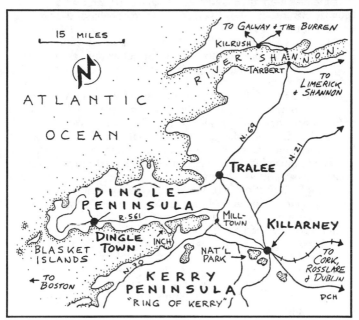

Street, by the water (March–October Monday–Saturday 9:00–19:00, Sunday 10:00–13:00 and 14:15–18:00, off-season shorter hours and closed Sunday, tel. 066/51188, Web site: www.dingle-peninsula.ie). In the summer the TI organizes town walks. For more creative help, drop by the Mountain Man shop (on Strand Street, see below).

Helpful Hints

Crowds: Dingle gets so crowded during summer holiday weekends that the police actually close down the road access. July 15 to August 30 is bad (you might consider the less-discovered Beara Peninsula, south of the Ring of Kerry). The absolute craziest are the Dingle Races (second weekend in August) and Dingle Regatta (third weekend in August). Dingle's dead before May 1: no music, activities, tours, or tourists.

 Banking: There are two banks in town, both uphill from the TI on Main Street (Monday–Friday 10:00–12:30 and 13:30–16:00). Both have cash machines.

 Supermarket: The Super Valu supermarket/department store is at the base of town (Monday–Saturday 8:00–21:00, Sunday 8:00–18:00, less off-season).

 Launderette: At this full-service shop you can drop off a load and pick it up three hours later (small-£3.50, large-£5.50, Monday–Saturday 9:00–17:30, on Green Street behind El Toro restaurant, tel. 066/51837).

Internet Café: Dingleweb, Monday–Saturday 10:00–22:00, less on Sunday, £5/hour, Main Street around the corner from Grapevine Hostel, tel. 066/52477, e-mail: postmaster @dingleweb.com).

Bike Rental: Bike rental shops abound in Dingle. You can get good mountain bikes at Paddy's Bike Hire (daily 9:00–19:00, £5/day, £6/24 hrs, on Dykegate next to Grapevine Hostel), Sciuird Tours, the Mountain Man, and the Ballintaggert Hostel. If you're biking the peninsula, get a bike with skinny street tires, not slow and fat mountain bike tires. Plan on leaving a credit card, driver's license, or passport as security.

Dingle Activities: The Mountain Man, a hiking shop run by two local guides, Con and Mike, is a clearinghouse for information, local tours, and excursions (located just off the harbor at Strand Street, tel. 066/52400, fax 066/52396). Pick up the free *Kerry Gems* booklet or, for longer outdoorsy stays, the more complete *Easy Guide to the Dingle Peninsula.* For bike rentals and ideas on biking, hiking, horse riding, climbing, peninsula tours (which they offer), and trips to the Blaskets, stop by here. They are the Dingle Town contact for the Dunquin–Blasket Islands boats (see Blasket Islands, below).

Sights—Dingle Town

▲**Oceanworld**—The only place charging admission in Dingle is worth considering. This new aquarium offers a little peninsula history, 160 different local fish and other sea creatures in thoughtfully described tanks (including a chance to walk under the fish in the "ocean tank"), and the easiest way to see Fungi the dolphin—on video (£4.50, £12 for families, daily 10:00–20:30 in summer, until 18:00 or earlier in off-season, just past the harbor on the west edge of town, tel. 066/52111).

Fungi—In 1983 a dolphin moved into Dingle Harbor and became a local celebrity. Fungi is now the darling of the town's tourist trade and one reason you'll find so many tour buses parked along the harbor. With a close look at Fungi as bait, tour boats are thriving—£6, book behind the TI. While she's too cute to kill, I'll happily give a free copy of the next edition of this book to anyone who can make Fungi leave.

▲**Short Harbor Walk from Dingle**—For an easy stroll along the harbor out of town (and a chance to see the dolphin) head east from the roundabout on R561. Just after Bambury's B&B, take a right following signs to Skelligs Hotel. At the beach, climb the steps over the wall and follow the seashore path to the mouth of Dingle harbor (marked by a tower—some 19th-century fat cat's

Dingle Town

1	SMEARA DUBHA	21	DICK MACK
2	OCEANWORLD	22	CAFE CEO
3	DINGLE SAILING CLUB	23	LAUNDRY
4	CRUISEBOAT OFFICES	24	EL TORO
5	MAIRE DE BARRA RESTAURANT	25	GRAPEVINE HOSTEL
6	MOUNTAIN MAN	26	BANK
7	BUS STATION	27	BIKE RENTAL
8	GREANY'S RESTAURANT	28	AN CAFE LITEARTA
9	SUPER VALUE	29	TOURIST INFORMATION
10	TIG LISE	30	CAPTAIN'S HOUSE B & B
11	O' FLAHERTY'S	31	CINEMA
13	BAMBURY'S B & B	32	ADAM'S BAR & RESTAURANT
14	TRAIL TO LIGHTHOUSE	33	SMALL BRIDGE BAR
15	BALLINTAGGERT HOSTEL	34	DOYLE'S & HALF DOOR RESTAURANTS
16	ALPINE HOUSE	35	SRAID EOIN B & B
17	SCIUIRD TOURS & KIRRARY B & B	36	KELLIHER'S BALLYEGAN HOUSE
18	CORNER HOUSE B & B	37	GREENMOUNT HOUSE
19	CONNORS B & B	38	HILLGROVE HOTEL
20	CITY PARK	39	ARD NA GREINE HOUSE B & B

folly). Ten minutes beyond that is a lighthouse. This is Fungi's neighborhood. If you see tourist boats out, you're likely to see her. If you continue walking, you'll get to a dramatic cliff.

The Harbor—The harbor is on land reclaimed (with imported Dutch expertise) five years ago. The new roundabout allows traffic to skirt the town center. The string of old stone shops facing the harbor was the loading station for the narrow-gauge railway that hauled the fish from Dingle to Tralee (1891–1953). The Esk Tower on the distant hill is a marker built in 1847 during the famine as a make-work project. In pre-radar days, it helped ships locate Dingle's hidden harbor. The fancy mansion across the harbor is Lord Ventry's 17th-century manor house.

Cruises—The Dingle Marina Center offers diving, sailing, and traditional currach rowing. One-man sailboats can be lent to those wanting to blow around the bay with a day membership in the Sailing Club (£15, tel. 066/52422). Currachs are Ireland's traditional lightweight fishing boats, easy to haul and easy to make: Cover a wooden frame with canvas and paint with tar. Stacked near the Sailing Club, the currachs are owned by the Dingle Rowing Club and go out most evenings. You can take a sailing trip to the Blaskets on the 41-foot cutter *Kimberly Laura* (£40, book in advance, tel. 066/59882). The beaches nearby are popular in the summer.

Entertainment

▲▲▲**Folk Music in Dingle Pubs**—Even if you're not into pubs, take a nap and then give these a whirl. Dingle is renowned among traditional musicians as a place to get work ("£30 a day, tax-free, plus drink"). The town has 50 pubs. There's music every night (and never a cover charge). The scene is a decent mix of locals, Americans, and Germans. Music normally starts around 21:30, and the last call for drinks is "half eleven" (23:30). For a seat near the music, arrive early. If the place is chockablock, power in and find breathing room in the back. By midnight the door is closed and the chairs are stacked. While two pubs, the Small Bridge Bar (An Droicheed) and O'Flahertys, are the most famous for their good beer and folk music, make a point to wander the town and follow your ear. Smaller pubs may feel a bit foreboding to a tourist, but people—locals as well as travelers—are out for the *craic*. Pubs are smoky and hot (leave your coat home). The more offbeat pubs are more likely to erupt into leprechaun karaoke.

The best pub crawl is along the Strand to O'Flaherty's (rough-and-tumble Murphy's is liveliest, offering rock as well as traditional music). Then head up Green Street. Dick Mack is a tiny leather shop by day and a pub by night with two snugs (private booths), reliably good beer, and a strangely fascinating ambience; notice the Hollywood-type stars on the sidewalk recalling famous visitors. Wander up and down Main Street (Small Bridge Bar at the bottom is best) and then up Spa Road a few doors to An Conair, a pub attracting a more alternative Celtic folk talent (often less crowded but with good music). During the day, music lovers will enjoy dropping by Danlann Gallery, a music shop on Dykegate Street (Monday–Saturday 10:00–22:00, Sunday 11:00–18:00, less off-season).

More Evening Fun—Somewhere almost every night, a pub hosts "Set Dancing" with live music (An Conair Bar does it on Monday after 21:30). The music office on Dykegate has the lastest on musical happenings. Hillgrove Hotel (up Spa Road a few hundred meters) is a modern hotel with traditional dances every Thursday and pop dancing other nights in summer. Locals say the Hillgrove "is a great time if you're pissed." Dingle has a great little theater (The Phoenix on Dykegate). The film club (50 or 60 locals) meets for coffee, cookies, and a film every Tuesday at 20:30 (October–June).

Sleeping in Dingle Town
(£1 = about $1.50, tel. code: 066, mail: Dingle, County Kerry)
Sleep Code: **S** = Single, **D** = Double/Twin, **T** = Triple, **Q** = Quad, **b** = bathroom, **t** = toilet only, **s** = shower only, **CC** = Credit Card (Visa, MasterCard, Amex).

Sraid Eoin B&B, on the quiet end of town with four spacious and modern pastel rooms and giant bathrooms, is warmly run by Kathleen and Maurice O'Connor (Sb-£25, Db-£34, family deals, CC:VM, John Street, tel. 066/51409, fax 066/52156). Maurice runs Galvin's Travel Agency on the ground floor (same phone number).

Kellihers Ballyegan House is a big, plain building with six comfortable rooms on the edge of town, run by friendly Mrs. Hannah Kelliher (Sb-£18, Db-£36, no CC or smokers, Upper John Street, tel. 066/51702).

Greenmount House sits among palm trees at the top of town, in the countryside with a commanding view of the bay and mountains but just three minutes' walk from the town center. John and Mary Curran run one of Ireland's classiest B&Bs with six fine rooms (Db-£40) and six sprawling suites (Db-£60) in a modern building with lavish public areas and breakfast in a solarium (no singles during high season or children under eight ever, lower prices off-season, CC:VM, up John Street to Gortonora, reserve in advance, tel. 066/51414, fax 066/51974).

Corner House B&B is my longtime Dingle home. It's a simple, traditional place with five rooms run with a twinkle and a smile by Kathleen Farrell (S-£18, D-£32, T-£45, plenty of plumbing but it's down the hall, no CC, reserve with a phone call and reconfirm a day or two ahead or risk losing your bed, central as can be on Dykegate Street, tel. 066/51516).

Captain's House B&B is a salty-feeling place in the town center with seven classy rooms (Sb-£30, Db-£44, CC:VMA, the Mall, tel. 066/51531, fax 066/51079, e-mail: captigh@tinet.ie, Jim and Mary Milhench).

Connors B&B, well-located and likely to have a room available, has 15 big, basic rooms (£25 per person in July and August,

£18 other months, CC:VMA, in the center on Dykegate Street, tel. 066/51598, fax 066/52376, Mrs. Connor).

Ard Na Greine House B&B is a charming, wind-blown, modern house on the edge of town. Mrs. Mary Houlihan rents four well-equipped, comfortable rooms to nonsmokers (Sb-£24, Db-£36, Tb-£50, CC:VM, on the edge of town a 10-minute walk up Spa Road, three doors beyond the Hillgrove Hotel, tel. 066/51113, fax 066/51898).

Ballintaggert Hostel is housed in a stylish old manor house used by Protestants during the famine as a soup kitchen (for those hungry enough to renounce their Catholicism). It comes complete with horse riding, bike rental, laundry service, kitchen, café, classy study, family room with a fireplace, a shuttle into town, and a resident ghost (166 beds, £7 in eight- to 12-bed dorms, £10 in quads, £13 in singles and doubles, breakfast extra, one mile east of town on Tralee Road, tel. 066/51454, fax 066/52207, e-mail: btaggert@iol.ie).

Grapevine Hostel is a clean and friendly establishment with a cozy fireplace lounge and a fine members' kitchen. Each four- to eight-bed dorm has its own bathroom. Dorms are coed but there's usually a girls' room established. No curfew or lockout (32 beds, £8–9 each, Dykegate Lane, tel. 066/51434).

Alpine House Guest House (tel. 066/51250) and **Bambury's B&B** (tel. 066/51244), both big, modern buildings on the main Tralee Road a block or so from the roundabout, might have a reasonable bed when the others are full.

Ocean View B&B rents three tidy rooms in a little waterfront rowhouse overlooking the the the bay (S-£15, D-£26, five-minute walk from the center, 100 meters past Ocean World at 133 The Wood, tel. 066/51659, Mrs. Brosnan).

Eating in Dingle Town
For a rustic little village, Dingle is swimming in high and fun cuisine. Many of the best values close after 18:00. Most pubs also stop serving food early (to make room for maximum beer). The town's grocery stores stay open until about 21:00.

Adam's Bar and Restaurant serves traditional food at great prices. Try their corned beef and cabbage (last meal at 20:30, earlier in low season, Upper Main Street).

Tig Lise offers a good, simple menu with a tasty lasagna-and-salad meal and good vegetarian selections (meals are £5, closed at 21:00, earlier off-season, near the roundabout at Holyground).

An Cafe Litearta, a popular and friendly eatery hiding behind an inviting bookstore, has good sandwiches, salads, and hot food (10:00–17:30, Dykegate Street).

Greany's Restaurant, just off the roundabout, is a local hit serving good, basic food at decent prices in a cheery, modern atmosphere (12:30–22:00, Holyground).

El Toro offers a candlelit splash of Italy with good seafood, salads, and pizzas (17:30–20:00, Green Street, tel. 066/51820). **Maire De Barra** has simple traditional food and seafood (£5, the Pier).

Smeara Dubha is a small vegetarian restaurant down by the harbor (evenings only, 18:00–21:00, The Wood, Dingle).

Dingle's long-established top-notch restaurants are **Doyle's Seafood Bar** (more famous, John Street, tel. 066/51174) and the **Half Door** (heartier portions, pay in cash to avoid VISA card scam, John Street, tel. 066/51600). Both offer three-course early-dinner specials for £15 between 18:00 and 18:30 and more expensive dining after that. Reservations are necessary in both places.

Transportation Connections—Dingle Town

The nearest train station is in Tralee. Buses connect Dingle and Tralee nine times a day in summer, less off-season and on Sunday (75 min, £6). Dingle has no bus station and only one stop, on the waterfront behind the Super Valu supermarket (bus info tel. 066/23566).

Drivers choose two roads into town, the easy southern route or the much more dramatic and treacherous Conor Pass. It's 30 miles from Tralee either way.

Dingle Peninsula:
Circular Tour by Bike or Car

A ▲▲▲ sight, the Dingle Peninsula loop trip is about 30 miles long (seven hours by bike, three hours by car, including stops; do only in clockwise direction). While you can take a guided tour of the peninsula (below), it's not necessary with the route described in this section. A fancy map is also unnecessary with my instructions. I've keyed in mileage to help locate points of interest. If you're driving, as you leave Dingle, reset your odometer at Oceanworld. Even if you get off track or are biking, derive distances between points from these numbers. To get the most out of your circle, read through this entire section before departing. Then go step by step (staying on R559 and following the "The Slea Head Drive" signs). Note: Roads are very congested in August.

The Dingle Peninsula is 10 miles wide and runs 40 miles from Tralee to Slea Head. The top of its mountainous spine is Mount Brandon—at 3,130 feet, the second-tallest mountain in Ireland. While only tiny villages lie west of Dingle Town, the peninsula is home to 500,000 sheep.

Leave Dingle Town west along the waterfront (0.0 miles at Oceanworld). There's an eight-foot tide here. The seaweed was used to nourish reclaimed land. Across the water the fancy Milltown House B&B was Robert Mitchum's home for a year during the filming of *Ryan's Daughter*.

Dingle Peninsula Tour

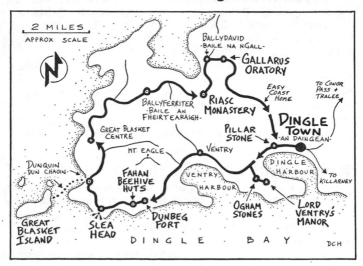

0.4 miles: Turn left over the bridge. The building on the right was a corn-grinding mill in the 18th century.

0.8 miles: The Milestone B&B is named for the pillar stone (*Gallaun* in Gaelic) in its front yard. This may have been a prehistoric grave marker or a boundary marker between two tribes. The stone goes down as far as it sticks up. Another pillar stone stands in the field across the street in the direction of the yellow manor house of Lord Ventry. The peninsula, literally an open-air museum, is dotted with more than 2,000 monuments dating from the Bronze Age through early Christian times.

2.1 miles: Pass through a rare grove of trees and turn left ("Leather Workshop" sign). After 100 yards enter the **Lord Ventry's Manor,** take the first left (unmarked, through white gate), and go up the long one-lane drive past small 18th-century estate houses and the palms, magnolias, fuchsias, and exotic flora introduced to Dingle by Lord Ventry. Because of the mild climate (cradled by the gulf stream), fuchsias line the roads all over the peninsula and fill the countryside with red from June to September. At the fork in the road, turn right. Fifty yards before the yellow mansion, stop at the six stones.

The **Ogham Stones** (dating from the third to seventh century, named for the Celtic goddess of writing) decorating the drive are rare examples of early Celtic writing. With variations on five straight lines, they could make 20 letters—the original bar code. Of the 380 known Ogham Stones, 80 are in Dingle. Lord Ventry, whose family came to Dingle as landlords in 1666, built this mansion in about 1750. Today it houses an all-Gaelic boarding school for 140 high school–age girls. Return to the main road and turn left (3.1 miles).

4.1 miles: Stay off the "soft margin" as you enjoy views of **Ventry Bay** and its four-mile-long beach. Mount Eagle (1,660 feet), the end of Ireland, is beyond. In the little town of Ventry, Gaelic is the first language.

6.0 miles: The rushes on either side of the road are the kind used to make the local thatched roofs. Thatching, which nearly died out because of the fire danger, is more popular now that anti-flame treatments are available. Magpies fly.

6.6 miles: The Irish football star Paidi O Se (Paddy O'Shea) is a household name in Ireland. He now trains the Kerry team and runs the pub on the left.

6.9 miles: The blue house hiding in the trees on the left (view through the white gate) was kept cozy by Tom Cruise and Nicole Kidman during the filming of *Far and Away*.

7.9 miles: "*Taisteaal go Mall*" means "go slowly"; there's a peach-colored schoolhouse on the right. On the left is the Celtic and Prehistoric Museum, a strange private collection of dinosaur eggs, Celtic and Viking tools, coins, weapons, and a very odd mechanical sheep (£3.50, closed Monday).

8.2 miles: The circular mound on the right is a late–Stone Age ring fort. In 500 B.C. it was a petty Celtic chieftain's headquarters, a stone-and-earth stockade filled with little stone houses. These survived untouched through the centuries because of superstitious beliefs that they were "fairy forts." While this is unexcavated, recent digging has shown that people have lived on this peninsula since 4000 B.C.

8.6 miles: The Hungarian red deer on the right are the work of the European Community (easier on the land, but higher fences are needed). Grass-fed deer (venison) are in the Euro cards, not more sheep.

9.0 miles: **Dunbeg Fort**, a series of defensive ramparts and ditches around a central *clochan*, while ready to fall into the sea, is open to tourists. While there are no carvings to be seen, the small (*beg*) fort (*dun*) is dramatic (£1, daily 9:00–20:00, descriptive handout). Forts like this are the most important relics left from Ireland's Iron Age (500 B.C. to A.D. 500). Since erosion will someday take this fort, it has been excavated.

9.6 miles: The Fahan group of **beehive huts**, or *clochans*, is a short walk uphill. These mysterious stone igloos cluster together within a circular wall (£1, daily 9:00–19:00, WC). These are a better sight than the Fahan beehive huts a mile down the road. Farther on, you'll ford a stream. There has never been a bridge here; the road was designed as a ford.

10.6 miles: Pull off to the left at this second group of beehive huts. Look downhill at the scant remains of the scant home that was burned as the movie equivalent of Lord Ventry tried to evict the tenants in *Far and Away*. Even without Hollywood, this is bleak, godforsaken land. Look above at the patches of land slowly reclaimed by the inhabitants of this westernmost piece of Europe. Rocks were moved and piled into fences. Sand and seaweed were laid on the clay and in time it was good for grass. The created land was generally not tillable. Much has fallen out of use now.

11.4 miles: At **Slea Head**, marked by a crucifix, a pullout, and great views of the Blasket Islands (described below), you turn the corner on this tour.

11.9 miles: Pull out here to view the Blaskets and Dunmore Head (the westernmost point in Europe) and to review the roadside map (which traces your route) in the parking lot. The scattered village of Dunquin has many ruined rock homes—abandoned during the famine. They were built with small windows to minimize taxation. Some have been fixed up, as this is a popular place these days for summer homes. (The lead singer of the Irish rock band The Cranberries has a huge home a mile or so down the road.) You can see more good examples of land reclamation, patch by patch, climbing up the hillside.

13.4 miles: The Blasket Islanders had no church or cemetery on the island. This was their cemetery. The famous Blasket storyteller Peig Sayers (1873–1958) is buried in the center. Just past a washed-out bit of road, a lane leads left (100 yards) to a marker remembering the 1588 shipwreck of the *Santa Maria de la Rosa* of the Spanish Armada. Below that is the often tempestuous Dunquin Harbor, from where the Blasket ferry departs.

13.5 miles: Back on the main road, follow signs to the Great Blasket Centre.

15 miles: Leave the Slea Head Road left for the modern Blasket Centre (described below).

15.7 miles: Back at the turnoff, head left (sign to Louis Mulcahy Pottery).

16.4 miles: Passing land that was never reclaimed, think of the work it took to pick out the stones, pile them into fences, and bring up sand and seaweed to nourish the clay and make soil for growing potatoes. On the left is a shadow of the main street of the fake poor village built to film *Far and Away*. Beyond that is the "Sleeping Giant" island—with hand resting happily on his beer belly.

16.8 miles: The view is spectacular, especially when the waves are "racing in like white horses." Ahead on the right, study the top fields, untouched since the planting of 1845, when the potatoes rotted in the ground. The vertical ridges of the potato beds can still be seen—a reminder of the famine. Before the famine, 60,000 people lived on this peninsula.

20.2 miles: Ballyferriter (Baile an Fheirtearaigh), established by a Norman family in the 12th century, is the largest town on this end of the peninsula. The pubs serve grub and the old schoolhouse is a museum (£1.50, daily in summer 10:00–17:30, off-season Monday–Friday 10:00–12:00 and 14:00–16:00). The early Christian cross looks real. Tap it . . . it's a fiberglass prop from *Ryan's Daughter*.

21.0 miles: At the T-junction, signs direct you to Dingle (An Daingean 11 km) either way. Go left, via Gallarus. Take a right over the bridge, still following signs to Gallarus.

21.4 miles: Just beyond the bridge and a few yards before the sign to Mainistir Riaise (Riasc Monastic enclosure), detour right up the lane. After .2 miles (the unsigned turnout on your right) you find the scant remains of the walled **Riasc Monastery** (dating from the fifth to 12th centuries). Step over the rocks and go inside. The inner wall divided the community into work and religious sections. The layer of black felt marks where the original rocks stop and the excavators' reconstruction begins. The pillar stone is Celtic (from 1000 B.C.). When the Christians arrived in the fifth century, they didn't throw out the Celtic society. Instead, they carved a Maltese-type cross over the Celtic scrollwork. The square building was an oratory (church). The round buildings would have been dwellings. The monasteries had cottage industries. Just outside the wall (opposite the oratory), find a stone hole with a passage facing the southwest wind. This was a kiln. Locals would bring their grain to be dried and ground. The monks would keep a "tithe." With the arrival of the Normans in the 12th century, these small religious communities were replaced by relatively big-time state and church governments.

21.9 miles: Back on the main road, continue to the right.

23.0 miles: At the big pink restaurant, turn left.

23.7 miles: At another restaurant, go right up an unmarked one-lane road.

24.0 miles: The Gallarus Oratory (£1), built about 1,300 years ago, is one of Ireland's best-preserved early-Christian churches. Its shape is reminiscent of an upturned boat, and the dry-stone walls are so perfectly fitted together that they are still waterproof. Notice the holes for some covering at the door and the fine alternating stonework on the corners. Your ticket includes a 17-minute *Story of the Dingle Peninsula* video, which gives an interesting overview of the historic sights. (Drivers can avoid the £3 parking fee by grabbing one of four spots up the hill and taking the public access path to the oratory (free, but no video). Continue up the rugged one-lane road.

24.6 miles: Turn left on the two-lane road, then right (to An Daingean, 7 km) where you'll crest and enjoy a three-mile coast back into Dingle Town in the direction of the Esk Tower.

27.6 miles: At the intersection just look for the happy dolphin.

Head that way, over the bridge and back into Dingle Town (28.4 miles). Well done.

Dingle Peninsula Tours

Sciuird Archaeology Tours are offered by the Sciuirds, a family that has Dingle history—and a knack for sharing it—in its blood. Tim Coileain (a retired Dingle policeman) and his son Michael give serious 2.5-hour, £7 minibus tours at 11:00 and 14:00, depending upon demand. Drop by the Kirrary B&B (at intersection of Dykegate and Grey's Lane in Dingle Town) or call 066/51937 or 066/51606 to put your name on the list. Call early. Tours fill quickly in summer. Off-season you may have to call back to see if the necessary four people signed up to make a bus go. While skipping the folk legends and the famous sights (such as Slea Head), your guide will drive down tiny farm roads (the Gaelic word for road is "cow path"), over hedges, and up ridges to hidden Celtic forts, mysterious stone tombs, and forgotten castles with sweeping seaside views. The running commentary gives an intimate peek into the history of Dingle. Sit as close to the driver as possible to get all the information. They do two completely different tours: west (Gallarus Oratory) and east (Minard Castle and a wedge tomb). I enjoyed both. Dress for the weather. In a literal gale with horizontal winds my guide kept saying, "You'll survive it."

Moran's Tour does three-hour guided minibus trips around the peninsula with a more touristic slant (£7, normally at 10:30 and 14:30 from the Dingle TI, tel. 066/51155). The **Mountain Man** also offers three-hour minibus tours of the peninsula (tel. 066/52400). **Guide Friday** makes the circuit about hourly in its familiar "hop on and off the topless bus" style.

Blasket Islands

This rugged group of six islands off the tip of Dingle Peninsula seems particularly close to the soul of Ireland. The population of Great Blasket Island, home to as many as 160 people, dwindled until the last handful of residents were moved by the government to the mainland in 1953. These people were the most traditional Irish community of the 20th century—the symbol of antique Gaelic culture. Their special closeness to their island—combined with their knack for vivid storytelling—is inspirational. From this poor, primitive but proud fishing/farming community came three writers of international repute whose Gaelic work—basically tales of life on Great Blasket—is translated into many languages. You'll find *Peig* (by Peig Sayers), *Twenty Years a-Growing* (Maurice O'Sullivan), and *The Islander* (Thomas O'Crohan) in shops all over the peninsula.

In the summer there may be a café, shop, and hostel on the island, but it's little more than a ghost town overrun with rabbits on a peaceful, grassy, three-mile-long poem. The ferry schedule is dictated by demand and weather. In 1999 there should be two or three buses a day from Dingle Town to Dunquin (usually around 9:00, 14:00, and 16:00, returning about 10:00, 14:30, and 18:00) coordinated with ferry departures; check at the Mountain Man shop in Dingle Town (£3 each way by bus, £10 round-trip with boat trip to Blasket, Dunquin ferry tel. 066/56455). There is a hostel in Dunquin.

▲▲**Great Blasket Centre**—This state-of-the-art Blasket and Gaelic heritage center gives visitors the best look possible at the language, literature, and way of life of the Blasket Islanders. See the fine video (shows on the half-hour), hear the sounds, read the poems, browse through old photos, and then gaze out the big windows at those rugged islands and imagine. Even if you never got past limericks, the poetry of these people—so pure and close to each other and nature—will have you dipping your pen into the cry of the birds (£2.50, daily 10:00–18:00 Easter–October, until 19:00 July and August, on the mainland facing the islands, well signposted, tel. 066/56444). Visit this center before visiting the islands.

ROME (ROMA)

Rome is magnificent and brutal at the same time. Your ears will ring, your nose will turn your handkerchief black, the careless will be run down or pickpocketed, you'll be frustrated by the kind of chaos that only an Italian can understand. You may even come to believe Mussolini was a necessary evil. But Rome is required.

If your hotel provides a comfortable refuge; if you pace yourself, accept and even partake in the siesta plan; if you're well-organized for sightseeing; and if you protect yourself and your valuables with extra caution and discretion, you'll do fine. You'll see the sights and leave satisfied.

Rome at its peak meant civilization itself. Everything was either civilized (part of the Roman Empire, Latin- or Greek-speaking) or barbarian. Today Rome is Italy's political capital, the capital of Catholicism, and a splendid . . . "junkpile" is not quite the right word . . . of Western civilization. As you peel through its fascinating and jumbled layers, you'll find its buildings, people, cats, laundry, and traffic endlessly entertaining. And then, of course, there are its magnificent sights.

Tour St. Peter's, the greatest church on earth, and scale Michelangelo's 100-yard-tall dome, the world's largest. Learn something about eternity by touring the huge Vatican Museum. You'll find paradise—bright as the day it was painted—in the newly restored Sistine Chapel. Do the "Caesar Shuffle" walk through ancient Rome's Forum and Colosseum. Take an early evening "Dolce Vita Stroll" down the Via del Corso with Rome's beautiful people. Enjoy an after-dark walk from Traste-vere to the Spanish Steps, lacing together Rome's Baroque and bubbling night spots.

Planning Your Time

For most travelers, Rome is best done quickly. It's a great city, but exhausting. Time is normally short, and Italy is more charming elsewhere. To "do" Rome in a day, consider it as a side trip from Orvieto or Florence and maybe before the night train to Venice. Crazy as that sounds, if all you have is a day, it's a great one.

Rome in a day: Vatican (two hours in the museum and Sistine Chapel, and one hour in St. Peter's), taxi over the river to the Pantheon (munch a bar-snack picnic on its steps), then hike over Capitoline Hill, through the Forum, and to the Colosseum. Have dinner on Campo dei Fiori and dessert on Piazza Navona.

Rome in two days (the optimal first visit): Do the "Caesar Shuffle" from the Colosseum and Forum, over the Capitoline Hill to the Pantheon. After a siesta, join the locals strolling from Piazza del Popolo to the Spanish Steps. Have dinner near your hotel. On the second day, see Vatican City (St. Peter's, climb the dome, tour the Vatican Museum). Spend the evening walking from Trastevere to Campo dei Fiori (atmospheric place for dinner) to the Trevi Fountain. With a third day, consider adding another museum and a side trip to Ostia.

Orientation

The modern sprawl of Rome is of no interest to us. Our Rome actually feels small when you know it. It's the old core—within the triangle formed by the train station, Colosseum, and Vatican. Get a handle on Rome by considering it in these chunks:

The ancient city had a million people. Tear it down to size by walking through just the core. The best of the classical sights stand in a line from the Colosseum to the Pantheon.

Medieval Rome was little more than a hobo-camp of 50,000—thieves, mean dogs, and the pope, whose legitimacy required a Roman address. The medieval city, a colorful tangle of lanes, lies between the Pantheon and the river.

Window-shoppers' Rome twinkles with nightlife and ritzy shopping near medieval Rome, on or near Rome's main drag, the Via del Corso.

Vatican City is a compact world of its own with two great sights: a huge basilica and the museum.

Trastevere, the seedy/colorful wrong-side-of-the-river neighborhood-village, is Rome at its crustiest—and perhaps most "Roman."

Baroque Rome is an overleaf that embellishes great squares throughout the town with fountains and church facades.

Since no one is allowed to build taller than St. Peter's dome, the city has no modern skyline. And the Tiber River is ignored.

It's not navigable and after the last floods (1870), the banks were built up very high and Rome turned its back on its naughty river.

Tourist Information

Rome has three main tourist information offices: airport (tel. 06-6595-6074), train station (daily 8:00-21:00, near track #1, very crowded, only one open on Sunday, marked with a large "i" in middle of station, tel. 06-487-1270 or 06-482-4078), and the central office (open Monday–Friday 8:15–19:15, Saturday 8:15–13:45, next to the SAAB dealership, Via Parigi 5, tel. 06-4889-9255 or 06-4889-9253, www.comune.roma.it, e-mail: mail@informaroma.it).

The central TI office, near Piazza della Republica's huge fountain, is a five-minute walk out the front of the train station. It's air-conditioned, less crowded and more helpful than the station TI, and has a table to plan on—or sit at to overcome your frustration. Ask for the better "long stay" city map and *L'Evento*, the bimonthly periodical entertainment guide for evening events and fun. (If all you need is a map, forget the TI and pick one up at your hotel.) All hotels list an inflated rate to cover the hefty commission any TI room-finding service charges. Save money by booking direct.

In addition to the above TIs there are smaller branches (Monday–Saturday 9:00–18:00) scattered around the city, including one near the entrance to the Forum (Piazza del Tempio della Pace), another at Via del Corso (Largo Goldoni), and another in Trastevere (Piazza Sonnino).

Romanc'e is a cheap little weekly entertainment guide with a helpful English section on musical events and the pope's schedule for the week. It's sold at newsstands. Fancy hotels carry a free English monthly, *Un Ospite a Roma* (A Guest in Rome).

Enjoy Rome is a free and friendly information service providing maps, museum hours, a free useful city guide, and a room-finding service (8:30–13:00, 15:30–18:00, closed Saturday afternoon and on Sunday, three blocks northeast of the station at Via Varese 39, tel. 06-445-1843, fax 06-445-0734, www.enjoyrome.it). They offer several English-only city walking tours daily (L30,000 per three-hour tour, L25,000 for those under 26, children under 15 go free). Ask about bike tours of Rome (L30,000 includes bike rental, helmet, and guide; three hours) or their air-conditioned bus to Pompeii (L60,000, offered every other day; tour and admission not included).

Guided Walks Through Rome: Several companies do guided walks through Rome. Tom Rankin (an American in love with Rome and his Roman wife) runs **Scala Reale**, a small company committed to sorting out the rich layers of Rome for small groups (with a longer-than-normal attention span). Their excellent walking tours vary in length from two to four hours and start at around L50,000 per person. It's best to book in advance since their small groups fill

Rome

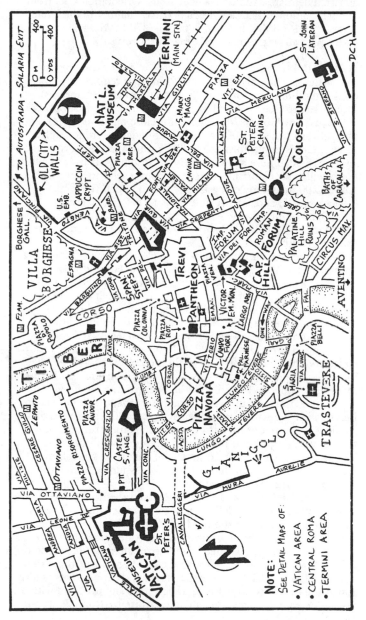

NOTE:
See Detail Maps of:
• Vatican area
• Central Roma
• Termini area

up fast. Their latest addition: a daily Rome Orientation walk from the train station to Piazza Venezia (toll-free number in the United States: 888/467-1986, Italy tel. & fax 06-4470-0898, Web site: www.scalareale.org, e-mail: scalareale@mail.nexus.it).

Helpful Hints

Plan Ahead: The only museum in Rome that requires reservations is the Borghese Museum (featuring Bernini's sculptures). Ideally, call to reserve ahead (see Sights—Villa Borghese, below).

Museum Hours: Most museums close on Monday (except the Vatican) and at 13:00 or 14:00 on Sunday. Outdoor sights like the Colosseum, Forum, and Ostia Antica are open roughly 9:00 to 18:00. There are absolutely no absolutes in Italy. These hours will vary. Confirm sightseeing plans each morning with a quick L200 telephone call asking, "Are you open today?" ("*Aperto oggi?*") and "What time do you close?" ("*A che ora chiuso?*"). I've included telephone numbers for this purpose. The last pages of the daily *Messaggero* newspaper list current events, exhibits, and hours.

Churches: Churches generally open early (around 7:00), close for lunch (roughly 12:00–15:00), and close late (around 19:00). Modest dress means no bare shoulders, miniskirts, or shorts (men or women). Kamikaze tourists maximize their sightseeing hours by visiting churches before 9:00 and seeing the major sights that stay open during the siesta (St. Peter's, Pantheon, Capitoline Museums, and the Forum) while all good Romans are taking it cool and easy.

Shop Hours: Usually 9:00 to 13:00 and 16:00 to 20:00. Groceries are often closed on Sunday. In the holiday month of August, many shops and restaurants close up for vacation and "*Chiuso per ferie*" signs decorate locked doors all over town.

Theft Alert: With sweet-talking con artists, pickpockets on buses and at the station, and thieving gangs at the ancient sights, Rome is a gauntlet of rip-offs. Other than getting run down, there's no great physical risk. But green tourists will be ripped off. Thieves strike when you're distracted. Don't trust kind strangers. Keep nothing important in your pockets. Assume you're being stalked. (Then relax and have fun.)

Buyer Beware: I carefully understand the final price before I order anything and I deliberately count my change. Expect the "slow count." Wait for the last bits of your change to straggle over to you. There are legitimate extras (café prices skyrocket when you sit down, taxis get L5,000 extra after 22:00, and so on) to which paranoid tourists wrongly take offense. But the waiter who charges you L70,000 for the pizza and beer assumes you're too polite to involve the police. If you have any problem with a restaurant, hotel, or taxi, get a cop to arbitrate. Rome is trying to civilize itself.

Staying Healthy: The siesta is a key to survival in summer-time Rome. Lie down and contemplate the extraordinary power of gravity in the eternal city. I drink lots of cold, refreshing water from Rome's many drinking fountains (the Forum has three). If you get sick, call Medi-Call (tel. 06-884-0113 or toll-free tel. 167-327-405, SE).

Arrival in Rome

By Train: The Termini train station is a minefield of tourist services: a late-hours bank, public showers, luggage lockers, 24-hour thievery, the city bus station, a subway stop, and a telephone office with lots of phones (Centro Telecomunicazioni, 8:00–21:45). Multilingual charts make locations fairly clear. The station is crawling with sleazy sharks with official-looking cards. Generally, avoid anybody selling anything at the station if you can. La Piazza, however, is a bright and cheery self-service restaurant (daily 11:00–22:30).

Most of my hotel listings are easily accessible by foot (near the train station) or by Metro (Colosseum and Vatican neighborhoods). The train station has its own Metro stop (Termini).

By Plane: If you arrive at the airport, catch a train (hrly, 30 min, L15,000) to Rome's train station or take a taxi to your hotel. For details see Transportation Connections, below.

Getting Around Rome

Sightsee on foot, by city bus, or by taxi. I've grouped your sightseeing into walkable neighborhoods. Public transportation is efficient, cheap, and part of your Roman experience. It starts running around 5:30 and stops around 23:30.

By Subway: The Roman subway system (Metropolitana) is simple, with two clean, cheap, fast lines. While much of Rome is not served by its skimpy subway, these stops are helpful: Termini (central train station, several recommended hotels, National Museum), Republica (main tourist office, several recommended hotels), Barberini (Cappuccin Crypt, Trevi Fountain), Spagna (Spanish Steps, Villa Borghese, classy shopping area), Flaminio (Piazza del Popolo, start of the Via del Corso Dolce Vita stroll), Ottaviano (the Vatican, recommended hotels), Colosseo (the Colosseum, Roman Forum, recommended hotels), and E.U.R. (Mussolini's futuristic suburb).

By Bus: Bus routes are clearly listed at the stops. Bus #64 is particularly useful, connecting the station, my recommended Via Nazionale hotels, Victor Emanuel Monument (near the Forum), Largo Argentina (near the Pantheon), and the Vatican. Ride it for a city overview and to watch pickpockets in action.

Buses and subways use the same ticket. You can buy tickets at newsstands, tobacco shops, or at major stations or bus stops, but

Metropolitana: Rome's Subway

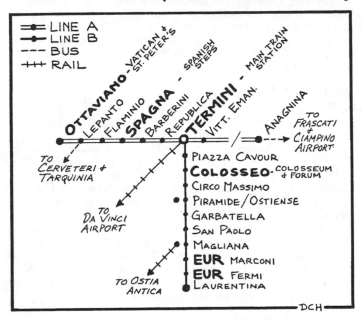

```
=●= LINE A
=●= LINE B
--- BUS
+++ RAIL
```

OTTAVIANO - VATICAN + ST. PETER'S
LEPANTO
FLAMINIO
SPAGNA - SPANISH STEPS
BARBERINI
REPUBLICA
TERMINI - MAIN TRAIN STATION
VITT. EMAN.
ANAGNINA
TO FRASCATI + CIAMPINO AIRPORT

TO CERVETERI + TARQUINIA

TO DA VINCI AIRPORT

PIAZZA CAVOUR
COLOSSEO - COLOSSEUM + FORUM
CIRCO MASSIMO
PIRAMIDE / OSTIENSE
GARBATELLA
SAN PAOLO
MAGLIANA
EUR MARCONI
EUR FERMI
LAURENTINA

TO OSTIA ANTICA

— DCH —

not on board (L1,500, good for 75 minutes—one Metro ride and unlimited buses, punch them yourself near back of bus as you board—or you are cheating; depart from front of bus). Buy a bunch of tickets so you can hop a bus without searching for an open tobacco shop. (Riding without a ticket, while relatively safe, is stressful. Inspectors fine even innocent-looking tourists L50,000 if found on a bus or subway without a ticket that has been stamped.) If you hop a bus without a ticket, locals who use tickets rather than a monthly pass can sell you a ticket from their wallet bundle. All-day bus/Metro passes cost L6,000. Learn which buses serve your neighborhood.

Buses, especially the touristic #64, and the subway, are havens for thieves and pickpockets. Assume any commotion is a thief-created distraction. Bus #64 gets extremely crowded.

By Taxi: Taxis start at about L5,000 (surcharges of L2,000 on Sunday, L5,000 for night hours of 22:00–7:00, L2,000 surcharge for luggage, L14,000 for airport). Sample fares: train station to Vatican, L16,000; train station to Colosseum, L10,000; Colosseum to Trastevere, L12,000. Three or four companions with more money than time should taxi almost everywhere. Rather than wave and wave, ask in local shops for the nearest taxi stand ("*Dové* [DOH-vay] *una fermata dei tassi?*"). Taxis with their telephone number on the door have fair meters—use them. If you or your hotel calls a taxi, the meter starts when the phone call is received.

Sights—Rome, near Forum

▲St. Peter-in-Chains Church (San Pietro in Vincoli)—The original chains and Michelangelo's able-to-stand-and-toss-those-tablets *Moses* are on exhibit in an otherwise unexceptional church, just a short walk uphill from the Colosseum (free, daily 6:30–12:30, 15:30–19:00, modest dress required).

▲▲Colosseum—This 2,000-year-old building is the great example of Roman engineering. Using concrete, brick, and their trademark round arches, Romans constructed much larger buildings than the Greeks. But in deference to the higher Greek culture, notice how they finished their no-nonsense megastructure by pasting all three orders of Greek columns (Doric, Ionic, and Corinthian) as exterior decorations. The Flavian Amphitheater's popular name "Colosseum" comes from the colossal statue of Nero that once stood in front of it.

Romans were into "big." By putting two theaters together, they created a circular amphitheater. They could fill and empty its 50,000 numbered seats as quickly and efficiently as we do our superstadiums. Teams of sailors hoisted canvas awnings over the stadium to give fans shade. This was where ancient Romans, whose taste for violence was the equal of modern America's, enjoyed their Dirty Harry and Terminator. Gladiators, criminals, and wild animals fought to the death in every conceivable scenario. They even waged mock naval battles (L10,000, Monday–Saturday 9:00–18:00, Sunday 9:00–13:00, off-season 9:00–15:00, tel. 06-700 4261). The stairs to the upper level are near the exit (north end).

In summer, tours led by history grads from America leave daily at 15:00 from the Colosseum metro stop (L5,000/1-hour tour of Colosseum, L15,000/3-hour tour of Colosseum, Forum, and Pantheon). These are informally run (no telephone number) and could be canceled; drop by only if you're in the neighborhood.

▲▲▲Roman Forum (Foro Romano)—Ancient Rome's birthplace and civic center, the Forum was the common ground between Rome's famous seven hills (free admission to Forum, L12,000 for Palatine Hill, Monday–Saturday 9:00–18:00, Sunday 9:00–13:00, off-season 9:00–15:00, tel. 06-699-0110). Just past the entry, there's a WC and a handy headless statue for you to pose behind.

To help resurrect this confusing pile of rubble, study the before-and-after pictures in the cheap city guidebooks sold on the streets. (Check out the small red *Rome, Past and Present* books with plastic overlays to un-ruin the ruins. They're priced at L25,000—pay no more than L15,000.) Follow this basic walk:

1. Start at the Basilica Aemilia (second century B.C., on your

The Forum Area

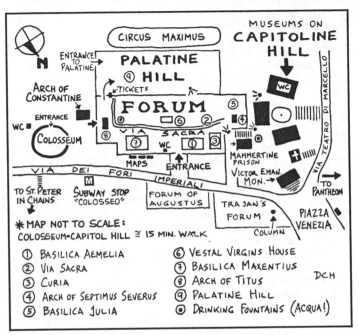

right as you walk down the entry ramp). Study the floorplan of the ancient palace. This pre-Christian "basilica" design was later adopted by medieval churches.

2. From the Basilica Aemilia, step out onto the Via Sacra (the Sacred Road), the main street of ancient Rome. It runs from the Arch of Septimus Severus on your right, past Basilica Aemilia, up to the Arch of Titus and the Colosseum on your left.

3. The plain, intact brick building near the Arch of Septimus Severus was the Curia where the Roman senate sat. (Peek inside.) Roman buildings were basically brick and concrete, usually with a marble veneer, which in this case has been long lost.

4. The Arch of Septimus Severus, from about A.D. 200, celebrates that emperor's military victories. In front of it a stone called the Lapis Niger covers the legendary tomb of Romulus. To the left of the arch, the stone bulkhead is the Rostra or speaker's platform. It's named for the ship's prows which used to decorate it as big shots hollered, "Friends, Romans, countrymen . . . "

5. The grand Basilica Julia, a first-century law court, fills the corner opposite the Curia. Ancient backgammon-type game boards are cut into the pavement.

6. Climb up toward the Palatine Hill, past the semicircular Temple of Vesta to the House of the Vestal Virgins. Here, the VVs kept the eternal flame lit. A set of ponds and a marble chorus line of Vestal Virgins mark the courtyard of the house.

7. Climb down to the Via Sacra and turn right toward the Colosseum. A path on the left leads up to the remains of the mammoth Basilica Maxentius. Only the giant barrel vaults remain, looming crumbly and weed-eaten. As you stand in the shadow of the Bas Max, reconstruct it in your mind. The huge barrel vaults were just side niches. Extend the broken nub of an arch out over the vacant lot and finish your imaginary Roman basilica with rich marble and fountains. People it with plenty of toga-clad Romans. Yeow.

8. Back on Via Sacra, continue climbing to the small Arch of Titus (drinking fountain opposite). The arch is carved with propaganda celebrating the A.D. 70 defeat of the Jews, which began the Diaspora that ended with the creation of Israel in 1947. Notice the gaggle of soldiers carrying the menorah.

9. From the Arch of Titus, walk up the Palatine Hill (L12,000 entry) to the remains of the Imperial palaces. We get our word "palace" from this hill, where the emperors chose to live. The newly-opened museum has sculptures and fresco fragments. From the pleasant garden, you'll get an overview of the Forum. On the far side, look down into an emperor's private stadium and then beyond at the dusty Circus Maximus, once a chariot course. Imagine the cheers, jeers, and furious betting.

▲**Thief Gangs**—If you know what to look out for, the gangs of children picking the pockets and handbags of naive tourists are no threat but an interesting, albeit sad, spectacle. Gangs of city-stained children, too young to prosecute but old enough to rip you off, troll through the tourist crowds around the Forum, Colosseum, and train and Metro stations. Watch them target tourists distracted with a video camera or overloaded with bags. The kids look like beggars and use newspapers or cardboard signs to confuse their victims. They scram like stray cats if you're onto them. A fast-fingered mother with a baby is often nearby.

▲**Mammertine Prison**—The 2,500-year-old converted cistern that once imprisoned Saints Peter and Paul is worth a look. On the walls are lists of prisoners (Christian and non-Christian) and how they were executed: *strangolati, decapitato, morto di fame* . . . (donation requested, daily 9:00–12:00, 14:30–18:00). At the top of the stairs leading to Capitoline Hill, you'll find a refreshing water fountain. Block the spout with your fingers; it spurts up for drinking.

Sights—Rome's Capitoline Hill
▲▲**Capitoline Hill (Campidoglio)**—This hill was the religious and political center of ancient Rome. It's still the home of the city's government. Michelangelo's Renaissance square is bounded

by two fine museums and the mayoral palace. Its centerpiece is a copy of his famous equestrian statue of Marcus Aurelius (behind glass in the adjacent museum). There's a fine view of the Forum from the terrace just past the mayor's palace on the right.

The two **Capitoline Museums** (Musei Capitolini) are in two buildings (one L10,000 ticket is good for both museums, free entrance on last Sunday of month, Tuesday–Sunday 9:00–19:00, closed Monday, tel. 06-671-02733).

The **Palazzo dei Conservatori** (the building nearest the river, on Marcus Aurelius' left side) is the world's oldest museum at 500 years old. Outside the entrance, notice the marriage announcements and, very likely, wedding-party photo ops. Inside the free courtyard, have a look at giant chunks of a statue of Emperor Constantine. (A rare public toilet hides near the museum ticket-taker.) The museum is worthwhile, with lavish rooms housing several great statues. Tops is the original (500 B.C.) Etruscan *Capitoline Wolf* (the little statues of Romulus and Remus were added in the Baroque age). Don't miss the *Boy Extracting a Thorn* or the enchanting *Commodus as Hercules*. The painting gallery (second floor) is forgettable except for one Carravagio.

Across the square, the **Palazzo Nuovo** houses mostly portrait busts of forgotten emperors. But it has two must-sees: the *Dying Gaul* (first floor) and the restored gilded bronze equestrian statue of Marcus Aurelius (behind glass in the museum courtyard). This greatest surviving equestrian statue of antiquity was the original centerpiece of the square. While most such statues were destroyed by Dark-Age Christians, Marcus was mistaken as Constantine (the first Christian emperor) and therefore spared.

To approach the great square the way Michelangelo wanted you to, walk halfway down the grand stairway toward Piazza Venezia, spin around, and walk back up. At the bottom of the stairs, look up the long stairway to your right (which pilgrims climb on their knees) for a good example of the earliest style of Christian church. While pilgrims find it worth the climb, sightseers can skip it.

From the bottom of the stairs, way down the street on your left, you'll see a condominium actually built around surviving ancient pillars and arches—perhaps the oldest inhabited building in Europe. Farther ahead (toward Piazza Venezia), look down into the ditch on your right, and see how everywhere modern Rome is built on the forgotten frescoes and mangled mosaics of ancient Rome.

Piazza Venezia—This vast square is the focal point of modern Rome. The Via del Corso, starting here, is the city's axis, surrounded by Rome's classiest shopping district. From the Palazzo Venezia's balcony above the square (to your left with back to Victor Emanuel Monument), Mussolini whipped up the nationalistic fervor of Italy. Fascist masses filled the square screaming, "Four more years!" or something like that. (Fifteen years later, they hung him from a meat hook in Milan.)

Victor Emanuel Monument—This oversized monument to an Italian king loved only by his relatives and the ignorant is known to most Romans as "the wedding cake," "the typewriter," or "the dentures." It wouldn't be so bad if it weren't sitting on a priceless acre of ancient Rome. Soldiers guard Italy's Tomb of the Unknown Soldier as the eternal flame flickers. Stand directly in front of it and see how Via del Corso bisects Rome.

▲**Trajan's Column**—This is the grandest column and best example of "continuous narration" from antiquity. Study the propaganda which winds up the column like a scroll, trumpeting Trajan's wonderful military exploits. You can view this close-up for free across Mussolini's busy Via dei Fori Imperiali from the Victor Emanuel Monument. In its day, for easier viewing, Trajan fans could study the scenes from the balconies of buildings which stood tall on either side.

Sights—Heart of Rome

▲▲▲**Pantheon**—For the greatest look at the splendor of Rome, antiquity's best-preserved interior is a must (free, Monday–Saturday 9:00–18:30, Sunday 9:00–13:00, tel. 06-683-00230). Since it became a church dedicated to the martyrs just after the fall of Rome, the barbarians left it alone and the locals didn't use it as a quarry. The portico is called Rome's umbrella—a fun local gathering in a rainstorm. Walk past its one-piece granite columns (biggest in Italy, shipped from Egypt) and through the original bronze doors. Sit inside under the glorious skylight and study it.

The dome, 140 feet high and wide, was Europe's biggest until the 20th century. Michelangelo's dome at St. Peter's, while much higher, is one meter smaller. The brilliance of its construction astounded architects through the ages. During the Renaissance, Brunelleschi was given permission to cut into the dome (see the little square hole above and to the right of the entrance) to analyze the material. The concrete dome gets thinner and lighter with height—the highest part is of volcanic pumice.

This wonderfully harmonious architecture greatly inspired the artists of the Renaissance, particularly Raphael. Raphael, along with Italy's first two kings, chose to be buried here. As you walk around the outside of the Pantheon, notice the "rise of Rome"— about 15 feet since it was built.

▲▲**Curiosities near the Pantheon**—The only Gothic church you'll see in Rome is Santa Maria sopra Minerva. On a little square behind the Pantheon to the east, past the Bernini statue of an elephant carrying an Egyptian obelisk, this Dominican church was built *sopra* (over) a pre-Christian temple of Minerva. Before

Heart of Rome

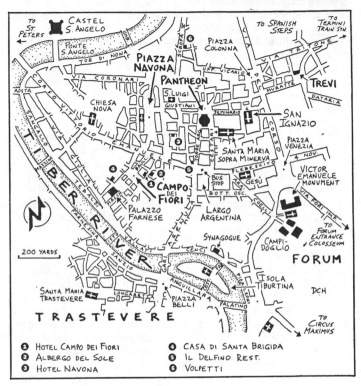

1 Hotel Campo dei Fiori   **4** Casa di Santa Brigida
2 Albergo del Sole   **5** Il Delfino Rest.
3 Hotel Navona   **6** Volpetti

stepping in, notice the high-water marks on the wall (right of door). Inside you'll see that the lower parts of the frescoes were lost to these floods.

Rome was at its low ebb, almost a ghost town, through much of the Gothic period. Little was built during this time. (And much of what was, was redone Baroque.) This church is a refreshing exception. St. Catherine's body lies under the altar (her head is in Siena). The patron saint of Italy, she convinced the pope to return from France to Rome, thus saving Italy from untold chaos.

Left of the altar stands a little-known Michelangelo statue, *Christ Bearing the Cross*. Michelangelo gave Jesus an athlete's or warrior's body (a striking contrast to the more docile Christ of medieval art) but left the face to one of his pupils. Fra Angelico's simple tomb is farther to the left, on the way to the back door. Before leaving, head over to the right (south transept), pop in a L500 coin for light, and enjoy a fine Filippo Lippi fresco showing scenes from the life of

St. Thomas Aquinas—founder of the Dominicans.

Exit the church via its rear door (behind the Michelangelo statue), walk down Fra Angelico lane (spy any artisans at work), turn left, and walk to the next square. On your right you'll find the **Chiesa di St. Ignazio** church, a riot of Baroque illusions. Study the fresco over the door and the ceiling in the back of the nave. Then stand on the yellow disk on the floor between the two stars. Look at the central (black) dome. Keeping your eyes on the dome, walk under and past it. Church building project runs out of money? Hire a painter to paint a fake, flat dome. (Both churches open early, take a siesta—Sopra Minerva closes at 12:00, St. Ignazio at 12:30; they reopen around 15:30 and close at 19:00. Modest dress recommended.)

A few blocks away, back across Corso Vittorio Emanuele, is the very rich and Baroque **Gesu Church**, headquarters of the Jesuits in Rome. The Jesuits powered the Church's Counter-Reformation. With Protestants teaching that all roads to heaven didn't pass through Rome, the Baroque churches of the late 1500s were painted with spiritual road maps that said they did.

Walk out the Gesu Church and two blocks down Corso V. Emanuele to the **Sacred Area** (Largo Argentina), an excavated square facing the boulevard, two blocks from the Pantheon. Walk around this square looking into the excavated pit at some of the oldest ruins in Rome. It was here that Caesar was assassinated. Today this is a refuge for cats. Some 250 cats are cared for by volunteers. You'll see them (and their refuge) at the far (west) side of the square.

Self-guided Walks—Rome

▲▲▲**The Dolce Vita Stroll down Via del Corso**—This is the city's chic and hip "cruise" from the Piazza del Popolo (Metro: Flaminio) down a wonderfully traffic-free section of the Via del Corso and up Via Condotti to the Spanish Steps each evening around 18:00. Shoppers, take a left on Via Condotti for the Spanish Steps and Gucci (shops open after siesta, 16:30–19:30). Historians, start with a visit to the Baroque Church of Santa Maria del Popolo (with Raphael's Chigi Chapel and two Caravaggio paintings, on the far side of Piazza del Popolo), and continue down the Via del Corso to the Victor Emanuel Monument. Climb Michelangelo's stairway to his glorious Campidoglio Square and catch the lovely view of the Forum (from past the mayor's palace on right) as the horizon reddens and cats prowl the unclaimed rubble of ancient Rome.

▲▲▲**Floodlit Rome Hike: Trastevere to the Spanish Steps**— Rome can be grueling. But a fine way to enjoy this historian's fertility rite is an evening walk lacing together Rome's floodlit night spots. Fine urban spaces, real-life theater vignettes, sitting close enough to the Bernini fountain to hear no traffic, water flickering its mirror on the marble, jostling with local teenagers to see all the gelato flavors, enjoying lovers straddling more than the bench, jay-walking past flak-vested *polizia*, marveling at the ramshackle elegance that softens this brutal city for those who were born here and can imagine living nowhere else—these are the flavors of Rome best tasted after dark.

Taxi or ride the bus (from Vatican area—#23, from Via Nazionale hotels—take #64, #70, #115, or #640 to Largo Argentina, then transfer to #8) to Trastevere, the colorful neighborhood across (*tras*) the Tiber (*tevere*). Start your hike at Santa Maria in Trastevere. Trastevere offers the best look at medieval-village Rome. The action all marches to the chime of the church bells. Go there and wander. Wonder. Be a poet. This is Rome's Left Bank.

Santa Maria in Trastevere (free, daily 7:30–13:00, 15:00–19:00), one of Rome's oldest churches, was made a basilica in the fourth century when Christianity was legalized. It was the first church dedicated to the Virgin Mary. Most of what you see today is from around the 12th century, but the ancient basilica floorplan (and ambience) survives and the portico (covered area just outside the door) is decorated with fascinating ancient fragments filled with early Christian symbolism. The 12th-century mosaics behind the altar are striking and notable for their portrayal of Mary—the first showing her at the throne with Jesus in Heaven. The ahead-of-their-time paintings (by Cavallini, from 1300) below scenes from the life of Mary predate the Renaissance by 100 years.

Don't leave Trastevere until you've wandered the back streets. From the square (see Eating, below), Via del Moro leads to the river and Ponte Sisto, a pedestrian bridge with a good view of St. Peter's dome. Cross the bridge and continue straight ahead for one block. Take the first left, which leads down Via di Capo di Ferro through the scary and narrow darkness to Piazza Farnese, with the imposing Palazzo Farnese. Michelangelo contributed to the facade of this palace, now the French embassy. The fountains on the square feature huge one-piece granite hot tubs from the ancient Roman Baths of Caracalla.

One block from there (opposite the palace) is **Campo dei Fiori** (Field of Flowers), which is my favorite outdoor dining room after dark (see Eating, below). The statue of Giordano Bruno, a heretic who was burned in 1600 for believing the world was round and not the center of the universe, marks the center of this great and colorful square. Bruno overlooks a busy produce market in the morning and strollers after dark. This neighborhood is still known for its free spirit. When the statue of Bruno was erected in 1889, local riots overcame Vatican protests against honoring a heretic. Bruno faces his executioner, the Vatican Chancellory (the big white building in the corner a bit to his right), while

on the pedestal the words say "and the flames rose up." The
square is lined and surrounded by fun eateries. Bruno also faces La
Carbonara, which gave birth to pasta carbonara. The Forno, next
door, is a popular place for hot and tasty take-out *pizza bianco*.

If Bruno did a hop, step, and jump forward and turned
right, he'd cross the busy Corso Vittorio Emanuele and find
Piazza Navona. Rome's most interesting night scene features
street music, artists, fire-eaters, local Casanovas, ice cream, outdoor cafés (splurge-worthy if you've got time to sit and enjoy the
human river of Italy), and three fountains by Bernini, the father
of Baroque art. Its Tartufo "death by chocolate" ice cream
(L5,000 to go, L11,000 at a table, closed Wednesday) made the
Tre Scalini café world-famous among connoisseurs of ice cream
and chocolate alike. This oblong square is molded around the
long-gone stadium of Domitian, an ancient chariot racetrack
that was often flooded so the masses could enjoy major water
games.

Leave Piazza Navona directly across from the Tre Scalini
café, go past rose peddlers and palm readers, jog left around the
guarded building, and follow the yellow sign to the Pantheon
straight down Via del Salvatore (cheap pizza place on left just
before the Pantheon). Sit for a while under the flood- and moonlit
Pantheon's portico.

With your back to the Pantheon, head right, passing Bar
Pantheon on your right. A blue-and-white arrow points down the
street past the Tazza d'Oro Casa del Caffè. The Tazza d'Oro, one
of Rome's top coffee shops, dates back to the days when this area
was licensed to roast coffee beans. Look back at the fine view of
the Pantheon from here.

Ahead is Piazza Capranica with the Florentine Renaissance–
style Palazzo Capranica. Big shots, like the Capranica family,
built stubby towers on their palaces—not of any military use . . .
just to show off. Leave the piazza to the right of the palace, following another white arrow. (These arrows, which I put here for
this tour in the late 1980s, are now accepted by local traffic.) Via
in Aquino leads to another arrow pointing to a sixth-century B.C.
Egyptian obelisk (taken as a trophy by Augustus after his victory
in Egypt over Mark Antony and Cleopatra). Approaching the
obelisk you'll find two arrows. Detour to the left for some of
Rome's best gelato. **Gelateria Caffè Pasticceria Giolitti** (just
behind Albergo Nazionale, Via Uffici del Vicario 40, open daily
until very late) is cheap to-go or elegant and splurge-worthy for
a sit among classy locals. Or head right, walking down Via della
Colonna Antonina to the big noisy main drag of downtown
Rome, Via del Corso.

Piazza Colonna features a huge second-century column
honoring Marcus Aurelius. The big important-looking palace is

the prime minister's residence. While pink, this is the closest thing in Italy to a "White House." Cross the street and take the right branch of the Y-shaped shopping gallery (1928) and exit, continuing straight down Via de Crociferi (or, if closed, head down Via dei Sabini) to the roar of the water, light, and people of the Trevi fountain.

The **Trevi fountain** is an example of how Rome took full advantage of the abundance of water brought into the city by its great aqueducts. This watery Baroque avalanche was built in 1762. Romantics toss two coins over their shoulder thinking it will give them a wish and assure their return to Rome. That may sound silly, but every year I go through this touristic ritual . . . and it actually seems to work.

Take some time to people-watch (whisper a few breathy *bellos* or *bellas*) before leaving. Facing the fountain, go past it on the right down Via delle Stamperia to Via del Triton. Cross the busy street and continue to the Spanish Steps (ask, "*Dové Piazza di Spagna?*") a few blocks and thousands of dollars of shopping opportunities away.

The **Piazza di Spagna** (rhymes with "lasagna"), with the very popular Spanish Steps, got its name 300 years ago when this was the site of the Spanish Embassy. It's been the hangout of many Romantics over the years (Keats, Wagner, Openshaw, Goethe, and others). The Boat Fountain at the foot of the steps was done by Bernini's father, Bernini. This is a thriving night scene.

Facing the steps, walk to your right about a block to tour one of the world's biggest and most lavish McDonald's. About a block on the other side of the steps is the subway, or Metropolitana, which (until 23:30) will zip you home.

Sights—Vatican City

This tiny independent country of just over 100 acres, contained entirely within Rome, has its own postal system, armed guard, helipad, mini-train station, and radio station (KPOP). Politically powerful, the Vatican is the religious capital of 800 million Roman Catholics. If you're not one already, become a Catholic for your visit. There's a helpful tourist office just to the left of St. Peter's Basilica (Monday–Saturday 8:30–19:00, tel. 06-6988-4466, Vatican switchboard 06-6982, Web site: www.vatican.va). Check out the glossy L5,000 guidebooklet (crowded piazza on cover), which doubles as a classy souvenir. Telephone the Vatican TI if you're interested in their sporadic but very good tours of the Vatican grounds or the church interior, or the pope's schedule (see below). If you don't care to see the pope, minimize crowd problems by avoiding these times.

Near the end of 1999 (or as soon as contruction work is completed within the Vatican grounds) the shuttle bus between St.

Vatican City, St. Peter's, and the Museum

Peter's and the Vatican Museum may begin running again (the stop is outside St. Peter's TI, to the left as you face the church). These little buses save you a 15-minute walk around the wall, give you a pleasant peek at the garden-filled Vatican grounds, and allow you to bypass the line outside the Vatican Museum. When running, the service costs L2,000 (2/hrly, 8:45–13:45, or 12:45 when museum closes early).

▲▲▲**St. Peter's Basilica**—There is no doubt: This is the richest and most impressive church on earth. To call it vast is like calling God smart. Marks on the floor show where the next-largest churches would fit if they were put inside. The ornamental cherubs would dwarf a large man. Birds roost inside, and thousands of people wander about, heads craned heavenward, hardly noticing each other. Don't miss Michelangelo's *Pietà* (behind bulletproof glass) to the right of the entrance. Bernini's altar work and seven-story-tall bronze canopy (*baldacchino*) are brilliant.

For a quick self-guided walk through the basilica, follow these points:

1. The atrium is larger than most churches. Notice the historic doors (the Holy Door, on the right, will be opened in the year 2000—see point 13 below). Guided tours depart from the desk nearby.

2. The purple circular porphyry stone marks the site of Charlemagne's coronation in A.D. 800. From here get a sense of the immensity of the church, which can accommodate 95,000 worshippers standing on its six acres.

3. Michelangelo planned to build a Greek cross church plan. A Greek cross, symbolizing the perfection of God, and by association the goodness of man, was important to the humanist Michelangelo. But accommodating large crowds was important to the Church in the fancy Baroque age, so the original nave length was doubled. Stand halfway up the nave and imagine the stubbier design Michelangelo had in mind.

4. View the magnificent dome from the statue of St. Andrew. See the vision of heaven above the windows: Jesus, Mary, a ring of saints, rings of angels, and, on the very top, God the Father.

5. The main altar sits directly over St. Peter's tomb and under Bernini's 70-foot-tall bronze canopy.

6. Take the stairs down to the crypt to see the foundation of St. Peter's chapels and tombs of popes.

7. The statue of St. Peter, with an irresistably kissable toe, is one of the few pieces of art which predate this church. It adorned the first St. Peter's church.

8. St. Peter's Throne and Bernini's star-burst dove window is the site of a daily Mass at 17:00.

9. St. Peter was crucified here (at the time the middle spot of a Roman racecourse) when this location was simply "the Vatican Hill."

10. For most, the treasury (in the sacristy) is not worth the admission.

11. The church is filled with mosaics, not paintings. Notice the mosaic version of Raphael's *Transfiguration*.

12. Blessed Sacrament Chapel.

13. Michelangelo sculpted this *Pietà* when he was 24 years old. A pietà is a work showing Mary with the dead body of Christ taken down from the cross. Michelangelo's mastery of the body is obvious in this powerfully beautiful masterpiece. Jesus is believably dead and Mary, the eternally youthful "handmaiden" of the Lord, still accepts God's will . . . even if it means giving up her son.

The Holy Door (piled high with plaster with a cross in its center, just to the right of the *Pietà*) will be opened in 2000, symbolizing the "Jubilee Year." Every 25 years the Church celebrates an especially festive year derived from the Old Testament idea of

St. Peter's Basilica

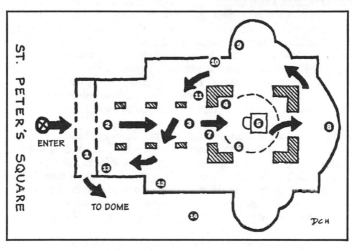

the Jubilee Year (originally every 50 years) which encourages new beginnings. Sins and debts are forgiven. The pope is tirelessly calling for this particularly monumental Jubilee Year to be one in which the World Bank and the world's rich countries will usher in the new millennium by forgiving or relieving the crippling debt burden which keeps much of the Third World in squalor.

14. An elevator leads to the roof and the stairway up the dome. The dome, Michelangelo's last work, is (you guessed it) the biggest anywhere. Taller than a football field is long, it's well worth the sweaty climb for a great view of Rome, the Vatican grounds, and the inside of the Basilica—particularly heavenly while there is singing. Look around—Rome has no modern skyline. No building is allowed to exceed the height of St. Peter's. The elevator (just outside the church to the right as you face it) takes you to the rooftop of the nave. From there a few steps bring you to a balcony at the base of the dome looking down into the church interior. After that the one-way 300-step climb (for some people, claustrophobic) to the cupola begins. The rooftop level (below the dome) has a gift shop, bathroom, drinking fountain, and a commanding view (L6,000 elevator, allow an hour to go up and down, daily 8:30–19:00 May–September, 8:30–18:00 October–April; ticket booth closes one hour earlier).

The church strictly enforces its dress code. Dress modestly—a dress or long pants, shoulders covered (men and women). You are usually required to check any bags at a free cloakroom near the entry. St. Peter's is open daily May through September from 7:00

to 19:00, until 18:00 October through April; ticket booth to treasury closes one hour earlier. All are welcome to join in the Mass at
the front altar (one hour, Monday–Saturday 17:00, Sunday 17:45).

The church is particularly moving at 7:00 while tourism is
still sleeping. Volunteers who want you to understand and appreciate St. Peter's give free 90-minute "Pilgrim Service" tours in
English usually at 10:00 and 12:30; these are usually excellent but
can lapse into preachiness. Check for the day's schedule at the
desk just after the dress-code check as you're entering. Seeing the
Pietà is neat; understanding it is divine.

▲▲▲**Vatican Museum**—Too often the immense Vatican
Museum is treated as an obstacle course, with four nagging miles
of displays, separating the tourist from the Sistine Chapel. Even
without the Sistine, this is one of Europe's top three or four
houses of art. It can be exhausting, so plan your visit carefully,
focusing on a few themes. Allow two hours for a quick visit, three
or four for time to enjoy it. The museum uses a nearly-impossible-
not-to-follow, one-way system.

You'll start as civilization did, in Egypt and Mesopotamia.
Next, the Pio Clementino collection features Greek and Roman
statues. Decorating its courtyard are some of the very best Greek
and Roman statues in captivity, including the *Laocoon* group (first
century B.C., Hellenistic) and the *Apollo Belvedere* (a second-century
Roman copy of a Greek original). The centerpiece of the next hall
is the *Belvedere Torso* (just a 2,000-year-old torso, but one which
had a great impact on the art of Michelangelo). Finishing off the
classical statuary are two fine fourth-century porphyry sarcophagi
(royal, purple stones for the coffins of Constantine's mother and
daughter). Crafted in Egypt at a time when a declining Rome was
unable to do such fine work, the details are fun to study.

After long halls of tapestries, old maps, broken penises, and
fig-leaves, you'll come to what most people are looking for: the
Raphael *stanza*, or rooms, and Michelangelo's Sistine Chapel.

These outstanding works are frescoes. A *fresco* (meaning
"fresh" in Italian) is not actually a painting. The color is mixed
into wet plaster and, when the plaster dries, the painting is actually
part of the wall. This is a durable but difficult medium requiring
speed and accuracy as the work is built slowly, one patch at a time.

After fancy rooms illustrating the "immaculate conception
of Mary" (a hard-to-sell, 19th-century Vatican doctrine) and the
triumph of Constantine (with divine guidance which led to his
conversion to Christianity), you enter the first room completely
done by Raphael and find the newly-restored *School of Athens*.
This is remarkable for its blatant pre-Christian classical orientation wallpapering the apartments of Pope Julius II. Raphael honors the great pre-Christian thinkers—Aristotle, Plato, and
company—who are portrayed as the leading artists of Raphael's

day. The bearded figure of Plato is Leonardo da Vinci. Diogenes, history's first hippie, sprawls alone in bright blue on the stairs, while Michelangelo broods in the foreground—supposedly added late. Apparently Raphael snuck a peek at the Sistine Chapel and decided that his arch-competitor was so good he had to put their personal differences aside and include him in this tribute to the artists of his generation. Today's St. Peter's was under construction as Raphael was working. In the *School of Athens*, he gives us a sneak preview of the unfinished church.

Next (unless you detour through the refreshingly modern Catholic art section) is the brilliantly restored Sistine Chapel. The Sistine Chapel, the pope's personal chapel, is where, upon the death of the ruling pope, a new pope is elected. The College of Cardinals meets here and votes four times a day until a two-thirds-plus-one majority is reached and a new pope is elected.

The Sistine is famous for Michelangelo's pictorial culmination of the Renaissance, showing the story of Creation with a powerful God weaving in and out of each scene through that busy first week. This is an optimistic and positive expression of the High Renaissance and a powerful example of the artistic and theological maturity of the 33-year-old Michelangelo, who spent four years at this work.

Later, after the Reformation wars had begun and after the Catholic army of Spain had sacked the Vatican, the reeling church began to fight back. As part of its Counter-Reformation, a much older Michelangelo was commissioned to paint the *Last Judgment* (behind the altar). Newly restored, the message is as brilliant and clear as the day Michelangelo finished it: Christ is returning, some will go to hell and some to heaven, and some will be saved by the power of the rosary.

In the recent (and controversial) restoration project no paint was added. Centuries of dust, soot (from candles used for lighting and Mass), and glue (added to make the art shine) were removed, revealing the bright original colors of Michelangelo.

The Vatican's small but fine collection of paintings, the Pinacoteca (with Raphael's *Transfiguration* and Caravaggio's *Entombment*), is near the entry/exit. The underrated early-Christian-art section is the final possible side trip before exiting via the souvenir shop.

Vatican Museum nitty-gritty: Just inside the entrance two huge elevators (*ascensore*) zip you past mobs climbing the fancy staircase. (Museum admission L18,000, April–mid-June and in September and October: open 8:45–16:30, Saturday 8:45–13:45, closed Sunday, except last Sunday of month when museum is free; the rest of the year it's open Monday–Saturday 8:45–13:45. Last entry 45 minutes before closing. The Sistine Chapel closes 30 minutes before the rest of the museum. Closed May 1, June 29, August 15, November 1, December 8, and on church holidays. Tel. 06-6988-3333.) The museum clearly marks out four color-coded visits of different lengths (A is shortest, D longest). The rentable CD-ROM tour (L8,000) is a great new system, letting you dial whichever piece of art you'd like commentary on as you come across numbered pieces in the museum. It offers a fine coverage of the Raphael rooms and Michelangelo's Sistine masterpiece. A small door at the rear of the Sistine Chapel allows tour groups and speedy individuals (without CD-ROM) to escape directly to St. Peter's Basilica (ignore sign saying "Tour Groups Only"). If you squirt out here you're done with the museum. The Pinacoteca is the only important part left. Consider doing it at the start. Otherwise it's a 10-minute heel-to-toe slalom through tourists from the Sistine to the entry/exit.

The museum's excellent book-and-card shop offers a priceless (L12,000) black-and-white photo book (by Hupka) of the *Pietà*— great for gifts. The Vatican post, with an office in the museum and one on Piazza San Pietro (comfortable writing rooms, Monday–Friday 8:30–19:00, Saturday 8:30–18:00), is the only reliable mail service in Italy. The stamps are a collectible bonus (Vatican stamps are good throughout Rome; Italian stamps are not good at the Vatican). The Vatican bank has sinful rates. The modern cafeteria is handy but comes with long lines and mediocre food.

To see the pope: The pope reads a prayer and blesses the gathered masses from his library window overlooking Piazza San Pietro each Sunday at noon. During the summer (when he's in town) the Holy Father blesses the masses from St. Peter's Square each Wednesday morning at 11:00 (10:00 if it's really hot). In the winter this is done in the 7,000-seat Aula Paola VI Auditorium (free, Wednesday at 11:00, call 06-698-83273 for details and reservations). Smaller ceremonies celebrated by the pope require reservations. The weekly entertainment guide *Romanc'e* always has a "Seeing the Pope" section.

Sights—Near Train Station
▲**National Museum of Rome (Museo Nazionale Romano)**— Directly in front of the train station, the Palazzo Massimo houses much of the greatest ancient Roman sculpture (L12,000, Tuesday–Saturday 9:00–14:00, Sunday 9:00–13:00, closed Monday, Via E. de Nicola 79, tel. 06-488-0530). The museum, which was closed much of 1998 for restoration, should reopen by January 1999.
▲**Baths of Diocletian**—At the far side of the National Museum, facing Piazza Republica, the Aula Ottagona (or Rotunda of Diocletian) is an impressive octagonal hall from A.D. 300 decorated with fine ancient statues and worth a quick peek (free, Tuesday–Saturday 9:00–14:00, Sunday 9:00–13:00, closed Monday, borrow the English description booklet).
Santa Maria Della Vittoria—This church houses Bernini's statue of a swooning *St. Theresa in Ecstasy* (free, daily 6:30–11:30,

16:30–19:00, Largo Susanna, about five blocks northwest of train station, Metro: Republica).

Sights—Villa Borghese and nearby Via Veneto

▲**Villa Borghese**—Rome's unkempt "Central Park" is great for people-watching (plenty of modern-day Romeos and Juliets). Take a row on the lake or visit its fine museums.

▲▲**Borghese Gallery**—This private museum uses a reservation system for admission to its collection of world-class Baroque sculpture, including Bernini's *David* and his excited statue of Apollo chasing Daphne, as well as paintings by Caravaggio, Giorgioni, Titian, and Rubens (L12,000, Tuesday–Saturday 9:00–22:00, Sunday 9:00–20:00, closed Monday, shorter hours off-season, located within Villa Borghese, tel. 06-854-8577). Entry times occur every two hours (e.g., 9:00, 11:00, etc.). To book a reservation, call 06-328 101 (if you get a recording in Italian, hang on, English will follow; booking office open Tuesday–Friday 9:00–19:00, Saturday 9:00–13:00; pick up tickets at least one hour before your scheduled time). If you want to book a reservation for a weekday, phone a week ahead. For a weekend visit, phone a month ahead. If you're in Rome without a reservation and you find the museum is booked up for days, go directly to the museum. You have two options. Plan A: Ask to be put on a waiting list; you'll get in if there are no-shows. Plan B: Try to tag along with a group (with their permission) that hasn't prepaid their admission. If they have prepaid, return to Plan A. Bring something to read or do while you wait. If nothing works, content yourself with seeing Bernini's fountains in the Piazza Navona and his *St. Theresa in Ecstacy* in the church Santa Maria Della Vittoria (on Largo Susanna, see above).

Also within the Villa Borghese is the **Museo di Villa Giulia**, a fine Etruscan museum (L8,000, Tuesday–Saturday 9:00–19:00, Sunday 9:00–13:30, closed Monday, tel. 06-320-1951).

▲**Cappuccin Crypt**—If you want bones, this is it: Below Santa Maria della Immaculata Concezione on Via Veneto, just off Piazza Barberini, are thousands of skeletons, all artistically arranged for the delight—or disgust—of the always-wide-eyed visitor. The monastic message on the wall explains that this is more than just a macabre exercise. Pick up a few of Rome's most interesting postcards (L1,000 donation, daily 9:00–12:00, 15:00–18:30, Metro: Barbarini). A bank with long hours and good exchange rates is next door, and the American Embassy and Federal Express are just up the street.

Sights—Away from Center

▲**E.U.R.**—Mussolini's planned suburb of the future (65 years ago) is a 10-minute subway ride from the Colosseum to Metro:

Magliana. From the Magliana subway stop, walk through the park uphill to the **Palace of the Civilization of Labor** (Pal. d. Civilta d. Concordia), the essence of Fascist architecture, with its giant, no-questions-asked, patriotic statues and its this-is-the-truth simplicity. On the far side is the **Museo della Civilta Romana**, a history museum which includes a large-scale model of ancient Rome (L5,000, Tuesday–Saturday 9:00–19:00, Sunday 9:00–13:30, closed Monday, Piazza G. Agnelli, Metro: E.U.R. Fermi, tel. 06-592-6041).

Pyramid—If you haven't been to Egypt, here's your chance to see a baby pyramid. Built in 12 B.C. as a tomb for the Roman Gaius Cestius, it's about 90 feet tall and was later incorporated into Rome's city wall. If you're taking the Metro to E.U.R., it's easy to surface at Metro: Piramide en route. It'll cost you only an extra Metro ticket (when you continue your journey).

▲▲**Ostia Antica**—Rome's ancient seaport (80,000 people in the time of Christ, later a ghost town, now excavated), less than an hour from downtown, is the next best thing to Pompeii. Start at the 2,000-year-old theater, buy a map, explore the town, and finish with its fine little museum. To get there take the subway's B Line to the Magliana stop, catch the Lido train to Ostia Antica (twice an hour), walk over the overpass, go straight to the end of that road, and follow the signs to (or ask for) "*scavi* Ostia Antica" (L8,000, Tuesday–Sunday 9:00–18:00, closed Monday, museum closes at 14:00; in winter open Tuesday–Sunday 9:00–16:00, tel. 06-5635-8099). Just beyond is Rome's filthy beach (*lido*).

Overrated Sights

The Spanish Steps (with Italy's first, and one of the world's largest, McDonald's—McGrandeur at its greatest—just down the street) and the commercialized Catacombs, which contain no bones, are way out of the city and are not worth the time or trouble. The venerable old Villa d'Este garden of fountains near Hadrian's Villa outside of town at Tivoli is now rundown, overpriced, and disappointing.

Sleeping in Rome
(L1,700 = about $1)

Sleep Code: **S** = Single, **D** = Double/Twin, **T** = Triple, **Q** = Quad, **b** = bathroom, **t** = toilet only, **s** = shower only, **CC** = Credit Card (Visa, MasterCard, Amex), **SE** = Speaks English, **NSE** = No English. Breakfast is normally included in the expensive places.

The absolute cheapest doubles in Rome are L70,000, without shower or breakfast. You'll pay L25,000 in a sleazy dorm or hostel. A nicer hotel (L120,000 doubles, L150,000 with bath, L190,000 with air-conditioning) provides an oasis and refuge, making it easier to enjoy this intense and grinding city. If you're going door to door, prices are soft—so bargain. Hotels list official prices which assume an agency or room-finding service kickback which, if you're coming direct, they avoid. Many hotels have high-season (mid-March–October) and low-season prices. Easter and September are the crowded times. In August, when temperatures climb, prices drop or get soft. Most of my recommended hotels are small, with huge, murky entrances that make you feel like a Q-Tip in a gas station. Most places speak English, but the amount of English spoken drops with the price. I've listed mostly places with minimal traffic noise, but you should always ask for a *tranquillo* room. Many prices here are promised only to people who show this book, don't use a credit card, and come direct without using a room-finding service. On Easter, April 25, and May 1 the entire city gets booked up.

Sleeping on/near Via Firenze

This is where I generally stay: It's tranquil, safe, handy, central, and a short walk from the central train station and airport shuttle, two blocks beyond the Piazza Republica and the TI. The first four are family-run. Parking is actually workable on Via Firenze. Double-park below the hotel until a space without yellow lines becomes available (confirm locally that it's still legal). The defense ministry is nearby, and you've got heavily armed guards all night. Virtually all the orange buses which rumble down Via Nazionale (#64, #70, #115, #640) take you to Largo Argentina. Beyond that, #8 goes to Trastevere (first stop after crossing the river) and #64 continues to the Vatican (last stop—jammed with people and thieves).

Hotel Oceania is a peaceful slice of air-conditioned heaven. This nine-room manor house–type hotel is spacious and quiet, with newly renovated and spotless rooms, run by a pleasant father-and-son team (Sb-L190,000, Db-L245,000, Tb-L310,000, Qb-L370,000, 10 percent off if you show this book, additional 15 percent off in August and winter, breakfast included, TVs, phones, CC:VMA, Via Firenze 38, 00184 Roma, tel. 06-482-4696, fax 06-488-5586, e-mail: hoceania@tin.it, son Stefano SE).

Residence Adler, with its wide halls, garden patio, and 16 big, quiet, and elegant rooms in a great locale, is a good deal, run by a charming family (D-L135,000, Db-L170,000, T-L170,000, Tb-L220,000, Q-L220,000, Qb-L280,000, including breakfast, CC:VMA, elevator, Via Modena 5, 00184 Roma, tel. 06-484-466, fax 06-488-0940, NSE).

Hotel Aberdeen is my classiest hotel listing and a good value for Rome. It has mini-bars, phones, TVs, and showers in its quiet, modern, wood-floored rooms; includes a first-class breakfast buffet; and is warmly run by Annamaria, with support from her cousins Sabrina and Cinzia, and trusty Reda on the late shift (Sb-L155,000, Db-L220,000, Tb-L260,000, with this book through 1999, L40,000 less per room in August and winter, air-conditioning for an extra L20,000/day, CC:VMA, garage-L40,000; reach up and swing those knockers at Via Firenze 48, 00184 Roma, tel. 06-482-3920, fax 06-482-1092, SE).

Hotel Cortina, run by the Aberdeen folks, is similarly quiet, classy, and comfortable. For the same prices as the Aberdeen, you get less soul but free air-conditioning (15 wood-floored rooms, Db-L210,000, breakfast included, Via Nazionale 18, 00184 Roma, tel. 06-481-9794, fax 06-481-9220, John Carlo SE).

Hotel Pensione Italia, in a busy, interesting, handy locale, placed safely on a quiet street next to the Ministry of the Interior, is comfortable, airy, bright, clean, and thoughtfully run by English-speaking Andrea and Abdul (31 rooms, Sb-L120,000, Db-L160,000, Tb-L220,000, Qb-L260,000, with breakfast, with cash and this book through 1999, all rooms one-third off in August, elevator, Via Venezia 18, just off Via Nazionale, tel. 06-482-8355, fax 06-474-5550, e-mail: hitalia.pronet.it). Nine of their rooms are across the street in a modern new annex. They sell stamps, mail postcards, and offer an airport pickup for L90,000.

Hotel Nardizzi Americana is the cheapest of my recommended hotels in this area. Traffic noise in the front rooms is a problem in the summer, when you'll want the window open; and the hotel won't win any cleanliness awards. The new roof garden is pleasant (D-L100,000, Db-L150,000, T-L140,000, Tb-L190,000, also four- and five-bed rooms, including breakfast; in summer and winter months they offer four nights for the price of three and discounts for longer stays; reservations are unreliable—they may book you elsewhere; CC:VMA, in same building as Oceania, Via Firenze 38, 00184 Roma, elevator, tel. 06-488-0368, fax 06-488-0035, SE).

The **YWCA Casa Per Studentesse** accepts women, couples, groups of men, and couples with children, but not single men. It's an institutional place, filled with white-uniformed maids, more-colorful Third World travelers, and 75 single beds. It's closed from midnight to 7:00 a.m. (L33,000 per person in three- and four-bed rooms, S-L50,000, Sb-L70,000, D-L80,000, Db-L100,000, breakfast included except on Sunday and in August, Via C. Balbo 4, 00184 Roma, tel. 06-488-0460, fax 06-487-1028.)

Sleeping near the Train Station

The cheapest hotels in town are north of the station. Avoid places on the seedy south (Colosseum) side of the station. The first four listings are closest in a safe and decent area (which gets a little weird and spooky late at night). With your back to the train tracks, turn right and walk two blocks out of the station. A self-serve *lavanderia* (Laundromat) is at Via Milazzo 8 (daily, 8:00–22:00, six kilos washed and dried for L12,000).

Albergo Sileo is a shiny-chandeliered, 10-room place with an

Rome's Train Station Neighborhood

TO VILLA BORGHESE

TO SPANISH STEPS

SANTA MARIA VITTORIA

RIST. DA GIOVANNI

1/4 MILE

NATIONAL MUSEUM

VENETO

CAPPUCCIN CRYPT

VIA BARBERINI

SETTEMBRE

PARIGI

PIAZZA INDEP.

PIAZZA BARB.

SANTA SUSANNA

QUATTRO

PIAZZA REP.

SANTA MARIA VITTORIA

DE NICOLA

HOST. ROMANA

QUIRNALE PALACE

FONTANE

SAN CARLINO

QUIRINALE

VIA

FIRENZE

TRITONE

PIAZZA CINQUE-CENTO

MARSALA

TERMINI STATION

TO TREVI FOUNTAIN + PANTHEON

NAZIONALE

DEPRETIS

GIOLITTI

VIA

CAVOUR

SANTA MARIA MAGGIORE

PANIS PERNA

SERPENTI

VIA LANZA

FORI IMPERIALI

CAVOUR

ST PETER IN CHAINS

FORUM

ARCH OF CONSTANTINE

COLOSSEUM

DCH

TO CIRCUS MAXIMUS

N

LODGING:
1. SILEO/FAWLTY
2. MAGIC/FENECIA
3. OCEANIA/NARDIZZI
4. ADLER
5. ABERDEEN
6. CORTINA/IRISH PUB
7. ITALIA
8. YWCA
9. DUCA D'ALBA
10. FLAVIO
11. SUORE SANT ANNA
12. DES ARTISTES
Ⓜ METRO STATIONS

elegant touch that has a contract to house train conductors who work the night shift. With maids doing double-time, they offer rooms from 19:00 to 9:00 only. If you can handle this it's a great value. During the day they store your luggage, and though you won't have access to a room, you're welcome to hang out in their lobby or bar (D-L70,000, Db-L85,000, Tb-L110,000, elevator, Via Magenta 39, tel. & fax 06-445-0246, Alessandro and Maria Savioli NSE).

Fawlty Towers is a backpacker-type place well-run by the

Aussies from Enjoy Rome. It's young, hip, and English-speaking, with a rooftop terrace, lots of information, and no curfew (shared co-ed, four-bed dorms for L30,000 per bed, S-L50,000, Sb-L70,000, D-L80,000, Db-L95,000, Tb-L120,000, reservations by credit card but pay in cash, elevator, Via Magenta 39, tel. & fax 06-445-0374).

Hotel Magic is a tiny, just-renovated place run by a mother-daughter team (Carmella and Rosanna). It's clean and high enough off the road to escape the traffic noise (10 rooms, Sb-L90,000, Db-L120,000, Tb-L160,000 with this book, tiny breakfast included, thin walls, midnight curfew, Via Milazzo 20, third floor, 00185 Roma, tel. & fax 06-495-9880, little English spoken, unreliable for reservations).

Hotel Fenicia, in the same building, also with lots of stairs, is eager for your business (Db-L130,000, Tb-L180,000, air-conditioning costs an extra L20,000/day, breakfast-L10,000, CC:VMA, Via Milazzo 20, tel. & fax 06-490-342, Anna and Georgio). Hotels Magic and Fenicia are in the same building but not related; reservations are not interchangeable.

Hotel Des Artistes has new, comfortable rooms—confirm price (Db-L180,000, Tb-L250,000, TV, phone, air-conditioning, CC:VMA, Via Villafranca 20, five blocks northeast of station, near National Library, tel. 06-445-4365, fax 06-446-2368, e-mail: artistes@tin.it). The same friendly owners, with the same reception desk and phone, run the inexpensive and dumpy **Hotel Matilde** (S-L65,000, D-L100,000, T-L135,000, e-mail: hmatilde@tin.it).

Sleeping near the Colosseum (zip code: 00184)

One stop on the subway from the train station (to Metro: Cavour), these places are buried in a very Roman world of exhaust-stained medieval ambience.

Hotel Duca d'Alba is a classy, tight, and modern place just half a block from the Metro station (Sb-L220,000, Db-L300,000, all air-conditioned and with breakfast buffet, extra bed-L40,000, CC:VMA, Via Leonina 14, tel. 06-484-471, fax 06-488-4840, e-mail: duca_dalba@venere.it, SE).

Hotel Flavio has an Old World TV-lounge/lobby, an elevator, and elegant furnishings throughout in a quiet setting. Its weaknesses are dim lights and lousy tub-showers down the hall for the five bath-less doubles (S-L85,000, Sb-L100,000, D-L140,000, Db-L180,000, family rooms available, breakfast extra, CC:VMA, hiding almost torchlit under vines on a tiny street a block toward the Colosseum from Via Cavour, Via Frangipane 34, Metro: Cavour, tel. 06-679-7203, fax 06-679-6246, indifferent staff speaks enough English).

Suore di Sant Anna was built for Ukrainian pilgrims. The sisters are sweet, but the male staff doesn't seem to care. It's clumsy and difficult (23:00 curfew), but once you're in, you've got a comfortable home in a classic Roman-village locale (S-L42,000, D-L84,000, including breakfast, consider a monkish dinner for L26,000 more, off the corner of Via dei Serpenti and Via Baccina at Piazza Madonna dei Monti 3, Metro: Cavour, tel. 06-485-778, fax 06-487-1064). Expect a price increase after remodeling.

Sleeping near the Campo dei Fiori and Piazza Navona (zip code: 00186)

Campo dei Fiori: Hotel Campo dei Fiori is an ideal location for wealthy bohemians who value centrality. It's just off the Campo dei Fiori, with comfortable rooms and an unreal rooftop terrace (D-L150,000, Db-L210,000, includes breakfast, CC:VM, lots of stairs and no elevator, Via del Biscione 6, tel. 06-6880-6865, fax 06-687-6003). They also have apartments nearby that can house five or six people; costs range from L210,000 to L250,000 for two people (extra person-L50,000).

The **Albergo del Sole** is impersonal and filled with German groups but well-located (D-L140,000, small Db-L170,000, Db-L180,000, no breakfast, Via del Biscione 76, tel. 06-6880-6873, fax 06-689-3787).

Casa di Santa Brigida is also near the characteristic Campo dei Fiori. With soft-spoken sisters gliding down polished hallways and pearly gates instead of doors, this lavish convent makes the exhaust-stained Roman tourist feel like he's died and gone to heaven. If you're unsure of your destiny, this is worth the splurge (twins with all the comforts-L250,000; walk-in address: Monserrato 54, mailing address: Piazza Farnese 96, tel. 06-6889-2596, fax 06-6889-1573, SE). Some of its 20 rooms overlook the Piazza Farnese.

Piazza Navona: Hotel Navona is a ramshackle 25-room hotel occupying an ancient building in a perfect locale a block off Piazza Navona and run by an Australian named Corry (S-L90,000, D-L130,000, Db-L160,000, Db with air-conditioning-L200,000, breakfast, family rooms, lots of student groups, Via dei Sediari 8, tel. 06-686-4203, fax 06-6880-3802, SE).

Sleeping near the Vatican Museum (zip code: 00192)

Pension Alimandi is a good value, run by the friendly and entrepreneurial Alimandi brothers: Paolo, Enrico, Luigi, and Germano (35 rooms, Sb-L140,000, Db-L190,000, Tb-L220,000, 5-percent discount with this book and cash, CC:VMA, elevator, grand breakfast-L15,000, great roof garden, self-service washing machines, pool table, parking-L30,000/day, down the stairs directly in front of the Vatican Museum, Via Tunisi 8, near Metro: Ottaviano—exit Metro at far left end of tunnel, tel. 06-3972-6300, fax 06-3972-3943, reserve by phone, no reply to fax means they are full, SE). They offer their guests free airport pickup and drop-off (saving you L80,000 if you were planning on taking a taxi), though you must reserve when you book your room and conform to their schedule (which can mean waiting).

Hotel Spring House offers decent rooms with balconies, TVs, and refrigerators; and an impersonal staff. Confirm prices and mention this book (Db-L250,000 with breakfast, 5 percent discount for cash payment, 15 percent discount in July and August, CC:VMA, air con, parking-L25,000/day, airport pickup-L70,000–90,000, Via Mocenigo 7, a block from Alimandi, tel. 06-3972-0948, fax 06-3972-1047, e-mail: Hotel.Spring.House@venere.it).

Hotel Gerber is sleek, modern, air-conditioned, business-like, and set in a quiet residential area (27 rooms, S-L120,000, Sb-L180,000, Db-L235,000, Tb-L285,000, Qb-L320,000, 10 percent discount with this book, includes breakfast buffet, CC:VMA, one block from Lepanto subway stop, Via degli Scipioni 241, tel. 06-321-6485, fax 06-321-7048, Peter SE).

Hotel Benjamin is a tiny family affair with seven simple but decent rooms on the third floor (D-L100,000, Db-L120,000, T-L110,000, Tb-L130,000, prices promised through 1999 with this book, no breakfast, no elevator, Metro: Ottaviano, corner of Via Terenzio at Via Boezio 31, tel. & fax 06-6880-2437, Sra Franca Fondi NSE). Faxes are expensive; they kindly ask you to expect only one fax in response, rather than a series of replies to a volley of faxes.

Suore Oblate dell Assunzione, a convent, rents clean, peaceful, and inexpensive rooms. No English is spoken and it's hard to get in (S-L55,000, D-L110,000, Db-L130,000, T-L150,000, Via Andrea Doria 42, three blocks from the Vatican Museum entrance, tel. 06-3973-7567, fax 06-3973-7020).

Sleeping in Hostels and Dorms

Rome has only one real youth hostel—it's big, institutional, and not central or worth the trouble. For cheap dorm beds, consider **Fawlty Towers** (above) or **Pensione Ottaviano**, which offers free showers, lockers, a mini-fridge in each room, a fun, laid-back clubhouse feel, and a good location near the Vatican (25 beds in two- to six-bed rooms, L25,000 per bed with sheets, D-L70,000, six blocks from Ottaviano Metro stop, Via Ottaviano 6, no reservations, call from the station, tel. 06-3973-7253). The same slum visionaries run the dumpier **Pensione Sandy** (L25,000 beds, south of station, up a million depressing stairs, Via Cavour 136, tel. 06-488-4585).

Eating in Rome

The cheapest meals in town are picnics (from *alimentari* shops or open-air markets), self-serve rotisseries, and stand-up or take-out meals from a *pizza rustica* (pizza slices sold by the weight, 100 grams is a hot cheap snack; 200 grams, or two *etti*, make a light meal). Most *alimentari* will slice and stuff your sandwich (*panini*) for you, if you buy the stuff there. For a fast/cheap/healthy lunch, find a bar with a buffet spread of meat and vegetables and ask for a mixed plate of vegetables with a hunk of mozzarella.

Eating in Trastevere

My best dinner tip is to go for Rome's Vespa street ambience and find your own place in Trastevere or on Campo dei Fiori (below). Guidebooks list Trastevere's famous places, but I'd wander the fascinating maze of streets near the Piazza Santa Maria in Trastevere and find a mom-and-pop place with barely a menu. Check out the tiny streets north of the church. At Piazza della Scala consider **Taverna della Scala** and the fine little *gelateria*. For the basic meal with lots of tourists, eat amazingly cheap at **Mario's** (closed Sunday, three courses with wine and service for L18,000, near the Sisto bridge at Via del Moro 53). On the same street, **Taverna del Moro** is inexpensive with efficient waiters (Via del Moro 43, tel. 06-580-9165). **Augusto Ristorante** (around the corner from Mario's) and **Ristorante Alle Fratte di Trastevere** (on Via dell Fratte di Trastevere) are also good. **La Cisterna** offers live music and tasty food in a pleasant setting (Via Della Cisterna 13, tel. 06-581-2543).

Eating on the Campo dei Fiori

For the ultimate romantic square setting, eat at whichever place looks best on Campo dei Fiori. Circle the square, considering each place. **La Carbonara** is the birthplace of pasta carbonara (Wednesday–Monday 12:30–15:00, 19:30–23:00, closed Tuesday). The **Forno**, next door, is popular for hot greasy snacks. Meals on small nearby streets are a better value but lack that Campo dei Fiori magic.

Nearby, on Piazza Farnese, **Da Giovanni Ar Galletto** has an ideal setting, moderate prices, and fine food (Monday–Saturday 12:30–15:00, 19:00–23:30, closed Sunday, tucked in a corner of Piazza Farnese at #102, tel. 06-686-1714).

For interesting bar munchies, try **Cul de Sac** on Piazza Pasquino (a block southwest of Piazza Navona).

Eating near the Pantheon

Il Delfino is a handy self-service cafeteria on the Largo Argentina square (daily 7:00–21:00, not cheap but fast). Across the side street, the **Frullati Bar** sells refreshing fruity frappés. The *alimentari* on the Pantheon square will make you a sandwich for a temple-porch picnic.

La Maddelena has good, affordable food (Piazza della Maddalena, with back to Pantheon entrance, take right around McDonald's, go one block, tel. 06-687-2316).

Volpetti is a lively *tavola calda* (deli) selling hot food by the weight for take-out or to be eaten in their air-conditioned basement dining room (across the street from Alfreddo's, at Via della Scrofa 31, where the famous fettucine was born, tel. 06-686-1940).

Eating near Hotels Oceania, Adler, and Aberdeen

Snack Bar Gastronomia is a great local hole-in-the-wall for lunch or dinner (open until 20:00, closed Sunday, really cheap hot meals dished up from under glass counter, tap water with a smile, Via Firenze 34). There's an *alimentari* (grocery store) across the street.

Pasticceria Dagnino, popular for its top-quality Sicilian specialties—especially pastries and ice cream—is where those who work at my recommended hotels eat (daily 7:00–22:00, in Galleria Esedra off Via Torino, a block from hotels, tel. 06-481-8660). Their *arancino*—a rice, cheese, and ham ball—is a greasy Sicilian favorite. Direct the construction of your meal at the bar, pay for your trayful at the cashier, and climb upstairs where you'll find the dancing Sicilian girls (free).

For an air-conditioned, classier, local favorite serving traditional Roman cuisine, run by a group of men who enjoy their work, eat at **Hostaria Romana** (closed Sunday, midway between the Trevi fountain and Piazza Barberini, Via del Boccaccio 1, at intersection with Via Rasella, tel. 06-474-5284).

Locals line up for **Ristorante da Giovanni** (L22,000 menu, Monday–Saturday 12:00–15:00, 19:00–22:30, closed Sunday, just off Via XX Septembre at Via Antonio Salandra 1, tel. 06-485-950).

Lon Fon serves reasonably priced Chinese food (18:30–23:00, closed Wednesday, Via Firenze 44, tel. 06-482-5261).

The **McDonald's** on Piazza della Republica (free piazza seating outside), **Piazza Barberini**, and **Via Firenze** offer air-conditioned interiors and a L7,000 salad bar that no American fast-food joint would recognize. **Greenpizz** is a lively place for good pizza (Via Cernaia 16, about five blocks north of the train station at intersection of Cernaia and Castelfidardo, tel. 06-474-1322). For pasta with Guinness or a late-night drink with live music, consider the lively **Irish Pub** (two blocks from recommended hotels at Via Nazionale 18, at intersection with Via Napoli, tel. 06-488-0418).

Eating near the Vatican Museum and Pension Alimandi

Viale Giulio Cesare is lined with cheap *pizza rusticas* and fun eateries (such as **Cipriani Self-Service Rosticceria** near the

Ottaviano subway stop at Viale Guilio Cesare 195, with pleasant outdoor seating).

Turn your nose loose in the wonderful **Via Andrea Doria** open-air market two blocks north of the Vatican Museum (between Via Tunisi and Via Andrea Doria, Monday–Saturday, open late on Friday, otherwise closed by 13:30). If the market is closed, try the nearby **Meta supermarket** on Via Francesco 18 (8:30–13:15, 16:15–19:30, closed Thursday afternoon and all day Sunday, one-half block straight out from the Via Tunisi entrance of the open-air market).

Antonio's Hostaria dei Bastioni is tasty and friendly with good sit-down meals (closed Sunday, L10,000–15,000 pastas, L18,000 *secondi*, no cover charge, at corner of Vatican wall, Via Leone IV 29, tel. 06-3972-3034). **La Rustichella** has a good antipasti buffet (L12,000, enough for a meal) and fine pasta dishes (arrive by 19:30 or wait to get in, closed Monday, opposite church at end of Via Candia, Via Angelo 1, tel. 06-3972-0649).

Transportation Connections—Rome

By train to: Venice (6/day, 5–8 hrs, overnight possible), **Florence** (12/day, 2 hrs), **Pisa** (8/day, 3–4 hrs), **Genova** (7/day, 6 hrs, overnight possible), **Milan** (12/day, 5 hrs, overnight possible), **Naples** (6/day, 2–3 hrs), **Brindisi** (2/day, 9 hrs), **Amsterdam** (2/day, 20 hrs), **Bern** (5/day, 10 hrs), **Frankfurt** (4/day, 14 hrs), **Munich** (5/day, 12 hrs), **Nice** (2/day, 10 hrs), **Paris** (5/day, 16 hrs), **Vienna** (3/day, 13–15 hrs). **Civita:** Take the Rome–Orvieto train (every 2 hrs, 75 min), catch the bus from Orvieto to Bagnoregio (8/day, 50 min, no service on Sunday), and walk to Civita. Train information: tel. 1478-88088.

Rome's Airport

A slick direct train link connects Rome's Leonardo da Vinci (a.k.a. Fiumicino) airport and the central Termini train station (L15,000 or free with first-class railpass, departures last year from train station at 20 minutes after every hour from 7:20–21:20, 30-minute ride). Your hotel can arrange a taxi to the airport at any hour for about L80,000.

Airport information (tel. 06-65951) can connect you directly to your airline. (British Air tel. 06-6595-4190, Alitalia tel. 06-65643, Delta tel. 06-6595-4104, KLM tel. 06-652-9286, SAS tel. 06-6501-0771, TWA tel. 06-6595-4901, Lufthansa tel. 06-6595-4156, Swiss Air tel. 06-6595-4099.)

Driving in Rome

Greater Rome is circled by the Grande Raccordo Anulare. This ring road has spokes that lead you into the center. Entering from the north, leave the autostrada at the Settebagni exit. Following

the ancient Via Salaria (and the black-and-white "Centro" signs),
work your way doggedly into the Roman thick-of-things. This will
take you along the Villa Borghese and dump you right on Via
Veneto (where there's an Avis office). Avoid rush hour. Drive
defensively: Roman cars stay in their lanes like rocks in an
avalanche. Parking in Rome is dangerous. Park near a police station or get advice at your hotel. The garage is L35,000 a day. The
Villa Borghese underground garage (Metro: Spagna) is handy.

Consider this: Your car is a worthless headache in Rome.
Avoid a pile of stress and save money by parking at the huge,
easy, and relatively safe lot behind the Orvieto station (follow
"P" signs from autostrada), and catch the train to Rome (every
two hours, 75 minutes).

FLORENCE (FIRENZE)

Florence, the home of the Renaissance and birthplace of our modern world, is a "supermarket sweep," and the groceries are the best Renaissance art in Europe.

Get your bearings with a Renaissance walk. Florentine art goes beyond paintings and statues—there's food, fashion, and handicrafts. You can lick Italy's best gelato while enjoying Europe's best people-watching.

Planning Your Time

If you're in Europe for three weeks, Florence deserves a well-organized day. Siena, an easy hour away by bus, has no awesome sights but is a more enjoyable home base. For a day in Florence, see Michelangelo's *David*, tour the Uffizi Gallery (best Italian paintings), tour the underrated Bargello (best statues), and do the Renaissance ramble (explained below). Art lovers will want to chisel another day out of their itinerary for the many other cultural treasures Florence offers. Shoppers and ice-cream lovers may need to do the same. Plan your sightseeing carefully. Mondays and afternoons can be sparse. You may very likely lose an hour or two in lines. If the line at the Uffizi depresses you, remind yourself that people think nothing of waiting an hour at Disneyland to see the Tiki Hut.

Orientation

The Florence we're interested in lies mostly on the north bank of the Arno River. Everything is within a 20-minute walk of the train station, cathedral, or Ponte Vecchio (Old Bridge). The less impressive but more characteristic Oltrarno (south bank) area is just over the bridge. Orient yourself by the huge red-tiled dome of the cathedral (the Duomo) and its tall bell tower (Giotto's Tower). This is the center of historic Florence.

Tourist Information

There are three TIs in Florence. The one at the train station may move to an easier-to-find location near track 16, but until then it's poorly located (exit the station near McDonald's, head across bus lane, then turn right down narrow median between streets). Avoid the Hotel Reservations TI near the McDonald's—it's geared toward hotels. The real TI is marked with an "i" (Monday–Saturday 8:15–19:15).

The TI near Santa Croce church is pleasant, helpful, and uncrowded (Monday–Saturday 8:30–19:15, Sunday 8:30–13:45, Borgo Santa Croce 29 red, tel. 055-234-0444). Another winner is the TI three blocks north of the Duomo (Monday–Saturday in summer 8:15–19:15, Sunday 8:15–13:45, only TI open Sunday, Via Cavour 1 red, tel. 055-290-832 or 055-290-833). There's a fine international bookstore (with American guidebooks) across the street at Via Cavour 20 red.

Pick up a map (ask for the better "long stay" map), a current museum-hours listing, and the periodical entertainment guide or tourist magazine at any TI. The free monthly *Florence Concierge Information* magazine lists the latest museum hours, markets, bus and train connections, and events; it's stocked by the TI (but given out only when requested) and by the expensive hotels (pick one up, as if you're staying there).

Arrival in Florence

By Train: The station feels crowded. Get out quickly if you can. (You can get onward tickets at American Express—see below.) With your back to the tracks, the train information office is to your right and the tourist information office is to your left (either at track 16 or just outside, see above). Straight ahead is the lobby and a cash machine which takes foreign bills (like dollars). Cash machines are sprinkled liberally throughout this market town.

Helpful Hints

Museums and Churches: See everyone's essential sight, *David*, right off. In Italy a masterpiece seen and enjoyed is worth two tomorrow; you never know when a place will unexpectedly close for a holiday, strike, or restoration. The Uffizi has one- to two-hour lines on busy days. During lunchtime (before 14:00), lines are shorter. By 17:00 lines are normally gone. Some museums close at 14:00 and stop selling tickets 30 minutes before that. The biggies (Uffizi and Accademia) close on Monday. The *Concierge Information* magazine thoughtfully lists which sights are open afternoons, Sundays, and Mondays (best attractions open Monday:

Michelangelo's Casa Buonarroti, Dante's House, Giotto's Tower, Museo dell' Opera del Duomo, and Palazzo Vecchio). Churches usually close from 12:30 to 15:00 or 16:00. Local guidebooks are cheap and give you a map and a decent commentary on the sights.

Addresses: Street addresses list businesses in red and residences in black or blue (color-coded on the actual street number and indicated by a letter following the number in printed addresses: n = black, r = red). *Pensioni* are usually black, but can be either.

Theft Alert: Florence has particularly hardworking thief gangs. They specialize in tourists and hang out where you do, near the train station, the station's underpass (especially where the tunnel surfaces), and major sights. American tourists, especially older ones, are considered the easiest targets.

Medical Help: For a doctor who speaks English call 055-475-411 (reasonable hotel calls, cheaper if you go to the clinic at Via L. Magnifico 59, 24-hour pharmacy at the train station).

American Express: It's near the Palazzo Vecchio on Via Dante Alighieri 22 red (Monday–Friday 9:00–17:30, Saturday 9:00–12:30, easy train tickets and reservations, CC:A!, tel. 055-50981).

Books: Paperback Exchange is at the corner of Via Fiesolana and Via dei Pilastri (six blocks east of the Duomo).

Getting Around Florence

If you organize your sightseeing with some geographic logic, you can do it all on foot. A L1,500 ticket gives you one hour on the buses, L2,500 gives you three hours, and L6,000 gets you 24 hours (tickets not sold on bus, buy in tobacco shops or newsstands, validate on bus). A taxi ride from the train station to the Ponte Vecchio costs about L15,000.

A Florentine Renaissance Walk

Even during the Dark Ages people knew they were in a "middle time." It was especially obvious to the people of Italy—sitting on the rubble of Rome—that there was a brighter age before them. The long-awaited rebirth, or "Renaissance," happened in Florence for good reason. Wealthy because of its cloth industry, trade, and banking; powered by a fierce city-state pride (locals would pee into the Arno with gusto, knowing rival city-state Pisa was downstream); and fertile with more than its share of artistic genius (imagine guys like Michelangelo and Leonardo attending the same high school)—Florence was a natural home for this cultural explosion.

Take a walk through the core of Renaissance Florence by starting at the Accademia (home of Michelangelo's *David*) and cutting through the heart of the city to the Ponte Vecchio on the Arno River. (A 10-page, self-guided tour of this walk is outlined in my museum guidebook, *Rick Steves' Mona Winks*. Otherwise, you'll find brief descriptions below.)

At the Accademia you'll look into the eyes of Renaissance man—humanism at its confident peak. Then walk to the cathedral (Duomo) to see the dome that kicked off the architectural Renaissance. Step inside the baptistery to view a ceiling covered with preachy, flat, 2-D, medieval mosaic art. Then, to learn what happened when art met math, check out the realistic 3-D reliefs on the doors. The painter, Giotto, designed the bell tower—an early example of how a Renaissance genius excelled in many areas. Continue toward the river on Florence's great pedestrian mall, Via de' Calzaioli (or "Via Calz"), which was part of the original grid plan given the city by the ancient Romans. Down a few blocks, compare medieval and Renaissance statues on the exterior of the Orsanmichele Church. Via Calz connects the cathedral with the central square (Piazza della Signoria), the city palace (Palazzo Vecchio), and the Uffizi Gallery, which contains the greatest collection of Italian Renaissance paintings in captivity. Finally, walk through the Uffizi courtyard—a statuary think-tank of Renaissance greats—to the Arno River and the Ponte Vecchio.

Sights—Florence

▲▲▲**Accademia (Galleria dell' Accademia)**—This museum houses Michelangelo's *David* and powerful (unfinished) *Prisoners*. Eavesdrop as tour guides explain these masterpieces. More than any other work of art, when you look into the eyes of *David*, you're looking into the eyes of Renaissance man. This was a radical break with the past. Man was now a confident individual, no longer a plaything of the supernatural. And life was now more than just a preparation for what happened after you died.

The Renaissance was the merging of art and science. In a humanist vein, *David* is looking at the crude giant of medieval darkness and thinking, "I can take this guy." Back on a religious track (and speaking of veins), notice *David*'s large and overdeveloped right hand. This is symbolic of the hand of God that powered David to slay the giant . . . and enabled Florence to rise above its crude neighboring city-states.

Beyond the magic marble are two floors of interesting pre-Renaissance and Renaissance paintings, including a couple of dreamy Botticellis (L12,000, Tuesday–Saturday 8:30–22:00, Sunday 8:30–20:00, closed Monday, shorter hours off-season, Via Ricasoli 60, tel. 055-238-8609).

Behind the Accademia, the Piazza Santissima Annunziata features lovely Renaissance harmony. Brunelleschi's Hospital of the Innocents (Spedale degli Innocenti, not worth going inside), with terracotta medallions by della Robbia, was built in the 1420s and is considered the first Renaissance building.

▲▲**Museum of San Marco**—One block north of the Accademia on Piazza San Marco, this museum houses the greatest collection

Florence

anywhere of medieval frescoes and paintings by the early Renaissance master Fra Angelico. You'll see why he thought of painting as a form of prayer and couldn't paint a crucifix without shedding tears. Each of the monks' cells has a Fra Angelico fresco. Don't miss the cell of Savonarola, the charismatic monk who rode in from the Christian right, threw out the Medici, turned Florence into a theocracy, sponsored "bonfires of the vanities" (burning books, paintings, and so on), and was finally burned himself when Florence decided to change channels (L8,000, daily 8:30–13:50 but closed the first, third, and fifth Sunday and the second and fourth Monday of each month).

▲▲**Duomo**—Florence's mediocre Gothic cathedral has the third-longest nave in Christendom (free, Monday–Saturday 10:00–17:00,

Sunday 13:00–17:00, first Saturday of month 10:00–15:30). The church's noisy neo-Gothic facade from the 1870s is covered with pink, green, and white Tuscan marble. Since nearly all of its great art is stored in the Museo dell' Opera del Duomo, behind the church, the best thing about the inside is the shade. The inside of the dome is decorated by what must be the largest painting of the Renaissance, a huge (and newly restored) *Last Judgment* by Vasari and Zuccari. The cathedral's claim to artistic fame is Brunelleschi's magnificent dome—the first Renaissance dome and the model for domes to follow (ascent L10,000, Monday–Friday 8:30–18:20, Saturday 9:30–17:00, first Saturday of month 9:30–15:20). When planning St. Peter's in Rome, Michelangelo said, "I can build a dome bigger, but not more beautiful, than the dome of Florence."

Giotto's Tower—Climbing Giotto's Tower (or Campanile) beats climbing the neighboring Duomo's dome because it's 50 fewer steps, faster, not so crowded, and offers the same view plus the dome (L10,000, daily 9:00–18:50).

▲▲**Museo dell' Opera del Duomo**—The underrated cathedral museum, behind the church at #9, is great if you like sculpture. It has masterpieces by Donatello (a gruesome wood carving of Mary Magdalene clothed in her matted hair; and the *cantoria*, a delightful choir loft bursting with happy children) and Luca della Robbia (another choir loft, lined with the dreamy faces of musicians praising the Lord); a late Michelangelo *Pietà* (Nicodemus, on top, is a self-portrait); Brunelleschi's models for his dome; and the original restored panels of Ghiberti's doors to the baptistery. This is one of the few museums in Florence open on Monday (L10,000, Monday–Saturday 9:00–18:50, Sunday 9:00–13:20, tel. 055-230-2885).

▲**Baptistery**—Michelangelo said its bronze doors were fit to be the gates of Paradise. Check out the gleaming copies of Ghiberti's bronze doors facing the Duomo, and the famous competition doors around to the right. Making a breakthrough in perspective, Ghiberti used mathematical laws to create the illusion of 3-D on a 2-D surface. Go inside Florence's oldest building and sit and savor the medieval mosaic ceiling. Compare that to the "new, improved" art of the Renaissance (L5,000 interior open Monday–Saturday 13:30–18:30, Sunday 8:30–13:30, bronze doors are on the outside so always "open"; original panels are in the Museo dell' Opera del Duomo).

▲**Orsanmichele**—Mirroring Florentine values, this was a combination church-granary. The best L200 deal in Florence is the machine which lights its glorious tabernacle. Notice the grain spouts on the pillars inside. Also study the sculpture on its outside walls. You can see man stepping out of the literal and figurative shadow of the church in the great Renaissance sculptor Donatello's *St. George* (free, daily 9:00–12:00, 16:00–18:00, on Via Calzaioli; if closed, as it often is due to staffing problems, try going through the back door).

▲**Palazzo Vecchio**—This fortified palace, once the home of the Medici family, is a Florentine landmark. But if you're visiting only one palace interior in town, the Pitti Palace is better. The Palazzo Vecchio interior is wallpapered with mediocre magnificence, worthwhile only if you're a real Florentine art and history fan (L10,000, 9:00–19:00, Sunday 8:00–13:00, closed Thursday, handy public WC inside on ground floor). Do step into the free courtyard (behind the fake *David*) just to feel the Medici. Until 1873 Michelangelo's *David* stood at the entrance, where the copy is today. While the huge statues in the square are important only as the whipping boys of art critics and reststops for pigeons, the nearby Loggia dei Lanzi has several important statues. Look for Cellini's bronze statue of Perseus (with the head of Medusa). The plaque on the pavement in front of the fountain marks the spot where Savonarola was burned in MCCCCXCVIII.

▲▲▲**Uffizi Gallery**—The greatest collection of Italian painting anywhere is a must, with plenty of works by Giotto, Leonardo, Raphael, Caravaggio, Rubens, Titian, and Michelangelo; and a roomful of Botticellis, including his *Birth of Venus*. There are no official tours, so buy a book on the street before entering (or follow *Mona Winks*). The long entrance line is a reasonable cost for an interior with no Louvre-style mob scenes. The museum is nowhere near as big as it is great: Few tourists spend more than two hours inside. The paintings are displayed (behind obnoxious reflective glass) on one comfortable floor in chronological order from the 13th through 17th centuries.

Essential stops are (in this order): the Gothic altarpieces (narrative, pre-realism, no real concern for believable depth); Giotto's altarpiece in the same room, which progressed beyond "totempole angels"; Uccello's *Battle of San Romano*, an early study in perspective (with a few obvious flubs); Fra Lippi's cuddly Madonnas; the Botticelli room, filled with masterpieces including a pantheon of classical fleshiness and the small *La Calumnia*, showing the glasnost of Renaissance free-thinking being clubbed back into the darker age of Savonarola; two minor works by Leonardo; the octagonal classical sculpture room with an early painting of Bob Hope and a copy of Praxiteles' *Venus de Medici*, considered the epitome of beauty in Elizabethan Europe; Michelangelo's only surviving easel painting, the round *Holy Family*; Raphael's noble *Madonna of the Goldfinch*; Titian's voluptuous *Venus of Urbino*; and views from the café terrace at the end (L12,000, Tuesday–Saturday 8:30–22:00, Sunday 8:30–20:00, closed Monday, shorter hours off-season, last ticket sold 45 minutes before closing, go late to avoid crowds and heat, elevator available).

To avoid having to wait in line, it's now possible to get a reservation (for L2,400) by paying in advance by phone (call 055-294-883). Credit cards are not accepted. When you call to reserve, ask where to pick up your tickets (likely at the Pitti Palace book-shop). Pay in cash when you pick up the tickets. If you're already in Florence, call to book, then pay at the train station TI. You can reserve from 48 hours to months in advance.

Enjoy the Uffizi square, full of artists and souvenir stalls. The surrounding statues honor the earthshaking: artists, philosophers (Machiavelli), scientists (Galileo), writers (Dante), explorers (Amerigo Vespucci), and the great patron of so much Renaissance thinking, Lorenzo (the Magnificent) de Medici.

▲▲▲**Bargello (Museo Nazionale)**—This underrated sculpture museum is behind Palazzo Vecchio in a former prison that looks like a mini-Palazzo Vecchio. It has Donatello's *David* (the very influential first male nude to be sculpted in a thousand years), works by Michelangelo, and more (L8,000, daily 8:30–13:50 but closed first, third, and fifth Sunday and second and fourth Monday of each month; Via del Proconsolo 4). Dante's house, across the street and around the corner, is interesting only to his Italian-speaking fans.

▲▲**Santa Croce Church**—This 14th-century Franciscan church, decorated by centuries of precious art, holds the tombs of great Florentines (free, Monday–Saturday 8:00–18:45, Sunday 15:00–17:30). The loud 19th-century Victorian Gothic facade faces a huge square ringed with tempting touristy shops and littered with tired tourists (and ice-cream cups—Vivoli's is two blocks away). Escape into the church.

Working counterclockwise from the entrance you'll find: the tomb of Michelangelo (with the allegorical figures of painting, architecture, and sculpture), a memorial to Dante (no body . . . he was banished by his hometown), the tomb of Machiavelli, a relief by Donatello of the Annunciation, and the tomb of the composer Rossini. To the right of the altar, step into the sacristy where you'll find the bit of St. Francis' cowl (he is supposed to have founded the church around 1290) and old sheets of music with the medieval and mobile C-clef (two little blocks on either side of the line determined to be middle C). In the bookshop notice the photos high on the wall of the devastating flood of 1966. Beyond that is a touristy—but mildly interesting—"leather school." The chapels lining the front of the church are richly frescoed. The Bardi Chapel (far left of altar) is a masterpiece by Giotto featuring scenes from the life of St. Francis. On your way out you'll pass the tomb of Galileo (allowed in by the church long after his death). The neighboring Pazzi Chapel (by Brunelleschi) is considered one of the finest pieces of Florentine Renaissance architecture.

▲**Medici Chapel (Cappelle dei Medici)**—This chapel, containing two Medici tombs, is drenched in incredibly lavish High Renaissance architecture and sculpture by Michelangelo (L10,000, daily 8:30–16:50 but closed the second and fourth Sunday and the first, third, and fifth Monday of each month). Behind San Lorenzo on Piazza Madonna is a lively market scene that I find more interesting. Don't miss a wander through the huge double-decker central market one block north.

Science Museum (Museo di Storia della Scienza)—This is a fascinating collection of Renaissance and later clocks, telescopes, maps, and ingenious gadgets. One of the most talked-about bottles in Florence is the one here containing Galileo's finger. English guidebooklets are available. It's friendly, comfortably cool, never crowded, and just downstream from the Uffizi (L10,000, Monday, Wednesday, and Friday 9:30–13:00, 14:00–17:00, Tuesday and Thursday 9:30–13:00, closed Sunday, Piazza dei Giudici 1).

▲**Michelangelo's Home, Casa Buonarroti**—Fans enjoy Michelangelo's house, which has some of his early, much-less-monumental works (L10,000, Wednesday–Monday 9:30–13:30, closed Tuesday, Via Ghibellina 70).

▲▲**Gelato**—Gelato is an edible art form. Italy's best ice cream is in Florence. Every year I repeat my taste test. And every year Vivoli's wins (8:00–01:00, closed Monday, the last three weeks in August, and winter, on Via Stinche, see map, cups only—no cones). These are also good: Gelateria Carrozze (30 yards from the Ponte Vecchio towards the Uffizi, Via del Pesce 3), Festival del Gelato (Via del Corso), and Perche Non! (Via Tavolini; Festival and Perche are both just off Via Calzaioli). Gelato is one souvenir that can't break and won't clutter your luggage. Get a free sample of Vivoli's *riso* (rice, my favorite) before ordering. (The Cinema Astro across the street from Vivoli's plays English/American movies in their original language, closed Mondays.)

Museum of Precious Stones (Museo delle Pietre Dure)—This unusual gem of a museum features mosaics of inlaid marble and semiprecious stones, along with oil-painting copies (L4,000, Tuesday–Saturday 9:00–14:00, closed Sunday and Monday, Via degli Alfani 78, around the corner from the Accademia).

Shopping—Florence is a great shopping town. Busy street scenes and markets abound, especially near San Lorenzo, on the Ponte Vecchio, and near Santa Croce. Leather, gold, silver, art prints, and tacky plaster "mini-*David*s" are most popular.

Scenic City Bus Ride to Fiesole—For a candid peek at a Florentine suburb, ride bus #7 (from Piazza Adua, near northeast entrance of station) for about 20 minutes through neighborhood gardens, vineyards, orchards, and large villas to the last stop— Fiesole. Fiesole is a popular excursion from Florence for its small eateries and good views of Florence. Catch the sunset from the terrace just below the La Reggia restaurant; from the Fiesole bus stop, face the square and take the very steep road on your left. Near the top of the hill you'll see the terrace on your left and the La Reggia restaurant farther ahead on your right (L25,000 menu).

Sights—Florence, South of the Arno River

▲▲**Pitti Palace**—From the Uffizi follow the elevated passageway (closed to non-Medicis) across the river to the gargantuan Pitti Palace which has five separate museums.

The **Palatine Gallery/Royal Apartments** features palatial room after chandeliered room, its walls sagging with paintings by the great masters. This Raphael collection is the biggest anywhere (first floor, L12,000, Tuesday–Saturday 8:30–22:00, Sunday 8:30–20:00, closed Monday, shorter hours off-season).

The **Modern Art Gallery** features 19th- and 20th-century art—mostly Romanticism, Neoclassicism, and Impressionism by Tuscan painters (second floor, L8,000, daily 8:30–13:50 but closed second and fourth Sunday and first, third, and fifth Monday).

The **Grand Ducal Treasures**, or Il Museo degli Argenti, is the Medici treasure chest entertaining fans of applied arts with jeweled crucifixes, exotic porcelain, gilded ostrich eggs, and so on (ground floor, L4,000, same hours as Modern Art Gallery).

Behind the palace, the huge semilandscaped **Boboli Gardens** offer a cool refuge from the city heat (L4,000, Tuesday–Sunday 9:00–17:30, closed Monday).

▲**Brancacci Chapel**—For the best look at the early Renaissance master Masaccio, see his restored frescoes here (L5,000, Monday and Wednesday–Friday 10:00–17:00, Sunday 13:00–17:00, closed Tuesday, cross the Ponte Vecchio and turn right a few blocks to Piazza del Carmine). The neighborhoods around here are considered the last surviving bits of old Florence.

▲**Piazzale Michelangelo**—Across the river overlooking the city (look for the huge statue of *David*), this square is worth the 30-minute hike, drive, or bus ride (either #12 or #13 from the train station) for the view. After dark it's packed with local schoolkids feeding their dates slices of watermelon. Just beyond it is the stark and beautiful, crowd-free, Romanesque San Miniato church.

Evening Side Trip to Siena

Connoisseurs of peace and small towns who aren't into art or shopping (and who won't be seeing Siena otherwise) should consider riding the bus to Siena for the evening (75 minutes if you take the "*corse rapide*" via the autostrada). Florence has no after-dark magic. Siena *is* after-dark magic. Confirm when the last bus returns.

Sleeping in Florence
(L1,700 = about $1)
Sleep Code: **S** = Single, **D** = Double/Twin, **T** = Triple, **Q** = Quad, **b** = bathroom, **s** = shower only, **CC** = Credit Card (Visa, Master-Card, Amex), **SE** = Speaks English, **NSE** = No English. Unless otherwise noted, breakfast is included (but usually optional). English is generally spoken.

The hotel scene in generally crowded and overpriced Florence isn't bad. With good information and a phone call ahead, you can find a stark, clean, and comfortable double with breakfast for L90,000, with a private shower for L120,000. You get roof-garden elegance for L140,000. Many places listed are old and rickety. I can't imagine Florence any other way. Virtually all of the places are central—the core of Florence is small and easily walkable.

Call direct to the hotel. Do not use the tourist office, which costs your host and jacks up the price. Except for Easter, Christmas, May, and October, there are plenty of rooms in Florence (dead winter and August are easiest). Budget travelers can call around and find soft prices. If you're staying for three or more nights, ask for a discount. The optional and overpriced breakfast can be a bargaining chip. Call ahead. I repeat, call ahead. Places will hold a room until early afternoon. If they say they're full, mention you're using this book.

Sleeping near the San Lorenzo Market (zip code: 50123)

East of the station a handy modern launderette is just off Via Cavour at Via Guelfa 22 red (daily 8:00–22:00, 12 pounds wash and dry for L12,000).

Hotel Accademia is an elegant one-star hotel with marble stairs, parquet floors, attractive public areas, pleasant rooms, and a floor plan that defies logic. This centrally-located hotel is just a few steps from the San Lorenzo market (S-L100,000, Sb-L110,000, Db-L170,000, Tb-L220,000, Qb-L270,000, CC:VMA, Via Faenza 7, tel. 055-293-451, fax 055-219-771).

Hotel Nuova Italia Firenze has 20 quiet, well-maintained rooms run by a likable English-speaking family with a sense of humor (Sb-L128,000, Db-L180,000, Tb-238,000, discount for paying cash, cheaper in winter, air-conditioning, triple-paned windows, CC:VMA, Via Faenza 26, tel. 055-268-430, fax 055-210-941).

Sleeping near the Central Market (zip code: 50129)

Casa Rabatti is the ultimate if you always wanted to be a part of a Florentine family. It's simple, clean, friendly, and run with motherly warmth by Marcella and her husband, Celestino, who speak minimal English (four rooms, D-L75,000, Db-L90,000, L35,000 per bed in shared quad or quint, prices good with this book, no breakfast, five blocks from station, Via San Zanobi 48 black, tel. 055-212-393).

Soggiorno Pezzati is another quiet little place with six homey rooms (Sb-L65,000, Db-L90,000, Tb-L126,000, no

Florence Hotels and Restaurants

1 - HOTEL ACCADEMIA	12 - HOTEL BELLETTINI	23 - PENSIONE BRETAGNA
2 - HOTEL NUOVA ITALIA	13 - ALBERGO CONCORDIA	24 - AILY HOME
3 - CASA RABATTI	14 - PENSIONE CENTRALE	25 - HOTEL TORRE GUELFA
4 - SOGGIORNO PEZZATI	15 - PENSIONE BURCHIANTI	26 - TRATTORIA IL CONTADINO
5 - HOTEL ENZA	16 - SOGGIORNO ABACO	27 - TRATTORIA DA GIORGIO
6 - SOGGIORNO MAGLIANI	17 - HOTEL PENDINI	28 - GROTTA DI LEO
7 - HOTEL LOGGIATO DEI SERVITI	18 - PENSIONE MAXIM	29 - TRATTORIA BURRASCA
8 - DUE FONTANE HOTEL	19 - HOTEL UNIVERSO	30 - HYDRA PIZZERIA
9 - OBLATE SISTERS	20 - HOTEL ELITE	31 - ROSTICCERIA GIULIANO
10 - SOGGIORNO LA PERGOLA	21 - ALBERGO MONTREALE	32 - OSTERIA SAPORI
11 - HOTEL IL PERSEO	22 - PENSIONE SOLE	33 - CANTINETTA VERRAZZANO

breakfast, marked only by small sign near door, Via San Zanobi 22, tel. 055-291-660, fax 055-287-145 Daniela SE). If you get an Italian recording when you call, hang on—your call is being transferred to a cell phone.

Hotel Enza, run by English-speaking Eugenia, who clearly enjoys her work, has 16 quirky, unpredictable rooms. While Eugenia's chihuahua, Tricky, is tiny, her rooms are particularly spacious—though sometimes dirty (S-L70,000, Sb-L75,000, D-L90,000, Db-L125,000, T-L125,000, Tb-L160,000, family loft, discounts for three nights off-season, no breakfast, six blocks from station, Via San Zanobi 45 black, tel. 055-490-990, fax 055-292-192).

Central and humble **Soggiorno Magliani** feels and smells like a great-grandmother's place (seven rooms, S-L52,000, D-L72,000, double-paned windows, at corner of Via Guelfa and Via Reparata, Via Reparata 1, tel. 055-287-378, run by Vincenza and her English-speaking daughter, Cristina).

Sleeping East of the Duomo

The first two listings are near the Accademia, on Piazza Annunziata (zip code: 50122).

Hotel Loggiato dei Serviti, at the most prestigious address in Florence on the most Renaissance (traffic-free) square in town, gives you Renaissance romance with a place to plug in your hair-dryer (29 rooms, Sb-L210,000, Db-L310,000, family suites from L500,000, book a month ahead, up to 30 percent off in August, elevator, CC:VMA, square noisy at night, Piazza S.S. Annunziata 3, tel. 055-289-592, fax 055-289-595, e-mail: loggiato_serviti@italyhotel.com, SE). Stone stairways lead you under open-beam ceilings through this 16th-century monastery's elegant public rooms. The cells, with air conditioning, TVs, mini-bars, and telephones, wouldn't be recognized by their original inhabitants. This place is my kind of classy.

Le Due Fontane Hotel faces the same great square but fills its old building with a modern, business-class ambience. Its air-conditioned rooms are big, modern, and stylish, but are less memorable and less expensive (57 rooms, Sb-L180,000, Db-L250,000, Tb-L360,000, prices promised by Sr. Borgia through 1999, CC:VMA, buffet breakfast, elevator, phones, TVs, Piazza S.S. Annunziata 14, tel. 055-210-185, fax 055-294-461, SE).

The **Oblate Sisters of the Assumption** run a 50-room hotel in a Renaissance building several blocks east of the Duomo (D-L110,000, Db-130,000, Borgo Pinti 15, 50121 Firenze, tel. 055-248-0582, fax 055-234-6291).

Another option is **Soggiorno La Pergola** di Letitia Barlozzi (Db-L120,000, air-conditioning, Via della Pergola 23, tel. 055-213-886).

Sleeping between the Station and Duomo (zip code: 50123)

Hotel Il Perseo is starkly clean, simple, and affordable. This centrally-located hotel, a block west of the Duomo, is run by Louise, a friendly Australian (one S-L75,000, D-L115,000, Db-L140,000, T-L155,000, Tb-L180,000, CC:VMA, add 3 percent if you pay with CC, phones in rooms, valet service for parking, Via Cerretani 1, tel. 055-212-504, fax 055-288-377).

Hotel Bellettini has 28 spacious, well-cared-for rooms with tile floors and a touch of class (Sb-L135,000, Db-L185,000, Tb-L245,000, CC:VMA, cheaper November through February, half the rooms have air-conditioning, Via de' Conti 7, tel. 055-213-561, fax 055-283-551, e-mail: hotel.bellettini@dada.it).

Albergo Concordia is a modern, well-run, and conveniently located place. Confirm prices (16 rooms, one fine Sb-L85,000, Db-L135,000, Tb-L180,000, CC:VMA, no elevator, filled with school groups February–April, Via dell'Amorino 14, tel. & fax 055-213-233, Fabrizio SE).

Pensione Centrale is indeed central, Old World comfortable, and run by Marie Therese Blot and Franco, who make you feel right at home (D-L160,000, Db-L190,000 with an "American" breakfast, often filled with American students, CC:VMA, elevator, Via de' Conti 3, tel. 055-215-761, fax 055-215-216).

Pensione Burchianti is old and noble yet rundown. Each of its 11 spacious rooms has a bit of old Florence surviving on its walls or ceilings (Sb-L70,000, D-L100,000, Ds-L120,000, Db-L130,000, extra bed-L35,000, breakfast-L5,000, prices promised with this book, reservations undependable, Via del Giglio 6, tel. & fax 055-212-796, Franco and Francesco SE).

Soggiorno Abaco is a bohemian, MTV kind of place listed in most of the student guidebooks and run by friendly, guitar-strumming Bruno (seven rooms, S-L70,000, Sb-L85,000, Ds-L110,000, Db-L130,000, extra roommate-L20,000, breakfast-L10,000, phones and TVs in room, Via Dei Banchi 1, tel. 055-238-1919, fax 055-282-289, SE).

Sleeping on/near Piazza Repubblica (zip code: 50123)

These are the most central of my recommendations, though given Florence's walkable core, nearly every hotel is central.

Hotel Pendini, a three-star hotel with 42 elegant rooms (eight with views of square), is popular and central, overlooking Piazza Repubblica (Sb-L140,000–170,000, Db-L190,000– 250,000; the cheaper prices are for low season: November through February and August; CC:VMA, Via Strozzi 2, reserve at least a month in advance, tel. 055-211-170, fax 055-281-807, Web site: www.tiac.net/users/pendini, e-mail: pendini@dada.it).

Pensione Maxim is big and as close to the sights as possible. You'll feel like a mouse in a maze navigating its narrow halls (23 rooms, Db-L130,000, Tb-L165,000, Qb-L200,000, CC:VMA but pay first night in cash, in-house laundry service for L18,000, nearby parking-L30,000/night, Via dei Medici 4, elevator entrance at Via dei Calzaiuoli 11, tel. 055-217-474, fax 055-283-729, e-mail: hotmaxim@tin.it).

Sleeping South of Station near Piazza Santa Maria Novella (zip code: 50123)

From the station, follow the underground tunnel to Piazza Santa Maria Novella, a pleasant square by day that becomes a little sleazy after dark. (Theft alert where the tunnel surfaces.) It's handy—only three blocks from the cathedral, it's near a good launderette (La Serena, Monday–Saturday 8:30–20:00, closed Sunday, L20,000 for 11 pounds, Via della Scala 30 red, tel. 055-218-183), cheap restaurants (on Via Palazzuolo, see below), and the bus and train station. There's a great Massaccio fresco (*The Trinity*) in the church on the square (free).

Hotel Universo, a big, group-friendly hotel with stark concrete hallways but fine rooms, is warmly run by a group of gentle men (D-L110,000, Db-L160,000, Tb-L200,000, Qb-L250,000, to get these discounted prices you must show this book, CC:VMA, elevator, right on Piazza S. M. Novella at #20, tel. 055-281-951, fax 055-292-335, SE).

Hotel Pensione Elite, with eight comfortable rooms, is a good basic value, run warmly by Maurizio and Nadia (Ss-L85,000, Sb-L110,000, Ds-L110,000, Db-L140,000, at south end of square with back to church, go right to Via della Scala 12, second floor, tel. & fax 055-215-395, SE).

The nearby **Albergo Montreal** is cheaper, with clean, airy, and comfortable rooms but less character (14 rooms, S-L60,000 Db-L96,000, Tb-L130,000, with this book through 1999, Via della Scala 43, tel. 055-238-2331, fax 055-287-491, SE).

Pensione Sole, a clean, cozy, family-run place with seven bright rooms, is just off Santa Maria Novella toward the river (S-L53,000, D-L73,000, Db-L93,000, Tb-L123,000, no breakfast, Via del Sole 8, third floor, lots of stairs, tel. & fax 055-239-6094, Anna NSE).

Sleeping on or near the Arno River and Ponte Vecchio (zip code: 50123)

Pensione Bretagna is an Old World–elegant place with thoughtfully appointed rooms. The hotel is run by the helpful, English-speaking Antonio, Maura, and Marco. Imagine eating breakfast under a painted, chandeliered ceiling overlooking the Arno River (S-L75,000, Ss-L80,000, Sb-L90,000, D-L110,000, Ds-L130,000,

Db-L155,000, Tb-L195,000, including optional L10,000 breakfast, family deals, prices special with this book through 1999, CC:VMA, elevator, just past Ponte San Trinita, Lungarno Corsini 6, tel. 055-289-618, fax 055-289-619, e-mail: hotelpens.bretagna @agora.stm.it). They also run a cheaper place, *Althea*, near Piazza San Spirito in the Oltrarno neighborhood (Db-L100,000, no breakfast, call Bretagna to book).

Aily Home is a humble, homey, grandmotherly, five-room place tucked away on a peaceful square a block from the Ponte Vecchio (three-night minimum, S-L35,000, D-L60,000, showers-L3,000, elevator, Piazza San Stefano 1, tel. 055-239-6505, Rosaria Franchis NSE).

Hotel Torre Guelfa is topped with a fun medieval tower with a panoramic rooftop terrace. Its 12 pricey rooms vary wildly in size, but cost virtually the same (Db-L250,000). Number 15, with a private terrace, is worth reserving several months in advance (elevator, air-conditioning, a couple blocks northwest of Ponte Vecchio, Borgo S.S. Apostoli 8, tel. 055-239-6338, fax 055-239-8577).

Sleeping in Oltrarno, South of the River (zip code: 50125)

Across the river in the Oltrarno area, between the Pitti Palace and the Ponte Vecchio, you'll still find small traditional crafts shops, neighborly piazzas and family eateries. Each of the following places is only a few minutes' walk from the Ponte Vecchio.

Hotel La Scaletta is elegant, friendly, and clean, with a dark, cool, labyrinthine floorplan and lots of Old World lounges. Owner Barbara, her son Manfredo, and daughters Bianca and Diana run this well-worn but loved place. Your journal becomes poetry when written on the highest terrace of La Scaletta's panoramic roof garden. Manfredo says, "From the garden you can visit the city without walking." If Manfredo is cooking dinner, eat here (Ss-L75,000, Sb-L120,000–140,000, D-L140,000, Db-L160,000–200,000, Tb-L200,000–240,000, Qb-L240,000–270,000, L20,000 extra for rooms on garden side, CC:VM, from L10,000–20,000 discount if you pay cash, elevator, Via Guicciardini 13 black, 150 yards up the street from the Ponte Vecchio, tel. 055-283-028, fax 055-289-562, Web site: www.alba.fi.it, e-mail: LaScaletta.htl@dada.it). Reserve well in advance by phone, then confirm your reservation with a fax and send a personal or traveler's check.

Hotel Silla, a classic three-star hotel with cheery, spacious, pastel and modern rooms, is a fine splurge. It faces the river overlooking a park opposite the Santa Croce church (32 rooms, Db-L250,000, CC:VMA, some rooms with air-conditioning, Via dei Renai 5, 50125 Florence, tel. 055-234-2888, fax 055-234-1437, manager Gabrielle SE).

Pensione Sorelle Bandini is a ramshackle 500-year-old

Florence's Oltrarno Neighborhood

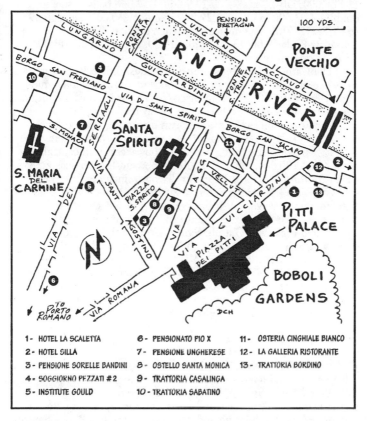

1 - HOTEL LA SCALETTA   6 - PENSIONATO PIO X   11 - OSTERIA CINGHIALE BIANCO
2 - HOTEL SILLA   7 - PENSIONE UNGHERESE   12 - LA GALLERIA RISTORANTE
3 - PENSIONE SORELLE BANDINI   8 - OSTELLO SANTA MONICA   13 - TRATTORIA BORDINO
4 - SOGGIORNO PEZZATI #2   9 - TRATTORIA CASALINGA
5 - INSTITUTE GOULD   10 - TRATTORIA SABATINO

palace on a perfectly Florentine square, with cavernous rooms, museum-warehouse interiors, a musty youthfulness, cats, a balcony lounge-loggia with a view, and an ambience that, for romantic bohemians, can be a highlight of Florence. Mimmo or Sr. Romeo will hold a room until 16:00 with a phone call (S-L131,000, Sb-L163,000, D-L146,000, Db-L178,000, T-L202,000, Tb-L245,000, includes breakfast, elevator, Piazza Santo Spirito 9, tel. 055-215-308, fax 055-282-761).

Soggiorno Pezzati #2, run by Daniela (who also manages the original Soggiorno Pezzati, listed above) offers five basic rooms in the Oltrarno neighborhood (Sb-L65,000, Db-L90,000, Tb-L126,000, tel. 055-291-660, fax 055-287-145, SE).

Institute Gould is a Protestant church–run place with 89 beds in 27 rooms and clean, modern facilities (S-L46,000, Sb-L53,000,

D-L68,000, Db-L76,000, Tb-L99,000, L37,000 beds in shared
doubles, L32,000 in quads, L27,000 in quints, Via dei Serragli 49,
tel. 055-212-576). You must arrive when office is open
(Monday–Friday 9:00–13:00, 15:00–19:00, Saturday 9:00–13:00, no
check-in on Sunday).

The Catholic-run **Pensionato Pio X-Artigianelli** is more
freewheeling and rundown, with 67 beds in 20 rooms and a midnight curfew (L22,000 beds in three- to five-bed rooms, minimum
two nights, Via dei Serragli 106, tel. & fax 055-225-044).

Pension Ungherese, warmly run by Sergio, is good for drivers. It's outside the city center (near Stadio, on route to Fiesole)
with easy free street parking and quick bus access into central Florence (Sb-L100,000, Db-L190,000, 20 percent less off-season, pay
cash with this book for a 7 percent discount, includes breakfast,
CC:VM, Via G. B. Amici 8, tel. & fax 055-573-474, NSE, e-mail:
hotel.ungherese@dada.it). It has great singles, a backyard garden
terrace, and just-renovated rooms (ask for one on the garden).

Last alternatives: **Ostello Santa Monaca** (L23,000 beds, 10-
bed rooms, no breakfast, midnight curfew, very well located a few
blocks past Ponte Alla Carraia, Via Santa Monaca 6, tel. 055-268-
338, fax 055-280-185) and the classy **Villa Camerata IYHF hostel** (L24,000 per bed and breakfast, four- to eight-bed rooms; ride
bus #17A or B then 500-meter walk, Via Righi 1, tel. 055-601-
451) are on the outskirts of Florence.

Eating in Florence

Eating in Oltrarno, South of the River
There are several good and colorful restaurants in Oltrarno on or
near Piazza Santo Spirito. **Borgo Antico** serves hearty portions to
a classy young and local clientele. It's right on a great square with
indoor and outdoor seating and worth the extra lire (Piazza Santo
Spirito 6 red, tel. 055-210-437). The Ricchi bar, #6 on the same
square, has fine homemade gelati and outdoor tables shaded by
trees (step inside to see the wallful of entries to finish the facade
of the Brunelleschi church on the square).

Trattoria Casalinga is an inexpensive and popular standby,
famous for its home-cooking (closed Sunday, just off Piazza
Santo Spirito, near the church at Via dei Michelozzi 9 red, tel.
055-218-624).

Good food and ambience at reasonable prices are also served
at **Trattoria Sabatino** at Borgo S. Frediano 17 blue and **Osteria
del Cinghiale Bianco** at Borgo S. Jacopo 43 red (open at 19:00,
closed Tuesday and Wednesday, arrive early or call 055-215-706
to reserve).

Trattoria Bordino is cozy and friendly and serves fine Florentine cuisine. Its prices aren't cheap, but it's an excellent value

(L40,000 dinners, closed Sunday, Via Stracciatella 9 red). Take the second left after crossing Ponte Vecchio and walk under the arch.

Eating North of the River
Near Santa Maria Novella and the Train Station

Two similar chow houses, each offering about a L20,000, hearty, family-style, fixed-price menu with a bustling working-class/budget-Yankee-traveler atmosphere, are **Trattoria il Contadino** (Monday–Saturday 12:00–14:30, 18:15–21:30, closed Sunday, Via Palazzuolo 69 red, a few blocks south of the train station, tel. 055-238-2673) and **Trattoria da Giorgio** (Monday–Saturday 12:00–15:00, 18:30–22:00, closed Sunday, across the street at Via Palazzuolo 100 red). Check each before choosing. Get there early or be ready to wait. The touristy **La Grotta di Leo** has a cheap, straightforward menu and edible food (Via della Scala 41 red, closed Wednesday, tel. 055-219-265).

Near the Central and San Lorenzo Markets

For mountains of picnic produce or just a cheap sandwich and piles of people-watching, visit the huge multistoried Central Market—**Mercato Centrale** (7:00–14:00, closed Sunday), a block north of the San Lorenzo street market.

Trattoria la Burrasca is a small inexpensive place serving local-style dishes to Italians in a characteristic setting (Friday–Wednesday 12:00–15:00, 19:00–22:00, closed Thursday, Via Panicale 6 red, Panicale borders the Central Market on the north, tel. 055-215-827).

Hydra Pizzeria Spaghetteria, two blocks south, is also good (across from Medici Chapel entrance amid San Lorenzo street market, Canto de' Nelli 38r, tel. 055-218-922).

A Quick Lunch near the Sights

I keep lunch in Florence fast and simple, eating in one of countless self-service places, *pizza rusticas* (holes-in-walls selling pizza by weight), or just picnicking (try juice, yogurt, cheese, and a roll for L8,000). For a reasonably priced pizza with a Medici-style view, try one of the pizzerias on Piazza della Signoria.

A few blocks east of the Palazzo Vecchio, the cozy **Rosticceria Guilano Centro** serves fine food to go or enjoy there (closed Sunday evening and all day Monday, Via Dei Neri 74 red).

Osteria Vini e Vecchi Sapori is a colorful hole-in-the-wall serving traditional food, including plates of mixed sandwiches, half a block north of the Palazzo Vecchio (Tuesday–Sunday 9:30–22:30, closed Monday, Via dei Magazzini 3 red, facing equestrian statue in Piazza della Signoria, go behind its tail to your left).

Cantinetta dei Verrazzano is a long-established bakery/café/winebar which serves elegant sandwich plates and hot focaccia sandwiches in an elegant old-time setting (open until 21:00, closed Sunday, just off Via Calzaiuoli at Via dei Tavolini 18, tel. 055-268-590).

Transportation Connections—Florence
By train to: Assisi (10/day, 2.5 to 3 hrs), **Orvieto** (6/day, 2 hrs), **Pisa** (2/hrly, 1 hr), **La Spezia** (for the Cinque Terre, 2/day direct, 2 hrs, or change in Pisa), **Venice** (7/day, 3 hrs), **Milan** (12/day, 3–5 hrs), **Rome** (hrly, 2.5 hrs), **Naples** (2/day, 4 hrs), **Brindisi** (3/day, 11 hrs with change in Bologna), **Frankfurt** (3/day, 12 hrs), **Paris** (1/day, 12 hrs overnight), **Vienna** (4/day, 9–10 hrs). Train info: tel. 1478-88088.

Buses: The SITA bus station, a block from the Florence train station, offers service to San Gimignano (hrly, 1.75 hrs) and Siena (hrly, 75-min fast buses or 2-hr slow buses, faster than the train). Bus info tel. 055-483-651; some schedules are in Florence's *Concierge* magazine.

Driving Florentine
From the autostrada (north or south) take the Certosa exit (follow signs to Centro, at Porta Romana go to the left of the arch and down Via Francesco Petrarca). After driving and trying to park in Florence, you'll understand why Leonardo never invented the car. Cars flatten the charm of Florence. Get near the *centro* and park where you can. Garages charge around L30,000 a day. The big underground lot at the train station charges L2,000 per hour. The cheapest parking is at Piazza della Liberta (about L15,000/day, northeast of city center). Another option is the garage at Fortezza di Basso (L20,000/day). White lines are free, blue are not. I got towed once in the town of Michelangelo—an expensive lesson.

PISA
Pisa was a regional superpower in her medieval heyday (11th, 12th, and 13th centuries), rivaling Florence and Genoa. Its Mediterranean empire, which included Corsica and Sardinia, helped make it a wealthy republic. But the Pisa fleet was beaten (1284, by Genoa) and its port silted up, leaving the city high and dry with only its Piazza of Miracles and its university keeping it on the map.

Pisa's three important sights (the cathedral, baptistery, and bell tower) float regally on the best lawn in Italy. Even as the church was being built, the Piazza del Duomo was nicknamed the Campo dei Miracoli, or "Field of Miracles," for the grandness of the undertaking. The style throughout is Pisa's very own "Pisan Romanesque" (surrounded by what may be Italy's tackiest ring of souvenir stands). This spectacle is tourism at its most crass. Wear gloves.

Planning Your Time

Seeing the tower and the square and wandering through the church are 90 percent of the Pisan thrill. Pisa is a touristy quickie. By train it's a joy. By car it's a headache. Train travelers may be changing trains in Pisa anyway. Hop on the bus and see the tower. Since you can't climb the tower, a look doesn't take very long and is worthwhile even after (or before) hours. Sophisticated sightseers stop more for the Pisano carvings in the cathedral and baptistery than for a look at the tipsy tower. There's nothing wrong with Pisa, but I'd stop only to see the "Piazza of Miracles" and get out. By car it's a 45-minute detour from the freeway.

Orientation

Tourist Information: TI offices are at the train station (Monday–Saturday 9:30–13:00, 15:00–18:30, closed Sunday, tel. 050-42291) and near the Leaning Tower (outside the medieval wall, to the left of the gate before you enter the Field of Miracles). The Pisa tourist board has a scheme to get you into its neglected secondary sights. Various sight combination tickets run from L10,000 for any two sights to L18,000 for the works. In comparison, the cathedral is a bargain (L3,000).

Arrival in Pisa

By Train: Train travelers bus easily from the station in the center, over the Arno River, and to the Duomo. Bus #1 (for Duomo) leaves from the bus circle to the right of the station every 10 minutes. Buy your L1,500 ticket from the tobacco/magazine kiosk in the station's main hall (good for one hour, round-trip OK).

   By Car: To get to the Leaning Tower, follow signs to the Duomo or the Piazza dei Miracoli. This is on the north edge of town. Drivers (coming from the Pisa Nord autostrada exit) don't have to mess with the city (although you will have to endure some terrible traffic). There's no option better than the L1,500-per-hour pay lot just outside the town wall near the Duomo.

Sights—Pisa

▲▲**Leaning Tower**—This most famous example of Pisan Romanesque architecture was leaning even before its completion. Notice how the architect, for lack of a better solution, kinked up the top section. The 294 tilted steps to the top are closed while engineers work to keep the bell tower from toppling. The formerly clean and tidy area around the tower is now a construction zone. Steam pipes drying out the subsoil and huge weights are working together to stop the leaning (but not straighten out the tower). For a quick lunch, the pizzeria/trattoria La Buca is a decent value (closed Friday, near tower at Via S. Maria and Via G. Tassi, tel. 050-560-660).

▲▲**Cathedral**—The huge Pisan Romanesque cathedral, with its carved pulpit by Giovanni Pisano, is artistically more important than its more famous bell tower (L3,000, summer: Monday–Saturday 10:00–19:20, Sunday 13:00–19:30; closes Monday–Saturday at 17:40 in spring and fall, at 16:40 in winter). Shorts are OK as long as they're not short shorts.

Baptistery—The baptistery, the biggest in Italy, with a pulpit by Nicolo Pisano (1260) which inspired Renaissance art to follow, is interesting for its great acoustics (L10,000 combination ticket for two sights, same hours as cathedral except open all day Sunday; located in front of the cathedral). If you ask nicely and leave a tip, the doorman uses the place's echo power to sing haunting harmonies with himself. Notice that even the baptistery leans about five feet. (The Nicolo Pisano pulpit and carvings in Siena were just as impressive to me—in a more enjoyable atmosphere.)

Other Sights—Pisa, of course, is more than the Campo dei Miracoli. Walking from the station to the Duomo shows you a classy Old World town with an Arno-scape much like its rival upstream. But for most, Pisa is just a cliché that needs to be seen and a chance to see the Pisano pulpits. For more Pisan art, see the **Museo dell' Opera del Duomo** (behind the tower) and the **Museo Nazionale di San Matteo** (on the river near Piazza Mazzini). The cemetery bordering the cathedral square is not worth the admission, even if its "Holy Land dirt" does turn a body into a skeleton in a day (same hours as cathedral, except open all day Sunday).

Transportation Connections—Pisa

By train to: Florence (hrly, one hour), **La Spezia** (hrly, 1 hr, milk-run from there into coastal villages), **Siena** (change at Empoli: Pisa–Empoli, hrly, 30 min; Empoli–Siena, hrly, 1 hr). Even the fastest trains stop in Pisa, and you'll very likely be changing trains here whether you plan to stop or not. Train info: tel. 1478-88088.

Route Tips for Drivers

To Florence and Siena: The drive from Pisa to Florence is that rare case where the non-autostrada highway (free, more direct, and at least as fast) is a better deal than the autostrada. When departing for Florence, San Gimignano, or Siena, follow the blue "superstrada" signs (green signs are for the autostrada) for the SS road (along the city wall east from the tower—away from the sea) for Florence (and later Siena).

To the Cinque Terre: From Pisa, catch the Genova-bound autostrada. The white stuff you'll see in the mountains as you approach La Spezia isn't snow—it's Carrara marble, Michelangelo's choice for his great art. From Pisa to La Spezia takes about an hour.

VENICE (VENEZIA)

Soak all day in this puddle of elegant decay. Venice is Europe's best-preserved big city. It's a car-free urban wonderland of 100 islands, laced together by 400 bridges and 2,000 alleys; and it's doing well on the artificial respirator of tourism.

Born in a lagoon 1,500 years ago as a refuge from barbarians, Venice is overloaded with tourists and slowly sinking (unrelated facts). In the Middle Ages, the Venetians, becoming Europe's clever middleman for east-west trade, created a great trading empire. By smuggling in the bones of St. Mark (San Marco, in about A.D. 830), Venice gained religious importance as well. With the discovery of America and new trading routes to the Orient, Venetian power ebbed. But as Venice fell, her appetite for decadence grew. Through the 17th and 18th centuries Venice partied on the wealth accumulated through earlier centuries as a trading power.

Today Venice is home to about 75,000 people in its old city, down from a peak population of around 200,000. While there are about 500,000 in greater Venice (counting the mainland, not counting tourists), the old town has a small-town feel. Locals seem to know everyone. To see small-town Venice through the touristic flak, explore the backstreets and try a Stand-Up Progressive Venetian Pub-Crawl Dinner.

Planning Your Time

Venice is worth at least a day on even the speediest tour. Hyperefficient train travelers take the night train in and/or out. Sleep in the old center to experience Venice at its best: early and late. For a one-day visit, cruise the Grand Canal, do the major San Marco sights (the square, Doge's Palace, St. Mark's Basilica), see the

Venice

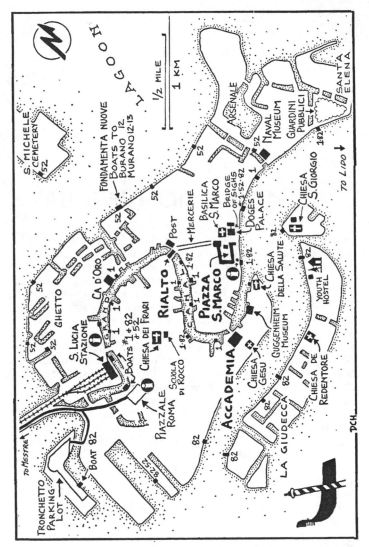

Church of the Frari for art, and wander the backstreets on a pub crawl (see Eating, below). Venice's greatest sight is the city itself. Make time to simply wander. While doable in a day, Venice is worth two. It's a medieval cookie jar, and nobody's looking.

Orientation

The island city of Venice is shaped like a fish. Its major thorough-fares are canals. The Grand Canal winds through the middle of the fish, starting at the mouth where all the people and food enter, passing under the Rialto Bridge, and ending at St. Mark's Square (San Marco). Park your 20th-century perspective at the mouth, and let Venice swallow you whole.

Venice is a carless kaleidoscope of people, bridges, and odorless canals. The city has no real streets, and addresses are hopelessly con-fusing. There are six districts: San Marco (most touristy), Castello (behind San Marco), Cannaregio (from the station to the Rialto), San Polo (other side of the Rialto), Santa Croce, and Dorsoduro. Each district has about 6,000 address numbers. Luckily it's easy to find your way, since many street corners have a sign pointing you to the nearest major landmark, such as San Marco, Accademia, Rialto, and Ferrovia (the train station). To find your way, navigate by land-marks, not streets. Obedient visitors stick to the main thoroughfares as directed by these signs and miss the charm of backstreet Venice.

Tourist Information

There are three tourist information offices: at the train station (daily 8:10–18:50, crowded and surly); at the far end of St. Mark's Square (daily 9:30–17:30, friendly, public WC nearby); and near St. Mark's Square at the San Marco *vaporetto* stop (Monday–Saturday 10:10–15:50, closed Sunday; helpful and uncrowded; from the church go to the lagoon, turn right, walk about 150 yards, and you'll run into it; public WC nearby). For TI info over the phone, call 041-529-8727 or 041-526-5721. At any TI, pick up a free city map, the week's events, and the latest museum hours, and confirm your sightseeing plans. The free periodical entertain-ment guide *Un Ospite de Venezia* (a monthly listing of events, nightlife, museum hours, train and *vaporetto* schedules, emergency telephone numbers, and so on) is at the TI or fancy hotel recep-tion desks. The cheap Venice map on sale at postcard racks has much more detail than the TI map. Also consider the little sold-with-the-postcards guidebook which comes with a city map and explanations of the major sights.

Walking Tours: The same people that run Enjoy Rome offer walking tours of Venice. You'll get a rundown on the Doges, Marco Polo, Casanova, casinos, canals, and building gondolas. Meet at 10:00 any day except Sunday in front of Thomas Cook, a few steps from the Rialto Bridge *vaporetto* stop (L30,000, L25,000 if under 26, three hours, toll-free tel. 167-274-819).

Arrival in Venice

A two-mile-long causeway (highway and train lines) connects Venice to the mainland. Mestre, the sprawling mainland industrial base of Venice, has fewer crowds, cheaper hotels, plenty of parking lots, but no charm. Don't stop here. Trains regularly connect Mestre with the Santa Lucia station (6/hrly, 5 min).

By Train: Venice's Santa Lucia train station plops you right into the old town on the Grand Canal, an easy *vaporetto* ride or fascinating 40-minute walk from San Marco. Upon arrival, skip the station's crowded TI (San Marco's are better), confirm your departure plan (good train info desk), consider stowing unnecessary heavy bags at the *deposito*, then walk straight out of the station to the canal. The dock for *vaporettos* #1 and #82 is on your left. Buy a L4,500 ticket at the window and hop on a boat for downtown (direction Rialto or San Marco).

By Car: At Venice, the freeway ends like Medusa's head. Follow the green lights directing you to a parking lot with space. The standard place is Tronchetto (across the causeway and on the right) with a huge new multistoried garage (L40,000 per day, half-price with a discount coupon from your hotel). From there you'll find travel agencies masquerading as tourist information offices and *vaporetto* docks for the boat connection (#82) to the town center. Don't let taxi boatmen con you out of the cheap *vaporetto* ride. Parking in Mestre is easy and much cheaper (open-air lots L6,000–8,000 per day, L10,000-a-day garage across from the Mestre train station).

By Plane: A handy shuttle bus (L3,000, 30 min, blue ATVO bus) or the cheaper bus #5 (L1,500, one hour, orange ICTV bus) connects the airport with the Tronchetto *vaporetto* stop. Those jetting in can get directly to San Marco by Alilaguna speedboat (L17,000, hrly, 80 min, running from 6:10 to midnight from airport, from 4:45 to 22:50 from San Marco).

Helpful Hints

The Venice fly-trap lures us in and takes our money any way it can. Count your change carefully. Accept the fact that Venice was a tourist town 400 years ago. It was, is, and always will be crowded. While 80 percent of Venice is actually an untouristy place, 80 percent of the tourists never notice. Hit the backstreets.

Get Lost: Venice is the ideal town to explore on foot. Walk and walk to the far reaches of the town. Don't worry about getting lost. Get as lost as possible. Keep reminding yourself, "I'm on an island and I can't get off." When it comes time to find your way, just follow the directional arrows on building corners, or simply ask a local, "*Dové San Marco*?" ("Where is St. Mark's?") People in the tourist business (that's most Venetians) speak some English. If they don't, listen politely, watching where their hands point, say "*Grazie*," and head off in that direction.

Rip-offs, Theft, and Help: While petty thieves work the crowded main streets, *vaporetto* boats, and docks, the dark, late-night streets of Venice are safe. A service called Venezia No Problem aids tourists who've been mistreated by any Venetian business (toll-free tel. 167-355-920).

Money: Bank rates vary. I like the Banca di Sicilia, a block toward San Marco from Campo San Bartolomeo. American Express, famous for its "no commission," makes up for that with mediocre rates (Monday–Friday 9:00–17:30, Saturday 9:00–12:30, San Marco 1471, tel. 041-520-0844). Thomas Cook waives its commission on Thomas Cook checks but charges 4.5 percent for others (at St. Mark's Square nearly under tower with digital clock, Monday–Saturday 9:00–20:00, Saturday 9:30–17:00; and at the Rialto *vaporetto* dock—Monday–Saturday 9:00–19:45, Sunday 9:30–17:00). Non-bank exchange bureaus like Exacto will cost you $10 more than a bank for a $200 exchange. A 24-hour cash machine near the Rialto *vaporetto* stop exchanges U.S. dollars and other currencies into lire at fair rates. Cash machines are plentiful.

Post Office: There's a large post office behind St. Mark's Square (on the side of square opposite church) and a branch near the Rialto (on St. Mark's side, Monday–Friday 8:10–13:30, Saturday 8:10–12:30).

The "Rolling Venice" Youth Discount Pass: This worthwhile L5,000 pass gives those under 30 discounts on sights and transportation, and information on cheap eating and sleeping (Monday–Friday 10:00–13:00, Tuesday and Thursday also open 15:00–18:00, closed Wednesday; from American Express head toward San Marco, take first left, first left again through "Contarina" tunnel, follow white sign to Commune di Venezia and see the sign; Corte Contarina 1529, third floor, tel. 041-274-7651).

Water: Venetians pride themselves on having pure, safe, and tasty tap water piped in from the foothills of the Alps (which you can actually see from Venice bell towers on crisp, clear winter days).

Pigeon Poop: If bombed by a pigeon, resist the initial response to wipe it off immediately—it'll just smear into your hair. Wait until it dries and flake it off cleanly.

Laundry: A handy *lavanderia* (Laundromat) near St. Mark's and near most of my hotel listings is the full-service Laundry Gabriella (Monday–Friday 8:00–19:00, 985 Rio Terra Colonne, one bridge off the Merceria near San Zulian church, down Calle dei Armeni, tel. 041-522-1758). The closest Laundromat to the Rialto is Lavanderia S.S. Apostoli (Monday–Saturday 8:30–12:00, 15:00–19:00, closed Sunday, on Campo S.S. Apostoli, tel. 041-522-6650). At either place you can get nine pounds of laundry washed and dried for L30,000— confirm price carefully. Drop it by in the morning, pick it up that afternoon. (Call to be sure they're open.) At either place, do not expect to get your clothes back folded, ironed, or even entirely dry.

Shopping: If you're buying a substantial amount from a glass/art shop, bargain. It's accepted and almost expected.

Downtown Venice

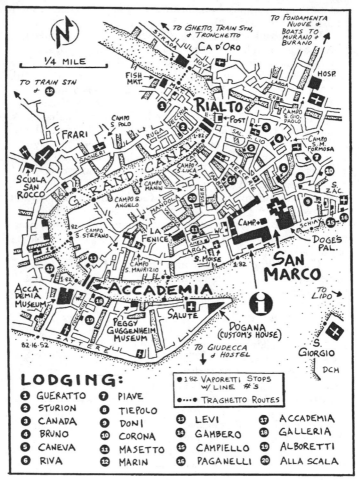

LODGING:

1. GUERATTO
2. STURION
3. CANADA
4. BRUNO
5. CANEVA
6. RIVA
7. PIAVE
8. TIEPOLO
9. DONI
10. CORONA
11. MASETTO
12. MARIN
13. LEVI
14. GAMBERO
15. CAMPIELLO
16. PAGANELLI
17. ACCADEMIA
18. GALLERIA
19. ALBORETTI
20. ALLA SCALA

● 1·82 VAPORETTI STOPS W/ LINE #'S
●····● TRAGHETTO ROUTES

Etiquette: Walk on the right and don't loiter on bridges. Picnicking is technically forbidden (keep a low profile). Dress modestly. Men should keep their shirts on. When visiting St. Mark's or other major churches, men and women should cover their knees and shoulders.

Getting Around Venice

The public transit system is a fleet of motorized bus-boats called *vaporetti*. They work like city buses except that they never get a flat, the stops are docks, and if you get off between stops, you may drown. For most, only two lines matter: #1 is the slow boat, taking 45 minutes to make every stop along the entire length of the Grand Canal; and #82 is the fast boat which zips down the Grand Canal in 25 minutes, stopping mainly at Tronchetto (car-park), Piazzale Roma (bus station), Ferrovia (train station), Rialto Bridge, and San Marco. Buy a L4,500 ticket before boarding or (for an extra fee) from a conductor on board. There are 24-hour (L15,000) and 72-hour (L30,000) passes, but I've never ferried enough to merit purchasing one (although it's fun to be able to hop on and off carelessly).

Only three bridges cross the Grand Canal, but *traghetti* (little L700 ferry gondolas, marked on better maps) shuttle locals and in-the-know tourists across the Grand Canal at seven handy locations (see downtown Venice map). Take advantage of these time-savers. They can also save money. For instance, while most tourists take the L4,500 *vaporetto* to connect St. Mark's with Salute Church, a L700 *traghetto* also does the job.

Grand Canal Tour of Venice

Grab a front seat on boat #82 (fast, 25 minutes) or #1 (slow, 45 minutes) to cruise the entire Canale Grande from Tronchetto (car-park) or Ferrovia (train station) to San Marco. If you can't snag a front seat, lurk nearby and take one when it becomes available, or find a seat outside at the very back of the boat. While Venice is a barrage on the senses that hardly needs a narration, these notes give the cruise a little meaning and help orient you to this great city. Some city maps (on sale at postcard racks) have a handy Grand Canal map on the back side.

Venice, built in a lagoon, sits on pilings—pine trees driven 15 feet into the mud. More than 100 canals—about 25 miles in length—drain the city, dumping like streams into the Grand Canal.

Venice is a city of palaces. The most lavish were built fronting this canal. This cruise is the only way to really appreciate the front doors of this unique and historic chorus line of mansions from the days when Venice was the world's richest city. Strict laws prohibit any changes in these buildings, so while landowners gnash their teeth, we can enjoy Europe's best-preserved medieval city—slowly rotting. Many of the grand buildings are now vacant. Others harbor chandeliered elegance above mossy ground floors.

Start at Tronchetto (the bus and car-park) or the train station (a good example of Fascist architecture built during Mussolini's time). F.S. stands for "Ferrovie dello Stato," the Italian state railway system. The bridge at the station is one of only three that cross the Canale Grande.

Vaporetto stop #4 (San Marcuola-Ghetto) is near the world's original **ghetto**, from when this area was set aside as the local Jewish quarter in 1516. This urban island developed into one of the most closely knit business and cultural quarters of any Jewish community in Italy.

As you cruise, notice the traffic signs. Venice's main thoroughfare is busy with traffic. You'll see all kinds of boats: taxis, police boats, garbage, even brown-and-white UPS boats. Venice's 500 sleek, black, graceful gondolas are a symbol of the city. They cost up to $35,000 apiece and are built with a slight curve so that one oar propels them in a straight line.

At the Ca d'Oro stop (stop #6), notice the lacy Gothic palace of the same name. Named the **"House of Gold,"** it's considered the most elegant Venetian Gothic palace on the canal. Unfortunately its art gallery interior shows nothing of its palatial origins.

After *vaporetto* stop #6, on the right, the outdoor **produce market** bustles with people in the morning, but is quiet the rest of the day. Can you see the *traghetto* gondola ferrying shoppers— standing like Washington crossing the Delaware—back and forth? The huge **post office**, usually with a postal boat moored at its blue posts, is on the left just before the Rialto Bridge.

A major landmark of Venice, the **Rialto Bridge** is lined with shops and tourists. Built in 1592, with a span of 42 meters, it was an impressive engineering feat in its day. Locals call the summit of this bridge the "icebox of Venice" for its cool breeze. But it's also a great place to kiss. *"Rialto"* means "high river." The restaurants lining the canal beyond the bridge feature high prices and low quality.

The Rialto, a separate town in the early days of Venice, has always been the commercial district, while San Marco was the religious and governmental center. Today a street called the Merceria connects the two, providing travelers with human traffic jams and a gauntlet of shopping temptations.

Take a deep whiff of Venice. What's all this nonsense about stinky canals? All I smell is my shirt. By the way, how's your captain? Smooth dockings? To get to know him, stand up in the bow and block his view.

Notice how the rich marble facades are just a veneer covering no-nonsense brick buildings. And notice the characteristic chimneys.

After the San Silvestro stop you'll see (on the right) a 13th-century admiral's palace. Venetian admirals marked their palaces with twin obelisks.

After the San Tomá stop look down the side canal (on the right) before the bridge to see the fire station and the fireboats ready to go.

The wooden Accademia Bridge crosses the Grand Canal and leads to the **Accademia Gallery**, filled with the best Venetian paintings. Put up in 1932 as a temporary fix for the original iron one, locals liked it, so it stayed.

Cruising under the bridge, you'll get a classic view of the **Salute Church**, built as a thanks to God when the devastating plague of 1630 passed. It's claimed that more than a million trees were used for the foundation alone. Much of the surrounding countryside was deforested by Venice. Trees were needed both to fuel the furnaces of its booming glass industry and to prop up this city in the mud.

The low white building on the right (before the church) is the **Peggy Guggenheim Gallery**. She willed the city a fine collection of modern art.

Just before the Salute stop (on the right), the house with the big view windows and the red and wild Andy Warhol painting on the living-room wall was lived in by Mick Jagger. In the 1970s this was famous as Venice's rock-and-roll-star party house.

The building on the right with the golden ball is the Dogana da Mar, a 16th-century customs house. Its two bronze Atlases hold a statue of Fortune riding the ball.

As you prepare to de-boat at stop #15—San Marco—look from left to right out over the lagoon. A wide harborfront walk leads past the town's most elegant hotels to the green area in the distance. This is the public garden, the only sizable park in town. Farther out is the *lido*, Venice's beach. It's tempting with its sand and casinos, but its car traffic breaks into the medieval charm of Venice.

The dreamy church that seems to float is the architect Palladio's San Giorgio. It's just a scenic *vaporetto* ride away. Find the Tintoretto paintings in the church (such as the *Last Supper*) and take the elevator up the bell tower for a terrific, crowd-free view (L3,000, daily 10:00–12:30, 14:30–17:30, tel. 041-522-7827). Beyond San Giorgio (to your right, if you're at San Marco) is a residential chunk of Venice called the Guidecca.

Get out at the San Marco stop. Directly ahead is Harry's Bar. Hemingway drank here when it was a characteristic no-name *osteria* and the gondoliers' hangout. Today, of course, it's the overpriced hangout of well-dressed Americans who don't mind paying triple for their drinks to make the scene. Piazza San Marco—a much better place to make the scene—is just around the corner.

For more *vaporetto* fun, ride a boat around the city and out into the lagoon and back (ask for the *circulare*). Plenty of boats leave from San Marco for the beach (*lido*), and speedboats offer tours of nearby islands: Burano is a quiet, picturesque fishing and lace town, Murano specializes in glassblowing, and Torcello has the oldest churches and mosaics, but is otherwise dull and desolate. Boat #12 takes you to these remote points slower and cheaper.

Sights—Venice, on St. Mark's Square

▲▲▲**St. Mark's Square (Piazza San Marco)**—Surrounded by splashy and historic buildings, Piazza San Marco is filled with

music, lovers, pigeons, and tourists by day and is your private rendezvous with the Middle Ages late at night. Europe's greatest
dance floor is the romantic place to be. This is the first place to
flood, has Venice's best TIs (with back to church, go to far corner
on your left; for other TI, go to lagoon, turn right), and offers fine
public restrooms (Albergo Diorno—"day hotel," L500 WC,
shower, between Piazza San Marco and American Express office).

With your back to the church, survey one of Europe's great
urban spaces and the only square in Venice to merit the title
"Piazza." Nearly two football fields long, it's surrounded by the
offices of the republic. On the right are the "old offices" (16th-
century Renaissance). On the left are the "new offices" (17th-
century Baroque). Napoleon enclosed the square with the more
simple and austere neoclassical wing across the far end and called
this "the most beautiful drawing room in Europe."

The clock tower, a Renaissance tower built in 1496, marks
the entry to the Mercerie, the main shopping drag connecting San
Marco with the Rialto. From the piazza you can see the bronze
men (Moors) swing their huge clappers at the top of each hour. In
the 17th century one of them knocked an unsuspecting worker off
the top and to his death—probably the first-ever killing by a
robot. Notice the world's first "digital" clock on the tower facing
the square (with dramatic flips every five minutes).

For a slow and pricey evening thrill, invest L15,000 (plus
L5,000 if the orchestra plays) in a beer or coffee in one of the elegant cafés with the dueling orchestras. If you're going to sit awhile
and savor the scene, it's worth the splurge. For the most thrills
L1,500 can get you in Venice, buy a bag of pigeon seed and
become popular in a flurry.

▲▲St. Mark's Basilica—Since about A.D. 830 it has housed the
saint's bones. The mosaic above the door at the far left of the
church shows two guys carrying Mark's coffin into the church.
Mark looks pretty grumpy after the long voyage from Egypt. The
church has 4,000 square meters of Byzantine mosaics. The best
and oldest are in the atrium (turn right as you enter and stop
under the last dome). Face the piazza, gape up (it's OK, no
pigeons), and study the story of Noah, the Ark, and the flood (two
by two, the wicked being drowned, Noah sending out the dove, a
happy rainbow, and a sacrifice of thanks). Now face the church
and read clockwise the story of Adam and Eve that rings the bottom of the dome. Step inside the church (stairs on right lead to
bronze horses) and notice the rolling mosaic marble floor. Stop
under the central dome and look up for the Ascension. (Modest
dress, no shorts or bare shoulders, free, Monday–Saturday
9:45–19:30, Sunday 14:00–17:00, tel. 041-522-5205.) See the
schedule board in the atrium listing two free English guided tours
of the church each week. The church is particularly beautiful when

lit at the 18:45 Mass on Saturday, from 14:00 to 17:00 on Sunday, and some middays.

In the museum upstairs (L4,000, daily 10:00–16:30), you can see an up-close mosaic exhibition, a fine view of the church interior, a view of the square from the horse balcony, and (inside, in their own room) the newly restored original bronze horses. These well-traveled horses, made during the days of Alexander the Great (fourth century B.C.), were taken to Rome by Nero, to Constantinople/Istanbul by Constantine, to Venice by crusaders, to Paris by Napoleon, back "home" to Venice when Napoleon fell, and finally indoors and out of the acidic air.

The treasury and altarpiece of the church (requiring two L4,000 admissions) give you the best chance outside of Istanbul or Ravenna to see the glories of Byzantium. Venetian crusaders looted the Christian city of Constantinople and brought home piles of lavish loot (until the advent of TV evangelism, perhaps the lowest point in Christian history). Much of this plunder is stored in the treasury of San Marco (*tesoro*). As you view these treasures, remember most were made in A.D. 500 while Western Europe was still rooting in the mud. Behind the high altar lies the body of St. Mark ("Marxus") and the Pala d'Oro, a golden altarpiece made (A.D. 1000–1300) with 80 Byzantine enamels. Each shows a religious scene set in gold and precious stones. Both of these sights are interesting and historic, but neither is as much fun as two bags of pigeon seed.

▲▲▲**Doge's Palace (Palazzo Ducale)**—The seat of the Venetian government and home of its ruling duke, or *doge*, this was the most powerful half-acre in Europe for 400 years (L17,000, daily 9:00–19:00, last entry at 17:30, shorter hours off-season). This L17,000 combo-ticket includes admission to a number of lesser museums: Museo Correr (see below), Ca' Rezzonico (see below), Palazzo Mocenigo (costumes), Museo Vetrario di Murano (glass museum on Murano), and Museo del Merletto di Burano (lace museum on Burano).

While each room in the Doge's Palace has a short English description, the fast-moving 90-minute tape-recorded guided tour wand is wonderfully done and worth the L7,000 if you don't have *Rick Steves' Mona Winks* and you're planning to really understand the Palace. (Vagabond lovers, sightseeing cheek to cheek, can crank up the volume and split one wand).

The palace was built to show off the power and wealth of the republic and remind all visitors that Venice was number one. Built in Venetian Gothic style, the bottom has pointy arches and the top has an Eastern or Islamic flavor. Its columns sat on pedestals, but in the thousand years since they were erected, the palace has settled into the mud, and they have vanished.

Enjoy the newly restored facades from the courtyard. Notice

a grand staircase (with nearly naked Moses and Paul Newman at the top). Even the most powerful visitors climbed this to meet the *doge*. This was the beginning of an architectural power trip. The *doge*, the elected-for-life king of this "dictatorial republic," lived near the halls of power with his family on the first floor. From his lavish quarters you'll follow the one-way tour through the public rooms of the top floor, finishing with the Bridge of Sighs and the prison. The place is wallpapered with masterpieces by Veronese and Tintoretto. Don't worry much about the great art. Enjoy the building.

In room 12, the Senate Room, the 200 senators met, debated, and passed laws. From the center of the ceiling, Tintoretto's *Triumph of Venice* shows the city in all her glory. Lady Venice, in heaven with the Greek gods, stands high above the lesser nations who swirl respectfully at her feet with gifts.

The Armory shows remnants of the military might the empire employed to keep the east-west trade lines open (and the local economy booming). Squint out the window at the far end for a fine view of Palladio's San Georgio Church and the *lido* (cars, casinos, crowded beaches) in the distance.

After the huge brown globes, you'll enter the giant Hall of the Grand Council (180 feet long, capacity 2,000) where the entire nobility met to elect the senate and *doge*. Ringing the room are portraits of 76 *doges* (in chronological order). One, a *doge* who opposed the will of the Grand Council, is blacked out. Behind the *doge's* throne, you can't miss Tintoretto's monsterpiece, *Paradise*. At 1,700 square feet, this is the world's largest oil painting. Christ and Mary are surrounded by a heavenly host of 500 saints.

Walking over the Bridge of Sighs, you'll enter the prisons. The *doges* could sentence, torture, and jail their opponents secretly and in the privacy of their own homes. As you walk back over the bridge, wave to the gang of tourists gawking at you.

▲**Museo Civico Correr**—The until-lately rarely visited city history museum is now included (whether you like it or not) with the Doge's Palace admission. It offers dusty bits of Venice's glory days (globes, flags, coins, paintings, and so on, all well-explained in English) and fine views of Piazza San Marco. The second floor is a lot of walking and worth a look only if you like musty old oil paintings (Pinacoteca—English descriptions) and exhibits on the unification of Italy (Risorgimento—no English). Entry is on the square opposite St. Mark's church (L17,000 combo ticket with Doge's Palace, daily 9:00–19:00, 9:00–17:00 November–May).

▲**Campanile di San Marco**—Ride the elevator 300 feet to the top of the bell tower for the best view in Venice. Photos on the wall inside show how this tower crumbled into a pile of bricks in 1902, 1,000 years after it was built. For an ear-shattering experience, be on top when the bells ring (L8,000, daily 9:00–19:30). The golden angel at its top always faces into the wind.

More Sights—Venice

▲▲**Galleria dell' Accademia**—Venice's top art museum is packed with the painted highlights of the Venetian Renaissance (Bellini, Veronese, Tiepolo, Giorgione, Testosterone, and Canaletto). It's just over the wooden Accademia Bridge (L12,000, Monday 9:00–14:00, Tuesday–Saturday 9:00–22:00, Sunday 9:00–20:00, shorter hours off-season, expect morning and midday delays as they allow only 300 visitors at a time, come late to miss crowds, tel. 041-522-2247). There's a decent pizzeria at the bridge (Snack Bar Accademia Foscarini; see Eating, below.)

▲**Peggy Guggenheim Collection**—This popular collection of far-out art, including works by Picasso, Chagall, and Dali, offers one of Europe's best reviews of the art styles of the 20th century (L12,000, Wednesday–Monday 11:00–18:00, closed Tuesday, near the Accademia).

▲▲**Chiesa dei Frari**—This great Gothic Franciscan church, an artistic highlight of Venice featuring three great masters, offers more art per lira than any other Venetian sight. Freeload on English-language tours to get the most out of the Titian *Assumption* above the high altar. Then move one chapel to the right to see Donatello's wood carving of St. John the Baptist almost live. And for the climax, continue right through an arch into the sacristy to sit before Bellini's *Madonna and the Saints*. The genius of Bellini, perhaps the greatest Venetian painter, is obvious in the pristine clarity, believable depth, and reassuring calm of this three-paneled altarpiece. Notice the rich colors of Mary's clothing and how good it is to see a painting in its intended setting. For many, these three pieces of art make a visit to the Accademia Gallery unnecessary (or they may whet your appetite for more). Before leaving, check out the neoclassical pyramid-shaped tomb of Canova and (opposite that) the grandiose tomb of Titian the Venetian. Compare the carved marble *Assumption* behind his tombstone portrait with the painted original above the high altar (L3,000, Monday–Saturday 10:00–17:30, Sunday 15:00–17:30).

▲**Scuola di San Rocco**—Next to the Frari church, another lavish building bursts with art, including some 50 Tintorettos. The best paintings are upstairs, especially the *Crucifixion* in the smaller room. View the neck-breakingly splendid ceiling paintings with one of the mirrors (*specchio*) available at the entrance (L8,000, daily 9:00–17:30). For *molto* Tiepolo (14 stations of the cross), drop by the nearby Church of San Polo.

Ca' Rezzonico—This 18th-century Grand Canal *palazzo* is now open as the Museo del '700 Veneziano, offering a good look at the life of Venice's rich and famous in the 1700s, along with frequent temporary exhibits for an additional admission fee (L12,000,

Saturday–Thursday 10:00–17:00, closed Friday, at a *vaporetto* stop
of the same name).
▲**Gondola Rides**—This is a rip-off for some but a traditional must
for romantics. Gondoliers charge about L120,000 for a 50-minute
ride (L150,000 at night, from 20:00 on). You can divide the cost—
and the romance—by up to six people (some take seven if you're
cute, blonde, and female). Glide through nighttime Venice with your
head on someone else's shoulder. Follow the moon as it sails past
otherwise unseen buildings. Silhouettes gaze down from bridges
while window glitter spills onto the black water. You're anonymous
in the city of masks as the rhythmic thrust of your striped-shirted
gondolier turns old crows into songbirds.

For a glimpse at a gondola workshop in the Accademia neighborhood, walk down the Accademia side of the canal Fondamente
Nani. As you approach Giudecca Canal you'll see the beached
gondolas on your right across the Nani Canal.

For cheap gondola thrills, stick to the L700 one-minute ferry
ride on a Grand Canal *traghetto*, or hang out on a bridge along the
gondola route and wave at (or drop leftover pigeon seed on)
romantics.
▲**Glassblowing**—Don't go all the way to Murano Island to see
glassblowing demonstrations. A demo's a demo. For the handiest
show, wait by one of several glassworks near St. Mark's Square and
follow any tour group into the furnace room for a fun and free
10-minute show. You'll usually see a vase and a "leetle 'orse" made
from molten glass. The commercial that always follows in the
showroom is actually entertaining. Prices around St. Mark's have a
sizable tour-guide commission built in. Serious glass-shoppers buy
at small shops on Murano Island.
Santa Elena—For a pleasant peek into a completely untouristy
residential side of Venice, catch the boat from San Marco to the
neighborhood of Santa Elena (at the fish's tail). This 100-year-
old suburb lives as if there were no tourism. You'll find a kid-
friendly park, a few lazy restaurants, and beautiful sunsets over
San Marco.
Old-Time Venetian Concerts—Vivaldi is as trendy here as Strauss
in Vienna and Mozart in Salzburg. In fact you'll find frilly young
Vivaldis all over town hawking concert tickets. The TI has a list of
this week's concerts (tickets from L30,000 up). The Venice Orchestra plays traditional Vivaldi concerts in 18th-century attire at the
Scuola Grande di San Giovanni Evengelista (L40,000–60,000,
performances at 20:30 on Wednesday, Friday, Saturday, and Sunday,
tel. 041-522-8125, e-mail: info@orchestra.venezia.it).

Sights—Venice Lagoon
Several interesting islands hide out in the Venice Lagoon.
Burano, famous for its lace-making, is a sleepy island with a

sleepy community—village Venice without the glitz. Lace fans enjoy Burano's Scuola di Merletti (L8,000, Wednesday–Monday 10:00–17:00, closed Tuesday, tel. 041-730-034). For a splurge lunch on Burano, consider Trattoria al Gatto Nero (tel. 041-730-120).

Torcello, another lagoon island, is dead except for its church, which claims to be the oldest in Venice (L2,000, daily 10:00–12:30, 14:00–17:00, tel. 041-730-084). It's impressive for its mosaics, but not worth a look on a short visit unless you really have your heart set on Ravenna but can't make it there.

The island of **Murano**, famous for its glass factories, has the Museo Vetrario, which displays the very best of 700 years of Venetian glassmaking (L8,000, Thursday–Tuesday 10:00–17:00, closed Wednesday, tel. 041-739-586). The islands are reached easily but slowly by *vaporetto* (from the Fondamente Nuove or San Zaccaria dock). Four-hour speedboat tours of these three lagoon destinations leave twice a day from the dock near the Doge's Palace.

Sleeping in Venice
(L1,700 = about $1)
Sleep Code: **S** = Single, **D** = Double/Twin, **T** = Triple, **Q** = Quad, **b** = bathroom, **t** = toilet only, **s** = shower only, **CC** = Credit Card (Visa, MasterCard, Amex), **SE** = Speaks English, **NSE** = No English. Breakfast is included unless otherwise noted. There are no elevators. Air conditioning, when available, is usually only turned on in summer.

Reserve a room as soon as you know when you'll be in town. Call first to see what's available. Follow up with a fax unless you're already on the road. Most places will take a credit card for a deposit. If everything's full, don't despair. Call a day or two in advance and fill in a cancellation. While many stay in a nearby less-crowded place and side trip to Venice, I can't imagine not sleeping downtown. If you arrive on an overnight train, your room may not be ready. Drop your bag at the hotel and dive right into Venice.

The prices I've listed here are for those who book direct. Prices may be cheaper (or soft) off-season. If on a budget, ask for a cheaper room or a discount. I've let location and character be my priorities. Rooms are clean, quiet, and generally stark, with high ceilings, slick little modern pre-fab shower/toilet/sink units, bare floors, and rickety freestanding furniture.

Sleeping near St. Mark's Square
(zip code: 30124)
Hotel Caneva is a funky, clean, vinyl-feeling place with plain, big and bright rooms, lots of canal ambience, and a wonderful family-run feeling. Seventeen of its 23 rooms overlook a canal (S-L70,000,

Venice Lagoon

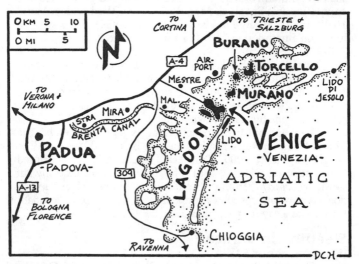

Sb-L110,000, Db-L160,000, Tb-L205,000, CC:VMA, prices are higher if you pay with a credit card; midway between Rialto and San Marco near Chiesa la Fava, Ramo Dietro La Fava #5515, 30122 Venezia, tel. 041-522-8118, fax 041-520-8676, Massimo and his family SE).

Hotel Riva, with gleaming marble hallways and bright modern rooms, is romantically situated on a canal along the gondola serenade route. You could actually dunk your breakfast rolls in the canal (but don't). Sandro may hold a corner (*angolo*) room if you ask. Reconfirm reservations you think you've made here. It's behind San Marco where the canals Rio di San Zulian and Rio del Mondo Nouvo hit Rio Canonica o Palazzo. Confirm prices (two fourth-floor view D with adjacent showers-L140,000, Db-L170,000, Tb-L250,000, Ponte dell' Angelo, tel. 041-522-7034, fax 041-528-5551, unenthusiastic receptionists don't speak English). Facing St. Mark's cathedral, go left to the farthest back corner of the square. Walk along the left side of the white building. Take first left (on Ramo in Canonica, see blue mozaic "Pauly & C" mozaic in street), continue straight, go over bridge, and angle right to hotel.

Locanda Piave, with 15 fine rooms above a bright and classy lobby, is newly remodeled and very comfortable (D-L160,000, Db-L230,000, family suites-L330,000–L400,000 for three to five people, air-conditioning, CC:VMA; from Campo Santa Maria Formosa—with Bar all' Orologio on your left and the church on your right—go straight ahead to the bridge at the far end of the square; the street is Ruga Giuffa, head over the bridge and walk 50 yards to Ruga

Giuffa #4838/40, Castello, 30122 Venezia, tel. 041-528-5174, fax
041-523-8512, Mirella and Paolo SE). Nearby they have a couple of
apartments for L250,000 to L300,000 (includes kitchenette). My
readers get discounts on any room—mention this book.

Albergo Tiepolo, a simple musty old seven-room place
tucked away down an alley just off Campo SS. Filippo e Giacomo,
is pricey but well-located (D-L100,000, Db-L150,000, T-L140,000,
Tb-L180,000, Q-180,000, Qb-L230,000, reservations unreliable;
Campo SS. F e G #4510, tel. & fax 041-523-1315).

Albergo Corona is a clean, confusing Old World place with
nine hard-to-get basic rooms (D-L75,000, showers L3,000, lots of
stairs, tel. 041-522-9174, SE). Coming from San Marco, find
Campo SS Filippo e Giacomo (behind St. Mark's church), go
down Calle Sacristia, take first right, then go left on Calle Corona
to #4464. Or, coming from Campo Maria di Formosa, go behind
the church down Ruga Giuffa and take third right at Pizzeria Can-
ton (see directions for Piave, above, to locate Ruga Giuffa).

Alloggi Masetto, well-located with four dirt-cheap rooms, is
a homey place filled with birds, goldfish, and stacks of magazines.
It's run by Irvana Artico, a rude landlady who surprises you with
pretty good English (D-L55,000, Db-L65,000, T-L75,000, Tb-
80,000, confirm prices carefully, no breakfast, shower *rapido* or
suffer Irvana's wrath; just off San Marco—from American Express
head toward San Marco, first left, first left again through "Contarina" tunnel, follow white sign to Commune di Venezia and see
her sign, Sotoportego Ramo Contarina 1520a, Frezzeria, tel.
041-523-0505). Irvana asks that if you can't make it to please call
to cancel your reservations.

Alloggi Alla Scala, a comfy and tidy seven-room place run by
Senora Andreina della Fiorentina, is very central and tucked away
on a quiet square that features a famous spiral stairway called Scala
Contarini del Bovolo (small Db-L110,000, big Db-L130,000, extra
bed-L35,000, breakfast-L10,000, send deposit of traveler's check
for first night, near Campo Manin #4306, San Marco, tel. 041-521-
0629, fax 041-522-8958, daughter SE). From Campo Manin follow signs to (on statue's left) "Scala Contarini del Bovolo."

Locanda Gambero, with 32 rooms, is the biggest one-
star hotel in the San Marco area (S-L80,000, D-L130,000,
Db-L190,000, T-L175,000, Tb-L220,000, CC:VM, rooms with
bath also have TV and air-conditioning; from Rialto *vaporetto* #1
dock go straight inland on Calle le Bembo—which becomes Calle
dei Fabbri; from Piazza San Marco it's a five-minute walk down
Calle dei Fabbri over two bridges to #4687, at intersection with
Calle del Gambero, tel. 041-522-4384, fax 041-520-0431, SE).
These prices are as firm as ripe bananas. Gambero runs the pleasant art-deco "La Bistrot" on the corner, which serves old-time
Venetian cuisine.

Sleeping near Waterfront and Doge's Palace

These places, about one canal down from the Bridge of Sighs on or just off the Riva degli Schiavoni waterfront promenade, rub drainpipes with Venice's most palatial five-star hotels. Each—while pricey for the location and not particularly friendly—is professional and comfortable.

Hotel Campiello is a lacy and bright little 16-room place, ideally located 50 yards off the waterfront (Sb-L160,000, Db-L220,000–270,000, CC:VMA, all air-conditioned, with satellite TV, safe, and phone; behind Hotel Savoia, up Calle del Vin off Riva Schiavoni, San Zaccaria #4647, tel. 041-520-5764, fax 041-520-5798, e-mail: campiello@hcampiello.it, SE).

Albergo Paganelli is right on the Riva degli Schiavoni with a few incredible view rooms (S-L120,000, Sb-L150,000, D-L150,000, small Db-L200,000, Db-L220,000 or L250,000 with canal view, T-L200,000, Tb-L300,000 or L340,000 with canal view, request "*con vista*" for view, most rooms are air-conditioned, CC:VMA, at the San Zaccaria *vaporetto* stop, Riva degli Schiavoni #4182, Castello, 30122 Venezia, tel. 041-522-4324, fax 041-523-9267, SE). With spacious rooms, carved and gilded headboards, chandeliers, and hair-dryers, this very hotelesque place is a good value. Seven of their 22 rooms are in a less interesting *dependencia* a block off the canal.

Albergo Doni is a dark, hardwood, clean, and quiet place with 12 dim-but-classy rooms run by a likable smart-aleck named Gina who promises my readers one free down-the-hall shower each day (D-L120,000, Db-L170,000, T-L170,000, Tb-L220,000, ceiling fans, prices good with this book, use credit card to secure telephone reservations but must pay in cash, Riva Schiavoni, San Zaccaria N. #4656 Calle del Vin, tel. & fax 041-522-4267, Nick and Gina SE). From the Bridge of Sighs walk east along Riva Degli Schiavoni, cross over another bridge, take the first left (Calle del Vin), and follow the signs.

Sleeping near the Rialto Bridge (zip code: 30125)

Locanda Sturion, with air-conditioning and all the modern comforts, is pricey because it overlooks the Grand Canal (Db-L295,000, Tb-380,000, Qb-L400,000, canal-view rooms cost extra, CC:VMA, miles of stairs, 100 yards from the Rialto Bridge opposite the *vaporetto* dock, San Polo, Rialto, Calle Sturion #679, 30125 Venezia, tel. 041-523-6243, fax 041-522-8378, e-mail: sturion@tin.it, SE). They require a personal check or traveler's check for a deposit.

Hotel Canada has 25 small, pleasant rooms (one Sb-L160,000, two D with adjacent bath-L200,000, Db-L230,000, CC:VM, Castello San Lio #5659, 30122 Venezia, tel. 041-522-

9912, fax 041-523-5852, SE). A couple of rooms are incredibly cramped—in particular, avoid "V" (the Roman numeral 5). Canada is ideally located on a small, lively square, just off Campo San Lio between the Rialto and San Marco.

Hotel da Bruno, 100 yards from Hotel Canada, has a central location, nice rooms, and all the comforts (Db-L250,000, CC:VMA, Salizzada S. Lio #5726, Castello, 30122 Venezia, tel. 041-523-0452, fax 041-522-1157, SE).

Albergo Guerrato, overlooking a handy and colorful produce market, one minute from the Rialto action, is run by friendly, creative, and hardworking Roberto and Piero Caruso. Georgio takes the night shift. Their 800-year-old building is Old-World simple, airy, and wonderfully characteristic (D-L120,000, Db-L165,000, T-L160,000, Tb-L220,000, Q-L190,000, Qb-L260,000, including a L4,000 city map, prices promised through 1999 with this book, no double beds, CC:VM; walk over the Rialto away from San Marco, go straight about three blocks, turn right on Calle drio la Scimia—not Scimia, the block before—and you'll see the hotel sign, Calle drio la Scimia #240a, 30125 San Polo, tel. & fax 041-522-7131 or 528-5927, e-mail: hguerrat@tin .it, SE). My tour groups book this place for 50 nights each year. Sorry. If you fax without calling first, no reply within three days means they are booked up. (It's best to call first.)

Sleeping near the Accademia

This quiet area with a guesthouse, three classy hotels, and a cheap monastery, next to the best painting gallery in town, is a 10-minute walk from any other sightseeing action.

Fonadazione Levi, a guesthouse run by a foundation that promotes research on Venetian music, offers 18 quiet, comfortable rooms (Sb-L100,000, Db-L170,000, Tb-L200,000, Qb-L230,000, San Vidal 2893, 30124 Venezia, tel. 041-786-711, fax 041-786-766, SE). At the base of the Accademia bridge (San Marco side), you're in Campo S. Vidal. Follow the sign to Palazzo Grassi; directly ahead is the door for the Fondazione—buzz the door on the right for the guesthouse.

Pension Accademia fills the 17th-century Villa Maravege. While its 27 comfortable and air-conditioned rooms are nothing extraordinary, you'll feel aristocratic gliding through its grand public spaces and lounging in its breezy garden (one S-L115,000, Sb-L180,000, standard Db-L270,000, superior Db-L330,000, or less off-season, family deals, CC:VMA, must send personal check or traveler's check to reserve; on corner of Rio della Toletta and Rio di San Trovaso 200 yards from gallery, Dorsoduro #1058, 30123 Venezia, tel. 041-523-7846, fax 041-523-9152, SE).

Hotel Galleria is a compact and velvety little 10-room place

(S-L90,000, Sb-L125,000, D-L130,000, Db-L160,000, bigger Db-L200,000, CC:VMA, breakfast in room, all rooms with views overlooking canal next to Accademia Gallery, Dorsoduro #878a, 30123 Venezia, tel. 041-523-2489, tel. & fax 041-520-4172, e-mail: galleria@tin.it, SE).

Hotel Agli Alboretti is a cozy, family-run, 25-room place in a quiet neighborhood a block behind the Accademia Museum (Sb-L160,000, two small Db-L200,000, Db-L250,000, Tb-L300,000, air-conditioning, CC:VMA; 100 yards from the Accademia *vaporetto* stop at #884 Accademia, tel. 041-523-0058, fax 041-521-0158, e-mail: alborett@gpnet.it, SE).

Sleeping near the Train Station
Hotel Marin is three minutes from the train station but completely out of the touristic bustle of the Lista di Spagna. Just renovated, cozy, and cheery, it seems like a 19-bedroom home the moment you cross the threshold (D-L105,000, Db-L135,000, T-L145,000, Tb-L175,000, Q-L180,000, Qb-L205,000, prices good with this book and if you pay cash, CC:VMA, San Croce #670b, tel. & fax 041-718-022 or 041-721-485, e-mail: htlmarin@gpnet.it). It's family-run by helpful, friendly English-speaking Bruno, Nadia, and son Samuel (they have city maps). It's across the canal from the train station behind the green dome (follow Rialto signs for 100 yards, look left).

Dormitory Accommodations
Foresteria della Chiesa Valdese, warmly run by a Protestant church, offers dorm beds at youth-hostel prices in a handy location (halfway between San Marco and Rialto). This rundown but charming old palace has elegant paintings on the ceilings (L30,000 dorm beds or L85,000 doubles with sheets and breakfast, more expensive for one-night stays, some larger "apartments" for families or small groups, office open 9:00–13:00, 18:00–20:00, Sunday 9:00–13:00, from Campo Santa Maria Formosa, walk past the Orologio bar to the end of Calle Lunga and cross the bridge, Castello #5170, tel. and fax 041-528-6797).

Near the Accademia, **Foresteria Domus Cavanis** is a simple church-run dorm offering cheap beds June 15 through September 15 only (S-L50,000, D-L75,000, breakfast-L5,000, next to Hotel Agli Alboretti, listed above, at #896 on Rio Antonio Foscarini, tel. & fax 041-528-7374).

The Venice **youth hostel**, on Giudecca Island, is crowded, cheap, and newly remodeled (L25,000 beds with sheets and breakfast in 10- to 16-bed rooms, membership required, office open 7:00–9:30, 13:30–23:00, catch boat #82 from station or San Marco to Zittele, tel. 041-523-8211). Their budget cafeteria welcomes non-hostelers (nightly 18:00–23:00).

Eating in Venice

Touristy restaurants are the scourge of Venice. I stick to small *cicchetti* bars (see Pub Crawl, below) or simple pizza-like dinners at scenic locations. You'll dine far better for less in other cities in Italy—go for the setting or the pub-crawl experience in Venice. For speed, value, and ambience, you can get a filling plate of local-style tapas at nearly any of the bars described below.

A key to cheap eating in Venice is bar snacks, especially stand-up mini-meals in out-of-the-way bars. Order by pointing. *Panini* (sandwiches) are sold fast and cheap at bars everywhere. Pizzerias are cheap and easy. Those that sell take-out by the slice or gram are cheapest. Fast food and self-serve places are easy to find.

The **produce market** that sprawls for a few blocks just past the Rialto Bridge (best 8:00–13:00, closed Sunday) is a great place to assemble a picnic. The nearby street, Ruga Vecchia, has good bakeries and cheese shops. Side lanes in this area are speckled with fine little hole-in-the-wall munchie bars.

The **Mensa DLF**, the public transportation workers' cafeteria, is cheap and open to the public (11:00–14:30, 18:00–21:30). Leaving the train station, turn right on the Grand Canal, walk about 150 yards, and you'll run into it.

The Stand-Up Progressive Venetian Pub-Crawl Dinner

A tradition unique to Venice in Italy is a *giro di ombre* (pub crawl)—ideal in a city with no cars. My favorite Venetian dinner is a pub crawl. I've listed plenty in walking order for a quick or extended crawl below. If you've crawled enough, most of the listed bars make a fine one-stop, sit-down dinner.

Venice's residential backstreets hide plenty of characteristic bars with countless trays of interesting toothpick-munchie food (*cicchetti*). This is a great way to mingle and have fun with the Venetians. Real *cicchetti* pubs are getting rare in these fast-food days, but locals appreciate the ones that survive. As always, the best way to find a landmark is to ask locals, "*Dové . . . ?*" and go where they point.

Try fried mozzarella cheese, blue cheese, calamari, artichoke hearts, and anything ugly on a toothpick. Ask for a *piatto misto* (mixed plate). Or try "*Un classico piatto di cicchetti misti da cinque mila lire*" (a plate of assorted appetizers for L5,000–10,000, depending upon how much food you want). Drink the house wines. A small glass of house red or white wine (*ombre rosso* or *ombre bianco*) or a small beer (*birrino*) costs about L1,000. *Vin bon*, Venetian for fine wine, may run you from L2,000 to L3,000 per little glass. Meat and fish (*pesce*: PAY-shay) munchies are expensive; veggies (*verdura*) are cheap, around L4,000 for a meal-sized plate. Bread sticks (*grissini*) are free for the asking. A good last drink is *fragolino*, the local sweet red wine. A liter of house wine costs around L7,000. Bars don't stay

Venice Pub Crawl

TO TRAIN STN. / STRADA / TO GHETTO / 200 YARDS / TO FONDAMENTA NUOVE
CA D'ORO / NUOVA / CAMPO SS. APOST.
FISH MARKET / CANAL / CAMPO SELVA / S. CANC. / CAMPO S. MARIA NUOVA / TESTA / LARGA / FOND. MERCANTI
MKT. / CAMPO BECC. / S. MATT / S. GIOV. / ORE/IC. / MKT. / RIALTO BRIDGE / POST / M. RACOS / LARGA / CAMPO S. GIOV. E PAOLO / HOSPITAL
CAMPO S. BART. / CAMPO MARINA / BERGALCCO / DANDALO / PRESS / COLLEONI STATUE
ROV / TO FRARI / FONDAMENTA / CARBON / FERRO / MAZZINI / 2 APRILE / STAGNERI / SAL. FAVA / SAN LIO / CAMPO S. MARIA FORMOSA / LUNGA / OSPEDALE
GRANDE / RIVA / CARBON / RIDO / FABRI / BALLOTTE / MERCERIA / BANDE / RUGA / GIUFFA / CAST.
CAMPO S. LUCA / REGINA / CAMPO ZUL / SPADARI / RIMEDIO / CAMPO FILIPPO
DCH / MERCERIA / PIAZZA SAN MARCO / SAN MARCO

❶ Do Mori
❷ All'Arco
❸ Ruga Rialto
❹ Do Ladroni
❺ Alla Botte
❻ San Barto.
❼ Portego
❽ Orologico
❾ Mascaron
❿ Mascareta
⓫ Ardenghi
⓬ Bepi
⓭ Alberto

open very late, and the *cicchetti* selection is best early, so start your evening by 18:30. Most bars are closed on Sundays. You can stand around the bar or grab a table in the back for the same price. (I'd appreciate any feedback on this plan.)

Cicchetteria near Rialto Bridge and Campo San Bartolomeo

Start your crawl near the Rialto Bridge. The first two places are on the San Polo side. Ai do Ladroni is a block past the bridge toward San Marco. And the last couple are a few blocks beyond the Campo.

Cantina Do Mori is famous with locals (since 1462) and savvy travelers (since 1962) as a classy place for fine wine and *frangobollo* (a spicy selection of 20 tiny sandwiches called "stamps"). Choose from the featured wines in the barrel on the bar. From Rialto Bridge walk 200 yards down Ruga degli Orefici away from San Marco—then ask (Monday–Saturday 17:00–20:30, closed Sunday, stand-up only, arrive early before *cicchetti* are gone, San Polo 429, tel. 041-522-5401). The rough-and-tumble **Cantina All' Arco** across the lane is worth a quick *ombra*.

Antica Ostaria Ruga Rialto is less expensive than Do Mori and offers tables, a busier/younger crowd, and a better selection of munchies (closed Monday, past the blue Chinese restaurant sign, on corner of Ruga Vecchia S. Giovanni and Ramo del Sturion, San Polo 692, tel. 041-521-1243). There are several other *cicchetti* bars within a block or two. You could track down: Ostaria Sora al Ponte (closed Monday, San Polo 1588, tel. 041-718-208), Cantina Do Spade, Vini da Pinto, and Osteria Enoteca Vivaldi (on Campo A. Aponal).

Cicchetteria on San Marco side of Rialto: **Hosteria Ai do Ladroni**, which specializes in *Veneziane piccola cucina*—mostly deep-fried munchies, is popular with locals and is half a block off the main Rialto-Campo San Bartolomeo drag (Monday–Saturday 8:00–24:00, closed Sunday, tel. 041-522-7741). They also serve acceptable L15,000 pasta plates.

Osteria "Alla Botte" Cicchetteria is an atmospheric place packed with a young, local, bohemian jazz clientele. It's good for a light meal or a *cicchetti* snack with wine (two short blocks off Campo San Bartolomeo in the corner behind the statue, tel. 041-520-9775, notice the "day after" photo showing a debris-covered Venice after the notorious 1989 Pink Floyd open-air concert).

If the statue on the Campo San Bartolomeo walked backward 20 yards, turned left, and went under a passageway, he'd hit **Rosticceria San Bartolomeo**. They have great fried *mozzarella e prosciutto* (L2,200) and L1,000 glasses of wine (for more info, see Eating near Campo San Bartolomeo, below). Continue over a bridge to Campo San Lio (a good landmark), go left at the Hotel Canada, and walk straight over another bridge into **Osteria Al Portego** (at #6015). This fine local-style bar has plenty of snacks and *cicchetti* (Monday–Saturday 9:00–22:00, closed Sunday, tel. 041-522-9038). From here, ask "*Dové Santa Maria di Formosa?*"

Cicchetteria near Campo Santa Maria di Formosa

Campo Santa Maria di Formosa is just plain atmospheric. For a balmy outdoor sit, you could split a pizza with wine on the square. Piero's **Bar all' Orologio**, opposite the canal, has the best setting and friendly service (closed Sunday). Or munch a slice of "pizza to go" on the square from Cip Ciap Pizza Rustica (over the bridge behind the SMF *gelateria* on Calle del Mondo Novo, open until 21:00, closed Tuesday). For your salad course there's a fruit-and-vegetable stand on the square next to the water fountain (open until about 20:00).

From Bar all' Orologio (on Campo S.M. di Formosa), with your back to the church, follow yellow sign to "SS Giov e Paolo" down Calle Longa Santa Maria di Formosa, and head down the street to **Osteria Mascaron** (Gigi's bar, best selection by 19:30, closes at 24:00 and on Sunday).

Gigi also runs **Enoteca Mascareta**, with less food and more wine, 30 yards farther down the street (#5183, closed Sunday, tel. 041-523-0744). The piano sounds like they dropped it in the canal, but the wine was saved. If you want more *cicchetti*, check out the two places described below in the Campo Santi Apostoli section. If you're feeling like the painting of Bacchus on the wall looks, it's time for . . .

Gelato: There's a decent *gelateria* on Campo di Formosa (closes at about 20:00 and on Thursday). There's a top-quality place two blocks away on the corner of Calle San Antonio and Calle Paradiso. Or head toward San Marco where the *gelaterias* stay open later (the best is opposite the Doge's Palace, by the two columns, on the bay).

You're not a tourist, you're a living part of a soft Venetian night . . . an alley cat with money. Streetlamp halos, live music, floodlit history, and a ceiling of stars make St. Mark's magic at midnight. Shine with the old lanterns on the gondola piers where the sloppy Grand Canal splashes at the Doge's Palace . . . reminiscing. Comfort the four frightened tetrarchs (ancient Byzantine emperors) under the moon where the Doge's Palace hits the basilica. Cuddle history.

Eating near Campo San Bartolomeo

The very local, hustling **Rosticceria San Bartolomeo Gislon** is a cheap—if confusing—self-service restaurant on the ground floor with a likably surly staff (good L7,000 pasta, prices listed at door, no cover or service charge). It's on Calle della Bissa #5424— starting from the statue in the San Bartolomeo square, it's 20 yards behind the statue to its left, under a passageway (daily 9:30–21:30, tel. 041-522-3569). Good but pricier meals are served at the full-service restaurant upstairs. Take out or grab a table.

Eating near Campo Santi Apostoli

Antiche Cantine Ardenghi de Lucia e Michael is a leap of local faith and an excellent splurge. Michael—an effervescent former Murano glass salesman—and his wife, Lucia, cook for 20 people a night by reservation only. You must call first. You pay L60,000 per person and trust them to wine, dine, and serenade you in Venetian class. The evening can be quiet or raucous depending on who and how many are eating. There's no sign and the door's locked. Find #6369 and knock. From Campo S. Giovanni e Paolo, pass the church-like hospital (notice the illusions painted on its facade), go over the bridge to the left, and take the first right to #6369 (8:30–2:00, closed Sunday, tel. 041-523-7691).

Two colorful *osterias* are good for *cicchetti*, wine-tasting, or a simple, rustic, sit-down meal surrounded by a boisterous local ambience: **Osteria da Alberto** (18:00–21:30, closed Sunday, midway between Campo Santi Apostoli and Campo S.S. Giovanni e Paolo, next to Ponte de la Panada on Calle larga Giacinto Gallina) and **Osteria Candela** on Calle de l'Oca. You'll find local pubs such as **Volante's** (next to Hotel Canada) and in the side streets opposite Campo St. Sofia across Strada Nuova.

Trattoria da Bepi caters to a local crowd and specializes in good seafood and Venetian cuisine. Bepi's son, Loris, speaks English and makes a mean licorice grappa (closed Thursday, allow L65,000 per person, midway between the Rialto Bridge and Ca d'Oro, next to the Santi Apostoli church and my recommended Laundromat, tel. 041-528-5031).

Eating near the Accademia

Snack Bar Accademia Foscarini, next to the Accademia Bridge and Galleria, offers decent L8,000 pizzas and offers canal-side or indoor seating (Wednesday–Monday 7:00–23:00, closed Tuesday, tel. 041-522-7281).

El Chef, with a fisherman's-shack design, has a good, cheap L20,000 menu (Campo S. Barnaba, seven-minute walk from Accademia, tel. 041-528-8422).

Transportation Connections—Venice

By train to: Verona (hrly, 90 min), **Florence** (6/day, 3 hrs), **Dolomites** (8/day to Bolzano, 4 hrs with one transfer; catch bus from Bolzano into mountains), **Milan** (hrly, 3–4 hrs), Rome (6/day, 5 hrs, slower overnight), **Naples** (change in Rome), **Brindisi** (3/day, 11 hrs), **Cinque Terre** (two La Spezia trains go directly to Monterosso al Mare daily, 6 hrs, at 9:58 and 14:58), **Bern** (4/day, change in Milan, 8 hrs), **Munich** (5/day, 8 hrs), **Paris** (3/day, 11 hrs), **Vienna** (4/day, 9 hrs). Train and *couchette* reservations (L30,500) are easily made at the American Express office near San Marco. Venice train info tel. 1478-88088.

HILL TOWNS OF CENTRAL ITALY

Break out of the Venice-Florence-Rome syndrome. There's more to Italy! Experience the slumber of Umbria, the texture of Tuscany, and the lazy towns of Lazio. For starters, here are a few of my favorites.

Siena seems to be every Italy connoisseur's pet town. In my office, whenever Siena is mentioned, someone moans, "Siena? I luuuv Siena!" San Gimignano is the quintessential hill town, with Italy's best surviving medieval skyline. Assisi—visited for its hometown boy, St. Francis, who made very good—is best after dark. Orvieto, one of the most famous hill towns, is an ideal springboard for a trip to tiny Civita. Stranded alone on its pinnacle in a vast canyon, Civita's the most lovable.

Planning Your Time

Siena, the must-see town, has the easiest train and bus connections. On a quick trip, consider spending three nights in Siena (with a whole-day side trip into Florence and a day to relax and enjoy Siena). Whatever you do, enjoy a sleepy medieval evening in Siena. After an evening in Siena, its major sights can be seen in half a day. San Gimignano is an overrun, pint-sized Siena. Don't rush Siena for San Gimignano.

Civita di Bagnoregio is the great pinnacle town. A night in Bagnoregio (via Orvieto bus) with time to hike to the town and spend three hours makes the visit worthwhile. Two nights and an entire day is a good way to keep your pain/pleasure ratio in order.

Assisi is the third most visit-worthy town. It has half a day of sightseeing and another half a day of wonder. While a zoo by day, it's a delight at night.

Hill Towns of Central Italy

SIENA

Seven hundred years ago, Siena was a major military power in a class with Florence, Venice, and Genoa. With a population of 60,000, it was even bigger than Paris. The town was weakened by a disastrous plague in 1348. In the 1550s her bitter rival Florence really salted her, making Siena forever a nonthreatening backwater. Siena's loss became our sightseeing gain, as its political and economic irrelevance pickled it purely Gothic. Today Siena's population is still 60,000 compared to Florence's 420,000.

Siena's thriving historic center, with red-brick lanes cascading every which way, offers Italy's best Gothic city experience. Most people do Siena, just 30 miles south of Florence, as a day trip, but it's best experienced after dark. While Florence has the blockbuster museums, Siena has an easy-to-enjoy soul: Courtyards sport flower-decked wells, alleys dead-end at rooftop views, and the sky is a rich blue dome. Right off the bat, Siena becomes an old friend.

For those who dream of a Fiat-free Italy, this is it. Sit at a café on the red-bricked main square. Take time to savor the first European city to eliminate automobile traffic from its main square (1966), and then, just to be silly, wonder what would happen if they did it in your city.

Orientation

Siena lounges atop a hill, stretching its three legs out from Il
Campo. This main square, the historic meeting point of Siena's
neighborhoods, is pedestrians-only. And most of those pedestrians
are students from the local university. Everything I mention is
within a 15-minute walk of the square. Navigate by landmarks, following the excellent system of street-corner signs. The typical visitor sticks to the San Domenico-Il Campo axis.

Tourist Information: Pick up the excellent and free topo-
graphical town map from the main TI on Il Campo (#56, look for
the yellow "Change" sign—bad rates, good information, open
mid-March–mid-November Monday–Saturday 8:30–19:30, open
some spring and fall Sundays 8:30–14:00, off-season Monday–
Saturday 8:30–14:00, tel. 0577-280-551). The little TI at San
Domenico is for hotel promotion only and sells a Siena map for
L500.

Arrival in Siena: From Siena's train station, buy a L1,400 bus
ticket from the blue machine near the exit (exact change needed),
cross the square, and board any orange city bus heading for Piazza
del Sale. Your hotel is probably within a 10-minute walk. The cost
of a taxi from the station to your hotel is about L15,000.

From the autostrada, drivers take the Porta San Marco exit
and follow the "Centro," then "Stadio" signs (stadium, soccer ball).
The soccer-ball signs take you to the stadium lot (L1,300/hour,
L15,000/day) at the huge bare-brick San Domenico church. You
can drive into the pedestrian zone (a pretty ballsy thing to do) only
to drop bags at your hotel. You can park free in the lot below the
Albergo Lea, white-striped spots behind Hotel Villa Liberty, and
behind the *fortezza*. (Note the L200,000 tow-fee incentive to learn
the days of the week in Italian).

Sights—Siena

Siena is one big sight. Its essential individual sights come in two
little clusters: the square (city hall, museum, tower) and the cathedral (baptistery, cathedral museum with its surprise viewpoint).
Check these sights off, and you're free to wander.

▲▲▲**Il Campo**—Siena's great central piazza is urban harmony at
its best. Like a people-friendly stage set, its gently tilted floor fans
out from the tower and city hall backdrop. It's the perfect invitation to loiter. Think of it as a trip to the beach without sand or
water. Il Campo was located at the historic junction of Siena's various competing districts, or *contrada*, on the old marketplace. The
brick surface is divided into nine sections, representing the council
of nine merchants and city bigwigs who ruled medieval Siena.
Don't miss the Fountain of Joy at the square's high point, with its
pigeons politely waiting their turn to gingerly tightrope down slippery snouts to slurp a drink, and with the two naked guys about to

Siena

1 - PICCOLO HOTEL ETRURIA
2 - ALBERGO TRE DONZELLE
3 - ALBERGO LA PERLA
4 - HOTEL DUOMO
5 - HOTEL CANNON D'ORO
6 - LOCANDA GARIBALDI
7 - ALBERGO BERNINI
8 - ALMA DOMUS
9 - HOTEL CHIUSARELLI
10 - ALBERGO LEA & HOTEL LIBERTY
11 - PIZZERIA SPADAFORTE
12 - CIAO CAFETERIA
13 - RISTORANTE GALLO NERO
14 - OSTERIA IL TAMBURINO
15 - OSTERIA DA DIVO
16 - IL VERROCHIO
17 - LAUNDROMAT
18 - TOURIST OFFICE

be tossed in. At the base of the tower, the Piazza's chapel was built in 1348 as a thanks to God for ending the Black Plague (after it killed more than a third of the population). The market area behind the city hall, a wide-open expanse since the Middle Ages, originated as a farming area within the city walls to feed the city in times of siege.

▲**Museo Civico**—The Palazzo Pubblico (City Hall), at the base of the tower, has a fine and manageable museum housing a good sample of Sienese art. You'll see, in the following order, the Sala Risorgimento with dramatic scenes of Victor Emanuel's unification of Italy (surrounded by statues that don't seem to care); the chapel with impressive inlaid wood chairs in the choir; and the Sala del Mappamondo, with Simone Martini's *Maesta* (Enthroned Virgin) facing the faded *Guidoriccio da Fogliano* (a mercenary providing a more concrete form of protection). Next is the Sala della Pace, which has two interesting frescoes showing "The Effects of Good and Bad Government." Notice the whistle-while-you-work happiness of the utopian community ruled by the utopian government (in the best-preserved fresco) and the fate of a community ruled by politicians with more typical values (in a terrible state of repair). The message: Without justice there can be no prosperity. Later you'll see a particularly gruesome *Slaughter of the Innocents*. The big stairs lead to a loggia with a nothing-special view (L8,000, Monday–Saturday 9:30–18:30, Sunday 9:30–13:30, off-season Monday–Saturday 10:00–17:00, tel. 0577-292-111).

▲**City Tower (Torre del Mangia)**—Siena gathers around its city hall, not its church. It was a proud republic and its "declaration of independence" is the tallest secular medieval tower in Italy, the 100-yard-tall Torre del Mangia (named after a hedonistic watchman who consumed his earnings like a glutton consumes food; his statue is in the courtyard, to the left as you enter). Its 300 steps get pretty skinny at the top, but the reward is one of Italy's best views (L7,000, Monday–Saturday 9:30–18:30, Sunday 9:30–13:30, off-season Monday–Saturday 10:00–17:00, limit of 30 towerists at a time, avoid the midday crowd).

The Palio—The feisty spirit of each of Siena's 17 *contrada* lives on. These neighborhoods celebrate, worship, and compete together. Each even has its own historical museum. *Contrada* pride is evident any time of year in the colorful neighborhood banners and parades. (If you hear distant drumming, run to it for the medieval action.) But *contrada* pride is most visible twice a year (July 2 and August 16) when they have their world-famous Palio di Siena. Ten of the 17 neighborhoods compete (chosen by lot), hurling themselves with medieval abandon into several days of trial races and traditional revelry. On the big day, Il Campo is stuffed to the brim with locals and tourists, as the horses charge wildly around the square in this literally no-holds-barred race. Of course, the winning neighborhood is the scene of grand celebrations afterward. The grand prize: simply proving your *contrada* is *numero uno*. All over town, sketches and posters depict the Palio. The TI has a free scrapbook-quality Palio brochure with English explanations. While the actual Palio really packs the city, you could side-trip in from Florence to see horse-race trials each of the three days before the big day (usually at 9:00 and 19:45).

▲**Palio al Cinema**—This fun, exciting 20-minute film helps re-create the craziness of the Palio. See it at the Galleria Odeon (L10,000, Monday–Friday 9:30–17:30, Saturday 9:30–15:00, closed Sunday, two blocks from the Campo, Via Banchi di Sopra 31, near intersection with B. Pier Pettinaio, tel. & fax 0577-247-372). Drop by and ask when the next English showing is scheduled—there are usually nine each day.

▲▲▲**Duomo**—Siena's cathedral is as Baroque as Gothic gets. The striped facade is piled with statues and ornamentation; the interior is decorated from top to bottom. The heads of 172 popes peer down from the ceiling over the fine inlaid art on the floor. This is one busy interior.

To orient yourself in this *panforte* of Italian churches, stand under the dome and think of the church floor as a big clock: You're the middle, the altar is high noon: you'll find the *Slaughter of the Innocents* roped off on the floor at 10:00, Pisano's pulpit between two pillars at 11:00, Bernini's chapel at 3:00, two mediocre Michelangelo statues (next to snacks, shop, and WC) at 7:00, the library at 8:00, and a Donatello statue at 9:00. Take some time with the floor mosaics in the front. Nicolo Pisano's wonderful pulpit is crowded but delicate Gothic story-telling from 1268. To understand why Bernini is considered the greatest Baroque sculptor, step into his sumptuous *Cappella della Madonna del Voto*. This last work in the cathedral, from 1659, is enough to make a Lutheran light a candle. Move up to the altar and look back at the two Bernini statues: St. Jerome playing the crucifix like a violinist lost in beautiful music, and Mary Magdalene in a similar state of spiritual ecstasy. The Piccolomini altar is most interesting for its two Michelangelo statues (the lower big ones). Paul, on the left, may be a self-portrait. Peter, on the right, resembles Michelangelo's more famous statue of Moses. Originally contracted to do 15 statues, Michelangelo left the project early (1504) to do his great *David* in Florence. The Piccolomini Library (worth the L2,000 entry), brilliantly frescoed with scenes glorifying the works of a pope from 500 years ago, contains intricately decorated, or "illuminated," music scores and a Roman copy of three Greek graces. Donatello's statue of St. John the Baptist is being restored (church open daily mid-March–October 9:00–19:30, off-season 10:00–13:00, 14:30–17:00, modest dress required).

Santa Maria della Scala—This newly opened and renovated old hospital (opposite the Duomo entrance) displays a rich treasury and a lavishly frescoed hall. The frescoes show medieval Siena's innovative healthcare and social welfare system in action. Unfortunately the high-tech gadgetry and signs are entirely in Italian (L8,000, daily 10:30–18:00, off-season 11:00–17:00).

▲**Baptistery**—Siena is so hilly that there wasn't enough flat ground on which to build a big church. What to do? Build a big church and prop up the overhanging edge with the baptistery. This dark and quietly tucked-away cave of art is worth a look (and L3,000) for its cool tranquility and the bronze carvings of Donatello (the six women, or angels) and Ghiberti on the baptismal font (mid-March–September daily 9:00–19:30, October 9:00–18:00, off-season 10:00–13:00, 14:30–17:00).

▲▲**Cathedral Museum (Museo dell'Opera Metropolitana)**—Siena's most enjoyable museum, on the Campo side of the church (look for the yellow signs), was built to house the cathedral's art. The ground floor is filled with the cathedral's original Gothic sculpture by Pisano (who spent 10 years here carving and orchestrating the decoration of the cathedral in the late 1200s) and a fine Donatello *Madonna and Child*. Upstairs to the left awaits a private audience with Duccio's *Maesta* (Enthroned Virgin). Pull up a chair and study one of the great pieces of medieval art. What was the flip side of the *Maesta* (displayed on the opposite wall), with 26 panels—the medieval equivalent of pages—shows scenes from the passion of Christ. At the end of the top floor, a little sign directs you to the "panorama." Climb to the first landing, then take the skinnier second spiral for Siena's surprise view. Look back over the Duomo, then consider this: When rival republic Florence began its grand cathedral, proud Siena decided to build the biggest church in all Christendom. The existing cathedral would be used as a transept. You're atop what would have been the entry. The wall below you, connecting the Duomo with the museum of the cathedral, was as far as Siena got before a plague killed the city's ability to finish the project. Were it completed, you'd be looking straight down the nave (L6,000, daily 9:00–19:30 mid-March–September, 9:00–18:00 October, off-season 9:00–13:30, tel. 0577-283-048).

Church of San Domenico—This huge brick church is worth a quick look. The simple, bland interior fits the austere philosophy of the Dominicans. Walk up the steps in the rear of the church for a look at various paintings from the life of Saint Catherine, patron saint of Siena and, since 1939, of all Italy. Halfway up the church on the right you'll find her head (free, daily 7:00–13:00, 15:00–17:30, less in winter).

Sanctuary of Saint Catherine—A few downhill blocks toward the center from San Domenico (follow signs to the Santuario di Santa Caterina), step into Catherine's cool and peaceful home. Siena remembers its favorite hometown girl, a simple, unschooled, but almost mystically devout girl who, in the mid-1300s, helped get the pope to return from France to Rome. Pilgrims have come here since 1464. Wander around to enjoy art depicting scenes from her life. Her room is downstairs (free, daily 9:00–12:30, 14:30–18:00, winter 9:00–12:00, 15:30–18:00, Via Tiratoio).

▲**Pinacoteca (National Picture Gallery)**—Siena was a power in Gothic art. But the average tourist, wrapped up in a love affair with the Renaissance, hardly notices. This museum takes you on a walk through Siena's art, chronologically from the 12th through 15th centuries. For the casual sightseer, the Sienese art in the city hall and cathedral museums is adequate. But art fans enjoy this opportunity to trace the evolution of Siena's delicate and elegant art (L8,000, Monday 8:30–13:30, Tuesday–Saturday 9:00–19:00, Sunday 8:30–13:00, tel. 0577-281-161). From the Campo, walk out Via di Citta to Piazza di Postierla and go left on San Pietro.

Tours by Roberto—Roberto Bechi, a hardworking Sienese tour guide, offers off-the-beaten-path tours of Siena and the region. After marrying an American and running a restaurant in the United States, Roberto communicates well with Americans. His passions are Sienese culture and local cuisine. Depending on the size of the group and type of tour, prices range from $50 to $90 per person for a full day, $20 to $50 per person for a half-day. (For more info or to book a tour, contact him at tel. & fax 0577-704-789, Web site: www.zaslon.si/roberto, e-mail: tourrob@tin.it, U.S.A. contact: Greg Evans, fax 540/434-4532.)

Sleeping in Siena
(L1,700 = about $1, zip code: 53100)
Sleep Code: **S** = Single, **D** = Double/Twin, **T** = Triple, **Q** = Quad, **b** = bathroom, **t** = toilet only, **s** = shower only, **CC** = Credit Card (Visa, MasterCard, Amex), **SE** = Speaks English, **NSE** = No English. Breakfast is generally not included. Have breakfast on Il Campo or in a nearby bar.

Finding a room is tough during Easter or for the Palio in early July and mid-August. Call ahead any time of year, as Siena's few budget places are listed in all the budget guidebooks. While day-tripping tour groups turn the town into a Gothic amusement park in midsummer, Siena is basically yours in the evenings and off-season. Nearly all listed hotels lie between Il Campo and the church of San Domenico.

Lavarapido Wash and Dry is a modern coin-op self-service Laundromat (L12,000 per eight-kilo load, takes an hour, daily 8:00–21:00, near the Campo at Via di Pantaneto 38).

Sleeping near Il Campo

Each of these first listings is forgettable but inexpensive and just a horse-wreck away from one of Italy's most wonderful civic spaces.

Piccolo Hotel Etruria, a good bet for a hotel with all the comforts but not much soul, is just off the square (S-L55,000, Sb-L65,000, Db-L103,000, Tb-L138,000, Qb-L173,000, breakfast-L7,000, CC:VMA, with back to the tower, leave Il Campo to the right at 2:00, Via Donzelle 1-3, tel. 0577-288-088, fax 0577-288-461).

Albergo Tre Donzelle is a plain, institutional, but decent place next door to Piccolo Hotel Etruria that makes sense only if you think of Il Campo as your terrace (S-L47,000, D-L70,000, Db-L90,000, Via Donzelle 5, tel. 0577-280-358, fax 0577-223-933, Senora Iannini SE).

Albergo La Perla is a funky, jumbled, 13-room place with a narrow maze of hallways, basic rooms, and a laissez-faire environment (Sb-L65,000, Db-L95,000, Tb-L130,000, rooms have tiny box showers, a block off the square on Piazza Independenza at Via della Terme 25, tel. 0577-47144). Attilio and his American wife, Deborah, take reservations only a day or two ahead. Ideally, call the morning you'll arrive.

Hotel Duomo is the best in-the-old-town splurge, a classy place with 23 spacious, elegant rooms (Sb-L140,000, Db-L220,000, Tb-L290,000, includes breakfast, CC:VMA, air-conditioning, elevator to first floor; follow Via di Citta, which becomes Via Stalloreggi, to Via Stalloreggi 38, tel. 0577-289-088, fax 0577-43043, e-mail: hduomo@comune.siena.it, SE). If you arrive by train, take a taxi (L15,000; if you drive, go to Porta San Marco and follow the signs to hotel, drop off bags, then park in nearby lot called "Il Campo").

Hotel Cannon d'Oro, a few blocks up Via Banchi di Sopra, is spacious and group-friendly (30 rooms, Sb-L100,000, Db-L120,000, prices promised through 1999 with this book, family deals, CC:VMA, Via Montanini 28, tel. 0577-44321, fax 0577-280-868, SE).

Locanda Garibaldi is a modest, very Sienese restaurant-*albergo*. Gentle Marcello wears two hats as he runs a busy restaurant with seven neglected doubles upstairs. This is a fine place for dinner but a bit noisy and dirty for some to sleep in (D-L85,000, T-L105,000, no credit cards, takes reservations only a few days in advance, half a block downhill off the square at Via Giovanni Dupre 18, tel. 0577-284-204, NSE).

Sleeping Closer to San Domenico Church

These hotels are listed in order of closeness to Il Campo—max 10-minute walk. The first two enjoy views of the old town and cathedral (which sits floodlit before me as I type). The first three are the best values in town.

Albergo Bernini makes you part of a Sienese family in a modest, clean home with nine newly renovated rooms. Friendly Nadia and Mauro, who welcome you to picnic on their spectacular view terrace for breakfast or dinner, get the "we try hardest in Siena" award. The mynah bird (Romeo) actually says *"ciao"* as you come and go from the terrace (Sb-L95,000, D-L110,000, Db-L130,000, family deals, prices drop in winter, midnight curfew, on main San Domenico-Il Campo drag at Via Sapienza 15, tel. & fax 0577-289-047, Alessandro SE).

Alma Domus is ideal—unless nuns make you nervous, you need a double bed, or you plan on staying out past the 23:30 curfew. This quasi-hotel (not a convent) is run with firm but angelic smiles by sisters who offer clean and quiet rooms for a steal and save the best views for foreigners. Bright lamps, quaint balconies, fine views, grand public rooms, top security, and a friendly atmosphere make this a great value. The checkout time is strictly 10:00, but they have a *deposito* for luggage. (Db-L95,000, Tb-L120,000, Qb-L140,000, from San Domenico walk downhill with church on your right toward the view, turn left down Via Camporegio, make a U-turn at the little chapel down the brick steps to Via Camporegio 37, tel. 0577-44177 and 0577-44487, fax 0577-47601, NSE).

Hotel Chiusarelli, a proper hotel in a fine location, is another wonderful value (50 rooms, one S-L65,000, Sb-L96,000, Db-L135,000, breakfast-L13,000, CC:VMA, pleasant garden terrace, tiny free parking lot; just outside the old town, across from San Domenico and overlooking the stadium at Viale Curtone 15, tel. 0577-280-562, fax 0577-271-177, SE).

Albergo Lea is a rundown but sleepable place in a residential neighborhood a few blocks away from the center (past San Domenico), with easy street parking (S-L70,000, Db-L120,000, Tb-L150,000, Qb-L180,000, with breakfast, CC:VMA, Viale XXIV Maggio 10, tel. & fax 0577-283-207, SE).

If you're traveling with rich relatives who want sterility away from the action, the **Hotel Villa Liberty** has big bright and comfortable rooms (Db-L200,000 with breakfast, CC:VMA, elevator, air-conditioning, TVs, mini-bars, etc., facing the fortress at Viale V. Veneto 11, tel. 0577-44966, fax 0577-44770, SE).

The tourist office lists private homes that rent rooms for around L25,000 per person. Many require a stay of several days, but some are central and a fine value. Siena's **Guidoriccio Youth Hostel** has 120 cheap beds, but given the hassle of the bus ride and the charm of downtown Siena at night, I'd skip it (office open 7:00–9:00, 15:00–23:30; L21,000 beds in doubles, triples, and dorms with sheets and breakfast, cheap meals, bus #10 from Piazza Gramsci or the train station to Via Fiorentina 89 in the Stellino neighborhood, tel. 0577-52212, SE).

Eating in Siena

Restaurants are reasonable by Florentine and Venetian standards. Budget eaters look for *pizza rustica* places, scattered throughout Siena, serving up cheap pizza-to-go (sold by the gram, 100 grams for a snack, 200 grams for a filling meal).

Even with higher prices and lower-quality food, consider eating on Il Campo. Eating in Il Campo ambience is a classic European experience. **Pizzeria Spadaforte** has a great setting, mediocre pizza, and tables steeper than its prices (daily 12:00–16:00, 19:30–22:30, tel. 0577-281-123).

For authentic Sienese dining at a fair price, eat at the **Locanda Garibaldi**, down Via Giovanni Dupre a few steps from the square (L26,000 menu, open at 12:00 for lunch and 19:00 for dinner, arrive early to get a table, closed Saturday). Marcello does a nice little L5,000 *piatto misto dolce*, featuring several local sweets with sweet wine. For a peasant's dessert, take your last glass of Chianti with a chunk of bread to the square, lean against a pillar, and sip Siena Classico. Picnics are royal on the Campo.

On the Campo, a **Ciao** cafeteria offers cheap meals, no ambience, and no views; the neighboring **Spizzicato** serves huge, inexpensive quarter-pizzas (daily 12:00–15:00, 19:00–21:00, to the left of the tower as you face it).

Ristorante Gallo Nero, a friendly "*grotto*" for authentic Tuscan cuisine, is good but uneven, with better food on some nights than others. This "black rooster" serves a mean *ribollita* (hearty Tuscan bean soup), offers a "medieval menu," and has cheap Chianti three blocks down Via del Porrione from the Campo at #65, tel. 0577-284-356). Just around the corner, **Il Verrochio** serves a decent L22,000 menu (Logge del Papa 1).

Osteria il Tamburino is small and intimate and serves up tasty meals (Monday–Saturday 12:00–14:30, 19:00–20:30, closed Sunday, follow Via Citta off Campo, becomes Stalloreggi, Via Stalloreggi 11, tel. 0577-280-306).

At **Antica Osteria Da Divo** the ambience is slippery as you climb deep into an Etruscan cellar to find your table. You'll pay a little extra here but the cuisine is local and good (daily 12:00–14:30, 19:00–22:00, facing baptistery door, take far right, Via Franciosa 29, tel. 0577-284-381).

Osteria la Chiacchera is a wonderfully medieval, tasty, and affordable hole-in-the-brick-wall (daily 12:00–15:00, 19:00–24:00, below Pension Bernini at Costa di San Antonio 4, tel. 0577-280-631).

For a chance to enjoy a treat on a balcony overlooking the Campo, stop by **Gelateria Artigiana La Costarella** (ice cream), **Bar Paninoteca** (sandwiches, near loggia on stairs leading to Campo), or **Bar Barbero d'Oro** (*panforte*—L3,500/100 grams—and cappuccino, best balcony open in summer), all of which are on Via di Citta.

Siena's claim to caloric fame is its *panforte*, a rich, chewy concoction of nuts, honey, and candied fruits that impresses even fruitcake-haters (although locals I met prefer a white macaroon and lemon cookie called *ricciarelli*). All over town Prodotti Tipici shops sell Sienese specialties.

Entertainment and Nightlife

Don't miss the evening *passeggiata* (peak strolling time is 19:00) along Via Banchi di Sopra with gelato in hand. **Nannini's at Piazza Salimbeni** has fine gelato (daily 10:30–24:00).

The **Enoteca Italia** is a good wine bar in the Fortezza (Monday 12:00–20:00, Tuesday–Saturday 12:00–1:00, closed Sunday, glasses cost L3,000–8,000, bottles and snacks available).

Sala di Te, a local late-night game and tearoom with a curiously welcoming atmosphere, is popular with visiting American students (Monday–Saturday 21:30–02:30, 50 yards past recommended Gallo Nero restaurant, turn right off Via del Porrione down the Vicolo del Vannello, go right at bottom of hill, take first left, go down stairs, then immediately go up stairs to wooden door, no sign).

Transportation Connections—Siena

To: Rome (by bus, 6/day, 3 hrs, L22,000; by train, 8/day, 3.5 hrs, including a 20-minute connection in Chiusi), **Viterbo** (for Civita, 1/day).

To Florence: Take the *rapide* SITA bus from Siena's Piazza San Domenico to downtown Florence's bus station (12/day, 75 min, L10,000, buy ticket before boarding at nearby *biglietteria* (or office on ground floor of church, 0577-204-111 or 0577-204-245). Don't confuse the blue (intercity) and orange (city) buses. You want blue. Don't panic if there are too many people. They generally add buses when necessary. The fastest buses are marked "*corse rapide*," the *diretto* makes two stops en route, and the misnamed *accellerata* stops everywhere. These milk-run buses are much slower but more scenic, offering an interesting glimpse of small-town and rural Tuscany.

Trains, which take a little longer than SITA buses, sometimes require a change in Empoli. Shuttle buses connect Siena's train station with its old town center (look for buses marked "Piazza del Sale" or "Piazza Gramsci").

SAN GIMIGNANO

The epitome of a Tuscan hill town with 14 medieval towers still standing (out of an original 72!), San Gimignano is a perfectly preserved tourist trap so easy to visit and visually pleasing that it's a good stop. In the 13th century, back in the days of Romeo and Juliet, towns were run by feuding noble families. They'd periodically battle things out from the protective bases of their respective family towers. Pointy skylines were the norm in medieval Tuscany. But in San Gimignano, fabric was big business and many of its towers were built simply to hang dyed fabric out for drying.

While the basic three-star sight here is the town of San Gimignano itself, there are a few worthwhile stops. From the town gate, shop straight up the traffic-free town's cobbled main drag to the Piazza del Cisterna (with its 13th-century well). The town sights cluster around the adjoining Piazza del Duomo.

The TI is in the old center on Piazza Duomo (daily March–October 9:00–13:00, 15:00–19:00, November–February 9:00–13:00, 14:00–18:00, changes money, tel. 0577-940-008, www.sangimignano.com, e-mail: prolocsg@tin.it).

Sights—San Gimignano

The **Collegiata**, with the round windows and wide steps, is a Romanesque church filled with fine Renaissance frescoes (free, daily 9:30–12:30, 15:00–17:30, closed during Mass). In Palazzo del Popolo (facing the same piazza) you'll find the city museum and San Gimignano's tallest tower, Torre Grossa. You can climb this 180-foot-tall tower for L8,000, but the free Rocca (castle), a short climb behind the church, offers a better view and a great picnic perch, especially at sunset.

The **Museo Civico** has a classy little painting collection with a 1422 altarpiece by Taddeo di Bartolo honoring Saint Gimignano. You can see him with the town in his hands surrounded by events from his life (L12,000-combined entry for Torre Grossa and Museo Civico, L8,000-tower only, L5,000-museum only, daily 9:30–19:20, November–February 9:30–12:50, 14:30–16:50 Tuesday–Sunday, closed Monday). Thursday is market day (8:00–13:00), but for local merchants, every day is a sales frenzy.

Sleeping and Eating in San Gimignano

Sra. Carla Rossi offers rooms—some with views—throughout the town (Db-from L90,000, Via di Cellole 81, 53037 San Gimignano, cellular 036-8352-3206, tel. 0577-955-041, fax 0577-941-268). For a listing of **private rooms**, stop by or call Associazione Strutture Extralberghiere (L50,000 per person, Piazza della Cisterna, tel. 0577-943-190). **Osteria del Carcere** has good food and prices (Via del Castello 13, just off Piazza della Cisterna, tel. 0577-941-905). Shops guarded by wild boar statues sell it by the gram; buy some wild boar (*cinghiale*—cheen-gah-lay), cheese, bread, and wine, and enjoy a picnic in the garden by the Rocca (castle).

Transportation Connections—San Gimignano

To: **Florence** (hrly departures, 75 min, change in Poggibonsi; or catch the frequent 20-min shuttle bus to Poggibonsi and train to

Florence), **Siena** (hrly, 90 min, change in Poggibonsi to bus or train), **Volterra** (6/day, 2 hrs, change in Poggibonsi and Colle di Val D'Elsa). Bus tickets are sold at the bar just inside the town gate. San Gimignano has no baggage-check service.

Drivers: You can't drive within the walled town of San Gimignano, but a car-park awaits just a few steps outside.

ASSISI

Around the year 1200, a simple friar from Assisi challenged the decadence of church government and society in general with a powerful message of nonmaterialism, simplicity, and a "slow down and smell God's roses" lifestyle. Like Jesus, Francis taught by example. A huge monastic order grew out of his teachings, which were gradually embraced (some would say co-opted) by the church. Clare, St. Francis' partner in poverty, founded the Order of the Poor Clares. Catholicism's purest example of simplicity is now glorified in beautiful churches. In 1939 Italy made Francis and Clare its patron saints.

Any pilgrimage site will be commercialized, and the legacy of St. Francis is Assisi's basic industry. In summer the town bursts with splash-in-the-pan Francis fans and Franciscan knick-knacks. Those able to see past the tacky friar mementos can actually have a "travel on purpose" experience. Francis' message of love and simplicity and sensitivity to the environment has a broad appeal.

Orientation

Assisi, crowned by a ruined castle, is beautifully preserved and rich in history. The upper part of the Basilica of St. Francis will be closed until Christmas '99 while the damage caused by the '97 earthquake is repaired. You might see scaffolding bracing some buildings and a crane hovering over the basilica, but it's back to business as the tourists return to Assisi. Most visitors are day-trippers. Assisi after dark is closer to a place Francis could call home.

Tourist Information: The TI is on Piazza del Comune (Monday–Saturday 9:00–13:00, 15:30–18:30, Sunday 9:00–13:00, tel. 075-812-534). Market day is Saturday on Piazza Mateotti.

Arrival in Assisi: Buses connecting Assisi's train station (near Santa Maria degli Angeli) with the old town center (L1,200, 2/hrly, 5 km) stop at Piazza Unita d'Italia (Basilica di San Francisco), Largo Properzio (Santa Chiara), and Piazza Matteotti (top of old town). Taxis into town run about L22,000.

Local Guide: Anne Robichaud, an American Elderhostel lecturer who has lived in Italy for 23 years, offers personalized tours of Assisi and the countryside, with a focus on history, art, crafts, folklore, and food—your choice (half-day tours are $65 apiece for four

Assisi

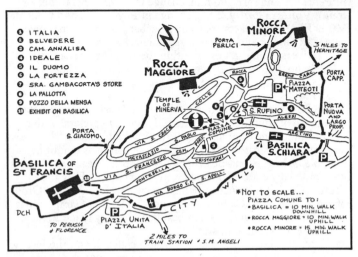

① ITALIA
② BELVEDERE
③ CAM. ANNALISA
④ IDEALE
⑤ IL DUOMO
⑥ LA FORTEZZA
⑦ SRA. GAMBACORTA'S STORE
⑧ LA PALLOTTA
⑨ POZZO DELLA MENSA
⑩ EXHIBIT ON BASILICA

ROCCA MINORE
PORTA PERLICI → 3 MILES TO HERMITAGE
ROCCA MAGGIORE
ROCCA
EREMO CARC. → PORTA CAPP.
P PIAZZA MATTEOTI
TEMPLE OF MINERVA
COLLE
PORTA NUOVA AND LARGO PROP.
S. RUFINO
ALESSI
PIAZZA COMUNE
PORTA S. GIACOMO
VIA S. CROCE
S. PAOLO
METASTASIO
SEM.
CRISTOFANI
AG.
ARETINO
BASILICA S. CHIARA
P
BASILICA OF ST FRANCIS
VIA S. FRANCESCO
FONTEBELLA
S. APOLL.
WALLS
CITY
DCH
TO PERUSIA & FLORENCE
P PIAZZA UNITA D'ITALIA
VIA BORGO S.P.
2 MILES TO TRAIN STATION & S.M. ANGELI

*NOT TO SCALE...
PIAZZA COMUNE TO:
• BASILICA = 10 MIN. WALK DOWNHILL
• ROCCA MAGGIORE = 10 MIN. WALK UPHILL
• ROCCA MINORE = 15 MIN. WALK UPHILL

people, $95 apiece for full day, prices drop for larger groups and multiple days, deposit required, tel. & fax 075-802-334—best from 6:30–7:30 and 20:00–23:00, e-mail: arobichaud@tecnonet.it).

Excursions: If you want to visit the sights near Assisi, Gino's car and van taxi service can help: one hour is L12,000 per person (four minimum), two hours about L20,000 per person (tel. 033-764-7780).

Sights—Assisi

▲▲▲**Basilica of St. Francis**—In 1226 St. Francis was buried outside of his town with the sinners on the "hill of the damned." Now called the "Hill of Paradise," this is one of the artistic highlights of medieval Europe. It's frescoed from top to bottom by Cimabue, Giotto, Simone Martini, and the leading artists of the day.

There are three parts to the church: upper basilica, lower basilica, and the saint's tomb (within the lower basilica). The upper basilica, closed for restoration, will re-open Christmas 1999. The lower basilica and crypt are open now (free, daily 7:00–19:00, sometimes closed for Mass, modest dress required, tel. 075-819-001). To get an idea of what the upper basilica looks like, head across the church courtyard to the free exhibit (up the stairs to the usually-open doors). Inside are brightly-lit pictures of Giotto's frescoes, videos showing the church before and after the earth-quake, and a bookshop (daily 9:00–12:30, 15:00–18:00).

The Basilica of St. Francis is a theological work of genius—

but difficult for the 20th-century tourist/pilgrim to appreciate. Since the basilica is the reason most visit Assisi and the message of St. Francis has even the least devout blessing the town Vespas, I've designed a *Mona Winks*–type tour with the stress on the place's theology rather than art history. It's adapted from the excellent little *The Basilica of Saint Francis—A Spiritual Pilgrimage* by Goulet, McInally, and Wood (L4,500 in the bookshop).

To follow along with the tour I've outlined below, head to the church itself for the beginning (lower basilica and crypt), and end at the exhibit on the upper basilica.

Enter the church from the parking lot at the lower level. At the doorway look up and see St. Francis who (sounding a bit like John Wayne) greets you with the Latin inscription saying the equivalent of "Slow down and be joyful, pilgrim. You've reached the Hill of Paradise and this church will knock your spiritual socks off." Start with the tomb (turn left into the nave and go down the "Tomba" stairs). Grab a pew right in front of his tomb.

The message: Francis' message caused a stir. He traded a life of power and riches for one of obedience, poverty, and chastity. The Franciscan existence (Brother Sun, Sister Moon, and so on) is a space where God, man, and the natural world frolic harmoniously. Franciscan friars, known as the "Jugglers of God," were a joyful part of the community. In an Italy torn by fighting between towns and families, Francis promoted peace and the restoration of order. (He set an example by reconstructing a crumbled chapel.) While the Church was waging bloody Crusades, Francis pushed ecumenism and understanding. Even today the leaders of the world's great religions meet here for summits.

This rich building seems to contradict the teachings of the poor monk it honors. But it was built as an act of religious and civic pride to remember the hometown saint. It was also designed and still functions as a pilgrimage center and a splendid classroom.

The tomb: Holy relics were the "ruby slippers" of medieval Europe. They gave you power—got your prayers answered and helped you win wars—and ultimately helped you get back to your eternal Kansas. For obvious reasons of security, you didn't flaunt your relics. In fact, Francis' tomb was hidden until 1818, when this crypt was opened to the public. The saint's remains are above the altar in the stone box with the iron ties. His four best friends are buried in the corners of the room. Opposite the altar, up four steps in between the entrance and exit, notice the remains of Francis' rich Roman patron, Jacopa dei Settesoli, in an urn behind the black metal grill.

The lower basilica is appropriately Franciscan, subdued and Romanesque. The nave was frescoed with parallel scenes from the lives of Christ and Francis—connected by a ceiling of stars. Unfortunately, after the church was built and decorated, the popularity of the Franciscans meant side chapels needed to be built. Huge arches were cut out of the scenes, but some scenes survive. The first panels show Jesus being stripped of his clothing, across the nave from the famous scene of Francis stripping off his clothes in front of his father. In the second arch fresco on the right wall, Christ is being taken down from the cross (just half his body can be seen) and it looks like the story is over. Defeat. But in the opposite fresco we see Francis preaching to the birds, reminding the faithful that through baptism, the message of the Gospel survives.

These stories directed the attention of the medieval pilgrim to the altar where, through the sacraments, he met God. The church was thought of as a community of believers sailing toward God. The prayers coming out of the nave (*navis*, or ship) fill the triangular sections of the ceiling—called *vele*, or sails—with spiritual wind. With a priest for a navigator and the altar for a helm, faith propelled the ship.

Stand behind the altar (toes to the bottom step) and look up. The three scenes in front of you are, to the right, "Obedience" (Francis wearing a yoke); to the left, "Chastity" (in a tower of purity held up by two angels); and straight ahead, "Poverty." Here, Jesus blesses the marriage as Francis slips a ring on Lady Poverty. In the foreground two "self-sufficient" merchants (the new rich of a thriving North Italy) are throwing sticks and stones at the bride. But Poverty, in her patched wedding dress, is fertile and strong, and even those brambles blossom into a rosebush crown.

Putting your heels to the altar and bending back like a drum major, look up at Francis, who traded a life of earthly simplicity for glory in heaven. Turn to the right and march . . .

St. Francis' patched robe is on display down the steps under the right transept. Back upstairs, look around at the painted scenes in this transept. In 1300 this was radical art—believable homespun scenes, landscapes, trees, real people. Check out the crucifix (by Giotto) with the eight sparrow-like angels. For the first time, holy people are expressing emotion—one angel turns her head sadly at the sight of Jesus; another scratches her hands down her cheeks, drawing blood. The up-until-now-in-control Mary has fainted in despair. The Franciscans, with their goal of bringing God to the people, found a natural partner in Europe's first modern painter, Giotto.

Francis' friend, "Sister Death," was really not all that terrible. In fact, Francis would like to introduce you to her now (to the right of the door leading into the bright courtyard). Go ahead, block the light and meet her. I'll wait for you in the courtyard.

From the courtyard you can enter the bookshop and the skipable Museum-Treasury (Gothic fine arts and paintings, no English explanations, L3,000). Monks in robes are not my idea of easy-to-approach people, but the Franciscans are still God's jugglers (and most of them speak English).

Head to the exhibit on the upper basilica. Or, if you're taking this tour after Christmas 1999, climb the stairs to the upper basilica. I'll also include directions for use within the church.

The upper basilica, built later than the lower, is brighter, Gothic, and nearly wallpapered by Giotto. This gallery of frescoes by Giotto and his assistants shows 28 scenes from the life of St. Francis.

Look for these scenes . . .

•**(Immediately to right of altar)** A common man, recognizing Francis as one who will do great things, spreads his cape before Francis as a sign of honor. Symbolized by the rose window, God looks over the 20-year-old Francis, a dandy imprisoned in his selfishness. A medieval pilgrim fluent in symbolism would understand this because the Temple of Minerva (which you'll see today on Assisi's Piazza del Comune) was a prison at that time. The rose window, which never existed, is symbolic of God's eye.

•**(Next panel)** Francis offers his cape to a needy stranger. Prior to this act of kindness, Francis had been captured in battle, held as a prisoner of war, and then released.

•**(Next panel)** He's visited by the Lord in a dream and told to leave the army and go home.

•**(Two panels down)** Francis gives his dad his clothes, his credit cards, and even his time-share condo on Capri. Naked Francis is covered by the bishop, symbolizing his transition from a man of the world to a man of the church.

•**The pope** has a vision of a simple man propping up his teetering church. This led to the papal acceptance of the Franciscan reforms.

•**(Other side of church, fourth panel from the door)** Christ appears to Francis being carried by a seraph (six-winged angel). For the strength of his faith, Francis is given the marks of his master, the "battle scars of love" . . . the stigmata. Throughout his life Francis was interested in chivalry; now he's joined the spiritual knighthood. The weeds in the foreground were an herb which, in olden days, "drove away sadness and made men merry and joyful." Pilgrims smiled.

•**(To the right of the exit)** Sans seraph, Francis is preaching to the birds. Francis was more than a nature lover. Notice that the birds are of different species. They represent the diverse flock of humanity and nature—all created and loved by God and worthy of each other's love.

This is a worthwhile message for pilgrims to take home. Near the outside of the upper basilica is the Latin Pax (peace) and the Franciscan tau cross in the grass. Tau, the last letter in the Hebrew alphabet, is symbolic of faithfulness to the end. Francis signed his name with this simple character. Tau and Pax.

(For more pax, take the high lane back to town, up to the castle or into the countryside.)

▲**Basilica di Santa Chiara (Saint Clare)**—Dedicated to the founder of the order of the Poor Clares, this Umbrian Gothic church is simple, in keeping with the Poor Clares' dedication to a life of contemplation. The church was built in 1265 and the huge buttresses were added in the next century. The interior's fine frescoes were whitewashed in the Baroque days. The Chapel of St. George on the right (actually an earlier church incorporated into this one) has the crucifix which supposedly spoke to St. Francis, leading to his conversion in 1206. In the back of that chapel are some important Franciscan relics, including Clare's robe. Stairs lead from the nave down to the tomb of Saint Clare. The attached cloistered community of the Poor Clares has flourished for 700 years (church open 7:00–12:00, 14:00–19:00, Sunday till 18:00). For a change of pace, cross the street behind the church at the arch and dip into the goofy mechanical and water-powered Biblical world of Silvano Gianbolina.

Piazza del Comune—This square is the center of town. You'll find the Roman temple of Minerva, a Romanesque tower, banks, the post office, the Pinacoteca (pathetic art gallery, not worth the admission), and the tourist information office. For a look at Assisi's Roman roots, tour the Roman Forum which is actually under the Piazza del Comune (Foro Romano, L4,000, daily 10:00–13:00, 15:00–19:00). The floor plan is sparse, and the odd bits and pieces obscure, but it's well explained in English, and it is ancient.

▲**Rocca Maggiore**—The "big castle" offers a good look at a 14th-century fortification and a fine view of Assisi and the Umbrian countryside (L5,000, daily 10:00–19:00, closes earlier off-season). If you're counting lire, the view is just as good from outside the castle and the interior is pretty bare—except for a model of a guillotine with an interesting history in English. For a picnic with the same birds and views that inspired St. Francis, leave all the tourists and hike to the Rocca Minore (small castle) above Piazza Matteotti.

▲▲**Santa Maria degli Angeli**—This huge Baroque church, towering above the buildings below Assisi, was built around the tiny but historic Porziuncola chapel. St. Francis took Jesus literally when he told him to "go and restore my house." Twenty-four-year-old Francis put the ruined and abandoned chapel back together. As you enter St. Mary of the Angels, notice the sketch on the door showing the original little chapel with the monks' huts around it, and Assisi before it had its huge basilica. Francis lived here after he founded the Franciscan Order in 1208, and this was where he consecrated St. Clare as the Bride of Christ. The other "sights" in the church (a chapel on the spot where Francis died, the rose garden, a museum which has a few monastic cells upstairs) are not very interesting (daily 7:00–18:30 May–October, 7:00–12:00 and 14:00–sunset November–April).

Sleeping in Assisi
(L1,700 = about $1, zip code: 06081)
Sleep Code: **S** = Single, **D** = Double/Twin, **T** = Triple, **Q** = Quad, **b** = bathroom, **s** = shower only, **CC** = Credit Card (Visa, Master-Card, Amex), **SE** = Speaks English, **NSE** = No English.

The town accommodates large numbers of pilgrims on religious holidays. Finding a room any other time should be easy.

Albergo Italia is clean and simple with great beds and delightful owners. Some of its 13 rooms overlook the town square (Ss-L37,000, D-L50,000, Db-L70,000, T-L63,000, Tb-L90,000, Qb-L100,000, CC:VM, just off the Piazza del Comune's fountain at Vicolo della Fortezza 2, tel. 075-812-625, fax 075-804-3749, SE).

Hotel Belvedere offers 16 comfortable rooms and good views and is run by friendly Enrico and his American wife, Mary (Db-L110,000, breakfast-L10,000, two blocks past St. Clare's church at Via Borgo Aretino 13, tel. 075-812-460, fax 075-816-812, SE). Their attached restaurant is also good.

Camere Annalisa Martini is a cheery home swimming in vines, roses, and bricks in the town's medieval core. Annalisa speaks English and enthusiastically accommodates her guests with a picnic garden, washing machine, refrigerator, and six homey, lived-in-feeling rooms (S-L38,000, Sb-L40,000, D-L58,000, Db-L65,000, T-L80,000, Q-L100,000, five rooms sharing three bathrooms, no breakfast, one block below the Piazza del Comune, then left on Via S. Gregorio to #6, tel. 075-813-536).

Hotel Ideale is on the far edge of town, overlooking the valley, with a peaceful garden, free parking, view balconies, all the modern comforts, and an English-speaking welcome (Sb-L65,000–80,000, Db-L105,000–125,000 depending on season, breakfast buffet-L10,000, CC:VMA, Piazza Matteotti 1, tel. 075-813-570, fax 075-813-020, Lara SE).

Albergo Il Duomo is tidy and quiet on a stairstep lane one block up from San Rufino (nine rooms, S-L39,000-47,000, Sb-L46,000–56,000, D-L54,000–67,000, Db-L69,000–81,000 depending on season, breakfast-L8,000, saggy beds, CC:VM, Vicolo S. Lorenzo 2, tel. 075-812-742, fax 075-812-762, e-mail: ilduomo@krenit.it, Carlo SE).

Hotel La Fortezza prompts a host of adjectives: small, clean, dim, tranquil, modern, cluttered, and quite comfortable (seven rooms, Db-L90,000, Qb-L140,000, half-pension available, CC:VMA, just up the lane from the Piazza del Comune at Vicolo della Fortezza 19b, tel. 075-812-993, fax 075-819-8035, e-mail: fortezza@krenet.it, SE).

La Pallotta has clean, bright rooms above its busy restaurant (see Eating, below). Rooms #12 or #18 have views (Db-L90,000, CC:VMA, Via San Ruffino 4, tel. & fax 075-812-307, SE).

Senora Gambacorta rents several decent rooms with a roof terrace on a quiet lane (Via Sermei 9) just above St. Chiara. There is no sign and no reception desk, so you'll need to check in at her shop one-half block off Piazza Comune at San Gabriele 17—look for the sign "Bottega di Gambacorta" (L35,000 per person, tel. 075-812-454, fax 075-813-186, e-mail: geo@krenet.it, NSE). She also has an apartment for longer stays.

Francis probably would have bunked with the peasants in Assisi's **Ostello della Pace** (L20,000 beds in four- to eight-bed rooms, two D-L50,000, a family room with bathroom-L25,000 apiece, breakfast included, a 15-minute walk below town at Via di Valethye 177, at the San Pietro stop on the station-town bus, tel. & fax 075-816-767, SE).

Eating in Assisi

For the best Assisian perch and fine regional cooking, relax on a terrace overlooking the Piazza del Comune at the **Taverna dei Consoli** (L24,000 menu, closed Wednesday, two steps straight across from the Albergo Italia, tel. 075-812-516, laid-back owner Moreno SE).

La Pallotta, run by a friendly hardworking family, is locally popular and offers excellent regional specialties such as *piccione* (pigeon), *coniglio* (rabbit), and much more (L27,000 menu, closed Tuesday, just one block up from the Piazza del Comune, Via San Rufino 4, tel. 075-812-649).

The **Pozzo della Mensa** has a good L20,000 menu with simple, hearty cooking (hidden down a quiet alley one block from San Rufino church at Via della Menza 11, tel. 075-816-247).

Transportation Connections—Assisi

By train to: Rome (9/day, 2.5 hrs with a change in Foligno), **Florence** (10/day, 2.5 hrs, sometimes changing at Terontola-Cortona), **Siena** (5/day, 4 hrs), **Orvieto** (4/day, 2–3 hrs). Train info tel. 1478-88088. There are one or two buses a day to Rome and Florence.

ORVIETO

Umbria's grand hill town, while no secret, is still worth a quick look. Just off the freeway, with three popular gimmicks (its ceramics, cathedral, and Classico wine), it's loaded with tourists by day and quiet by night. Drinking a shot of wine in a ceramic cup as you gaze up at the cathedral lets you experience all of Orvieto's claims to fame at once.

Ride the back streets of Orvieto into the Middle Ages. The

Orvieto

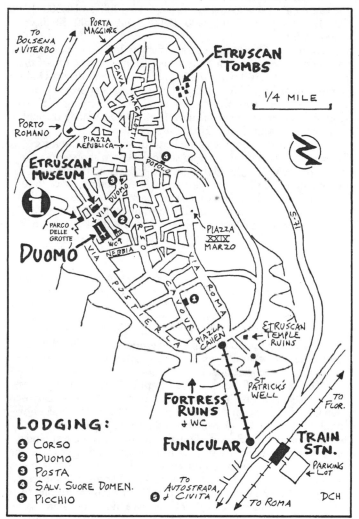

LODGING:

- ❶ CORSO
- ❷ DUOMO
- ❸ POSTA
- ❹ SALV. SUORE DOMEN.
- ❺ PICCHIO

town sits majestically on tufa rock. Streets lined with buildings made from the exhaust-stained volcanic stuff seem to grumble Dark Ages.

Piazza Cahen is only a transportation hub at the entry to the hilltop town. It has a ruined fortress with a garden, a commanding view, and a popular well which is an impressive, although over-priced, double helix carved into tufa rock.

Tourist Information: The TI is at #24 Piazza Duomo on the cathedral square (Monday–Friday 8:15–13:50 and 16:00–19:00, Saturday 10:00–13:00 and 16:00–19:00, Sunday 10:00–12:00 and 16:00–18:00).

Arrival in Orvieto: A handy funicular/bus shuttle takes visitors quickly from the train station and car-park to the top of the town (4/hrly, L1,500 ticket includes Piazza Cahen–Piazza Duomo minibus transfer, where you'll find everything that matters; or L1,200 for funicular only—best choice if you're staying at Hotel Corso). The funicular runs from 7:15 to 20:30 Monday through Saturday and from 8:00 to 20:30 on Sunday.

Buy your ticket at the entrance to the funicular (look for "*biglieterria*" sign) or at the train station tobacco shop across the street. At the top of the funicular, walk right onto the waiting orange bus. The shuttle bus drops you at the tourist office (last stop, in front of the Duomo). Drivers park at the base of the hill at the huge, free lot behind the Orvieto train station (follow the "P" and "*funicolare*" signs), or at the pay lot to the right of Orvieto's cathedral (L1,500 for first hour, L1,000/hrly thereafter).

Sights—Orvieto

▲▲**Duomo**—Orvieto's cathedral has Italy's most striking facade (from 1330). Grab a gelato (to the left of the church) and study this fascinating mass of mosaics and sculpture (daily 7:30–12:45 and 14:30–19:15 April–September, closes at 18:15 March and October, closes at 17:15 November–February). Inside the cathedral notice how the downward-sloping floor diminishes the perspective, giving it an illusion of being shorter than it is. Notice also the alabaster windows.

To the right of the altar, the **Chapel of St. Brizio** features Signorelli's brilliantly lit and restored frescoes of the Apocalypse. Step into the chapel and you're surrounded by vivid scenes showing the Preaching of the Antichrist, the End of the World, the Resurrection of the Bodies, the Last Judgment, and a gripping pietà. For a bonus, check out Fra Angelico's painting of Jesus, the angels, and the prophets on the ceiling. This room is Orvieto's artistic must-see (get L3,000 ticket at the TI across the square, see TI hours above; chapel sometimes free 7:30–10:00—drop by to check). Public toilets are just off the square, down the stairs from the left transept. To find the viewpoint park, face the cathedral and go right (past parking lot) for one minute.

Archeological Museum (Museo Civico)—Across from the entrance of the cathedral is a fine Etruscan art museum combined with a city history museum (L7,000, April–September Tuesday–Sunday 10:00–13:00 and 14:00–18:00, closed Monday; October–March Tuesday–Sunday 10:00–13:00 and 14:30–17:00).

Underground Orvieto Tours (Parco delle Grotte)—Guides

weave a good archeological history into an hour-long look at about 100 meters of caves (L10,000, tours daily at 11:00, 12:15, 16:00, and 17:15 from the TI, tel. 0763-375-084 or the TI). Orvieto is honeycombed with Etruscan and medieval caves. You'll see only the remains of an old olive press, two impressive 40-meter-deep Etruscan well shafts, and the remains of a primitive cement quarry, but if you want underground Orvieto, this is the place to get it.

Wine Tasting—Orvieto Classico wine is justly famous. For a peek into a local winery, visit Tenuta Le Velette, where English-speaking Corrado and Cecilia Bottai welcome those who call ahead to set up an appointment for a look at their winery (L15,000 for tour and tasting, Monday–Friday 8:30–12:00 and 14:00–17:00, Saturday 8:30–12:00, closed Sunday, tel. 0763-29090, fax 0763-29114). From their sign (five minutes past Orvieto at top of switchbacks just before Canale, on Bagnoregio road) cruise down a long tree-lined drive then park at the striped gate (call ahead; no drop-ins).

Sleeping in Orvieto
(L1,700 = about $1, zip code: 05018)

Here are six places in the old town and one in a more modern neighborhood near the station.

Hotel Virgilio is a decent hotel with bright and modern—if overpriced—rooms shoe-horned into an old building ideally located on the main square facing the cathedral (Sb-L130,000, small Db-L169,000, Db-L175,000, includes breakfast, send personal or traveler's check for first night's deposit, CC:VM, elevator, Piazza Duomo 5, tel. 0763-341-882, fax 0763-343-797, SE). They also have a cheaper "*dependence*"—a double and quad in a one-star hotel a few doors away (Db-L110,000, Qb-L200,000).

Hotel Corso is small, clean, and friendly, with comfy modern rooms, some with balconies and views (Sb-L100,000, Db-L140,000, 10 percent discount if you show this book, CC:VM, elevator, garage on the main street up from the funicular toward the Duomo at Via Cavour 339, tel. & fax 0763-342-020).

Hotel Duomo is a funky, brightly colored, Old World place with not-quite-clean rooms and a great location (17 rooms, S-L40,000, D-L60,000, Db-L85,000, a block from the Duomo, behind the *gelateria* at Via di Maurizio 7, tel. 0763-341-887, fax 0763-341-105).

Hotel Posta is a five-minute walk from the cathedral into the medieval core. It's a big, old, formerly elegant, but well-cared-for-in-its-decline building with a breezy garden, a grand old lobby, and spacious, clean, plain rooms with vintage rickety furniture and springy beds (20 rooms, D-L75,000, Db-L95,000, Via Luca Signorelli 18, tel. 0763-341-909).

The sisters of the **Instituto Salvatore Suore Domenicane**

rent 15 spotless twin rooms in their heavenly convent (Sb-
L40,000, Db-L80,000, two-night minimum, just off Piazza del
Populo at Via del Populo 1, tel. & fax 0763-342-910).

Hotel Picchio is a concrete-and-marble place, more comfortable but with less character than others in the area. It's family-run
by Marco and Picchio. It's in the lower, plain part of town, 300
yards from the train station (D-L50,000, Db-L70,000, Tb-L90,000,
Via G. Salvatori 17, 05019 Orvieto Scalo, tel. 0763-301-144 or
0763-90246). A trail leads from here up to the old town.

For a long list of rural B&Bs, farms, and apartments in
Canale, Bagnoregio, and Lubriano, contact Cecilia Bottai at the
winery (Db-L80,000, tel. 0763-29090, fax 0763-29114, SE).

Transportation Connections—Orvieto
By train to: Rome (14/day, 75 min, consider leaving your car at
the large car-park behind the Orvieto station), **Florence** (14/day,
90 min), **Siena** (10/day, 2–3 hrs, change in Chiusi).

By bus to Bagnoregio: It's a 50-minute L3,000 bus ride
(1998 departures from Orvieto's Piazza Cahen on blue Cotral bus:
9:10, 12:40, 13:55, 15:45, 17:40, and 18:35, each bus stops at Orvieto's train station five minutes later, runs daily except Sunday, buy
tickets on bus or from "café snack bar" at station, confirm return
times with the conductor, tel. 0763-792-237). If the bus is empty,
develop a relationship with your driver. He may let you jump out
in Lubriano for a great photo of distant Civita.

CIVITA DI BAGNOREGIO
Perched on a pinnacle in a grand canyon, the traffic-free village of
Civita is Italy's ultimate hill town. Curl your toes around its Etrus-
can roots.

Civita is terminally ill. Only 15 residents remain as, bit by bit,
it's being purchased by rich big-city Italians who escape here.
Apart from its permanent (and aging) residents and those who
have weekend homes here, there is a group of Americans—introduced to the town through a small University of Washington
architecture program—who have bought into the rare magic of
Civita. When the program is in session, 15 students live with residents and study Italian culture and architecture.

Civita is connected to the world and the town of Bagnoregio
by a long pedestrian bridge. While Bagnoregio lacks the pinnacle-
town romance of Civita, it is a pure and lively bit of small-town
Italy. It's actually a healthy, vibrant community (unlike Civita, the
suburb it calls "the dead city"). Get a haircut, sip a coffee on the
square, walk down to the old laundry (ask, *"Dové la lavanderia vecchia?"*). A lively market fills the parking lot each Monday.

From Bagnoregio, yellow signs direct you along its long,
skinny spine to its older neighbor, Civita. Enjoy the view as you

Civita

head up the bridge to Civita. A shuttle bus runs from the base of the Civita bridge to Bagnoregio and sometimes as far as Al Boschetto (see Sleeping, below) about twice hourly in season—though not during the siesta time of 13:00 to 15:00 (L1,100). Be prepared for the little old ladies of Civita who have become aggressive at getting lire out of visitors; tourists are their only source of support. Off-season Civita, Bagnoregio, and Al Boschetto are all deadly quiet—and cold. I'd side-trip in quickly from Orvieto or skip the area altogether.

Civita Orientation Walk

Civita was once connected to Bagnoregio. The saddle between the separate towns eroded away. Photographs around town show the old donkey path, the original bridge. It was bombed in World War II, then replaced in 1965 with the new bridge you'll climb today. The town's hearty old folks hang on the bridge's hand railing when fierce winter weather rolls through.

Entering the town you'll pass through a cut in the rock (made by Etruscans 2,500 years ago) and under a 12th-century Romanesque arch. This was the main Etruscan road leading to the Tiber Valley and Rome.

Inside the town gate, on the left, notice the old Laundromat (in front of the WC). On the right a fancy door and windows lead to thin air. This was the facade of a Renaissance palace—one of five which once graced Civita. It fell into the valley riding a chunk of the ever-eroding rock pinnacle. Today the door leads to a remaining chunk of the palace—complete with Civita's first hot tub—owned by the "Marchesa," a countess who married into Italy's biggest industrialist family.

Poke through the museum next door and check out the viewpoint around the corner near the long-gone home of Civita's one famous son, St. Bonaventura.

Now wander to the town square in front of the church where you'll find Civita's only public phone, bar, and restaurant—and a wild donkey race on the first Sunday of June and the second Sunday of September. The church marks the spot where an Etruscan temple, and then a Roman temple, once stood. The pillars which stand like giants' barstools are ancient—Roman or Etruscan.

Go into the church and find Anna. She'll give you a tour, proudly pointing out frescoes and statues from "the school of Giotto" and "the school of Donatello," a portrait of the patron saint of your teeth (notice the scary-looking pincers), and an altar dedicated to Marlon Brando (or St. Ildebrando). Tip her and buy your postcards from her.

The basic grid street plan of the ancient town survives. Just around the corner from the church, on the main street, is Rossana and Antonio's cool and friendly wine cellar. Pull up a stump and let them or their children, Arianna and Antonella, serve you *panini* (sandwiches), *bruschetta* (garlic toast with tomato), wine, and a local cake called *ciambella*. Climb down into the cellar and note the traditional wine-making gear and the provisions for rolling huge kegs up the stairs. Tap on the kegs in the cool bottom level to see which are full.

The ground below Civita is honeycombed with ancient cellars (for keeping wine at the same temperature all year) and cisterns (for collecting rainwater, since there was no well in town). Many of these date from Etruscan times.

Explore farther down the street but remember, nothing is abandoned. Everything is still privately owned. After passing an ancient Roman tombstone on your left, you'll come to Vittoria's **Antico Mulino**, an atmospheric collection of old olive presses (donation requested, give about L1,500). Her sons Sandro and Felice, running the local equivalent of a lemonade stand, toast delicious *bruschetta* on weekends and holidays. Choose your topping (chopped tomato is super) and get a glass of wine for a fun, affordable snack.

Farther down the way, Maria (for a donation of about L1,500) will show you through her garden with a grand view (Maria's Giardino) and historical misinformation (she says Civita and Lubriano were once connected).

At the end of town the main drag peters out and a trail leads you down and around to the right to a tunnel that has cut through the hill under the town since Etruscan times. It was widened in the 1930s so farmers could get between their scattered fields easier.

Evenings on the town square are a bite of Italy. The same people sit on the same church steps under the same moon, night after night, year after year. I love my cool late evenings in Civita. If you visit in the cool of the early morning, have cappuccino and rolls at the small café on the town square.

Whenever you visit, stop halfway up the donkey path and listen to the sounds of rural Italy. Reach out and touch one of the monopoly houses. If you know how to turn the volume up on the crickets, do so.

Sleeping in Civita, Bagnoregio, and Beyond
(L1,700 = about $1, zip code: 01022)
When you leave the tourist crush, life as a traveler in Italy becomes easy and prices tumble. Room-finding is easy in small-town Italy.

Franco, who runs Civita's only restaurant, **Antico Forno**, rents three newly-remodeled rooms on Civita's main square. Call a minimum of two days in advance. Franco will meet you at the base of the bridge to beam up your luggage (D-L100,000, small D-L80,000, the more expensive rooms overlook square, L20,000 more for optional half-pension, CC:VM, Piazza Del Duomo Vecchio s.n.c., 01022 Civita di Bagnoregio, tel. 0761-760-016, cell phone: 0347-611-5426, Franco Sala SE).

For information about a two-bedroom, fully furnished and equipped Civita **apartment** with terrace and cliffside garden, rentable May through October ($700/week, $2,200/month, one week minimum), call Carol Watts in Kansas (tel. 785/539-0815, evenings).

Hotel Fidanza, in Bagnoregio near the bus stop, is tired but decent, and the only hotel in town. Of its 25 rooms, #206 and #207 have views of Civita (Sb-L70,000, Db-L100,000, breakfast-L20,000, attached restaurant, Via Fidanza 25, Bagnoregio/Viterbo, tel. & fax 0761-793-444).

Just outside Bagnoregio is **Al Boschetto**. The Catarcia family speaks no English. Have an English-speaking Italian call for you (D-L85,000, Db-L95,000, breakfast L6,000, CC:V, Strada Monterado, Bagnoregio/Viterbo, tel. 0761-792-369, walking and driving instructions below). Most rooms, while very basic, have private showers (no curtains, slippery floors—be careful not to flood the place; sing in search of your shower's resonant frequency). The Catarcia family (Angelino, his wife Perina, sons Gianfranco and Domenico, daughter-in-law Giuseppina, and the grandchildren) offer a candid look at rural Italian life. Meals are sometimes hearty and the men are often tipsy. If the men invite you down deep into the gooey, fragrant bowels of the cantina, be warned: The theme song is "Trinka Trinka Trinka," and there are no rules unless the female participants set them. The Orvieto bus drops you at the town gate. (Remember, no bus service at all on Sunday.) Al Boschetto is a 15-minute walk out of town past the old arch (follow "Viterbo" signs); turn left at the pyramid monument and right at the first fork (follow "Montefiascone" sign). Civita is a pleasant 45-minute walk (back through Bagnoregio) from Al Boschetto.

Casa San Martino, in the village of Lisciano Niccone (near Cortona and Perugia), is a 250-year-old farmhouse run as a B&B by American Italophile Lois Martin. Using this comfortable hilltop countryside as a home base, those with a car can tour Assisi, Orvieto, and Civita. While Lois reserves the summer for one-week stays, she'll take guests staying a minimum of two nights for the rest of the year (Db-$100, includes breakfast, views, pool, washer/dryer, house rental available, Casa San Martino 19, Lisciano Niccone, tel. 075-844-288, fax 075-844-422).

Eating in and near Civita
In Civita, try **Trattoria Antico Forno**, which serves up a variety of pastas at affordable prices (daily for lunch at 12:30 and dinner at 19:30, on the main square, tel. 0761-793-651).

Hostaria del Ponte offers light, creative cuisine at the carpark at the base of the bridge to Civita (12:30–16:00 and 19:30–24:00, closed Sunday evening and all of Monday, great view terrace, tel. 0761-793-565).

In Bagnoregio, check out **Ristorante Nello il Fumatore** (Piazza Fidanza, closed Friday). You'll get hearty country cooking—such as bunny—served at **Al Boschetto** (see above), just outside of Bagnoregio.

Transportation Connections—Bagnoregio
To Civita: It's a 30-minute walk. Taking the shuttle bus from Bagnoregio (10-min ride, first bus at 7:45, last at 17:50, twice hourly except during 13:00–15:00 siesta) still involves a 15-minute walk up the donkey path from the bus stop.

To Orvieto: Public buses (8/day, 50 min) connect Bagnoregio to the rest of the world via Orvieto (1998 departures from Bagnoregio: 5:30, 6:35, 6:55, 9:30, 10:15, 13:00, 13:35, 14:25, 16:40, 17:20, runs daily except Sunday, see Connections—Orvieto, above). While there's no official baggage-check service in Bagnoregio, I've arranged with Laurenti Mauro, who runs the Bar Enoteca just outside the Bagnoregio old-town gate, to let you leave your bags there (open 6:00–24:00 with a short lunch break, closed Thursday, from the Orvieto bus stop walk downhill and turn right on first street). Pay him L2,000 per bag or buy breakfast there.

Driving from Orvieto to Bagnoregio: Orvieto overlooks the autostrada (and has its own exit). The shortest way to Civita from the freeway exit is to turn left (below Orvieto) and follow the signs to Lubriano and Bagnoregio. The more winding and scenic route takes 20 minutes longer: From the freeway, pass under hillcapping Orvieto (on your right, signs to Lago di Bolsena, on Viale I Maggio); take the first left (direction: Bagnoregio), winding up past great Orvieto views, the Orvieto Classico vineyard (see above), through Canale, and through farms and fields of giant shredded wheat to Bagnoregio, where the locals (or rusty old signs) will direct you to Al Boschetto, just outside town. Either way, just before Bagnoregio, follow the signs left to Lubriano and pull into the first little square by the church on your right for a breathtaking view of Civita. Then return to the Bagnoregio road. Drive through Bagnoregio (following yellow "Civita" signs) and park at the base of the steep donkey path up to the traffic-free, 2,500-year-old, canyon-swamped pinnacle town of Civita di Bagnoregio.

THE CINQUE TERRE

The Cinque Terre (CHINK-wuh TAY-ruh), a remote chunk of the Italian Riviera, is the traffic-free, low-brow, under-appreciated alternative to the French Riviera. There's not a museum in sight. Just sun, sea, sand (well, pebbles), wine, and pure unadulterated Italy. Enjoy the villages, swimming, hiking, and evening romance of one of God's great gifts to tourism. For a home base, choose among five villages, each of which fills a ravine with a lazy hive of human activity. Vernazza is my favorite.

The area was first described in medieval times as "the five castles." Tiny communities grew up in the protective shadows of the castles ready to run inside at the first hint of a Turkish "Saracen" pirate raid. Many locals were kidnapped and ransomed or sold into slavery somewhere far to the east. As the threat of pirates faded, the villages grew with economies based on fish and grapes. Until the advent of tourism in this generation, they were very remote. Even today, traditions survive and each of the five villages comes with a distinct dialect and proud heritage.

Planning Your Time

The ideal minimum stay is two nights and a completely uninterrupted day. The Cinque Terre is served by the milk-run train from Genoa and La Spezia. Speed demons arrive in the morning, check their bag in La Spezia, take the five-hour hike through all five towns, laze away the afternoon on the beach or rock of their choice, and zoom away on the overnight train to somewhere back in the real world. Each town has its own character, and all are a few minutes apart by an hourly train. There's no checklist of sights or experiences; just the hike, the towns, and your fondest vacation desires.

For a good Cinque Terre day consider this: Pack your beach

Cinque Terre

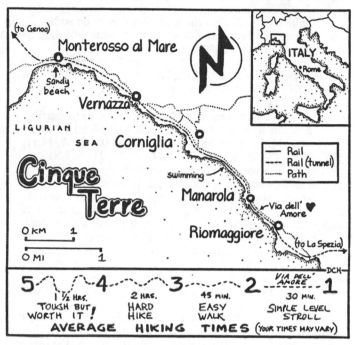

and swimming gear, wear your walking shoes, and catch the train to town #1: Riomaggiore. (Since I still get the names mixed up, I think of the five Cinque Terre towns by number.) Walk the cliff-hanging Via dell' Amore to Manarola (#2) and buy food for a picnic, then hike to Corniglia (#3) for a rocky but pleasant beach. Swim here or in the more resorty Monterosso (#5, a 10-minute train ride away). From #5, hike or catch the boat home to Vernazza (#4).

If you're into *il dolce far niente* (the sweetness of doing *nada*) and don't want to hike, you could enjoy the blast of cool train-tunnel air that announces the arrival of every Cinque Terre train and go directly to Monterosso al Mare, where a sandy "front door"–style beach awaits. The Cinque Terre has a strange way of messing up your momentum.

Getting Around the Cinque Terre

The city of La Spezia is the gateway to the Cinque Terre. In La Spezia's train station, the milk-run Cinque Terre train schedule is posted at the information window. Take the L2,000 half-hour train ride into the Cinque Terre town of your choice. Though the emphasis of this section is on trains, boats are getting more and more reliable (see below).

Cinque Terre Train Schedule: Since the train is the Cinque Terre lifeline, many shops and restaurants post the current schedule (train info tel. 1478-88088).

Trains leave La Spezia for the Cinque Terre villages (last year's schedule) at 6:00, 7:17, 8:10, 9:25, 10:00, 10:57, 11:43, 12:41, 13:15, 14:05, 15:00, 15:40, 17:15, 17:40, 19:10, 19:40, 21:10, and 23:00.

Trains leave Monterosso al Mare for La Spezia (departing Vernazza about 10 minutes later, last year's schedule) at 5:07, 6:30, 7:04, 8:30, 9:14, 10:14, 10:58, 11:31, 12:19, 13:09, 14:09, 14:52, 15:20, 16:10, 17:27, 18:25, 19:08, 20:09, 21:22, 21:39, 22:19.

Do not base your happiness on these train times. You must confirm at the station—look for the posted schedule.

To orient yourself, remember that directions are "*per* (to) Genoa" or "*per* La Spezia," and any train that stops at any of the villages other than Monterosso will stop at all five. (Note that many trains leaving La Spezia skip them all or stop only in Monterosso.) The five towns are just minutes apart by train. Know your stop. After leaving the town before your destination, go to the door to slip out before mobs pack in. Since the stations are small and the trains are long, you might need to get off the train deep in a tunnel, and you might need to open the door yourself.

If the train station is not staffed (which is usually the case in Vernazza, Corniglia, and Manarola), buy your ticket from the nearest newsstand or tobacco shop (in Vernazza, near the harbor) or on board from the conductor. If you buy from the conductor, explain, "*La stazione era chiusa*" ("the station was closed"); otherwise you'll pay a bit more.

Since a one-town hop costs the same as a five-town hop (L1,700), and every ticket is good for six hours with stopovers, save money and explore the region in one direction on one ticket. Stamp the ticket at the station machine before you board. Stations sell a L5,000 all-day Five-Terre pass. Don't spend a railpass flexiday on the Cinque Terre.

Boats: From Easter to late October the most frequent boat service is between Monterosso and Vernazza (L6,000 one way, L10,000 round-trip, nearly hourly from 10:00 to around 18:30, canceled when windy, tel. 0187-732-987). Aquavision runs red boats between Riomaggiore, Manarola, Vernazza, and Monterosso. Their much-hyped glass-bottomed boats are a disappointment if you expect to see anything other than water (L5,000 for one-town hop, L9,000 for Cinque Terre journey one way, 45 min total, 4/day each way, tel. 0187-817-456). Boat schedules may be posted at docks, harbor bars, or even at your hotel. The trains are more dependable and run year-round, but boats are a fun alternative.

VERNAZZA

With the closest thing to a natural harbor—overseen by a ruined castle and an old church—and only the occasional noisy slurping up of the train by the mountain to remind you these are the 1990s, Vernazza is my Cinque Terre home base.

The action is at the harbor, where you'll find a kids' beach, plenty of sunning rocks, outdoor restaurants, a bar hanging on the edge of the castle (great for evening drinks), the tiny town soccer field, and a tailgate-party street market each Tuesday morning.

The town's 500 residents, proud of their Vernazzan heritage, brag that "Vernazza is locally owned. Portofino has sold out." Fearing the change it would bring, they stopped the construction of a major road into the town and region. Families are tight and go back centuries; several generations stay together. Leisure time is spent wandering lazily together up and down the main street. Sit on a bench and study Vernazza's *passeggiata*. Then explore the characteristic alleys called *carugi*. In October the cantinas are draped with drying grapes. In the winter the population shrinks, as many people move to more comfortable big-city apartments.

A steep five-minute hike in either direction from Vernazza gives you a classic village photo op (for the best light, head toward Corniglia in the morning, toward Monterosso in the evening). Franco's Bar, with a panoramic terrace, is at the tower on the trail toward Corniglia.

The banks at the top of the town have decent rates. The Blue Marlin bar, which offers slow Internet access, opened a self-service laundry next door (L18,000 to wash and dry, Via Roma 49, a few steps from train station on main street, toward harbor). Accommodations are listed at the end of this chapter.

Sights—Vernazza

▲▲**Vernazza Town Top-Down Orientation Walk**—Walk uphill until you hit the parking lot, two banks, and post office. The tidy new square is called "Fontana Vecchia" after a long-gone fountain. Older locals remember the river filled with townswomen doing their washing. Begin your saunter downhill to the harbor.

Just before the "Pension Sorriso" sign you'll see the ambulance barn on the right. A group of volunteers are always on call for a dash to the hospital, 30 minutes away in La Spezia. Opposite that is a big empty lot behind Pension Sorriso. Like many landowners, Sr. Sorriso had plans to expand but the government said no. The old character of these towns is carefully protected.

Across from the "Pension Sorriso" sign is the honorary clubhouse for the ANPI (members of the local WWII resistance). Only five ANPI old-timers survive. Cynics consider them less than

Vernazza

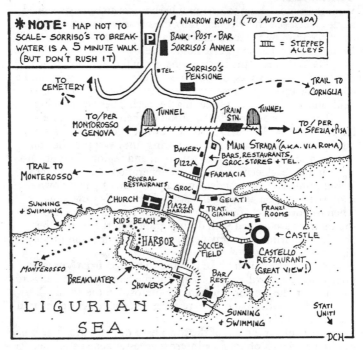

✳ NOTE: MAP NOT TO SCALE- SORRISO'S TO BREAK-WATER IS A 5 MINUTE WALK. (BUT DON'T RUSH IT)

↑ NARROW ROAD! (TO AUTOSTRADA)

BANK · POST · BAR
SORRISO'S ANNEX

IIII = STEPPED ALLEYS

P

• TEL.

SORRISO'S PENSIONE

TO CEMETERY ↑

TRAIL TO CORNIGLIA

TUNNEL   TRAIN STN.   TUNNEL

TO/PER MONTOROSSO & GENOVA ←   → TO/PER LA SPEZIA & PISA

BAKERY

"MAIN STRADA" (A.K.A. VIA ROMA)
← BARS, RESTAURANTS, GROC. STORES & TEL.

PIZZA

TRAIL TO MONTEROSSO ←

SEVERAL RESTAURANTS

FARMACIA

GROC.

CHURCH

SUNNING & SWIMMING

PIAZZA MARCONI

GELATI

TRAT. GIANNI

FRANZI ROOMS

KIDS BEACH →

← CASTLE

HARBOR

SOCCER 'FIELD'

CASTELLO RESTAURANT (GREAT VIEW!)

TO MONTEROSSO

BREAKWATER   SHOWERS ↗

BAR/ REST.

L I G U R I A N

S E A

SUNNING & SWIMMING

STATI UNITI ↓

—DCH—

heroes. After 1943 Hitler called up any boy over 15. Like any reasonably smart person, they escaped to the hills rather than fight for Hitler on the front. Only to remain free did they become "resistance fighters."

A few steps farther you'll see a monument to those killed in WWII. Not a family was spared. The tiny monorail *trenino* is parked quietly here except in September and October when it's busy helping locals bring down the grapes. From here the path leads to Corniglia. The school bus picks up children from the many tiny neighboring villages. Today only about 25 children attend the Vernazza elementary school. At this point, Vernazza's tiny river goes underground.

Under tracks you'll find posters for various volunteer organizations. The second track was recently renovated to lessen the disruptive noise.

Until the 1950s Vernazza's river ran open through the center of town from here to the *gelateria*. You can see where it once flowed.

Wandering through the main business center you'll pass

many locals doing their *vasca* (laps) past the tiny Chapel of Santa Marta where Mass is celebrated only on Palm Sunday, the Blue Marlin bar (a good breakfast place and the only night spot in town), the bakery, grocery, and pharmacy. Tiny lanes lead up in both directions (the best *carugi* are on the right).

To the left of the *gelateria* an arch leads to what was a beach and where the river used to flow out of town. Continue on down to the harbor square and breakwater or follow the trail (second path above the church toward Monterosso) to the classic view of Vernazza (best photos just before sunset).

▲▲▲**The Burned-Out Sightseer's Visual Tour of Vernazza**—Sit on the harbor breakwater (perhaps with a glass of local white wine from the Cantina del Molo, last door on left), face the town, and see . . .

The harbor: In a moderate storm you'd be soaked as waves routinely crash over the *molo* (breakwater, built in 1972). The train line, built 130 years ago to tie a newly-united Italy together, linked Turin and Genoa with Rome. A second line (hidden in a tunnel at this point) was built in the 1960s. The yellow building was Vernazza's first train station. You can see the four bricked-up waiting alcoves. Vernazza's fishing fleet is down to three small fishing boats (with the net spools)—the town's restaurants buy up everything they catch. Vernazzans are more likely to own a boat than a car. In the '70s tiny Vernazza had one of the top water polo teams in Italy and the harbor was their "pool." Later, when a real pool was required, Vernazza dropped out of the league.

The castle: On the far right, the castle (now a pleasant park, L2,000, open daily 9:00 or 10:00–19:00) still guards the town. The Belforte Bar (the fort was named *bea forte* or "loud screams," for the warnings it made back in pirating days) is a great and grassy perch. The lowest deck (follow the rope) is great for a glass of wine. (Inside the submarine-strength door, a photo of a major storm shows the entire tower under a wave.) The highest umbrellas mark the recommended Castello restaurant (see Eating, below).

The town: From the lower castle the houses were interconnected with an interior arcade—ideal for fleeing attacks. The pastel colors are regulated by a commissioner of good taste in the community government. The square before you is locally famous for some of the region's finest restaurants. The big red central house, the 12th-century site where Genoan ships were built, used to be a kind of guardhouse.

Above the town: The ivy-covered tower, another part of the city fortifications, reminds us of Vernazza's importance in the Middle Ages, when it was an important ally of Genoa (whose arch enemies were the other maritime republics of Pisa, Amalfi, and Venice). Franco's Bar (closed Tuesday), just behind the tower, welcomes hikers finishing, starting, or simply contemplating the

Corniglia–Vernazza hike with great town views. Vineyards fill the mountainside beyond the town. Wine production is down nowadays, as the younger residents choose less physical work. But locals still work their plots and proudly serve their family wine. A single steel train line winds up the gully behind the tower. This is for the vintner's *trenino*, the tiny service train.

The church and city hall: Vernazza's Ligurian Gothic church dates from 1318. The grey and red house above and to the left of the spire is the school. The red building to the right is the former monastery and present city hall. Vernazza and Corniglia function as one community. In 1995 they elected their popular mayor, a Communist, to his second five-year term. The party's banner (now the PDS or "people's democratic party of the left") decorates town walls. High school is in the "big city," La Spezia. Finally, on the top of the hill, with the best view of all, is the town cemetery where most locals plan to end up (*tutto completo* . . . but a new wing is under construction).

Cinque Terre Experiences

▲▲▲**Hiking**—All five towns are connected by good trails. Experience the area's best by hiking from one end to the other. The entire hike can be done in about four hours, but allow five for dawdling. While you can detour to hilltop sanctuaries, I'd keep it simple by following the easy red-and-white-marked low trails between the villages. A good L7,000 hiking map (sold in all the towns, not necessary for this described walk) covers the expanded version of this hike from Porto Venere through all five Cinque Terre towns to Levanto.

Riomaggiore–Manarola (20 min): Facing the front of the train station in Riomaggiore (town #1), go up the stairs to the right, following signs for the Via dell' Amore. The film-gobbling promenade—wide enough for baby strollers—leads down the coast to Manarola. While there's no beach here, stairs lead down to sunbathing rocks.

Manarola–Corniglia (45 min): From the Manarola (#2) waterfront it's easiest to take the high trail out of town. The broad and scenic low trail ends with steep stairs leading to the high road. The walk from #2 to #3 is a little longer and a little more rugged than that from #1 to #2. The high alternative via the hamlet of Volastra takes two hours and offers sweeping views and a closer look at the vineyards. Ask locally about the more difficult six-mile inland hike to Volastra. This tiny village, perched between Manarola and Corniglia, offers great views and the Five-Terre wine co-op; stop by the Cantina Sociale.

Corniglia–Vernazza (90 min): The hike from Corniglia (#3) to Vernazza (#4)—the wildest and greenest of the coast—is most rewarding. From the Corniglia station and beach, zigzag up to the town. Ten minutes past Corniglia toward Vernazza you'll see the well-hung Guvano beach far below (see below). The trail leads past a bar and picnic tables, through lots of fragrant and flowery vegetation, and scenically into Vernazza.

Vernazza–Monterosso (90 min): The trail from Vernazza to Monterosso (#5) is a scenic up-and-down-a-lot trek. Trails are rough (and some readers report "very dangerous") but easy to follow. Camping at the picnic tables midway is frowned upon. The views just out of Vernazza are spectacular.

▲**Swimming**—Wear your walking shoes and pack your swim gear. Each beach has showers that may work better than your hotel's. (Bring soap and shampoo.) Monterosso's beaches, immediately in front of the train station, are easily the best (and most crowded). It's a sandy resort with everything rentable . . . lounge chairs, umbrellas, paddleboats, and usually even beach access (L2,000). Vernazza has a sandy children's cove, sunning rocks, and showers by the breakwater. The tiny "Acque Pendente" (waterfall) cove that locals call their *laguna blu* between Vernazza and Monterosso is accessible only by small hired boat. Forget Manarola or Riomaggiore for beaches. I do my Cinque Terre swimming on the pathetic but peaceful man-made beach below the Corniglia station. Unfortunately, much of it has washed away, and it's almost nonexistent when the surf's up. What's left is clean and less crowded than the Monterosso beach, and the beach bar has showers, drinks, and snacks.

The nude Guvano (GOO-vah-noh) beach (between Corniglia and Vernazza) made headlines in Italy in the 1970s as clothed locals in a makeshift armada of dinghies and fishing boats retook their town beach. But big-city nudists still work on all-around tans in this remote setting. From the Corniglia train station (follow the road north, zigzag below the tracks, follow signs to tunnel) travelers buzz the intercom and the hydraulic *Get Smart*–type door is opened from the other end. After a 15-minute hike through a cool, moist, and dimly-lit unused old train tunnel, you'll emerge at the Guvano beach—and be charged L5,000 (L4,000 with this guidebook, water, no WC). A steep (free) trail also leads from the beach up to the Corniglia–Vernazza trail.

The crowd is Italian counterculture: pierced nipples, tattooed punks, hippie drummers in dreads, and nude exhibitionist men. The ratio of men to women is about three to two. About half the people on the pebbly beach keep their swimsuits on.

▲▲**Pesto**—This is the birthplace of pesto. Try it on spaghetti, *trofie*, or *trenette*. Basil, which loves the temperate Ligurian climate, is mixed with cheese (half *parmigiano* cow cheese and half *pecorino* sheep cheese), garlic, olive oil, and pine nuts, then poured over pasta. If you become addicted, small jars of it are sold in the local grocery stores.

▲▲**Wine**—The *vino delle Cinque Terre*, famous throughout Italy,

flows cheap and easy throughout the region. If you like sweet,
sherry-like wine, the local *sciacchetrà* wine is worth the splurge
(L5,000 per glass, often served with a cookie). While 10 kilos of
grapes yield seven liters of local wine, *sciacchetrà* is made from
near-raisins, and 10 kilos of grapes make only 1.5 liters of *sciacchetrà*. If your room is up a lot of steps, be warned: *sciacchetrà* is
18 percent alcohol, while regular wine is only 11 percent. In the
cool, calm evening, sit on the Vernazza breakwater with a glass
of wine and watch the phosphorous in the waves. While red wine
is sold as Cinque Terre wine, it's a fantasy designed to please
the tourists.

Cinque Terre Towns

(Note: Readers of this book fill Vernazza. For this reason you
might prefer to stay in one of these towns with fewer Americans.
See Sleeping, below.)

▲▲**Riomaggiore (town #1)**—The most substantial non-resort
town of the group, Riomaggiore is a disappointment from the train
station. But walk through the tunnel next to the train tracks (or
take the scenic high road, straight up and to the right) and you land
in a fascinating tangle of pastel homes leaning on each other as if
someone stole their crutches. There's homemade gelato at the Bar
Central on main street and, if Ivo is there, you'll feel right at home.
Riomaggiore's beach is just out of town (from the main street follow the "Marina" sign through the tunnel, then the "Spiaggia" sign
up the stairs to the left and around the cliff. The beach is more
rocky than sandy, but it's pleasant without Monterosso's crowds). A
cliff-hanging trail leads from the beach to a hilltop botanical garden and old WWII bunkers. Another climbs scenically to the
Madonna di Montenero sanctuary high above the town.

▲**Manarola (town #2)**—Like town #1, #2 is attached to its station by a 200-yard-long tunnel. Manarola is tiny and rugged, a
tumble of buildings bunny-hopping down its ravine to the tiny
harbor. Buy a picnic (stores close from 13:00–17:00) before walking to the beaches of Corniglia.

▲▲**Corniglia (town #3)**—From the station a footpath zigzags up
370 stairs to the only town of the five not on the water. Originally
settled by a Roman farmer who named it for his mother, Cornelia,
its ancient residents produced a wine so famous that vases found at
Pompeii touted its virtues. Today its wine is still its lifeblood. Follow the pungent smell of ripe grapes into an alley cellar and get a
local to let you dip a straw into her keg. Remote and less visited,
Corniglia has cooler temperatures, a windy belvedere, a few restaurants, and more than enough private rooms for rent. Past the train
station is the Corniglia beach and Albergo Europa, a bungalow village filled with Italians doing the Cinque Terre in 14 days.

▲▲**Monterosso al Mare (town #5)**—This is a resort with cars, hotels, rentable beach umbrellas, and crowds. Walk east of the station through the tunnel for the Old World charm (and the nearly hourly boats to Vernazza, 1998 departures: 10:15, 11:15, 12:15, 14:15, 15:45, 16:45, 17:45, 18:45). If you want a sandy beach, this is it. Adventurers may want to rent a rowboat or paddleboat and find their own private cove. The TI is open 10:00–12:00 and 15:30–19:30, and closed Sunday afternoon (exit station and go left, tel. 0187-817-506).

Sleeping and Eating on the Cinque Terre
(L1,700 = about $1, tel. code: 0187)
Sleep Code: **S** = Single, **D** = Double/Twin, **T** = Triple, **Q** = Quad, **b** = bathroom, **t** = toilet only, **s** = shower only, **CC** = Credit Card (Visa, MasterCard, Amex), **SE** = Speaks English, **NSE** = No English. Breakfast is included only in real hotels.

If you're trying to avoid my readers, stay away from Vernazza and Mama Rosa's. Rich, sun-worshipping softies like Monterosso. Winos and mountain goats prefer Corniglia. Students sleep cheap in Riomaggiore. Sophisticated Italians and Germans take stuffy Manarola.

While the Cinque Terre is too rugged for the mobs that ravage the Spanish and French coasts, it's popular with Italians, Germans, and Americans in the know. Room-finding is difficult on Easter, in August, and on summer Fridays and Saturdays. August weekends are worst.

Ideally, reserve ahead (a minimum of a couple of days) for summer visits. If you don't have reservations, arrive in the morning. Off-season, empty rooms abound: For the best value, arrive in the morning, ask around, visit three private rooms, and snare the best. Going direct cuts out a middleman and softens prices. Private rooms are generally bigger and more comfortable than those offered by the pensions.

Sleeping in Vernazza
(tel. code: 0187, zip code: 19018)
Vernazza, the essence of the Cinque Terre, is my favorite town. There is just one real pension, but two restaurants have about a dozen simple rooms each, and many locals rent extra rooms. Anywhere you stay here will require some climbing. Night noises can be a problem if you're near the station or the church bell tower. Address letters to 19018 Vernazza, Cinque Terre, La Spezia.

Trattoria Gianni rents 21 small rooms just under the castle. The funky ones are artfully decorated à la shipwreck, up lots of tight, winding, spiral stairs mostly with tiny balconies and grand views. The new comfy rooms lack views but have modern bathrooms and a super-scenic, cliff-hanger private garden. The Franzi family splits the work: Gianni maintains the restaurant's good reputation, and Anna and stoic Marisa (who doles out smiles like a rich gambler on a losing streak) run the rooms (two-night minimum required, S-L60,000, D-L90,000, Db-L110,000, Tb-L150,000, CC:VMA, Piazza Marconi 5, closed January–February, tel. & fax 0187-812-228, tel. 0187-821-003). Pick up your keys at the restaurant/reception on the harbor square and hike up the stairs to #41 (funky) or #47 (new) at the top. Communication can be difficult. No reply to your fax means they don't want to make a reservation (they get piles of requests and my tour company books this place 50 nights of the season). Telephone three days in advance and leave your first name and time of arrival.

Pension Sorriso knows it's the only real pension in town. Don't expect an exuberant welcome. Prices include breakfast and an obligatory, uninspired dinner (D-L150,000, Db-L180,000, cash only, 50 yards up from station, closed November–February, tel. 0187-812-224, fax 0187-821-198, no answer to your fax means they're full, some English spoken). While train sounds rumble through the front rooms of the main building, the annex up the street is quieter.

Albergo Barbara, on the harbor square, is run by kindly Giuseppe and his Swiss wife, Patricia. The nine rooms share three public showers and WCs (S-L60,000, tiny loft D-L80,000, bigger D-L90,000, family deals, loads of stairs, closed December–January, Piazza Marconi 21, tel. & fax 0187-812-398, SE). The big doubles come with grand harbor views and are the best value. The office is on the top floor of the big, red, vacant-looking building facing the harbor.

Affitta Camere: Vernazza is honeycombed year-round with pleasant, rentable private rooms and apartments (cheap for families, with kitchens). They are reluctant to reserve rooms far in advance. To minimize frustration call a day or two in advance, or simply show up by morning and look around. All are comfortable and inexpensive (L30,000–40,000 per person depending on the view). Some are lavish with killer views, and cost the same as a small dark place on a back lane over the train tracks. Little or no English is spoken at these places. Any main-street business has a line on rooms for rent.

Affitta Camere da Filippo is a good network of 15 rooms and apartments run by Antonio and his mother, Rita (D-L70,000, Db-L80,000, apartments-L100,000, Via A. Del Santo 62—take stairs across from the phone booths by railroad tracks—or ask at the Blue Marlin bar, tel. 0187-812-244). For rooms with some of the best harbor views in town, see the snooty harborfront **Gambero Rosso** restaurant (closed Monday, tel. 0187-812-265). Or try **Affitta Camere da Anna-Maria** (Db-L100,000 with view or terrace; turn left at pharmacy, climb via Carattino to #64, tel. 0187-821-082). Anna-Maria's German-speaking husband, Franco, runs the "Bar la Torre" (closed Tuesday) and rents noisy rooms at the top of the town. The lady at the grocery store across from the *gelateria* has a line on rooms (Giuseppina's villa is a modern, deluxe apartment without a view, Db-L80,000, Qb-L140,000, Via S. Giovanni Battista 7, tel. 0187-812-026).

Eating in Vernazza

If you're into Italian cuisine, Vernazza's restaurants are worth the splurge. All seem good and have similar prices. At about 20:00 wander around and compare the ambience. The **Castello**, run by gracious and English-speaking Monica and her family, serves great food with great views just under the castle (12:00–22:00, closed Wednesday and November–April, tel. 0187-812-296). On the harborfront, **Trattoria Franzi** and **Trattoria del Capitano** are more atmospheric and famous. **Gambero Rosso**, considered Vernazza's best restaurant, feels classy and costs only a few thousand lire more than the others. **Trattoria da Sandro**, which makes tasty meals, and the more off-beat and intimate **Trattoria da Piva** (closed Monday) may come with late-night guitar-strumming.

You can get good pizza by the slice on the main street. Grocery stores make inexpensive sandwiches to order (7:30–13:00, 17:00–19:30, closed Sunday afternoon). The town's only *gelateria* is good, and most harborside bars will let you take your glass on a breakwater stroll.

Locals take breakfast about as seriously as flossing. A cappuccino and a pastry or a piece of focaccia bread does it. The two harborfront bars offer the most ambience. The bakery is open early and makes ham and cheese on toast. Vernazza's only cybercafé, the **Blue Marlin** bar, offers the best selection of sandwiches, salads, and *bruschetta* (Friday–Wednesday 6:30–1:00, closed Thursday, just below the station, tel. 0187-821-149).

Sleeping in Riomaggiore
(tel. code: 0187, zip code: 19017)

Riomaggiore is bursting with private rooms. It's a very competitive scene. **Mar Mar Rooms** is a well-organized network of private rooms run by English-speaking Mario Franceschetti (Db-L80,000, bunky family deals, you can request kitchen, balcony, open year-round, Via Malborghetto 8, tel. & fax 0187-920-932).

Michielini Anna rents three rooms (Db-L80,000) and two apartments with kitchens (L40,000 apiece, up to five; across from the Central Bar at Colombo 143, tel. 0187-920-950, tel. & fax 0187-920-411, e-mail: camichie@tin.it, Daniela SE).

Luciano and Roberto Fazioli have five apartments, nine rooms, and a slummy seven-bed mini-hostel. You can pay as little as L25,000 for a bed in a shared apartment or up to L100,000 for a double room with bath; prices depend on views, amenities, and

the season (Via Colombo 94, tel. 0187-920-587 or 0187-920-904).
Edi has a similar network of rooms (Via Colombo 111, tel. 0187-920-325, fax 0187-920-325, cell phone: 033-8619-0434).

If friendly Ivo or Alberto are on duty at the **Bar Central**,
they'll help you find a room (tel. 0187-920-208). Ivo lived in San
Francisco and speaks great English. His Bar Central is a good stop
for breakfast, prize-winning gelato, and e-mail and Internet access
(e-mail: barCENTR@tin.it, L10,000 for half-hour). It's the only
lively late-night place in town.

Youth Hostel Mama Rosa is run with a splash of love and
craziness by Rosa Ricci (an agressively friendly character who
snares backpackers at the train station); her husband, Carmine
(a.k.a. "Papa Rosa"); and their English-speaking son, Silvio. This
unique comedy of errors creates a special bond among the young,
rugged, and poor who sleep here. Many consider it a slum. It's a
chaotic but manageable jumble with the ambience of a YMCA
locker room filled with bunk beds (L25,000 beds—price promised
through 1999; 20 yards directly in front of the station; no curfew;
just show up without a reservation—the earlier the better; no telephone). The nine co-ed rooms, with four to ten beds each, are
plain, basic, and poorly ventilated. But a family atmosphere rages
with hand-wash laundry facilities, trickle-down showers (best in
afternoon), and Silvio's five cats. This is one of those rare places
where perfect strangers become good friends with the slurp of
spaghetti, and wine supersedes the concept of ownership. For sanity, sleep at the new Manarola hostel. For value, spend a few extra
lire and find a private room. For new friends, the aroma of cat pee,
and memories you'll be unable to forget, it's Mama Rosa's.

Eat well at **La Lampara** (check out the *frutti di mare* pizza,
trenete al pesto, and the rice with seafood; closed Tuesday) on Via
Colombo. The Pizzeria at Via Colombo 26 serves thick and delicious pizza by the slice.

Sleeping in Manarola
(tel. code: 0187, zip code: 19010)
The first place is near the harbor, and the rest (in the order in which
you will encounter them) are up the hill above the train tracks.

Marina Piccola has 10 bright, modern rooms on the water,
so they figure a warm welcome is unnecessary (Db-L130,000,
requires dinner in July and August, CC:VMA, tel. 0187-920-103,
fax 0187-920-966).

Up the hill and a five-minute walk from the station, the
utterly normal **Albergo ca' d'Andrean** is quiet, comfortable,
modern, and very hotelesque, with 10 big sunny rooms and a cool
garden oasis complete with orange trees (Db-L110,000, closed
November, Via A. Discovolo 101, tel. 0187-920-040, fax 0187-
920-452, Simone SE).

Farther up the street, **Casa Capellini** rents four rooms (D-L70,000; the *alta camera* on the top with a kitchen, private terrace, and knockout view-L100,000; take a hard right on the church square, then two doors down the hill on your right, Via Ettore Cozzani 12, tel. 0187-920-823 or 0187-736-765, run by a quiet older man and his daughter, who speak no English).

La Torretta, on the church square, has two compact apartments with kitchens (L90,000), two doubles (L65,000), and a single (L40,000), all designed by English-speaking architect/ manager Gabriele Baldini (views, big garden, breakfast-L8,000, open year-round; with back to church, look left across square, Piazza della Chiesa, Vico Volto 14, tel. & fax 0187-920-327).

Ostello 5-Terre, Manarola's new youth hostel, is just off the church square at the top of the town (beds-L25,000, 48 beds in four- to six-bed rooms, closed 10:00–17:00 and all November, Via B. Riccobaldi 21, tel. 0187-920-215, fax 0187-920-218, Web site: www.cinqueterre.net/ostello/, e-mail: ostello@cdh.it).

Sleeping and Eating in Corniglia
(tel. code: 0187, zip code: 19010)
Private rooms run about L70,000 for a double without bath and L80,000 with bath. **Maria Guelfi** (tel. 0187-812-178) and **Senora Silvana** (tel. 0187-513-830) offer rooms (from the main square, Largo Tarago, head past Bar Trattoria La Lanterna) at the town-end promontory. The **Lanterna** also rents rooms (tel. 0187-812-291). **Affittasi Vista Mare** has rooms scattered all over town (Via Villa 3, tel. 0187-812-293). Try Domenico Spora (Via Villa 19, tel. 0187-812-293) or **Pellegrini**, which has three rooms (Via Solferino 34, tel. 0187-812-184), or **Villa Sandra** (Via Fieschi 212, tel. 0187-812-384). **Villa Cecio** is more of a hotel (on main road 212 yards toward Vernazza, views, tel. 0187-812-043). There is a slim chance someone will be waiting for stray travelers at the station with a car to run you up to their place in the town—otherwise, prepare for a 15-minute uphill hike.

Ristorante Cecio is a tasty splurge (closed Wednesday); **Bar Trattoria La Laterna** is disappointing in comparison.

Sleeping in Monterosso
(tel. code: 0187, zip code: 19016)
Monterosso al Mare, the most beach-resorty of the five Cinque Terre towns, offers maximum comfort and ease. There are plenty of hotels, rentable beach umbrellas, shops, and cars. The TI (Pro Loco) can find you a L40,000-per-person room in a private home (below station, open 10:00–12:00 and 15:30–19:30, closed Sunday afternoon, tel. 0187-817-506). If driving to Monterosso, leave the freeway at the Carrodano exit (30 minutes from there to Monterosso) and park (L10,000/day) in the huge beachfront guarded lot.

The following hotel listings are in the order you'll see them as you leave the station heading right (two hotels) or left (the rest of the hotels).

Turn right leaving the station to the grumpy, money-grubbing **Hotel Baia**. Facing the beach, more than half of the Baia's 30 comfortable rooms come with great beachfront balconies—confirm prices (Db-L180,000–200,000 including breakfast, CC:VM, Via Fegina 88, tel. 0187-817-512, fax 0187-818-322, SE). Farther on, **Hotel Cinque Terre** is a slick new building with 54 similar rooms (Db-L180,000–200,000, breakfast included, open April–October, CC:VM, reconfirm reservations, easy parking, Via IV Novembre 21, tel. 0187-817-543, fax 0187-818-380). From beach road, turn right at the "Il Gigante" restaurant sign. Drivers will find the hotel on the big road into (not out of) town; signs say "Hotel 5 Terre."

Turn left out of the station to the bright, airy **Pension Agavi** (eight rooms, Db-L110,000–130,000, tel. 0187-817-171, fax 0187-818-264, Claudia SE). The tunnel then leads to the old town and three unexceptional places that require dinner mid-June through mid-September: the neglected but cheap **Albergo Marina** (Db-L110,000, open March–October, Via Buranco 40, tel. & fax 0187-817-242 or 0187-817-613), the fancy and more expensive **Albergo degli Amici** (no views, next door at Via Buranco 36, tel. 0187-817-544, fax 0187-817-424), and **Ristorante/Pensione al Carugio** (two D-L90,000, Db-L105,000-145,000, modern, blocky, no-view apartment at top of town, Via S. Pietro 15, tel. & fax 0187-817-453).

Farther on, the lovingly managed **Hotel Villa Steno** features great view balconies, private gardens off some rooms, TVs, telephones, all the comforts, and the friendly help of English-speaking Matteo. Of his 16 rooms, 12 have view balconies (Sb-L120,000, Db-L180,000, Tb-L210,000, Qb-L250,000, with hearty buffet breakfast, L10,000 discount per room per night if you pay with cash and show this book; 10-minute hike from the station at the top of the old town at Via Roma 109, tel. 0187-817-028 or 0187-818-336, fax 0187-817-056, Web site: www.pasini.com, e-mail: steno@pasini.com). Readers get a free glass of the local sweet wine, *sciacchetrà*, when they check in—ask. The Steno has a tiny parking lot (free, but call to reserve a spot). The same family runs the **Albergo Pasquale**, a decent place with less character but comfortable and closer to the beach. While Villa Steno is quieter, it's a climb from the beach and station. If Steno is full, they'll honor Steno prices at Pasquale (first place after tunnel, air-conditioning, Via Fegina 4, tel. 0187-817-550 or 0187-817-477, fax 0187-817-056, Felicita and Matteo SE).

Sleeping near the Cinque Terre

La Spezia: When all else fails, you can stay in a noisy, bigger town like La Spezia. Each of the following places is within a block of the train station. The elegant, old, newly restored **Hotel Firenze e Continentale** has all the classy comforts but no parking (Db-L190,000, maybe L170,000 in slow time, includes buffet breakfast, good group rates, CC:VMA, air-conditioning, elevator, Via Paleocapa 7, 19122 La Spezia, tel. 0187-713-200, fax 0187-714-930, SE). **Albergo Parma**, bright and bleachy clean with TVs and folding metal furniture in the rooms, is located just below the station, down the stairs (D-L75,000, Db-L90,000, CC:VM, Via Fiume 143, 19100 La Spezia, tel. 0187-743-010, fax 0187-743-240). **Hotel Terminus** has filthy rooms with worn-out carpets, yellow walls, and old plumbing (D-L50,000, Db-L70,000, Via Paleocapa 21, just down from the station, tel. 0187-703-436). Friday morning a huge open-air market sprawls for about a mile from the station. The Museo Amedeo Lia displays Italian paintings from the 13th to 18th centuries (L12,000, Tuesday–Sunday 10:00–13:00 and 17:00–20:00, Via Prione 234, tel. 0187-731-100).

Santa Margherita Ligure: If you need the movie-star's Riviera, park your yacht at Portofino. Or you can settle down in Santa Margherita Ligure (20 minutes by bus from Portofino and an hour by train north of the Cinque Terre). While Portofino's velour allure is tarnished by snobby residents and a nonstop traffic jam in peak season, Santa Margherita tumbles easily downhill from its huggable train station. The town has a fun resort character with a breezy promenade (TI: tel. 0185-287-485). Buses go from the station and the harborfront to Portofino (3/hrly, L1,700), but the boat does it with more class and without the traffic jams. Hikers count the SM–PF hike as one of the best on the Riviera. The Sabini family offers 12 nonsmoking rooms in the stately old **Hotel Nuova Riviera** (D-L115,000, Db-L150,000, T-L150,000, Tb-L180,000, CC:V, cramped parking, peaceful garden; 10-minute walk from the station; walking or driving, follow signs to hospital, on Piazza Mazzini see hotel signs, Via Belvedere 10-2, 16038 S. Margherita Ligure, tel. & fax 0185-287-403, son John Carlo SE). **Hotel Terminus**, right at the station, works hard to keep its travelers happy (Db-L150,000 with huge breakfast, CC:VMA, good meals, tel. 0185-286-121, fax 0185-282-546; son Angelo SE).

Transportation Connections—Cinque Terre

The five towns of the Cinque Terre are on a milk-run train line described earlier in this chapter. Hourly trains connect each town with the others, La Spezia, and Genoa. While a few of the milk-run trains go to more distant points (Milan or Pisa), it's faster to change in La Spezia to a bigger train.

From La Spezia by train to: Rome (10/day, 4 hrs), **Pisa** (hrly, 1 hr), **Florence** (hrly, 2.5 hrs, change at Pisa), **Milan** (hrly, 3 hrs, change in Genoa), **Venice** (2 direct 6-hr trains/day—also from Monterosso).

AMSTERDAM

Amsterdam is a progressive way of life housed in Europe's most 17th-century city. It's a city built on good living, cozy cafés, great art, street-corner jazz, stately history, and a spirit of live and let live. It has 800,000 people and as many bikes, with more canals than Venice—and as many tourists. While Amsterdam may box your Puritan ears, this great, historic city is an experiment in freedom.

Planning Your Time

While I'd sleep in nearby Haarlem, Amsterdam is worth a full day of sightseeing on even the busiest itinerary. While the city has a couple of must-see museums, its best sight is its own breezy ambience. Here are the essential stops for a day in Amsterdam (while it's easily doable on foot with a few hops on tram #20, lacing these sightseeing highlights together by bike—as described below—affords a more vivid experience):

Start the day by touring the Anne Frank House. Finish your morning at the city's two great art museums: Rijksmuseum (cafeteria for lunch) and Van Gogh.

Spend mid-afternoon taking a relaxing hour-long canal cruise (from the dock at Spui). Near Spui consider seeing the idyllic Begijnhof, the Amsterdam Historical Museum, and the flower market.

In the late afternoon, walk from Spui down the busy Kalverstraat pedestrian street to Dam Square, the heart of Amsterdam (palace, church, monument). From Dam Square the Red Light District is several blocks northeast (see map), or walk down Damrak a few blocks to get back to the train station.

With extra time: With two days in Holland, I'd side-trip by bike, bus, or train to an open-air folk museum and visit

Haarlem. With a third day I'd do the other great Amsterdam museums. With four days I'd visit the Hague.

Orientation (tel. code: 020)

The central train station is your starting point (TI, bike rental, and trolleys and buses fanning out to all points). Damrak is the main street axis, connecting the station with Dam Square (people-watching and hangout center) and its Royal Palace. From this spine the city spreads out like a fan, with 90 islands, hundreds of bridges, and a series of concentric canals (named "Prince's," "Gentleman's," and "Emperor's") laid out in the 17th century, Holland's Golden Age. The city's major sights are within walking distance of Dam Square.

Tourist Information

Try to avoid Amsterdam's inefficient VVV office across from the train station. ("VVV" is Dutch for tourist information office; daily 9:00–17:00; TI in train station open Monday–Saturday 7:45–20:00, Sunday 8:00–17:00). Most people wait 30 minutes just to pick up the information brochures and get a room. Avoid this line by studying the wall display of publications for sale and going straight to the sales desk (where everyone ends up anyway, since any information of substance will cost you). Consider buying a city map (f4), *What's On* (f4, monthly entertainment calendar), *Amsterdam: Your Favorite Capital* (f5 for two booklets covering attractions, museums, restaurants, and bars), and any of the walking tour brochures (f4, "Discovery Tour Through the Center," "The Former Jewish Quarter," "Walks Through Jordaan"). The "Amsterdam Culture & Leisure Pass," offering free or discounted admissions to some sights and boat rides, isn't worth the clutter or cost (f36.75, doesn't include Anne Frank House). Nor does it make sense to stand in line at the VVV to buy prepaid same-cost admissions to various Amsterdam sights.

The TI on Leidsestraat is much less crowded (daily 9:00–20:00, closing at 19:00 on Saturday and 17:00 on Sunday). But for f1 a minute you can save yourself a trip by calling the tourist information toll-line at 06-3403-4066 (Monday–Saturday 9:00–17:00). If you're staying in nearby Haarlem, use the helpful Haarlem TI (see Haarlem section, below) to answer most of your Amsterdam questions and provide you with the brochures.

At Amsterdam's Central Station, GWK Change has two hotel reservations windows that sell phone cards and cheaper city maps (f3), and answer basic tourist questions. The lines are short and move quickly. They also change money, including coins, for a hefty f5 fee (near the lockers, at the right end of the station as you leave the platform).

Don't use the TI (or GWK) to book a room. The phone

system is easy, everyone speaks English, and the listings in this book are a better value than the potluck booking you'd be charged for at the TI.

Helpful Hints
Many shops close all day Sunday and Monday morning. A *plein* is a square, *gracht* means canal, and most canals are lined by streets with the same name. Handy telephone cards (f10, f25, or f50) are sold at the TI, the GVB public transit office, tobacco shops, the post office, and train stations. The Dutch go *"surfen"* at the Internet Center a couple blocks east of the Rijksmuseum (9:00–18:00, closed Sunday, Monday morning, and Saturday by 17:00, Weteringschans 165, tel. 0800-0403, Web site: www.eteringschans.com). Beware of the bogus telephone offices dressed up like government outlets but ready to rip you off. Tourists are considered green and rich, and the city has more than its share of hungry thieves.

Arrival in Amsterdam
By Train: Amsterdam swings, and the hinge that connects it to the world is its perfectly central Central Station. Walk out the door and you're in the heart of the city. You'll nearly trip over trams ready to take you anywhere your feet won't. Straight ahead is Damrak street, leading to Dam Square. With your back to the entrance of the station, the TI and GVB public transit office are to your left, just across the train tracks.

By Plane: From Schiphol Airport, take the train to Amsterdam (6/hrly, 20 min, f6). If you'll be staying in Haarlem, take a direct express bus from the airport to Haarlem (#236 or #362, 2/hrly, 30 min, f7).

Getting Around Amsterdam
The helpful transit-information office (GVB) is next to the TI (in front of the train station). Its free multilingual *Tourist Guide to Public Transport* includes a transit map and explains ticket options and tram connections to all the sights. Ask for the free "Circle Tram 20" brochure listing all of the stops (and nearby sights) of this handy tram that makes a loop around Amsterdam (#20A goes clockwise, #20B goes counterclockwise).

By Bus, Tram, and Metro: Individual tickets cost f3 and give you an hour on the buses, trams, and metro system (on trams and buses pay as you board; on the metro buy tickets from machines before boarding). **Strip cards** are cheaper than buying individual tickets. Any downtown ride costs two strips (good for an hour of transfers). A card with 15 strips costs f11.50 at the GVB public transit office, train stations, post offices, airport, or tobacco shops throughout the country (senior discount available); shorter strip tickets (two, three, and eight strips) are also sold on some buses and trams. Strip cards are good on buses all over Holland (e.g., six strips for Haarlem to the airport), and you can share them with your partner. An f12 **Day Card** gives you unlimited transportation on the buses and metro for a day in Amsterdam; you'll almost break even if you take three trips (valid until 6:00 the following morning; buy when you board or at the GVB public transit office, which also sells a two-day version for f15). If you get lost in Amsterdam, 10 of the city's 17 trams take you back to the central train station.

By Foot: The longest walk a tourist would take is 45 minutes from the station to the Rijksmuseum. Watch out for silent but potentially painful bikes, trams, and curb posts.

By Bike: One-speed bikes, with "brrringing" bells and two locks (use them both; bike thieves are bold and brazen here), rent for f9.5 per day at the central train station (daily 8:00–22:00; deposit of f200, $120, or your credit-card imprint required; entrance to the left down the ramp as you leave the station, tel. 020/624-8391). In the summer, arrive early or make an easy telephone reservation.

By Boat: While the city is great on foot or bike, there is a "Museum Boat" and a similar "Canal Bus," with an all-day ticket that permits tourists to shuttle from sight to sight. Tickets cost f22 (with discounts that will save you about f5 on admissions). The sales booths in front of the central train station (and the boats) offer handy free brochures with museum times and admission prices. The narrated ride takes 90 minutes if you don't get off (every 30 minutes in summer, every 45 minutes off-season, seven stops, live quadrilingual guide, departures 10:00–17:00, discounted after 13:00 to f15, tel. 020/622-2181).

Sights—Amsterdam's Museum Neighborhood

▲▲▲**Rijksmuseum**—Focus on the Dutch masters: Rembrandt, Hals, Vermeer, and Steen. For a list of the top 20 paintings, pick up the cheap f1 leaflet "A Tour of the Golden Age" and plan your attack (or follow the self-guided tour, one of 20, in my *Mona Winks* guidebook). Audiotaped tours are available (f7.50, more than 200 paintings described, shortcuts advisable).

Follow the museum's chronological layout to see painting evolve from narrative religious art, to religious art starring the Dutch love of good living and eating, to the Golden Age, when secular art dominates. With no local church or royalty to commission big canvases in the post-1648 Protestant Dutch republic, artists specialized in portraits of the wealthy city class (Hals), pretty still lifes (Claesz), and nonpreachy slice-of-life art (Steen). The museum has four quietly wonderful Vermeers. And, of course, a thoughtful brown soup of Rembrandt, including the *Night Watch*. Works by Rembrandt show his excellence as a portraitist for hire (*De Staalmeesters*) and offer some powerful psychological

Amsterdam

studies, such as *St. Peter's Denial*—with Jesus in the murky background (f15, daily 10:00–17:00, great bookshop, decent cafeteria; tram #2, #5, or #20 from the station; Stadhouderskade 42, tel. 020/673-2121).

▲▲▲**Van Gogh Museum**—Next to the Rijksmuseum, this outstanding and user-friendly museum is a stroll through a beautifully displayed garden of van Gogh's work and life (f12.50, daily 10:00–17:00, Paulus Potterstraat 7, tel. 020/570-5200). The museum also focuses on the late 19th-century art that influenced van Gogh (it happened to be in his brother Theo's collection).

The f7 audioguides include insightful commentaries about van Gogh's paintings including related quotes from Vincent himself.

Note: This museum, which has been closed for renovation, will reopen in May '99. If you visit prior to May, look for van Gogh's art in the south wing of the Rijksmuseum.

Stedelijk Modern Art Museum—Next to the Van Gogh Museum, this place is fun, far-out, and refreshing. It has mostly post-1945 art, but also a sometimes-outstanding collection of Monet, van Gogh, Cézanne, Picasso, and Chagall, and a lot of special exhibitions (f9, daily 11:00–19:00, closes at 17:00 November–March, tel. 020/573-2737).

Sights—Near Dam Square

▲▲**Anne Frank House**—This house offers a fascinating look at the hideaway where young Anne hid when the Nazis occupied the Netherlands. Pick up the English pamphlet at the door. An expanded exhibit, new for 1999, offers more thorough coverage of the Frank family, the diary, the stories of others who hid out, and the Holocaust (f10, daily 9:00–21:00 April–August, closes daily at 17:00 September–March, 263 Prinsengracht, tel. 020/556-7100). For an interesting glimpse of Holland under the Nazis, rent the powerful movie *Soldier of Orange* before you leave home.

Westerkerk—Near Anne Frank's House, this landmark church, with a barren interior and Amsterdam's tallest steeple, is worth climbing for the view (f3, ascend only with a guide, departures on the hour, Monday–Saturday 10:00–16:00 April–September, closed Sunday, tel. 020/612-6856).

Royal Palace (Koninklijk Paleis)—The palace, right on Dam Square, was built when Amsterdam was feeling its global oats. It's worth a look (f5, daily 12:30–17:00 June–August, less off-season).

▲**Begijnhof**—Step into this tiny, idyllic courtyard in the city center to escape the crazy 1990s and feel the charm of old Amsterdam. Notice house #34, a 500-year-old wooden structure (rare since repeated fires taught city fathers a little trick called brick). Peek into the hidden Catholic church, opposite the English Reformed church, where the pilgrims worshiped while waiting for their voyage to the New World (marked by a plaque near door). Be considerate of the people who live here (free, on Begijnensteeg Lane, just off Kalverstraat between #130 and #132, pick up English info flier at office near entrance).

Amsterdam Historical Museum—Offering the town's best look into the age of the Dutch masters, this creative and hardworking museum features Rembrandt's paintings, fine English descriptions, and a carillon loft. The loft comes with push-button recordings of the town bell tower's greatest hits and a self-serve carillon "keyboard" to ring a few bells yourself. The museum is

next to the Begijnhof, Kalverstraat 92 (f11, Monday–Friday
10:00–17:00, Saturday and Sunday 11:00–17:00, good-value
restaurant, tel. 020/523-1822). Its free pedestrian corridor is a
powerful teaser.

Sights—East Amsterdam

Rembrandt's House—This place is interesting only to Rembrandt's fans. There are 250 etchings (f7.5, Monday–Saturday
10:00–17:00, Sunday 13:00–17:00, 15-minute English audiovisual
presentation upon request, Jodenbreestraat 4, tel. 020/638-4668).
Holland Experience—With the slogan "Experience Holland in
30 minutes," this show combines footage of Holland with multivisual effects (e.g., as you see a boat sailing, you feel wind on your
face). It's fun but pricey, and focuses more on goofy tourists than
on the wonders of Holland (f17.50, daily 10:00–18:30, Jodenbreestraat 8, near Rembrandt's House and Waterlooplein street
market, metro: Waterlooplein, tel. 020/422-2233).
▲Tropenmuseum (Tropical Museum)—As close to the Third
World as you'll get without lots of vaccinations, this imaginative
museum offers wonderful re-creations of tropical-life scenes and
explanations of Third World problems (f10, Monday–Friday
10:00–17:00, Saturday and Sunday 12:00–17:00, tram #9 to Linnaeusstraat 2, tel. 020/568-8215).
Netherlands Maritime (Scheepvaart) Museum—This kid-friendly museum is fascinating if you're into Henry Hudson or
scheepvaarts (f12.50, daily 10:00–17:00, closed Monday
October–April, English explanations, bus #22 or #28 to Kattenburgerplein 1, tel. 020/523-2222).

Sights—Red Light District

Our Lord in the Attic (Amstelkring)—Near the station, in the
red light district, you'll find a 17th-century merchant's house
turned museum, with a fascinating hidden church. This dates from
1661, when post-Reformation Dutch Catholics were not allowed
to worship in public. The church fills the attics of several homes
(f7.50, Monday–Saturday 10:00–17:00, Sunday 13:00–17:00, O.Z.
Voorburgwal 40, tel. 020/624-6604).
▲Red Light District—Europe's most high-profile ladies of the
night shiver and shimmy in display-case windows between the
Oude Zijds Achterburgwal and Oude Zijds Voorburgwal, surrounding the Oude Kerk (Old Church). It's dangerous late at
night but a fascinating walk at any other time after noon.

According to CNN statistics, more than 60 percent of Amsterdam's prostitutes are HIV-positive (but a naive tourist might
see them as just hardworking girls from Latin America or Africa
trying their best to build up a bank account—f50 at a time).

Amsterdam has two sex museums, one in the red light district and one a block in front of the train station on Damrak. While visiting one can be called sightseeing, visiting both is a bit obsessive. Here's a comparison:

The red light district sex museum is less offensive, with five sparsely decorated rooms relying heavily on badly-dressed dummies acting out the roles that women of the neighborhood play. It also has videos, phone-sex phones, and a lot of uninspired paintings, old photos, and sculpture (f5, along the canal at Oude Zijds Achterburgwal 54).

The Damrak sex museum goes much deeper, with many more rooms. It tells the story of pornography from the 1860s through today, starting with early French pornographic photos. Every sexual deviation is uncovered in its various displays, and the nude and pornographic art is a cut above the other sex museum's. Also interesting is the international sex art and memorabilia from Europe, India, and Asia. You'll find a Marilyn Monroe tribute and some S&M displays, too (f4, Damrak 18, a block in front of the station).

More Sights—Amsterdam

▲**Herengracht Canal Mansion** (Willet Holthuysen Museum)—This 1687 patrician house offers a fine look at the old rich of Amsterdam, with a good 15-minute English introductory film and a 17th-century garden in back (f7.50, Monday–Friday 10:00–17:00, Saturday and Sunday 11:00–17:00, tram #4 or #9 to Herengracht 605, tel. 020/523-1870).

Vondelpark—This huge and lively city park gives a fragrant look at today's Dutch youth, especially on sunny summer weekends.

Leidseplein—Brimming with cafés, this people- and pigeon-watching square is an impromptu stage for street artists, accordionists, jugglers, and unicyclists. Sunny afternoons are the liveliest. Stroll nearby Lange Leidsedwarsstraat (one block north) for a taste-bud tour of ethnic eateries from Greece to Indonesia.

Shopping—Amsterdam brings out the browser even in those who were not born to shop. Ten general markets, open six days a week, keep folks who brake for garage sales pulling U-ies. Shopping highlights include Waterlooplein (flea market); the huge Albert Cuyp street market; various flower markets (daily along Singel Canal near the mint tower, or Munttoren); diamond dealers (free cutting and polishing demos at shops behind the Rijksmuseum and on Dam Square); and Kalverstraat, Amsterdam's teeming walking/shopping street (parallel to Damrak).

Tours of Amsterdam

▲▲**Canal-Boat Tour**—These long, low, tourist-laden boats leave continually from several docks around the town for a good, if uninspiring, one-hour quadrilingual introduction to the city (f13, 2/hrly, more frequent in summer). One very central company is at the corner of Spui and Rokin, about five minutes from Dam Square (9:30–22:00, tel. 020/623-3810). No fishing allowed, but bring your camera for this relaxing orientation. Some prefer to cruise at night when the bridges are illuminated.

Biking and Walking Tours—The Yellow Bike Tour company offers bike tours (f29 for three-hour city tour, f42.50 for 6.5-hour 35-kilometer countryside tour) as well as city walking tours for groups by arrangement (f15, 1.75 hours) daily April through November (Nieuwezijds Kolk 29, near train station, tel. 020/620-6940).

Do-It-Yourself Bike Tour of Amsterdam—A day enjoying the bridges, bike lanes, and sleepy off-the-beaten-path canals on your own one-speed is the essential Amsterdam experience. Do it Dutch-style: on two wheels. The real joys of Europe's best-preserved 17th-century city are the countless intimate glimpses it offers: the laid-back locals sunning on their porches under elegant gables, rusted bikes that look as if they've been lashed to the same lamppost since the '60s, wasted hedonists planted on canalside benches.

For a good day, rent a bike at the station. Head west down Haarlemmerstraat, working your wide-eyed way through the Prinsengracht (along the canal) and gentrified Jordaan area to Westerkerk, with the tallest spire in the city. Tour Anne Frank's House.

Pedal past the palace, through Dam Square, down Kalverstraat (the city's bustling pedestrian mall), and poke into the sleepy Begijnhof. Roll down tacky Leidsestraat. Lunch near Spui or at the Leidseplein (see Eating, below). Catch the hour-long cruise at Spui. Pedal to the Rijksmuseum and Van Gogh Museum, inhale art, then pedal back to the train station. For a detour through seedy, sexy, pot-smoking Amsterdam, roll down Damstraat, then down Oudezijds Voorburgwal through the land of Rastafarian "coffee shops," red lights over black tights, and sailors lost without the sea.

To escape to the countryside, hop on the free ferry for both pedestrians and bikes behind the Amsterdam station. In five minutes Amsterdam will be gone and you'll be rolling through your very own Dutch painting. (See Getting Around Amsterdam, above, for info on bike rental.)

Brewery Tour—The infamous Heineken brewery tours are in full slosh Monday through Friday from 9:30 to 11:00 (f2; also open 13:00 and 14:30 mid-June–mid-September, and 11:00, 13:00, and 14:30 Saturdays July–August; Stadhouderskade 78, near the Rijksmuseum). Try to arrive a little early.

Sleeping in Amsterdam
(f1 = about 60 cents, tel. code: 020)
Sleep Code: S = Single, **D** = Double/Twin, **T** = Triple, **Q** = Quad, **b** = bathroom, **t** = toilet only, **s** = shower only, **CC** = Credit Card (Visa, MasterCard, Amex). Nearly everyone speaks English

in the Netherlands, and prices include breakfast unless noted.

While I prefer sleeping in cozy Haarlem (see below), those into more urban charms will find that Amsterdam has plenty of beds. For a f5 fee, the VVV (tourist office) can find you a room in the price range of your choice.

Sleeping near the Station

Amstel Botel, the city's only remaining "boat hotel," is a ship-shape, bright, and clean floating hotel with 175 rooms (Sb-f125, Db-f143, Tb-f180, worth the extra f10 for canalside view, breakfast-f11, f30/day parking pass, CC:VMA, 400 yards from the station, on your left as you leave, you'll see the sign, Oosterdokskade 2-4, 1011 AE Amsterdam, tel. 020/626-4247, fax 020/639-1952).

Sleeping between Dam Square and Anne Frank's House

Hotel Toren is a chandeliered historic mansion in a pleasant, canalside setting in downtown Amsterdam. This splurge is classy, quiet, and two blocks northeast of Anne Frank's (S-f85, Sb-f185–200, three unadvertised D-f170, Db-f200–275, Tb-f240, pay for canalside rooms—it's worth it; bridal suites for f285–400 make you want to get married; prices vary according to season; CC:VMA, Keizersgracht 164, 1015 CZ Amsterdam, tel. 020/622-6352, fax 020/626-9705, e-mail: hotel.toren@tip.nl).

Well-heeled readers will prefer the pricier, fancier 17th-century **Canal House Hotel**, a few doors down, for its beautiful antique interiors, candlelit evenings, and soft music (Sb-from f215, Db-f235–280, CC:VMA, elevator, Keizersgracht 148, 1015 CX Amsterdam, tel. 020/622-5182, fax 020/624-1317, e-mail: canalhousehotel@compuserve.com).

Cheap hotels line the noisy main drag between the town hall and Anne Frank's House. Expect a long, steep, and depressing stairway, with quieter rooms in the back. **Hotel Aspen**, a good value for a budget hotel, is tidy, simple, and well-maintained, with firm beds (S-f55, D-f80, Db-f120, Tb-f130-150, Qb-f180, CC:MA, ideally reserve by fax using credit-card number, Raadhuisstraat 31, 1016 DC Amsterdam, tel. 020/626-6714, fax 020/620-0866). A few doors away, **Hotel Pax** has large, plain, but airy rooms, carefully managed by Mr. and Mrs. Veldhuizen (tiny D-f75, large D-f90, T-f105, showers down the hall, Raadhuisstraat 37, tel. 020/624-9735).

$54

Sleeping in the Leidseplein Area

The area around Amsterdam's museum square (Museumplein) and the rip-roaring nightlife center (Leidseplein) is colorful, comfortable, convenient, and affordable.

Hotel Keizershof is a wonderfully Dutch place, with six bright,

Amsterdam Hotels

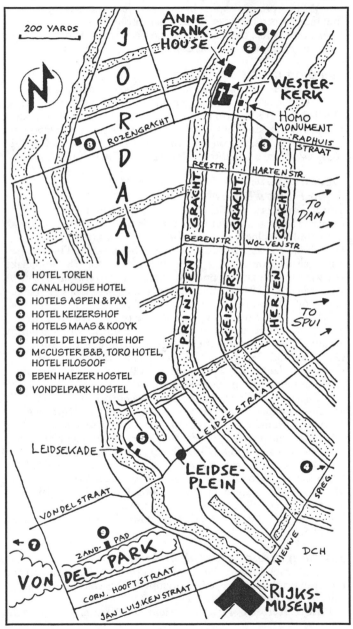

200 YARDS

JORDAAN

ANNE FRANK HOUSE

WESTER-KERK

HOMO MONUMENT

RADHUIS STRAAT

ROZENGRACHT

REESTR.   HARTENSTR.

PRINSENGRACHT

KEIZERSGRACHT

HERENGRACHT

TO DAM

BERENSTR.   WOLVENSTR.

TO SPUI

❶ HOTEL TOREN
❷ CANAL HOUSE HOTEL
❸ HOTELS ASPEN & PAX
❹ HOTEL KEIZERSHOF
❺ HOTELS MAAS & KOOYK
❻ HOTEL DE LEYDSCHE HOF
❼ McCUSTER B&B, TORO HOTEL,
   HOTEL FILOSOOF
❽ EBEN HAEZER HOSTEL
❾ VONDELPARK HOSTEL

LEIDSE STRAAT

LEIDSEKADE

LEIDSE-PLEIN

VONDELSTRAAT

NIEUWE SPIEG.

VON DEL PARK

ZAND- PAD

DCH

CORN. HOOFT STRAAT

JAN LUIJKEN STRAAT

RIJKS-MUSEUM

airy rooms in a 17th-century canal house. You'll climb a steep spiral staircase to rooms named after old-time Hollywood stars. The friendly De Vries family has made this place a treat for 38 years and offers its guests plenty of fine eating advice (S-f75, D-f125, Ds-f135, Db-f150, T-f175, Tb-f200, nonsmoking, includes classy breakfast, nice garden, CC:VM, where Keizers canal crosses Spiegelstraat at Keizersgracht 618, 1017 ER Amsterdam, tel. 020/622-2855, fax 020/624-8412). It's a 10-minute walk from Leidseplein.

The next two hotels are on a quiet street, easy to reach from the central station (tram #1, #2, #5, or #20 to Leidseplein, then head west a block along the north side of canal), and within easy walking distance of the Rijksmuseum.

Hotel Maas, with a phone, TV, and coffeepot in every room, is a big, well-run, elegant, quiet, and hotelesque place (S-f110, one D-f125, Db-f225–275, prices vary with view and room size, extra person-f50, suite-f375, CC:VMA, hearty breakfast, air-conditioning, elevator, Leidsekade 91, 1017 PN Amsterdam, tel. 020/623-3868, fax 020/622-2613, e-mail: maas@worldaccess.nl).

Kooyk Hotel is a dumpy but cheap dive, with 17 rooms, four on the ground floor. Halls are narrow, some top rooms are disappointing, bedspreads and furnishings are faded, but the canalside rooms are bright (S-f75, D-f120, T-f165, Q-f200, Quint-f225, CC:VM, Leidsekade 82, 1017 PM Amsterdam, tel. 020/623-0295, fax 020/638-8337, run by Pierre).

Hotel Seven Bridges, decorated with antiques, is a lot nicer than my house. The 11 rooms feature fine draperies, woven carpets, and beautifully crafted furniture, though some may find the big mirrors above the beds on the walls a bit weird (Sb-f170–230, two D-f150, Db-f200–300, prices vary with quality, ask for room #5 for a splurge, CC:VMA, near Rembrandtplein, Reguliersgracht 31, 1017 LK Amsterdam, reserve three to four weeks in advance, tel. 020/623-1329). Take trams #16, #24, or #25 from the station and get off at "Keizersgracht."

Hotel De Leydsche Hof is canalside with simple, quiet rooms. Its peaceful demeanor almost helps you overlook the flimsy cots and old carpets (D-f85, Db-f95–110, Tb-f130, Qb-f170, no breakfast, Leidsegracht 14, 10-minute walk from Leidseplein, 1016 CK Amsterdam, tel. 020/623-2148, run by friendly Mr. Piller).

Sleeping near Vondelpark

These options connect you with the sights via an easy tram ride or a pleasant 15-minute walk or short bike ride through Vondelpark.

Karen McCuster, a friendly Englishwoman, rents cozy rooms in her home as a B&B without the breakfast. Rooms are clean, white, and bright with red carpeting and green plants; one room has a private rooftop patio. Advance reservations are necessary (D-f80–110 per night). Tram #2 from the station gets you to Zeilstraat 22 (third floor, 1075 SH Amsterdam, tel. 020/679-2753, fax 020/670-4578); get off at "Amstelveenseweg" and cross street in same direction that tram runs (every 10 minutes; buy ticket or day card on board).

Toro Hotel, in a peaceful residential area at the edge of Vondelpark, is your personal turn-of-the-century hotel/mansion, with an elegant dining hall and 22 rooms with TVs, safes, and phones. Rooms in the back overlook the park, canal, and terrace, which is yours for relaxing. Mr. Plooy fusses over his guests (Ss-f165, Sb-f200, Db-f250, Tb-f300, CC:VMA, elevator, easy parking, Koningslaan 64, 1075 AG Amsterdam, tel. 020/673-7223, fax 020/675-0031). Take tram #2 from the station; get off at "Koningslaan."

Hotel Filosoof greets you with Aristotle and Plato in the foyer and classical music in its lobby. Its 25 rooms are subtly decorated with themes; the Egyptian room has a frieze of hieroglyphics. Philosophers' sayings hang on walls, professors wander down the halls, and on Thursday evenings in fall, guests meet to discuss philosophy—in Dutch. The rooms are small (and split between two buildings), but the hotel is endearing and the terrace is made for pondering (Sb-f155, Db-f185, Tb-f235, Qb-f275, CC:VMA, cheaper off-season, all rooms with TV and phone, reserve three weeks in advance for summer weekends, Anna Vondelstraat 6, five-minute walk from tram #6 line, get off at "Constantyn Huygenstraat," tel. 020/683-3013, fax 020/685-3750).

Hostels

Christian Youth Hostel Eben Haezer is scruffy, with 20-bed women's dorms and a 40-bed men's dorm. Friendly, well-run, and in a great neighborhood, it has Amsterdam's best rock-bottom budget beds (f22.50 per bed with sheets and breakfast, maximum age 35, near Anne Frank's House, Bloemstraat 179, tel. 020/624-4717, e-mail: eben@globalxs.nl). It serves cheap, hot meals, runs a snack bar, offers lockers to all, leads nightly Bible studies, and closes the dorms from 10:00 to 14:00. The hostel will happily hold a room for a phone call (three to seven days in advance in the summer). Its sister Christian hostel, **The Shelter** (in the red light district, open to any traveler, f22.50 for a bed, tel. 020/625-3230), is similar but definitely not preaching to the choir.

The city's two IYHF hostels are **Vondelpark**, Amsterdam's top hostel (f34.50 with breakfast, S-f72, D-f90, nonmembers pay f5 extra, lots of school groups, 6–22 beds per dorm, right on the park at Zandpad 5, tel. 020/683-1744, fax 020/589-8955); and Stadsdoelen YH (f25.25 with breakfast, f5 extra without YH card, f6.25 for sheets, just past Dam Square, closed January, Kloveniersburgwal 97, tel. 020/624-6832, fax 020/639-1035).

Eating in Amsterdam

Dutch food is basic and hearty. *Eetcafés* are local cafés serving budget sandwiches, soup, eggs, and so on. Cafeterias, *broodje* (sandwich shops), and automatic food shops are also good bets for budget eaters. Picnics are cheap and easy. A central supermarket is **Albert Heijn** near the flower market, at the corner of Koningsplein and Singel canal (Monday–Saturday 10:00–20:00, Sunday 12:00–18:00).

Eating near Spui in the Center

The city university's **Atrium** is a great, budget cafeteria (f9 meals, Monday–Friday 12:00–14:00 and 17:00–19:30; from Spui, walk west down Landebrug Steeg past the canalside Café 't Gasthuys three blocks to Oudezijds Achterburgwal 237, go through arched doorway on the right, tel. 020/525-3999). **Café 't Gasthuys**, one of Amsterdam's many "brown" cafés (named for their smoke-stained walls), makes good sandwiches and offers indoor or canal-side seating (daily 12:00–1:00, walk west down Landebrug Steeg to Grimburgwal 7).

La Place, a cafeteria on the ground floor of the Vroom Dreesmann department store, has islands of entrées, veggies, fruits, desserts, and beverages (Monday–Saturday 10:00–21:00, Thursday until 22:00, Sunday 11:00–21:00, near Mint Tower, corner of Rokin and Muntplein). The locals splurge for Dutch food at **Restaurant Haesje Claes** (f25 entrées, daily 12:00–22:00, Spuistraat 275, tel. 020/624-9998). **Blincker Theatercafé** is popular with the younger crowd (open from 19:00, St. Barberenstraat 7-9, tel. 020/627-1938).

Eating in or near the Train Station

Keuken van 1870 has been cooking basic, cheap cafeteria meals in a simple setting since, you guessed it, 1870 (Monday–Friday 12:30–20:00, weekends 16:00–21:00, Spuistraat 4, several blocks west of station, tel. 020/624-8965). The train station has a surprisingly classy budget self-service Stationsrestauratie on platform 1 (Monday–Saturday 7:00–22:00, Sunday from 8:00).

Eating near Anne Frank's House

For pancakes in a family atmosphere, try the **Pancake Bakery** (f11 pancakes, splitting is OK, offers an Indonesian pancake for those who want two experiences in one, daily 12:00–21:30, Prinsengracht 191, one block north of A.F. House, tel. 020/625-1333). Across the canal, DeBolhoed serves great vegetarian food (daily 12:00–22:00, Prinsengracht 60, tel. 020/626-1803).

Eating near the Rijksmuseum, on Leidseplein

The art deco **American Hotel** dining room serves an elegant all-you-can-eat f12 salad bar (available 12:00–14:30 and 18:00–20:30, where Leidseplein hits Singel Canal). **De Smoeshaan** offers classy and tasty f25 meals (next to Hotel Maas, 50 meters down Singel canal from the American Hotel). On the café-packed street called Lange Leidsedwarsstraat, **Bojo** is a reasonably-priced Indonesian restaurant at #51 (Monday–Wednesday 16:00–1:30, Thursday–Sunday 12:00–1:30, 020/622-7434). If hunger hits in the **Rijksmuseum,** head for the cafeteria in the west wing's ground floor.

Bars

Try a *jenever* (Dutch gin), the closest thing to an atomic bomb in a shot glass. While cheese gets harder and sharper with age, *jenever* grows smooth and soft. Old *jenever* is best.

Drugs

Amsterdam, Europe's counterculture mecca, thinks the concept of a "victimless crime" is a contradiction. While hard drugs are definitely out, marijuana causes about as much excitement as a bottle of beer. A "pot man" with a worldly menu of f25 baggies is a fixture in many bars (walk east from Dam Square on Damstraat for a few blocks, then down to Nieuwmarkt). While several touristy Bulldog cafés are very popular with tourists, less-glitzy smaller places (farther from the tourists) offer a better value and a more comfortable atmosphere. Near the corner of Leidsestraat and Prinsengracht, the **Easy Times** rasta coffee shop dangles its menu from a string at the bar. At the brighter **Tops** coffee shop next door, you can use the Internet to say high to your friends back home. **Homegrown Fantasy** coffee shop and gallery, about two blocks northwest of Dam Square, has a gentle Dutch atmosphere and cosmic restroom (daily 9:00–24:00, Nieuwe Zijds Voorburgwal 87a, tel. 020/627-5683). They also have a grow shop next door.

The tiny **Grey Area** coffee shop is a cool, welcoming, and smoky hole-in-the-wall appreciated among local aficionados as a seven-time winner of Amsterdam's Cannabis Cup award. Judging by the proud autographed photos on the wall, many of America's most famous heads have dropped in. You're welcome to just nurse a bottomless cup of coffee (open high noon to 22:00, closed Monday, between Dam Square and Anne Frank's House at Oude Leliestraat 2, tel. 020/420-4301, e-mail: greyarea@xs4all.nl).

▲**Marijuana and Hemp Museum**—This is a collection of dope facts, history, science, and memorabilia (f8, daily 11:00–22:00, Oudezijds Achterburgwal 148, tel. 020/623-5961). While quite small, it has a shocker finale: the high-tech grow room in which dozens of varieties of marijuana are cultivated in optimal hydroponic (among other) environments. Some plants stand five feet tall and shine under the intense grow lamps. The view is actually through glass walls into the neighboring "Sensi Seed Bank" Grow Shop (which sells carefully cultivated seeds and all the gear needed to grow them). Pot should never be bought on the street in Amsterdam. Well-established coffee shops are considered much safer. Up to five grams of marijuana can be sold in coffee shops per person per day. Minimum age for purchase: 18 years.

Transportation Connections—Amsterdam

Amsterdam's train-information center requires a long wait. Save lots of time by getting train tickets and information in a small-town station or travel agency. For phone information, call 0900-9292 for local trains or 0900-9296 for international (75 cents/min, daily 7:00–24:00, wait through recording and hold . . . hold . . . hold . . .).

By train to: Schiphol Airport (6/hrly, 20 min, f6.25), Haarlem (6/hrly, 15 min, f10.50 round-trip), The Hague (4/hrly, 45 min), Rotterdam (4/hrly, 1 hr), Brussels (hrly, 3 hrs), Oostende (hrly, 4 hrs, change in Roosendaal), Paris (5/day, 5 hrs, required fast train from Brussels with f21 supplement), London (4/day, 10–12 hrs), Copenhagen (5/day, 11 hrs), Frankfurt (10/day, 5 hrs), Munich (8/day, 8 hrs, change in Mannheim), Bonn (10/day, 3 hrs), Bern (8/day, 9 hrs, change in Basel).

Amsterdam's Schiphol Airport: The airport, like most of Holland, is English-speaking, user-friendly, and below sea level. Its banks offer fair rates (24 hours daily, in arrivals). Schiphol Airport has easy bus and train connections (seven miles) into Amsterdam or Haarlem. The airport also has a train station of its own. (You can validate your Eurailpass and hit the rails immediately or, to stretch your train pass, buy the short ticket today and start the pass later.) Schiphol flight information (tel. 06-350-34050 or 0900-503-0141) can give you flight times and your airline's Amsterdam number for reconfirmation before going home (f1 per minute to climb through its phone tree).

HAARLEM

Cute, cozy yet real, and handy to the airport, Haarlem is a fine home base, giving you small-town, overnight warmth with easy access (15 minutes by train) to wild and crazy Amsterdam.

Haarlem is a busy Dutch market town, buzzing with shoppers biking home with fresh bouquets. Enjoy Saturday (general) and Monday (clothing) market days, when the square bustles like a Brueghel painting with cheese, fish, flowers, and families. You'll feel comfortable here. Buy some flowers to brighten your hotel room.

Orientation (tel. code: 023)

Tourist Information: Haarlem's VVV, at the train station, is friendlier, more helpful, and less crowded than Amsterdam's. Ask your Amsterdam questions here (Monday–Friday 9:00–17:30, Saturday 10:00–14:00, closed Sunday, tel. 0900-616-1600, f1 a minute).

Arrival in Haarlem: As you walk out of the train station, the TI is on your right and the bus station is across the street. Two parallel streets flank the train station (Kruisweg and Jansweg). Head up either one and you'll reach the town square and church within 10 minutes. If uncertain of the way, ask a local person, "Grote Markt?" ("Main Square?"), and they'll point you in the right direction.

Helpful Hints: The handy GWK change office at the station offers decent exchange rates (Monday–Saturday 8:00–20:00, Thursday and Friday until 21:00, Sunday 9:00–17:00). The train station rents bikes cheaply and easily (f9.50/day, f100 deposit, Monday–Saturday 6:00–1:00, Sunday 7:30–24:30). Haarlem lacks a cyber café, but even non-guests are welcome to use Hotel Amadeus' computer (f7.50/30 minutes). My Beautiful Laundrette is handy, self-service, and cheap (f10 wash and dry, daily 8:30–20:30, near Vroom Dreesman department store at Boter Markt 20). The VVV and local hotels have a helpful parking brochure.

Sights—Haarlem

▲▲**Frans Hals Museum**—Haarlem is the hometown of Frans Hals, and this delightful museum displays many of his greatest paintings in a glorious old building (f8, Monday–Saturday 11:00–17:00, Sunday 13:00–17:00, tel. 023/516-4200). Enjoy take-me-back paintings of old-time Haarlem. Peter Brueghel the Younger's painting *Proverbs* (outside room #24) shows 72 old Dutch proverbs; the handy English-language key gives you a fascinating peek into the Dutch old days. The museum across the street features the architecture of old Haarlem.

Corrie Ten Boom House—As many Americans (but few Dutch) know, Haarlem is also home to Corrie Ten Boom (popularized by *The Hiding Place*, an inspirational book and movie about the Ten Boom family's experience hiding Jews from the Nazis). The Ten Boom House, at Barteljorisstraat 19, is open for 45-minute English tours (donation requested, Tuesday–Friday 10:00–16:00, Saturday until 15:30; open Tuesday–Saturday 11:00–15:00 November–April; only one tour/day off-season, tel. 023/531-0823). Some of the guides do more preaching than teaching.

Grote Kerk (Church)—You'll see (and maybe hear) Holland's greatest pipe organ (regular free concerts mid-May–mid-October on Tuesdays at 20:15; additional concerts in July and August on Thursdays at 15:00; confirm schedule at TI). The church is open and worth a look, if only to see its Oz-like organ (f2.50, Monday–Saturday 10:00–16:00; closes at 15:00 in winter). Note how the organ, which fills the west end, seems to steal the show from the altar. To enter the church, look for the small entrance marked "*Entree*" behind the church, kitty-corner from La Plume restaurant. (There is a handy public WC in the east end of the church.) The new church (Kathedrale Basiliek Sint Bavo at Leidsevaart 146) offers free concerts on Saturdays at 15:00 from April through September.

▲**Teylers Museum**—Famous as the oldest museum in Holland, it used to be interesting mainly as a look at a 200-year-old museum. New exhibition halls (with rotating exhibits) and a café have brought life to the dusty exhibits. Stop by if you enjoy mixing, say, Renaissance sketches with pickled coelacanths (f7.50, Tuesday–Saturday 10:00–17:00, Sunday 12:00–17:00, Spaarne 16, tel. 023/531-9010).

Red Lights—For a little red light district precious as a Barbie doll, wander around the church in Haarlem's cutest Begijnhof (two blocks northeast of the big church, off Lange Begijnestraat, no

Haarlem

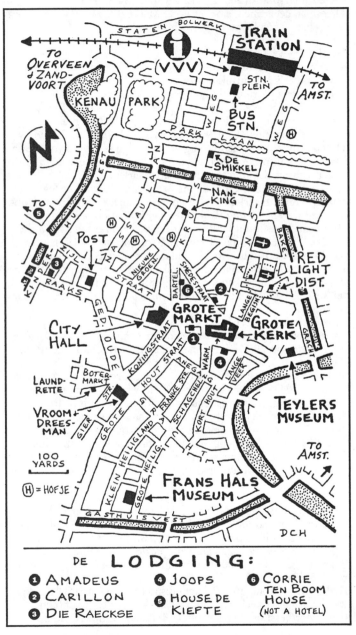

STATEN BOLWERK

TRAIN STATION

TO OVERVEEN & ZANDVOORT

(VVV)

STN. PLEIN

TO AMST.

BUS STN.

KENAU PARK

PARK LAAN

DE SMIKKEL

NAN-KING

TO 5

Post

H

RED LIGHT DIST.

City Hall

GROTE MARKT

GROTE KERK

Laundrette

BOTER-MARKT

VROOM DREES-MAN

TEYLERS MUSEUM

TO AMST.

100 YARDS

H = HOFJE

FRANS HALS MUSEUM

GASTHUIS VEST

DCH

DE LODGING:

1 AMADEUS
2 CARILLON
3 DIE RAECKSE
4 JOOPS
5 HOUSE DE KIEFTE
6 CORRIE TEN BOOM HOUSE (NOT A HOTEL)

senior or student discounts). Don't miss the mall marked by the red neon sign, t'Steegje. The nearby t'Poortje ("office park") costs f7.50.

Nightlife in Haarlem

Haarlem's evening scene is great. The bars around the Grote Kerk and Lange Veerstraat are colorful, lively, and always full of music.

The **Studio**, jammed with Haarlem's 30-something crowd, has a pleasant ambience (on the square, next to Hotel Carillon). **Café Brinkman**, also on the square, is a good people-watching perch. **Café 1900** (across from the Corrie Ten Boom House) is classy by day and draws a young crowd with live music on Sunday nights. **Lange Veerstraat** (behind the church) is probably the best bar street in town. The **Crack** (Lange Veerstraat 32) is the wild and leathery place to go for loud music and smoking. Across the street at **High Times** (#47), smokers can choose from 16 varieties of joints in racks behind the bar (neatly prepacked in trademarked "Joint Packs", f2.50 to f7.50). The **Imperial Café and Bar** has live music every Monday, Wednesday, Thursday, and Friday (a few doors down from the Crack, at Korte Veerstraat 3).

Don't be shocked if locals drop into a bar, plunk down f25 for a baggie of marijuana, and casually roll a joint. (If you don't like the smell of pot, avoid "coffee shops" sporting Rastafarian yellow, red, and green colors; wildly painted walls; or plants in the windows.)

Sleeping in Haarlem
(f1 = about 60 cents, tel. code: 023)
Sleep Code: S = Single, **D** = Double/Twin, **T** = Triple, **Q** = Quad, **b** = bathroom, **t** = toilet only, **s** = shower only, **CC** = Credit Card (Visa, MasterCard, Amex).

The helpful Haarlem tourist office ("VVV" at the train station, Monday–Friday 9:00–17:30, Saturday 10:00–14:00, tel. 0900-616-1600, f1/minute) can nearly always find you a f32.50 bed in a nearby private home (for a f9-per-person fee plus a cut of the hotel's money).

Haarlem is most crowded in April, on Easter weekend, May, and August, but if you phone ahead, my recommended hotels will happily hold a room without a deposit (though they may ask for a credit-card number). Nearly every Dutch person you'll encounter speaks English. The listed prices include breakfast (unless otherwise noted) and usually include the f3.50 per-person-per-day tourist tax. To avoid this town's louder-than-normal street noises, forego views for a room in the back. Don't needlessly use the TI's room-finding service. Call direct.

Hotel Amadeus, on the town square, has 15 small, bright rooms, all with simple modern furnishings, TVs, private showers, and toilets. Some have views of the square. This characteristic hotel, ideally located above a turn-of-the-century dinner café, is relatively quiet and has an elevator. The lush old lobby is on the second floor in a "*pianola* bar" (Sb-f90, Db-f120, Tb-f165, nicer rooms go to earliest reservations, seconds-on-everything buffet breakfast, kid-friendly, a 12-minute walk from train station, CC:VMA, use credit card to secure reservations, Grote Markt 10, 2011 RD Haarlem, tel. 023/532-4530, fax 023/532-2328, e-mail: info@amadeus-hotel.com, Web site: www.amadeus.com, brothers Dave and Mike run the place for their family).

Hotel Carillon, also right on the town square, has an ideal location. Many of the well-worn rooms are small, the stairs are ste-e-e-p, and front rooms come with great town-square views, lots of street noise, and double-paned windows (22 rooms, tiny loft sin-gles-f57.50, Db-f137, Tb-f180.50, Qb-f194, no elevator, 12-minute walk from train station, CC:VMA, Grote Markt 27, 2011 RC Haarlem, tel. 023/531-0591, fax 023/531-4909). The Carillon also runs the nearby **Die Raeckse Hotel**, which has fewer stairs, less character, more traffic noise, smoky halls, and decent rooms (Sb-f92.50–110, Db-f135–160, CC:VMA, attached restaurant, Raaks 1, 2011 VA Haarlem, tel. 023/532-6629, fax 023/531-7937).

Hotel Joops is an innovative concept. A well-organized central office, just behind the church in the town center, administers a cor-ral of 80 rooms in different buildings (all within three blocks of the church). They have cheap, run-down, spacious rooms (S-f55, D-f95, T-f130); and new, elegant suites with kitchenettes (Db-f125–145, Tb-f165–195, CC:V, get one day free if you stay a week, office at Oude Groenmarkt 20, 2011 HL Haarlem, tel. 023/532-2008, fax 023/532-9549, e-mail: joops@hotelinformation.com).

Bed and Breakfast House de Kiefte, your get-into-a-local-home budget option, epitomizes the goodness of B&Bs. Marjet (mar-yet) and Hans, a young Dutch couple who speak fluent Eng-lish, rent four bright, cheery, nonsmoking rooms (with good breakfast and travel advice) in their quiet, 100-year-old home (S-f50, Ds-f90, T-f130, Qs-f165, Quint/s-f190, cash only, minimum two nights, family loft sleeps up to five, very steep stairs, kid-friendly, Coornhertstraat 3, 2013 EV Haarlem, tel. 023/532-2980, cellular phone 06/5474-5272). It's a 15-minute walk or f12 taxi ride from the train station, and a five-minute walk from the cen-ter. From Grote Markt (main square) walk straight out Zijlstraat, over the bridge, and take a left on the fourth street.

Family Dekker B&B is in a fine, quiet neighborhood near the station. For 25 years Mrs. Dekker has given her guests a cheery welcome in her clean but well-worn place (small D-f60, D-f70, T-f105, Q-f140, three-night minimum, closed 12:00–18:00 and October–March, one block from the station at Ripperdastraat 9, 2011 KG Haarlem, tel. 023/532-0554).

Hotel Lion D'Or is a classy business hotel with all the pro-fessional comforts, an attached restaurant, and a handy location.

Don't expect a warm welcome (Sb-f203, Db-f272, extra beds-f50, request a "weekend package" at least three days in advance to get substantial weekend discounts June–September and in winter months, some nonsmoking rooms, CC:VMA, across the street from the station at Kruisweg 34, 2011 LC Haarlem, tel. 023/532-1750, fax 023/532-9543).

The 300-room, very American **Hotel Haarlem Zuid** is sterile but a good value for those interested only in sleeping and eating (Db-f127, Tb-f150.50, breakfast-f13.50, elevator, easy parking, inexpensive hotel restaurant, in an industrial zone, a 20-minute walk from the center on the road to the airport, CC:VMA, Toekenweg 2, 2035 LC Haarlem, tel. 023/536-7500, fax 023/536-7980). Buses #70, #72, and #75 connect the hotel to the station and town square every 10 minutes.

Sleeping near Haarlem

Pension Koning, a 15-minute walk north of the station or quick hop on bus #71, has five simple rooms in a rowhouse in a residential area (S-f40, D-f80, T-f120, two-night minimum, includes breakfast, Kleverlaan 179, 2023 JC Haarlem, tel. 023/526-1456).

Hostel Jan Gijzen charges f24.75 for beds in six-bed dorms (f5 extra for nonmembers), f6.50 for sheets, and includes breakfast (daily 7:00–24:00, closed November–February, Jan Gijzenpad 3, two miles from the Haarlem station—take bus #2, or a five-minute walk from the Santpoort Zuid train station, tel. 023/537-3793, fax 023/537-1176).

Eating in Haarlem

Eating between Grote Markt (Main Square) and Train Station

Enjoy an Indonesian *rijsttafel* feast at the **Nanking Chinese-Indonesian Restaurant** (Kruisstraat 16, a few blocks off Grote Markt, tel. 023/532-0706, daily 12:30–22:00). Couples eat plenty, heartily, and more cheaply by splitting a f24.50 Indonesian rice table for one. (Each eater should order a drink.) Say hi to gracious Ai Ping and her daughter, Fan. Don't let them railroad you into a Chinese (their heritage) dinner. They also do cheap and tasty take-out.

Going Dutch? How about pancakes for dinner at **Pannekoekhuis "De Smikkel"**? Dinner and dessert pancakes cost f12 each; there's a f2.50-per-person cover charge, so splitting pancakes is OK (daily until 20:00, two blocks in front of station, Kruisweg 57, tel. 023/532-0631).

Eat well and surrounded by trains in the classy Station Restaurant (between tracks #3 and #4) in Old World atmosphere in the Netherlands' oldest train station (kitchen 12:00–20:00, also serves continental breakfast from 6:30 weekdays and 8:00 on weekends).

Eating on or near Zijlstraat

Eko Eet Café is great for a cheery, tasty vegetarian meal (f18 menu, daily 17:30–21:30, Zijlstraat 39).

For a "bread line" experience with basic/bland food, well-worn company, and the cheapest price in town (f9), eat at **Eethuis St. Vincent** (Monday–Friday 12:00–13:30 and 17:00–19:00, Nieuwe Groenmarkt 22).

The friendly **De Buren** offers traditional Dutch food and handlebar mustache fun (such as *draadjesvlees*—beef stew with applesauce; and *oma's kippetje*—grandmother's chicken) to happy locals (daily 17:00–22:00, Brouwersvaart 146, near intersection with Zijlsingel, across the canal from Die Raeckse Hotel and close to House de Kiefte B&B, tel. 023/534-3364).

Eating between Church and Frans Hals Museum

For good food, classy atmosphere, and f30 dinners, try the **Bastiaan** (opens at 18:00, closed Monday, CC:VMA, Lange Veerstraat 8, off Grote Markt, behind the church). Nearby, **La Plume** is a less expensive steak house (open daily at 17:30, CC:VMA, Lange Veerstraat 1). Popular with locals, **Jacobus Pieck** offers a varied menu selection (daily 10:00–22:00, Sundays from 12:00, Warmoesstraat 18, tel. 023/532-6144). For a (f2) cone of old-fashioned local French fries, drop by **Friethuis de Vlaminck** on Warmoesstraat 3 (closed Sunday and Monday).

Dine at the Indonesian **De Lachende Javaan** ("The Laughing Javanese," opens at 17:00, closed Monday, Frankestraat 25, tel. 023/532-8792) or get Indonesian take-out from the **Toko Nina** deli (Koningstraat 48, just off Grote Markt).

For a candlelit dinner of cheese and wine, consider **In't Goede Uur** (opens at 17:30, closed Monday, Korte Houtstraat 1).

For a healthy budget lunch with Haarlem's best view, eat at **La Place**, on the top floor or roof garden of the Vroom Dreesman department store (Monday–Saturday 9:30–18:00, Thursday until 21:00, closed Sunday, on the corner of Grote Houtstraat and Gedempte Oude Gracht).

Picnic-shoppers head to the **DekaMarkt** (Monday–Saturday 8:30–20:00, closed Sunday, Gedemple Oude Gracht 54, between Vroom Dreesman department store and the post office).

Transportation Connections—Haarlem

By train to: Amsterdam (6/hrly, 15 min, f10.50 same-day return), **Delft** (2/hrly, 38 min), **Hoorn** (4/hrly, 1 hr), **The Hague** (4/hrly, 35 min), **Alkmaar** (2/hrly, 30 min), **Schiphol Airport** (2/hrly, 40 min, f10, transfer at suburban Amsterdam-Sloterdijk); the direct buses #236 (use a strip card) and #362 (buy ticket at the train station ticket windows) to the airport are faster (2/hrly, 30 min, f6.25); by taxi it's a f70 ride.

Sights—Near Haarlem and Amsterdam

▲**Zaanse Schans**—At this 17th-century Dutch village turned open-air folk museum, you can see and learn about everything Dutch, from cheese-making to wooden-shoe carving. Take an inspiring climb to the top of a whirring windmill (get a group of people together and ask for a tour) and buy a small jar of fresh ground mustard for your next picnic. Located in the town of Zaandijk, this is your easiest one-stop look at traditional Dutch culture and the Netherlands' best collection of windmills (free, daily 8:30–18:00, until 17:00 in winter, parking-f7.50 = 1 hr, tel. 075/616-8218). Fifteen minutes by train north of Amsterdam: Take the Alkmaar-bound train to Station Koog-Zaandijk, then walk following signs—past a fragrant chocolate factory—for 10 minutes.

▲▲**Aalsmeer Flower Auction**—Get a bird's-eye view of the huge Dutch flower industry. Visitors are welcome to wander on elevated walkways (through what is claimed to be the biggest building on earth), over literally trainloads of fresh-cut flowers. About half of all the flowers exported from Holland are auctioned off here in six huge auditoriums (f7.5, Monday–Friday 7:30–11:00; the auction is pretty dead after 9:30 but the warehouse swarms; gift shop, cafeteria; bus #172 from Amsterdam's station, 2/hrly, 1 hr; from Haarlem, take bus #140, 2/hrly, 1 hr, tel. 0297/393-939). Aalsmeer is close to the airport and a handy last fling before catching a morning weekday flight.

▲▲▲**Keukenhof**—This is the greatest bulb-flower garden on earth. Each spring 6 million flowers conspire to make even a total garden-hater enjoy them. In 1999 the Keukenhof gardens will celebrate their 50th birthday with a special exposition from August 19 to September 19. This 100-acre park is packed with tour groups daily from about March 25 to May 20 (f17.50, 8:00–19:30, last tickets sold at 18:00; if you bus from Haarlem, transfer at Lisse; tel. 0252/465-555). Go very late in the day for the best light and the fewest groups.

▲**Alkmaar**—Holland's cheese capital is especially fun (and touristy) during its weekly cheese market (Friday 10:00–12:00).

▲▲**The Hague (Den Haag)**—Locals say the money is made in Rotterdam, divided in the Hague, and spent in Amsterdam. The Hague is the Netherlands' seat of government and the home of several engaging museums. The Mauritshuis' delightful, easy-to-tour art collection stars Vermeer and Rembrandt (f12.50, Tuesday–Sunday 11:00–17:00, Korte Vijverberg 8, tel. 070/302-3456). Across the pond, the Torture Museum (Gevangenpoort) shows the medieval mind at its worst (f6, Tuesday–Friday 10:00–16:00, weekends 12:00–16:00, closed Monday, required tours on the hour; confirm with ticket-taker if film and talk will be in English before committing, tel. 070/346-0861). For a look at the 19th century's attempt at virtual reality, tour Panorama

Mesdag, a 360-degree painting of the nearby town of Scheveningen in the 1880s, with a 3-D sandy-beach foreground (f6, Monday–Saturday 10:00–17:00, Sunday 12:00–17:00, Zeestraat 65, tel. 070/310-6665). The nearby Peace Palace, a gift from Andrew Carnegie, houses the International Court of Justice (f5, Monday–Friday open only for required guided tours at 10:00, 11:00, 14:00, or 15:00; tram #7 or #8 from the station; tel. 070/302-4137; closes without warning, call ahead or check at TI). Scheveningen, the Dutch Coney Island, is liveliest on sunny summer afternoons (take tram #7); and Madurodam, a mini-Holland amusement park, is a kid-pleaser (f19.50, discounts for kids, daily 9:00–17:00, until 21:00 in June, until 22:00 in July and August, tram #1 or #9, tel. 070/355-3900). The Hague's TI is at the train station (Monday–Saturday 9:00–17:30, later in summer, Sunday 10:00–17:00, tel. 06/3403-5051, f1 a minute).

▲▲**Arnhem's Open-Air Dutch Folk Museum**—An hour east of Amsterdam, Arnhem has a home show in a time tunnel: Holland's first and biggest folk museum. You'll enjoy a huge park of windmills, old farms, traditional crafts in action, and a pleasant education-by-immersion in Dutch culture. The English guidebook (f7.50) explains each historic building (f17, daily 10:00–17:00 April–October, tel. 026/357-6111). The park has several good budget restaurants and covered picnic areas. Its rustic **Pancake House** serves hearty (splittable) Dutch flapjacks.

Trains make the 70-minute trip from Amsterdam to Arnhem twice an hour (likely transfer in Utrecht). At Arnhem station, take bus #3 or #13 (faster, four/hr, 15 min) to the Openlucht Museum. By car from Haarlem, skirt Amsterdam to the south on E9, following signs to Utrecht, then take A12 east to Arnhem. Just before Arnhem, take the Arnhem Nord exit (you'll see the white "Openluchtmuseum" sign) and follow the signs to the nearby museum. For the Kröller-Müller Museum, follow the white signs to Hoge Veluwe.

▲▲**Kröller-Müller Museum and Hoge Veluwe National Park**—Also near Arnhem, the Hoge Veluwe National Park is Holland's largest (13,000 acres), and is famous for its Kröller-Müller Museum. This huge and impressive modern-art collection, including 55 paintings by van Gogh, is set deep in the wilderness. The park has lots more to offer, including hundreds of white bikes you're free to use to make your explorations more fun. After paying f8.50 at the park entrance, the museum is "free" (f8.50, Tuesday–Sunday 10:00–17:00, easy parking, tel. 055/378-1441). Pick up more information at the Amsterdam or Arnhem TI (tel. 026/442-6767). Bus #12 connects the Arnhem train station with the Kröller-Müller Museum (March–October). Consider combining a visit to the park and the open-air museum for a great day trip from Amsterdam.

LISBON

Lisbon is a ramshackle but charming mix of now and then. Old wooden trolleys shiver up and down its hills, bird-stained statues mark grand squares, taxis rattle and screech through cobbled lanes, and well-worn people sip coffee in Art Nouveau cafés.

Lisbon, like Portugal in general, is underrated. The country seems somewhere just beyond Europe. The pace of life is noticeably slower than in Spain. Roads are rutted. Prices are cheaper. While the unification of Europe is bringing sweeping changes, the traditional economy is based on fishing, cork, wine, and textiles. Be sure to balance your look at Iberia with enough Portugal.

While Lisbon's history goes back to the Romans and the Moors, the glory days were the 15th and 16th centuries, when explorers such as Vasco da Gama opened new trade routes around Africa to India, making Lisbon one of Europe's richest cities. (Da Gama has a higher profile these days in the wake of the 500th anniversary of his 1498 voyage.) Portugal's "Age of Discovery" fueled an economic boom which fueled the flamboyant art boom called the Manueline period—named after Portugal's King Manuel I (ruled 1495–1521). Later, in the early 18th century, the gold and diamonds of Brazil, one of Portugal's colonies, made Lisbon even wealthier.

Then, on All Saints' Day in 1755, while most of the population was in church, the city was hit by a tremendous earthquake. Candles quivered as far away as Ireland. Lisbon was dead center. Two-thirds of the city was leveled. Fires started by the many church candles raged throughout the city, and a huge tidal wave blasted the waterfront. Thirty thousand of Lisbon's 270,000 people were killed.

Under the energetic and eventually dictatorial leadership of Prime Minister Marques de Pombal—who had the new city planned within a month of the quake, Lisbon was rebuilt in a progressive grid plan with broad boulevards and square squares. Remnants of pre-earthquake Lisbon charm survive in Belém, the Alfama, and the Baírro Alto district.

The heritage of Portugal's Age of Discovery was a vast colonial empire. Except for Macao and the few islands off the Atlantic coast, the last bits of the empire disappeared with the 1974 revolution that delivered Portugal from the right-wing Salazar dictatorship. Emigrants from former colonies such as Mozambique and Angola have added diversity and flavor to the city, making it more likely that you'll hear African music than Portuguese fado these days.

But Lisbon's heritage survives. The city seems better organized, cleaner, and more prosperous and people-friendly than ever. With its elegant outdoor cafés, exciting art, entertaining museums, a hill-capping castle, the saltiest sailors' quarter in Europe, and the boost given the city after hosting the 1998 World's Fair, Lisbon is a world-class city. And with some of Europe's lowest prices, enjoying Lisbon is easy on the budget.

Planning Your Time

With three weeks in Iberia, Lisbon is worth two days.

Day 1: Start by touring Castle São Jorge, at the top of the Alfama, and surveying the city from its viewpoint. Hike down to another fine viewpoint, Miradouro de Santa Luzia, and descend into the Alfama. Explore. Back in the Baixa (bai-shah; lower city), have lunch on or near Rua Augusta and walk to the funicular near Praça dos Restauradores. Start the described walk through the Baírro Alto with a ride up the funicular. Take a joyride on trolley #28. If it's not later than 15:00, art-lovers can metro or taxi to the Gulbenkian Museum. Consider dinner at a fado show in the Baírro Alto. If one of your nights is a summer Thursday, consider a bullfight.

Day 2: Trolley to Belém and tour the Tower, Monastery, and Coach Museum. Have lunch in Belém. You could catch the train or drive to Sintra to tour the Pena Palace and explore the ruined Moorish castle. If you're itchy for the beach, drive four hours from Sintra to the Algarve.

A third day could easily be spent at the Museum of Ancient Art and browsing through the Rossio, Baírro Alto, and Alfama neighborhoods.

Orientation (tel. code: 01)

Greater Lisbon has around 3 million people and some frightening sprawl, but for the visitor, Lisbon can be a delightful small-town series of parks, boulevards, and squares bunny-hopping between two hills down to the waterfront. The main boulevard, Avenida da Liberdade, goes from the high-rent district downhill, ending at the grand square called Praça dos Restauradores. From here the

Baixa—the post-earthquake, grid-planned lower town, with three fine squares—leads to the riverfront. Rua Augusta is the grand pedestrian promenade running through the Baixa to the river.

Most travelers focus on the three characteristic neighborhoods that line the downtown harborfront: Baixa (in the middle), the Baírro Alto (literally "high town," Lisbon's "Latin Quarter" on a hill to the west), and the tangled, medieval Alfama (topped by the castle on the hill to the east).

From all this ye olde Lisbon, Avenida da Liberdade storms into the no-nonsense real world where you find the airport, bullring, popular fairgrounds, Edward VII Park, and breezy botanical gardens.

Tourist Information

Lisbon's city TI is under the green ticket kiosk at the bottom of Praça dos Restauradores (daily 9:00–18:00, Rua Jardim do Regedor 50, tel. 01/343-3672). The Portugal Tourist Office, which also has info on Lisbon, is across the same square in the Palacio Foz (daily 9:00–20:00, tel. 01/346-6307). The free city map lists all museums and has a helpful inset of the town center. The free monthly *What's on in Lisbon* (with more English, sometimes only available at hotels) is better than the TI's *Cultural Agenda*. The Falk Map, sold for 1,200$ at bookstores (*liveiros*), is excellent. Each summer cheery little "Ask me about Lisbon" info booths, staffed by tourism students, pop up all over town (less busy and jaded, actually eager to help you enjoy their town). The city has no regular walking tours, but for a private guide you can call the Guides' Union (13,000$/four hrs, 21,000$ full-day, tel. 01/346-7170). Angela da Silva is a good local guide (tel. 01/479-3597, cellular tel. 0936-605-9518).

Arrival in Lisbon

By Train: Lisbon has four train stations—Santa Apolonia (to Spain and most points north), Rossio (for Sintra, Obidos, and Nazaré), Barreiro (for Algarve), and Cais do Sodre (Cascais and Estoril). If leaving Lisbon by train, see if your train requires a reservation (boxed "R" in timetable).

Santa Apolonia Station covers international trains and nearly all of Portugal (except the south). It's just past the Alfama, and includes foreign-currency change machines and good bus connections to the town center (buses #9, #39, #46, and #90 go from station through center, up Avenida da Liberdade). A taxi from Santa Apolonia to any hotel I recommend should cost around 700$. If there's a long taxi-stand lineup, walk a block away and hail one off the street.

Rossio Station is in the town center (within walking distance of most of my hotel listings) and handles trains from Sintra (and

Óbidos and Nazaré, with transfers at Cacém). It has a handy all-Portugal train information office on the ground floor (Monday–Friday 9:00–18:00, weekends 10:00–19:00).

Barreiro Station, a 30-minute ferry ride across the Tagus River (Rio Tejo) from Praça do Comércio, is for trains to the Algarve and points south (the 170$ ferry ticket is generally sold to you with a train ticket).

Caís do Sodre Station handles the 30-minute rides to Cascais and Estoril.

By Bus: Lisbon's bus station is at Arco do Cego (200 meters from Metro: Saldanha, tel. 01/354-5439 and 01/357-7715).

By Plane: Lisbon's easy-to-manage airport is eight kilometers northeast of downtown, with a 24-hour bank, ATM and bill-changer machines, a tourist office, reasonable taxi service (1,200$ to center), good city bus connections into town (#44 and #45, 160$), and an airport bus.

The Aero-Bus runs from the airport to Restauradores, Rossio, and Praça do Comércio (430$, 3/hrly, 30 min, operates 7:00–21:00, buy ticket on bus). Your ticket is actually a one-day Lisbon transit pass that covers bus, tram, and elevator rides. If you fly in on TAP airline, show your ticket at the TAP welcome desk on the arrivals level to get a free one-way voucher for the Aero-Bus (TAP tel. 01/841-6990). A Lisbon transit pass (sold in one-day and three-day versions) covers the Aero-Bus trip to the airport if you're flying out of Lisbon. (Airport information: tel. 01/841-3500; flight info: tel. 01/841-3700.)

Getting Around Lisbon

By Metro: Lisbon's simple, fast, 80$-per-ride subway is handy for trips to the Gulbenkian Museum, fairgrounds, bullfight, Colombo shopping mall, Expo '98 site, and long-distance bus station. Bring change for the ticket machines, as many stations are not staffed. Remember to stamp your ticket in the machine. Metro stops are marked with a red "M." *Saida* means exit.

By Trolley, Funicular, and Elevator: For fun and practical public transport, use the trolley system, the funicular, and the Eiffelesque elevator (tickets at the door, going every few minutes) that connect the lower and upper towns. One ride on any of these costs 160$ (no transfers). The 430$ day pass and the 1,000$ three-day transit pass cover all public transportation (including the extensive city bus system) except for the Metro.

The 155$ *Bilhete Unico de Coroa* gives you two trips on the tram, bus, or elevator for the cost of one. Buy these tickets at green-and-yellow Carris booths (on Praça Figueira or at the base of the Santa Justa elevator—up a few stairs and behind the elevator).

By Taxi: Lisbon taxis are good-humored, abundant, and use their meters. Rides start at 250$ and you can go anywhere in the

Lisbon

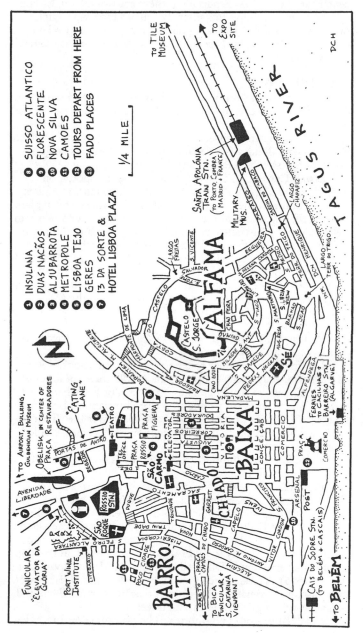

center for under 500$. Especially if there are two of you, Lisbon cabs are a great, cheap time-saver. For an average trip, couples save less than a dollar by taking public transport and spend an extra 20 minutes to get there—bad economics. If time is limited, taxi everywhere.

Helpful Hints

Bullfights are most summer Thursdays in Lisbon and most Sundays nearby. Tuesday and Saturday are flea-market days in the Alfama.

Museums: Most museums are free on Sunday until 14:00 and closed all day Monday (a good day to explore Lisbon's neighborhoods or Sintra's Pena Palace and Moorish ruins).

LisboaCard: This card covers all public transportation (including the Metro), allowing free entrance to most museums and discounts on others, plus discounts on city tours. If you plan to museum-hop, the card is a good value, particularly for a day in Belém (covers your transportation and every worthwhile sight in Belém). Don't use one on a Monday, when virtually all sights are closed, or on a Sunday, when many sights are free until 14:00 (24-hour card/1,700$; 48-hour card/2,800$; 72-hour card/3,600$; includes excellent explanatory guidebook). Buy it at the city tourist office (Rua Jardím do Regedor 50, see above) or at the Monastery of Jerónimos in Belém (see below). You can choose what date and time you want it to "start."

Pedestrian Warning: Sidewalks are narrow and drivers are daring; cross streets with care.

Language: Remember to try to start conversations in Portuguese. Fortunately, many people in the tourist trade speak some English. Otherwise, try Portuguese, Spanish, or French, in that order. Lisbon comes with some tricky pronunciations. Locals call their city "Lisboa" (LEEZH-bo-ah) and their river the "Tejo" (TAY-zhoo). Squares are major navigation points and are called "*praça*" (PRA-sah).

Time Zone Change: Portuguese time is usually one hour earlier than Spanish time.

Banking: Banks offer fine rates but high fees to change checks or cash. Shop around and minimize trips to the bank by changing large amounts (bank hours are generally Monday–Friday 8:30–11:45 and 13:00–15:00). American Express cashes any kind of traveler's check at a decent rate without a commission, but is not central (Monday–Friday 9:30–13:00 and 14:30–18:30, in the Top Tours office at Avenida Duque de Loule 108, Metro: Rotunda, tel. 01/315-5885). ATMs (which give more escudos per dollar) are all over Lisbon. Automatic bill-changing machines are available and seductive, offering fair rates but high fees.

Post Office and Telephones: The post office, at Praça dos

Restauradores 58, has easy-to-use metered phones (Monday–Friday 8:00–22:00, weekends 9:00–18:00). The telephone center, on the northwest corner of Rossio Square, sells phone cards and also has metered phone booths (daily 8:00–23:00, accepts credit cards).

Do-It-Yourself Walking Tours

▲▲**The Baírro Alto and Chiado Stroll**—This colorful upper-city walk starts at the funicular and ends with the elevator, each a funky 160$ experience in itself. Leave the lower town on the funicular, called Elevator da Gloria, near the obelisk at Praça dos Restauradores. (Notice the plaque inside near the ceiling from the car's 100th birthday in 1985.) Leaving the funicular on top, turn right to enjoy the **city view** from Miradouro de São Pedro Alcantara (San Pedro Park belvedere). Wander over to the tile map which helps guide you through the view, stretching from the castle birthplace of Lisbon on the right to the towers of the new city in the distance on the left. The centerpiece of the park is a statue honoring a 19th-century local writer. This district is famous for its writers, poets, and bohemians.

If you're into port (the fortified wine that takes its name from the city of Oporto), you'll find the world's greatest selection directly across the street from the lift at Solar do Vinho do Porto (run by the Port Wine Institute, 10:00–23:30, less on Saturday, closed Sunday, Rua São Pedro de Alcantara 45). In a plush air-conditioned living room you can, for 200$ to 3,000$ per glass poured by an English-speaking bartender, taste any of 300 different ports—though you may want to try only 150 or so and save the rest for the next night. Fans of port describe it as "a liquid symphony playing on the palate."

Follow the main street (Rua São Pedro de Alcantara) downhill a couple of blocks; it turns into the Rua Misericordia. The grid plan of streets to your right is 16th-century Renaissance town planning—predating the earthquake and grid plan of the lower town by two centuries.

São Roque Church is on your left at Largo Trindade Coelho (open 8:00–17:00). It looks like just another church, but wander slowly under its flat, painted ceiling and notice the rich side chapels. The highlight is the Chapel of St. John the Baptist (left of altar, gold and blue), which looks like it came right out of the Vatican. It did. Made in Rome out of the most precious materials, it was the site of one papal Mass; then it was taken down and shipped to Lisbon—probably the most costly chapel per square inch ever constructed. Notice the beautiful mosaic floor and the three paintings that are actually intricate mosaics—a Vatican specialty. The São Roque Museum (with some impressive old paintings and church riches, 150$, 10:00–17:00, closed Monday) is not as interesting as the church itself.

After a visit with the poor pigeon-drenched man in the church square (TI and WC), continue downhill along Rua da Misericordia into the more elegant shopping district called the Chiado (SHEE-ah-doo).

When you reach Praça Luis de Camões (named after Portugal's best-loved poet), turn left to a small square (Largo Chiado) past **A Brasileira** café and the classy Rua Garrett. The statue is of a famous local poet (Fernando Pessoa) who was a regular at Brasileira. Coffeehouse aficionados enjoy this grand old café, reeking with smoke and the 1930s (open daily). Drop in for a *bica* (Lisbon slang for an espresso) and a *pastel de Belém* (140$ cream cake—a local specialty).

Browse downhill for two blocks on Rua Garrett, peeking into the classy shops. Notice the lamps with the symbol of Lisbon: a ship, or caravel—with the remains of St. Anthony—guarded by two ravens. This street was one of Lisbon's best shopping streets before the fire of 1988.

At Calle Sacramento, go left uphill to another pleasant square, Largo dos Carmo, with the ruins of the **Convento do Carmo** (if open, pop in to see the elegant, earthquake-ruined Gothic arches for free, or pay 300$ to get all the way in and see the museum; Monday–Saturday 10:00–17:30, closed Sunday).

Trolley tracks lead from the square past the church to the Santa Justa elevator. At the elevator, climb the spiral stairs one floor to the small observatory deck or to the top of this Eiffelian pimple for a great view café (daily, English spoken, reasonable coffee, expensive eats). The elevator (built by a pupil of Eiffel) takes you down into the Baixa.

▲▲▲**Alfama Stroll**—Europe's most colorful sailors' quarter goes back to Visigothic days. It was a rich district during the Arabic period and finally the home of Lisbon's fisherfolk (and of the poet Luis de Camões, who wrote, "our lips meet easily high across the narrow street"). The tangled street plan is one of the few aspects of Lisbon to survive the 1755 earthquake, helping make the Alfama a cobbled playground of Old World color. A visit is best during the busy midmorning market time or in the late afternoon/early evening, when the streets teem with locals.

Consider riding a taxi, or bus #37 from Praça Figueira, to the castle—the highest point in town—and walking from there down to the Alfama viewpoint and into the Alfama.

Start at **Castle São Jorge**. Lisbon's castle is boring as far as castles go. But it's the birthplace of the city, offers a fine view, and it's free (open daily until sunset). Straddle a cannon, enjoy the view and park, and wander the sterile ramparts if you like. Within the castle, **Olisiponia** (the Roman name for Lisbon), is a new high-tech syrupy multimedia presentation offering a sweeping video overview of the city's history in English (600$, daily 10:00–18:00).

It's a five-minute walk downhill to another great Alfama view-point, at Largo Santa Luzia. (This square is a stop for trolleys #12 and #28; some prefer to start their Alfama exploration here, and take the steep but worthwhile 10-minute uphill hike to the castle.) Admire the panoramic view from the square's small terrace, Miradouro de Santa Luzia, where old-timers play cards in the shade of the bougainvillea amid lots of tiles. Probably the most scenic cup of coffee in town is enjoyed from the nearby Cerca Moura bar/café terrace (after 11:30, Largo das Portas do Sol 4).

The **Museum of Decorative Arts**, next to the Cerca Moura bar, offers a unique (but nearly meaningless with its lack of decent English descriptions) stroll through aristocratic households richly decorated in 16th- to 19th-century styles (800$, Tuesday–Sunday 10:00–17:00, closed Monday, Largo das Portas do Sol 2, tel. 01/886-2183).

From the Largo das Portas do Sol (Cerca Moura bar), stairs lead deep into the Alfama. To descend from the viewpoint: behind the Santa Luzia church, take Rua Norberto de Araujo down a few stairs, go left under the arch, and you'll hook up with Beco Santa Helena, an alley of steps leading downhill.

The Alfama's urban jungle roads are squeezed into tangled and confusing alleys; bent houses comfort each other in their romantic shabbiness; and the air drips with laundry and the smell of clams and raw fish. Get lost. Poke aimlessly, sample ample grapes, peek through windows, buy a fish. Don't miss Rua de São Pedro, the liveliest street around. On Tuesday and Saturday mornings the fun Feira da Ladra flea market rages on the Campo de Santa Clara (a good 20-minute walk; worth it only if it's flea-market day).

Tours—Lisbon

▲▲**Ride a Trolley**—Lisbon's vintage trolleys, most from the 1920s, shake and shiver all over town, somehow safely weaving within inches of parked cars, climbing steep hills, and offering sightseers breezy wide-open-window views of the city. Line #28 is a Rice-A-Roni Lisbon joyride. Tram #28 stops from west to east include: Estrela (the 18th-century late-Baroque Estrela Basilica and Estrela Park—cozy neighborhood scene with pond-side café and even a "garden library kiosk"), top of Bica funicular (dropping steeply through a rough-and-tumble neighborhood to the river-front), Chiado square (Lisbon's café and "Latin Quarter"), Baixa (on Rua da Conceicão between Augusta and Prata), the cathedral (Sè), the Alfama viewpoint (Santa Luzia Belvedere), Portas do Sol, the Santa Clara church (flea market), and the pleasant and untouristy Graca district. Just pay the conductor as you board, sit down, and catch the pensioners as they lurch at each stop. For a quicker circular Alfama trolley ride, catch #12 on Praça da

Figueira (departures every few minutes for the 20-minute circle; driver can tell you when to get out for the viewpoint near the castle—about three-quarters through the ride).
City Bus Tours—Two tours give tired tourists a lazy overview of the city. Neither is great, but both are handy, daily, and inexpensive. **Tagus Tour** lets you hop on and off their topless double-decker buses (2,000$, hrly departures start at 11:00 May–September, the 90-minute tour covers the town and Belém, taped commentary in English, Portuguese, and French). On the **Hills Tour** you follow the rails on restored turn-of-the-century trams through the Alfama and Baírro Alto (2,800$; live, trilingual guide; four or five departures daily in summer, less off-season). While the ride is a scenic joy, the information is sparse. Both tours leave from the same info kiosk on Praça do Comércio (tel. 01/363-2021).

Sights—Lisbon
▲▲▲**Gulbenkian Museum**—This is the best of Lisbon's 40 museums. Gulbenkian, an Armenian oil tycoon, gave his art collection (or "harem," as he called it) to Portugal in gratitude for the hospitable asylum granted him there during World War II. This great collection, spanning 2,000 years in a classy and comfortable modern building, offers the most purely enjoyable museum experience in Iberia. It's cool, uncrowded, gorgeously lit and easy to grasp, displaying only a few select and exquisite works from each epoch.

Savor details as you stroll chronologically through the ages past the delicate Egyptian, vivid Greek (fascinating coins), exotic Oriental sections, and the well-furnished Louis land. There are masterpieces by Rembrandt, Rubens, Renoir, Rodin, and artists whose names start with other letters. The nubile finale is a dark room filled with Art Nouveau jewelry by the French designer Rene Lalique (500$, free Sunday, daily 10:00–17:00, pleasant gardens; good, air-conditioned cafeteria; Metro from Rossio to São Sebastião and walk 200 meters, or 500$ taxi from downtown, Berna 45, tel. 01/793-5131).
▲▲**Museum of Ancient Art (Museu Nacional de Arte Antiga)**—This is the country's best for Portuguese paintings from her glory days, the 15th and 16th centuries. (Most of these works were gathered in Lisbon after the dissolution of the abbeys and convents in 1834.) You'll also find the great European masters (such as Bosch, Jan van Eyck, and Raphael) and rich furniture, all in a grand palace. Highlights include: the Temptations of St. Anthony (another three-paneled altarpiece fantasy by Bosch, c. 1500); St. Jerome (by Dürer); the Adoration of St. Vincent (a many-paneled altarpiece by the late-15th-century Portuguese master, Nuno Goncalves, showing everyone from royalty to sailors and beggars surrounding Portugal's patron saint); and the curious Namban screens (16th-century Japanese depictions of Portuguese

traders in Japan). The museum has a good cafeteria with seating in a shady garden overlooking the river (500$, Tuesday 14:00–18:00, Wednesday–Sunday 10:00–18:00, closed Monday, tram 15, bus #40, or #60 from Praça Figueira, Rua das Janeles Verdes 9, tel. 01/397-6002).

▲**National Tile Museum (Museu Nacional do Azulejo)**—This museum, filling the Convento da Madre de Deus, features piles of tiles which, as you've probably noticed, are an art form in Portugal. The presentation is very low-tech but the church is sumptuous and the tile panorama of pre-earthquake Lisbon (upstairs) is fascinating (350$, Tuesday 14:00–18:00, Wednesday–Sunday 10:00–18:00, closed Monday, 10 minutes on bus #59 or #105 from Praça Figueira, Rua da Madre de Deus 4, tel. 01/814-7747).

Cathedral (Sè)—Just a few blocks east of Praça do Comércio, it's not much on the inside, but its fortress-like exterior is a textbook example of a stark and powerful Romanesque fortress of God. Started in 1150, after the Christians reconquered Lisbon from the Islamic Moors, its crenellated towers made a powerful statement: The Reconquista was here to stay. St. Anthony—the patron saint of Portugal but known to most of us as the saint in charge of helping you find lost things—is buried in the church. In the 12th century his remains were brought to Lisbon on a ship, as the legend goes, guarded by two sacred black ravens . . . the symbol of the city. The cloisters are peaceful and an archaeological work in progress—uncovering Roman ruins (100$). The humble treasury shows off relics of St. Anthony but is worthwhile only if you want to support the church and climb some stairs (400$).

Expo '98 Grounds—Lisbon celebrated the 500th anniversary of Vasco da Gama's voyage to India by hosting Expo '98. The theme was "The Ocean and the Seas" with an emphasis on importance of healthy, clean waters in our environment. The riverside fairgrounds are east of the Santa Apolonia train station in an area suddenly revitalized with luxury condos and crowd-pleasing terraces and restaurants. Ride the Metro to the last stop (Oriente—meaning east end of town) to join the riverside promenade and visit Europe's biggest aquarium.

Vasco da Gama Bridge—The second-longest bridge in Europe (14 km) was opened in 1998 to connect the Expo grounds with the south side of the Tagus, and to alleviate the traffic jams on Lisbon's only other bridge over the river. As the 25th of April Bridge (see below) was modeled after the Golden Gate bridge in San Francisco (same company built it and was paid off by years of tolls), this new Vasco da Gama Bridge was designed with engineering help from the people building the new San Francisco Bay Bridge.

▲**25th of April Bridge**—At a mile long, this is one of the longest suspension bridges in the world. Built in 1966, it was originally named for the dictator Salazar but renamed for the date of Portugal's 1974 revolution and freedom. For over 30 years locals could show their political colors by choosing what name to use. While conservatives called it the Salazar Bridge, liberals called it the 25th of April Bridge. Those who preferred to keep their politics private simply called it "the bridge over the river." With the opening of the second bridge over the Tagus, everyone will have to choose a name . . . and show their politics. In 1999 the bridge will become a double-decker as a much-needed commuter train line will be added.

Cristo Rei—A huge statue of Christ (à la Rio de Janeiro)—with outstretched arms symbolically blessing the city—overlooks Lisbon from across the Tagus River. It was built as a thanks to God, funded by Lisboetas grateful that Portugal stayed out of WWII. While it's designed to be seen from a distance, a lift takes visitors to the top for a great view (250$, daily 9:30–18:00). Catch the ferry from downtown Lisbon (six/hrly, from Praça do Comércio) to Cacilhas, then take a bus marked "Cristo Rei" (4/hrly, from ferry dock). Because of bridge tolls, taxis to or from the site are expensive. For drivers, the most efficient visit is a quick stop on your way south to the Algarve.

Sights—Lisbon's Belém District

Three miles from downtown Lisbon, the Belém District is a sprawling pincushion of important sights from Portugal's Golden Age, when Vasco da Gama and company made it Europe's richest power. Belém was the send-off point for voyages from the Age of Discovery. Sailors would stay and pray here before embarking. The tower would welcome them home. For some reason, the grand buildings of Belém survived the great 1755 earthquake. Consequently, this is the only place to experience the grandeur of pre-earthquake Lisbon. Safety-conscious royalty lived here after the earthquake and the modern-day president of Portugal has his house here today. To celebrate the 300th anniversary of independence from Spain, a grand exhibition was held here in 1940 resulting in the fine parks, fountains, and monument.

While the monastery is great, Belém's several museums are somewhere between good and mediocre, depending upon your interests. All of Belém's sights are closed on Monday.

Get to Belém by taxi (800$ from downtown), bus (#s 27, 28, 29, 43, 49, and 51), or the sleek new tram #15 from Praça da Figueira (buy 160$ tickets from machine on board, no change). The first Belém stop is the Coach Museum, the second stop is the monastery. Consider doing Belém in this order: tram or taxi to the Coach Museum, pastry and coffee break, Monastery of Jerónimos, (Maritime Museum if interested), Monument to the Discoveries, the Belém Tower.

▲▲**Coach Museum (Museu dos Coches)**—In 1905 the Queen of Portugal decided to use the palace's riding school building to preserve this fine collection of royal coaches. Claiming to be the most visited sight in Portugal, it is impressive, with more than 70 dazzling carriages (well-described in English). The oldest (on left as you enter) is the crude and simple coach used by King (of Spain and Portugal) Philip II to shuttle between Madrid and Lisbon around 1600. Imagine how slow and rough the ride would be with rough roads and no suspension. Study the evolution of suspension and the highly symbolic ornamentation of the coaches. The newly restored "Ocean Coach" has figures symbolizing the Atlantic and Indian Oceans holding hands, in recognition of Portugal's mastery of the sea (450$, Tuesday–Sunday 10:00–17:00, closed Monday, tel. 01/363-8022).

Rua de Belém leads from the coach museum and the monastery past the guarded entry to Portugal's presidential palace, some fine pre-earthquake buildings, and a famous pastry shop. This shop, **Casa Pasties de Belém** is the birthplace of the wonderful cream tart called *pastel del Nata* throughout Portugal. In Lisbon they're called *pastel del Belém*. Since 1837 locals have come here to get them warm out of the oven (Rua de Belém 88). Sit down and order one with a *café com leite*. Sprinkle on the cinnamon and powdered sugar.

▲▲▲**Monastery of Jerónimos**—This is Portugal's most exciting building. King Manuel (who ruled from 1495) had this giant church and its cloisters built (starting in 1501) with "pepper money"—a 5 percent tax on spices brought back from India—as a thanks for the discoveries. Sailors would spend their last night here in prayer before embarking on their frightening voyages.

1. The ornate **south portal**, facing the street, is a great example of the Manueline style. Manueline—like Spain's Plateresque but with motifs from the sea—bridged Gothic and Renaissance. Henry the Navigator stands in the middle of the door with his patron saint, St. Jerome (with the lion), up in the tympanum. This door is only used when a Mass lets out.

2. The **church interior** is best viewed from the high altar in the middle. Look back down the nave to see how Manueline is a transition between Gothic and Renaissance. While in Gothic architecture huge columns break the interior into a nave with low-ceilinged ambulatories on either side, here the slender palm tree-like columns don't break the interior space and the ceiling is all one height. Find some of the Manueline motifs from the sea: the shells providing ceilings for the niches, the rope-like arches, the ships, coral, and seaweed. The sea, after all, brought Portugal its 16th-century wealth and power and made this art possible.

3. Now turn 180 degrees toward the front and see how the rest of the church is Renaissance. Everything but a cupola and the stained glass (replacement glass is from 1940) survived the

Belém

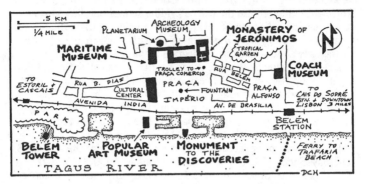

earthquake. In the **apse** lions support two kings and two queens
(King Manuel I is front left).

4. The rear of the nave sports two fine **memorial tombs.**
Closest to the street is the one for Portugal's much-loved poet
Camões (he's buried elsewhere). Vasco da Gama might be buried
in the other. Check out its richly symbolic carving: The proud
sailboat is a Portuguese caravel (a technological marvel in its day
with a sail that could pivot to efficiently catch the wind). The
sphere is a common Manueline symbol. Some say the diagonal
slash is symbolic of the unwritten pact and ambition of Spain and
Portugal to split the world evenly. Even the ceiling—a Boy Scout
handbook of rope and knots—comes with a whiff of the sea.

5. Leave the church (turn right, buy a ticket) and enter the
cloisters. These cloisters, my favorite in all of Europe, are the
architectural highlight of Belém. The lacy lower arcade is textbook
Manueline, the simpler top floor is Renaissance. Study the carvings. The 12 doors lead to confessionals in the church. Traditionally girls put their right hand on the left paw of St. Jerome's lion
(in the corner of the courtyard) and were married within six
months. Upstairs you'll find better views and the bookshop
(church free, 400$ for cloisters; Tuesday–Sunday 10:00–17:00,
closed Monday; women's WC upstairs, men's downstairs).

Maritime Museum (Museu de Marinha)—If you're interested
in the ships and navigational tools of Portugal's Age of Discovery,
this museum, which fills the east wing of the monastery, is worth a
look. Sailors love it (300$, free on Wednesday, Tuesday–Sunday
10:00–18:00, closed Monday, Praça do Império).

▲Monument to the Discoveries—This giant riverside monument was built in 1960 to honor Prince Henry the Navigator on
the 500th anniversary of his death. Huge statues of Henry, Magel-
lan, Vasco da Gama, and other heroes of Portugal's Age of Dis-

covery line the giant concrete prow of a caravel. Note the marble map chronicling Portugal's empire-building (on the ground in front). Follow the years as Portuguese explorers gradually worked their way around Africa. In 1999 Portugal grants Macau its independence, leaving only the Azores and Madeira (whose original inhabitants were Portuguese) as Portuguese possessions. Inside a TV plays footage of the 1940 Expo and you can ride a lift to a fine view (330$, Tuesday–Sunday 9:30–18:45, closed Monday).

▲**Belém Tower**—The only purely Manueline building in Portugal (built 1515–1520), this tower protected Lisbon's harbor and today symbolizes the voyages that made it powerful. This was the last sight sailors saw as they left and the first when they returned loaded with gold, spices, and social diseases. When built, the river went nearly to the walls of the monastery and this tower was in mid-river. Its interior is pretty bare but the view from its top is fine (400$, Tuesday–Sunday 10:00–18:30, closed Monday, tel. 01/361-0850). The floatplane on a pedestal is a monument to the first flight across the South Atlantic (Portugal to Brazil) in 1922. The original plane is across the street in the Maritime Museum.

Popular Art Museum (Museu de Arte Popular)—This museum takes you through Portugal's folk art one province at a time, providing a sneak preview of what you'll see throughout the country (300$, Tuesday–Sunday 10:00–12:30 and 14:00–17:00, closed Monday, between the monument and tower on Avenida Brasilia).

Shopping

Flea Market—On Tuesday and Saturday, the Feira da Ladra flea market hops in the Alfama on Campo de Santa Clara.

Colombo Shopping Mall—While Lisbon offers decaying but still elegant department stores, a teeming flea market, and classy specialty shops, nothing is as impressive as the enormous Centro Colombo, the largest shopping center in Spain and Portugal. More than 400 shops, 10 cinemas, 60 restaurants, and a health club sit atop Europe's biggest underground car park and under a vast and entertaining play center (daily until midnight, pick up a map at the info desk, Metro: Colegio Militar takes you right there, tel. 01/711-3600).

Nightlife

Nightlife in the Baixa seems to be little more than loitering prostitutes and litter stirred by the wind. But head up into the Baírro Alto and you'll find plenty of action. The Jardím do São Pedro is normally festive and the Rua Diario de Noticias is lined with busy bars.

▲**Fado**—Fado is the folk music of Lisbon's back streets. Since the mid-1800s it's been the Lisbon blues—mournfully beautiful, haunting ballads about lost sailors, broken hearts, and sad romance. The singer longs for what's been lost to the lilting accompaniment of the Portuguese *guitarra*—like a 12-string mandolin.

These days, the fado songs come with a new casualty—a tourist's budget. Fado has become one of Lisbon's favorite late-night tourist traps but it can still be a great experience. The Alfama has a few famous touristy fado bars, but the Baírro Alto is better (and safer late at night). Wander around Rua Diario de Noticias and neighboring streets either for a late dinner (after 21:30) or later for just drinks and music. Homemade "fado tonight" signs in Portuguese are good news, but even a restaurant filled with tourists can come with good food and fine fado. Prices for a fado performance vary greatly. Many have a steep cover charge while others have a minimum purchase. Any place a hotel sends you to has a bloated price for the kickback.

Canto do Camões is my favorite, run by friendly Gabriel (1,800$ minimum, 3,700$ menu, Travessa da Espera 38, call ahead to reserve—ask for Mr. Rick's table, tel. 01/346-5464). The meal is punctuated with sets of three fado songs with different singers. Relax, spend some time, make eye contact with the singer. Let the music and wine work together.

▲▲▲**Portuguese Bullfight**—If you always felt sorry for the bull, this is Toro's Revenge—in a Portuguese bullfight, the matador is brutalized along with the bull. After an exciting equestrian prelude in which the horseman (*cavaleiro*) skillfully plants barbs in the bull's back while trying to avoid the padded horns, a colorfully clad, eight-man team (suicide squad called a *forcado*) enters the ring and lines up single file facing the bull. The leader prompts the bull to charge, then braces himself for a collision that can be heard all the way up in the cheap seats. As he hangs onto the bull's head, his buddies then pile on, trying to wrestle the bull to a standstill. Finally, one guy hangs on to *el toro*'s tail and "water-skis" behind him. Unlike at the Spanish *corrida*, the bull is not killed in front of the crowd at the Portuguese *tourada* (yet it is killed later).

You're most likely to see a bullfight in Lisbon, Estoril, or on the Algarve (Easter–October, schedules at TI). In Lisbon's Campo Pequeno, fights are on Thursday mid-June through September at 22:00. Tickets range from 1,000$ to 10,000$. The ring is small. There are no bad seats. To get close to the action, the cheapest *bancada* seat gets you into the generally half-empty and un-moni-tored main floor where you can sit nearly at ringside.

Note: Half the fights are simply Spanish-type *corridas* without the killing. For the real slam-bam Portuguese-style fight, confirm that there will be *grupo de forcados*. Tickets are nearly always avail-able at the door (no surcharge, tel. 01/793-2143 to confirm). For an 11 percent surcharge you can buy them at the green ABEP kiosk above Lisbon's central TI (bottom of Praça dos Restauradores).

▲**People's Fair (Feira Popular)**—Consider spending a lowbrow evening at Lisbon's Feira Popular, which bustles on weekends with Portuguese families at play. Pay the entry fee, then enjoy rides, munchies, people-watching, and music—basic Portuguese fun. Have dinner among the chattering families, with endless food and wine paraded frantically in every direction. Fried ducks drip, barbecues spit, and dogs squirt the legs of chairs while, somehow, local lovers ignore everything but each other's eyes. (300$, nightly 19:00–midnight May–September, on Avenida da República at Metro: Entre-Campos.)

Movies—Lisbon reels with theaters and, unlike in Spain, most films are in the original language with subtitles. Many of Lisbon's theaters are classy, complete with assigned seats and ushers, and the normally cheap tickets go for half-price on Monday. Check the cinema listings in the monthly magazine *Lisboaem* (free at TI).

Sleeping in Lisbon
(180$ = about $1, tel. code: 01)
Sleep Code: **S** = Single, **D** = Double/Twin, **T** = Triple, **Q** = Quad, **b** = bathroom, **t** = toilet only, **s** = shower only, **CC** = Credit Card (Visa, MasterCard, Amex), **SE** = Speaks English, **NSE** = No English. Breakfast is usually included.

With the exception of a few splurges, rooms downtown feel like Lisbon does downtown: tired and well-worn. To sleep in a well-located place with local character, you'll be climbing dark stairways into a world of cracked plaster, taped handwritten signs, dingy carpets, cramped and confusing floor plans, and ramshackle plumbing. If you're on a tight budget, arrive without a reservation and bargain. While old Lisbon seems a little sleazy at night, with normal discretion my listings are safe.

Singles cost nearly the same as doubles. As in France, bathtubs and twin beds can cost more than showers and double beds. Addresses like 26-3 stand for street #26, third floor (which is fourth floor in American terms). Never judge a place by its entryway.

Sleeping Downtown in Baixa
(zip code: 1100)
Central as can be, this area bustles with lots of shops, traffic, people, buskers, pedestrian areas, and urban intensity.

Lisboa Tejo is an oasis, newly and tastefully refurbished, with 58 comfortable rooms and an attentive and welcoming staff (Sb-14,000–16,000$, Db-16,000–18,000$, prices vary according to room size, includes huge buffet breakfast, 8 percent discount with this book, air-conditioning, CC:VMA, Poço do Borratém 4, from southeast corner of Praça da Figueira, walk one block down Rua Dos

Condes de Monsanto and turn left, tel. 01/886-6182, fax 01/886-5163, SE). Manolo Carrera is proud of his historic fountain and wine shop.

Albergaria Residencial Insulana, on a pedestrian street, is very professional with 32 quiet and comfortable—if a bit smoky—rooms (Sb-8,500$, Db-10,000$, Tb-14,000$, includes breakfast, elevator, air-conditioning, CC:VMA, Rua da Assuncão 52, tel. & fax 01/342-3131, SE).

Pensão Aljubarrota is a fine value if you can handle the long climb up four floors, claustrophobic hallways, and the black-vinyl flooring. Once on top it's a happy world of small rustically furnished rooms with cute take-my-photo balconies from which to survey the Rua Augusta scene (S-3,300–4,500$, D-5,400–7,000$, Ds-7,000–8,500$, T-7,200–10,800$, 10 percent discount with cash and this book, includes breakfast, all but singles have balconies, CC:VM, Rua da Assuncão 53-4, tel. & fax 01/346-0112, Pino and lovely Rita SE).

Hotel Metropole, right on Rossio Square, offers 1920s-style elegance and 36 big, beautiful rooms, some of which overlook the square (Sb-16,000–19,000$, Db-19,000–21,000$, extra bed-4,000$, includes breakfast, air-conditioning, elevator, double-paned windows, CC:VMA, Rossio 30, tel. 01/346-9164, fax 01/346-9166, SE).

Pensão Residencial Gerês, a good budget bet downtown, has bright, basic, cozy rooms. Recently remodeled, it lacks the dingy smokiness that pervades Lisbon's cheaper hotels (S-6,500$, Sb-8,000$, D-8,000$, Db-10,000$, T-9,500$, Tb-12,000$, Qb-14,000$, 10 percent discount for cash with this book, CC:VMA, Calçada do Garcia 6, uphill a block off the northeast corner of Rossio, tel. 01/881-0497, fax 01/888-2006, Nogueira family speaks some English).

Sleeping Uptown along Avenida da Liberdade

Pensão Residencial 13 da Sorte, a simple but cheery place, has full bathrooms in each of its 23 rooms and bright, small-town tiles throughout (Sb-6,000$, Db-7,000–9,000$, Tb-10,000$, no breakfast, elevator, CC:VM, just off Avenida da Liberdade near Hotel Sofitel at Rua do Salitre 13, 1200 Lisbon, 50 meters from Metro: Avenida, tel. 01/353-9746, fax 01/353-1851, SE).

Hotel Lisboa Plaza, a four-star gem, is by far my classiest Lisbon recommendation. It's a spacious and plush mix of traditional style with bright pastel modern elegance, offering a warm welcome without the stuffiness you'd expect in this price range (Db-27,000–30,000$, CC:VMA, air-conditioning, well-located on a quiet street off busy Avenida da Liberdade, a block from Metro: Avenida at Travessa do Salitre, 1250 Lisboa, tel. 01/346-3922, fax 01/347-1630, e-mail: plaza.hotels@mail.telepac.pt).

Hotel Suisso Atlantico is formal, hotelish, and stuffy, with tour groups and drab carpets throughout, but it's a functional hotel with a practical location (Sb-9,000$, Db-13,500$, Tb-15,000$, includes breakfast, no fans or air-conditioning, CC:VMA, Rua da Gloria 3-19, 1200 Lisbon, behind the funicular station, on a quiet street near a peep show one block off Praça dos Restauradores, tel. 01/346-1713, fax 01/346-9013, SE).

Residencial Florescente rents 72 rooms on a thriving pedestrian street a block off Praça dos Restauradores. It's a slumber mill, but rooms are clean and some are nearly charming (S-4,000$, Ss-6,000$, Sb-7,000$, D-5,000$, Ds-7,000$, Db-8,000$, no breakfast, most Db with air-conditioning, CC:VMA, Rua Portas S. Antão 99, 1100 Lisbon, tel. 01/346-3517, fax 01/342-7733, SE).

Hotel Ibis Lisboa-Centro, big, concrete, modern, and practical in a soulless area far from the center but near a Metro station, offers plain modern comforts and no stress for a good price (Db-9,300$ without breakfast, CC:VMA, air-conditioning, next to Novotel and Metro: Palhava, Avenida Jose Malhoa, tel. 01/727-3181, fax 01/727-3287, SE). Forgive me.

Sleeping in Baírro Alto
(zip code: 1200)
Just west of downtown, this area is a bit seedy but full of ambience, good bars, local fado clubs, music, and markets. The area may not feel comfortable for women alone at night, but the hotels themselves are safe.

Residencial Nova Silva is a quiet, ramshackle place on the crest of the Baírro Alto overlooking the river. The five borderline dumpy rooms with grand little river-view balconies give you bird noises rather than traffic noises (priority for longer stays). It's three blocks from the heart of Chiado on the scenic #28 tram line, with the easiest street parking of all my listings (S-4,500$, Ss-5,000$, Sb-6,000$, D-5,000$, Ds-5,500$, Db-6,000–7,000$, T-6,500$, Ts-7,000$, Tb-8,500$, breakfast-400$, no elevator, Rua Victor Cordón 11, tel. 01/342-4371, fax 01/342-7770, Fatima SE).

Residencial Camões lies right in the seedy thick of the Baírro Alto but offers sleepable rooms (S-3,000$, D-6,000$, Db-7,500$, includes breakfast, Travessa Poco da Cidade 38, one block south of São Roque Church and to the right, tel. 01/346-7510, fax 01/346-4048, some English spoken).

Eating in Lisbon

Eating in the Alfama
This gritty chunk of pre-earthquake Lisbon is full of interesting eateries, especially along Rua San Pedro (the lower main drag) and on Largo de São Miguel. Before or after your castle visit, eat fast, cheap, and healthy at **Comidas de Santiago**, a clever little salad bar with great gazpacho (choose two salads on a small plate for

530$ or four on a big plate for 860$, open from 11:00, one block uphill from Santa Luzia viewpoint terrace, Largo do Contador Mor 21, tel. 01/887-5805).

For a seafood feast, consider dining high in the Alfama at the **Farol de Santa Luzia** restaurant (2,600$ dinner menu, closed Sunday, Largo Santa Luzia 5, across from Santa Luzia viewpoint terrace, no sign but many window decals, tel. 01/886-3884). For cheap and colorful dinners, walk past Portas do Sol and follow the trolley tracks along Rua da São Tome to a square called Largo Rodrigues Freitas, where **Nossa Churrasqueira** is busy feeding chicken to finger-lickin' locals on rickety tables and meager budgets (closed Monday).

While in the Alfama, brighten a few dark bars. Have an aperitif, taste the *branco seco* (local dry white wine). Make a friend, pet a chicken, read the graffiti, pick at the humanity ground between the cobbles.

Eating in Baírro Alto

Lisbon's "high town" is full of small, fun, and cheap places. Fishermen's bars abound. Just off São Roque's Square you'll find two fine eateries: the very simple and cheap **Casa Trans-Montana** (closed Sunday) down the steps of Calcada do Duque at #43; and the bright and touristy **Cervejaría da Trindade**, a Portuguese-style beer hall covered with historic tiles and full of seafood (2,000$ meals, daily 12:00–24:00, CC:VMA, one block down from São Roque at Rua Nova da Trindade 20C, tel. 01/342-3506). You'll find many less-touched restaurants deeper into the Baírro Alto on the other (west) side of Rua Misericordia.

Eating in Rossio and Beyond

In Rossio: For cod and vegetables prepared faster than a Big Mac and served with more energy than a soccer team, stand or sit at **Restaurant Beira-Gare** (a greasy spoon in front of Rossio train station at the end of Rua 1 de Dezembro, Monday–Saturday 6:00–24:00, closed Sunday). To get a simple fish sandwich, ask for a *filete pescada no pão*. Farther down the same street is **Celeiro**, a handy and bigger-than-it-looks supermarket (weekdays 8:30–20:00, until 19:00 Saturday, closed Sunday, Rua 1 de Dezembro 67-68). Across the street at #65 (same hours), Celeiro runs a health-food store with a bleak but healthy cafeteria in its basement. The Rossio's Rua dos Correeiros is lined with competitive local cafés.

The **"eating lane"** is a galaxy of eateries with small zoos hanging from their windows for you to choose from (opposite Rossio station, just off Praça dos Restauradores down Rua do Jardím do Regedor and Rua das Portas de St. Antão). The seafood is some of Lisbon's best. **Restaurant da Casa do Alentejo**, part of a cultural and social center for people from the traditional southern province of Portugal who are living in Lisbon, fills an ornate old ballroom and specializes in dry and salty meat and potatoes—Alentejo cuisine (three-course 2,500$ menu, open from 19:30, Rua das Portas de St. Antao 58).

On **Praça Figueria: Casas Suissa** is popular with locals because it's classy but affordable (cheap at the bar, reasonable at tables, good salads and fruit cups, open 7:00–22:00, entries on both Praça Figueria and Rossio square). For a gritty snack, stand with the locals at **Pastelaria Tentacão** (daily 7:00–22:00, east side of Praça Figueria) and munch one of their *prato do dia* (daily specials, all under 1,000$). The house specialty to try (or avoid) is *leitão*, a suckling pig sandwich. Pick up the tally sheet as you enter, eat what you like, and turn it in to pay up as you leave. A few doors down, **Mercado da Figueira** is a great indoor supermarket.

Eating Elsewhere in Lisbon

Up Avenida da Liberdade: Cerevejaria Ribadouro is popular with locals for seafood. The menu is simple with many items listed at per-kilo prices. The waiter will explain the price per portion (3000$ meals, Avenida da Liberdade 155, at intersection with Rua do Salitre, Metro: Avenida, tel. 01/354-9411).

At Feira Popular: For a chance to go purely local, join hundreds of Portuguese families having salad, fries, chicken, and wine at the **Feira Popular** (nightly from 19:00 May–September, Avenida da República, Metro: Entre-Campos).

Drinks

Ginjinha is the diminutive name for a favorite Lisbon drink. *Ginjinha* (geen-szeen-nyah) is a sweet liquor made from the sour cherry-like *ginja* berry, sugar, and schnapps. It's sold for 150$ a shot in funky little hole-in-the-wall shops throughout town. The only choices are: with or without berries (*com* or *sem fruta*) and *gelada* if you want it from a chilled bottle out of the fridge (very nice). In Portugal, when someone is impressed by the taste of something, they say, "*Sabe melhor que nem ginjas*" ("It tastes better even than *ginja*").

Transportation Connections—Lisbon

Remember to reserve ahead if your train requires a reservation.

By train to: Madrid (2/day, overnight 22:00–8:35), **Faro** (4 fast trains/day, 3.5 hrs), **Paris** (1/day, 18:03–15:00, 21 hrs), **Porto** (12/day, 3.5 hrs), **Évora** (5/day, 2 hrs), **Lagos** (5/day, 3.5 hrs, overnight possible, likely transfer in Tunes), **Coimbra** (17/day, 2.5 hrs), **Nazaré Valado** (9/day, 2.5 hrs), **Sintra** and **Cascais** (4/hrly, 45 min). Train information tel. 01/888-4025 or 01/888-5092.

To Salema: Both bus and train take about five hours from Lisbon to Lagos. Trains from Lisbon to the **south coast** leave from the Barreiro station across the Tagus from downtown. Boats shuttle train travelers from Praça do Comércio to the Barreiro train station with several departures each hour (160$, 30-min ride, note that schedule times listed are often when the boat sails, not when train departs). The 23:00-to-6:45 night train, while no fun, allows you to enjoy the entire day on the Algarve.

By bus to: Coimbra (12/day, 2.5 hrs, 1,400$), **Nazaré** (8/day, 2.25 hrs), **Fatima** (9/day, 2.5 hrs), **Alcobaça** (5/day, 2 hrs), **Óbidos** (5/day, 2 hrs, transfer in Caldas de Rainha), **Évora** (12/day, 2.5 hrs), **Lagos** (8/day, 5 hrs, 2,000$, easier than the train, must book ahead, get details at TI). Buses leave from Lisbon's Arco do Cego bus station (Metro: Saldanha, tel. 01/354-5439). Buses to Spain leave from the same station but are through a different company (tel. 01/317-4992).

COPENHAGEN

Copenhagen (København) is Scandinavia's largest city. With over a million people, it's home to more than a quarter of all Danes. A busy day cruising the canals, wandering through the palace, taking a historic walking tour, and strolling the Strøget (Europe's greatest pedestrian shopping mall) will get you oriented, and you'll feel right at home. Copenhagen is Scandinavia's cheapest and most fun-loving capital, so live it up.

Planning Your Time
A first visit deserves two days.

Day 1: If staying in Christianshavn, start the day browsing through the neighborhood, called Copenhagen's "Little Amsterdam." Catch the 10:30 city walking tour. After a Riz-Raz lunch, visit the Use It information center and catch the relaxing canal boat tour out to *The Little Mermaid*. Spend the rest of the afternoon tracing Denmark's cultural roots in the National Museum and/or touring the Ny Carlsberg Glyptotek art gallery; spend the evening strolling or biking Strøget (follow "Heart and Soul" walk described below) or Christianshavn.

Day 2: At 10:00 explore the subterranean Christiansborg Castle ruins under today's palace. At 11:00 take the 50-minute guided tour of Denmark's royal Christiansborg Palace. The afternoon is free, with many options, including a *smørrebrød* lunch, tour of the Rosenborg Castle/crown jewels, brewery tour, or Nazi Resistance museum (free tour often at 14:00). Evening at Tivoli Gardens before catching a night train out.

With a third day, side-trip out to Roskilde and Frederiksborg. Remember the efficiency of sleeping in-and-out by train. If flying in, most flights from the States arrive in the morning. After that,

head for Stockholm and Oslo. Kamikaze sightseers see Copenhagen as a Scandinavian bottleneck. They sleep in-and-out heading north and in-and-out heading south, with two days and no
nights in the city. Considering the joy of Oslo and Stockholm, this
isn't that crazy if you have limited time. You can check your bag at
the station and take a 10-kr shower in the Interail Center.

You can set yourself up in my best rooms for your entire
Scandinavian tour with a quick trip to a pay phone. This is probably a wise thing to do.

Orientation

Nearly all of your sightseeing is in Copenhagen's compact old
town. By doing things by bike or on foot you'll stumble into
some surprisingly cozy corners, charming bits of Copenhagen
that many miss. Study the map. The medieval walls are now
roads that define the center: Vestervoldgade (literally, "western
wall street"), Nørrevoldgade, and Østervoldgade. The fourth
side is the harbor and the island of Slotsholmen where København ("merchants' harbor") was born in 1167. The next of the
city's islands is Amager, where you'll find the local "Little Amsterdam" district of Christianshavn. What was Copenhagen's
moat is now a string of pleasant lakes and parks, including Tivoli
Gardens. To the north is the old "new town," where the
Amalienborg Palace is surrounded by streets on a grid plan, and
The Little Mermaid poses relentlessly, waiting for her sailor to
return and the tourists to leave.

The core of the town, as far as most visitors are concerned, is
the axis formed by the train station, Tivoli Gardens, the Rådhus
(city hall) square, and the Strøget pedestrian street. It's a great
walking town, bubbling with street life and colorful pedestrian
zones. But be sure to get off the Strøget.

The character in Copenhagen's history who matters most is
Christian IV, who ruled from 1588 to 1648. He was Denmark's
Renaissance king, the royal Danish party animal whose personal
energy kindled a Golden Age when Copenhagen prospered and
many of the city's grandest buildings were built. Locals love to
tell great stories of everyone's favorite king.

Tourist Information

The tourist office is now run by a for-profit consortium called
"Wonderful Copenhagen." This colors the advice and information it provides. Still, it's worth a quick stop for the top-notch
freebies it provides, such as a city map and *Copenhagen This Week*
(a free, handy, and misnamed monthly guide to the city, worth
reading for its good maps, museum hours with telephone numbers, sightseeing tour ideas, shopping suggestions, and calendar of
events, including free English tours and concerts). The TI is

Copenhagen

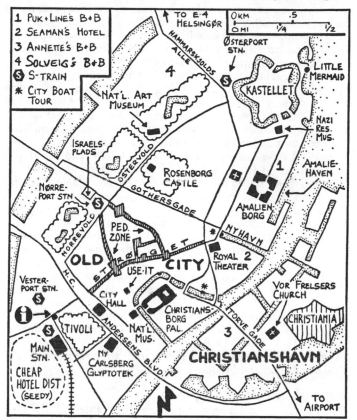

1 PUK+LINE'S B+B
2 SEAMAN'S HOTEL
3 ANNETTE'S B+B
4 SOLVEIG'S B+B
S S-TRAIN
* CITY BOAT
TOUR

TO E·4 HELSINGØR

0 KM · .5
0 MI ¼ ½

ØSTERPORT STN.

LITTLE MERMAID

KASTELLET

NAZI RES. MUS.

NAT'L. ART MUSEUM

4

HAMMARSKJOLDS ALLE

ISRAELS-PLADS

ROSENBORG CASTLE

ØSTERVOLD

AMALIE-HAVEN

1

NØRRE-PORT STN.

GOTHERSGADE

+

AMALIEN-BORG

NØRREVOLD

PED. ZONE

NYHAVN

OLD   S T R Ø G E T   CITY

ROYAL THEATER

2

VESTER-PORT STN.

H.C.

USE·IT

VOR FRELSERS CHURCH

CITY HALL

CHRISTIANS-BORG PAL

CHRISTIANIA

+

i

ANDERSENS BLVD.

TIVOLI

NAT'L MUS.

TORVE GADE

3

MAIN STN.

NY CARLSBERG GLYPTOTEK

CHRISTIANSHAVN

CHEAP HOTEL DIST. (SEEDY)

TO AIRPORT

across from the train station, near the corner of Vesterbrogade and Bernstorffsgade, next to the Tivoli entrance (daily May through mid-September 9:00–21:00; mid-September to April weekdays 9:00–17:00, Saturday 9:00–14:00, closed Sunday; tel. 33 11 13 25). Corporate dictates prohibit the TI from freely offering other brochures (such as walking-tour schedules and brochures on any sights of special interest), but ask and you shall receive. The TI's room-finding service charges you and the hotel a fee and cannot give hard opinions. Do not use it. Get on the phone and call direct—everyone speaks English.

Use It is a better information service. This "branch" of Huset, a hip, city government–sponsored, student-run cluster of cafés, theaters, and galleries, caters to Copenhagen's young but welcomes travelers of any age. It's a friendly, driven-to-help, energetic, no-nonsense source of budget travel information, with a free budget room-finding service, ride-finding board, free luggage lockers, pen-pals-wanted scrapbook, free condoms, and Copenhagen's best free city maps. Their free *Playtime* publication is full of Back Door–style travel articles on Copenhagen and the Danish culture, special budget tips, and events. They have brochures on just about everything, including self-guided tours for bikers, walkers, and those riding scenic bus #6. They have a list of private rooms (250-kr doubles without breakfast). Use It is a 10-minute walk from the station: head down Strøget, then turn right on Rådhustræde for three blocks to #13 (daily June– September 9:00–19:00; off-season open weekdays 10:00–16:00 and closed weekends; tel. 33 15 65 18, fax 33 15 75 18). After hours, their computer touch screen lists the cheapest rooms available in town.

The **Copenhagen Card** covers the public transportation system and admissions to nearly all the sights in greater Copenhagen, which stretches from Helsingør to Roskilde. It includes virtually all the city sights, Tivoli, and the bus from the airport. Available at any tourist office (including the airport's) and the central station: 24 hours, 140 kr; 48 hours, 230 kr; 72 hours, 295 kr. It's hard to break even, unless you're planning to side trip on the included (and otherwise expensive) rail service. It comes with a handy book explaining the 60 included sights, such as: Christiansborg Palace (normally 35 kr), Castle Ruins (20 kr), National Museum (30 kr), Ny Carlsberg Glyptotek (15 kr), Rosenborg Castle (40 kr), Tivoli (39 kr), Frederiksborg Castle (40 kr), and Roskilde Viking Ships (40 kr), plus round-trip train rides to Roskilde (70 kr) and Frederiksborg Castle (70 kr).

Arrival in Copenhagen

By Train: The main train station, Hovedbanegården (HOETH-ban-gorn; learn that word—you'll need to recognize it) is a temple of travel and a hive of travel-related activity. You'll find lockers (25 kr/day), a *garderobe* (35 kr/day per rucksack), a post office, a grocery store (daily 8:00–24:00), 24-hour thievery, and bike rentals. The Interail Center, a service the station offers to mostly young travelers (but anyone with a Eurailpass, Scanrail, student BIGE or Transalpino ticket, or Interail pass is welcome) is a pleasant lounge with 10-kr showers, free (if risky) luggage storage, city maps, snacks, information, and other young travelers (June through mid–September 6:30–22:00). If you just need the map and *Playtime*, a visit here is quicker than going to the TI.

Most travelers arrive in Copenhagen after an overnight train ride. The station has two long-hours money exchange desks. Den Danske Bank is fair—charging the standard 40-kr minimum or 20-kr-per-check fee for traveler's checks (daily 7:00–20:00).

FOREX, which has a worse rate but charges only 10 kr per traveler's check with no minimum, is better for small exchanges (daily 8:00–21:00). On a $100 exchange, I saved 22 kr at FOREX. (The American Express office—a 20-minute walk away, off Strøget—may be even better; see Helpful Hints, below). While you're in the station, reserve your overnight train seat or couchette out (at Rejse-bureau). International rides and all IC trains require reservations (usually 20 kr). Bus #8 (in front of the station on the station side of Bernstorffsgade) goes to Christianshavn B&Bs. Note the time the bus departs, then stop by the TI (across the street on the left) and pick up a free Copenhagen city map that shows bus routes.

By Plane: Copenhagen's International Airport is a traveler's dream, with a tourist office, bank (standard rates), post office, telephone center, shopping mall, grocery store, and bakery. You can use American cash at the airport and get change back in kroner. (Phone service for all airline offices is split between two switchboards: SAS services—tel. 31 54 17 01 and Copenhagen Air Service—tel. 32 47 47 47. SAS ticket hotline—tel. 32 32 68 00.) If you need to kill a night at the airport, try the fetal rest cabins, the *hvilekabiner* (Sb-270 kr, Db-405 kr, rented by the eight-hour period; reception open 6:00–22:00; easy telephone reservations, CC:VMA, tel. 32 31 32 31, fax 32 31 31 09).

Getting Downtown from the Airport: Taxis are fast and easy, accept credit cards, and, at about 150 kr to the town center, are a good deal for foursomes. The SAS **shuttle bus** zips between the central train station and airport in 20 minutes for 35 kr. **City bus** #250s gets you downtown (City Hall Square, TI) in 30 minutes for 17 kr (12/hour, across the street and to the right as you exit the airport). If you're going from the airport to Christianshavn, ride #9 just past Christianshavn Torv to the last stop before Knippels Bridge.

Helpful Hints

Ferries: Book any ferries you plan to use in Scandinavia now. Any travel agent can book the boat rides you plan to take later on your trip, such as the Denmark–Norway ferry (ask for special discounts on this crossing) or the Stockholm–Helsinki–Stockholm cruise (the Silja Line office is directly across from the station at Nyhavn 43A, open Monday–Friday 9:00–17:00, tel. 33 14 40 80). Drivers heading to Sweden by ferry should call for a reservation (two competing Helsingør lines: 33 15 15 15 and 49 26 01 55, and the often cheaper Dragør line: 32 53 15 85). Reservations are free and easy and assure that you won't be stuck in a long line.

Jazz Festival: The Copenhagen Jazz Festival—10 days starting the first Friday in July (July 3–12 in 1998)—puts the town in a rollicking slide-trombone mood. The Danes are Europe's jazz enthusiasts and, more than most music festivals, this one fills the town with happiness. The TI prints up an extensive listing of each year's festival events (as well as a listing of other festivals).

Telephones: Use the telephone liberally. Everyone speaks English, and *This Week* and this book list phone numbers for everything you'll be doing. All telephone numbers in Denmark are eight digits, and there are no area codes. Calls anywhere in Denmark are cheap; calls to Norway and Sweden cost 6 kr per minute from a booth (half of that from a private home). Coin-op booths are often broken. Get a phone card (from newsstands, starting at 20 kr).

Traveler's Checks: The American Express Company does not charge any fee on their checks and only 15 kr per transaction on any other checks and cash (Strøget at Amagertorv 18, Monday–Friday 9:00–17:00, summer Saturdays 9:00–14:00, tel. 33 12 23 01).

Getting Around Copenhagen

By Bus and Subway: Take advantage of the fine bus (tel. 36 45 45 45) and subway system called S-tog (Eurail valid on S-tog, tel. 33 14 17 01). A joint fare system covers greater Copenhagen. You pay 11 kr as you board for an hour's travel within two zones, or buy a blue two-zone *klippekort* from the driver (75 kr for 10 one-hour "rides"). A 24-hour pass costs 70 kr. Don't worry much about "zones." Assume you'll be within the middle two zones. Board at the front, tell the driver where you're going, and he'll sell you the appropriate ticket. Drivers are patient, have change, and speak English. City maps list bus and subway routes. Locals are friendly and helpful. Copenhagen is a bit torn up as it puts together a slick new subway system to celebrate the year 2000.

By Bus Tour: The city tour bus scene is in flux, but there are always tours leaving from the City Hall Square (under the statue of the two Lur Blowers, in front of Palace Hotel, one-hour blitz overview—with a short stop only at the *Mermaid*, two departures per hour, 100 kr, also longer tours, tel. 31 54 06 06). There is a new "hop-on-hop-off" tour bus making a general circuit of the town's top sights (daily 9:00–18:00, 100 kr, tel. 36 77 77 66). Budget do-it-yourselfers simply ride city bus #6: from the Carlsberg Brewery, it stops at Tivoli, town hall, national museum, palace, Nyhavn, Amalienborg castle, the Kastellet, and the *Mermaid* (11 kr for one stop-and-go hour). The entire tour is clearly described in a free Use It brochure.

By Taxi: Taxis are plentiful and easy to call or flag down (22-kr drop charge, then 9 kr per km). For a short ride, four people can travel cheaper by taxi than by bus (e.g., 50 kr from train station to Christianshavn B&Bs). Taxis accept all major credit cards. Calling 31 35 35 35 will get you a taxi within minutes.

Free Bikes! Copenhagen's radical "city bike" program is great for sightseers. Two thousand clunky but practical little bikes are scattered around the old town center (basically the terrain covered in the Copenhagen map in this chapter). Simply locate one of the 150 racks, unlock a bike by popping a 20-kr coin into the handlebar, and pedal away. When you're done, park the bike at any other rack, pop in the lock and you get your deposit coin back (if you can't find a rack, leave the bike on the street anywhere and a bum will take it back and pocket your coin). These simple bikes come with "theft-proof" parts (unusable on regular bikes) and—they claim—computer tracer chips embedded in them so bike patrols can retrieve strays. These are constructed with prison labor and funded by advertisements painted on the wheels and by a progressive electorate. Try this once and you'll find Copenhagen suddenly a lot smaller and easier.

For a serious bike tour, rent a more comfortable bike. Use It has a great biking guide brochure and information about city bike tours (50 kr including bike, two hours, grunge approach). You can rent bikes at Central Station's Cykelcenter (50 kr/day, weekdays 8:00–18:00, Saturday 9:00–13:00, summer Sundays 10:00–13:00, closed Sunday off-season, tel. 33 33 86 13) and Dan Wheel (35 kr/day, 60 kr/2 days, weekdays 9:00–18:00, Saturday and Sunday 9:00–14:00, 2 blocks from the station at 3 Colbjørnsensgade, on the corner of Vesterbrogade, tel. 31 21 22 27).

Do-It-Yourself Orientation Walk: "Strøget and Copenhagen's Heart and Soul"

Start from Rådhuspladsen (City Hall Square), the bustling heart of Copenhagen, dominated by the city hall spire. This used to be the fortified west end of town. The king cleverly quelled a French Revolution–type thirst for democracy by giving his people Europe's first great public amusement park. Tivoli was built just outside the city walls in 1843. When the train lines came, the station was placed just beyond Tivoli. The golden girls high up on the building on the square opposite the Strøget's entrance tell the weather: on a bike (fair) or with an umbrella. These two have been called the only women in Copenhagen you can trust. Here in the traffic hub of this huge city you'll notice . . . not many cars. Denmark's 200 percent tax on car purchases makes the bus or bike a sweeter option.

Old Hans Christian Andersen sits to the right of the city hall, almost begging to be in another photo (as he did in real life). On a pedestal left of the city hall, note the Lur-Blowers sculpture. The *lur* is a horn that was used 3,500 years ago. The ancient originals (which still play) are displayed in the National Museum.

The American trio of Burger King, 7-Eleven, and McDonald's marks the start of the otherwise charming Strøget (stroy-et). Copenhagen's 25-year-old experimental, tremendously successful, and most-copied pedestrian shopping mall is a string of lively (and individually named) streets and lovely squares that bunny-hop through the old town from the city hall to Nyhavn, a 15-minute stroll (or "strøget") away.

As you wander down this street, remember that the commercial focus of a historic street like Strøget drives up the land value, which generally tears down the old buildings. While Strøget has become quite hamburgerized, charm lurks in adjacent areas and many historic bits and pieces of old Copenhagen are just off this commercial cancan.

After one block you can side-trip two blocks left up Larsbjørnsstræde into Copenhagen's colorful university district. Formerly the old brothel area, today this is Soho-chic.

Back on Strøget, the first segment, Frederiksberggade, ends at Gammel Torv and Nytorv (Old Square and New Square). This was the old town center. The Oriental-looking kiosk was one of the city's first community telephone centers before phones were privately owned. The squirting woman and boy on the very old fountain was so offensive to people from the Victorian age that the pedestal was added, raising it—they hoped—out of view. The brick church at the start of Amager Torv is the oldest building you'll see here.

Side-trip two blocks north of Amager Torv to the leafy and caffeine-stained Gråbrødretorv (Grey Brothers' Square). At the next big intersection, Kobmagergade—an equally lively but less-touristy pedestrian street—is worth exploring.

The final stretch of Strøget leads past the American Express office, Pistolstræde (a cute street of shops in restored 18th-century buildings leading off Strøget to the right from Ostergade), McDonald's (good view from top floor), and major department stores (Illum and Magasin, see below) to a big square called Kongens Nytorv, where you'll find the Royal Theater.

Nyhavn, a recently gentrified sailors' quarter, is just opposite Kongens Nytorv. This formerly sleazy harbor is an interesting mix of tattoo parlors, taverns, and trendy (mostly expensive) cafés lining a canal filled with glamorous old sailboats of all sizes. Any historic sloop is welcome to moor here in Copenhagen's ever-changing boat museum. Hans Christian Andersen lived and wrote his first stories here.

Continuing north, along the harborside (from end of Nyhavn canal, turn left), you'll pass a huge ship that sails to Oslo every evening. Follow the water to the modern fountain of Amaliehave Park. The Amalienborg Palace and Square (a block inland, behind the fountain) is a good example of orderly Baroque planning. Queen Margrethe II and her family live in the palace to your immediate left as you enter the square from the harbor side. Her son and heir to the throne, Frederik, recently moved into the

Central Copenhagen

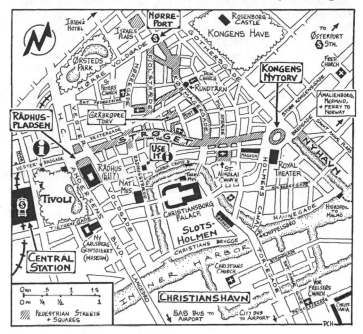

palace directly opposite his mother's. While the guards change with royal fanfare at noon only when the queen is in residence, they shower every morning.

Leave the square on Amaliegade, heading north to Kastellet (Citadel) Park and a small museum about Denmark's World War II resistance efforts. A short stroll, past the Gefion fountain (showing the mythological story of the goddess who was given one night to carve a chunk out of Sweden to make into Denmark's main island, Zealand—which you're on) and a church built of flint and along the water, brings you to the overrated, over-fondled, and over-photographed symbol of Copenhagen, *Den Lille Havfrue— The Little Mermaid.*

You can get back downtown on foot, by taxi, or on bus #1, #6, or #9 from Store Kongensgade on the other side of Kastellet Park (a special bus may run from the *Mermaid* in summer).

Tours of Copenhagen

▲**Walking Tours**—Once upon a time, American Richard Karpen visited Copenhagen and fell in love with the city (and one of its women). He gives daily two-hour walking tours of his adopted hometown covering its people, history, and contemporary scene. His entertaining walks (there are three—each about 1.5 miles with breaks—covering different parts of the city center) leave daily at 10:30 Monday–Saturday, May–September, from in front of the TI (40 kr, kids under 12 free, pick up schedule at the TI or call Richard at tel. 32 97 14 40). All of Richard's tours, while different, complement each other and are of equal "introduction" value. Richard and local historian Helge "Jack" Jacobsen (tel. 31 51 25 90) give reasonably priced private walks and tours. Use It also offers walking tours (40 kr, 15:30 on Wednesday).

▲▲**Harbor Cruise and Canal Tours**—Two companies offer basically the same live, four-language, 60-minute tours through the city canals (2/hour, daily 10:00–17:00, later in July; runs May to mid-September). They cruise around the palace and Christianshavn area, into the wide-open harbor, and out to the *Mermaid*. Both leave from near Christiansborg Palace. It's a pleasant way to see the *Mermaid* and take a load off those weary feet. Dress warmly; boats are open-top.

The low-overhead 20-kr Netto-Bådene Tour boats (tel. 31 87 21 33) leave from Holmens Kirke across from the Borsen (stock exchange), just over Knippels Bridge. The competition, Canal Tours Copenhagen, does a 40-kr harbor tour with a hop-on-and-hop-off version. It leaves from Gammel Strand near Christiansborg Palace and the National Museum (tel. 33 13 31 05). Don't be confused. If you don't plan to get off the boat, go with Netto. There's no reason to pay double. Tour boats also start at Nyhavn.

Sights—Copenhagen
▲**Copenhagen's Town Hall (Rådhus)**—This city landmark, between the station/Tivoli/TI and Strøget pedestrian mall, offers private tours and trips up its 350-foot-high tower. It's draped, inside and out, in Danish symbolism. Bishop Absalon (the city's founder) stands over the door. The polar bears climbing on the rooftop symbolize the giant Danish protectorate of Greenland. The city hall is free and open to the public (Monday–Friday 10:00–15:00). Tours are given in English and get you into other-wise-closed rooms (20 kr, 45 minutes, Monday–Friday at 15:00, Saturday at 10:00). Tourists are allowed to romp up the tower's 300 steps for the best aerial view of Copenhagen (10 kr, Monday–Friday 10:00, 12:00, and 14:00; Saturday 12:00; off-season Monday–Saturday 12:00, tel. 33 66 25 82).

▲**Christiansborg Palace**—This modern *slot*, or palace, built on the ruins of the original 12th-century castle, houses the parliament, supreme court, prime minister's headquarters, and royal reception rooms. Guided 40-minute English tours of the queen's reception rooms let you slip-slide on protect-the-floor slippers through 22 rooms and gain a good feel for Danish history, royalty, and politics in this 100-year-old, still-functioning palace (35 kr, June–August daily at 11:00, 13:00, 15:00; off-season Tuesday, Thursday, and Sunday 11:00 and 15:00; tel. 33 92 64 92). For a rundown on contemporary government, you can also tour the parliament building. From the equestrian statue in front, go through the wooden door, past the entrance to the Christiansborg Castle ruins, into the courtyard, and up the stairs on the right.

▲Christiansborg Castle ruins—An exhibit in the scant remains of the first castle built by Bishop Absalon—the 12th-century founder of Copenhagen—lies under the palace (20 kr, daily 9:30–15:30, closed off-season Monday and Saturday, good 1-kr guide). Early birds note that this sight opens 30 minutes before other nearby sights.

▲▲▲National Museum—Focus on the excellent and curiously enjoyable Danish collection, which traces this civilization from its ancient beginnings. Exhibits are laid out chronologically and well-described in English. Pick up the museum map and consider the 10 kr mini-guide which highlights the top stops. Find room 1 opposite the new entrance and begin your walk following the numbers through the "prehistory" section on the ground floor—oak coffins with still-clothed and armed skeletons from 1300 B.C., ancient and still playable lur horns, the 200-year old Gunderstrup Cauldron of art textbook fame, lots of Viking stuff, and a bitchin' collection of well-translated rune stones. Then go upstairs, find room 101 and carry on—fascinating dirt on the Reformation, everyday town life in the 16th and 17th centuries and, in room 126, a unique "cylinder perspective" of the royal family (from 1656) and two peep shows. The next floor takes you into modern times (30 kr, Tuesday–Sunday 10:00–17:00, free on Wednesday, closed Monday, enter from Ny Vestergade 10, tel. 33 13 44 11). Occasional free English tours are offered in the summer—call first).

▲Ny Carlsberg Glyptotek—Scandinavia's top art gallery, with especially intoxicating Egyptian, Greek, and Etruscan collections, the best of Danish Golden Age (early 19th century) painting, and a heady, if small, exhibit of 19th-century French paintings (in the new "French Wing," including Géricault, Delacroix, Manet, Impressionists, Gauguin before and after Tahiti) is an impressive example of what beer money can do. Linger with marble gods under the palm leaves and glass dome of the very soothing winter garden. Designers, figuring Danes would be more interested in a lush garden than classical art, used this wonderful space as leafy bait to cleverly introduce locals to a few Greek and Roman statues. (It works for tourists too.) One of the original Rodin *Thinker*s (wondering how to scale the Tivoli fence?) can be seen for free in the museum's backyard. This collection is artfully displayed and thoughtfully described—good even after a visit to Rome (15 kr, Tuesday–Sunday 10:00–16:00, free on Wednesday and Sunday,

2-kr English brochure/guide, classy cafeteria under palms, behind Tivoli, Dantes Plads 7, tel. 33 41 81 41).

▲▲**Rosenborg Castle**—This impressively furnished Renaissance-style castle houses the Danish crown jewels and 500 years of royal knickknacks. It's musty with history (including some great Christian IV lore . . . like the shrapnel he pulled from his eye after a naval battle and made into earrings for his girlfriend) and would be fascinating if anything was explained in English. Consider purchasing the guide. The castle is surrounded by the royal gardens, a rare plant collection, and on sunny days, a minefield of sunbathing Danish beauties and picnickers (40 kr, daily June–August 10:00–16:00; May, September, and October 11:00–15:00; there's no electricity inside, so visit at a bright time; Richard Karpen—see Walking Tours, above—does two Rosenborg tours a week; S-train: Nørreport, tel. 33 15 32 86). There is a daily changing of the guard mini-parade from Rosenborg Castle (at 11:30) to Amalienborg Castle (at 12:00). The King's Rosegarden (across the canal from the palace) is a fine place for a picnic (for cheap open-face sandwiches to go, walk a couple of blocks to Lorraine's at the corner of Borgergade and Dronningenstværgade). The fine statue of Hans Christian Andersen in the park, actually erected in his lifetime (and approved by H.C.A.), is meant to symbolize how his stories had a message even for adults.

▲**Denmark's Resistance Museum (Frihedsmuseet)**—The fascinating story of a heroic Nazi resistance struggle (1940–1945) is well-explained in English (free, between the Queen's Palace and the *Mermaid*, daily May–mid-September 10:00–16:00, closed Monday; off-season 11:00–15:00; bus #1, #6, or #9, tel. 33 13 77 14). If prioritizing, the Resistance Museum in Oslo is more interesting.

▲**Our Savior's (Vor Frelsers) Church**—The church's bright Baroque interior is worth a look (free, daily June–August 9:00–16:30, Sunday 13:30–16:30; closes an hour early in spring and fall; closed in winter, bus #8, tel. 31 57 27 98). The unique spiral spire that you'll admire from afar can be climbed for a great city view and a good aerial view of the Christiania commune below. It's 311 feet high, claims to have 400 steps, and costs 20 kr.

Lille Mølle—This tiny intimate museum shows off a 1916 house in Christianshavn (Monday–Friday 11:00–14:00, just off south end of Torvgade, tel. 33 47 38 38). A fine café serves light lunches and dinners in its terrace garden.

Carlsberg Brewery Tour—Denmark's beloved source of legal intoxicants, Carlsberg, provides free one-hour brewery tours followed by 30-minute "tasting sessions" (Monday–Friday 11:00 and 14:00; bus #6 to 140 Ny Carlsberg Vej, tel. 33 27 13 14).

Museum of Erotica—This museum's focus: the love life of *Homo sapiens*. Better than the Amsterdam equivalents, it offers a chance to visit a porno shop and call it a museum. It took some digging, but they've documented a history of sex from Pompeii to present day. Visitors get a peep into the world of 19th-century Copenhagen prostitutes and a chance to read up on the sex lives of Martin Luther, Queen Elizabeth, Charlie Chaplin, and Casanova. After reviewing a lifetime of *Playboy* centerfolds, visitors sit down for the arguably artistic experience of watching the "electric *tabernakel*," a dozen silently slamming screens of porn seething to the gentle accompaniment of music (worth the 49-kr entry fee only if fascinated by sex, daily May–September 10:00–23:00; 11:00–20:00 the rest of the year, a block north of Strøget at Købmagergade 24, tel. 33 12 03 11). For the real thing—unsanitized but free—wander Copenhagen's dreary little red light district along Istedgade behind the train station.

Hovedbanegården—The great Copenhagen train station is a fascinating mesh of Scandinanity and transportation efficiency. Even if you're not a train traveler, check it out (fuller description under Orientation, above).

Nightlife—For the latest on Copenhagen's hopping jazz scene, pick up the *Copenhagen Jazz Guide* at the TI or the more "alternative" *Playtime* magazine at Use It.

Tivoli Gardens

The world's grand old amusement park—which just turned 150 years old—is 20 acres, 110,000 lanterns, and countless ice-cream cones of fun. You pay one admission price and find yourself lost in a Hans Christian Andersen wonderland of rides, restaurants, games, marching bands, roulette wheels, and funny mirrors. Tivoli is wonderfully Danish. It doesn't try to be Disney (39 kr regular admission, 30 kr entry before 13:00 and after 22:00, open daily from April–mid-September 10:00–24:00, closed off-season, tel. 33 15 10 01). Rides are 15 kr, or 1,148 kr for an all-day pass. All children's amusements are in full swing by 11:30—the rest of the amusements are open by 13:30.

Entertainment in Tivoli: Upon arrival, go right to the Tivoli Service Center (through main entry, on left) to pick up a map and events schedule. Take a moment to sit down and plan your entertainment for the evening (events on the half-hour 18:30–23:00; 19:30 concert in the concert hall can be free or cost up to 500 kr, depending on the performer). Free concerts, mime, ballet, acrobats, puppets, and other shows pop up all over the park, and a well-organized visitor can enjoy an exciting evening of entertainment without spending a single krone (though occasionally the schedule is a bit sparse). The children's theater, Valmuen, plays excellent traditional fairy tales (daily except Monday, 12:00, 13:00, and 14:00). If the Tivoli Symphony is playing, it's worth paying for. Friday evenings feature a 22:00 rock or pop show. On

Wednesday and Saturday at 23:45, fireworks light up the sky. If you're taking an overnight train out of Copenhagen, Tivoli (across from the station) is the place to spend your last Copenhagen hours.

Eating at Tivoli: Generally, you'll pay amusement-park prices for amusement park quality food inside. **Søcafeen**, by the lake, allows picnics if you buy a drink. The *pølser* (sausage) stands are cheap. **Færgekroen** is a good lakeside place for a beer or some typical Danish food. The Croatian restaurant, **Hercegovina**, is a decent value (100-kr lunch buffet, 140-kr dinner buffet). For a cake and coffee, consider the **Viften** café.

Christiania

In 1971 the original 700 Christianians established squatters right in an abandoned military barracks just a ten-minute walk from the Danish parliament building. A generation later this "free city"—an ultra-human mishmash of 1,000 idealists, anarchists, hippies, dope fiends, non-materialists, and people who dream only of being a Danish bicycle seat—not only survives, it thrives. This is a communal cornucopia of dogs, dirt, soft drugs, and dazed people—or haven of peace, freedom, and no taboos, depending on your perspective. Locals will remind judgmental Americans that a society must make the choice: allow for alternative lifestyles . . . or build more prisons.

For 25 years Christiania was a political hot potato . . . no one in the Danish establishment wanted it—or had the nerve to mash it. Now that Christiania is no longer a teenager, it's making an effort to connect better with the rest of society. The community is paying its utilities and even offering daily walking tours (see below).

Passing under the city gate you'll find yourself on "Pusher Street" . . . the main drag. This is a line of stalls selling hash, pot, pipes, and souvenirs leading to the market square and a food circus beyond. Make a point of getting past this "touristy" side of Christiania. You'll find a fascinating ramshackle world of moats and earthen ramparts, alternative housing, unappetizing falafel stands, carpenter shops, hippie villas, children's playgrounds, and peaceful lanes. Be careful to distinguish between real Christianians and Christiania's uninvited guests—motley lowlife vagabonds from other countries who hang out here in the summer, skid row–type Greenlanders, and gawking tourists.

Soft Drugs: While hard drugs are out, hash and pot are sold openly (huge joints for 20 kr, senior discounts) and smoked happily. While locals will assure you you're safe within Christiania, they'll remind you that it's risky to take pot out—Denmark is required by Uncle Sam to make a token effort to snare tourists leaving the "free city" with pot. Beefy marijuana plants stand on proud pedestals at the market square. Beyond that an open-air food circus (or the canal-view perch above it, on the earthen ramparts) creates just the right ambience to lose track of time. Graffiti on the wall declares "a mind is a wonderful thing to waste."

Nitty-Gritty: Christiania is open all the time and visitors are welcome (follow the beer bottles and guitars down Prinsessegade behind Vor Frelsers' spiral church spire in Christianshavn). Photography is absolutely forbidden on Pusher Street (if you value your camera, don't even sneak a photo). Otherwise, you are welcome to snap photos, but ask residents before you photograph them. Christiania's free English/Dansk visitor's magazine, *Nitten* (available at Use It), is good reading, offering a serious explanation about how this unique community works and survives. It suggests several do-it-yourself walking tours. Guided tours leave from the front entrance of Christiania at 15:00 (daily June–August, 20 kr, in English and Danish, tel. 32 95 65 07 to confirm). Morgenstedet is a cheap and good vegetarian place (left after Pusher Street). Spiseloppen is the classy good-enough-for-Republicans restaurant (see Eating, below).

More Sights—Copenhagen

Thorvaldsen's Museum features the early 18th-century work of Denmark's greatest sculptor (free, Tuesday–Sunday 10:00–17:00, closed Monday, next to Christiansborg Palace). The noontime **changing of the guard** at the Amalienborg Palace is boring: All they change is places. **Nyhavn**, with its fine old ships, tattoo shops (pop into Tattoo Ole at #17—fun photos, very traditional), and jazz clubs, is a wonderful place to hang out. The **Round Tower**, built in 1642 by Christian IV, connects a church, library, and observatory (the oldest functioning observatory in Europe) with a ramp which spirals up to a fine view of Copenhagen (15 kr, daily 10:00–17:00, later in summer, less on Sunday, nothing to see but the ramp and the view, just off Strøget on Købmagergade).

Copenhagen's **Open Air Folk Museum (Frilandsmuseet)** is a park filled with traditional Danish architecture and folk culture (30 kr, Tuesday–Sunday April–October 10:00–17:00, closed Monday; shorter hours off-season, outside of town in the suburb of Lyngby, tel. 45 85 02 92). From Copenhagen, hop on the S-train to Sorgenfri; then either take a 20-minute walk to the museum (as you exit the station, turn right and walk about one kilometer to next traffic light, turn left and go two blocks to museum) or catch bus #184 from the north end of Nørreport station (this bus takes a circuitous route through several towns before stopping at museum).

Danes gather at Copenhagen's other great amusement park, **Bakken** (free, daily April–August 14:00–24:00, 30 minutes by S-train to Klampenborg, then walk through the woods, tel. 39 63 35 44).

If you don't have time to get to the idyllic island of Ærø, consider a trip to the tiny fishing village of **Dragør** (30 minutes on bus #30 or #33 from Copenhagen's City Hall Square).

Shopping

Copenhagen's colorful flea market is small but feisty and surprisingly cheap (summer Saturdays 8:00–14:00 at Israels Plads). More flea markets are listed in *Copenhagen This Week*. An antique market enlivens Nybrogade (near the palace) every Friday and Saturday. For a streetful of shops selling "Scantiques," wander down Ravnsborggade from Nørrebrogade. The city's top department stores (Illum at 52 Østergade, tel. 33 14 40 02, and Magasin at 13 Kongens Nytorv, tel. 33 11 44 33) offer a good, if expensive, look at today's Denmark. Both are on Strøget and have fine cafeterias on their top floors.

Danes shop cheaper at Dælls Varehus (corner of Krystalgade and Fiolstræde). At UFF on Kultorvet you can buy nearly new clothes for peanuts and support charity. Shops are open Monday–Friday 10:00–19:00; Saturday 9:00–16:00.

The department stores and the Politiken Bookstore on the Rådhus Square have a good selection of maps and English travel guides.

If you buy more than 300 kr ($50) worth of stuff, you can get 80 percent of the 25 percent VAT (MOMS in Danish) back if you buy from a shop displaying the Danish Tax-Free Shopping emblem. If you have your purchase mailed, the tax can be deducted from your bill. Call 32 52 55 66 (8:30–16:00 weekdays), see the shopping-oriented *Copenhagen This Week*, or ask a merchant for specifics.

Sleeping in Copenhagen
(7 kr = about $1)

Sleep Code: **S** = Single, **D** = Double/Twin, **T** = Triple, **Q** = Quad, **b** = bathroom, **CC** = Credit Card (Visa, MasterCard, Amex). Breakfast is often included at hotels and rarely included with private rooms and hostels.

I've listed the best budget hotels in the center (with doubles for 400–600 kr), rooms in private homes an easy bus ride or 15-minute walk from the station (around 350 kr per double), and dormitory options (100 kr per person).

Hotel Sankt Jørgen has big, friendly-feeling rooms with plain old wooden furnishings. Brigitte and Susan offer a warm welcome and a great value (S-375 kr, D-475 kr with this book through 1998, third person-125 kr extra, five-bed family rooms, 10 percent less in winter, breakfast served in your room, elevator, a 12-minute walk from the station or catch bus #13 to the first stop after the lake, Julius Thomsensgade 22, DK-1632 Copenhagen V, tel. 35 37 15 11, fax 35 37 11 97. Unfortunately, each room smells musty from smokers.

Webers Best Western Hotel is my best fine hotel by the train station. Just a five-minute walk down Vesterbrogade from the station, it offers breakfast in a peaceful garden courtyard (if sunny); a classy, modern but inviting interior; and generous weekend/summer rates (May–September and Friday, Saturday, and Sunday all year: Sb-695 kr, Db-995 kr, 1,095 kr, and 1,195 kr depending on size/grade of room; high season: Sb-from 1,080 kr, Db-from 1,280 kr, CC:VMA, sauna/exercise room, Vesterbrogade 11B, DK-1620 Copenhagen, tel. 31 31 14 32, fax 31 31 14 41, e-mail: Webers@webers-hotel.dk).

Excelsior Hotel is a big, mod, normal, tour-group hotel a block behind the station, in a sleazy but safe area just half a block off the decent, bustling Vesterbrogade (small Db-770 kr, bigger Db-865 kr, CC:VMA, Colbjørnsensgade 4, DK-1652 Copenhagen, tel. 31 24 50 85, fax 31 24 50 87).

Ibsen's Hotel is modern, soul-less, and central. Rates are cheaper Friday–Sunday (Sb-455 kr weekends/695 kr weekdays, Db-590 kr/900 kr, CC:VMA, Vendersgade 23, DK-1363 Copenhagen, bus #5, #7E, #16, or #40 from the station, or S-train: Nørreport, tel. 33 13 19 13, fax 33 13 19 16, e-mail: hotel@nicholls.dk).

Hotel KFUM Soldaterhjem, originally for soldiers, rents eight singles and three doubles on the fifth floor, with no elevators (S-215 kr, S plus hideabed-315 kr, D-340 kr, no breakfast, Gothersgade 115, Copenhagen K, tel. 33 15 40 44). The reception is on the first floor up (weekdays 8:30–23:00, weekends 15:00–23:00) next to a budget cafeteria.

Cab-Inn is a radical innovation: 86 identical, mostly collapsible, tiny but comfy, cruise ship–type staterooms, all bright, molded, and shiny with TV, coffeepot, shower, and toilet. Each room has a single bed that expands into a twin with one or two fold-down bunks on the walls. The staff will hardly give you the time of day, but it's tough to argue with this efficiency (S-395 kr, D-495 kr, T-595 kr, Q-695 kr, breakfast-40 kr, easy parking-30 kr, CC:VMA). There are two virtually identical Cab-Inns in the same neighborhood: **Cab-Inn Copenhagen** has a bit nicer locale (Danasvej 32-34, 1910 Frederiksberg C, five minutes on bus #29 to center, tel. 31 21 04 00, fax 31 21 74 09). **Cab-Inn Scandinavia** has a bit bigger building with a bigger cafeteria. Some rooms come with a real double bed for 100 kr extra (Vodroffsvej 55, tel. 35 36 11 11, fax 35 36 11 14). E-mail either at: cabinn@inet.uni-c.dk.

Sleeping in Rooms in Private Homes

Following are a few leads for Copenhagen's best accommodations values. Most are in the lively Christianshavn neighborhood. While each TI has its own list of B&Bs, by booking direct you'll save yourself and your host the tourist-office fee. *Always* call ahead; they book in advance. Most are run by single professional women supplementing their income. All speak English and afford a fine peek into Danish domestic life. Generally no sinks and no breakfast.

In Christianshavn: This area—my adopted Copenhagen home—is a never-a-dull-moment hodgepodge of the chic, artistic, hippie, and hobo, with beer-drinking Greenlanders littering streets in the shadow of fancy government ministries. Colorful with lots of shops, cafés, and canals, it's an easy 10-minute walk to the center, and has good bus connections to the airport and downtown.

Annette and Rudy Hollender enjoy sharing their 300-year-old home with my readers. Even with a long skinny staircase, sinkless rooms, and three rooms sharing one toilet/shower, it's a comfortable and cheery place to call home—which you will by day two (S-225 kr, D-300 kr, T-400 kr, Wildersgade 19, 1408 Copenhagen K, closed November–April, tel. 32 95 96 22, fax 31 57 24 86). Take bus #9 from the airport, bus #8 from the station, or bus #2 from the city hall. From downtown, push the button immediately after crossing Knippels Bridge, and turn right off Torvegade down Wildersgade.

Morten Frederiksen, a laid-back, ponytailed sort of guy, rents five spacious rooms and two four-bed suites in a mod-funky-pleasant old house. The furniture is old-time rustic but elegant. The posters are Mapplethorpe. It's a clean, comfy, good look at today's hip Danish lifestyle and has a great location right on Christianshavn's main drag (D-275 kr, T-375 kr, Q-475 kr, no breakfast, two minutes from Annette's, Torvegade 36, tel. 32 95 32 73, cell phone 20 41 92 73).

Britta Krogh-Lund rents two spacious doubles in an old Christianshavn house (S-225 kr, D-300 kr, T-400 kr, kitchen for self-serve breakfast only, Amagergade 1, C-1423 Copenhagen K, tel. 32 95 55 85). **Loni Føgh** rents two rooms in her modern apartment in the same area (D-300 kr, no breakfast, Strandgade 41, third floor, tel. 32 95 44 77).

South of Christianshavn, **Gitte Kongstad** rents two apartments, each taking up an entire spacious floor in her flat. You'll have a kitchenette, little garden, and your own bike (D-300 kr, family deals, no breakfast, bus #9 from airport, bus #12 or #13 from station, a 10-minute ride past Christianshavn to Badensgade 2, 2300 Copenhagen, tel. and fax 32 97 71 97, cell phone 20 74 21 17). While the neighborhood is inconvenient, you'll feel very at home here and the bike ride into town is a snap.

Private Rooms in Central Copenhagen
Lone (loan-nuh) **Hardt** rents two white woody rooms, each with a double mattress on the floor and nearly no furniture, in a 300-year-old half-timbered building a stone's throw from the Round Tower in the old center of town. If you want to stow away in the very center of town, this can't be beat (D-300 kr, no breakfast, St. Kannikestræde 5, tel. 33 14 60 79).

Solveig Diderichsen rents three rooms in her comfortable, high-ceilinged, ground-floor apartment home. She serves no breakfast but offers kitchen facilities, and there's a good bakery around the corner. Located in a quiet embassy neighborhood next to a colorful residential area with fun shops and eateries behind the Østre Anlæg park (S-275 kr, D-325 kr, T-450 kr, bus #9 direct from the airport or three stops on the subway from the central station, to Østerport, then a three-minute walk to Upsalagade 26, 2100 Copenhagen Ø, tel. 35 43 39 58, fax 35 43 22 70, cell phone 40 11 39 58). If her place is full, she can find you a room in a B&B nearby. An avid sledder, Solveig shares her home with her sled-dog, Maya.

Annette Haugballe rents three modern, pleasant rooms in the quiet, green, residential Frederiksberg area (D-300 kr, no breakfast, easy parking, Hoffmeyersvej 33, 2000 Frederiksberg, on bus line #1 from station or City Hall Square, and near Peter Bangsvej S subway station, tel. 38 74 87 87). Her parents and her friends also rent rooms.

Near the Amalienborg Palace: This is a stately embassy neighborhood—no stress but a bit bland and up lots of stairs. You can look out your window to see the queen's palace (and the guards changing). It's a 10-minute walk north of Nyhavn and Strøget. **Puk** (pook) **De La Cour** rents two rooms in her mod, bright, and easygoing house (D-325 kr with no breakfast but tea, coffee, and a kitchen/family room available, Amaliegade 34, fourth floor, tel. 33 12 04 68). Puk's friend **Line** (lee-nuh) **Voutsinos** offers a similar deal June through September only (D-325 kr, 125 kr/extra bed, each room comes with a small double bed, no breakfast, long-term parking—5 kr/hour or 50 kr/day on street, Amaliegade 34, third floor, tel. 33 14 71 42).

Sleeping in Hostels

Copenhagen energetically accommodates the young vagabond on a shoestring. The Use It office is your best source of information. Each of these places charges about 100 kr per person for bed and breakfast. Some don't allow sleeping bags, and if you don't have your own hostel bedsheet, you'll normally have to rent one for around 30 kr. IYHF hostels normally sell non-cardholders a "guest pass" for 22 kr.

The modern **Copenhagen Hostel** (IYHF) is huge, with 60 220-kr doubles, five-bed dorms at 80 kr/bed, sheets extra, no curfew, excellent facilities, cheap meals, and a self-serve laundry. Unfortunately, it's on the edge of town: bus #10 from the station to Mozartplads, then #37; or, daytime only, ride bus #46 direct from the station (breakfast not included, Vejlands Alle 200, 2300 Copenhagen S, tel. 32 52 29 08, fax 32 52 27 08).

The Danish **YMCA/YWCA**, open only in July and August, is a 10-minute walk from the train station or a short ride on bus #6

(dorm bed-65 kr, four- to 10-bed rooms, breakfast-30 kr, Valde-
marsgade 15, tel. 31 31 15 74).

The **Sleep-In** is extremely popular with the very desperate
or the very adventurous (100 kr with sheets, July–August, four-
bed cubicles in a huge 452-bed co-ed room, no curfew or breakfast, pretty wild, lockers, always has room and free condoms;
Blegdamsvej 132; bus #1 or #6 to "Triangle" stop and look for
sign, tel. 35 26 50 59). In the summer, **Jørgensens Hotel** rents
beds to backpackers in small dorms (100 kr/bed, four- to six-bed
rooms, no reservations for dorm beds, no breakfast, extra for
sheets, near Nørreport, Rømersgade 11, tel. 33 13 81 86, fax 33
15 51 05).

Eating in Copenhagen
Copenhagen's many good restaurants are well listed by category
in *Copenhagen This Week*. Since restaurant prices include 25 percent tax, your budget may require alternatives. These survival
ideas for the hungry budget traveler in Copenhagen will save
lots of money.

Picnics
Irma (in arcade on Vesterbrogade next to Tivoli) and **Brugsen** are
the two largest supermarket chains. **Netto** is a cut-rate outfit with
the cheapest prices. The little grocery store in the central station
is expensive but handy (daily 8:00–24:00).

Viktualiehandler (small delis) and bakeries, found on nearly
every corner, sell fresh bread, tasty pastries (a *wienerbrød* is what
we call a "Danish"), juice, milk, cheese, and yogurt (drinkable, in
tall liter boxes). Liver paste (*leverpostej*) is cheap and a little better
than it sounds.

Smørrebrød
While virgins no longer roll around carts filled with delicate
sandwiches, Denmark's 300-year-old tradition of open-face
sandwiches survives. Open-face sandwiches cost a fortune in
restaurants, but the many *smørrebrød* take-out shops sell them for
8 kr to 30 kr. Drop into one of these often-no-name, family-run
budget savers, and get several elegant OFSs to go. The tradition
calls for three sandwich courses: herring first, then meat, then
cheese. It makes for a classy—and cheap—picnic.

Downtown you'll find these handy local alternatives to Yankee fast-food chains: **Centrum** (open long hours, Vesterbrogade
6C, across from station), **Tria Cafe** (Monday–Friday 8:00–
14:00, closed weekends, Gothersgade 12, near Kongens Nytorv),
Domhusets Smørrebrød (Monday–Friday 7:00–14:30, Katte-
sundet 18), and one in Nyhavn, on the corner of Holbergsgade
and Peder Skrams Gade.

The Pølse

The famous Danish hot dog, sold in *pølsevogn* (sausage wagons) throughout the city, is one of the few typically Danish institutions to resist the onslaught of our global fast-food culture. "Hot dog" is a Danish word for wienie—study the photo menu for variations. These are fast, cheap, tasty, easy to order, and almost worthless nutritionally. Even so, the local "dead man's finger" is the dog kids love to bite.

By hanging around a *pølsevogn* you can study this institution. Denmark's "cold feet café" is a form of social care: only people who have difficulty finding jobs, such as the handicapped, are licensed to run these wiener-mobiles. As they gain seniority they are promoted to work at more central locations. Danes like to gather here for munchies and *pølsesnak* ("sausage talk"), the local slang for empty chatter.

Inexpensive Restaurants

Riz-Raz, around the corner from Use It at Kompagnistræde 20, serves a healthy, all-you-can-eat, 49-kr Mediterranean/vegetarian buffet lunch (daily 11:30–17:00), and an even bigger 59-kr dinner buffet (until 24:00, tel. 33 15 05 75), which has to be the best deal in town. And they're happy to serve free water with your meal. Department stores serve cheery, reasonable meals in their cafeterias (such as **Illum,** an elegant top-floor circus of reasonable food under a glass dome, just past the American Express office; **Magasin;** or **Dælls Varehus,** at Nørregade 12). At **El Porron,** you'll find good Spanish tapas (Vendersgade 10, 1 block from Ibsen's Hotel).

Det Lille Apotek, the "little pharmacy," is a reasonable, candlelit place which has been popular with locals for 200 years (reasonable sandwich lunches, bigger dinners, just off Strøget, between the Frue Church and the Round Tower at St. Kannikestræde 15, tel. 33 12 56 06). The **Chicago Pizza Factory,** next door, serves a cheap lousy pizza buffet and salad bar (49 kr).

To explore your way through a world of traditional Danish food, try a Danish *koldt bord* (an all-you-can-eat buffet). The central station's **Bistro Restaurant** is handy but touristy (154-kr dinner, served daily 11:30–21:30, tel. 33 14 12 32).

Good Eating in Christianshavn

This neighborhood is so cool, it's worth combining an evening wander with dinner even if you don't live here. **Café Wilder** serves creative and hearty dinner salads by candlelight to a trendy local clientele (corner of Wildersgade and Skt. Annæ Gade, a block off Torvegade, open until 22:00). To avoid having to choose just one of their interesting salads, try their three-salad plate (60 kr with bread). They also feature a budget dinner plate for around 75 kr and are happy to serve free water.

Across the street, the **Luna Café** is also good and serves a slower-paced meal. Choose one of three good dinner salads and bread for 40 kr.

The **Ravelin Restaurant**, on a tiny island on the big road just south of Christianshavn, serves good traditional Danish-style food at reasonable prices to happy local crowds. Its lovely lakeside terrace is open on sunny days (100–170-kr dinners, Torvegade 79, tel. 32 96 20 45).

A block away, at the little windmill (Lille Mølle), **Bastionen & Loven** serves Scandinavian nouveau cuisine on a Renoir terrace or in its Rembrandt interior (40-kr lunch specials, 50-kr dinner salads, 80–120-kr dinners, menu is small but fresh, Voldgade 54, up on the bastion off Torvegade at south end of Christianshavn, tel. 32 95 09 40).

In Christiania, the wonderfully classy **Spiseloppen** (meaning "the flea eats") serves great 100-kr vegetarian meals and 140-kr meaty ones by candlelight. Christiania is the free city/squatter town, located three blocks behind the spiral spire of Vor Frelser's church (restaurant open Tuesday–Sunday 17:00–22:00, closed Monday, on the top floor of an old brick warehouse, turn right just inside Christiania's gate, reservations often necessary on weekends, tel. 31 57 95 58).

Morten, who runs a local B&B, recommends: **Dhaka Town** (for good, inexpensive Bangladesh cuisine, south end of Torvegade), **Era Ora** (sophisticated Italian, south end of Torvegade), **Long Feng** (good, cheap Chinese, south end of Torvegade), and **Skipperkroen** (cheap Danish, east end of Strandgade). Right on the community square you'll find a huge grocery store, fruit stands under the Greenlanders monument, and a delightful bakery (facing the square at Torvegade 45).

Transportation Connections—Copenhagen

By train to: Hillerød/Frederiksborg (40/day, 30 min), **Louisiana Museum** (Helsingør train to Humlebæk, 40/day, 30 min), **Roskilde** (16/day, 30 min), **Odense** (16/day, 2 hrs), **Helsingør** (ferry to Sweden, 40/day, 50 min), **Stockholm** (8/day, 8 hrs), **Oslo** (4/day, 10 hrs), **Växjö** (via Alvesta, 6/day, 5 hrs), **Kalmar** (6/day, via Alvesta and Växjö, 7 hrs), **Berlin** (via Gedser, 2/day, 9 hrs), **Amsterdam** (2/day, 11 hrs), **Frankfurt/Rhine** (4/day, 10 hrs). National train info tel. 33 14 17 01. International train info tel. 70 13 14 16.

Cheaper **bus trips** are listed at Use It. All Norway- and Sweden-bound trains go right onto the Helsingør–Helsingborg ferry. (You get 20 minutes to romp on the deck, eat the wind, grab a bite, and change money.) The crossing is included in any train ticket. There are convenient overnight trains from Copenhagen directly to Stockholm, Oslo, Amsterdam, and Frankfurt.

A quickie cruise from Copenhagen to Oslo: A luxurious cruise ship leaves daily from Copenhagen (departs 17:00, returns by 9:15 two days later; 16 hours sailing each way and seven hours in Norway's capital). Special packages give you a bed in a double cabin, a fine dinner, and two smørgåsbord breakfasts for around $170 in summer ($200 for single, Friday and Saturday cost more). Call DFDS Scandinavian Seaways (tel. 33 42 30 00). It's easy to make a reservation in the U.S.A. (tel. 800/5DF-DS55).

STOCKHOLM

If I had to call one European city home, it would be Stockholm. Surrounded by water and woods, bubbling with energy and history, Sweden's stunning capital is green, clean, and underrated.

Crawl through Europe's best-preserved old warship and relax on a canal-boat tour. Browse the cobbles and antique shops of the lantern-lit Old Town and take a spin through Skansen, Europe's first and best open-air folk museum. Marvel at Stockholm's glittering city hall, modern department stores, and art museums.

While progressive and sleek, Stockholm respects its heritage. In summer, mounted bands parade daily through the heart of town to the royal palace, announcing the changing of the guard, and turning the most dignified tourist into a scampering kid. The Gamla Stan (Old Town) celebrates the Midsummer festivities (late June) with the vigor of a rural village, forgetting that it's part of a gleaming 20th-century metropolis.

Planning Your Time

On a two- to three-week trip through Scandinavia, Stockholm is worth two days. Efficient train travelers sleep in and out for two days in the city with only one night in a hotel. (The Copenhagen train arrives at about 7:00 and departs at about 23:30.) To be even more economical and efficient, you could use the luxury Stockholm–Helsinki boat as your hotel for two nights (spending a day in Helsinki) and have two days in Stockholm without a hotel (e.g., Copenhagen; night train to Stockholm, day in Stockholm; night boat to Helsinki, day in Helsinki; night boat to Stockholm, day in Stockholm; night train to Copenhagen). That may sound crazy, but it gives you three interesting and inexpensive days of travel fun.

Spend two days in Stockholm this way:

Day 1: Arrive by train (or the night before by car), do station chores (reserve next ride, change money, pick up map, *Stockholm This Week*, and a Stockholm Card at the Hotellcentralen TI), check into hotel. At 10:00 catch one-hour bus tour from Opera; 11:00 tour *Vasa* warship and have a picnic; 13:00 tour Nordic Museum; 15:00 Skansen (ask for an open-air folk museum tour); 19:00 folk dancing, possible smørgåsbord, and popular dancing, or wander Gamla Stan.

Day 2: Do the 10:00 city hall tour and climb the city hall tower for a fine view; 12:00 catch the changing of the guard at the palace, tour royal palace and armory, explore Gamla Stan, or picnic on one-hour city boat tour; 16:00 browse the modern city center around Kungsträdgården, Sergels Torg, Hötorget market and indoor food hall, and Drottninggatan area.

Orientation (tel. code: 08)

Greater Stockholm's 1.8 million residents live on 14 islands that are woven together by 50 bridges. Visitors need only concern themselves with five islands: **Norrmalm** is downtown, with most of the hotels, shopping areas, and the train station. **Gamla Stan** is the old city of winding lantern-lit streets, antique shops, and classy, glassy cafés clustered around the royal palace. **Södermalm**, aptly called Stockholm's Brooklyn, is residential and untouristy. **Skeppsholmen** is the small, very central traffic-free park island with the Museum of Modern Art and two fine youth hostels. **Djurgården**, literally "deer garden" and now officially a national city park, is Stockholm's wonderful green playground with many of the city's top sights (bike rentals just over the bridge as you enter the island).

Tourist Information

Hotellcentralen is primarily a room-finding service (in the central train station), but its friendly staff adequately handles all your sightseeing and transportation questions. This is the place for anyone arriving by train to arrange accommodations, buy the Tourist Card or Stockholm Card (see below), and pick up a city map, *Stockholm This Week* (which lists opening hours and directions to all the sights, special events, and all the tedious details: lost and found, embassies, post offices, etc.), and brochures on whatever else you need (city walks, parking, jazz boats, excursions, bus routes, shopping, and so on). While *This Week* has a decent map of the sightseeing zone, the 15-kr map covers more area and bus routes. It's worth the extra money if you'll be using the buses (daily June–August 7:00–21:00; May and September 8:00–19:00; off-season 9:00–18:00; tel. 08/789-2425, fax 08/791-8666, e-mail: hotels@stoinfo.se).

Sverige Huset (Sweden House), Stockholm's official tourist information office (a short walk from the station on Kungsträdgården), is very good but usually more crowded than Hotellcentralen.

Greater Stockholm

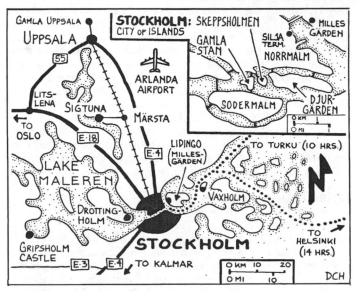

They've got pamphlets on everything; an "excursion shop" for transportation, day-trip, and bus-tour information, and tickets; and an English library and reading room upstairs with racks of 5-kr information on various aspects of Swedish culture and one state's attempt at cradle-to-grave happiness (July–September Monday–Friday 9:00–18:00, Saturday–Sunday 9:00–17:00; off-season weekdays 9:00–18:00, weekends 9:00–15:00; Hamngatan 27, tel. 08/789-2490 for info, 08/789-2415 for tickets; T-bana: Kungsträdgården).

The **City Hall TI** is smaller but with all the information and a bit less chaos (daily 9:00–17:00, May–October only, at the Stadshuset or City Hall, tel. 08/5082-9000).

Arrival in Stockholm

By Train: Stockholm's central train station is a wonderland of services, shops, and people going places. The Hotellcentralen TI is as good as the city TI nearby. If you're sailing to Finland, check out the Viking Line office. The FOREX long-hours exchange counter changes traveler's checks for only a 15-kr fee (two offices, upstairs and downstairs, in the station).

By Plane: Stockholm's Arlanda Airport is 45 kilometers north of town. Shuttle buses run between the airport and the City Terminal next to the station (6/hrly, tel. 08/600-1000). Airport information tel. 08/797-6000 (SAS tel. 08/910-150, British Air tel. 08/679-7800).

Helpful Hints

The Kulturhus on Sergels Torg has a cyber café (Monday–Saturday 11:00–18:00, 20 kr for 30 minutes with assistance, 30 kr same with coffee and a roll). There are three kinds of public phones: coin-op, credit card, and phone card. For operator assistance, call 0018. Numbers starting with 020 are toll-free. For medical help, call 08/644-9200. There's a 24-hour pharmacy near the central station at Klarabergsgatan 64 (tel. 08/454-8100). To get a taxi within three minutes, call Taxi Stockholm (tel. 08/150-000) or Taxi Kurir (tel. 08/300-000).

Getting Around Stockholm

By Bus and Subway: Stockholm complements her many sightseeing charms with great information services, a fine bus and subway system, and special passes that take the bite out of the city's cost (or at least limit it to one vicious budgetary gash).

Buses and the subway work on the same tickets. Ignore the zones since everything I mention (except Drottningholm and Carl Millesgården) are in Zone One. Each 14-kr ticket is valid for one hour (10-packs cost 95 kr). The subway, called T-bana or Tunnelbana, gets you where you want to go very quickly. Ride it just for the futuristic drama of being a human mole and to check out the modern public art (for instance, in the Kungsträdgården station, transit info tel. 08/600-1000). The Tourist Card, which gives you free use of all public transport and the harbor ferry (24 hours/60 kr, 72 hours/120 kr, sold at TIs and newsstands), is not necessary if you're getting the Stockholm Card (see below). The 72-hour pass includes admission to Skansen, Gröna Lund, and the Kaknäs Tower.

It seems too good to be true, but each year I pinch myself and the **Stockholm Card** is still there. This 24-hour, 185-kr pass (sold at TIs and ship terminals) gives you free run of all public transit, free entry to virtually every sight (70 places), free parking, a handy sightseeing handbook, and the substantial pleasure of doing everything without considering the cost (many of Stockholm's sights are worth the time but not the steep individual ticket costs). This pays for itself if you do Skansen, the *Vasa*, and the Royal Palace and Treasury tour. If you enter Skansen on your 24th hour (and head right for the 50-kr aquarium), you get a few extra hours. (Parents get an added bonus: two children under 18 go along for free with each adult pass.) The same pass comes in 48-hour (350-kr) and 72-hour (470-kr) versions.

By Harbor Shuttle Ferry: Throughout the summer, ferries connect Stockholm's two most interesting sightseeing districts. They sail from Nybroplan and Slussen to Djurgården, landing next to the *Vasa* and Skansen (15 kr, not covered by Stockholm Card, every 20 min).

Sights—Downtown Stockholm

▲**Kungsträdgården**—The King's Garden Square is the downtown people-watching center. Watch the life-sized game of chess and enjoy the free concerts at the bandstand. Surrounded by the Sweden House, the NK department store, the harborfront, and tour boats, it's the place to feel Stockholm's pulse (with discretion).

▲▲**Sergels Torg**—The heart of modern Stockholm, between Kungsträdgården and the station, is worth a wander. Enjoy the colorful, bustling underground mall and dip into the Gallerien mall. Visit the Kulturhuset, a center for reading, relaxing, and socializing designed for normal people (but welcoming tourists), with music, exhibits, hands-on fun, and an insight into contemporary Sweden (free, Tuesday–Sunday 11:00–17:00, often later, tel. 08/700-0100). From Sergels Torg, walk up the Drottninggatan pedestrian mall to Hötorget (see Eating, below).

▲▲**City Hall**—The Stadshuset is an impressive mix of 8 million bricks, 19 million chips of gilt mosaic, and lots of Stockholm pride. One of Europe's most impressive public buildings (b. 1923) and site of the annual Nobel Prize banquet, it's particularly enjoyable and worthwhile for its entertaining tours (30 kr, daily June–August at 10:00, 11:00, 12:00, and 14:00; off-season at 10:00 and 12:00; just behind the station, bus #48 or #62, tel. 08/5082-9059). Climb the 350-foot tower (an elevator takes you halfway) for the best possible city view (15 kr, daily 10:00–16:30, May–September only). The City Hall also has a TI and a good cafeteria with complete lunches for 60 kr (11:00–14:00, Monday–Friday).

▲**Orientation Views**—Try to get a bird's-eye perspective on this wonderful urban mix of water, parks, concrete, and people from the City Hall tower (see above), the Kaknäs Tower (at 500 feet, the tallest building in Scandinavia, 20 kr, daily May–August 9:00–22:00, daily September–April 10:00–21:00, bus #69 from Nybroplan or Sergels Torg, tel. 08/789-2435), the observatory in Skansen, or the Katarina elevator (5 kr, daily 7:30–21:00, circa 1930s, ride 40 meters to the top, near Slussen subway stop, then walk behind Katarinavagen for grand views, a classy residential neighborhood, and the lively Mosebacke evening scene— strolling, dancing, and beer gardens).

▲**Quickie Orientation Bus Tour**—Several different city-bus tours leave from the Royal Opera House: 50 minutes for 85 kr with a Swedish/English guide (mid-June through mid-August at 10:30, 11:30, 12:30, 13:30, 14:30) or 90 minutes for 130 kr (mid-April–October at 10:00, 12:00, 14:00, 17:00, tel. 08/411-7023). They also organize 75-minute Old Town walks (75 kr, daily in

Stockholm Center

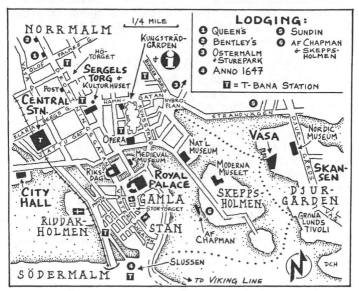

LODGING:
① QUEEN'S   ⑤ SUNDIN
② BENTLEY'S   ⑥ AF CHAPMAN
③ ÖSTERMALM   + SKEPPS-
   + STUREPARK   HOLMEN
④ ANNO 1647

Ⓣ = T-BANA STATION

1/4 MILE

NORRMALM
KUNGSTRÄD-
GÅRDEN
HÖ-
TORGET
SERGELS
TORG +
KULTURHUSET
CENTRAL
STN.
POST
OPERA
MEDIEVAL
MUSEUM
RIKS-
DAG
CITY
HALL
RIDDAR-
HOLMEN
ROYAL
PALACE
GAMLA
STORTORGET
STAN
AF
CHAPMAN
SLUSSEN
SÖDERMALM
TO VIKING LINE
NAT'L
MUSEUM
MODERNA
MUSEET
SKEPPS-
HOLMEN
STRANDVÄGEN
VASA
NORDIC
MUSEUM
SKANSEN
DJUR-
GÅRDEN
GRÖNA
LUNDS
TIVOLI
DCH

summer at 11:30 and 14:30). For a free self-guided tour, follow the Gamla Stan walk laid out below.

▲**City Boat Tour**—For a good floating look at Stockholm, and a pleasant break, consider a sightseeing cruise. Tour boats leave regularly from in front of the Grand Hotel (tel. 08/240-470). The "Historical Canals of Stockholm" tour offers the best informative introduction (80 kr, one hour, departing on the half-hour 10:30–16:30 from mid-June–mid-August). The "Under the Bridges" tour goes through two locks and under 15 bridges (live guide, 130 kr, 2 hours, hourly departures mid-April–mid-October). The "Royal Canal" tour is a scenic joyride through lots of greenery (80 kr, one-hour tape-recorded spiel, departs at half-past each hour from mid-May–August).

▲**National Museum**—Though mediocre by European standards, this museum is small, central, uncrowded, and very user-friendly. The highlights of the collection are several Rembrandts, Rubens, a fine group of Impressionists, and works by the popular and good-to-get-to-know local artists Carl Larsson and Anders Zorn (60 kr, Tuesday–Sunday 11:00–17:00, Tuesday and Thursday until 20:00, closed Monday, tel. 08/666-4250). A worthwhile audiotape (20 kr) guides you through a 50-minute tour of the collection's highlights.

Museum of Modern Art—Newly reopened after a major renovation, this bright and cheery gallery is as far out as can be, with

Picasso, Braque, and lots of goofy Dada art (such as the *Urinal* and the *Goat with Tire*). It's in a pleasant park on Skeppsholmen (60 kr, Tuesday–Thursday 11:00–22:00, Friday–Sunday 11:00–18:00, closed Monday, tel. 08/666-4363).

Sights—Stockholm's Gamla Stan

▲▲**Gamla Stan self-guided walk**—Stockholm's old island core is charming, fit for a film, and full of antique shops, street lanterns, painted ceilings, and surprises. While many will happily just wander around, take this guided walk first:

Slottsbacken: Start at the base of the palace (bottom of Slottsbacken) where a statue of King Gustav III gazes at the palace, formerly the site of Stockholm's first castle. Walk up the broad cobbled boulevard. Behind the obelisk stands the Storkyrkan, Stockholm's cathedral (and most interesting church, which we'll visit later in the walk). Opposite the palace (orange building on left) is the Finnish church (Finska Kyrkan), which originated as the royal tennis hall. Walk behind the church into the shady churchyard where you'll find the three-inch-tall "iron boy," the tiniest statue in Stockholm (often with a little gift). Continue through the yard onto Tradgardsgatan, which leads (turn right) to the old stock exchange.

Stortorget: Left of the stock exchange is the oldest square in town, Stortorget. The town well is now dry but this is still a popular meeting point. Scan the fine old facades. This square has a notorious history. It was the site of Stockholm's bloodbath of 1520—during a royal power-grab, most of the town's aristocracy was beheaded. Rivers of blood were said to have run through the streets. Later, this was the location of the town's pillory. At the far end of the square (under the finest gables) turn right and follow Trangsund toward the cathedral.

Cathedral: Just before the church you'll see my favorite phone booth (Rikstelefon) and the gate to the churchyard being guarded by statues of Caution and Hope. Enter the cathedral (10 kr, daily 9:00–18:00, until 16:00 off-season, pick up the free English flier describing interior). The fascinating interior is paved with centuries-old tombstones; more than 2,000 people are buried under the church. In front on the left is an impressive sculpture of *Saint George and the Dragon* made of oak, gilded metal, and elk horn (1489). Near the exit is a painting with the oldest existing depiction of Stockholm (from 1535, showing a walled city filling only today's Gamla Stan).

Prastgatan: Exiting through the churchyard, continue down Trangsund. At the next corner go downhill on Storkyrkobrinken and take the first left—where the priests used to—on Prastgatan. Enjoy a quiet wander down this peaceful lane. After 2 blocks (at Kakbrinken) you'll see a cannon on the corner guarding a prehistoric rune stone. (In case you can't read ancient Nordic script, it says: "Torsten and Trogun erected this stone in memory of their son.") Continue farther down Prastgatan until you see the German-strength brick steeple of the Tyska Kyrkan (German church). This is a reminder of the days when German merchants worked here. Wander through its churchyard and out the back onto Svartmangatan. Follow it downhill to its end at a couple of benches and an iron railing overlooking Østerlånggatan.

Østerlånggatan: From this perch, survey the street to the left and right. Notice how it curves. This marks the old shoreline. In medieval times piers stretched out like many fingers into the harbor. Gradually, as land was reclaimed and developed, these piers were extended and what were originally piers became lanes leading to piers farther away. Walk left along Østerlånggatan. At the cobbled Y in the road head uphill (up Kopmanbrinken) past a copy of *George and the Dragon*. (Or, for a quick finish, Østerlånggatan takes you back to your starting point at the palace.)

Shopping, Jazz, and Food: From Kopmantorget (the statue), Kopmangatan leads past fine antique shops (some with their medieval painted ceilings still visible) back to Stortorget. Crossing the square, follow the crowds downhill 2 blocks to Stora Nygatan. This is Gamla Stan's main commercial drag, a festival with all the distractions which keep most visitors from seeing the historic charms of the old town—which you just did. Now you can shop and eat.

▲▲**Military Parade and Changing of the Guard**—Starting at the Army Museum (daily at 12:00), the parade marches over either Norrbro Bridge or Strombron Bridge and up to the palace courtyard where the band plays and the guard changes (every other day the band is mounted . . . on horses). These days, the royal family lives out of town at Drottningholm, but the guards are for real. If the guard by the cannon in the semicircular courtyard looks a little lax, try wandering discreetly behind him.

▲▲**Royal Palace**—The palace is a complex of sights. Drop by the info booth in the semicircular courtyard (at the top where the guard changes) for an explanatory brochure with a map marking the different entrances. In a nutshell: The apartments of state are lavish, as worthwhile as any; the treasury is the best in Northern Europe; the chapel is no big deal; Gustav III's museum of antiquities—skip it; and the Royal Armoury is awesome—plan to spend some time. An 80-kr combo ticket covers the apartments, treasury, and antiquities (more info below).

▲▲**Apartments of State**—The stately palace exterior encloses 608 rooms (one more than Britain's Buckingham Palace) of glittering Baroque and rococo decor. Clearly the palace of Scandinavia's superpower, it's richly decorated (18th century) and steeped in royal history. The guided tour is heavy and tedious; the place is more interesting on your own—pick up English descriptions where available and don't miss the Bernadotte rooms (45 kr, daily June–August 10:00–16:00; off-season Tuesday–Sunday 12:00–15:00, closed Monday; free English-language tours at 12:00 and 13:15).

▲▲**Royal Treasury**—You'll find great crowns, scepters, jeweled robes, and plenty of glitter that's gold. Nothing is explained, so get the 2-kr description at the entry (40 kr, same hours as above, no samples, often tours at 11:00 and 14:15, tel. 08/402-6000).

Gustav III's Museum of Antiquities—In the 1700s, Gustav III traveled through Italy and brought home an impressive gallery of classical Roman statues. This was a huge deal if you'd never been out of Sweden. It's worth a look only if you've never been to the rest of Europe. Nothing is explained in English (40 kr, same hours).

▲▲▲**Royal Armoury (Livrust Kammaren)**—This, the oldest museum in Sweden, has the most interesting and best displayed collection of medieval royal armor I've seen anywhere in Europe. The incredible, original 17th-century gear includes royal baby wear, outfits kings wore when they were killed in battle or assassinated, and five centuries of royal Swedish armor—all wonderfully described in English. An added bonus is a basement lined with royal coaches, including coronation coaches, all beautifully preserved and richly decorated (40 kr, daily 11:00–16:00, closed winter Mondays, tours daily in summer at 13:00, entry at the bottom of Slottsbacken at the base of the palace, tel. 08/666-4475).

Riksdaghuset—You can tour Sweden's parliament buildings if you'd like a firsthand look at its government (free hourly tours in English from June through August, usually Monday–Friday at 11:00, 12:30, and 14:00, enter at Riksgatan 3a, but call 08/786-4000 to confirm times).

Museum of Medieval Stockholm (Medeltidsmuseet)—While grade-schoolish, this gives you a good look at medieval Stockholm (30 kr, daily July–August 11:00–16:00, Tuesday, Wednesday, Thursday until 18:00; Monday–Saturday September–June 11:00–16:00, closed Monday; free 30-minute English tours at 14:00 daily in summer enlivens the exhibits; enter from the park in front of the Parliament, tel. 08/700-0593). The Stromparterren park, with its Carl Milles statue of the *Sun Singer* greeting the day, is a pleasant place for a sightseeing break (but an expensive place for a potty break—use the free WC in the museum).

Riddarholm Church—This final resting place for about 600 years of Sweden's royalty is pretty lifeless (20 kr, daily June–August 11:00–16:00, less in May and September, closed in winter, tel. 08/402-6000). In a futile attempt to make this more interesting, they'll loan you the church guidebooklet. The cathedral next to the palace (see Gamla Stan walk, above) is far more interesting.

Sights—Stockholm's Djurgården

▲▲▲**Skansen**—Europe's original and best open-air folk museum, Skansen is a huge park gathering more than 150 historic buildings (homes, churches, shops, and schoolhouses) transplanted from all corners of Sweden. Tourists can explore this Swedish-culture-on-a-lazy-Susan, seeing folk crafts in action and wonderfully furnished old interiors (lively only in the summer). In the town quarter (top of the escalator), craftspeople such as potters are busy doing their traditional thing in a re-created Old World Stockholm. Don't miss the glassblowers if you'll be missing Sweden's Glass Country to the south.

Spreading out from there, the sprawling park is designed to show northern Swedish culture and architecture in the northern part of the park (top of park map) and southern Sweden in the south (bottom of map). Excellent, free one-hour guided walks (from Bollnästorget info stand at top of escalator) paint a fine picture of old Swedish lifestyles (usually daily at 14:00 and 16:00 June–August). There's fiddling nightly (except Sunday) at 18:15, folk dancing demonstrations daily in summer at 19:00, Sunday at 14:30 and 16:00, and public dancing to live bands weeknights (20:30–23:30, call for evening theme—jazz, folk, rock, or disco, nightly except Sunday). Admission to the aquarium is the only thing not covered on your entry ticket (45 kr, 10:00–20:00, shorter hours off season).

Kids love Skansen, especially its zoo (ride a life-size wooden Dala-horse and stare down a hedgehog) and Lill' Skansen (Punch 'n' Judy, mini-train, and pony ride fun daily from 11:00 till at least 16:00). There are lots of special events and several restaurants. The main restaurant serves a grand smørgåsbord (200 kr) and the Ekorren café offers the least expensive self-service lunches with a view. Tre Byttor (next to Ekorren) serves 18th-century-style food in a candlelit setting. Another cozy inn, the old-time Stora Gungan Krog, at the top of the escalator, has better food (60-kr indoor or outdoor lunches with a salad and cracker bar).

Skansen is great for people-watching and picnicking, with open and covered benches all over (especially at Torslunden and Bollnästorget, where peacenik local toddlers don't bump on the bumper cars). Get the map or the 30-kr museum guidebook that has the same map, and check the live crafts schedule at the information stand at Bollnästorget to confirm your Skansen plans.

Use the west entrance (Hazeliusporten) if you're heading to or from the Nordic Museum. (55-kr entry, 30-kr in winter; daily May–August 9:00–22:00, buildings 11:00–17:00; winter 9:00–17:00, some buildings 11:00–15:00; take bus #47 or #44 from the station; call 08/5789-0005 for a recording of the day's tour, music, and dance schedule, or 08/442-8000.) You can miss Gröna Lund, the second-rate amusement park across the street.

▲▲▲*Vasa*—Stockholm turned a titanic flop into one of Europe's
great sightseeing attractions. This glamorous but unseaworthy
warship—top-heavy with a tacked-on extra cannon deck—sank 20
minutes into her 1628 maiden voyage when a breeze caught the
sails and blew her over in the Stockholm harbor. After 333 years
she rose again from the deep (with the help of marine archaeologists) and today is the best-preserved ship anywhere, housed in a
state-of-the-art museum. The masts on the roof are placed to
show their actual height.

Catch the 25-minute English-subtitled movie (at the top of
each hour, dubbed versions often play at 11:30 and 13:30), and for
more information, take the free 25-minute English tours (at the bottom of each hour from 10:30, every other hour off-season) to best
enjoy and understand the ship. Learn about ship's rules (bread can't
be older than eight years), why it sank (heavy bread?), how it's preserved, and so on. Private tours are easy to freeload on, but the displays are so well described that a tour is hardly necessary. (50 kr,
daily mid-June–mid-August 9:30–19:00; off-season 10:00–17:00,
winter on Wednesday until 20:00, tel. 08/666-4800.) Take bus #47
to the big brick Nordic Museum or catch the boat from Nybroplan
or Slussen, or walk from Skansen.

▲▲**Nordic Museum**—This museum, built to look like a Danish palace, offers a look at how Sweden lived over the last 500
years. Highlights include the Food and Drink section, with its
stunning china and crystal table settings; the Nordic folk art
(second and third floors); the huge statue of Gustav Vasa, father
of modern Sweden, by Carl Milles (top of second flight of stairs);
and the Sami (Lapp) exhibit in the basement (Tuesday–Sunday
11:00–17:00, summer Tuesdays and Thursdays until 21:00,
closed Monday, tel. 08/666-4600). Worth your time if you have
the Stockholm Card, but it's overpriced at 60-kr admission. The
30-kr guidebook isn't necessary, but pick up the English
brochure at the entrance.

▲**Thielska Galleriet**—If you liked the Larsson and Zorn art in
the National Gallery and/or if you're a Munch fan, this charming mansion on the water at the far end of the Djurgården park
is worth the trip (40 kr, Monday–Saturday 12:00–16:00, Sunday
13:00–16:00; bus #69 from the central station, tel. 08/662-5884).

Sights—Outer Stockholm

▲▲**Carl Millesgården**—The home and garden housing a
museum and the major work of Sweden's greatest sculptor is dramatically situated on a cliff overlooking Stockholm. Milles' entertaining, unique, and provocative art was influenced by Rodin.
There's a classy café and a great picnic spot (50 kr, daily May–
September 10:00–17:00; off-season Tuesday–Sunday 12:00–16:00,
closed Monday; tel. 08/446-7590.) Catch the T-bana to Ropsten,

then take any bus (except #203 and #213) to the first stop (Torsvik). It's a five-minute walk from there (follow the signs).

▲▲**Drottningholm**—The queen's 17th-century summer castle and present royal residence has been called, not surprisingly, Sweden's Versailles. The adjacent, uncannily well-preserved Baroque theater is the real highlight, especially with its 40-kr guided tours (English theater tours normally depart 12:30, 13:30, 14:30, 15:30, and 16:30 May–September). Get there by a relaxing but over-priced boat ride (70 kr round-trip, two hours) or take the subway to Brommaplan and bus #301 or #323 to Drottningholm. (40-kr entry, palace open daily May–August 11:00–16:30; September weekdays 13:00–15:30, weekends 12:00–15:30; tel. 08/402-6280 for palace tours in English, scheduled often at 11:00.)

The 18th-century Drottningholm court theater performs perfectly authentic operas (about 30 performances each summer). Tickets to these very popular and unique shows go on sale each March. Prices for this time-tunnel musical and theatrical experience are 100 kr to 470 kr. For information, write to Drottningholm's Theater Museum, Box 27050, 10251 Stockholm, or phone 08/660-8225, fax 08/665-1473.

▲▲**Archipelago**—The world's most scenic islands (24,000 of them!) surround Stockholm. Europeans who spend entire vacations in and around Stockholm rave about them. If you cruise to Finland, you'll get a good dose of this island beauty. Otherwise, consider the pleasant hour-long cruise (90 kr each way) from Nybroplan downtown to the quiet town of Vaxholm. The tourist office has a free archipelago guide booklet.

Sauna

Sometime while you're in Sweden or Finland, you'll have to treat yourself to Scandinavia's answer to support hose and a face-lift. (A sauna is actually more Finnish than Swedish.) Simmer down with the local students, retired folks, and busy executives. Try to cook as calmly as the Swedes. Just before bursting, go into the shower room. There's no luke-cold, and the trickle-down theory doesn't apply—only one button, bringing a Niagara of liquid ice. Suddenly your shower stall becomes a Cape Canaveral launch pad, as your body scatters to every corner of the universe. A moment later you're back together. Rejoin the Swedes in the cooker, this time with their relaxed confidence; you now know that exhilaration is just around the corner. Only very rarely will you feel so good.

Any tourist office can point you toward the nearest birch twigs. Good opportunities include a Stockholm–Helsinki cruise, any major hotel you stay in, some hostels, or cheapest, a public swimming pool. In Stockholm, consider the Eriksdalsbadet (Hammarby Slussvag 8, near Skanstull T-bana, tel. 08/643-0673). Use of its 50-meter indoor/outdoor pool and first-rate sauna costs 35 kr.

For a classier experience, the newly refurbished Central-badet lets you enjoy an extensive gym, "bubblepool," sauna, steam room, and an elegant Art Nouveau pool from 1904 (79 kr, long hours, last entry 20:30, closed Sunday, Drottningsgatan 88, five minutes up from Sergels Torg, tel. 24 24 03). Bring your towel into the sauna; the steam room is mixed, the sauna is not. Massage and solarium cost extra, and the pool is more for floating than for jumping and splashing. The leafy courtyard is an appropriately relaxing place to enjoy their restaurant (reasonable and healthy light meals).

Shopping

Modern design, glass, clogs, and wooden goods are popular targets for shoppers. Browsing is a free, delightful way to enjoy Sweden's brisk pulse. Cop a feel at the Nordiska Kompaniet (NK, also meaning "no kroner left") just across from the Sweden House or close by in the Gallerian mall. The nearby Åhlens is less expensive. Swedish stores are open 9:30 to 18:00, until 14:00 on Saturday, and closed Sunday. Some of the bigger stores (like Åhlens and NK) are open later on Saturday and on Sunday afternoon. Take a short walk to Norrmalms Torg to the new bank branch of Scandia Insurance for its ATMs, clean design, Internet access, and free coffee, tea, or chocolate.

For a smørgåsbord of Scanjunk, visit the Loppmarknaden (northern Europe's biggest flea market) at the planned suburb of Skarholmen (free on weekdays, 10 kr on weekends, Monday–Friday 11:00–18:00, Saturday 9:00–15:00, Sunday 10:00–15:00, busiest on weekends, T-bana: Skarholmen, tel. 08/710-0060).

Sleeping in Stockholm
(7 kr = about $1, tel. code: 08)

Sleep Code: **S** = Single, **D** = Double/Twin, **T** = Triple, **Q** = Quad, **b** = bathroom, **CC** = Credit Card (Visa, MasterCard, Amex). "Summer rates" mean mid-June to mid-August, and Friday and Saturday (sometimes Sunday) the rest of the year. Prices include breakfast unless otherwise noted.

Stockholm has plenty of money-saving deals for the savvy visitor. Its hostels are among Europe's best ($15 a bed), and plenty of people offer private accommodations ($50 doubles). Peak season for Stockholm's expensive hotels is business time—workdays outside of summer. Rates drop by 30 to 50 percent in the summer or on weekends, and if business is slow, occasionally any night—ask. To sort through all of this, the city has helpful, English-speaking room-finding services with handy locations and long hours (see Hotellcentralen and Sweden House, above).

The **Stockholm Package** offers business-class doubles with buffet breakfasts from 790 kr, includes two free Stockholm Cards, and lets two children up to 18 years old sleep for free. This is limited from mid-June to mid-August, and Friday and Saturday throughout the year. Assuming you'll be getting two Stockholm Cards anyway (370 kr), this gives you a $200 hotel room for about $50. This is for real (summertime is that dead for business hotels). The procedure (through either tourist office) is easy: a 100-kr advance booking fee (you can arrange by fax, pay when you arrive) or a 40-kr in-person booking fee if you just drop in. Arriving without reservations in July is never a problem. It gets tight during the Water Festival (ten days in early August) and during a convention stretch for a few days in late June.

My listings are a good value only outside of Stockholm Package time, or if the 790 kr for a double and two cards is out of your range and you're hosteling. Every place listed here has staff who speak English and will explain their special deals to you on the phone. If money is limited, ask if they have cheaper rooms. It's not often that a hotel will push their odd misfit room that's 100 kr below all the others. And at any time of year, prices can be soft.

About the only Laundromat in central Stockholm is Tvättomaten, at Våstmannagatan 61 on Odenplan, bus route #53 from Upplandsgaten to Central Station (60 kr, 80 kr full-serve, weekdays 8:30–18:30, Saturday 9:30–15:00, closed Sunday, across from Gustav Vasa church, helpful manager, tel. 08/346-480).

Sleeping in Hotels

Queen's Hotel is cheery, clean, and just a 10-minute walk from the station, located in a great pedestrian area across the street from the Centralbadet (city baths, listed on all maps). With a TV and piano lounge, evening coffee, and a staff that enjoys helping its guests, this is probably the best cheap hotel in town (summer and Friday-Saturday rates: S-450 kr, Ss-480 kr, Sb-595 kr, D-550 kr, Ds-580 kr, Db-695–895 kr, winter rates: D-550–680 kr, Ds-580–780 kr, Db-1,050–1,150 kr, CC:VMA, Drottninggatan 71A, tel. 08/249-460, fax 08/217-620, e-mail:queenshotel@queenshotel.se, run by the Bergman family). Their simple rooms have no sinks. If you're arriving early from the train or boat, you're welcome to leave your bags and grab a 45-kr breakfast.

Bentley's Hotel is an interesting option with old English flair and renovated rooms (summer rates include winter Sundays: very small Db-590 kr, Db-775 kr, suite Db-915 kr, winter Db-1,175 kr, CC:VMA, a block up the street from Queen's at Drottninggatan 77, 11160 Stockholm, tel. 08/141-395, fax 08/212-492). Klas and Agi Kallstrom attempt to mix elegance, comfort, and simplicity into an affordable package. Each room is tastefully decorated with antique furniture but has a modern full bathroom.

The proud little **Stureparkens Gästvåning** is a carefully run, traditional-feeling place with lots of class and 10 thoughtfully

appointed rooms. It's a better value during the high season (July
rates: S-400 kr, D-600 kr, Db-700 kr; high season: S-460 kr, D-660
kr, Db-760 kr, two-night minimum, elevator, CC:VM, near T-bana:
Stadion, across from Stureparken at Sturegatan 58, tel. 08/662-
7230, fax 08/661-5713).

Hotel Gustav Vasa has classy Old World rooms in a listed
building with a family-run feel on a convenient square a 15-minute
walk from the center (Sb-550 kr, D-550 kr, Db-650 kr, rates
100–150 kr higher outside of summer and weekends, they have
some cheaper very small doubles, family deals, CC:VMA, elevator,
subway to Odenplan, exit Våstmannagatan, to Våstmannagatan 61,
tel. 08/343-801, fax 08/307-372).

Drottning Victorias Orlogshem, formerly a hotel for Navy
personnel, now accepts the public, offering functional quiet rooms
with hardwood floors and naval decor in a great neighborhood just
a block off the central harbor behind the National Museum (35
rooms, Sb-450 kr, Db-650 kr, Tb-750 kr, Qb-1,000 kr, family
deals, same prices all year, breakfast-35 kr, no double beds—only
twins, Teatergatan 3, 11148 Stockholm, tel. 08/611-0113, fax
08/611-3150).

Prize Hotel is unique—a super-modern, happy place with
tight 'n' tidy rooms two blocks from the station in Stockholm's
World Trade Center. Designed for business travelers, it has
mostly singles (with wall-beds which fold down to make doubles)
and major summer and weekend discounts (not worth the high-
season price, low prices Friday, Saturday, and June 8 through
August 10: Sb-550 kr, Db-650 kr, they have a few real doubles for
the same price as their wall-bed doubles—worth asking for, low
rates offered during slow winter times—ask, breakfast-55 kr,
CC:VMA, Kungsbron 1, tel. 08/566-2200, fax 08/5662-2444, e-
mail: prize.sth@prize.se, www.prize.se).

City Hotel is also unique. Filling the top floors of a downsized
department store and a leader in environmental friendliness, this
modern place offers hardwood floors and all the comforts in a "one-
star delux" package (200 rooms, discount rates for Friday, Saturday,
and June 20–August 15: Sb-550 kr, Db-790 kr, Qb-990 kr, some Db
with no windows but good ventilation-690 kr, all D are twins
shoved together, high season Db-1,100 kr, breakfast included,
CC:VMA, free loaner bikes, overlooking Hotorget market at
Kungsgatan 47, tel. 08/723-7220, fax 08/723-7299).

Sleeping in Rooms in Private Homes

Stockholm's centrally located private rooms are nearly as expensive as discounted hotels—a deal only in the high season. More
reasonable rooms are a few T-bana stops just minutes from the
center. Stockholm's tourist offices refer those in search of a
room in a private house to **Hotelljånst** (near station, Vasagatan

15, tel. 08/104-467, fax 08/213-716). They can set you up for about 430 kr per double without breakfast for a minimum two-night stay. Go direct—you'll save your host the listing service's fee. Be sure to get the front door security code when you call, as there's no intercom connection with front doors.

Else Mari Sundin is an effervescent retired actress who rents her homey apartment, beautifully located just two blocks from the bridge to Djurgården (D-600 kr for up to four people, bus #47 or #69 to Torstenssonsgatan 7, go through courtyard to "garden house" and up to second floor, tel. 08/665-3348, 0884 door code). Since she lives out of town, this can be complicated. But once you're set up, it's great.

Mrs. Lichtsteiner offers rooms with kitchenettes and has a family room with a loft (Sb-300 kr, Db-400 kr without breakfast, a block from T-bana: Rådhuset, exit T-bana direction Polishuset, at Bergsgatan 45, once inside go through door on left and up elevator to second floor, tel. 08/746-9166, call ahead to get the security code, e-mail: lichtsteiner@monitor-akuten.se).

Sleeping in Hostels

Stockholm has Europe's best selection of big-city hostels offering good beds in simple but interesting places for 100 kr. If your budget is tight, these are right. Each has a helpful English-speaking staff, pleasant family rooms, good facilities, and good leads on budget survival in Stockholm. All will hold rooms for a phone call. Hosteling is cheap only if you're a member (guest membership: 35 kr a night necessary only in IYHF places); bring your own sheet (paper sheets rent for 30 kr), and picnic for breakfast (breakfasts cost 40 kr). Several of the hostels are often booked up well in advance but hold a few beds for those who are left in the lurch.

Af Chapman (IYHF), Europe's most famous youth hostel, is a permanently moored cutter ship. Just a five-minute walk from downtown, this floating hostel has 140 beds—two to eight per stateroom. A popular but compassionate place, it's often booked far in advance, but saves some beds each morning for unreserved arrivals (given out at 7:00) and gives away unclaimed rooms each evening after 18:00. If you call at breakfast time and show up before 12:00, you may land a bed, even in summer (110 kr per bed, D-240 kr, open April–mid-December, sleeping bags allowed, has a lounge and cafeteria that welcomes non-hostelers, reception open 24 hours, rooms locked up 11:00–15:00, STF Vandrarhem Af Chapman, Skeppsholmen, 11149 Stockholm, tel. 08/679-5015 for advance booking or 08/679-5016).

Skeppsholmen Hostel (IYHF), just ashore from the Af Chapman, is open all year. It has better facilities and smaller rooms (120 kr per bed in doubles, triples, and quads, only 90 kr in dorms, nonmembers pay 40 kr extra, tel. 08/679-5016), but it isn't as romantic as its seagoing sister.

Zinken Hostel (IYHF) is a big, basic hostel in a busy suburb, with 120-kr dorm beds (40 kr extra for sheets and nonmembers), plenty of 355-kr doubles without sheets, a Laundromat, and the best hostel kitchen facilities in town (STF Vandrarhem Zinken, open 24 hours all year, Zinkens Väg 20, T-bana: Zinkensdamm, tel. 08/616-8100 or 08/616-8188 in evenings). This is a great no-nonsense, user-friendly value.

Vandrarhemmet Brygghuset, in a former brewery near Odenplan, is small (57 beds in 12 spacious rooms), bright, clean, and quiet, with a Laundromat and a kitchen. Since this is a private hostel, its two- to six-bed rooms are open to all for 125 kr per bed (no sleeping bags allowed, sheets rent for 35 kr). Sheetless doubles are 310 kr. (Open June–mid-September 7:00–12:00, 15:00–23:00, 02:00 curfew, good lockers, Norrtullsgatan 12 N, tel. 08/312-424.)

Café Bed and Breakfast is Stockholm's newest cozy hostel, with only 30 beds (130 kr per bed in eight- to 12-bed rooms, breakfast-30 kr, sheets-30 kr, near Radmansgatan T-bana stop, just off Sveavägen at Rehnsgatan 21, tel. & fax 08/152-838). Bjorn and Daniela also offer three 335-kr doubles and a free sauna.

Stockholm has 12 **campgrounds** (located south of town) that are a wonderful solution to your parking and budget problems. The TI's "Camping Stockholm" brochure has specifics.

Eating in Stockholm

Stockholm's elegant department stores (notably NK and Åhlens, near Sergels Torg) have cafeterias for the kroner-pinching local shopper. Look for the 50-kr "rodent of the day" (*dagens rett*) specials. Most museums have handy cafés. The café at the **Af Chapman hostel** (open to the public in summer daily 11:30–18:00) serves a good salad/roll/coffee lunch in an unbeatable deck-of-a-ship atmosphere (if the weather's good).

The Old Town (Gamla Stan) has lots of restaurants. Try the wonderfully atmospheric **Kristina Restaurang** (Västerlånggatan 68, Gamla Stan, tel. 08/200-529). In this 1632 building, under a leather ceiling steeped in a turn-of-the-century interior, you'll find good dinners from 145 kr, including a salad and cracker bar and a cheaper "summer" menu. They serve a great 55-kr lunch (from 11:00 to 15:00) that includes an entrée, salad bar, bread, and a drink. The place is best Wednesday through Saturday 20:00 to 23:00, when live jazz accompanies your meal (silent in July and August). You can enjoy the music over just a beer or coffee, too. **Hermans** has good vegetarian food and daily specials (Stora Nygatan 11, also in Gamla Stan).

Picnics

With higher taxes almost every year, Sweden's restaurant industry is suffering. You'll notice many fine places almost empty. Swedes joke that the "local" cuisine is now Chinese, Italian, and hamburgers. Here more than anywhere, budget travelers should picnic.

Stockholm's major department stores and the many small corner groceries are fine places to assemble a picnic. **Åhlens** department store has a great food section (open until 21:00, near Sergels Torg). The late-hours supermarket downstairs in the central train station is picnic-friendly, with fresh, ready-made sandwiches (weekdays 7:00–23:00, weekends 9:00–23:00).

The market at **Hötorget** is a fun place to picnic shop, especially in the indoor, exotic ethnic Hötorgshallen (fun café and restaurant in fish section). The outdoor market closes at 18:00, and many merchants put their unsold produce on the push list (earlier closing and more desperate merchants on Saturday).

For a classy vegetarian buffet lunch (70 kr, Monday–Friday until 17:00), often with a piano serenade, or dinner (85 kr, evenings and weekends), eat at **Örtagården** (literally, "the herb garden," Nybrogatan 31, tel. 08/662-1728), above the colorful old Østermalms food market at Østermalmstorg.

Transportation Connections—Stockholm

By train to: **Uppsala** (30/day, 45 min), **Kalmar** (12/day, 5 hrs, including evening service 18:18–23:06), **Copenhagen** (6/day, 8 hrs, night service 22:30–7:00), **Oslo** (3/day, 7 hrs). For train information, call 020/757-575 (toll-free in Sweden) for domestic trains, 08/227-940 for international trains.

By boat to: **Helsinki** (daily/nightly boats, 14 hrs via Viking–U.S. tel. 800/688-3876 or Silja–U.S. tel. 800/323-7436; **Turku** (daily/nightly boats, 10 hrs).

Estline runs a regular ferry from Stockholm to **Tallinn, Estonia** (every other night at 17:30, arriving at 9:00 the next morning, 445 kr each way, 590 kr round-trip with breakfasts and a bed in a quad, cheaper off-season). It offers a 36-hour tour (no visa necessary, round-trip, simple two-bed cabins, two breakfasts, two dinners) for 1,030 kr per person (tel. 08/667-0001).

Parking in Stockholm: Only a Swedish meatball would drive his car in Stockholm. Park it and use the public transit. But parking is confusing, a major hassle, and expensive. Unguarded lots generally aren't safe. Take everything into your hotel or hostel, or pay for a garage. The tourist office has a "Parking in Stockholm" brochure. Those hosteling on Skeppsholmen feel privileged with their 25-kr-a-day island parking passes. Those with the Stockholm Card can park free in a big central garage or at any meter for the duration of the ticket. Ask for your parking card and specifics when you get your Stockholm Card.

OSLO

Oslo is the smallest and least earth-shaking of the Nordic capitals, but this brisk little city offers more sightseeing thrills than you might expect. Sights of the Viking spirit—past and present—tell an exciting story. Prowl through the remains of ancient Viking ships and marvel at more peaceful but equally gutsy modern boats like the *Kon-Tiki*, *Ra*, and *Fram*. Dive into the country's folk culture at the open-air folk museum and get stirred up by Norway's heroic spirit at the Nazi resistance museum.

For a look at modern Oslo, browse through the new yuppie-style harbor shopping complex, tour the striking city hall, take a peek at sculptor Vigeland's people pillars, and climb the towering Holmenkollen ski jump.

Situated at the head of a 60-mile-long fjord, surrounded by forests, and populated by more than 500,000 people, Oslo is Norway's cultural hub and an all-you-can-see smørgåsbord of historic sights, trees, art, and Nordic fun.

Planning Your Time

Oslo offers an exciting two-day slate of sightseeing thrills. Ideally, arrive on the overnight train from Copenhagen, spend two days, and leave on the day train to Stockholm or on the scenic train to Bergen the third morning. Spend the two days like this:

Day 1: Set up. Visit the TI. Tour the Akershus Castle and Norwegian Resistance Museum. Take a picnic on the ferry to Bygdøy and enjoy a view of the city harbor. Tour the *Fram*, *Kon-Tiki*, and Viking ships. Finish the afternoon at the Norwegian Open Air Folk Museum. Boat home. For evening culture, consider the folk music and dance show (20:30 Monday and Thursday).

Day 2: At 10:00 catch the city hall tour, then browse through the National Gallery. Spend the afternoon at Vigeland Park and at the Holmenkollen ski jump and museum. Browse Karl Johans Gate (all the way to the station) and Aker Brygge harbor in the early evening for the Norwegian *paseo*. Consider munching a fast-food dinner on the harbor mini-cruise.

Orientation

Oslo is easy to manage, with nearly all its sights clustered around the central "barbell" street (Karl Johans Gate, with the Royal Palace on one end and the train station on the other), or in the Bygdøy district, a ten-minute ferry ride across the harbor.

Tourist Information

The **Norwegian Information Center** displays Norway as if it were a giant booth at a trade show (on the waterfront between the city hall and Aker Brygge, daily 9:00–20:00, shorter hours off-season, tel. 22 83 00 50). Stock up on brochures for Oslo and all of your Norwegian destinations, especially the *Bergen Guide*. Pick up the free Oslo map, Sporveiskart transit map, *What's on in Oslo* monthly (for the most accurate listing of museum hours and special events), *Streetwise* magazine (hip, fun to read, and full of offbeat ideas), and the free annual *Oslo Guide* (with plenty of details on sightseeing, shopping and eating). Consider buying the Oslo Card (unless your hotel provides it for free, see below). The info center has a rack of free pages on contemporary Norwegian issues and life (near the door); a 30-minute "multi-vision" slideshow taking you around Norway (free, top of the hour, in theater in the back); a 30-minute video called *Look to Norway* that runs all day; a handy public toilet; and rooms showcasing various crafts and ways you can spend your money. The tourist information window in the central station is much simpler and deals only with Oslo but can handle your needs just as well (daily in summer 8:00–23:00, less off-season).

Use It is a hardworking youth information center, providing solid, money-saving, experience-enhancing information to young, student, and vagabond travelers (mid-June–mid-August Monday–Friday 7:30–18:00, Saturday 9:00–14:00, closed Sunday; Monday–Friday 11:00–17:00 the rest of the year, Møllergata 3, tel. 22 41 51 32, Web site: www.unginfo.oslo.no). They have telephones and e-mail, and can find you the cheapest beds in town for no fee. Read their free *Streetwise* magazine for ideas on eating and sleeping cheap, good nightspots, best beaches, and so on.

The **Oslo Card** gives you free use of all city public transit and boats, free entry to all sights, a free harbor mini-cruise tour, free parking, and many more discounts—and is also a handy handbook (24 hours-130 kr, 48 hours-200 kr, or 72 hours-240 kr).

Almost any two-day visit to Oslo will be cheaper with the Oslo Card (which costs less than three Bygdøy museum admissions, the ski jump, and one city bus ride). Students with an ISIC card may be better off without the Oslo Card. The TI's special Oslo Package hotel deal (described under Sleeping, below) includes this card with your discounted hotel room.

Arrival in Oslo
Oslo S, the modern central train station, is slick and helpful, with a late-hours TI (daily in summer 8:00–23:00, less off-season), room-finding service, late-hours bank (fair rates, normal fee), and a super-market (daily 6:30–23:30). While you're at the station, pick up information leaflets on the Flåm and Bergen Railway.

Getting Around Oslo
By Public Transit: Oslo's transit system is made up of buses, trams, ferries, and a subway. Tickets cost 18 kr and are good for one hour of use on any combination of the above. Flexicards give eight rides for 105 kr. Buy tickets as you board (bus info tel. 22 17 70 30, daily 8:00–23:00). **Trafikanten,** the public transit informa-tion center, is under the ugly tower immediately in front of the station. Their free "Sporveiskart for Oslo" transit map is the best city map around and makes the transit system easy. The similar but smaller "Visitor's Map Oslo" (available at TI) is easier to use and also free. The **Dagskort Tourist Ticket** is a 40-kr, 24-hour transit pass that pays for itself on the third ride. The Oslo Card (see Tourist Information, above) gives you free run of the entire transit system. Note how gracefully the subway lines fan out after huddling at Stortinget. Take advantage of the way they run like clockwork, with schedules clearly posted and followed.

    By Bike: Oslo is a good biking town, especially if you'd like to get out into the woods or ride a tram uphill out of town and coast for miles back. Vestbanen organizes tours and rents bikes (three hours/90–130 kr, six hours/140–180 kr depending on bike, in-line skates 100 kr/3 hours, 20 percent discount for readers of this book; May–September weekdays 7:00–22:00, weekends 10:00–18:00, closes earlier off-season; on the harbor next to the Norway Information Center; tel. 23 11 51 00).

Helpful Hints
To get a taxi, call 22 38 80 70, then dial 1. To get on the Internet, try the new cyber café in the east hall of the train station and the Velvet café nearby (10 kr per hour, Monday–Thursday 14:00–20:00, Friday 14:00–18:00, Nedre Slottsgate 2). Jernbanetorgets Apotek is a 24-hour pharmacy directly across from the train station (on Jern-banetorget, tel. 22 41 24 82). Kilroy Travel has student and dis-counted air tickets (Nedre Slottsgate 23, tel. 23 10 23 10).

Oslo Center

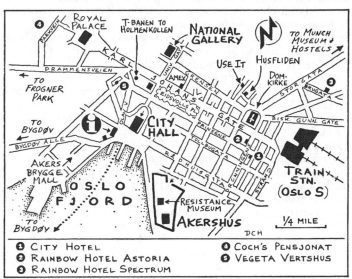

Map legend:
- ❶ City Hotel
- ❷ Rainbow Hotel Astoria
- ❸ Rainbow Hotel Spectrum
- ❹ Coch's Pensjonat
- ❺ Vegeta Vertshus

Sights—Downtown Oslo

Note: Because of Norway's passion for minor differences in opening times from month to month, I've generally listed only the peak-season hours. Assume opening hours shorten as the days do. The high season in Oslo is mid-June to mid-August. (I'll call that "summer" in this chapter.)

▲▲City Hall—Construction on Oslo's richly decorated Rådhuset began in 1931. Finished in 1950 to celebrate the city's 900th birthday, Norway's leading artists (including Edvard Munch) all contributed to what was an avant-garde thrill in its day. The interior's 2,000 square yards of bold and colorful "socialist modernism" murals (which take you on a voyage through the collective psyche of Norway, from its simple rural beginnings through the scar tissue of the Nazi occupation and beyond) are meaningful only with the excellent, free guided tours (20 kr, tours offered Monday–Friday at 10:00, 12:00, and 14:00; open Monday–Saturday 9:00–17:00, Sunday 12:00–17:00, until 16:00 in off-season, entry on the Karl Johans side, tel. 22 86 16 00). Ever notice how city halls rather than churches are the dominant buildings in the your-government-loves-you northern corner of Europe? The main hall of Oslo's city hall actually feels like a temple to good government (the altar-like mural celebrates "work, play, and civic administration"). The Nobel Peace Prize is awarded each December in this room.

▲**Akershus Fortress Complex**—This park-like complex of sites scattered over Oslo's fortified center is still a military base. But dodging patrolling guards and vans filled with soldiers you'll see war memorials, the castle, prison, Nazi resistance museum, armed forces museum, and cannon-strewn ramparts affording fine harbor views and picnic perches. Immediately inside the gate is an information center with an interesting exhibit on medieval Oslo's fortifications. In summer, free 45-minute tours of the grounds leave from the center (10:00, 12:00, 14:00, 16:00, daily but not Sunday morning, tel. 23 09 39 17). There's a small changing of the guard daily at 13:30. The prison, which is visited on the guided walk, will open as a museum in 1998.

Akershus Fortress—One of the oldest buildings in town, this castle overlooking Oslo's harbor is mediocre by European standards. The big, empty rooms remind us of Norway's medieval poverty. Behind the chapel altar, steps lead down to the tombs of some Norwegian kings. The castle is interesting only with the tour (20 kr for castle entry, May to mid-September Monday–Saturday 10:00–16:00, Sunday 12:30–16:00; open Sunday only in spring and fall; closed in winter; free 50-minute English tours offered in summer from Monday–Saturday at 11:00, 13:00, and 15:00, Sunday at 13:00 and 15:00; tel. 22 41 25 21).

▲▲**Norwegian Resistance Museum (Norges Hjemmefrontmuseum)**—A stirring story about the Nazi invasion and occupation is told with wonderful English descriptions. This is the best look in Europe at how national spirit endured total German occupation (20 kr, Monday–Saturday 10:00–17:00, Sunday 11:00–17:00, closes one hour earlier off-season, next to castle in building overlooking the harbor, tel. 23 09 31 38).

Armed Forces Museum—Across the fortress parade ground, a large museum traces Norwegian military from Viking days to post-WWII. The early stuff is very sketchy but the WWII story is fascinating (free, Monday–Friday 10:00–18:00, weekends 11:00–16:00, shorter hours September–May, tel. 22 40 35 82).

▲**National Gallery**—Located downtown, this easy-to-handle museum gives you an effortless tour back in time and through Norway's most beautiful valleys, mountains, and villages, with the help of its romantic painters (especially Dahl). The gallery also has several Picassos, a noteworthy Impressionist collection, some Vigeland statues, and a representative roomful of Munch paintings, including the famous *Scream*. His paintings here make a trip to the Munch museum unnecessary for most. For an entertaining survey of 2,500 years of sculpture, go through the museum gift shop and down the stairs to the right for a room filled with plaster copies of famous works (free, Monday, Wednesday, Friday 10:00–18:00; Thursday 10:00–20:00; Saturday 10:00–16:00; Sunday 11:00–15:00; closed Tuesday; Universitets Gata 13, tel. 22 20 04 04).

▲▲**Browsing**—Oslo's pulse is best felt along and near the central Karl Johans Gate (from station to palace), between the city hall and the harbor, and in the trendy new harborside Aker Brygge Festival Market Mall—a glass-and-chrome collection of sharp cafés and polished produce stalls just west of the city hall (trams #10 and #15 to/from train station). The buskers are among the best in Europe. Aker Brygge is very lively late evenings.

▲▲▲**Vigeland Sculptures and the Vigeland Museum in Frogner Park**—The 75-acre park contains a lifetime of work by Norway's greatest sculptor, Gustav Vigeland. From 1924 through 1942, he sculpted 175 bronze and granite statues—each nude and unique. Walking over the statue-lined bridge you'll come to the main fountain. Trace the story of our lives in the series of humans intertwined with trees around the fountain. The maze in the pavement around the fountain starts opposite the monolith and comes out, 3 kilometers later, closest to the monolith. Try following it . . . you can't go wrong. Vigeland's 60-foot-high tangled tower of 121 bodies called "the monolith of life" is the centerpiece of the park. While it seems the lower figures are laden with earthly concerns and the higher ones are freed to pursue loftier, more spiritual adventures, Vigeland gives us permission to interpret it any way we like. Pick up the free map from the box on the kiosk wall as you enter. The park is more than great art. It's a city at play. Enjoy its urban Norwegian ambience. Then visit the Vigeland Museum to see the models for the statues and more in the artist's studio. Don't miss the photos on the wall showing the construction of the monolith (20 kr for museum, Tuesday–Saturday 10:00–18:00, Sunday 12:00–19:00, closed Monday; off-season Tuesday–Sunday 12:00–16:00 and free, tel. 22 44 11 36). The park is always open and free. Take T-bane #2, bus #20 or #45, or tram #12 or #15 to Frogner Plass.

Oslo City Museum—Located in the Frogner Manor farm in Frogner Park, this museum tells the story of Oslo. A helpful free English brochure guides you through the exhibits (20 kr, Tuesday–Friday 10:00–18:00, Saturday and Sunday 11:00–17:00, closed Monday; shorter hours off-season, tel. 22 43 06 45).

▲▲**Edvard Munch Museum**—The only Norwegian painter to have had a serious impact on European art, Munch (monk) is a surprise to many who visit this fine museum. The emotional, disturbing, and powerfully expressionist work of this strange and perplexing man is arranged chronologically. You'll see paintings, drawings, lithographs, and photographs. Don't miss *The Scream*, which captures the fright many feel as the human "race" does just that (50 kr, daily 10:00–18:00; off-season closes as early as 16:00 and all day Monday; take the T-bane from the station to "Tøyen," tel. 22 67 37 74). If the price or location is a problem, you can see a roomful of Munch paintings in the free National Gallery downtown.

Greater Oslo

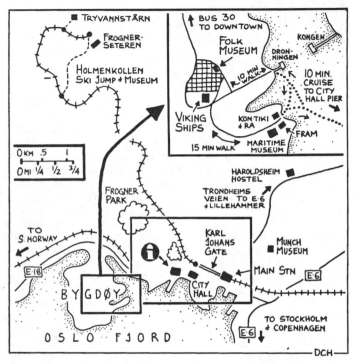

Sights—Oslo's Bygdøy Neighborhood

▲▲▲**Bygdøy**—This exciting cluster of sights is on a park-like peninsula just across the harbor from downtown. To get to Bygdøy, either take bus #30 from the station and National Theater or, more fun, catch the ferry from City Hall (18 kr, free with transit pass or Oslo Card, 3/hour, 8:30–21:00). The Folk Museum and Viking ships are a ten-minute walk from the ferry's first stop, Dronningen. The other museums are at the second stop, Bygdøynes. (See Bygdøy inset in "Greater Oslo" map above.) All Bygdøy sights are within a 15-minute walk of each other. While a handy tourist train shuttles visitors around Bygdøy (3/hour, 20 kr for an all-day pass) the *Fram*-Viking ships walk gives you a fine feel for rural Norway.

▲▲**Norwegian Folk Museum**—Brought from all corners of Norway, 150 buildings have been reassembled on these 35 acres. While Stockholm's Skansen was the first to open to the public, this museum is a bit older, starting in 1885 as the king's private collection. You'll find craftspeople doing their traditional things;

security guards disguised in cute, colorful, and traditional local costumes; endless creative ways to make do in a primitive log-cabin-and-goats-on-the-roof age; a 12th-century stave church; and a museum filled with toys and fine folk costumes. The place hops in the summer but is dead off-season. Catch the free one-hour guided walks at 10:00, 12:00, and 14:00 (call to confirm schedule). Otherwise, glean information from the 10-kr guidebook and the informative attendants who look like Rebecca Boone's Norwegian pen pals (50 kr, daily June–August 9:00–18:00; off-season 10:00–17:00 or less). For folk dance performances, tour, and crafts demonstration schedules, call 22 12 37 00.

▲▲**Viking Ships**—Three great ninth-century Viking ships are surrounded by artifacts from the days of rape, pillage, and—ya sure, yu betcha—plunder. There are no museum tours, but everything is well described in English, and it's hard not to hear the English-speaking bus tour guides. There was a time when much of a frightened Europe closed every prayer with "And deliver us from the Vikings, Amen." Gazing up at the prow of one of these sleek, time-stained vessels, you can almost hear the screams and smell the armpits of those redheads on the rampage (30 kr, daily summer 9:00–18:00, off-season 11:00–15:00, tel. 22 43 83 79). To miss the tour-group crowds, come early, late, or at lunchtime.

▲▲**The *Fram***—This great ship took modern-day Vikings Amundsen and Nansen deep into the Arctic and Antarctic, farther north and south than any ship before. For three years the *Fram* was part of an Arctic ice drift. The exhibit is fascinating. Read the ground-floor displays, then explore the boat (20 kr, daily summer 9:00–18:45, shorter hours off-season). You can step into the lobby and see the ship's hull for free.

The **Polar Sloop *Gjøa*** is dry-docked next to the ferry dock. This is the boat Amundsen and a crew of six used from 1903 to 1906 to "discover" the Northwest Passage (*Fram* ticket gets you aboard).

▲▲**The *Kon-Tiki* Museum**—Next to the *Fram* are the *Kon-Tiki* and the *Ra II*, the boats Thor Heyerdahl built and sailed 4,000 and 3,000 miles, respectively, to prove that early South Americans could have sailed to Polynesia and Africans could have populated Barbados. Both are well-displayed and described in English. A short "adventures of Thor Heyerdahl" movie plays constantly (25 kr, daily 9:30–17:45, off-season 10:30–16:45).

▲**Norwegian Maritime Museum**—If you like the sea, this museum is a salt lick, providing a fine look at Norway's maritime heritage (30 kr, 60 kr for a family, daily 10:00–19:00, off-season 10:30–16:00 and sometimes later). Consider viewing the wide-screen nature film on Norway's coast called *The Ocean, A Way of Life* (free, 20 minutes, on the half-hour).....

Other Oslo Sights and Activities

▲**Henie-Onstad Art Center**—Norway's best private modern art collection, donated by the famous Norwegian Olympic skater/movie star Sonja Henie (and her husband), combines modern art, a stunning building, a beautiful fjord-side setting, and the great café/restaurant Pirouetten. Don't miss her glittering trophy room near the entrance of the center (40 kr, Monday 11:00–17:00, Tuesday–Friday 9:00–21:00, weekends 11:00–19:00, tel. 67 54 30 50). It's in Høvikodden, 8 miles southwest of Oslo (catch bus #151, #153, #251, or #252 from the Oslo train station or from Universitets Plass by the National Theater).

▲▲**Holmenkollen Ski Jump and Ski Museum**—Overlooking Oslo is a tremendous ski jump with a unique museum of skiing. The T-bane #1 gets you out of the city, into the hills and forests that surround Oslo, and to the jump. After touring the history of skiing in the museum, ride the elevator and climb the 100-step stairway to the thrilling top of the jump for the best possible view of Oslo—and a chance to look down the long and frightening ramp that has sent so many tumbling into the agony of defeat.

The **ski museum** is a must for skiers—tracing the evolution of the sport from 4,000-year-old rock paintings, to crude 1,500-year-old skis, to the slick and quickly evolving skis of our century (50 kr, ski jump and museum open daily 9:00–20:00 in June, 9:00–22:00 in July and August, closes earlier off-season).

For a special thrill, step into the **Simulator** and fly down the French Alps in a Disneyland-style downhill ski-race simulator. My legs were exhausted after the four-minute terror. This stimulator, parked in front of the ski museum, costs 35 kr. (Japanese tourists, who wig out over this one, are usually given a free ride after paying for four.)

To get to the ski jump, ride the T-bane line #1 to the Holmenkollen stop and hike up the road 10 minutes. For a longer walk, ride to the end of the line (Frognerseteren) and walk 10 minutes down to the **Frognerseteren Hovedrestaurant**. This classy, traditional old place, with a terrace that offers a commanding view of the city, is a popular stop for apple-cake and coffee or a splurge dinner (daily 11:00–22:30, tel. 22 14 37 36). From the restaurant it's a 30-minute walk downhill through the woods on a gravel path that runs generally parallel to Holmenkollenveien.

The nearby **Tryvannstårnet observatory tower** offers a lofty 360-degree view of Oslo in the distance, the fjord, and endless forests, lakes, and soft hills. It's impressive but not necessary if you climbed the ski jump, which gives you a much better view of the city (daily 10:00–19:00 in June, 9:00–22:00 in July, and 9:00–20:00 in August, less off-season, 10-minute walk from Voksenkollen T-bane stop, tel. 22 14 67 11).

Forests, Lakes, and Beaches—Oslo is surrounded by a vast forest dotted with idyllic little lakes, huts, joggers, bikers, and sun-worshipers. Mountain-bike riding possibilities are endless (as you'll discover if you go exploring without a guide or good map). For a quick ride, you can take the T-bane (with your bike; it needs a ticket too) to the end of line #1 (Frognerseteren, 30 minutes from the National Theater, gaining you the most altitude possible) and follow the gravelly roads (mostly downhill but with some climbing) past several dreamy lakes to Sognsvann at the end of T-bane line #3 (a one-hour ride, not counting time lost). Farther east, from Maridalsvannet, a bike path follows the Aker River all the way back into town. For plenty of trees and none of the exercise, ride the T-bane #3 to Sognsvann (with a beach towel rather than a bike) and join in the lakeside scene. Other popular beaches (such as Bygdøy Huk—direct boat from city hall pier, and others on islands in the harbor) are described in Use It's *Streetwise* magazine.

Harbor and Fjord Tours—Several tour boats leave regularly from Pier 3 in front of the city hall. A relaxing and scenic 50-minute mini-cruise with a boring three-language commentary departs hourly and costs only 70 kr (free with Oslo Card, daily 11:00–20:00, tel. 22 20 07 15). They won't scream if you bring something to Munch. The cheapest way to enjoy the scenic Oslo fjord is to simply ride the ferries that regularly connect the nearby islands with downtown (free with the Oslo Card or transit pass).

▲▲▲**Folk Entertainment**—A group of amateur musicians and dancers (called "Leikarringen Bondeungdomslaget"—Oslo's country youth society) gives a sweet, caring, and vibrant 90-minute show at the Oslo Concert Hall. Several traditional instruments are explained and demonstrated. While folk dancing seems hokey to many, if you think of it as medieval flirting set to music and ponder the complexities of village social life back then, the experience takes you away (140–180 kr, Monday and Thursday from July through early September at 20:30; tel. 22 83 45 10 or 81 53 31 33). Look for the big, brown, glassy overpass on Munkedamsveien; the recommended Vegata Vertshus restaurant is just up the street. For their off-season concert schedule (different locales), call 22 41 40 70.

Tusenfryd/Vinkinglandet—A giant amusement complex just out of town offers a world of family fun—sort of a combo Norwegian Disneyland/Viking Knott's Berry Farm. It's one big company. While the Tusenfryd entry includes the Vikings, you can do just the Viking park if you like. Tusenfryd offers more than 50 rides, plenty of entertainment, family fun, and restaurants. Vikinglandet is a Viking theme park. A coach shuttles fun-seekers to the park from behind the train station (20 kr, 2/hr, 20-minute ride). The entry, 180 kr, is not covered by the Oslo Card (daily 10:30–19:00

in summer, closed in winter). For Viking Land only, tickets cost 95 kr (55 kr for kids under 4'7", tel. 64 94 63 63).

Wet Fun—Oslo offers lots of water fun for about 35 kr (kids half-price). In Frogner Park, the Frognerbadet has a sauna, outdoor pools, high dives, a cafeteria, and lots of young families (free with Oslo Card, daily mid-May–late August 11:00–17:45, Middelthunsgate 28, tel. 22 44 74 29). Kriskis and Svettis (tel. 22 83 25 40) organize free community exercise sessions at Frognerpark. Toyenbadet is a modern indoor pool complex with mini-golf and a 100-yard-long water slide (free with Oslo Card, open at odd hours throughout the year, Helgengate 90, a ten-minute walk from Munch Museum, tel. 22 68 24 23). Oslo's free botanical gardens are nearby. (For more ideas on swimming, pick up *Streetwise* magazine.)

Nightlife—They used to tell people who asked about nightlife in Oslo that Copenhagen was only an hour away by plane. Now Oslo has sprouted a nightlife of its own. The scene is always changing. The tourist office has information on Oslo's many cafés, discos, and jazz clubs. It is the best source of information for local hot spots.

Shopping—For a great selection (but high prices) in sweaters and other Norwegian crafts, shop at Husfliden, the retail center for the Norwegian Association of Home Arts and Crafts (Sunday–Friday 10:00–17:00, Saturday until 15:00, Den Norske Husflidsforening, Møllergata 4, behind the cathedral, tel. 22 42 10 75). Shops are generally open 10:00 to 18:00. Many stay open until 20:00 on Thursday and close early on Saturday and all day Sunday.

Sleeping in Oslo
(7 kr = about $1)
Sleep Code: **S** = Single, **D** = Double/Twin, **T** = Triple, **Q** = Quad, **b** = bathroom, **CC** = Credit Card (Visa, MasterCard, Amex).

Yes, Oslo is expensive. In Oslo, the season dictates the best deals. In low season (July–mid-August, and Friday, Saturday, and Sunday the rest of the year), fancy hotels are the best value for softies, with 600 kr for a double with breakfast. In high season (business days outside of summer), your affordable choices are dumpy-for-Scandinavia (but still nice by European standards) doubles for around 500 kr in hotels and 350 kr in private homes. For experience and economy (but not convenience), go for a private home. Oslo's new Albertine hostel (see below) is well-located and normally has space available (100 kr per bed, 300-kr doubles).

Like those in its sister Scandinavian capitals, Oslo's hotels are designed for business travelers. They're expensive during our off-season (fall through spring), full in May and June for conventions (get reservations), and empty otherwise. Only the TI can sort through all the confusing hotel "specials" and get you the best deal possible on a fancy hotel—push-list rooms at about half-price. Half-price is still 600 kr to 700 kr, but that includes a huge breakfast and a lot of extra comfort for a few extra kroner over the cost of a cheap hotel. Cheap hotels, whose rates are the same throughout the year, are a bad value in summer but offer real savings in low season.

The TI's **Oslo Package** advertises 700-kr discounted doubles in business-class (normally priced at 1,200 kr) rooms and includes a free Oslo Card (worth 130 kr/day). The Oslo Package is a good deal for couples and an incredible deal for families with children under 16 who are traveling in late-June through mid-August or on weekends. Two kids under 16 sleep free, breakfast included, and up to four family members get Oslo Cards, covering free admission to sights and all public transportation. The clincher is that the cards are valid for four days, even if you only stay at the hotel for one night (technically, you should stay two nights, but this is not enforced). Buy this through your travel agent at home, ScanAm World Tour at 800/545-2204, or, easier, upon arrival in Oslo (at the tourist information office).

Use the TI only for these push-list deals, not for cheap hotels or private homes. Some of the cheaper hotels (my listings) tell the TI (which gets a 10 percent fee) they're full when they're not. Go direct. A hotel getting 100 percent of your payment is more likely to have a room. July and early August are easy, but June can be crammed by conventions and September can be tight.

Sleeping in Hotels near the Train Station

Each of these places is within a five-minute walk of the station, in a neighborhood your mom probably wouldn't want you hanging around in at night. The hotels themselves, however, are secure and comfortable. Leave nothing in your car. The Paleet parking garage is handy but not cheap—120 kr per 24 hours.

City Hotel, clean, basic, very homey, and with a wonderful lounge, originated 100 years ago as a cheap place for Norwegians to sleep while they waited to sail to their new homes in America. It now serves the opposite purpose with good if well-worn rooms and a great location (S-380 kr, Sb-495 kr, D-550 kr, Db-680 kr, includes breakfast, CC:VMA, Skippergata 19, enter from Prinsens Gate, tel. 22 41 36 10, fax 22 42 24 29).

Rainbow Hotel Astoria is a comfortable, modern place, and part of the quickly growing Rainbow Hotel chain that understands which comforts are worth paying for. There are umbrellas, televisions, telephones, and full modern bathrooms in each room. Ice machines! Designed for businessmen, the place has mostly singles. Most "twins" are actually "combi" rooms with a regular bed and a fold-out sofa bed (Sb-395–595 kr, Twin/Db-540–695 kr, Db-640–795 kr, rates vary with season, included buffet breakfast, CC:VMA, 3 blocks in front of the station, 50 yards off Karl Johans Gate, Dronningensgate 21, 0154 Oslo, tel. 22 42 00 10, fax 22 42 57 65).

Rainbow Hotel Spectrum is also conveniently located and a good value (discounted prices Friday, Saturday, Sunday, and throughout July: "combi" Twin/b-570–695 kr, full doubles— actually two twins shoved together—100 kr more, CC:VMA, 4 blocks to the right as you leave the station on Lilletorget, Brugata 7, 0186 Oslo, tel. 22 17 60 30, fax 22 17 60 80). **Rainbow Hotel Terminus** is similar and closer to the station, but has a less exciting low-season deal (Friday, Saturday, or Sunday anytime or reservations within 48 hours any day during the May–August period: Sb-420 kr, small bed Db-580 kr, Db-680 kr, regular Db rate-810 kr, includes breakfast, Stenersgate 10, tel. 22 05 60 00, fax 22 17 08 98).

Sleeping in the West End
Cochs Pensjonat has 68 plain rooms (plus nine remodeled doubles) with fresh paint and stale carpets. It's right behind the palace (S-310 kr, Sb-390 kr, D-420 kr, Db-530–580 kr, all Dbs have kitchenettes, no breakfast, CC:VM, tram #11, #13, #17, or #18 to Parkveien 25, tel. 22 60 48 36, fax 22 46 54 02).

Ellingsen's Pensjonat has no lounge, no breakfasts, and dreary halls. But its rooms are great, with fluffy down comforters. It's located in a residential neighborhood 4 blocks behind the Royal Palace (a lot of S-240 kr, S with extra bed-340 kr, D-380 kr, Db-470 kr, extra bed-100 kr, call well in advance for doubles, Holtegata 25, 0355 Oslo 3, tel. 22 60 03 59, fax 22 60 99 21). Located near the Uranienborg church, it's #25 on the east side of the street (T-bane #19 from the station).

Sleeping in Rooms in Private Homes
The TI can find you a 300-kr double for a 20-kr fee (minimum two-night stay). My listings are pretty funky, but full of memories.

Mr. Naess offers big, homey old rooms overlooking a park, and the use of a fully-equipped kitchen. This is a flat in a big ramshackle building, in a borderline-rough neighborhood with workaday shops and eateries nearby (special prices for two or more nights: S-150 kr, D-250 kr, T-375 kr, add 40 kr extra per person for one night stay, no breakfast, plenty of stairs, Toftegate 45, tel. & fax 22 37 58 94). Walk 20 minutes from the station, or take bus #30 from the tower in front of the station to Olaf Ryes Plass (five stops). Three people (or two with lots of luggage) should take a taxi.

Marius Meisfjord, a retired teacher deeply interested in imparting Norse culture, rents rooms behind the palace. Beds are 145 kr per person in a house stuffed with ancient furniture and pictures of European royalty. This eccentric place feels more like a museum than a B&B, and friendly Mr. Meisfjord looks more like Ibsen than a B&B host (breakfast extra, take tram #12 or #15 to

Elisensbergveien, walk 2 blocks to Thomas Heftes Gate 46, tel. 22 55 38 46).

The **Caspari family** rents four comfortable rooms in their home (D-280 kr, breakfast-45 kr). Loosely run, it's set in a lush green yard in a peaceful suburb behind Frogner Park, a quick T-bane ride away (get off at Borgen and walk 100 yards more on the right-hand side of the tracks, Heggelbakken 1, tel. 22 14 57 70).

Sleeping in Hostels

Albertine Hostel, a huge student dorm newly opened to travelers of any age, offers the best cheap doubles in town. It feels like a bomb shelter but each room is spacious, simple, and clean. There are kitchens, free parking, and elevators (Sb-225 kr, Db-300 kr, beds in quads-125 kr, beds in six-bedded rooms-95 kr, sheets-35 kr, towel-15 kr, breakfast-45 kr; catch tram #11, #12, #15, or #17, or bus #27 or #30 from the station; Storgata 55, N-0182 Oslo, tel. 22 99 72 00, fax 22 99 72 20, Web site: www.anker.oslo.no/Anker/turist/Engelsk/turistuk.html). In winter they use the adjacent Anker hotel reception desk.

Haraldsheim Youth Hostel (IYHF), a huge, modern hostel, is open all year, situated far from the center on a hill with a grand view, laundry, and self-service kitchen. Its 270 beds (four per room) are often completely booked. Beds in the new fancy quads with private showers and toilets are 175 kr per person, including buffet breakfast. (Beds in simple quads-155 kr, includes breakfast, sheets-35 kr, guest membership-25 kr; tram #10 or #11 from station to Sinsen, 4 km out of town, five-minute uphill hike; Haraldsheimvcien 4; tel. 22 15 50 43, fax 22 22 10 25.) Eurailers can train (2/hour, to Gressen) to the hostel for free.

YMCA Sleep-In Oslo, located near the train station, offers the cheapest mattresses in town in three large rooms with 15 to 30 mattresses each, plus a left-luggage room, kitchen, and piano lounge (earplugs for sale). It's as pleasant as a sleep-in can be (100 kr, no bedding provided, you must bring a sleeping bag, reception open daily 8:00–11:00 and 17:00–24:00 July to mid-August only, Møllergata 1, entry from Grubbegata, 1 block beyond the cathedral behind Use It, tel. 22 20 83 97). They take no reservations, but call to see if there's a place.

Sleeping on the Train

Norway's trains offer 100-kr beds in triple compartments and 200-kr beds in doubles. Eurailers who sleep well to the rhythm of the rails have several very scenic overnight trips to choose from (it's light until midnight for much of the early summer at Oslo's latitude). If you have a train pass, use the station's service center (across from the ticket windows) and avoid the long lines.

Eating in Oslo

My strategy is to splurge for a hotel that includes breakfast. A 50-kr Norwegian breakfast is fit for a Viking. Have a picnic for lunch or dinner, using one of the many grocery stores. Basements of big department stores have huge first-class supermarkets with lots of picnic dinner-quality alternatives to sandwiches. The little yogurt tubs with cereal come with a collapsible spoon. The train station has a late-hours grocery.

Oslo is awash with clever little budget eateries (modern, ethnic, fast food, pizza, department store cafeterias). Here are three places for those who want to eat like my Norwegian grandparents:

Kaffistova is an alcohol-free cafeteria serving simple, hearty, and typically Norwegian (read "bland") meals for the best price around. You'll get your choice of an entrée (meatballs) and all the salad, cooked vegetables, and "flat bread" you want (or, at least, need) for around 80 kr (open Monday–Friday 12:00–20:30, until 17:00 Saturday and 18:00 Sunday in summer, closes earlier off-season, 8 Rosenkrantzgate).

Norrøna Cafeteria is another traditional budget-saver (70-kr *dagens rett*, before 14:00 you'll get the same thing for 60 kr with a cup of coffee tossed in; Monday–Friday until 18:00, later off-season; central at 19 Grensen). For a classier traditional meal with a grand view, consider the Frognerseteren restaurant (described above with the ski jump).

Vegeta Vertshus, which has been keeping Oslo vegetarians fat, happy, and low on the food chain for 60 years, serves a huge selection of vegetarian food that would satisfy a hungry Viking. Fill your plate once (small plate-73 kr, large plate-83 kr) or eternally for 114 kr. How's your balance? One plate did me fine (daily 11:00–23:00, no smoking, no meat, Munkedamsveien 3B, near top of Stortingsgata between palace and city hall, tel. 22 83 42 32).

The **Aker Brygge** (harborfront mall) development isn't cheap, but it has some cheery cafés, classy delis, open-'til-22:00 restaurants, and markets.

For a grand and traditional breakfast, consider the elegant spread at the **Bristol Hotel** (90 kr, a block off Karl Johans Gate behind the Grand Hotel).

Transportation Connections—Oslo

For train info, call 81 50 08 88 (7:00–23:00, press 1 and wait).

By train to Bergen: Oslo and Bergen are linked by a spectacularly scenic seven-hour train ride. Reservations (20 kr) are required on all long and IC (express) trains. Departures are roughly at 7:45, 10:45, 14:45, 16:00, and 23:00 daily in both directions (500 kr, or 380 kr if you buy a day early and don't travel at peak times like Friday or Sunday).

By boat to Copenhagen: Consider the cheap quickie cruise that leaves daily from Copenhagen (departs 17:00, returns 9:15 two days later; 16 hrs sailing each way and seven hrs in Norway's capital). See Copenhagen chapter for specifics.

By plane: Oslo's new Gardermoen Airport is far from town (30 miles to the north) but is connected by a slick shuttle train to the central train station.

BARCELONA

Barcelona is Spain's second city and the capital of the proud and distinct region of Catalunya (Catalonia). With Franco's fascism now history, Catalunyan flags wave once again. The local language and culture are on a roll in Spain's most cosmopolitan and European corner.

Barcelona bubbles with life in its narrow Gothic Quarter alleys, along the grand boulevards, and throughout the chic, grid-planned new town. While Barcelona had an illustrious past as a Roman colony, Visigothic capital, 14th-century maritime power, and, in more modern times, a top Mediterranean trading and manufacturing center, it's most enjoyable to throw out the history books and just drift through the city. If you're in the mood to surrender to a city's charms, let it be in Barcelona.

Planning Your Time

Sandwich Barcelona between flights or overnight train rides. There's little of earth-shaking importance within eight hours by train. It's as easy to fly into Barcelona as into Madrid, Lisbon, or Paris for most travelers from the United States. Those renting a car can cleverly start here, sleep on the train or fly to Madrid, see Madrid, then pick up the car there.

On the shortest visit Barcelona is worth one night, one day, and an overnight train out. The Ramblas is two different streets by day and by night. Stroll it from top to bottom at night and again the next morning, grabbing breakfast on a stool in a café in the market. Wander the Gothic Quarter, see the cathedral, and have lunch in Eixample (ay-SHAM-pla). The top two sights in town, Gaudí's Sacred Family Church and the Picasso Museum, are usually open until 20:00. The illuminated foun-

Barcelona

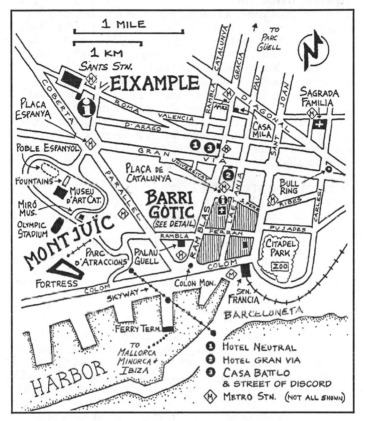

1 MILE

1 KM

SANTS STN.

EIXAMPLE

TO PARC GÜELL

COBERTA

PLAÇA ESPANYA

ROMA

VALENCIA

D. ARAGO

POBLE ESPANYOL

GRAN

VIA

UNIVERSITAT

PLAÇA DE CATALUNYA

PARALLEL

BARRI GÒTIC (SEE DETAIL)

FOUNTAINS

MUSEU D'ART CAT.

MIRÓ MUS.

OLYMPIC STADIUM

MONTJUÏC

PARC D'ATRACCIONS

PALAU GÜELL

RAMBLA

FERRAN

RAMBLAS

FORTRESS

COLOM

COLOM

SKYWAY

COLON MON.

STN. FRANCIA

BARCELONETA

FERRY TERM.

TO MALLORCA MINORCA & IBIZA

HARBOR

RAMBLA CATALUNYA

GRACIA

PAU

DIAGONAL

CASA MILA

JOAN

SANT

SAGRADA FAMILIA

BULL RING

RIBES

CARLES I

PUJADES

CITADEL PARK

ZOO

1 HOTEL NEUTRAL
2 HOTEL GRAN VIA
3 CASA BATLLO & STREET OF DISCORD
Ⓜ METRO STN. (NOT ALL SHOWN)

---

tains (on Montjuïc, near Plaça Espanya) are a good finale for your day.

Of course, Barcelona in a day is a dash. To better appreciate the city's ample charm, spread your visit over two days.

Orientation

Orient yourself mentally by locating these essentials on the map: Barri Gòtic/Ramblas (Old Town), Eixample (fashionable modern town), Montjuïc (hill covered with sights and parks), and Sants Station (train to Madrid). The soul of Barcelona is in its compact core—the Barri Gòtic (Gothic Quarter) and the Ramblas (main boulevard). This is your strolling, shopping, and people-watching nucleus. The city's sights are widely scattered, but with a map and a willingness to figure out the sleek subway system, all is manageable.

Tourist Information

There are three useful TIs in Barcelona: at the Sants train station, at the airport, and on (actually, under) Plaça de Catalunya
across from the Corte Inglés store (TI open Monday–Saturday
9:00–21:00, Sunday 9:00–21:00, no telephone for the public; the
TI exchange desk has fair rates). The Sants Station's TI is
located at the access to platform 6 (daily 8:00–20:00, off-season
8:00–14:00, tel. 93-491-4431). Pick up the large city map and
brochures on Gaudí, Miró, Dalí, Picasso, and the Barri Gòtic.
Ask for the free quarterly Barcelona guide with practical information (transportation, museum hours, restaurants) and cultural
information (history, festivals, and points of interest grouped by
neighborhood).

Arrival in Barcelona

By Train: Although many international trains use the França Station, all domestic (and some international) trains use Sants Station.
Both França and Sants have subway stations: França's is
"Barceloneta" (two blocks away) and Sants' is "Sants Estacio"
(under the station). Both stations have baggage lockers. Sants Station has a good TI, a world of handy shops and eateries, and a
classy "Sala Euromed" lounge for travelers with first-class reservations (quiet, plush, TV, free drinks, study tables, coffee bar).
There is nothing of interest within easy walking distance of either
train station. Subway or taxi to your hotel.

By Plane: Barcelona's El Prat de Llobregat Airport is 12
kilometers southwest of town and connected cheaply and quickly
by Aerobus (immediately in front of arrivals lobby, 4/hrly, 20 min
to Plaça de Catalunya, buy 475-pta ticket from driver, tel. 93-412-
0000) or by RENFE train (walk the tunnel overpass from airport
to station, 2/hrly, 20 min to Sants Station and Plaça de Catalunya,
310 ptas). A taxi to or from the airport costs about 3,000 ptas.

Getting Around Barcelona

Barcelona's subway, among Europe's best, can be faster than a taxi
and connects just about every place you'll visit. It has five color-
coded lines (L1 is red, L2 is lilac, L3 is green, L4 is yellow, L5 is
blue). Rides cost 140 ptas each. A T-1 Card gives you 10 tickets
good for the bus or Metro (subway) for 760 ptas. Pick up the TI's
guide to public transport.

The handy Tourist Bus (Bus Turistic) shuttles tourists on an
18-stop circuit covering the must-sees, with stops at the funicular
and *teleférico* to Montjuïc (9:00–21:30 April–December, buy tickets
on bus). The one-day (1,700 ptas) and two-day (2,300 ptas) tickets
include some serious discounts on the city's major sights. Buses run
every 10 to 20 minutes and take 2.5 hours to do the entire circuit.

Taxis are plentiful and honest (300 ptas drop charge, 100

ptas/km). You can go from the Ramblas to Sants Station for 600 ptas (300 ptas extra for luggage).

Helpful Hints

Theft Alert: Barcelona, after recently illuminating many of its seedier streets, is not the pickpocket paradise it was a few years back, but it's good to be alert—especially on the Ramblas.

American Express: AmEx offices are at Paseo de Gràcia 101 (weekdays 9:30–18:00, Saturday 10:00–12:00, tel. 93-415-2371, Metro: Diagonal) and on the Ramblas opposite the Liceu Metro station (weekdays 9:00–20:30, Saturday 10:00–19:00, Sunday 9:00–14:00, with a small TI).

U.S. Consulate: Passeig Reina Elisenda 23, tel. 93-280-2227.

Pharmacy: At corner of Ramblas and Carrer de la Portaferrissa (daily 9:00–22:00).

Language: Although Spanish is understood here (and the basic survival words are the same), Barcelona speaks a different language—Catalan. (Most place names in this chapter are listed in Catalan.) Here are the essential Catalunyan phrases:

Hello	*Hola*	(OH-lah)
Please	*Si us plau*	(see oos plow)
Thank you	*Gracies*	(GRAH-see-es)
Goodbye	*Adeu*	(ah-DAY-oo)
Exit	*Sordida*	(sor-DEE-dah)
Long live Catalunya!	*Visca Catalunya!*	(BEE-skah . . .)

Sights—The Ramblas

More than a Champs-Élysées, this grand boulevard called the Ramblas takes you from rich at the top to rough at the port, a 20-minute walk. You'll find the grand opera house, ornate churches, plain prostitutes, pickpockets, con men, artists, street mimes, an outdoor bird market, elegant cafés, great shopping, and people willing to charge more for a shoeshine than you paid for the shoes. Take 15 minutes to sit on a white metal chair for 50 ptas and observe. When Hans Christian Andersen saw this street more than 100 years ago, he wrote that there could be no doubt that Barcelona was a great city.

Rambla means "stream" in Arabic. The Ramblas was a drainage ditch along the medieval wall that used to define what is now called the Gothic Quarter. It has five separately named segments, but addresses treat it as a mile-long boulevard.

Walking from Plaça de Catalunya downhill to the harbor, Ramblas highlights are:

▲**Plaça de Catalunya**—This vast central square is the divider between old and new, and the hub for the Metro, bus, and airport shuttle. The grass around its fountain is considered the best public place in town for serious necking. Overlooking the square, the

huge El Corte Inglés department store offers everything from
banzai trees to a travel agency, plus one-hour photo developing,
haircuts, and cheap souvenirs (Monday–Saturday 10:00–21:30,
closed Sunday, supermarket in basement, ninth-floor terrace cafeteria with great city view—take elevator from west entrance, tel.
93-302-1212). Four great boulevards start here: the Ramblas, the
fashionable Passeig de Gràcia, the cozier but still fashionable
Rambla Catalunya, and the stubby, shop-filled, pedestrian-only
Portal de L'Angel.

▲▲**La Boqueria**—This lively produce market (a.k.a. Mercat de
Sant Josep) is an explosion of chicken legs, bags of live snails, stiff
fish, delicious oranges, and sleeping dogs (Monday–Saturday
8:00–20:00, best in the morning after 9:00, closed Sunday).
Straight in (near the back, on the right), the Conserves shop sells
25 kinds of olives (100-gram minimum, 40–70 ptas). Full legs of
ham (*jamón serrano*) abound; *Paleta Iberica de Bellota* are best—
strictly acorn-fed, about 15,000 ptas ($100) each. Beware: *Heuvos
de toro* are bull testicles—surprisingly inexpensive . . . but oh so
good. Drop by Mario and Alex's Café Central for breakfast or an
espresso con leche (far end of main aisle on left).

Café de L'Òpera—One of Barcelona's mainstays, this serves a good
café con leche (daily 9:00–02:30, La Rambla 74, tel. 93-317-7585).

Gran Teatre del Liceu—Spain's only real opera house is luscious
but closed for a few years for renovation because of a 1994 fire
(tourable when it reopens).

Plaça Reial—This elegant, neoclassical square comes complete
with old-fashioned taverns, a Sunday coin and stamp market
(10:00–14:00), and characters who don't need the palm trees to be
shady. Escudellers, a street one block toward the water from the
square, is lined with bars whose counters are strewn with vampy
ladies. The area is well-policed, but if you tried, you could get into
trouble.

▲**Palau Güell**—The only look at a Gaudí Art Nouveau interior, and
for me, it's the most enjoyable look at Barcelona's organic architect
(300 ptas, combo ticket for 1,500 ptas covers six modernist sights
plus English guidebook—worthwhile for fans; usually open Monday–Friday 10:00–14:00 and 16:00–20:00, maybe Saturday, Carrer
Nou de la Rambla 3-5, tel. 93-317-3974). If you're tired and will
see/have seen Casa Milà, skip the climb to the rooftop.

Chinatown (Barri Xines)—Farther downhill, on the right-hand
side, is the world's only Chinatown with nothing even remotely
Chinese in or near it. Named this for the prejudiced notion that
Chinese immigrants go hand in hand with poverty, prostitution,
and drug dealing, the actual inhabitants are poor Spanish, Arab,
and Gypsy people down on their luck. At night the area is full of
prostitutes, many of them transvestites, who cater to sailors wandering up from the port. Don't venture in at night.

Barcelona's Gothic Quarter

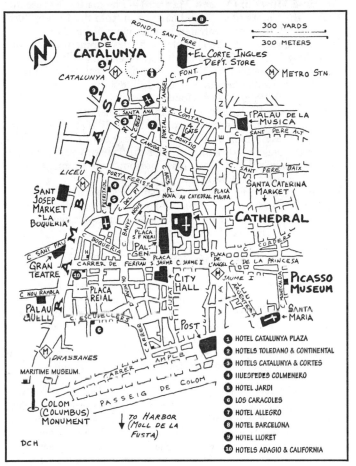

300 YARDS

300 METERS

Ⓜ METRO STN

PLACA DE CATALUNYA

CATALUNYA Ⓜ

RONDA SANT PERE

←EL CORTE INGLES DEP'T. STORE

C. FONT

PALAU DE LA MUSICA

C. SANTA ANA

COMTAL

4 GATS

SANT PERE ALT

AV PORTAL DE L'ANGEL

C. MONTSIO

SANT PERE BAIX

LICEU

PORTAFERISSA

PL. NOVA AV CATEDRAL MAURA

SANTA CATERINA MARKET

SANT JOSEP MARKET "LA BOQUERIA"

PLACA S F NERI

CATHEDRAL

CORDERS

PAL. GEN.

PLACA GEN.

CARRER DE FERRAN S JAVME C. JAVME I

PLACA DE L'ANGEL C. DE LA PRINCESA

PICASSO MUSEUM

GRAN TEATRE

BOQUERIA

Ⓜ JAUME I

C NOV RAMBLA

PLACA REIAL

CITY HALL

SANTA MARIA

PALAU GUELL

C. ESCUDELLERS

Post

DRASSANES Ⓜ

MARITIME MUSEUM

CARRER

AMPLE

CARRER

COLOM (COLUMBUS) MONUMENT

PASSEIG DE COLOM

↓ TO HARBOR (MOLL DE LA FUSTA)

DCH

❶ HOTEL CATALUNYA PLAZA
❷ HOTELS TOLEDANO & CONTINENTAL
❸ HOTELS CATALUNYA & CORTES
❹ HUESPEDES COLMENERO
❺ HOTEL JARDI
❻ LOS CARACOLES
❼ HOTEL ALLEGRO
❽ HOTEL BARCELONA
❾ HOTEL LLORET
❿ HOTELS ADAGIO & CALIFORNIA

Columbus Monument (Monument a Colóm)—Marking the point where the Ramblas hits the harbor, this 50-meter-tall monument built for an 1888 exposition offers an elevator-assisted view from its top (250 ptas, daily 9:00–21:00; off-season 10:00–14:30 and 15:30–19:30; skip the ascent if you plan on riding the harbor gondola to Montjuïc, which offers a far better view). It's interesting that Barcelona would so honor the man whose discoveries ultimately led to its downfall as a great trading power. It was here in Barcelona that Ferdinand and Isabel welcomed Columbus home after his first trip to America.

Maritime Museum (Museo Maritim)—The maritime museum displays the history of ships and navigation from the 13th to 20th centuries. Its 45-minute infrared headphone multimedia tour in English shows off the Catalan role in the development of maritime technology (e.g., the first submarine was Catalan). With fleets of seemingly unimportant replicas of old boats explained in Catalan and Spanish, landlubbers may find it dull (800 ptas, Tuesday–Sunday 10:00–19:00, closed Monday).

Golondrinas—Little tourist boats make a half-hour tour of the harbor every 20 to 30 minutes from 11:00 to 20:00 at the foot of the Columbus Monument (300 ptas one-way to other side of harbor, or 480 ptas round-trip). Consider this ride or the harbor steps here for a picnic. They offer a glass-bottom, four-language, 30-minute port tour for 1,300 ptas.

Maremagnum—This modern Spanish monstrosity of a mall (with a cinema, aquarium, and restaurants) offers fine city views. It's connected to the waterfront by a slick wooden pedestrian drawbridge next to the *golondrina* boats.

Sights—Gothic Quarter (Barri Gòtic)

The Barri Gòtic is a bustling world of shops, bars, and nightlife packed between hard-to-be-thrilled-about 14th- and 15th-century buildings. Except for the part closest to the port, the area now feels safe, thanks to police and countless streetlights. There is a tangled grab bag of undiscovered courtyards, grand squares, schoolyards, Art Nouveau storefronts, baby flea markets, musty junk shops, classy antique shops, and balconies with domestic jungles behind wrought-iron bars. Go on a cultural scavenger hunt. Write a poem.

▲**Cathedral**—The colossal cathedral, a fine example of Catalan Gothic, was started in about 1300 and took 600 years to complete. Rather than stretching toward heaven, it makes a point to be simply massive (similar to the Gothic churches of Italy). Under towering arches, 28 richly ornamented chapels ring the finely carved 15th-century choir (*coro*). While you can see the *coro* from the back for free, paying the 120-ptas entry fee turns on the lights and lets you get close up to the ornately carved stalls and the emblems representing the various Knights of the Golden Fleece who once sat here. Don't miss the cloister with its wispy garden, protective geese, and WC, or the dark, barrel-vaulted Romanesque Chapel of Santa Lucia with a great old tombstone floor. The tiny 100-ptas museum is one plush room with a dozen old religious paintings (cathedral 8:00–13:30 and 16:00–19:30; cloisters 9:00–13:00 and 16:00–19:00; museum 10:00–13:00; tel. 93-315-1554).

▲**Sardana Dances**—The stirring and patriotic Sardana dances are held at the cathedral (18:30 Saturday and noon on Sunday) and at Plaça de Sant Jaume (18:30 Sunday). Locals of all ages seem to spontaneously appear. They gather in circles after putting their things in the center—symbolic of community and sharing. Then they raise and hold hands as they hop and sway gracefully to the band. The band (*cobla*) consists of a long flute, tenor and soprano oboes, strange-looking brass instruments, and a tiny bongo-like drum (*tambari*). The rest of Spain mocks this lazy circle dance, but it is a stirring display of local pride and patriotism.

Shoe Museum (Museu del Calcat)—Shoe-lovers enjoy this two-room shoe museum (with a we-try-harder attendant) on the delightful Plaça Sant Felip Neri (200 ptas, Tuesday–Sunday 11:00–14:00, closed Monday, one block beyond the outside door of the cathedral cloister behind Plaça de G. Bachs).

Royal Palace (Palau Reial)—Several museums are in the old Royal Palace complex next to the cathedral. The city history museum shows off Barcelona's Roman and medieval history, along with piles of medieval documents in the *Arxiu de la Corona d'Aragon* (Archives of the Kingdom of Aragon). The Frederic Mares Museum combines a classy collection of medieval religious art with a quirky bundle of more modern artifacts—old pipes, pin-ups, toys, and so on (both museums are open Tuesday–Saturday 10:00–14:00 and 16:00–20:00, Sunday 10:00–14:00, closed Monday).

Plaça de Sant Juame—On this stately central square of the Gothic Quarter, two of the top governmental buildings in Catalan face each other: the Barcelona city hall (*Ayuntamento*) and the seat of the autonomous government of Catalan (*Palau de la Generalitat*). Sardana dances take place here Sunday at 18:30 (see Sardana Dances, above).

▲▲Picasso Museum—Far and away the best collection of Picasso's (1881–1973) work in Spain, and the best collection of his early works anywhere, is scattered through two Gothic palaces a short walk from the cathedral. This is a great chance to see his earliest sketches and paintings and better understand his genius. You'll find no English information inside but if you follow the rooms in numerical order you can trace the evolution of his work. Picasso lived in Barcelona from 1895 to 1904. The first rooms show the 14-year-old hard at work. Room 13 holds a museum highlight: Science and Charity. Pablo painted this in 1897 at age 16. Note the tiny studies inside the doorway. The man in the painting is Pablo's first teacher—his dad. The baby was rented. From this point on, young Pablo Ruiz calls himself Picasso, moves to Paris in 1900, and sharpens the cutting edge. The next rooms show Picasso romping through various styles and into his popular Blue Period (named for the tone and tint of his works from 1901 to 1904). After the Rose Period (1904 and 1905) we see Picasso the cubist (1917, room 21). Much later in life—in 1957—Picasso begins a series of variations on Velázquez' famous *Las Meninas*. Study the copy of the realistic Velázquez original and the

Velázquez/Picasso comparison chart. Then see if you can follow Picasso as he plays paddleball with perspective in the next few rooms. Before leaving, drop by the video room (opposite the café) to see Picasso at work. (600 ptas, Tuesday–Saturday 10:00–20:00, Sunday 10:00–15:00, closed Monday, Montcada 15-19, Metro: Jaume, tel. 93-319-6310.)

Textile and Garment Museum (Museu Textil i de la Indumentaria)—If fabrics from the fourth to 16th century leave you cold, have a *café con leche* on the museum's beautiful bourgeois patio (museum, 400 ptas, Tuesday–Saturday 10:00–20:00, Sunday 10:00–15:00, closed Monday; patio is outside museum but within the walls, 30 meters from Picasso Museum at Montcada 12-14).

▲Catalana Concert Hall (Palau de la Música Catalana)—This colorful hall is an extravagant burst of modernisme, with a floral ceramic ceiling, colored glass columns, and detailed mosaics. Admission is by tour only (one hour, in English, 500 ptas; Monday–Friday at 14:00, 15:00, and 16:00 through the tourist season, Tuesday and Thursday 15:00–16:00 October–May; call to reserve, tel. 93-268-1000).

Sights—Eixample

Uptown Barcelona is a unique variation on the common grid-plan city. Barcelona snipped off the building corners to create light and spacious eight-sided squares at every intersection. Wide sidewalks, hardy shade trees, chic shops, and plenty of Art Nouveau fun make the Eixample a refreshing break from the Old Town. For the best Eixample example, ramble Rambla Catalunya (unrelated to the more famous Ramblas) and pass through Passeig de Gràcia (described below, Metro: Passeig de Gràcia).

The 19th century was a boom time for Barcelona. By 1850 it was busting out of its medieval walls. A new town was planned to follow a grid-like layout. The intersection of three major thoroughfares—Gran Vía, Diagonal, and the Meridiana—would shift the city's focus uptown.

The Eixample, or "Enlargement," was a progressive plan in which everything was accessible to everyone. Each 20-block square district would have its own hospital and large park, each 10-block-square area would have its own market and general services, and each five-block-square grid would house its own schools and day-care centers. The hollow space found inside each "block" of apartments would form a neighborhood park.

While much of that vision never quite panned out, the Eixample was an urban success. Rich and artsy bigshots bought plots along the grid. The richest landowners built as close to the center as possible. For this reason, the best buildings are near the Passeig de Gràcia. Adhering to the height, width, and depth limitations, they built as they pleased—often in the trendy new moderniste style.

Modernisme

The Renaixenca (Catalan cultural revival) gave birth to Modernisme (Catalan Art Nouveau) at the end of the 19th century. Barcelona is the capital of modernisme. Meaning "a taste for what is modern," it lasted from 1888 to 1906. This free-flowing organic style broke with tradition and experimented with glass, tile, iron, and brick. Decoration became structural.

Antonio Gaudí is the most famous moderniste artist. From four generations of metalworkers, a lineage of which he was quite proud, he incorporated his ironwork into his architecture and came up with novel approaches to architectural structure and space.

Two other moderniste architects famous for their unique style are Lluís Domènech i Muntaner and Josep Puig i Cadafalch. You'll see their work on the "Street of Discord" (described in Sights—Gaudí's Art and Architecture).

Barcelona's Eixample neighborhood shimmies with the colorful, leafy, flowing, blooming shapes of modernisme in doorways, entrances, facades, and ceilings.

Modernisme fans appreciate the "Ruta del Modernisme" combo ticket (1,500 ptas for entry to six main sites, an English guidebook, and some guided tours; virtually pays for itself if you go only to Sagrada Familia and Casa Milà; sold at Palau Güell and Casa Lleo Morera).

Sights—Gaudí's Art and Architecture

Barcelona is an architectural scrapbook of the galloping gables and organic curves of hometown boy Antonio Gaudí. A devoted Catalan and Catholic, he immersed himself in each project, often living on-site. He called Parc Güell, La Pedrera, and the Sagrada Familia all home.

▲**Sagrada Familia (Sacred Family) Church**—Gaudí's most famous and persistent work is this unfinished landmark. He worked on the church from 1891 to 1925; your 800 ptas admission helps pay for the ongoing construction (daily 9:00–20:00, off-season 9:00–18:00, Metro: Sagrada Familia, tel. 93-455-0247).

When finished, 12 100-meter spires (representing the Apostles) will stand in groups of four marking the three ends of the building. The center tower (honoring Jesus), reaching 170 meters up, will be flanked by 125-meter-tall towers of Mary and the four Evangelists. A unique exterior ambulatory will circle the building like a cloister turned inside out.

The nativity facade really shows the vision of Gaudí. It was finished in 1904, before Gaudí's death, and shows scenes from the birth and childhood of Jesus along with angels playing musical instruments. (Because of ongoing construction, you may need to access this area—opposite the entrance, viewed from outside—by walking through the museum. Don't miss it.)

The little on-site museum displays physical models used for the church's construction. Gaudí lived on the site for more than a decade and is buried in the crypt. When he died in 1926, only one spire stood. Judge for yourself how the controversial current work fits in with Gaudí's original formulation.

With the cranking cranes, rusty forests of rebar, and scaffolding requiring a powerful faith, the Sagrada Familia offers a fun look at a living, growing, bigger-than-life building. Take the lift (200 ptas) or the stairs (free but can be miserably congested) up to the dizzy lookout bridging two spires. You'll get a great city view and a gargoyle's-eye perspective of the loopy church. If there's any building on earth I'd like to see, it's the Sagrada Familia—finished.

▲**Palau Güell**—This is the best chance to enjoy a Gaudí interior (see above under Ramblas). Curvy.

▲**Casa Milà (La Pedrera)**—This house and nearby Casa Battlo have Gaudí exteriors that laugh down on the crowds filling Passeig de Gràcia. Casa Milà, also called La Pedrera (The Quarry), has a much-photographed roller coaster of melting-ice-cream eaves. This is Barcelona's quintessential Moderniste building. An elevator whisks you to the top where you can wander under brick arches, frolic on the fanciful rooftop, and enjoy the fascinating new *Espai Gaudí*, a multimedia exhibit of models, photos, and videos of Gaudí's works in English (500 ptas, daily 10:00–20:00; Friday and Saturday evenings 21:00–24:00 for 1,000 ptas with a glass of wine; Passeig del Gràcia 92, Metro: Diagonal, tel. 93-484-5995). Take this opportunity to actually get inside the many playful (and otherwise private) Gaudí buildings via the many video screens of Espai Gaudí.

At the ground level of Casa Milà is the entrance courtyard for the Fundacio Caixa de Cataluyna, dreamily painted in pastels. It's original and can be seen free of charge.

The Street of Discord—Four blocks from Casa Milà you can survey a noisy block of competing turn-of-the-century facades. Several of Barcelona's top moderniste mansions line Passeig de Gràcia (Metro: Passeig de Gràcia). As if they are trying to outdo each other in creative twists, locals nicknamed the block (between Consell de Cent and Arago) "the street of discord." First (at #43) and most famous is Gaudí's **Casa Battlo** with skull-like balconies and a tile roof of cresting waves . . . or is it a dragon's back? (If you're tempted to frame your photos from the middle of the street, be careful—Gaudí died under a streetcar.) Next door, at Casa Amatller (#41), check out architect Puig i Cadafalch's creative mix of Moorish and Gothic and iron grillwork. **Casa Lleo**

Morera (on the corner at #35, by Lluís Domènechi Muntaner) offers more of a sense of a moderniste interior—you can nose into the lobby and often climb to the first floor. The perfume shop halfway down the street has a free and interesting little perfume museum in the back.

Parc Güell—Gaudí fans find the artist's magic in this colorful park (free, daily 10:00–20:00) and small **Gaudí Museum** (200 ptas, Sunday–Friday 10:00–14:00 and 16:00–18:00, closed Saturday, Metro: Vallarca but easier by bus #24 from Plaça de Catalunya; 1,000 ptas by taxi). Gaudí didn't intend this to be a park but a planned garden city. As a high-income housing project, it flopped. As a park . . . even after reminding myself that Gaudí's work is a careful rhythm of color, shapes, and space, I was disappointed.

Bus Tour—A four-hour guided Gaudí bus tour runs daily from April through September (5,000 ptas, departs Casa Milà at 10:00 and 15:00, in English and Spanish, tel. 93-484-8909). The TI has specifics on this and lots of information on Gaudí.

Modern Art Museum (Museu d'Art Modern)—East of the França train station in Parc de la Ciutadella, this manageable museum exhibits Catalan sculpture, painting, glass, and furniture by Gaudí, Casas, Llimona, and others (300 ptas, Tuesday–Sunday 10:00–19:00, closed Monday).

Sights—Barcelona's Montjuïc

The Montjuïc (Mount of the Jews), overlooking Barcelona's hazy port, has always been a show-off. Ages ago it had the impressive fortress. In 1929 it hosted an international fair from which most of today's sights originated. And in 1992 the Summer Olympics directed the world's attention to this pincushion of sightseeing attractions.

There are many ways to reach Montjuïc: on the Bus Turistic (see Getting Around Barcelona, above); bus #61 from Plaça Espanya (150 ptas, every 10 minutes); subway to Metro: Parallel and catch the funicular (250 ptas one-way, 350 ptas round-trip, daily 10:45–20:00, later in summer); or taxi. The first three options leave you at the *teleférico*, which you can take to the Castle of Montjuïc (425 ptas one-way, 625 ptas round-trip). Alternatively, from the same spot, you can walk uphill 20 minutes though the pleasant park. Only a taxi gets you doorstep delivery. From the port, the fastest and most scenic way to Montjuïc is via the 1929 Trasbordador Aereo (at the tower in the port, ride an elevator up to catch the dangling gondola, 800 ptas one way, 4/hrly, daily 12:00–20:00).

Amusement Park (Parc d'Atraccions de Montjuïc)—Your best chance to eat, whirl, and hurl with local families (700 ptas to get in, 2,000 ptas for entry with unlimited rides—otherwise 300 ptas per ride, open daily in summers until late, access by the skyway from the port or by Metro: Parallel, from which you can walk or ride the Montjuïc *teleférico*, which stops here on its way up to the castle).

Castle of Montjuïc—This offers great city views and a military museum (200 ptas, Tuesday–Sunday 9:30–19:30, closed Monday). The seemingly endless museum houses a dull collection of guns, swords, and toy soldiers. An interesting section on the Spanish-American war covers Spain's valiant fight against American aggression (from its perspective). Unfortunately, there are no English descriptions. Those interested in Jewish history will find a fascinating collection of ninth-century Jewish tombstones.

▲**Fountains (Fonts Lluminoses)**—Music, colored lights, and impressive amounts of water make an artistic and coordinated splash on summer nights (Thursday–Sunday, four 30-minute shows start on the half-hour, 22:00–23:30, from Metro: Plaça Espanya, walk toward huge towering National Palace).

Spanish Village (Poble Espanyol)—This tacky five-acre model village uses fake traditional architecture from all over Spain as a shell to contain gift shops. Craftspeople do their clichétic thing only in the morning (9:00–19:30 but dead after 13:00, not worth the time or the 950 ptas). After hours it becomes a popular local nightspot.

▲▲**Catalonian Art Museum (Museo Nacional d'Art de Catalunya)**—Often called "the Prado of Romanesque art," this is a rare, world-class collection of Romanesque art collected mostly from remote Catalan village churches in the Pyrenees (saved from unscrupulous art dealers).

The Romanesque wing features frescoes, painted wooden altarfronts, and ornate statuary. This classic Romanesque art—with flat 2-D scenes, each saint holding his symbol, and Jesus (easy to identify by the cross in his halo)—is now impressively displayed on replicas of the original church ceilings.

In the Gothic wing, fresco murals give way to vivid 14th-century paintings of Bible stories on wood. A roomful of paintings by the Catalan master Jaume Huguet (1412–1492) deserves a very close look.

Before you leave, ice skate under the huge dome over to the air-conditioned cafeteria. This was the prime ceremony room and dance hall for the 1929 International Exposition (800 ptas, Tuesday–Saturday 10:00–19:00, Thursday until 21:00, Sunday 10:00–14:30, closed Monday, tel. 93-423-7199). The museum is in the massive National Palace building above the fountains, near Plaça Espanya (Metro: Plaça Espanya, then hike up or ride the bus; the tourist bus and #61 stop close by).

▲**Fundació Joan Miró**—For something more up-to-date, this museum showcases the modern art talents of yet another Catalunyan artist and is considered the best collection of Joan Miró art anywhere. You'll also see works by other modern Spanish artists; don't miss the Mercury Fountain by Calder. This museum leaves those who don't like abstract art scratching their head (800 ptas, 10:00–20:00, Sunday 10:30–14:30, Thursday until 21:30, closed Monday and at 19:00 off-season).

Sleeping in Barcelona
(150 ptas = about $1)
Sleep Code: **S**=Single, **D**=Double/Twin, **T**=Triple, **Q**=Quad, **b**=bathroom, **t**=toilet only, **s**=shower only, **CC**=Credit Card (Visa, MasterCard, Amex), **SE**=Speaks English, **NSE**=No English.

Barcelona is Spain's most expensive city. Still, it has reasonable rooms. A few places raise their rates for "high season" (August) and deal in off-season. Assume prices listed do not include the 7 percent tax or breakfast. While many recommended places are on pedestrian streets, night noise is a problem almost everywhere. Most places charge more for a balcony overlooking a people-filled street. To save money and gain sleep ask for "*tranquilo*" rather than "*con vista.*"

Sleeping near the Ramblas and in the Gothic Quarter
(zip code: 08002)
These accommodations are listed in roughly geographical order downhill from Plaça de Catalunya. See map on page 631.

Hotel Allegro, which opened in 1998, fills a renovated old palace with wide halls, marble and hardwood floors, and elegant, modern rooms with all the comforts. It overlooks a busy pedestrian boulevard (Db-16,900 ptas plus tax and breakfast, 3,000 ptas more for view balcony or third bed, price promised by Carles with this book through 1999, CC:VMA, family rooms, satellite TV, air-conditioning, elevator, a block down from Placa Catalunya at Portal de l'Angel 17, tel. 93-318-4141, fax 93-301-2631, SE).

Catalunya Plaza, a business hotel, has all the air-conditioning and mini-bar comforts (Sb-17,000 ptas, Db-22,000 ptas including breakfast, CC:VMA, elevator, free nuts at the desk, on the plaza at Plaça de Catalunya 7, tel. 93-317-7171, fax 93-317-7855, SE).

Hotel Barcelona is another big American-style hotel (Sb-15,000 ptas, Db-23,000 ptas, 26,000 ptas with a terrace, CC:VMA, air-conditioning, one block away at Caspe 1-13, tel. 93-302-5858, fax 93-301-8674).

Nouvel Hotel, an elegant Victorian-style building on a fine pedestrian street, has royal lounges and comfy rooms (Sb-8,800 ptas, Db without balcony-14,000 ptas, Db with balcony-17,000 ptas, including breakfast, manager Gabriel promises 10-percent discount with this book, no balcony = quieter and cheaper, air-conditioning, CC:VMA, Carrer de Santa Ana 18, tel. 93-301-8274, fax 93-301-8370, SE).

Hotel Toledano's elevator takes you high above the noise and into the *zona bella vista*. View balcony rooms overlook the Ramblas. This small and folksy hotel is run by the helpful English-speaking owner Juan Sanz, his son Albert, and Jordi (Sb-3,900 ptas, Db-6,900 ptas, Tb-8,600 ptas, Qb-9,600 ptas, cheaper off-season, CC:VMA, Rambla de Canaletas 138, tel. 93-301-0872, fax 93-412-3142, e-mail: Toledano@idgrup.ibernet.com). They run **Hostal Residencia Capitol** one floor above—quiet, plain, cheaper, and appropriate for backpackers (S-2,900 ptas, D-4,600 ptas, Ds-5,200 ptas, cheap five-bedded room).

Hotel Continental has comfortable rooms, double-thick mattresses, wildly clashing carpets and wallpaper, an all day complimentary coffee bar, and a good location at the top of the Ramblas (Db-8,000–10,000 ptas with breakfast, CC:VMA, fans in rooms, elevator, Las Ramblas 138, tel. 93-301-2570, fax 93-302-7360, e-mail: hotel_continental@seker.es).

Hotel Lloret is a big, dark, Old World place on the Ramblas with plain, air-conditioned rooms—confirm prices first (Sb-6,000 ptas, Db-8,500 ptas, extra beds-1,000 ptas each up to quints, buffet breakfast-450 ptas, choose between a noisy Ramblas balcony or *tranquilo* in the back, elevator dominates the stairwell, CC:VMA, Rambla de Canaletas 125, tel. 93-317-3366, fax 93-301-9283, SE).

Hotel Jardi is a hardworking, clean, plain place on the happiest little square in the Gothic Quarter. Room prices vary with newness, views, and balconies (Sb-3,500–4,000 ptas, Db-5,500–6,600 ptas, Tb-6,500–9,200 ptas, enjoy a view-terrace breakfast-700 ptas, no elevator, CC:VMA, halfway between the Ramblas and the cathedral on Plaça Sant Josep Oriol #1, tel. 93-301-5900, fax 93-318-3664, NSE). Rooms with balconies enjoy a classic plaza setting and minimal noise.

These sister hotels straddle a pedestrian street in buildings that reek of concrete. Run by the same company, they have good but plain rooms with mod bathrooms (Sb-5,600 ptas, Db-9,300 ptas including tax and breakfast, CC:VMA, elevator): **Hotel Cataluña** (Carrer de Santa Ana 24, tel. 93-301-9120, fax 93-302-7870) and **Hotel Cortes** (Carrer de Santa Ana 25, tel. 93-317-9112, fax 93-302-7870).

Deeper in the Gothic Quarter, these two new, modern neighbors suffer from street noise but keep business people happy with TV, telephone, and air-conditioning: **Hotel Adagio** (Sb-7,000 ptas, Db-8,500 ptas, Tb-11,000 ptas, saggy beds, includes breakfast, elevator, CC:VMA, Ferran 21, tel. 93-318-9061, fax 93-318-3724) and, across the street, the **Hotel California** (Sb-5,500 ptas, Db-9,000 ptas, Tb-12,000 ptas, includes breakfast, CC:VMA, Raurich 14, tel. 93-317-7766, fax 93-317-5474, Web site:

www.seker.es/hotel_california). Hike halfway down the Ramblas (just past Metro: Liceu), then turn left at McDonald's. The California lacks an elevator but has bigger and brighter halls and bathrooms.

Humble Places Buried in Gothic Quarter with Youth Hostel Prices

Pensio Vitoria has loose tile floors and 12 humble rooms, each with a tiny balcony. It's a fine line between homey and dumpy but consider the price (D-3,000, Db-3,500 ptas, CC:VM, a block off the day-dreamy Plaça dei Pi at Carrer la Palla 8, tel. & fax 93-302-0834).

Hostal Campi, big, quiet, and ramshackle, is a few doors off the Ramblas (D-4,000 ptas, Db-5,000 ptas, no elevator, Canuda 4, tel. 93-301-3545, NSE). **Huéspedes Santa Ana** is plain and claustrophobic with head-to-toe twins (S-2,600 ptas, D-4,200 ptas, Db-6,000 ptas, T-6,000 ptas, Carrer de Santa Ana 23, tel. 93-301-2246). **Hostal Residencia Lausanne**, filled with backpackers, has only its location and price going for it (S-2,500 ptas, D-3,500 ptas, Ds-5,000 ptas, Db-6,500 ptas, TV room, Avenida Portal de l'Angel 24, tel. 93-302-1139, SE). **Hostal Residencia Rembrandt** keeps countless backpackers happy with simple rooms and a good locale (S-2,900 ptas, Sb-3,800 ptas, D-4,000 ptas, Db-5,500 ptas, T-7,000 ptas, breakfast-350 ptas, Portaferriso 23, tel. & fax 93-318-1011, SE). **Huéspedes Colmenero**, on a noisy pedestrian street, is a homey little place with five rooms, each with a tiny balcony (S-3,000 ptas, D-5,000 ptas, Db-6,000 ptas, less off-season, two streets toward the cathedral from the Ramblas at Petritxol 12, tel. 93-302-6634, fax: What's that?, Rosa speaks no English).

Sleeping in Eixample

For a more elegant and boulevardian neighborhood, sleep on or near Gran Vía de les Corts Catalanes in Eixample, a 10-minute walk from the Ramblas action.

Hotel Gran Vía, filling a palatial mansion built in the 1870s, offers Botticelli and chandeliers in the public rooms, a sprawling peaceful sun-garden, and spacious, comfy, air-conditioned rooms. It's an excellent value (Sb-9,000 ptas, Db-12,000 ptas, tax and breakfast extra, prices promised by Juan Gomez the desk manager through 1999 with this book, CC:VMA, book long in advance, elevator, Gran Vía de les Corts Catalanes 642, 08008 Barcelona, tel. 93-318-1900, fax 93-318-9997, SE).

Hotel Residencia Neutral, with a classic Eixample location, 35 cheery rooms, plush public rooms, and a passion for cleanliness, is the poor man's Hotel Gran Vía (tiny Sb-3,000 ptas, big Sb-4,400 ptas, Ds-4,500 ptas, Db-5,400 ptas, Ts-5,100 ptas, Tb-6,200 ptas,

tax and breakfast extra, CC:VM, elevator, elegantly located two
blocks north of Gran Vía at Rambla Catalunya 42, 08007
Barcelona, tel. 93-487-6390, SE).

Eating in Barcelona

Barcelona, the capital of Catalunyan cuisine, offers a tremendous
variety of colorful places to eat. The harbor area, especially
Barceloneta, is famous for fish. Good tapas bars are all over the
Gothic Quarter. Many restaurants are closed in August.

Eating in the Gothic Quarter

Taverna Basca Irati serves 20 kinds of hot and cold Basque
pintxos for 130 ptas each. These are open-face sandwiches—like
Basque sushi but on bread. Muscle in through the hungry local
crowd. Get an empty plate from the waiter then help yourself. It's
a Basque honors system: You'll be charged by the number of
toothpicks left on your plate when you're done. Wash it down
with a glass of *sidra* (apple wine, 120 ptas) poured from on high
into a delicate glass to bring out the flavor (12:00–15:00 and
19:00–23:00, closed Sunday night and Monday, a block off the
Ramblas, behind the noisy amusement arcade at Calle Cardenal
Casanyes 17, near Metro: Liceu, tel. 93-302-3084). **Juicy Jones**,
next door, is a tutti-fruity vegetarian place with an extremely hip
menu (#7, great fresh juices).

Els **Quatre Gats**, Picasso's hangout and still popular with
locals, calls itself a "Cervesteria Modernista." Before it was
founded in 1897, the idea of a café for artists was mocked as a
place where only *quatre gats* ("four cats," meaning nobody) would
go (3,000 ptas meals, Monday–Saturday 8:30–1:30, Sunday
17:00–1:30, live piano nightly from 21:00, CC:VMA, Montsio 3,
tel. 93-302-4140).

Two popular but touristy places are side by side, just down
from the Plaça Reial: **Los Caracoles** is a pricey Spanish wine cellar
dripping in atmosphere (daily 13:00–24:00, Escudellers 14, a block
toward the harbor from Plaça Reial in red-light bar country,
Metro: Drassanes, tel. 93-302-3185). The neighboring **La Fonda** is
brighter and more modern, with quality traditional cuisine at better
prices and even more tourists. Arrive early or make a reservation to
avoid the very long waits (Escudellers 10, tel. 93-301-7515).

The owner of the wildly successful La Fonda has opened **La
Dolca Herminia** using the same "good local food, good prices,
classy modern bistro" ambience formula. Already popular but not
yet touristy, it's two blocks toward the Ramblas from the Palau de
la Música at Magdalenes 27 (tel. 93-317-0676).

A fine place for local-style food in a local-style setting is
Restaurant Agut (inexpensive, closed in July or August, huge
servings, Calle Gignas 16, tel. 93-315-1709).

Egipte, with its late-19th-century ambience, attracts the opera crowd. Local stars' portraits are on the walls. Try the *pebrots amb bacalao*—red bell peppers stuffed with cod and served over rice (daily 13:00–16:00 and 20:00–24:00, Rambla 79, downhill from the Boqueria, Metro: Liceu, tel. 93-317-7480).

Eating near Plaza Catalunya

Self Naturista is a bright and cheery buffet that will make vegetarians and health-food-lovers feel right at home. Others may find a few unidentifiable plates and drinks. The food's already out—pick what you like and microwave it (Monday–Saturday 11:30–22:00, closed Sunday, near several recommended hotels, just off the top of Ramblas at Carrer de Santa Ana 13). Another vegetarian choice is **Bio Center** (9:00–23:00, closed Sunday, Pintor Fortuny 25, Metro: Catalunya, tel. 93-301-4583).

Julivert Meu teams up regional specialties like *pan con tomate* (bread with tomato and olive oil), *jamón serrano* (cured ham), and *escalivadas* (grilled vegetables) in a rustic interior (Monday–Saturday 13:00–1:00, Sunday 13:00–16:00 and 20:00–1:00, off the Ramblas at Bonsuccés 7, Metro: Catalunya, tel. 93-318-0343).

Eating Elsewhere in Barcelona

In the Eixample at **La Bodegueta**, have a *carajillos* (coffee with rum) and a *flauta* (sandwich on flute-thin baguette) in this authentic below-street-level bodega (Monday–Saturday 8:00–1:30, Sunday 7:00–13:00, Rambla Catalunya 100, at intersection with Provenza, Metro: Diagonal, tel. 93-215-4894); or slip into the classy **Quasi Queviures** for upscale tapas, sandwiches, or the whole nine yards—classic food with modern decor (Passeig de Gràcia 24).

El Café de Internet provides an easy way to munch a sandwich while sending e-mail messages to Mom (600 ptas for a half-hour, Monday–Saturday 10:00–24:00, closed Sunday, Gran Vía 656, Metro: Passeig de Gràcia, tel. 93-412-1915, Web site: www.cafeinternet.es).

For a quick meal, pick up a healthy sandwich at **Pans & Company**. This Catalan chain puts the food back in fast food. Its sister establishment, **Pastafiore**, dishes up salads and pasta at a fair price (500–800 ptas). Both are lifesavers on Sunday, when many restaurants are closed (daily 8:00–24:00, opens at 9:00 on Sunday, located on Plaza Urquinaona, Provenza, La Rambla, Portal de l'Angel, and just about everywhere else).

Eating in Barceloneta

This charming little beach suburb of the big city has long been famous for its fresh fish restaurants. Lately, the big money has shifted to new, more trendy locales and Barceloneta has gone back to being a big, easygoing neighborhood. A grid plan of long,

narrow, laundry-strewn streets surrounds the central Plaça Poeta
Boscan. For an entertaining evening, start here (15-minute walk or
Metro: Barceloneta). During the day, a lively produce market fills
one end of the square. In the evening kids play Ping-Pong.

Cova Fumada is the neighborhood eatery. Josep Maria and
his family serve famously fresh fish (Monday–Friday 17:30–20:30,
Carrer del Baluarte 56, on the corner at Carrer Sant Carles closest
to downtown, tel. 93-221-4061). Their *sardinas a la plancha* (grilled
sardines, 350 ptas) are fresh and tasty. *Bombas* (potato croquets
with pork, 150 ptas) are the house specialty. It's macho to have it
picante (spicy with chili sauce); feminine taste buds prefer it with
garlic cream (pron: all-i-oli). If you're not sure how you like it, get
it *marica*. Catalunyan bruschetta is *pan tôstado* (toast with oil and
garlic, 140 ptas). Wash it all down with a glass of *vino tinto* (house
red wine, 80 ptas).

At **Bar Electricidad**, Arturo Jordana Barba is the neighborhood source for cheap wine. Drop in. It's 180 ptas per liter; the
empty plastic water bottles are for take-away. Try a 75-ptas glass
of Torroja Tinto, the best local red; or Priorato Dulce, a wonderfully sweet red (18:00–21:00, across the square from Cova
Fumada, at corner with Carrer Sant Carles, #61, NSE).

If you're looking for a real restaurant, humble local places
abound. For dessert, consider a walk along the sandy beach board-
walk for a Mediterranean breeze.

Tapas

Tapas may not be as popular in Catalunya as they are in the rest of
Spain, but Barcelona boasts some great *tascas*—colorful local tapas
bars. Get small plates (for maximum sampling) by asking for "tapas,"
not "*raciones*." For the most fun and flavorful route through the
Gothic Quarter, go to the Plaza de la Merce (Metro: Drassanes),
then follow the small street that runs along the right side of the
church (Carrer Merce), stopping at whichever *tascas* look fun. Con
sider these: **La Jarra** is known for its tender *jamón canario con patatas*
(baked ham with salty potatoes). Across the street, **La Pulperia**
serves up fried fish. **La Socarrena** serves North Spain mountain
favorites (*queso de cabrales*—very moldy cheese) with *sidra* (apple
wine). **Tasca El Corral** makes one of the neighborhood's best
chorizo al diablo (hell sausage), which you sauté yourself. It's great
with the regional specialty *pan con tomate*. Across the street, **La Plata**
keeps things wonderfully simple, serving extremely cheap plates of
sardines and small glasses of keg wine. You can smell **Las Cam-
panas'** fragrant sausage a block away. Have a chat with the parrot at
Bar la Choza del Sopas. At the end of Carrer Merce, **Bar
Vendimia** serves up tasty clams and mussels. Carrer Ample, the
street paralleling Carrer Merce, has ample additional bar-hopping
possibilities in more refined confines.

In the Gothic Quarter, **La Cava del Palau** is a great wine bar, bubbling with Spain's sparkling wine (Verdaguer i Callis 10, near Palau de la Música Catalana, tel. 93-310-0938).

Transportation Connections—Barcelona

By train to: Lisbon (1/day, 15 hrs with change in Madrid), **Madrid** (6/day, 7–9 hrs, $50 with a *couchette*), **Paris** (3/day, 11–15 hrs, $70 night-train reservation required), **Sevilla** (4/day, 11 hrs), **Málaga** (3/day, 14 hrs), **Nice** (1/day, 12 hrs, change in Cerbere). Train info tel. 93-490-0202; international train info tel. 93-490-1122.

By bus to: Madrid (6/day, 8 hrs, half the price of a train ticket).

By flight to: Madrid—to avoid 10-hour train trips, those continuing to Madrid or Sevilla should check the reasonable flights from Barcelona: Iberia Air (tel. 93-412-5667) and Air Europe (tel. 90-224-0042) offer $80 flights to Madrid. Airport information tel. 93-298-3838.

MADRID

Today's Madrid is upbeat and vibrant, still enjoying a post-Franco renaissance. You'll feel it. Even the statue-maker beggars have a twinkle in their eyes.

Madrid is the hub of Spain. This modern capital—Europe's highest, at more than 2,000 feet—has a population of more than 4 million and is young by European standards. Only 400 years ago, King Philip II decided to move the capital of his empire from Toledo to Madrid. One hundred years ago Madrid had only 400,000 people, so nine-tenths of the city is modern sprawl, surrounding an intact, easy-to-navigate historic core.

Dive headlong into the grandeur and intimate charm of Madrid. The lavish Royal Palace, with its gilded rooms and frescoed ceilings, rivals Versailles. The Prado has Europe's top collection of paintings. The city's huge Retiro Park invites you for a shady siesta and a hopscotch through a mosaic of lovers, families, skateboarders, pets walking their masters, and expert bench-sitters. Make time for Madrid's elegant shops and people-friendly pedestrian zones. Enjoy the shade in an arcade. On Sundays, cheer for the bull at a bullfight or bargain like mad at a mega–flea market. Lively Madrid has enough street singing, barhopping, and people-watching vitality to give any visitor a boost of youth.

Planning Your Time

Madrid's top two sights, the Prado and the palace, are worth a day. If you hit the city on a Sunday, allot extra time for a bullfight. Ideally, give Madrid two days and spend them this way:

Day 1: Breakfast of *churros* (see Eating, below) before a brisk, good-morning-Madrid walk for 20 minutes from Puerta del Sol to the Prado; 9:00–12:00 at the Prado; afternoon siesta in Retiro

Park or lap up the modern art at Reina Sofia (Guernica) and/or the Thyssen-Bornemisza Museum; 19:30 historic walking tour followed by tapas for dinner around Plaza Santa Ana.

Day 2: Follow this book's Puerta del Sol to Royal Palace walk (see below); tour Royal Palace, lunch near Plaza Mayor; afternoon free for other sights, shopping, or side trip to El Escorial (open until 19:00). Note that the Prado and Thyssen-Bornemisza Museum are closed on Monday.

Orientation

The historic center can easily be covered on foot. No major sight is more than a 20-minute walk from the Puerta del Sol, Madrid's central square. Your time will be divided between the city's two major sights—the Royal Palace and the Prado—and its barhopping, car-honking, contemporary scene.

The Puerta del Sol is at the dead center of Madrid and of Spain itself; notice the "kilometer zero" marker, from which all of Spain is surveyed (southwest corner). The Royal Palace to the west and the Prado Museum and Retiro Park to the east frame Madrid's historic center.

Southwest of Puerta del Sol is a 17th-century district with the slow-down-and-smell-the-cobbles Plaza Mayor and plenty of relics from pre-industrial Spain.

North of Puerta del Sol runs the Gran Vía, and between the two are lively pedestrian shopping streets. The Gran Vía, bubbling with business, expensive shops, and cinemas, leads to the impressively modern Plaza de España. North of Gran Vía is the gritty Malasana quarter, with its colorful small houses, shoemakers' shops, sleazy-looking hombres, milk vendors, bars, and hip night scene.

Tourist Information

Madrid has four handy Turismos: one on the Plaza Mayor at #3 (Monday–Friday 10:00–20:00, Saturday 10:00–14:00, closed Sunday, tel. 91-588-1636); another near the Prado Museum, across from the front door of the giant Palace Hotel (weekdays 9:00–19:00, Saturday 9:00–13:00, Duque de Medinaceli 2, tel. 91-429-4951); and smaller offices at the Chamartin train station (weekdays 8:00–20:00, Saturday 9:00–13:00, closed Sunday, tel. 91-315-9976) and at the airport (same hours, tel. 91-305-8656). During the summer you'll also find small temporary stands with yellow umbrellas and yellow-shirted student guides happy to help out lost tourists (there's a handy such booth on Puerta del Sol). Confirm your sightseeing plans and pick up a map and *Enjoy Madrid*, the free monthly city guide. (The TI's free guide to city events, *En Madrid*, is not as good as the easy-to-decipher Spanish weekly entertainment guide, *Guía del Ocio*, on sale at streetside

Madrid

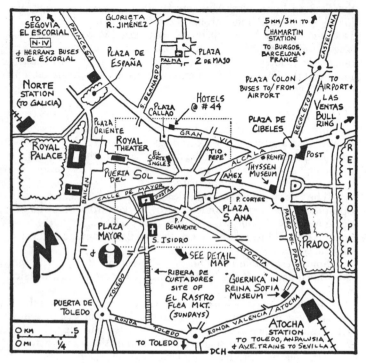

newsstands for 125 ptas.) If interested, ask at the TI about bull-fights and Zarzuela (the local light opera). The free and amazingly informative *Mapa de Comunicaciones España* lists all the Turismos and highway SOS numbers, with a road map of Spain. (If they're out, ask for the Paradores Hotel chain-sponsored route map.) If you're heading to other destinations in Spain, see if the Madrid TI has free maps and brochures. Since many small-town TIs keep erratic hours and run out of these pamphlets, get what you can here. Get bus schedules, too, to avoid unnecessary trips to the various bus stations.

Arrival in Madrid

By Train: The two main rail stations, Atocha and Chamartin, are both on subway lines with easy access to downtown Madrid. Each station has all the services, though there is no TI at Atocha. In Spain, train rides longer than about three hours require reservations, even if you have a Eurailpass. To avoid needless running around, arrange your departure upon arrival.

Chamartin handles most international trains, and Atocha runs AVE trains to Sevilla. Both stations offer *largo recorrido* (long-distance) trains as well as *cercanías* (local trains to nearby destinations). Atocha is more clearly split into two halves (local and long-distance trains) with separate schedules; this can be confusing if you're in the wrong side of the building. Atocha also has two helpful (necessary) customer-service offices called *Atencion al Cliente* (daily 7:00–23:00)—one office for each half of the building. The Chamartin station is less confusing. Its customer-service office is called *Atención al Viajero* (beside the ticket windows, in the middle of the building) and the helpful TI is opposite track #20.

Club AVE in Atocha (upstairs) is a lounge reserved solely for AVE business or first-class ticketholders or Eurailers with a reservation (free drinks, newspapers, showers, info service, and so on). Club Intercity in Chamartin is less exclusive—you can get in if you have a first-class railpass and first-class seat or sleeper reservations.

Both train stations have Metro stops (Chamartin and Atocha RENFE). Note that there are two Atocha Metro stops in Madrid. The train station's Metro station is "Atocha RENFE." If you're traveling between Chamartin and Atocha, use the *Cercanias* trains (6/hrly, 12 min, free with railpass—show it at ticket window in middle of all the turnstiles); they're far quicker than the subway. Trains depart from Atocha's track #2. At Chamartin, check the *Salidas Immediatas* board for the next departure.

At the downtown RENFE office, you can get train information, reservations, and tickets (Monday–Friday 9:30–19:00, credit cards accepted, best to go in person, two blocks north of the Prado Museum at Calle Alcala 44, tel. 91-328-9020).

By Bus: Madrid's three key bus stations are all connected by Metro: La Sepulvedana (handles Segovia and Avila, Metro: Príncipe Pío), the brand-new Estación Sur Autobuses (covers Toledo and Granada, Metro: Ménedez Alvaro), and Estación Herranz (serves El Escorial, Metro: Moncloa). For details, see Transportation Connections at the end of this chapter.

By Plane: Madrid's Barajas Airport, 10 miles east of downtown, comes well-equipped to help new arrivals. It has a 24-hour bank with fair rates, an ATM, a TI, a telephone office where you can buy a phone card, a RENFE desk for rail information, a pharmacy, on-the-spot car-rental agencies, and easy public transportation into town. Airport info: tel. 91-305-8343. Use your phone card to call and confirm your hotel, then head into town. Taxis are easiest. By public transport, take the yellow bus into Madrid (to Plaza Colón, 4/hrly, 20 min, 380 ptas). From Plaza Colón, take a taxi or subway to your hotel (walk up the stairs and face the blue "URBIS" sign high on a building—the subway stop, M. Serrano, is 50 yards to your right). If you take a taxi (easily available from the airport bus station at Plaza Colón), insist on the meter. For a taxi to or from the airport, allow at least 3,000 ptas. (5,000 ptas is a rip off.) To get a rough idea of the price before you hop in, ask "*¿Cuanto cuesta a Madrid, más o menos?*" ("How much is it to Madrid, more or less?")

Getting Around Madrid

By Subway: Madrid's subway is simple, speedy (outside of rush hour), and cheap (130 ptas/ride). For 670 ptas, buy the 10-ride "*bono*" ticket, which can be shared by several travelers and works on both the Metro and buses (available at kiosks, tobacco shops, or in Metro). The city's broad streets can be hot and exhausting. A subway trip of even a stop or two can save time and energy. Pick up a free map (*Plano del Metro*) at most stations. Navigate by subway stops (shown on city maps). To transfer, follow signs to the next subway line (numbered and color-coded). End stops are used to indicate directions. Insert your ticket in the turnstile, then retrieve it as you pass through. Green *Salida* signs point to the exit. Use the neighborhood maps and street signs to exit smartly.

By Bus: City buses, while not as easy as the Metro, can be useful. If interested, get a bus map at the TI or the info booth on Puerta del Sol. Tickets are 130 ptas (buy on bus), or 670 ptas for a pack of 10 bus/Metro tickets (buy at kiosks, tobacco shops, or in Metro). The Madrid Vision bus provides transportation and a tour (see Tours of Madrid, below).

By Taxi: While taxis are easy to hail and reasonable (175 ptas drop, 85 ptas per km, late night 115 ptas per km; supplements for airport, train station, and bags), you'll go just as fast and a lot cheaper by subway.

Helpful Hints

Theft Alert: Be wary of pickpockets, anywhere, anytime, but particularly on Puerta del Sol (main square), the subway, and crowded streets. Wear your money belt. In crowds, keep your daybag in front of you. Some thieves "accidentally" spill ketchup on your clothes, then pick your pocket as they help you clean up. The small streets north of Gran Vía are particularly dangerous even before nightfall. Fortunately, violent crime against tourists is very rare.

Museum Pass: If you plan to visit the Prado, Reina Sofia (Guernica), and Thyssen-Bornemisza museums, save 33 percent by buying the Paseo del Arte pass (1,050 ptas, available at all three museums). The Prado and Reina Sofia are free on Saturday afternoon, Sunday, and for those over 65.

Monday Plans: If you're in Madrid on a Monday (when the Prado is closed), you can visit the Royal Palace and Reina Sofia (Guernica), rent a boat at Retiro Park, tour the nearby botanical gardens, shop, or café-hop.

Travel Agency and Free Maps: The grand department store, El Corte Inglés has a travel agency (Monday–Saturday 10:00–21:30, just off Puerta del Sol) and gives free Madrid maps (at the information desk, just inside the door at northwest intersection of Preciados and Tetuan).

Telephones: The telephone office, centrally located at Gran Vía 30, has metered phones and accepts credit cards for charges over 500 ptas (daily 10:00–23:00).

American Express: The Amex office is at Plaza Cortes 2 (opposite Palace Hotel, six blocks from Metro: Sevilla, Monday–Friday 9:00–17:30, Saturday 9:00–12:00, tel. 91-322-5455).

Embassies: The U.S. Embassy is at Serrano 75 (tel. 91-587-2200); the Canadian Embassy is at Nuñez de Balboa 35 (tel. 91-431-4300).

Tours of Madrid

Walking Tour—British expatriate Stephen Drake-Jones gives entertaining and informative walks of historic old Madrid almost nightly (along with several other more specialized tours). A historian with a passion for the memory of Wellington (the man who stopped Napoleon), Stephen is the founder of Madrid's Wellington Society. For 2,500 ptas you become an honorary member of the society and get a free two-hour tour which includes stops at two bars for local drinks and tapas. Stephen, in his almost eccentric style, takes you back in time to sort out the Habsburg and Bourbon history of this under-appreciated city. Tours start at the statue on Puerta del Sol nearly nightly at 19:30 (tel. 60-914-3203—a cell phone number that will cost you 200 ptas—to confirm tour and reserve a spot; Stephen also does inexpensive private tours for small groups; e-mail: sdrake_jones@hotmail.com).

Bus Tour—The Madrid Vision Bus takes tourists on a big hop-on and hop-off sightseeing loop with a multilingual tape-recorded narration (1,700 ptas for all-day pass, departures from Gran Vía 32 9:45–17:15, tel. 91-302-4526).

Sights—From Madrid's Puerta del Sol to the Royal Palace

Connect the sights with the following walking tour. Allow an hour for this half-mile walk, not including your visit to the palace.

▲▲**Puerta del Sol**—Even without its "kilometer zero" plaque, Puerta del Sol is ground zero for Madrid. Standing by the statue of Charles III, survey the square. Because of his enlightened urban policies, King Charles III (who ruled until 1788) is affectionately called the "best mayor of Madrid." He decorated the city squares with fine fountains, got the meddlesome Jesuits out of city government, established a public education system, made the Retiro a

Heart of Madrid

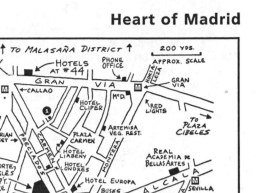

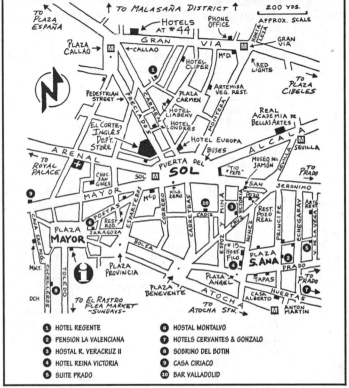

❶ HOTEL REGENTE	❻ HOSTAL MONTALVO
❷ PENSION LA VALENCIANA	❼ HOTELS CERVANTES & GONZALO
❸ HOSTAL R. VERACRUZ II	❽ SOBRINO DEL BOTIN
❹ HOTEL REINA VICTORIA	❾ CASA CIRIACO
❺ SUITE PRADO	❿ BAR VALLADOLID

public park rather than a royal retreat, and generally cleaned up Madrid. The huge palace he faces was the first post office (which he established in the 1760s). Today the building is remembered for being a police headquarters during the reign of Franco. An amazing number of those detained and interrogated by the Franco police "tried to escape" by flying out the windows to their deaths. You'll see civil guardsmen at the entry. (It's said their hats have square backsides so they can lean against the wall while enjoying a cigarette.)

On New Year's Eve, crowds gather on this square; and, as the big clock atop the post office chimes 12 times, Madrillinos eat one grape for each ring to bring good luck through the coming year.

A plaque on the post office wall marks the spot where the war against Napoleon started. Napoleon wanted his brother to be king of Spain. Trying to finagle this, Napoleon brought nearly the entire Spanish royal family (the Bourbons) to Paris for negotiations. An anxious crowd gathered outside the post office awaiting word of the fate of their royal family. This was just after the French Revolution and there was a general nervousness between France and Spain. The French guard appeared and the second of May, 1808, massacre took place. Goya, who lived just up the street, observed the massacre and captured the tragedy in his paintings—*2nd of May, 1808* and *3rd of May, 1808*—that you'll see in the Prado.

Puerta del Sol is a hub for the Metro, buses, and pickpockets. Look up at the surveillance camera. In summer you'll see a yellow-umbrella TI booth with student tour guides helping visitors. The statue of the bear pawing the strawberry bush is the symbol of Madrid.

Walking from Puerta del Sol to Plaza Mayor: On the corner of Calle Mayor and Puerta del Sol, step into the busy Confiteria. It's famous for its savory, meat-filled *agujas* pastries (175 ptas); notice the racks with goodies hot out of the oven. Look back toward the entrance and notice the tile above the door with the 18th-century view of the Puerta del Sol. Compare this with the view out the door. This was before the square was widened, when a church stood where the Tio Pepe sign stands today. This church was where the French kept local patriots awaiting execution.

Continue down Calle Mayor. At McDonald's veer left up the pedestrian alley called Calle de Postas. The street sign shows the post coach heading for that famous first post office. Take a left up Calle San Cristobal. At the square notice the big brick 17th-century Ministry of Foreign Affairs building—originally a prison for rich prisoners who could afford the best cells. Look right and walk under the arch into . . .

Plaza Mayor—This square, built in 1619, is a vast, cobbled, traffic-free chunk of 17th-century Spain. Each side of the square is uniform, as if a grand palace were turned inside out. The statue is of Felipe III who ordered the square's construction. Upon this stage, much Spanish history was played out: bullfights, fires, royal pageantry, and events of the gruesome Inquisition. Carved reliefs under the lampposts tell the story. During the Inquisition, many were tried here. The guilty would parade around the square (bleachers were built for bigger audiences) with billboards listing their many sins. They were then burned. Some were slowly strangled with a garrotte; they'd hold a crucifix and hear the reassuring words of a priest as this life was squeezed out of them. The square is painted a lovely shade of burgundy—the result of a city-wide vote. Since Franco's 1975 death, there's a passion for voting here. Three different colors were painted as samples on the walls of this square and the city voted for its favorite. Under the fanciest facade (the Casa de la Panaderia—Royal Bakery), visit the subterranean museum of city history (free, weekdays 10:00–13:30 and 18:00–20:20, weekends 10:00–13:30).

Throughout Spain, lesser *plazas mayores* provide peaceful pools for the river of Spanish life. A stamp-and-coin market bustles here on Sundays from 10:00 to 14:00, and on any day it's a colorful and affordable place to enjoy a cup of coffee. The TI is at #3.

Finish your Plaza Mayor visit with a drink at the Torre del Oro Bar Andalu. This is Madrid's temple to bullfighting. When you order a beer or wine you may get a free tapa—often gazpacho or paella. (Warning: They tend to order for tourists, serving them expensive dishes they didn't order; I ended up with a $10 plate I didn't want. To ask if the food is free, ask, "*¿Libero?*") The ambience is "Andalu" . . . Andalusian. Look under the stuffed head of "Barbero" the bull. At eye level you'll see a *puntilla*, the knife used to put a bull out of its misery at the arena. This was the knife used to kill Barbero.

Notice the incredible action caught in the bar's many photographs. Near Barbero, follow the photo series of a wannabe bull fighter who jumped into the ring and was killed by the bull. Below that is a series of photos showing the scandalous fight in which a *bandillero* (the guy who puts the arrows into the bull's back) was in trouble and his partners just stood by watching in horror as the man was killed. At the end of the bar in a glass case is the "suit of lights" El Cordobes wore in his ill-fated 1967 fight. With Franco in attendance, El Cordobes went on and on, long after he could have ended the fight, until finally the bull gored him. El Cordobes survived, the bull didn't. Find Franco with El Cordobes at the far end.

Walking from Plaza Mayor to the Royal Palace: Leave the Plaza Mayor on Calle Cuidad Rodrigo (left of Royal Bakery), passing a series of fine turn-of-the-century storefronts. From the archway you'll see Mercado de San Miguel, covered since 1900 (on left). Wander through this produce market, leaving on the downhill side and following the street left. At the corner, turn right continuing downhill. A right on Calle de Punonrostro gives a feeling of medieval Madrid and eventually becomes Calle del Codo (where those in need of bits of armor shopped), before hitting Plaça de la Villa, the city hall square. Notice the Moorish arch where Calle del Codo hits the square. Ahead the flags of city, state, and nation grace the city hall. In the lovely garden there's a statue of Don Bazan—mastermind of the Christian victory over the Muslims at the naval battle of Levanto in 1571. This pivotal battle ended the Muslim threat to Christian Europe.

From here Calle Mayor leads downhill a couple more blocks to the Royal Palace. Halfway down there's a tiny square opposite the recommended Casa Ciriaco restaurant (#84). The statue memorializes the 1906 anarchist bombing that killed about 50 people as the royal couple paraded by on their wedding day.

While the crowd was throwing flowers, an anarchist threw a bomb from the top floor of #84 (which was a pension at the time). Amazing photos of the event are on the wall in the dining room of the restaurant.

▲▲▲**Royal Palace (Palacio Real)**—Europe's third-greatest palace (after Versailles and Vienna) is packed with tourists and royal antiques. After a fortress burned down on this site, King Phillip V commissioned this huge 18th-century palace as a replacement. How huge is it? Two thousands rooms with miles of lavish tapestries, a king's ransom of chandeliers, priceless porcelain, and paintings. Nowadays it's used only for formal state receptions and tourist's daydreams.

You can wander on your own or join an English tour (get time of next tour and decide as you buy your ticket; tours depart about every 20 minutes). The museum guidebook and the tour guides are equally dry, each showing a passion for meaningless data (850 ptas without a tour, 950 ptas with a tour, Monday–Saturday 9:00–18:00, Sunday 9:00–15:00, October–March 9:30–17:00, Sunday 9:00–14:00, Metro: Opera, tel. 91-542-0059). Your ticket includes the impressive armory (most likely closed for restoration) and the pharmacy, both on the courtyard.

Sights—Madrid's Museum Neighborhood

These three worthwhile museums are in east Madrid. From Prado to the Thyssen-Bornemisza Museum is a five-minute walk; Prado to Reina Sofia a 10-minute walk.

▲▲▲**Prado Museum**—The Prado is my favorite collection of paintings anywhere. With more than 3,000 canvases, including entire rooms of masterpieces by Velázquez, Goya, El Greco, and Bosch, it's overwhelming. Take a tour or buy a guidebook (or bring me along by ripping out and packing the Prado chapter from *Rick Steves' Mona Winks*). Focus on the Flemish and northern (Bosch, Dürer, Rubens), the Italian (Fra Angelico, Raphael, Botticelli, Titian), and the Spanish art (El Greco, Velázquez, Goya).

Follow Goya through his stages, from cheery (*The Parasol*), to political (*2nd of May, 1808* and *3rd of May, 1808*), to dark (*Negras de Goya*: e.g., *Saturn Devouring His Children*). In each stage, Goya asserted his independence from artistic conventions. Even the standard court portraits from his "first" stage reflect his politically liberal viewpoint, subtly showing the vanity and stupidity of his royal subjects by the looks in their goony eyes. His political stage, with paintings like the *3rd of May*, depicting a massacre of Spaniards by Napoleon's troops, makes him one of the first artists with a social conscience. Finally, in his gloomy "dark stage," Goya probed the inner world of fears and nightmares, anticipating the 20th-century preoccupation with dreams. Also, don't miss Bosch's *The Garden of Earthly Delights*. The art is constantly rearranged by the Prado's fidgety management so even the Prado's own maps and guidebooks are out of date. Regardless of the latest location, most art is grouped by painter, and any guard can point you in the right direction if you say "*¿Dónde está . . . ?*" and the painter's name as Españoled as you can (e.g., Titian is "Ticiano" and Bosch is "El Bosco"). Show up 30 minutes after it opens to avoid the flood. The Prado is quietest at lunchtime from 14:00 to 16:00 (500 ptas; free on Saturday after 14:30, all day Sunday, and anytime if your passport says you're over 65; Tuesday–Saturday 9:00–19:00, Sunday 9:00–14:00, closed Monday; Paseo de Prado, Metro: Banco de España or Atocha—each a 15-minute walk from the museum, tel. 91-330-2800 or 91-420-2836).

▲▲**Thyssen-Bornemisza Museum**—This stunning new museum displays the impressive collection that Baron Thyssen (a wealthy German married to a former Miss Spain) sold to Spain for $350 million. It's basically minor works by major artists and major works by minor artists (the real big guns are over at the Prado). But art lovers appreciate how the good baron's art complements the Prado's collection filling in where the Prado is weak (Impressionism). For a fine walk through art history, ride the elevator to the top floor and do the rooms in numerical order. It's located across from the Prado at Paseo del Prado 8 in the Palacio de Villahermosa (700 ptas, Tuesday–Sunday 10:00–19:00, closed Monday, Metro: Banco de España or Atocha, tel. 91-369-0151). Tired ones can hail a cab at the gate and zip straight to Centro Reina Sofia.

▲▲**Centro Reina Sofia**—This exceptional modern art museum covers the art of our century. Ride the elevator to the second floor and follow the room numbers for art from 1900 to 1950. The fourth floor continues the collection from 1950 to 1980. The museum is most famous for Picasso's *Guernica*, a massive painting showing the horror of modern war. Guernica, a village in northern Spain, was the target of the world's first saturation-bombing raid, approved by Franco and carried out by Hitler. Notice the two rooms of studies for *Guernica* filled with iron-nail tears and screaming mouths. Franco's death ended *Guernica*'s exile in America, and now it reigns as Spain's national piece of art. The museum also houses an easy-to-enjoy collection of other modern artists, including more of Picasso (three rooms divided between his pre–civil war work, *Guernica*, and his post–civil war art) and a mind-bending room full of Dalís. Enjoy a break in the shady courtyard before leaving. (500 ptas, free on Saturday after 14:30, all day Sunday, and for those over 65 with a passport; Monday and Wednesday–Friday 10:00–21:00, Sunday 10:00–14:30, closed Tuesday, Santa Isabel 52, Metro: Atocha, across from the Atocha train station, look for the exterior glass elevators, tel. 91-467-5062.)

More Sights—Madrid

Chapel San Antonio de la Florida—Goya's tomb stares up at a splendid cupola filled with his own frescoes (free, Tuesday–Friday 10:00–14:00 and 16:00–20:00, weekends 10:00–14:00, closed Monday, Glorieta de San Antonio de la Florida, Metro: Principe Pio, tel. 91-547-0722).

▲**Royal Tapestry Factory (Real Fabrica de Tapices)**—Have a look at the traditional making of tapestries (250 ptas, Monday–Friday 9:00–14:00, closed August, cheap tours in Spanish only, Calle Fuenterrabia 2, Metro: Menendez Pelayo, take Gutenberg exit, tel. 91-551-3400).

▲▲**Retiro Park**—Siesta in this 350-acre green and breezy escape from the city. At midday on Saturday and Sunday the area around the lake becomes a street carnival with jugglers, puppeteers, and lots of local color. These peaceful gardens offer great picnicking and people-watching. From the Retiro Metro stop, walk to the big lake (*El Estanque*) where you can rent a rowboat (450 ptas for 45 min). Past the lake, a grand boulevard of statues leads to the Prado. Charles III's Botanical Garden (*Real Jardín Botánico*) is a pleasant extension of Retiro Park (entry just opposite the Atocha end of the Prado). For 200 ptas you can escape all the commotion of Madrid and wander through a lush forest with trees from around the world (daily 10:00–sunset, Plaza de Murillo 2, Metro: Atocha or Retiro).

Parque de Atracciones—This colorful amusement park comes complete with Venetian canals, dancing, eating, games, free shows, and top-notch people-watching (free admission to park, Super Napy all-inclusive ticket for rides-2,200 ptas, 1,225 ptas for kids, July–September Tuesday–Friday 12:00–21:00 or 22:00, Saturday until midnight, closed Monday, winter Saturday and Sunday only, Metro: Batan, tel. 91-463-2900 for exact times). This fair and Spain's best zoo (600 ptas, daily 10:00–21:00, dolphin shows, tel. 91-711-9950) are in the vast Casa de Campo Park just west of the Royal Palace.

Shopping

Shoppers can focus on the colorful pedestrian area between Gran Vía and Puerta del Sol. The giant Spanish department store, El Corte Inglés, is a block off Puerta del Sol and a handy place to pick up just about anything you may need (Monday–Saturday 10:00–21:00, closed Sunday, free maps at info desk, supermarket in basement).

▲**El Rastro**—Europe's biggest flea market is a field day for shoppers, people-watchers, and thieves (Sundays and holidays 9:00–15:00, best before 12:00). Thousands of stalls titillate more than a million browsers with mostly new junk. If you brake for garage sales, you'll pull a U-turn for El Rastro. Start at the Plaza

Mayor and head south, or take the subway to Tirso de Molina. Hang on to your wallet. Munch on a *relleno* or *pepito* (meat-filled pastry). Europe's biggest stamp market thrives simultaneously on Plaza Mayor.

Nightlife

▲▲▲**Bullfight**—Madrid's Plaza de Toros hosts Spain's top bull-fights on most Sundays and holidays from Easter through October and nearly every day mid-May through early June. Top fights sell out in advance. Fights usually start punctually at 19:00. Tickets range from 500 to 10,000 ptas. There are no bad seats at Plaza de Toros; paying more gets you in the shade and/or closer to the gore (*filas* 8, 9, and 10 tend to be closest to the action). Booking offices add 20 percent and don't sell the cheap seats (Plaça del Carmen 1, tel. 91-531-2732). If you want to save money, buy your ticket at the bullring. Tickets go on sale the day of the fight at 10:00; 10 percent of the seats are kept available to be sold two hours before the fight (Calle Alcala 231, Metro: Ventas, tel. 91-356-2200). The bullfight-ing museum (Museo Taurino) is next to the bullring (free, Mon-day–Friday 9:30–14:30, Calle Alcala 237, tel. 91-725-1857).

▲▲**Zarzuela**—For a delightful look at Spanish light opera that even English-speakers can enjoy, try an evening of Zarzuela. Gui-tar-strumming Napoleons in red capes, buxom women with masks and fans, castanets and stomping feet, Spanish-speaking pharaohs, melodramatic spotlights, aficionados singing along from the cheap seats where the acoustics are best—this is the people's opera. That's Zarzuela. Madrid's Theater Zarzuela is at Jovellanos 4 (Metro: Banco de Espana, tel. 91-524-5400). The TI's monthly guide has a special Zarzuela listing.

Flamenco—Save this for Sevilla if you can. In Madrid, Taberna Casa Patas is small, intimate, smoky, and powerful, with one drink included and no hassling after that (tickets around 3,000 ptas, shows at 22:30 and 24:00, Canizares 10, near Plaza Santa Ana, reservations tel. 91-369-0496). The Flamenco House is more touristic (Calle Torija 7, just off Plaza Mayor).

Sleeping in Madrid
(150 ptas = about $1)

Sleep Code: **S** = Single, **D** = Double/Twin, **T** = Triple, **Q** = Quad, **b** = bathroom, **t** = toilet only, **s** = shower only, **CC** = Credit Card (Visa, MasterCard, Amex), **SE** = Speaks English, **NSE** = No Eng-lish. Breakfast is not included unless noted. In Madrid, the 7 per-cent IVA tax is generally, but not always, included in the price.

Madrid has plenty of centrally located budget hotels and *pen-siónes*. You'll have no trouble finding a sleepable double for $30, a good double for $60, and a modern air-conditioned double with all the comforts for $100. Prices are the same throughout the year and it's almost always easy to find a place. The accommodations I've listed are all within a few minutes' walk of Puerta del Sol. Competition is stiff. Those on a budget can bargain. Nighttime Madrid's economy is brisk. Even decent areas are littered with shady-looking people after dark. Just don't invite them in.

Sleeping in the Pedestrian Zone between Puerta del Sol and Gran Vía
(zip code: 28013)

Predictable and away from the seediness, these are good values for those wanting to spend a little more. Especially for these hotels, call first to see if the price is firm. Their formal prices may be inflated and some offer weekend deals. Use Metro: Sol for these five hotels.

Hotel Europa has red-carpet charm: a quiet courtyard, royal salon, plush halls with happy Muzak, polished wood floors, attentive staff, and 70 squeaky-clean rooms with balconies overlooking the pedestrian zone or an inner courtyard. All rooms have TVs (CNN) and big, modern bathrooms. Many rooms face an inner courtyard which amplifies voices and TV noise. Caution, your words will travel. For a better night's sleep, feel free to remove their rubber-coated undersheets—then toss them into the hallway to make a statement (Sb-6,100 ptas, Db-8,200 ptas, Tb-11,100 ptas, Qb-13,200 ptas, breakfast-600 ptas, fine lounge on second floor, elevator, fans in rooms, easy phone reservations with no deposit, CC:VM, Calle del Carmen 4, tel. 91-521-2900, fax 91-521-4696, e-mail: hoteleuropa@genio.infor.es, Sr. Garaban and his very helpful staff SE). The convenient Europa cafeteria next door is a good value.

Hotel Regente is a big, traditional, and impersonal place with 145 plain but comfortable air-conditioned rooms and a great location (Sb-5,500 ptas, Db-8,700 ptas plus tax, CC:VMA, midway between Puerta del Sol and Plaza del Callao at Mesonero Romanos 9, tel. 91-521-2941, fax 91-532-3014).

Nearby, the **Hotel Cliper** is faded-elegant, with character and comfortable rooms on a fairly quiet street (Sb-5,200 ptas, Db-7,500 ptas, includes breakfast and tax, most rooms have air-conditioning, elevator, CC:VMA, Chincilla 6, near Plaza Carmen, tel. 91-531-1700, fax 91-531-1707, SE).

The huge **Hotel Liabeny** feels classy and new, with 222 plush, spacious rooms and all the comforts. It's a business-class hotel that decided to lower its prices to get the tourist trade (Sb-11,500 ptas, Db-16,000 ptas, CC:VMA, air-conditioned, if one room is smoky they can usually switch you to another, off Plaza Carmen at Salud 3, tel. 91-531-9000, fax 91-532-7421, Web site: www.apunte.es/liabeny, e-mail: liabeny@apunte.es, SE).

Hotel Londres is a sad business-class hotel: dark, stark, air-conditioned, and a little smoky (Db-9,500 ptas, renovated

Db-11,000 ptas, CC:VMA, elevator, don't trust their safes, Galdo
2, tel. 91-531-4105, fax 91-531-4101, some English spoken).

Sleeping at Gran Vía #44
(zip code: 28013)
The pulse (and noise) of today's Madrid is best felt along the Gran
Vía. This main drag in the heart of the city stays awake all night.
Despite the dreary pile of prostitutes just a block north, there's a
certain urban decency about it. My choices (all at Gran Vía #44)
are across from Plaza del Callão, which is four colorful blocks (of
pedestrian malls) from Puerta del Sol. Although many rooms are
high above the traffic noise, cooler and quieter rooms are on the
back side. The Café & Te next door provides a classy way to
breakfast. The Callão Metro stop is at your doorstep, and the
handy Gran Vía stop (direct to Atocha) is two blocks away.
    Hostal Residencia Miami is clean and quiet, with lovely,
well-lit rooms, padded doors, and plastic-flower decor throughout.
It's like staying at your eccentric aunt's in Miami Beach. The bubbly landlady, Sra. Sanz, and her too-careful husband, who dresses
up each day for work here, speak no English (S-2,500–3,000 ptas,
D-3,500 ptas, Db-4,500 ptas, closed mid-July–August—if they
take reservations then, they're booking you elsewhere; eighth
floor, tel. 91-521-1464).
    Across the hall, **Hostal Alibel**, like Miami with less sugar,
rents eight big, airy, quiet rooms (D-3,500 ptas, Ds-4,200 ptas,
Db-4,500 ptas, tel. 91-521-0051, grandmotherly Terese NSE).
Downstairs, **Hostal Josefina** has junkyard doors but strong beds
in museum-warehouse rooms (Ss-3,000 ptas, Ds-4,000 ptas, Ts-
6,000 ptas, seventh floor, tel. 91-521-8131 or 91-531-0466, NSE).
    Hostal Residencia Valencia is run like a hotel with 32 big
stark rooms. The friendly manager, Antonio Ramirez, speaks English (Sb-4,000 ptas, big Sb-4,500 ptas, Ds-5,300 ptas, Db-5,800
ptas, Tb-7,500 ptas, Qb-8,500 ptas, CC:VM, fifth floor, tel. 91-
522-1115, fax 91-522-1113). Also a good value but a bit smoky
and with less character is **Hostal Residencia Continental** (Sb-
3,800 ptas, Db-5,200 ptas, CC:VMA, fourth floor, tel. 91-521-
4640, fax 91-521-4649, SE).

Sleeping on or near Plaza Santa Ana
(zip code: 28012)
The Plaza Santa Ana area has plenty of small, cheap places. While
well-worn and noisy at night, it has a rough but charming ambience, with colorful bars and a very central location (three minutes
from Puerta del Sol's "Tío Pepe" sign; walk down Calle San
Jeronimo and turn right on Principe; Metro: Sol). At most of these
hotels, fluent Spanish is spoken, bathrooms are usually down the
hall, and there's no heat during winter.

Hopeless romantics might enjoy playing corkscrew up the rickety cut-glass elevator to the very simple yet homey **Pensión La Valenciana's** old and funky rooms with springy beds. All rooms have balconies; three of them overlook the square (S-1,600 ptas, D-3,500 ptas, Principe 27, fourth floor, right on Plaza Santa Ana next to the theater with flags, tel. 91-429-6317, Esperanza NSE).

In the beautifully tiled building at Plaza Santa Ana 15, up a dark wooden staircase, are two good places. Unfortunately, a disco thumps on Thursday, Friday, and Saturday. **Hostal Filo** is squeaky clean with a nervous but helpful management and 20 rooms hiding in a confusing floor plan (S-2,000 ptas, Ss-3,000 ptas, D-3,500 ptas, Ds-4,500 ptas, T-4,500 ptas, Ts-5,400 ptas, closed in August, second floor, tel. 91-522-4056). **Hostal Delvi** is simple, clean, and very homey (S-1,800–2,000 ptas, D-3,000 ptas, Ds-3,500 ptas, Ts-4,500 ptas, third floor, tel. 91-522-5998, Marie NSE). Marie promises these discounted prices to those with this book.

The cheapest beds are across the street at **Hostal Lucense** (S-1,500 ptas, D-2,300 ptas, Ds-3,000 ptas, T-3,500 ptas, 200 ptas per shower, cheaper for two nights, Nuñez de Arce 15, tel. 91-522-4888; run by Sr. and Sra. Muñoz, both interesting characters; Sr. SE) and **Casa Huéspedes Poza** (same prices and owners, Nuñez de Arce 9, tel. 91-222-4871). Because of these two places, I list no Madrid youth hostels.

Hostal R. Veracruz II, between Plaza Santa Ana and Puerta del Sol, rents decent, quiet rooms (Sb-3,700 ptas, Db-5,200 ptas, Tb-6,900 ptas, elevator, air-conditioning, CC:VM, Victoria 1, third floor, 28012 Madrid, tel. 91-522-7635, fax 91-522-6749, NSE).

Splurges: To be on the same square and spend in a day what others spend in a week, luxuriate in **Hotel Reina Victoria** (Sb-20,500 ptas, Db-27,000 ptas, includes breakfast, prices generally discounted to Db-15,000 in July and August when this becomes a fine value, ask about "corporate rates," CC:VMA, Plaza Santa Ana 14, tel. 91-531-4500, fax 91-522-0307, e-mail: hotel@tryp.es, SE). For a royal, air-conditioned breather and some cheap entertainment, spit out your gum, step into its lobby, grab a sofa, and watch the bellboys push the beggars back out of the revolving doors.

Suite Prado, two blocks toward the Prado from Plaza Santa Ana, is a better value, offering 18 sprawling, air-conditioned suites with a homier feel (Db suite-17,000 ptas is "corporate rate" with this book through 1999, suites are modern and comfortable with fridges and sitting rooms, two extra kids sleep for free or one extra adult for 3,000 ptas, elevator, CC:VMA, Manuel Fernandez y Gonzalez 10, at the intersection with Venture de la Vega, 28014 Madrid, tel. 91-420-2318, fax 91-420-0559, Sylvia SE).

Sleeping Elsewhere in Central Madrid
Just off Plaza Mayor, **Hostal Montalvo** is sprawling, family-run, comfortable, and just half a block east of the elegant Plaza Mayor on a quiet, traffic-free street (S-2,700 ptas, Sb-3,700 ptas, D-4,000 ptas, Db-5,000 ptas, Tb-7,500 ptas, elevator, CC:VM, Zaragoza 6, 28012 Madrid, third floor, Metro: Opera, tel. 91-365-5910, some English spoken).

Halfway between the Prado Museum and Plaza Santa Ana are two good places in the same building. At #34 Cervantes (28014 Madrid, Metro: Anton Martin), you'll find the spotless, friendly, and comfortable **Hotel Cervantes** (Sb-4,500 ptas, Db-6,000 ptas, CC:VM, second floor, tel. & fax 91-429-2745, NSE); and the equally polished and friendly **Hotel Gonzalo** (Sb-4,000 ptas, Db-5,200 ptas, CC:VM, third floor, tel. 91-429-2714, fax 91-420-2007, NSE).

Eating in Madrid
In Spain only Barcelona rivals Madrid for taste-bud thrills. You have three dining choices: an atmospheric sit-down meal in a well-chosen restaurant, an unmemorable basic sit-down meal, or a stand-up meal of tapas in a bar or (more likely) in several bars. Many restaurants are closed in August.

Eating between Puerta del Sol and Gran Vía
Restaurante Puerto Rico has fine food, great prices, and few tourists. Try it now before the menu has English translations (13:00–16:30 and 20:30–24:00, closed Sunday, Chinchilla 2, off Gran Vía, on same street as Hotel Cliper, tel. 91-532-2040).

Artemisa II is a hit with vegetarians who like good healthy food in a smoke-free room (closed Sunday night and August, CC:VMA, Tres Cruces 4, just off Plaza Carmen, tel. 91-521-8721).

Eating between Puerta del Sol and Plaza Santa Ana
For an inexpensive, local-style dinner that won't make you sick, consider **Restaurante Pozo Real** (two blocks off Puerta del Sol). It's friendly and popular with locals, with quiet tables in the back and unremarkable 900-ptas meals (daily 9:00–24:30, Calle del Pozo 6, one block behind Museo del Jamón, tel. 91-521-7951). **Artemesia I**, like its partner described above, serves fine vegetarian meals in smoke-free comfort (daily 13:30–16:00 and 21:00–midnight, non-veggie options available, CC:VMA, Via de la Vega 4 off San Jeronimo, tel. 91-429-5092).

Eating near Plaza Mayor
At **Restaurante Rodriguez**, the food's not fancy but hearty (closed in July, San Cristobal 15, one block toward Puerta del Sol

from Plaza Mayor, tel. 91-231-1136). Many Americans are drawn
to Hemingway's favorite, **Sobrino del Botín** (daily 13:00–16:00
and 20:00–24:00, Cuchilleros 17, a block downhill from Plaza
Mayor, tel. 91-366-4217). It's touristy, pricey, and the last place
he'd go now, but still, people love it and the food is excellent. If
phoning to make a reservation, ask for downstairs (for dark,
medieval cellar ambience) or upstairs (for a still-traditional but
airier and lighter elegance). Those in need of a dirt-cheap but
tasty *bocadillo* (sandwich) or *calamares* (squid) line up at the **Casa
Rua** on Plaza Mayor's southwest corner (behind and to the right
of the horse statue). Picnic shoppers forage at the San Miguel
market (see Picnics, below). For a great scene and reasonable
prices, consider eating right on the Plaza Mayor.

For a fine meal with no tourists and locals who appreciate
good local-style cooking, eat at **Casa Ciriaco** (2,000-ptas meals,
Thursday–Tuesday 13:30–16:00 and 20:30–24:00, closed Wednesday, halfway between Puerta del Sol and the Royal Palace at Calle
Mayor 84, tel. 91-548-0620). It was from this building in 1906 that
an anarchist threw a bomb at the royal couple on their wedding
day. Photos of the carnage are on the wall in the dining room.

Eating near the Prado
Each of the big three art museums has a decent cafeteria. After a
long visit to the Prado, consider a meal on the tiny Plaza de
Platarias de Matinez (directly across the busy highway from the
Atocha end of the Prado) where two little eateries share the square
and shade. **La Plateria** is a hardworking little café/wine bar with a
good menu for light meals or a hearty salad. The chalkboard
shows a list of items in three different sizes (daily 13:00–15:00 and
17:00–24:00). The **Bar Museu**, a simpler place, serves tapas and
sandwiches.

Tapas: The Madrid Pub Crawl Dinner
For maximum fun, people, and atmosphere, go mobile and do the
"tapa tango," a local tradition of going from one bar to the next,
munching, drinking, and socializing. Tapas are the toothpick
appetizers, salads, and deep-fried foods served in most bars.
Madrid is Spain's tapa capital—tapas just don't get any better.
Grab a toothpick and stab something strange—but establish the
prices first. Some items are very pricey, and most bars offer larger
raciónes rather than smaller tapas. *Un pincho* is a bite-sized serving
(not always available), *una tapa* is a snack, and *una ración* is half a
meal. Say "*un bocadillo*" and it comes on bread as a sandwich. A
caña is a small glass of draft beer.

Prowl the area between Puerta del Sol and Plaza Santa Ana.
There's no ideal route, but the little streets (in this book's map)
between Puerta del Sol, San Jeronimo, and Plaza Santa Ana hold

tasty surprises. Below is an eight-stop tapa crawl. These places are good, but don't be blind to making a discovery or two on your own.

1. From Puerta del Sol, head east down Carrera de San Jeronimo to the corner of Victoria street. Across from Museo del Jamón you'll find **La Tourina Cervecería**, a bullfighters' Planet Hollywood. Wander among trophies and historic photographs. Each stuffed bull's head is named along with its farm, awards, and who killed him. Among the photos you can see Che Guevara, Orson Welles, and Salvador Dalí all enjoying a good fight. Find the Babe Ruth of bullfighters, El Cordobes, wounded in bed. The photo below shows him in action. Kick off your pub crawl with *rabo del toro* (bull-tail stew) and a glass of red wine. Across the street at San Jeronimo 6 is . . .

2. Museo del Jamón (Museum of Ham), which is tastefully decorated, unless you're a pig. This frenetic, cheap, stand-up bar is an assembly-line of fast and deliciously simple *bocadillos* and *raciónes*. Options are shown in photographs with prices. For a small sandwich, ask for a *bocadilla chiquito* (95 ptas). Just point and eat (daily 9:00–24:00, sit-down restaurant upstairs). Next, head halfway up Calle Victoria to the tiny . . .

3. La Casa del Abuelo, for shrimp-lovers who savor sizzling plates of tasty little *gambas*. Try *gambas a la plancha* (fried shrimp, 560 ptas) and *gambas al ajillo* (shrimp version of escargot . . . cooked in oil and garlic and ideal for bread dipping—700 ptas) and a 150-ptas glass of red wine (daily 11:30–15:30 and 18:30–23:30, Calle Victoria 12). Continue uphill and around the corner to . . .

4. Casa Toni for refreshing bowls of gazpacho (200 ptas, Calle Cruz 14). This cold tomato and garlic soup is slurped by locals throughout the summer. Backtrack halfway down Calle Victoria and turn left, walking through an alley littered with dining tables to . . .

5. El Rocio, a tapas bar, which sells plates of 10 mussels—toss the shells on the floor as you smack your lips (19:00–23:00, Pasaje Matheu 5). *Mejillones picantes* is spicy (430 ptas). Wash each down with the crude, dry, white Ribeiro wine from Galicia. It's served in a ceramic bowl to disguise its lack of clarity. The place is draped in mussels. Notice the photo showing the floor filled with litter—a reminder that mussel bars have seen better days. In the 1970s they sold 14 tons a month. Now—with other more trendy evening activities entertaining the cruising youth—it takes a year to sell 14 tons.

6. Jump to stop #7 or, for a classy side trip, follow Nuñez de Arce up to Plaza Santa Ana. Cross the square (past lots of trendy pubs) and continue one block down Calle Principe to the venerable **Casa Alberto**. It's been serving tasty tapas since 1827 (11:00–1:00; closed Sunday evening, all day Monday, and most of August; Huertas 18, tel. 91-429-9356). It's hard to stop at just one *canape de salmon ahumado* (smoked salmon appetizer, 275 ptas). The popular dining room in the back has a different, pricier menu (lunch starts at 13:30, dinner at 21:00).

7. Head to Plaza Mayor for **La Torre del Oro Bar Andalu** (26 Plaza Mayor, tel. 91-366-5016). Bullfight aficionados hate the gimmicky Bull Bar across from Museo del Jamón (stop #1). This one has more soul. The walls are lined with grisly bullfight photos from annual photo competitions. Read the complete description above in the Plaza Mayor section. A free tapa often comes with your drink. Be careful not to let the aggressive staff bully you into food you don't want (they served me a 1,600-ptas plate of shrimp I didn't ask for).

8. The classy **Chocolatería San Ginés** is much loved locally for its *churros* (greasy cigar-shaped fritters) and chocolate. Open from 22:00 to 7:00 nightly, it caters to the late-night crowd (mostly disco—the famous "Joy" disco is next door). Finish off your crawl with this sweet treat, dunking your *churros* into the pudding-like hot chocolate as locals have done here for over 100 years (from Plaza Mayor, cross Calle Mayor and go down Calle P. de San Ginés to #5, off Calle Arenal, tel. 93-365-6546).

Fast Food, Picnics, and Breakfast

Fast Food: For an easy, light, cheap meal, try **Rodilla**—a popular sandwich bar on the northeast corner of Puerta del Sol at #13 (daily 8:30–20:30). **Pans & Company**, a chain with shops throughout Madrid, offers healthy, tasty sandwiches and great chef's salads (daily 9:00–24:00, on Puerta del Sol, Plaza Callão, Gran Vía 30, and many more).

Picnics: The department store El Corte Inglés has a well-stocked deli, but its produce is sold only in large quantities (10:00–21:00, closed Sunday). A perfect place to assemble a cheap picnic is downtown Madrid's neighborhood market, Mercado de San Miguel. How about breakfast surrounded by early morning shoppers in the market's café? Get a couple of oranges to go (9:00–14:00 and 16:00–19:00, closed Saturday afternoon and Sunday; from Plaza Mayor, face the colorful building and exit from the upper left-hand corner).

Churros con chocolate **for breakfast:** If you like hash browns and eggs in American greasy-spoon joints, you must try the Spanish equivalent: greasy *churros* dipped in pudding-like chocolate at **Bar Valladolid** (open from 7:00, closed Sunday, two blocks off the Tío Pepe end of Puerta del Sol, south on Espoz y Mina, turn right on Calle de Cadiz). If you arrive early, it's *churros* and hookers. You'll see the changing of the guard, as workers of the night finish their day by downing a cognac, and workers of the day start theirs by dipping *churros* or *porras* (simply fatter *churros*) into chocolate. (One serving is often plenty for two.) With luck, the *churros* machine in the back will be cooking. Throw your napkin on the floor like you own the place. For something with less grease and more substance, ask for a *tortilla española* (potato omelet), *zumo de naranja* (orange juice), and *café con leche*. Notice the expressive WC signs.

Transportation Connections—Madrid

By train to: Toledo (9/day, 75 min, from Madrid's Atocha station), **Segovia** (9/day, 2 hrs, both Chamartin and Atocha stations), **Ávila** (1/hrly, 1 hr, from Chamartin and Atocha), **Salamanca** (3/day, 3 hrs, from Chamartin), **Barcelona** (7/day, 8 hrs, mostly from Chamartin), **Granada** (6–9 hrs, a daily day train from Chamartin and a nightly train from Atocha), **Sevilla** (15/day, 2.5 hrs by AVE, 3.5 hrs by Talgo, from Atocha), **Córdoba** (16 AVE trains/day, 2 hrs, from Chamartin and Atocha), **Lisbon** (1/day, 10 hrs, overnight from Chamartin), **Paris** (4/day, 12–16 hrs, one direct overnight, from Chamartin). Train information: tel. 91-328-9020.

Spain's new AVE bullet train opens up some good itinerary. options. Pick up the brochure at the station. Prices vary with times and class. The basic Madrid-to-Sevilla fare is 8,100 ptas (1,100 ptas less on the almost-as-fast Talgo). AVE is now 85-percent covered by Eurail (so the Madrid–Sevilla–Madrid round-trip costs Eurailers about 2,400 ptas). So far AVE only covers Madrid–Córdoba–Sevilla. Consider this exciting day trip from Madrid: 7:00 depart, 8:45–12:40 in Córdoba, 13:30–21:00 in Sevilla, 23:30 back in Madrid. Reserve each AVE segment.

By bus to: Segovia (hrly, 90 min), **Ávila** (7/day, 2 hrs), **Toledo** (2/hrly, 75 min); buses depart from Estación sur Autobuses (Metro: Méndez Alvaro, tel. 91-530-4800).

GIMMELWALD AND THE BERNER OBERLAND

Frolic and hike high above the stress and clouds of the real world. Take a vacation from your busy vacation. Recharge your touristic batteries up here in the Alps, where distant avalanches, cowbells, the fluff of a down comforter, and the crunchy footsteps of happy hikers are the dominant sounds. If the weather's good (and your budget's healthy), ride a gondola from the traffic-free village of Gimmelwald to a hearty breakfast at Schilthorn's 10,000-foot revolving Piz Gloria restaurant. Linger among Alpine whitecaps before riding, hiking, or hang gliding down (5,000 feet) to Mürren and home to Gimmelwald.

Your gateway to the rugged Berner Oberland is the grand old resort town of Interlaken. Near Interlaken is Switzerland's open-air folk museum, Ballenberg, where you can climb through traditional houses from every corner of this diverse country.

Ah, but the weather's fine and the Alps beckon. Head deep into the heart of the Alps and ride the gondola to the stop just this side of heaven—Gimmelwald.

Planning Your Time

Rather than tackling a checklist of famous Swiss mountains and resorts, choose one region to savor—the Berner Oberland. Interlaken is the administrative headquarters (fine transportation hub, banking, post office, laundry, shopping). Use it for business and as a springboard for Alpine thrills. With decent weather, explore the two areas (south of Interlaken) that tower above either side of the Lauterbrunnen Valley: Kleine Scheidegg/Jungfrau and Schilthorn/Mürren. Ideally, home-base three nights in the village of Gimmelwald and spend a day in each area. On a speedy train trip, you can overnight into and out of Interlaken. For the fastest look, consider a night in Gimmelwald, breakfast at the Schilthorn, an afternoon doing the Männlichen-to-Wengen hike, and an evening or night train out. What? A nature lover not spending the night high in the Alps? Alpus-interruptus.

Getting Around the Berner Oberland

For more than 100 years, this has been the target of nature-worshiping pilgrims. And the Swiss have made the most exciting Alpine perches accessible by lift or train. Part of the fun (and most of the expense) here is riding the many lifts. Generally, scenic trains and lifts are not covered on train passes (but a Eurail or Europass gets you a 25 percent discount on even the highest lifts). Ask about discounts for early birds, youths, seniors, families, groups, and those staying awhile. The Family Card pays for itself on the first hour of trains and lifts: children under 16 travel free with parents, children ages 16 to 23 pay half-price (20 SF at Swiss train stations but not gondola stations). Get a list of discounts and the free fare and time schedule at any train station. Study the Alpine Lifts in the Berner Oberland chart in this chapter. Lifts generally go at least twice an hour, from about 7:00 to about 20:00 (sneak preview: www.jungfrau.ch).

INTERLAKEN

When the 19th-century Romantics redefined mountains as something more than cold and troublesome obstacles, Interlaken became the original Alpine resort. Ever since then, tourists have flocked to the Alps "because they're there." Interlaken's glory days are long gone, its elegant old hotels eclipsed by the new, more jet-setty Alpine resorts. Today its shops are filled with chocolate bars, Swiss Army knives, and sunburned backpackers.

Orientation (tel. code: 033)

Efficient Interlaken is a good administrative and shopping center. Take care of business, give the town a quick look, view the live TV coverage of the Jungfrau and Schilthorn weather in the window of the Schilthornbahn office on the main street (at Höheweg 2, also on TV in most hotel lobbies). Then head for the hills. Stay in Interlaken only if you suffer from alptitude sickness (see Sleeping, below).

   Tourist Information: The TI has good information for the whole region, advice on Alpine lift discounts, and a room-finding service (July–September Monday–Friday 8:00–12:00, 13:30–18:30, Saturday 8:00–17:00, Sunday 17:00–19:00; off-season weekdays 8:00–12:00, 14:00–18:00, Saturday 8:00–12:00, closed Sunday, tel. 033/822-2121, on main street, five-minute walk from West station). While the Jungfrau region map costs 2 SF, a perfectly good mini-version is included in the free Jungfrau region train timetable. Pick

Interlaken

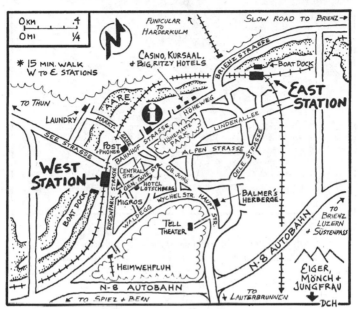

up a Bern map if that's your next destination. The TI organizes daily town walks in English (10 SF, 18:00, 60 minutes, from the TI).

Arrival in Interlaken: Interlaken has two train stations: East and West. Most major trains stop at the Interlaken-West station. The station's train information desk answers tourist questions and has a fair exchange desk (daily 8:00–12:00, 14:00–18:00). Ask at the station about discount passes, special fares, Eurail discounts, and schedules for the scenic mountain trains (tel. 033/826-4750). An open-late Migros supermarket is across the street with a self-service cafeteria upstairs (Monday–Thursday 8:00–18:30, Friday 8:00–21:00, Saturday 7:30–16:00, closed Sunday).

It's a pleasant 15-minute walk between the West and East stations, or an easy, frequent train connection. From the Interlaken-East station, private trains take you deep into the mountainous Jungfrau region (see Transportation Connections, below).

Helpful Hints

Telephone: Phone booths cluster outside the post office in the center of town. Inside the office, you'll find metered phone booths (talk first, pay later; Monday–Friday 7:45–18:15, Saturday 8:30–11:00, closed Sunday). For efficiency, buy a phone card from a newsstand. (There's a card phone—which doesn't take coins—in Gimmelwald.)

Gimmelwald

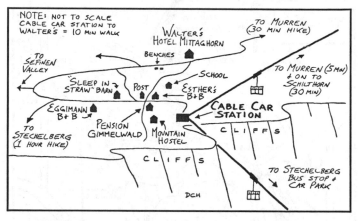

Laundry: Helen Schmocker's *Wäscherei* (laundry) has a change machine, soap, English instructions, and a pleasant riverside locale (daily 7:00–22:00 for self-service, or Monday–Saturday 8:00–12:00, 13:30–18:00 for full service: drop off 10 pounds and 12 SF in the morning and pick up clean clothes that afternoon, from post office, follow Marktgasse over two bridges to Beatenbergstrasse, tel. 033/822-1566).

Activities: For the adventurer with money, Alpin Raft offers high-adrenaline trips such as rafting, canyoning (rappeling down watery gorges), bungee jumping, and paragliding (Postfach 78, tel. 033/823-4100, Web site: www.alpinraft.ch). Most adventure trips cost from 80 to 140 SF.

GIMMELWALD

Saved from developers by its "avalanche zone" classification, Gimmelwald is one of the poorest places in Switzerland. Its economy is stuck in the hay, and its farmers, unable to make it in their disadvantaged trade, are subsidized by the Swiss government (and work the ski lifts in the winter). For some travelers, there's little to see in the village. Others enjoy a fascinating day sitting on a bench and learning why they say, "If heaven isn't what it's cracked up to be, send me back to Gimmelwald."

Take a walk through the town. This place is for real. Most of the 130 residents have the same last name—von Allmen. They are tough and proud. Raising hay in this rugged terrain is labor intensive. One family harvests enough to feed only 15 or 20 cows. But they'd have it no other way and, unlike absentee landlord Mürren, Gimmelwald is locally owned. (When word got out that urban planners wished to develop Gimmelwald into a town of 1,000,

Lauterbrunnen Valley: West Side Story

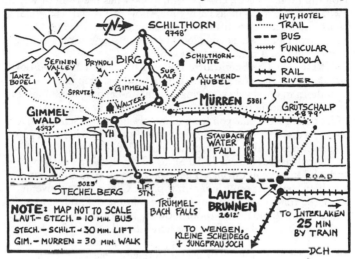

locals pulled some strings to secure the town's bogus "avalanche zone" building code.)

Notice the traditional log cabin architecture and blond-braided children. The numbers on the buildings are not addresses, but fire insurance numbers. The cute little hut near the station is for storing and aging cheese, not hostelers. In Catholic-Swiss towns, the biggest building is the church. In Protestant towns, it's the school. Gimmelwald's biggest building is the school (one teacher, 17 students, and a room that doubles as a chapel when the pastor makes his monthly visit). Do not confuse obscure Gimmelwald with touristy and commercialized Grindelwald just over the Kleine Scheidegg ridge.

Evening fun in Gimmelwald is found at the youth hostel (lots of young Alp-aholics and a good chance to share information on the surrounding mountains) or at the Pension Gimmelwald's terrace restaurant next door (see Sleeping, below).

Walter's bar is a local farmers' hangout. When they've made their hay, they come here to play. They look like what we'd call "hicks" (former city-slicker Walter still isn't fully accepted by the gang), but they speak some English and can be fun to get to know. Sit outside (benches just below the rails, 100 yards down the lane from Walter's), and watch the sun tuck the mountaintops into bed as the moon rises over the Jungfrau.

Alpine Hikes

There are days of possible hikes from Gimmelwald. Many are a fun combination of trails, mountain trains, and gondola rides.

Don't mind the fences, cross at will; a hiker has the right of way in Switzerland. But as late as early June, snow can curtail your hiking plans (the Männlichen lift doesn't even open until June 6). Get advice from a knowledgeable local before setting out on any hike to confirm that it is safe and accessible.

▲▲▲**Hike 1: The Schilthorn: Hikes, Lifts, and a 10,000-Foot Breakfast**—If the weather's good, have breakfast atop the Schilthorn in the slowly revolving, mountain-capping restaurant (of James Bond movie fame). The early bird–special gondola tickets (rides before 9:00) take you from Gimmelwald to the Schilthorn and back at a discount. Nag the Schilthorn station in Mürren for a gondola souvenir decal (Schilthorn info: tel. 033/8231-444).

Breakfast costs from 13.50 SF to 22 SF. Expect slow service, and ask for more hot drinks if necessary. If you're not revolving, ask them to turn it on. Linger on top. Piz Gloria has a souvenir shop, the rocks of the region on the restaurant wall, telescopes, and a "touristorama" film room showing a multi-screen slideshow and explosive highlights from the James Bond thriller that featured the Schilthorn (free and self-serve; push the button for slides or, after a long pause for the projector to rewind, push for 007).

Watch hang gliders set up, psych up, and take off, flying 30 minutes with the birds to distant Interlaken. Walk along the ridge out back. This is a great place for a photo of the "mountain-climber you." For another cheap thrill, ask the gondola attendant to crank down the window, stick your head out, and pretend you're hang gliding, ideally over the bump going down from Gimmelwald.

Lifts go twice an hour, and the ride (including two transfers) to the Schilthorn takes 30 minutes. Watch the altitude meter in the gondola. (The Gimmelwald-Schilthorn hike is free, if you don't mind a 5,000-foot altitude gain.) You can ride up to the Schilthorn and hike down, but I wouldn't (weather can change; have good shoes). For a less scary hike, go halfway down by cable car and walk down from the Birg station. Buy the round-trip excursion early-bird fare (cheaper than the Gimmelwald-Schilthorn-Birg ticket) and decide at Birg if you want to hike or ride down.

Hiking down from Birg is very steep and gravelly. Just below Birg is the Schilthorn-Hutte. Drop in for soup, cocoa, or a coffee schnapps. You can spend the night in the hut's crude loft (40 mattresses, 60 SF for bed, breakfast, and dinner, open July–September, tel. 033/855-1167). Youth hostelers scream down the ice fields on plastic-bag sleds from the Schilthorn. (English-speaking doctor in Mürren.)

The most interesting trail from Birg to Gimmelwald is the high one via Grauseewli Lake and Wasenegg Ridge to Brünli, down to Spielbodenalp, and the Sprutz waterfall. From the Birg lift, hike toward the Schilthorn, taking your first left down to the little, newly made Grauseewli Lake. From the lake a gravelly trail leads down the rough switchbacks until it levels out. When you see a rock painted with arrows pointing to "Mürren" and "Rotstockhütte," follow the path to Rotstockhütte, traversing the cow-grazed mountainside. Follow Wasenegg Ridge left/down and along the barbed wire fence, which dead-ends at Brünli below. (For maximum thrills, stay on the ridge and climb all the way to the knobby little summit where you'll enjoy an incredible 360-degree view and a chance to sign your name on the register stored in the little wooden box.) A steep trail winds directly down from Brünli towards Gimmelwald, soon hitting a bigger, easy trail. The trail bends right (just before the popular restaurant/mountain hut at Spielbodenalp) leading to Sprutz. Walk under the Sprutz waterfall, and a steep wooded trail deposits you in a meadow of flowers at the top side of Gimmelwald.

For an expensive thrill, you can bungee-jump from the Stechelberg–Mürren service gondola (100 SF for a 330-foot drop, 220 SF for 590 feet, drop head-first or feet-first, have photos taken, daily 8:00–18:00, tel. 033/826-7711).

▲▲▲**Hike 2: The Männlichen–Kleine Scheidegg Hike**—This is my favorite easy Alpine hike, entertaining you all the way with glorious Jungfrau, Eiger, and Mönch views. (That's the Young Maiden being protected from the Ogre by the Monk.)

If the weather's good, descend from Gimmelwald bright and early. Catch the post bus to the Lauterbrunnen train station (synchronized to depart with the arrival of each lift—3.60 SF; or drive, parking at the large multi-storied pay lot behind the Lauterbrunnen station). Buy a ticket to Männlichen and catch the train. Ride past great valley views to Wengen, where you'll walk across town (buy a picnic, but don't waste time here if it's sunny), and catch the Männlichen lift (departing every 15 minutes, after June 6) to the top of the ridge high above you.

From the tip of the Männlichen lift, hike 20 minutes north to the little peak for that king- or queen-of-the-mountain feeling. It's an easy hour's walk from there to Kleine Scheidegg for a picnic or restaurant lunch. (For accommodations, see Sleeping, below.) If you've got an extra 100 SF and the weather's perfect, ride the train from Kleine Scheidegg through the Eiger to the towering Jungfraujoch and back. Check for discount trips up to Jungfraujoch (three trips a day—early or late, tel. 033/826-4750, trilingual weather info: tel. 033/855-1022). Jungfraujoch crowds can be frightening. The price has been jacked up to reduce the mobs, but sunny days are still a mess.

From Kleine Scheidegg, enjoy the ever-changing Alpine panorama of the north faces of the Eiger, Jungfrau, and Mönch, probably accompanied by the valley-filling mellow sound of Alphorns and distant avalanches, as you ride the train or hike downhill (30 gorgeous minutes to Wengeralp, 90 more steep minutes from there into the town of Wengen). If the weather turns bad or you

Berner Oberland

NOTE: THIS BIRD'S EYE VIEW LOOKS SOUTH...

EIGER 13026'   MONCH 13449'   JUNGFRAU 13692'

SCHILT-HORN 9748'

JUNG-FRAU-JOCH

TUNNEL

KLEINE SCHEIDEGG 6762'

GIMMEL-WALD 4593'

BIRG 8784'

HIKE #1

HIKE #2

W. ALP

MÜRREN 5381'

GRINDEL-WALD 3393'

MÄNN-LICHEN 7317'

STECHEL-BERG 3025'

← NICE WALK

GRÜTSCHALP 4879'

TO FIRST →

GRUND

WENGEN 4180'

LAUTERBRUNNEN 2612'

ISENFLUH

HIKE #3

SCHYNIGE PLATTE 6454'

ISELT-WALD

WILDERSWIL 1916'

TO LUZERN

E.

W.

SPIEZ

LAKE BRIENZ

BRIENZ

BALLENBERG

INTER-LAKEN 1860'

LAKE THUN

TO BERN →

┼─┼ PRIVATE RAIL – EURAIL NOT VALID
┼─┼ OTHER RAIL – EURAIL VALID
○─○ MTN. LIFTS

- - - BUS
•••• BOAT
········ TRAIL

NOT TO SCALE!

— DCH —

run out of steam, catch the train early at the little Wengeralp station along the way. After Wengeralp, the trail to Wengen is steep and, while not dangerous, requires a good set of knees. Wengen is a fine shopping town. (For accommodations, see Sleeping, below.) The boring final descent from Wengen to Lauterbrunnen is knee-killer steep—catch the train. Trails may be snowbound into early June. Ask about conditions at the lift stations or local TI. If the Männlichen lift is closed, take the train straight from Lauterbrunnen to Kleine Scheidegg. Many take the risk of slipping and enjoy the Kleine Scheidegg-to-Wengeralp hike even with a little snow.

▲▲**Hike 3: Schynige Platte to First**—The best day I've had hiking in the Berner Oberland is the demanding six-hour ridge walk high above Lake Brienz on one side and all that Jungfrau beauty on the other. Start at Wilderswil train station (just above Interlaken), where you catch the little train up to Schynige Platte (2,000 meters). Walk through the Alpine flower display garden and into the wild Alpine yonder. The high point is Faulhorn (2,680 meters, with its famous mountaintop hotel). Hike to a small gondola called "First" (2,168 meters), where you descend to Grindelwald and

Alpine Lifts in the Berner Oberland

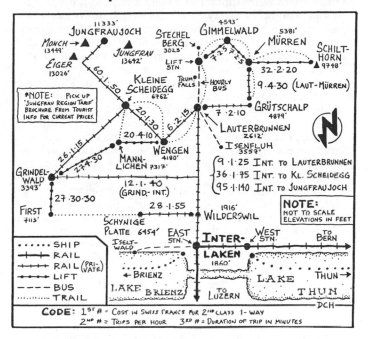

catch a train back to your starting point, Wilderswil—or, if you have a regional train pass or no car but endless money, return to Gimmelwald via Lauterbrunnen from Grindelwald over Kleine Scheidegg. For an abbreviated ridge walk, consider the Panoramaweg, a short loop from Schynige Platte to Daub Peak.

▲▲**Hike 4: Cloudy Day Lauterbrunnen Valley Walk**—For a smell-the-cows-and-flowers lowland walk, ideal for a cloudy day, weary body, or tight budget, follow the riverside trail five kilometers from Lauterbrunnen's Staubach Falls (just after the town church) to the Schilthornbahn station at Stechelberg. Detour to Trümmelbach Falls en route (see below).

If you're staying in Gimmelwald: To get to Lauterbrunnen, walk up to Mürren (30 min), walk or ride the train to Grütschalp (60-min hike), ride the funicular down to Lauterbrunnen (10 min), walk through town, and take the riverside trail ending up at Stechelberg (75 min)—where you can ride the lift back up to Gimmelwald (10 min).

Also consider biking around the valley. Imboden Bike rents bikes on the main street of Lauterbrunnen (20–40 SF/day, tel. 033/855-2114, see Rainy Day Options below).

▲**Other Hikes near Gimmelwald**—For a not-too-tough three-hour walk (but there's a scary 20-minute stretch that comes with ropes) with great Jungfrau views and some mountain farm action, ride the funicular from Mürren to Allmendhübel (1,934 meters), and walk to Marchegg, Saustal, and Grütschalp (a drop of about 500 meters), where you can catch the panorama train back to Mürren. An easier version is the lower Bergweg from Allmenhübel to Grütschalp via Winteregg. For an easy family stroll with grand views, walk from Mürren just above the train tracks to either Winteregg (40 min, restaurant, playground, train station) or Grütschalp (60 min, train station), and catch the panorama train back to Mürren. An easy, go-as-far-as-you-like trail from Gimmelwald is up the Sefinen Valley. Or you can wind from Gimmelwald down to Stechelberg (one hour).

You can get specifics at the Mürren TI. For a description of six diverse hikes on the west side of Lauterbrunnen, pick up the fine and free *Mürren-Schilthorn Hikes* brochure (at stations, hotels, and TIs). The 3-D map of the Mürren mountainside, which includes hiking trails, makes a useful, attractive souvenir (2 SF at TI and lift station). For an extensive rundown on the region, get Don Chmura's fine 5-SF Gimmelwald guidebook (includes info on hikes, flora, fauna, culture, and travel tips; available at Hotel Mittaghorn in Gimmelwald).

Rainy Day Options

If clouds roll in, don't despair. They can roll out just as quickly, and there are some good bad-weather options. There are easy trails and pleasant walks along the floor of the Lauterbrunnen Valley (see above). If all the waterfalls have you intrigued, sneak a behind-the-scenes look at the valley's most powerful one, **Trümmelbach Falls** (10 SF, daily April–November 9:00–17:00, July–August 8:00–18:00, on the Lauterbrunnen-Stechelberg road, tel. 033/855-3232). You'll ride an elevator up through the mountain and climb through several caves to see the melt from the Eiger, Mönch, and Jungfrau grinding like God's band saw through the mountain at the rate of up to 20,000 liters a second (nearly double the beer consumption at Oktoberfest). The upper area, chutes 6 to 10, are the best, so if your legs ache, you can skip the lower ones and ride the lift down.

You can rent bikes at the Interlaken station. For 5 SF extra you can take your bike on the train to the top of Lauterbrunnen Valley and enjoy a scenic ride downhill back into Interlaken via a peaceful bike path over the river from the road.

Lauterbrunnen's **Heimatmuseum** shows off the local folk culture (3 SF, mid-June–September, Tuesday, Thursday, Saturday, and Sunday 14:00–17:30, just over the bridge).

Mürren's slick **Sports Center** (Sportzentrum) offers a world of indoor activities (12 SF for use of the swimming pool and whirlpool, 7 SF for Mürren hotel guests, pool open Monday–Saturday afternoon, mid-June–October). Mürren also has plenty of shops, bakeries, banks, a TI, and accommodations (see Sleeping, below).

Boat Trips from Interlaken—"Interlaken" means "between the lakes." Lazy boat trips explore these lakes (8/day, fewer off-season, free with Eurail, schedules at TI). The Lake Thun boat stops at Beatushöhlen (interesting caves, 30 min from Interlaken) and two visit-worthy towns: Spiez (1 hr from Interlaken) and Thun (1.75 hrs away). The Lake Brienz boat stops at the super-cute and quiet village of Iseltwald (45 min away), and Brienz (1.25 hrs away, near Ballenberg Open-Air Folk Museum).

▲▲**Swiss Open-Air Folk Museum at Ballenberg**—Near Interlaken, the Swiss Open-Air Museum of Vernacular Architecture, Country Life, and Crafts in the Bernese Oberland is a rich collection of traditional and historic farmhouses from every region of the country. Each house is carefully furnished, and many feature traditional craftspeople at work. The sprawling 50-acre park, laid out roughly as a huge Swiss map, is a natural preserve providing a wonderful setting for this culture-on-a-lazy-Susan look at Switzerland.

The Thurgau house (#621) has an interesting wattle-and-daub (half-timbered construction) display and house #331 has a fun bread museum. Use the 2-SF map/guide. The more expensive picture book is a better souvenir than guide. (14-SF entry, half-price after 16:00, daily mid-April–October 10:00–17:00, houses close at 17:00, park stays open later, craft demonstration schedules are listed just inside the entry, tel. 033/951-1123.) There's a reasonable outdoor cafeteria inside the west entrance, and fresh-baked bread, sausage, mountain cheese, and other goodies on sale in several houses. Picnic tables and grills with free firewood are scattered throughout the park. The little wooden village of Brienzwiler (near the east entrance) is a museum in itself with a lovely little church. Trains run frequently from Interlaken to Brienzwiler, an easy walk from the museum.

Sleeping and Eating in the Berner Oberland
(1.4 SF = about $1, tel. code: 033)
Sleep Code: **S** = Single, **D** = Double/Twin, **T** = Triple, **Q** = Quad, **b** = bathroom, **t** = toilet only, **s** = shower only, **CC** = Credit Card (Visa, MasterCard, Amex), **SE** = Speaks English, **NSE** = No English. Unless otherwise noted, breakfast is included.

Sleeping and Eating in Gimmelwald
(4,500 feet, tel code: 033, zip code: 3826)
To inhale the Alps and really hold it in, sleep high in Gimmelwald. Poor but pleasantly stuck in the past, the village has a creaky

hotel, happy hostel, decent pension, and a couple of B&Bs. The bad news is that the lift costs 7.20 SF each way to get there.

Hotel Mittaghorn, the treasure of Gimmelwald, is run by Walter Mittler, a perfect Swiss gentleman. Walter's hotel is a classic, creaky, Alpine-style place with memorable beds, ancient down comforters (short and fat; wear socks and drape the blanket over your feet), and a million-dollar view of the Jungfrau Alps. The Yodelin' Seniors' loft has a dozen real beds on either side of a divider, with several sinks, down comforters, and a fire ladder out the back window. The hotel has one shower for 10 rooms (1 SF for five minutes). Walter is careful not to let his place get too hectic or big and enjoys sensitive Back Door travelers. He runs the hotel alone with the help of Rosemary from the village, keeping it simple, but with class. This is a good place to receive mail from home (check the mail barrel in entry hall).

To some, Hotel Mittaghorn is a fire waiting to happen—with a kitchen that would never pass code, lumpy beds, teeny towels, and nowhere near enough plumbing—run by an eccentric old grouch. These people enjoy Interlaken, Wengen, or Mürren, and that's where they should sleep. Be warned, you'll see more of my readers than locals here, but it's a fun crowd—an extended family (D-60–70 SF, T-85 SF, Q-105 SF, Yodelin' Seniors' loft beds-25 SF, all with breakfast, 3 SF surcharge for one-night stays, CH-3826 Gimmelwald/Bern, tel. 033/855-1658, closed November–April). Reserve by telephone only, and then you must reconfirm by telephone the day before your arrival. Walter usually offers his guests a simple 15-SF dinner. Off-season only, lofters pay just 20 SF for a bed with breakfast. Hotel Mittaghorn is at the top of Gimmelwald, a five-minute climb up the steps from the village intersection.

Mountain Hostel is goat-simple, as clean as its guests, cheap, and very friendly. Its 50 dorm beds are often taken, so call ahead. Petra only takes reservations the day before or the day of arrival (after 9:30). Simply call and leave your name. The hostel has low ceilings, a self-service kitchen (pack in groceries), and new plumbing. Petra Brunner has filled the place with flowers. This relaxed hostel survives with the help of its guests. Please read the signs, respect Petra's rules, and leave it cleaner than you found it. Guests do a small duty. The place is one of those rare spots where a family atmosphere spontaneously combusts, and spaghetti becomes communal as it softens (15 SF per bed in six- to 15-bed rooms, showers-1 SF, no breakfast and no sheets—bring your own, hostel membership not required, 20 yards from the lift station, tel. & fax 033/855-1704).

Next door, **Pension Restaurant Gimmelwald** serves meals and offers 12 basic rooms under low creaky ceilings (D-90 SF, Db-110 SF) and sheetless backpacker beds (25 SF in D, T, and Q rooms), including breakfast. The pension has a scenic terrace over-looking the Jungfrau and the hostel: great for camaraderie but not for peace (closed November and first half of May, 50 meters from gondola station, non-smoking, CC:VM, tel. & fax 033/855-1730). Nicole speaks English and runs the pension. Her husband, Francois, runs the kitchen. Reserve by phone, obligatory reconfirmation by phone two or three days in advance of arrival.

Maria and Olle Eggimann rent two rooms—Gimmelwald's most comfortable—in their Alpine-sleek chalet. Twelve-year town residents Maria and Olle, who job-share the village's only teaching position and raise three kids of their own, offer visitors a rare inside peek at this community (D-100 SF, Db with kitchenette-180 SF for two or three people, optional breakfast-18 SF, no CC, last check-in 18:30, three-night minimum for advance reservations; from gondola continue straight 100 meters past town's only intersection, B&B on left, CH-3826 Gimmelwald, tel. 033/855-3575, e-mail: oeggimann@bluewin.ch, SE fluently).

Esther's B&B, overlooking the main intersection of the village, rents basic rooms in a creaky old home (St-40 SF, Dt-72 SF, Tt-90 SF, with breakfast, two-night minimum stay, tel. 033/855-5488, fax 033/855-5492, a little English spoken).

Schalf im Stroh ("Sleep in Straw") offers exactly that—in an actual barn. After the cows head for higher ground in the summer, the friendly von Allmen family hoses out their barn and fills it with straw and budget travelers. Blankets are free, but bring your own sheet, sleep sack, or sleeping bag. No beds, no bunks, no mattresses, no kidding (19 SF, 13 SF for kids under 12, breakfast included, showers-2 SF, open mid-June–mid-October, depending on grass and snow levels; from lift, continue straight through intersection, barn marked "1995" on right, tel. 033/855-5488, fax 033/855-5492).

Eating in Gimmelwald: Pension Gimmelwald, the only restaurant in town, serves a hearty breakfast buffet for 11 SF and 15-SF dinners featuring a sampling of organic produce from the local farmers and a fine *Rösti*. The hostel has a decent members' kitchen but serves no food. There are no groceries in town. The wise and frugal pack in food from the Co-op stores in Mürren or Lauterbrunnen or the Migros in Interlaken. Hotel Mittaghorn serves dinner only to its guests (15 SF). Follow dinner with a Heidi Cocoa (cocoa *mit* peppermint schnapps) or a Virgin Heidi. The local farmers sell their produce. Esther (at the main intersection of the village) makes by far Gimmelwald's best yogurt—but only until the cows go up in June.

Sleeping and Eating in Mürren
(5,500 feet, tel. code: 033, zip code: 3825)
Mürren—pleasant as an Alpine resort can be—is traffic-free, filled with bakeries, cafés, souvenirs, old-timers with walking sticks, GE

employees enjoying incentive trips, and Japanese making movies of each other with a Fujichrome backdrop. Its chalets are prefab-rustic. Sitting on a ledge 2,000 feet above the Lauterbrunnen Valley, surrounded by a fortissimo chorus of mountains, it has all the comforts of home and then some, with Alp-high prices. All prices are higher during the ski season and from July 15 to August 15. Mürren has an ATM.

Mürren's TI can find you a room, give hiking advice, rent mountain bikes (20 SF/half-day, 30 SF/full day), and change money (in Sportzentrum, open mid-July–mid-September 9:00–12:00, 13:00–18:30, Thursday until 20:30, Saturday 13:00–18:00, Sunday 13:00–17:30, less off-season, tel. 033/856-8686, Web site: www.muerren.ch, e-mail: info@muerren.ch).

Guesthouse Belmont offers good budget rooms. This is a friendly, creaky, very wooden home away from home (S-45 SF, D-90 SF, Db-130 SF, 39-SF beds in two-, four- and six-person bunkrooms, with sheets and breakfast, closed November, CC:VMA, across from the train station, tel. 033/855-3535, fax 033/855-3531, well-run by Verena). The Belmont serves good, reasonably-priced dinners and its poolroom is a popular local hangout.

Hotel Alpina is a simple modern place with comfortable rooms and a concrete feeling—comforting, given its cliff-edge position (Sb-75 AS, Db-130 AS with awesome cliff-hanging Jungfrau views and balconies, "no view" special: Db-90 SF with this book, CC:VMA, exit left from station, walk two minutes downhill, tel. 033/855-1361, fax 033/855 1049, Frau Taugwalder).

Chalet Fontana, run by an Englishwoman, Denise Fussell, is worn and basic (the rooms, not Denise) but a rare budget option in Mürren (35–45 SF per person in small doubles or triples with break-fast, 5 SF cheaper without breakfast, one three-bed room with kitch-enette-45 SF per person, open mid-May through October, across street from Stägerstübli restaurant in town center, tel. 033/855-2686, e-mail: 106501.2731@compuserve.com). If no one's home, check at the Ed Abegglen shop next door (tel. 033/855-1245).

Hotel Jungfrau offers an array of options: **Hotel** with pricey, modern, and comfortable rooms (Db-160 SF with view, 140 SF without, elevator); **Lodge** in a basic, blocky 20-room annex with well-worn but fine rooms and actually better Jungfrau views (Db-110 SF, family apartments); and the **Staff House.** Outside of ski season, half the industrial-strength employees' quarters are empty and rented to budget travelers—stark and basic with only sinks in the rooms (S-48 SF, D-76 SF). All rooms include the same fancy buffet breakfast and free entrance to the Sports Center pool. Without breakfast deduct 10 SF per person (CC:VMA, near TI and Sportzentrum, tel. 033/855-4545, fax 033/855-4549, Web site: www.muerren.ch/jungfrau, e-mail: jungfrau@muerren.ch).

Hotel Alpenruh—expensive and yuppie-rustic—is about the only hotel in Mürren open year-round. The comfortable rooms come with views and some balconies (Sb-80–100 SF, Db-140–200 SF depending on season, elevator, attached restaurant, sauna, free tickets for breakfast atop Schilthorn, CC:VMA, 10 yards from gondola station, tel. 033/856-8800, fax 033/856-8888, e-mail: alpruh@tcnet.ch). Hotel Bellevue-Crystal also offers reasonable rooms (Db-110 SF, tel. 033/855-1401).

Eating in Mürren: For a rare bit of ruggedness, eat at the Stägerstübli (10–30 SF lunches and dinners, closed Tuesday). The Kandhar Snack Bar at the Sport Center has fun, creative, and inexpensive light meals and a good selection of teas and pastries. Mürren's bakery is excellent. For picnic fixings, shop at the Co-op (normally open 8:00–12:00, 14:00–18:30, closed afternoons on Tuesday and Saturday and all day Sunday).

Sleeping in Wengen
(4,200 feet, tel. code: 033, zip code: 3823)
Wengen, a fancy Mürren on the other side of the valley, has more tennis courts than budget beds. This traffic-free resort is an easy train ride above Lauterbrunnen and halfway up to Kleine Scheidegg and Männlichen.

Reasonable beds can be found at: Hotel Bernerhof (D-90 SF, Db-130 SF, includes breakfast, dorm bed-29 SF with sheets and breakfast, 17 SF without breakfast, tel. 033/855-2721, fax 033/855-3358). Chalet Bergheim (some doubles and six 28-SF dorm beds with sheets, opens in June, tel. 033/855-2755). Chalet Schweizerheim Garni (Db-120 SF, summer only, tel. 033/855-1581). Hotel Eden (S-62 SF, D-116 SF, Db-144 SF, tel. 033/855-1634, fax 033/855-3950, Kerstin Bucher SE); the same hotel runs Eddy's Hostel, a block away, with 33-SF dorm beds. Clare and Andy's B&B Chalet (Chalet Trogihalten, one Db-74SF, one Qb-156SF, breakfast 7-SF, four night minimum preferred, tel. & fax 033/855-1712, Clare's English, Andy's Swiss).

Sleeping in Kleine Scheidegg
(6,762 feet, tel. code: 033, zip code: 3801)
For dorm beds with breakfast high in the mountains, sleep at Kleine Scheidegg's Bahnhof Buffet (D-106 SF, 38 SF per bed in dorm, breakfast included, tel. 033/855-1151) or at Restaurant Grindelwaldblick (32 SF for bed in 12-bed room, no sheets, open June–October, tel. 033/855-1374). Confirm price and availability before ascending.

Sleeping near the Stechelberg Lift
(2,800 feet, tel. code: 033, zip code: 3824)
Stechelberg is a hamlet at the end of the valley (bus stop at the post

office). **Nelli Beer**, renting three rooms in a quiet, scenic, and folksy setting, is your best Stechelberg option (S-27 SF, D-50 SF, minimum two nights, over river behind Stechelberg post office at big "Zimmer" sign, tel. 033/855-3930, some English spoken). **Hotel Stechelberg** has 20 clean and quiet rooms (S-45 SF, D-78 SF, Db-112 SF, CC:VMA, tel. 033/855-2921, fax 033/855-4438, e-mail: hotel.stechelberg@tcnet.ch). The local **Naturfreundehaus Alpenhof** is a rugged Alpine lodge for hikers (60 co-ed beds, four to eight per room, 17.60 SF per bed, breakfast-8 SF, dinner-14 SF, no sheets, closed November, tel. 033/855-1202).

Here's a wild idea: **Mountain Hotel Obersteinberg** is a working Alpine farm—cheese, cows, a mule shuttling up food once a day, and an American (Vickie) who fell in love with a mountain man. It's a 2.5-hour hike either from Stechelberg or from Gimmelwald. They rent 12 primitive rooms and a bunch of loft beds: no shower, no hot water, meager solar-panel electricity. Candles light up the night, and you can take a hot-water bottle to bed if necessary (S-74 SF, D-148 SF, including linen, breakfast, and dinner, dorm beds without sheets-17 SF or 57 SF with dinner and breakfast, open June–September, tel. 033/855-2033). The place is filled with locals and Germans on weekends but all yours on weekdays. Why not hike there from Gimmelwald and leave the Alps a day later?

Sleeping in Lauterbrunnen
(2,600 feet, tel. code: 033, zip code: 3822)
Lauterbrunnen—with a train station, TI (tel. 033/855-1955), bank, shops, and lots of hotels—is the valley commercial center. This is the jumping-off point for Jungfrau and Schilthorn adventures. It's idyllic in spite of the busy road and big buildings.

Valley Hostel is new, concrete, and practical, offering cheap and comfortable beds two blocks up the valley from the Lauterbrunnen station (D-44 SF, beds in larger family-friendly rooms-20 SF each, breakfast extra, non-smoking, laundry service, tel. & fax 033/855-2008, Martha and Alfred Abegglen).

Crystal Gästehaus is another new, concrete-feeling hotel offering comfort at a good price and location (Db-120 SF, 50 SF per bed in larger rooms, two blocks up valley from station, tel. 033/856-9090, fax 033/856-9099). **Chalet im Rohr** is a creaky old fire-waiting-to-happen place offering 26-SF beds in one- to four-bed rooms and plenty of character (near the church, tel. 033/855-1507).

Masenlager Stocki is rustic and humble with the cheapest beds in town (12 SF with sheets in an easygoing little 30-bed co-ed dorm with a kitchen, tel. 033/855-1754).

Two campgrounds just south of town provide 15- to 25-SF beds (in dorms, two-, four-, and six-bed bungalows, no sheets, kitchen facilities, and big English-speaking tour groups). **Camping**

Jungfrau, romantically situated beyond Staubach Falls, is huge and well organized (tel. 033/855-2010). It also has fancier cabins (18 SF per person). **Schützenbach Campground**, on the left just past Lauterbrunnen toward Stechelberg, is simpler (tel. 033/855-1268).

Sleeping in Isenfluh
(3,560 feet, tel. code: 033, zip code: 3807)
In the tiny hamlet of Isenfluh, which is smaller than Gimmelwald and offers even better views, **Pension Waldrand** rents six reasonable rooms (Db-110 SF, tel. 033/855-1227, hourly shuttle bus from Lauterbrunnen).

Sleeping in Interlaken
(tel. code: 033, zip code: 3800)
I'd head for Gimmelwald. Interlaken is not the Alps. But if you must stay, here are some good choices.

Hotel Lotschberg, with a sun terrace and wonderful rooms, is run by English-speaking Susi and Fritz and is the best real hotel value in town. Information abounds, and Fritz organizes wonderful adventures (Sb-100 SF, Db-145–180 SF, extra bed 20–25 SF, family deals, cheaper November–May, CC:VMA, elevator, bar, laundry service-8 SF, free e-mail access, non-smoking, four-minute walk from the West Station, on General Guisanstrasse 31, tel. 033/822-2545, fax 033/822-2579, Web site: www.beoswiss .ch/lotschberg, e-mail: lotschberg@interlakentourism.ch).

Guest House Susi's B&B is Hotel Lotschberg's no-frills annex, run by the same people (same address and phone number). It has simple, cozy, cheaper rooms (Db-110 SF, apartments with kitchenettes for two people-100 SF; for four to five people-175 SF, cheaper off-season).

Villa Margaretha B&B, warmly mothered by English-speaking Frau Kunz-Joerin, offers the best cheap beds in town for those staying two nights and wishing to be in a private home. It's a big house in a garden on a quiet residential street three blocks directly in front of the West Station (D-75 SF, T-115 SF, minimum two night stay, no breakfast but kitchenette, Aarmühlestrasse 13, tel. 033/822-1813).

Hotel Aarburg offers 13 plain peaceful rooms in a beautifully located but run-down old building five minutes' walk from the West Station (D-80 SF, Db-100 SF, near recommended Laundromat at Beatenbergstrasse 1, tel. 033/822-2615, fax 033/822-6397).

Backpackers' Villa Sonnenhof is a new, creative guesthouse run by a Methodist Church group. It's fun and youthful but without the frat-party ambience of Balmer's. Rooms are comfortable, and most come with Jungfrau-view balconies (D-86 SF, dorm beds in four- to six-bed rooms with individual lockers and sheets-30 SF each, cheaper if you provide your own sheets, breakfast included, kitchen, garden, Internet access, game room, no curfew, 10-minute walk from either station, Alpenstrasse 16, tel. 033/826-7171, fax 033/826-7172, Web site: www.villa.ch, e-mail: backpackers@villa.ch).

Happy Inn Lodge has cheap rooms a five-minute walk from the West Station (D-60 SF, dorm bed-20 SF, breakfast-7 SF, their bar is a dive, Rosenstrasse 17, tel. 033/822-3225, fax 033/822-3268).

For many, **Balmer's Herberge** is backpacker heaven. This Interlaken institution comes with movies, ping-pong, a Laundromat, bar, restaurant, swapping library, Internet stations, tiny grocery, bike rental, currency exchange, rafting excursions, a shuttle-bus service (which meets every arriving train), and a friendly, hardworking, mostly American staff. This little Nebraska is home for those who miss their fraternity (20-SF dorm beds, 22–28 SF in D, T, or Q, 12 SF in overflow on-the-floor accommodations, all with breakfast and sheets, no reservations, non-smoking, open year-round, CC:VMA, Hauptstrasse 23, in Matten, 15-minute walk from either Interlaken station, tel. 033/822-1961, fax 033/823-3261, SE).

Transportation Connections—Interlaken

By train to: Spiez (2/hrly, 15 min), **Brienz** (hrly, 20 min), **Bern** (hrly, 1 hr). While there are a few long trains from Interlaken, you'll generally connect from Bern.

By train from Bern to: Lausanne (hrly, 70 min) **Zurich** (hrly, 75 min), **Salzburg** (4/day, 8 hrs, transfers include Zurich), **Munich** (4/day, 5.5 hrs), **Frankfurt** (hrly, 4.5 hrs, transfers in Basel and Mannheim), **Paris** (4/day, 4.5 hrs).

Interlaken to Gimmelwald: Take the train from the Interlaken East (Ost) Station to Lauterbrunnen, then cross the street to catch the funicular to Mürren. You'll ride up to Grütschalp, where a special scenic train (*Panorama Fahrt*) rolls you along the cliff into Mürren. From there, either walk an easy, paved 30 minutes downhill to Gimmelwald or walk 10 minutes across Mürren to catch the gondola (7.20 SF and a five-minute steep uphill backtrack) to Gimmelwald. A good bad-weather option (or vice versa) is to ride the post bus from Lauterbrunnen (hourly departure generally coordinated with arrival of train) to Stechelberg and the base of the Schilthornbahn (a big, gray gondola station, tel. 033/823-1444 or 033/555-2141), which will whisk you in five thrilling minutes up to Gimmelwald.

By car it's a 30-minute drive from Interlaken to Stechelberg. The pay parking lot (5 SF/day) at the gondola station is safe. Gimmelwald is the first stop above Stechelberg on the Schilthorn gondola (7.20 SF, two trips/hrly at :25 and :55; get off at first stop). Note that for a week in early May and from mid-November through early December, the Schilthornbahn is closed for servicing.

APPENDIX

National Tourist Offices in the U.S.A.
Austrian National Tourist Office: Box 1142, New York, NY 10108, tel. 212/944-6880, fax 212/730-4568, Web site: www .anto.com. Ask for their Vacation Kit map. Fine hikes and Vienna material.

Belgian National Tourist Office: 780 3rd Ave. #1501, New York, NY 10017, tel. 212/758-8130, fax 212/355-7675, Web site. www.visitbelgium.com. Good country map.

British Tourist Authority: 551 5th Ave., 7th floor, New York, NY 10176, tel. 800/462-2748 or 212/986-2200, Web site: www.visitbritain.com. Free maps of London and Britain. Meaty material, responsive to individual needs.

Czech Tourist Authority: 1109 Madison Ave., New York, NY 10028, tel. 212/288-0830, fax 212/288-0971, Web site: www.czech.cz/new_york. To get a weighty information package (12 lbs, no advertising), send a check for $3 to cover postage and specify places of interest.

Denmark (see Scandinavia)

French Tourist Office: 444 Madison Ave., 16th floor, New York, NY 10022; 676 N. Michigan Ave. #600, Chicago, IL 60611; 9454 Wilshire Blvd. #715, Beverly Hills, CA 90212. General information number (in Washington D.C.): tel. 202/659-7779. Web site: www.francetourism.com.

German National Tourist Office: 122 E. 42nd St., 52nd floor, New York, NY 10168, tel. 212/661-7200, fax 212/661-7174, Web site: www.germany-tourism.de. Maps, Rhine schedules, events; very helpful.

Irish Tourist Board: 345 Park Ave., 17th floor, New York, NY 10154, tel. 800/223-6470 or 212/418-0800, fax 212/371-9052 Web site: www. ireland.travel.ie.

Italian Government Travel Office: 630 5th Ave. #1565, New York, NY 10111, tel. 212/245-4822, fax 212/586-9249; 401 N. Michigan Ave. #3030, Chicago, IL 60611, tel. 312/644-9448, fax 312/644-3019; 12400 Wilshire Blvd. #550, Los Angeles, CA 90025, tel. 310/820-0098, fax 310/820-6357. Web site: www .italiantourism.com.

Netherlands National Tourist Office: 225 N. Michigan Ave. #1854, Chicago, IL 60601, tel. 888/GO-HOLLAND (automated) or 312/819-1500 (live), fax 312/819-1740, Web site: www .goholland.com. Great country map.

Norway (see Scandinavia)

Portuguese National Tourist Office: 590 5th Ave., 4th floor, New York, NY

10036, tel. 212/354-4403, fax 212/764-6137, Web site: www
.portugal.org.
Scandinavian Tourism: P.O. Box 4649, Grand Central Station,
New York, NY 10163, tel. 212/885-9700, fax 212/885-9710, Web
site: www.goscandinavia.com. Good general booklets on all the
Scandinavian countries, but be sure to ask for city maps and
specifics.
Spanish National Tourist Office: 666 5th Ave., 35th floor, New
York, NY 10103, tel. 888/OKSPAIN or 212/265-8822, fax
212/265-8864; 845 N. Michigan Ave., Chicago, IL 60611, tel.
312/642-1992, fax 312/642-9817; 1221 Breckell Ave. #1850,
Miami, FL 33131, tel. 305/358-1992, fax 305/358-8223; San
Vicente Plaza Bldg., 8383 Wilshire Blvd. #960, Beverly Hills, CA
90211, tel. 213/658-7188, fax 213/658-1061. Web site: www
.okspain.org.
Sweden (see Scandinavia)
Swiss National Tourist Office: 608 5th Ave., New York, NY
10020, tel. 212/757-5944, fax 212/262-6116; 222 N. Sepulveda
Blvd. #1570, El Segundo, CA 90245, tel. 310/640-8900, fax
310/335-0131. Web site: www.switzerlandtourism.com. Great
maps, rail, and hiking material.

Let's Talk Telephones

In Europe, you can make your calls from public phone booths
using a phone card or coins. At post offices in major cities,
you'll sometimes find easy-to-use "talk now-pay later" metered
phones.

Avoid using hotel room phones, which are major rip-offs
for anything other than local calls or calling-card calls (see
below).

Dialing Direct

Calling Between Countries: Dial the international access code
(of the country you're calling from), the country code (of the
country you're calling), the area code (if it it starts with zero, drop
the zero), and then the local number. See the chart below for
international access codes and country codes.

Calling Long Distance Within a Country: First dial the
area code (including its zero), then the local number.

Europe's Exceptions: France, Italy, Spain, Norway, and
Denmark don't use area codes. To make an international call to
these countries, dial the international access code, the country
code, then the local number in its entirety. The exception to this
exception: for France, drop the initial zero of the local number.
To make long-distance calls within any of these countries, simply
dial the local number whether you're calling across the country or
within the city.

International Access Codes

When dialing direct, first dial the international access code of the country you're calling from. For most countries, it's "00." Only the exceptions are noted below.

Estonia 800	Russia 810
Finland 990	Spain 07
Latvia 800	Sweden 009
Lithuania 810	U.S.A./Canada 011

Country Codes

After you've dialed the international access code, then dial the code of the country youre calling.

Austria 43	Germany 49	Portugal 351
Belgium 32	Greece 30	Russia 7
Britain 44	Ireland 353	Spain 34
Czech Rep. 420	Italy 39	Sweden 46
Denmark 45	Latvia 371	Switzerland 41
Estonia 372	Lithuania 370	U.S.A./Canada 1
Finland 358	Netherlands 31	
France 33	Norway 47	

Calling Card Operators

	AT&T	MCI	SPRINT
Austria	022-903-011	022-903-012	022-903-014
Belgium	0800-100-10	0800-100-12	0800-100-14
Britain	0800-89-0011	0800-89-0222	0800-89-0877
Czech Rep.	00420-00101	00420-00112	00420-87187
Denmark	8001-0010	8001-0022	8001-0877
France	0800-990-011	0800-990-019	0800-990-087
Germany	0130-0010	0800-888-8000	0130-0013
Ireland	1800-550-000	1800-551-001	1800-552-001
Italy	172-1011	172-1022	172-1877
Netherlands	0800-022-9111	0800-022-9122	0800-022-9119
Norway	800-19-011	800-19-912	800-19-877
Portugal	0-0800-111-1111	050-171-234	0800-800-187
Spain	900-990-011	900-99-0014	900-99-0013
Sweden	020-795-611	020-795-922	020-799-011
Switzerland	0800-89-0011	0800-89-0222	0800-89-9777

Numbers and Stumblers

•Europeans write a few of their numbers differently than we do.
1 = 1 , 4 = 4 , 7 = 7 . Learn the difference or miss your train.
•In Europe, dates appear as day/month/year, so Christmas is
25/12/99.
•Commas are decimal points and decimals commas. A dollar and a
half is 1,50 and there are 5.280 feet in a mile.
•When pointing, use your whole hand, palm downward.
•When counting with fingers, start with your thumb. If you hold
up your first finger to request one item, you'll probably get two.
•What we Americans call the second floor of a building is the first
floor in Europe.
•Europeans keep the left "lane" open for passing on escalators and
moving sidewalks. Keep to the right.

Weather Chart

Here is a list of average temperatures and days of no rain. This can be
helpful in planning your itinerary, but I have never found European
weather to be particularly predictable, and these charts ignore humidity.

(1st line, avg. daily low; 2nd line, avg. daily high; 3rd line, days of no rain)

	J	F	M	A	M	J	J	A	S	O	N	D
France	32°	34°	36°	41°	47°	52°	55°	55°	50°	44°	38°	33°
Paris	42°	45°	52°	60°	67°	73°	76°	75°	69°	59°	49°	43°
	16	15	16	16	18	19	19	19	19	17	15	14
Germany	29°	31°	35°	41°	48°	53°	56°	55°	51°	43°	36°	31°
Frankfurt	37°	42°	49°	58°	67°	72°	75°	74°	67°	56°	45°	39°
	22	19	22	21	22	21	21	21	21	22	21	20°
Great Britain	35°	35°	37°	40°	45°	51°	55°	54°	51°	44°	39°	36°
London	44°	45°	51°	56°	63°	69°	73°	72°	67°	58°	49°	45°
	14	15	20	16	18	19	18	18	17	17	14	15
Italy	39°	39°	42°	46°	55°	60°	64°	64°	61°	53°	46°	41°
Rome	54°	56°	62°	68°	74°	82°	88°	88°	83°	73°	63°	56°
	23	17	26	24	25	28	29	28	24	22	22	22
Netherlands	34°	34°	37°	43°	50°	55°	59°	59°	56°	48°	41°	35°
Amsterdam	40°	41°	46°	52°	60°	65°	69°	68°	64°	56°	47°	41°
	12	13	18	16	19	18	17	17	15	13	11	12
Switzerland	29°	30°	35°	41°	48°	55°	58°	57°	52°	44°	37°	31°
Geneva	39°	43°	51°	58°	66°	73°	77°	76°	69°	58°	47°	40°
	20	19	21	19	19	19	22	21	20	20	19	21

Road Scholar Feedback for
BEST OF EUROPE 1999

We're all in the same travelers' school of hard knocks. Your feedback helps us improve this guidebook for future travelers. Please fill this out (attach more info or any tips/favorite discoveries if you like) and send it to us. As thanks for your help, we'll send you our quarterly travel newsletter free for one year. Thanks! **Rick**

Of the recommended accommodations/restaurants used, which was:

Best _____

    Why? _____

Worst _____

    Why? _____

Of the sights/experiences/destinations recommended by this book, which was:

Most overrated _____

    Why? _____

Most underrated _____

    Why? _____

Best ways to improve this book:

_____

I'd like a free newsletter subscription:

___ Yes   ___ No   ___ Already on list

_____
Name
_____
Address
_____
City, State, Zip
_____
E-mail Address

Please send to: ETBD, Box 2009, Edmonds, WA 98020

Jubilee 2000—Let's Celebrate the Millennium by Forgiving Third World Debt

Let's ring in the millennium by convincing our government to forgive the debt owed to us by the world's poorest countries. Imagine spending over half your income on interest payments alone. You and I are creditors and poor countries owe us more than they can pay.

Jubilee 2000 is a worldwide movement of concerned people and groups—religious and secular—working to cancel the international debts of the poorest countries by the year 2000.

Debt ruins people: In the poorest countries, money needed for health care, education, and other vital services is diverted to interest payments.

Mozambique, with a per capita income of $90 and life expectancy of 40, spends over half its national income on interest. This poverty brings social unrest, civil war, and often costly humanitarian intervention by the U.S.A. To chase export dollars, desperate countries ruin their environment. As deserts grow and rain forests shrink, the world suffers. Of course, the real suffering is among local people born long after some dictator borrowed (and squandered) that money. As interest is paid, entire populations go hungry.

Who owes what and why? Mozambique is one of 41 countries defined by the World Bank as "Heavily Indebted Poor Countries." In total, they owe $200 billion. Because these debts are unlikely to be paid, their market value is only a tenth of the face value (about $20 billion). The U.S.A.'s share is under $2 billion.

How can debt be canceled? This debt is owed mostly to the U.S.A., Japan, Germany, Britain, and France either directly or through the World Bank. We can forgive the debt owed directly to us and pay the market value (usually 10 percent) of the debts owed to the World Bank. We have the resources. (Norway, another wealthy creditor nation, just unilaterally forgave its Third World debt.) All America needs is the political will . . . people power.

While many of these poor nations are now democratic, corruption is still a concern. A key to Jubilee 2000 is making certain that debt relief reduces poverty in a way that benefits ordinary people: women, farmers, children, and so on.

Let's celebrate the new millennium by giving poor countries a break. For the sake of peace, fragile young democracies, the environment, and countless real people, forgiving this debt is the right thing for us in the rich world to do.

Tell Washington, DC.: If our government knows this is what we want, it can happen. Learn more, write letters, lobby legislators, or even start a local Jubilee 2000 campaign. For details, contact Jubilee 2000 (tel. 202/783-3566, www.j2000usa.org). For information on lobbying Congress on J2000, contact Bread for the World (tel. 800/82-BREAD, www.bread.org).

Faxing Your Hotel Reservation

Most hotel managers know basic "hotel English." Faxing is the preferred method for reserving a room. It's more accurate and cheaper than telephoning and much faster than writing a letter. Use this handy form for your fax. Photocopy and fax away.

One-Page Fax

To: _____ @ _____
     hotel   *fax*

From: _____ @ _____
        name   *fax*

Today's date: ____ / ____ / ____
              day *month* *year*

Dear Hotel _____,

Please make this reservation for me:

Name: _____

Total # of people: _____   # of rooms: _____   # of nights: _____

Arriving: ____ / ____ / ____   My time of arrival (24-hr clock): _____
          day *month* *year*   (I will telephone if I will be late)

Departing: ____ / ____ / ____
           day *month* *year*

Room(s): Single___ Double___ Twin___ Triple___ Quad___
With: Toilet___ Shower___ Bath___ Sink only___
Special needs: View___ Quiet___ Cheapest Room___

Credit card: Visa___ MasterCard___ American Express___
Card #: _____
Expiration Date:_____
Name on card: _____

You may charge me for the first night as a deposit. Please fax or mail me confirmation of my reservation, along with the type of room reserved, the price, and whether the price includes breakfast. Thank you.

_____
Signature

_____
Name

_____
Address

_____
City   *State*   *Zip Code*   *Country*

_____
E-mail Address

INDEX

A new book from Rick!

1978   1998

Rick Steves' Postcards from Europe
25 Years of Travel Tales from America's Favorite Guidebook Writer

TRAVEL GURU RICK STEVES has been exploring Europe through the Back Door for 25 years, sharing his tricks and discoveries in guidebooks and on TV. Now, in *Rick Steves' Postcards from Europe*, Rick shares his favorite stories and his off-beat European friends.

Postcards takes you on the fantasy trip of a lifetime. While goofy and inspirational, it's informative, too—giving you a close-up look at contemporary Europeans.

You'll meet Marie-Alice, the Parisian restaurateur who sniffs a whiff of moldy cheese and says, "It smells like zee feet of angels." In an Alpine village, meet Olle, the schoolteacher who lets Rick pet his edelweiss, and Walter, the innkeeper who schemes with Rick to create a fake Swiss tradition. In Italy, cruise with Piero through his "alternative Venice" and learn why all Venetian men are mama's boys.

Postcards also tracks Rick's passion for wandering—from his first "Europe-through-the-gutter" trips, through his rocky early tours, to his career as a travel writer and host of a public television series.

These 272 pages of travel tales are told in that funny, down-to-earth style that makes Rick his Mom's favorite guidebook writer.

Rick Steves' Phrase Books

Unlike other phrase books and dictionaries on the market, my well-tested phrases and key words cover every situation a traveler is likely to encounter. With these books you'll laugh with your cabby, disarm street thieves with insults, and charm new European friends.

Each book in the series is 4" x 6", with maps.

RICK STEVES' FRENCH PHRASE BOOK & DICTIONARY
U.S. $6.95/Canada $10.75

RICK STEVES' GERMAN PHRASE BOOK & DICTIONARY
U.S. $6.95/Canada $10.75

RICK STEVES' ITALIAN PHRASE BOOK & DICTIONARY
U.S. $6.95/Canada $10.75

RICK STEVES' SPANISH & PORTUGUESE PHRASE BOOK & DICTIONARY
U.S. $8.95/Canada $13.95

RICK STEVES' FRENCH, ITALIAN & GERMAN PHRASE BOOK & DICTIONARY
U.S. $8.95/Canada $13.95